The

Bed & Breakfast
Book

New Zealand 2005

*New Zealand's leading guide to
accommodation with character.
We have inspected every one.*

Okari Lake Hideaway, Westport

Fyffe Country Lodge, Kaikoura

PUBLISHED BY...

Moonshine Press
P.O. Box 6843
Wellington
New Zealand
Tel: +64 4 385-2615
Fax: +64 4 385-2694
Web: www.bnb.co.nz
Email: info@bnb.co.nz

© Moonshine Press, 2004

ISBN 0-9582569-0-X

Cover photo by Stirling Images, Nelson,
www.stirlingimages.com

INTRODUCTION

Welcome to this edition of The Bed & Breakfast Book

Bed & breakfast in New Zealand means a warm welcome and a unique holiday experience. Most B&B accommodation is in private homes with a sprinkling of guesthouses and small hotels. Each listing in the guide has been written by the host themselves and you will discover their warmth and personality through their writing. *The Bed & Breakfast Book* is not just an accommodation guide – it is an introduction to a uniquely New Zealand holiday experience.

The best holidays are often remembered by the friends one makes. How many of us have loved a country because of one or two memorable individuals we encountered? For the traveller who wants to experience the real New Zealand and get to know its people, bed and breakfast offers an opportunity to do just that.

We recommend you don't try to travel too far in one day. Take time to enjoy the company of your hosts and other local people. You will find New Zealand hosts friendly and generous, and eager to share their local knowledge with you.

All properties inspected

B&B Approved - All B&Bs in The Bed & Breakfast Book have been inspected on joining. They conform to the Schedule of Standards on page 508. As important as the requirement of meeting a physical standard, we expect that all of our properties will offer excellent hospitality. Some hosts who are members of associations or marketing groups, which also undertake inspections, have chosen to display the logos below.

The **@home NEW ZEALAND** logo represents the largest organisation of hosted accommodation providers in New Zealand. It assures you of a warm welcome from friendly, helpful hosts. Accommodations displaying this logo are regularly assessed every two years and have met the quality standards set by the Association.

Qualmark - Qualmark™ is New Zealand tourism's official mark of quality. All Qualmark™ licenced accommodation listed in this directory means they have been independently assessed as professional and trustworthy, so you can book and buy with confidence. They will meet your essential requirements of cleanliness, safety, security and comfort; and offer a range and quality of services appropriate to their star grade.

Heritage Inns - A collection of luxury historic hosted character bed and breakfast lodges across NZ, are superior and often recommended by tourists. Our B&Bs have knowledgeable and friendly hosts. Our luxury accommodation ranges from the quiet honeymoon lodge in boutique romantic locations to central city accommodation - rivaling superior apartments, hotels or motels. Alternatively, enjoy the genuine NZ experience of an idyllic farmstay, lodge or luxury country B&B.

Superior Inns - Superior Inns of New Zealand properties are specially selected. All offer a true bed and breakfast experience, highlights of your visit to New Zealand. The specially selected bed and breakfast properties offer spacious bedrooms with bathrooms, luxury fittings, private guest lounges, fabulous delectable breakfasts and a chance to meet other visitors or be on your own. Our hosts can organise airport pickups, rental cars, restaurant bookings, honeymoon packages and short stay options.

Finding your way around - using *The Bed & Breakfast Book*

We travel from north to south listing the towns as we come to them. In addition, we've divided New Zealand into geographical regions, a map of which is included at the start of each chapter. In some regions, such as Southland, our listings take a detour off the north-to-south route, and follow their nose - it will soon become obvious.

Happy Travelling

The B&B Book Team

Your Comments

We welcome your views on *The Bed & Breakfast Book* and the hosts you meet.

Please visit our website www.bnb.co.nz or write to us at:

PO Box 6843, Wellington, New Zealand.

Comment Forms

Please help us to maintain our high standards by sending us comments about where you stayed. Guest Comments forms are available from your hosts.

*   You may submit your comment on our website www.bnb.co.nz
*   Or your hosts will give you a comment form.
*   Or simply cut one from the back of the book.
*   Each comment returned will be in our ongoing monthly draw for a free night's B&B.
*   Each person staying can submit a comment for an increased chance of success.
*   Guest comments are displayed on the hosts' pages at: www.bnb.co.nz

The Perfect Guest

Our hosts try to be the perfect hosts, to make your stay with them memorable.

Here's how you can help them do this -

Advise them of your time of arrival as accurately as you can. If you're held up, phone to give them a new arrival time. The reason is that your hosts have to be at home when you arrive. That means planning their day around you, because unlike a motel or hotel, they don't have staff. And of course they don't want to be cooking or eating dinner when you arrive, because they want to give all their attention to welcoming you and settling you in. So please make it easy for them by arriving when they expect you or letting them know if you can't.

Hansel & Gretels B&B, Cambridge

ABOUT BED & BREAKFAST

Our B&Bs range from homely to luxurious, but you can always be assured of generous hospitality.

Types of accommodation

Traditional B&B
Generally small owner-occupied home accommodation usually with private guest living and dining areas.

Homestay
A homestay is a B&B where you share the family's living area.

Farmstay
Country accommodation, usually on a working farm.

Self-contained
Separate self-contained accommodation, with kitchen and living/dining room. Breakfast provisions usually provided at least for the first night.

Separate/suite
Similar to self-contained but without kitchen facilities. Living/dining facilities may be limited.

Bathrooms

Ensuite and private bathrooms are for your use exclusively.
Guests share bathroom means you will be sharing with other guests.
Family share means you will be sharing with the family.

Tariff

The prices listed are in New Zealand dollars and include GST. Prices listed are subject to change, and any change to listed prices will be stated at time of booking. Some hosts offer a discount for children - this applies to age 12 or under unless otherwise stated. Most of our B&Bs will accept credit cards.

Reservations

We recommend you contact your hosts well in advance to be sure of confirming your accommodation. Most hosts require a deposit so make sure you understand their cancellation policy. Please let your hosts know if you have to cancel, they will have spent time preparing for you. You may also book accommodation through some travel agents or via specialised B&B reservation services.

Breakfast & Dinner

Breakfast is included in the tariff, with each host offering their own menu. You'll be surprised at the range of delicious breakfasts available, many using local produce. If you would like dinner most hosts require 24 hours notice.

Smoking

Most of our B&Bs are non-smoking, but smoking is permitted outside. Listings displaying the no smoking logo do not permit smoking anywhere on the property. B&Bs which have a smoking area inside mention this in their text.

Accessibility

  Certified as being wheelchair accessible

  Can accommodate guests in wheelchairs, but not certified.

The difference between a hotel and a B&B...
is that you don't hug the hotel staff when you leave.

NEW ZEALAND – REGIONS
Main cities in black

Northland

Whangarei

Auckland

Coromandel

Bay of Plenty

Tauranga

Waikato, King Country

Hamilton

Rotorua

Gisborne

Taranaki, Wanganui,
Ruapehu, Rangitikei

Gisborne

New Plymouth

Napier

Manawatu, Horowhenua

Hawkes Bay

Nelson, Golden Bay

Palmerston North

Wairarapa

Nelson

Masterton

Blenheim

Wellington

West Coast

Greymouth

Marlborough

Canterbury

Christchurch

South Canterbury,
North Otago

Timaru

Queenstown

Chatham Islands

Dunedin

Otago, North Catlins

Invercargill

Southland,
South Catlins

Stewart Island

CONTENTS

Northland

Houhora
Cape Karikari
Coopers Beach
10
Mahinepua
Kaitaia
Kaeo
Ahipara
Kerikeri
Okaihau
Paihia
Russell
Kohukohu
Opua
Rawene
Pakaraka
Opononi
12
Oakura Bay
Omapere
12
Whangarei
Onerahi
Parua Bay
14
Whangarei Heads
Dargaville
Ruakaka
Waipu
Waipu Cove
Paparoa
Langs Beach
Matakohe
Maungaturoto

Te Hana
Wellsford
Warkworth
Sandspit
Snells Bea
Puhoi
Orewa
Kaukapakapa
Whangapa
Helensville
Silverdale
Albany
Auckland

Towns listed generally follow
a north to south route. Refer
to the index if required.

0   Kilometres   45
0   Miles   27

HOUHORA   *44km N of Kaitaia*

Houhora Lodge & Homestay   *Homestay*
Jacqui & Bruce Malcolm
3994 Far North Road, Houhora, RD 4, Kaitaia

Tel (09) 409 7884   Fax (09) 409 7884
Mob 021 926 992   houhora.homestay@xtra.co.nz
www.topstay.co.nz

Double $125-$155   Single $90-$100   (Full Breakfast)
Dinner $35 by arrangement   Credit cards accepted
Children welcome
3 King/Twin 3 Single (3 bdrm)
Bathrooms: 2 Ensuite 1 Private

We have fled our largest city to live on the shores of Houhora Harbour, and look forward to sharing this special part of New Zealand with you. Come and enjoy remote coastal walks, shell-collecting, Cape Reinga, Ninety Mile Beach and other attractions. We can arrange 4x4 trips, sport or game fishing and provide relaxed and quality accommodation on your return. Home-made bread, home-grown fruit, home-pressed olive oil, vegetables and eggs. Fresh or smoked fish a speciality. Email, internet, fax and laundry facilities available.

CAPE KARIKARI - WHATUWHIWHI   *30min SE of Kaitaia*

Riviera Lodge   *B&B & 3 Bedroom Holiday Home*
Janine & Rex Honeyfield
69 Whatuwhiwhi Road, RD 3, Cape Karikari, Kaitaia

Tel (09) 406 7596   Fax (09) 406 7581   Mob 027 277 2510
riviera.lodge@xtra.co.nz
www.bnb.co.nz/rivieralodge.html

Double $120-$200   Single $100-$160
(Continental Breakfast)   Child over 12 years $40
High rate 20 Dec to 31 Jan incl public holidays
Credit cards accepted   Children welcome
1 Queen (bdrm) 1 Dble/Twin (In Lounge)   Bathrooms: 1 Private

Opening in October 2004. Riviera Lodge a new B&B nestled on the edge of Doubtless Bay set alongside native bush, 15 minutes off Highway 10 Whatuwhiwhi, Cape Karikari. Recreational activities: rock fishing, diving, swimming, also fishing trips by arrangement. Handy to Matai Bay, Rangiputa and Tokerau beach, where you can take a walk. Just minutes from Carrington Club which has a 18 hole golf course, winery and restaurant. Whatuwhiwhi has a service station and dairy. Janine, Rex, our dog Duke and cat Brandy welcome you to the winterless north.

AHIPARA - NINETY MILE BEACH   *16km W of Kaitaia*

Siesta Lodge   *B&B Self-contained Guesthouse*
Carole & Alan Harding
PO Box 30, Ahipara, Northland

Tel (09) 409 2011   Fax (09) 409 2011   Mob 021 965 085
ninetymile@xtra.co.nz
www.ahipara.co.nz/siesta

Double $150-$190   (Continental Breakfast)
Dinner by arrangement   2 apartments $150-$250
Credit cards accepted
1 King 3 Queen 1 Twin (5 bdrm)
Bathrooms: 3 Ensuite 1 Guests share

The Siesta is a Mediterranean style house set in private grounds with panoramic views overlooking the sheltered Ahipara Bay, sand-dune wilderness and the magnificent Ninety Mile Beach. Each room has private balcony, queen-size bed and ensuites. Sleep to the sound of the sea with sea views from your bed, enjoy spectacular sunsets from your balcony. The adjacent Ocean Vista apartments have two luxury self-contained, spacious apartments with spectacular views, and are an ideal base for longer stays. We have a very friendly cat and dog. Phone for directions.

KAITAIA - PAMAPURIA *10 kms S of Kaitaia*

Plane Tree Lodge *B&B Homestay Self-contained*
Rosemary & Mike Wright
Pamapuria, RD 2, Kaitaia, Northland

Tel (09) 408 0995 Fax (09) 408 0995 Mob 025 338 859
reservationsplanetreelodge@xtra.co.nz
www.plane-tree-lodge.net.nz

Double $130-$160 Single $100-$125
(Special Breakfast) Child neg
Self-contained cottage sleeps 4 $180-$220
Credit cards accepted Children welcome
3 Queen 1 Twin 1 Single (5 bdrm)
Bathrooms: 3 Ensuite 1 Private

At Plane Tree Lodge you can experience the best of both worlds - the peace and tranquility of a rural retreat, only a short drive to Ninety Mile Beach. We offer park-like gardens, bordered by paddocks & a river, with our own fresh-water swimming hole. Breakfasts are an event, with home made conserves, muesli, yoghurt & garden produce, plus a cooked course to boast about (try our Plane Tree Lodge Special). Visit us for an unforgetable experience, & become part of the family, without having to wash the dishes!

COOPERS BEACH *3km N of Mangonui*

Mac'n'Mo's *B&B Separate/Suite*
Maureen & Malcolm MacMillan
PO Box 177, Mangonui

Tel (09) 406 0538 Fax (09) 406 0538
MacNMo@xtra.co.nz
www.bnb.co.nz/macnmos.html

Double $80-$90 Single $50-$60
(Continental Breakfast)
Dinner $25 by arrangement
1 Queen 1 Double 1 Twin (3 bdrm)
Bathrooms: 2 Ensuite 1 Private

Enjoy a "million dollar" view of Doubtless Bay while you enjoy Mac's smoked fish on your toast. The bus to Cape Reinga stops at our gate, you may go on a craft or wine trail, swim with dolphins, go fishing, diving or just relax on our unpolluted uncrowded beaches, there's one across the road. There are several fine restaurants and the "world famous" fish and chip shop nearby. Have a memorable stay with Mac'n'Mo, they will take good care of you.

COOPERS BEACH *2km N of Mangonui*

Bella Vista Swiss Inn Guesthouse *B&B Homestay*
Rudi Heinzelmann
47 Spicer Road, Coopers Beach, Mangonui 0557

Tel (09) 406 2035 Fax (09) 406 2035
Mob 021 154 9813 Heinz.Rud@xtra.co.nz
www.bnb.co.nz/heinzelmann.html

Double $65-$140 Single $50
(Full Breakfast) Dinner $20-$35
Sleep-out / tent site $20pp
1 King 2 Queen 1 Twin 1 Single (5 bdrm)
Bathrooms: 2 Ensuite 1 Private

The Bella Vista guesthouse is located on the hilltop of Coopers Beach. We are first to see the sun! Our commanding views take your eyes over the whole Doubtless Bay area, it's totally relaxing. Visitors are most welcome to share all this beauty with us. A range of sports and leisure activities are waiting for you and we can arrange this for you. Stroll the beach and watch the sunset, dine out with your best friend. Enjoy your stay at Bella Vista. We'll take care of you.

COOPERS BEACH *31km NE of Kaitaia*

Doubtless Bay Lodge *B&B*
33 Cable Bay Road,
Coopers Beach, Mangonui

Tel (09) 406 1661 Fax (09) 406 1662
Mob 021 824 571
enquiries@doubtlessbaylodge.co.nz
www.bnb.co.nz/doubtless.html

Double $98 Single $73 (Full Breakfast) Child $20
Credit cards accepted Children welcome
3 Queen 1 Twin (4 bdrm)
Bathrooms: 4 Ensuite

A mini motel type B&B with a personal touch, situated 800 metres north of Coopers Beach Shops and an hour north of Paihia. Each room has an ensuite bathroom, Sky TV, fridge, tea and coffee making facilities. There is a guest laundry and barbeque. Scenic bus tours to Cape Reinga, fishing trips and dolphin watching can be arranged. Visit the many historic places and isolated beaches in the area. Relax and enjoy the expansive sea and rural views from the breakfast room and balcony.

MAHINEPUA - KAEO *22km E of Kaeo*

Waiwurrie *Homestay Cottage on the beach*
Vickie & Rodger Corbin
Mahinepua, RD 1, Kaeo/ Whangaroa, Northland

Tel (09) 405 0840 Fax (09) 405 0854
Mob 021 186 7900 wai.wurrie@xtra.co.nz
www.coastalfarm-lodge.co.nz

Double $175-$200 Single $150 (Full Breakfast)
Dinner $40pp Credit cards accepted
1 King 1 Queen (2 bdrm)
Bathrooms: 1 Ensuite 1 Private

Want something a little special? Have we the place for you! A bit more expensive but worth it. Situated on Northland's east coast surrounded by forestry and private farmland magnificent views, Cavalli Islands and deep sea fishing grounds. Golfers paradise, Kauri Cliffs, Waitangi, sightsee to Cape Reinga, visit the Bay of Islands, Kerikeri, Whangaroa Habour or just relax. We have Benson the dog and Moppet the cat. We love to entertain and would enjoy meeting you. Good Kiwi hospitality! For more information please phone us.

KERIKERI *3km E of Kerikeri*

Matariki Orchard *B&B Homestay*
Alison & David Bridgman
14 Pa Road, Kerikeri, Bay of Islands

Tel (09) 407 7577 Fax (09) 407 7593
Mob 027 408 0621 matarikihomestay@xtra.co.nz
www.kerikeri.co.nz/matariki

Double $120-$140 Single $70 (Full Breakfast)
Child neg Dinner $40pp Credit cards accepted
Children welcome
1 King 1 Queen 2 Single (3 bdrm)
Bathrooms: 1 Ensuite 1 Private

We welcome guests to our home, large garden,
swimming pool and subtropical orchard, within walking distance to historic area. 4 minutes by car to township. David has a vintage car that is used for personalised tours. A short complimentary tour of historic areas is offered to guests. We are retired farmers and David a local tour operator for 9 years loves to help with 'where to go and what to do'. Can arrange tour bookings. We enjoy providing dinner with NZ wine. No pets or children. Phone for directions .

KERIKERI - OKAIHAU *12km W of Kerikeri*

Clotworthy Farmstay *B&B Farmstay*
Shennett & Neville Clotworthy
Wiroa Road, RD 1, Okaihau, Bay of Islands

Tel (09) 401 9371 Fax (09) 401 9371
www.bnb.co.nz/clotworthyfarmstay.html

Double $80 Single $40 (Full Breakfast)
Dinner $25 by arrangement Credit cards accepted
1 Queen 2 Single (2 bdrm)
Bathrooms: 1 Guests share

We farm cattle, sheep, and horses on our 310 acres. There are panoramic views of the Bay of Islands area from our home 1,000 foot above sea level. Of 1840's pioneering descent, our interests are travel, farming, genealogy and equestrian activities. We have an extensive library on Northland history and families. Directions: SH10 take Wiroa/Airport Road at the Kerikeri intersection, 9km on the right. Or SH1, take Kerikeri Road just south of Okaihau. We are fourth house on the left, past the golf course (8km).

KERIKERI *8km S of Kerikeri*

Puriri Park *B&B Self-contained Orchardstay*
Charmian & Paul Treadwell
Puriri Park Orchard, State Highway 10,
Box 572, Kerikeri

Tel (09) 407 9818 Fax (09) 407 9498
Mob 027 471 4932 puriri@xtra.co.nz
www.bnb.co.nz/puriripark.html

Double $95 Single $75 (Full Breakfast)
Child $10 Dinner $30 Children welcome
1 Queen 2 Double 2 Twin 1 Single (4 bdrm)
Bathrooms: 2 Private 1 Guests share

Puriri Park has long been known for its hospitality in the Far North. Guests are welcome to wander around our large garden, explore the orange and kiwifruit orchards, sit by the lilypond or feed our flock of fantail pigeons. We have 5 acres of bird-filled native bush, mostly totara and puriri. We are in an excellent situation for trips to Cape Reinga and sailing or cruising on the beautiful Bay of Islands. We can arrange tours for you or pick you up from the airport.

KERIKERI *10km Kerikeri Central*

Kerikeri Inlet View *B&B Farmstay Homestay*
Trish & Ryan Daniells
99C Furness Road, RD 3, Kerikeri

Tel (09) 407 7477 Fax (09) 407 7478
Mob 025 612 0021 kerikeri_inlet_view@hotmail.com
www.bnb.co.nz/kerikeriinletview.html

Double $70 Single $45 (Full Breakfast)
Child $15 Dinner $18 by arrangement
Backpackers (no water view) $15, no breakfast
Credit cards accepted Children welcome
1 Queen 2 Double 2 Single (3 bdrm)
Bathrooms: 1 Ensuite 1 Private 1 Guests share

We welcome you to our spacious home on top of our 1100 acre beef and sheep farm. Enjoy the superb views of the Kerikeri Inlet and the Bay of Islands while you relax in our spa pool. Join us for breakfast consisting of seasonal fruit, home-made bread and butter, free-range chook eggs, our own sausages, before exploring the many attractions around Kerikeri. Backpackers has private lockable bedrooms, lounge, kitchen/laundry. Note: please phone first for bookings, detailed directions or pick up. We can speak Japanese.

KERIKERI
7km N of Kerikeri

Sunrise Homestay B&B   *B&B Homestay*
Judy & Les Remnant
140 Skudders Road, Skudders Beach,
RD 1, Kerikeri

Tel (09) 407 5447   Fax (09) 407 8448
Mob 021 774 941   sunrisehomestay@xtra.co.nz
www.bnb.co.nz/sunrisehomestaybb.html

Double $90   Single $60   (Full Breakfast)
Dinner $30pp by arrangement   Credit cards accepted
1 Double 4 Single (3 bdrm)
Bathrooms: 1 Ensuite 1 Guests share

A warm welcome awaits you at our restful homestay ovelooking Kerikeri inlet, magnificent water views
and often spectacular sunrises and sunsets. Occasional visits from dolphins. Plenty to see and do in
Bay of Islands. We are only too happy to help arrange your trips. Tea and coffee available at all times.
Laundry facilities available. Courtesy pick up from bus or airport. Phone, fax or leave phone number
on answer phone, we will call you back. One of the best locations in Kerikeri. Do come and share it
with us. Non-smokers. We have no pets.

KERIKERI
2.6km N of Kerikeri

Glenfalloch   *B&B Homestay*
Evalyn & Rick Pitelen
48 Landing Road, Kerikeri

Tel (09) 407 5471   Fax (09) 407 5473
Mob 025 280 0661   glenfall@ihug.co.nz
www.bnb.co.nz/glenfalloch.html

Double $80-$95 Single $65   (Full Breakfast)
Child $25   Dinner $30pp by arrangement
Credit cards accepted   Children welcome
1 King 1 Queen 1 Double 1 Single (3 bdrm)
Bathrooms: 2 Ensuite 1 Private

Venture down Glenfalloch's tree lined driveway to a peaceful garden paradise. Evalyn and Rick
welcome guests with refreshments to be enjoyed in the lounges or outdoors on the decks. You are
welcome to wander about the garden, use the swimming pool and tennis court, or just relax in our
private retreat. Breakfast can be enjoyed at your leisure outdoors, weather permitting. Laundry
facilities available. Directions: travel 0.6km from the Stone Store to second driveway on left after
Department of Conservation sign.

KERIKERI
12km E of Kerikeri

Oversley   *Homestay Coastal*
Maire & Tone Coyte
Doves Bay Road, RD 1, Kerikeri

Tel (09) 407 8744   Fax (09) 407 4487
Mob 025 959 207   oversley@xtra.co.nz
www.bnb.co.nz/oversley.html

Double $120-$160   Single $90-$130   (Full Breakfast)
Dinner by arrangement   Credit cards accepted
1 King/Twin 1 Queen 2 Single (3 bdrm)
Bathrooms: 2 Ensuite 1 Private

Oversley offers magnificent panoramic water views, sweeping lawns and private native bush walks to
the water. Our spacious, comfortable home, set in 18 acres, has a friendly relaxed atmosphere with
quality accommodation. Laundry facilities available. We are an easy going, well travelled, retired
couple, enjoy all sports, sailing and fishing on our 13 metre yacht, golfing on Kerikeri's first class course
15 minutes away (Kauri Cliffs course only 35 minutes) and are animal lovers. Your company at dinner,
to share good food and wine with us, is most welcome.

KERIKERI *2km S of Kerikeri*

Gannaway House *B&B Homestay*
Jill & Roger Gardner
Kerikeri Road, RD 3, Kerikeri

Tel (09) 407 1432 Fax (09) 407 1431
Mob 025 798 115 gannaway@xtra.co.nz
www.bnb.co.nz/gannawayhouse.html

Double $85-$115 Single $55-$85 (Full Breakfast)
Child $30 Dinner $35 by arrangement
Credit cards accepted
2 Queen 1 Twin (3 bdrm)
Bathrooms: 1 Ensuite 1 Guests share

Jill and Roger welcome you to Gannaway House. Our comfortable home, set in 2 acres of garden and orchard is situated down a tree-lined driveway, close to town but in the quiet of the country. We offer one large ground floor room with ensuite and private entrance. Upstairs, 2 rooms (1 queen and 1 twin) with shared facilities. Enjoy our beautiful tranquil garden - also the sheep and lambs in the orchard. We are also breeders of very sociable burmese cats. Directions: From SH10 - first driveway on left past Makana Chocolate Factory.

KERIKERI

Pukanui Lodge B&B *Homestay*
Dale Simkin & Dale Hutchinson
322 Kerikeri Road, Kerikeri

Tel (09) 407 7003 Fax (09) 407 7068
Mob 027 444 4955 accom@pukanui.co.nz
www.bnb.co.nz/pukanui2.html

Double $120-$160 Single $70-$90
(Full Breakfast) Dinner $40 Credit cards accepted
2 Queen 2 Twin (3 bdrm)
Bathrooms: 3 Ensuite

Tranquility 400 metres from Kerikeri township.
Subtropical gardens and citrus orchard have influenced both decor and cuisine of Pukanui. Generous breakfast can be served on private decks off your ensuite bedroom in garden setting or overlooking pool in summer. Cosy lounge in winter. Local produce features significantly in our culinary delights with dinner by prior arrangement. Friendly hosts will help plan your visit to make it memorable. Fax and email facilities available. Complimentary airport/bus transfers.

KERIKERI CENTRAL *800m N of kerikeri*

Peacock Gardens Bed & Breakfast
B&B Separate/Suite Self-contained
Sally & Ken Climo
1 Peacock Gardens Drive, Kerikeri, Bay of Islands

Tel (09) 407 5070 Fax (09) 407 5070
Mob 027 4311 312 ksclimo@paradise.net.nz
www.bnb.co.nz/peacockgardens.html

Double $90 Single $70 (Continental Breakfast)
Credit cards accepted
1 Queen (1 bdrm)
Bathrooms: 1 Ensuite

800 metres from Kerikeri township offering a tranquil location with rural views. Enjoy a short walk to quality cafés and restaurants, a variety of shops, historical Stone Store and Maori Pa. 20 minutes to Paihia/Waitangi, fishing, golf, beaches, tourist attractions. Amenities include off-street parking, own entrance, TV, microwave, fridge, tea/coffee making facilities, private ensuite, iron, hairdryer. View the sunset from the decks or relax in the spa pool. Continental breakfast provisions supplied daily to enjoy at your leisure. Winter rates apply.

PAKARAKA

15km from Pahia/ Kerikeri/Kaikohe

B&B
Approved

Jarvis Family Farmstay & Equestrian Centre
B&B Farmstay Separate/Suite private bathrooms / spa bath room
Frederika & Douglas Jarvis
State Highway 1, Pakaraka, RD 2 Ohaeawai, Bay of Islands

Tel (09) 405 9606 Fax (09) 405 9607 Mob 021 259 1120
baystay@igrin.co.nz www.nzbaystay.com

Double $100-$120 Single $60 (Special Breakfast)
Child half price Dinner $30 by arrangement
Credit cards accepted Children welcome
Pets welcome Smoking area inside

1 Queen 1 Double 1 Twin (2 bdrm) Bathrooms: 3 Private

Beautiful subtropical gardens with water features surround our
spacious family home where you can choose between indoor and
outdoor living.

Our four-poster suite includes its own lounge with two single
beds, TV/video plus a private deck in the 'wishing well' garden.
Fredi and Douglas emigrated from the UK in 1990, where they
ran one of England's top country inns: so they are no strangers
to hospitality. We have 30 acres for you to enjoy with extensive
equestrian facilities and walks. Just bring a smile with you.

Here are some quotes from our visitors book: *"Wow! What
a fabulous time. Fredi's musical talent, a sing-a-long on the
porch. The food, the dogs & horses, wanted to take everyone
home."* USA. *"Lovely stay, perfect surroundings for our
honeymoon."* UK. *"Thank you for sharing your little bit of
heaven."* USA

Pakaraka is centrally based for touring the bay, west and
north coasts with all the popular tourist, dolphin and marine
discoveries. We are a pet friendly country stay.

For a charming and relaxing break, look no further!

PAKARAKA - PAIHIA *10km N of Kawakawa*

Approved

Bay of Islands Farmstay - B&B Highland Farm
B&B Farmstay
Glenis & Ken Mackintosh
Pakaraka, 6627 State Highway 1, RD 2, Kaikohe 0400

Tel (09) 404 0430 Fax (09) 404 0430
Mob 027 249 8296 Ken@infobiz.co.nz
www.bnb.co.nz/bayofislandfarmstaybb.html

Double $90 Single $60 (Full Breakfast) Child $10
Dinner $20-$30 (byo & comp) Twin room $90
Credit cards accepted Children welcome
1 Double 1 Twin 3 Single (2 bdrm) Bathrooms: 2 Ensuite

Beautiful 51 acres, stone walls, barberry hedges. Sheep, cattle. Ken a sheep-dog trialist, trains dogs and pups daily! Enjoy watching, help shift animals. Meet and photograph with animals on your farm walk. Enjoy your visit. Swimming pool or cosy warm home in winter. Access to internet. Good central base! 5 golf courses, beaches, hot pools, shopping! Situated 15 minutes from Paihia, Kerikeri, Kaikohe. Welcome to Bay of Islands. Book early or take pot luck! (10 minutes north of Kawakawa, 2 south of Pakaraka Junction). "Highland Farm" on entrance.

PAIHIA *4km N of Paihia*

Approved

Lakeview Homestay *Homestay*
Heather and Maurice Pickup
12 The Anchorage, Watea RD 1, Paihia

Tel (09) 402 8152 Fax (09) 402 8152
Mob 025 260 7058
Lakeviewwatea@xtra.co.nz
www.bnb.co.nz/lakeview.html

Double $120 Single $90 (Full Breakfast)
Dinner $35 Credit cards accepted
1 Queen (1 bdrm)
Bathrooms: 1 Private

Our modern wooden home is set in quiet countryside. A small lake at the bottom of the garden which is home to many native birds and black swans. We are of English/NZ origins, but have American connections too. The guest bedroom has a view of the lake. We are close to Haruru Falls, Waitangi, beaches, walks, golf and historic places. Breakfasts feature homemade breads and preserves and more. We can book tours and cruises. Complimentary refreshments on arrival. We have 2 dogs and 1 cat.

PAIHIA *7km N of Paihia*

Approved

Lily Pond Estate B&B (Est 1989) *Countrystay*
Allwyn & Graeme Sutherland

725 Puketona Road, RD 1, Paihia,
Lily Pond Estate sign at gate

Tel (09) 402 7041
www.bnb.co.nz/lilypondorchardbb.html

Double $85-$105 Single $50
(Full Breakfast)
1 Double 1 Twin 1 Single (3 bdrm)
Bathrooms: 1 Private 1 Guests share

Drive in through an avenue of mature liquid amber trees to our comfortable timber home on our 5 acre country estate growing citrus and pip fruit. The guest wing has views of the fountain, bird aviary, small lake and black swan with the double and twin rooms having private verandah access. Fresh orange juice, fruit and home-made jams are served at breakfast. We are born New Zealanders, sailed thousands of miles living aboard our 50 foot yacht in the Pacific and will gladly share our Bay of Island knowledge to make your visit most memorable.

PAIHIA *1.5km S of Paihia*

home NEW ZEALAND

Te Haumi House *B&B Homestay*
Enid & Ernie Walker
12 Seaview Road, Paihia

Tel (09) 402 8046 Fax (09) 402 8046
enidanderniewalker@xtra.co.nz
www.bnb.co.nz/tehaumihouse.html

Double $80-$90 Single $60 (Continental Breakfast)
Credit cards accepted
2 Queen 1 Single (2 bdrm)
Bathrooms: 2 Guests share 1 Host share

Millennium Sunrise. Welcome to our modern waterfront home, set amongst subtropical gardens with expansive harbour views, just minutes from tourist activities and town centre. Guests enjoy privacy through a clever split-level design. Buffet breakfast with a choice of dining room, garden deck or courtyard. Laundry facilities, ample off-street parking and courtesy pickup from bus available. Descendants of early settlers, we have a good knowledge of local history. Ernie is a Masonic Lodge member.

PAIHIA *Paihia Central*

home NEW ZEALAND

Castle Spas *Separate/Suite Self-contained*
Jo & Peter Nisbet
Unit 2, Treetops, Paihia, Bay of Islands, 0252

Tel (09) 402 8516 Fax (09) 402 8555
Mob 025 969 281 enquiry@castlespas.co.nz
www.castlespas.co.nz

Double $120-$150 Single $120-$150
Breakfast provisions available $21
Agency bookings, extra 5% Credit cards accepted
2 Queen 1 Double 2 Single¯ (3 bdrm)
Bathrooms: 3 Ensuite

'Castle Spas', formerly 'Cedar Suite Spas', offers first class accommodation, with beautiful sea views from our self-catering character cottage, and majestic bush at The Keep, our new garden apartment. Very close to central Paihia and minutes to bay trips, beaches, shops and cafés, both suites have kitchens, private spa pools and superior ensuite bathrooms. 'Seaview Cottage' for romance of the past, or 'The Keep', (opening September 2004), for up to the minute design. The choice is yours. Recommended Lonely Planet and English Rough Guide.

PAIHIA *Paihia Central*

Approved

Craicor Accommodation *Self-contained*
Garth Craig & Anne Corbett
PO Box 15, 49 Kings Road, Paihia, Bay of Islands

Tel (09) 402 7882 Fax (09) 402 7883
craicor@actrix.gen.nz
www.craicor-accom.co.nz

Double $130 Single $95
(Continental breakfast optional $7.50 each)
Credit cards accepted
2 King 2 Single (2 bdrm)
Bathrooms: 2 Ensuite

The perfect spot for those seeking a quiet, sunny and central location. Discover the Garden Suite and Tree House. Self-contained modern units nestled in a garden setting with trees that almost hug you, native birds and sea views. Each unit has ensuite bathroom, fully equipped kitchen for self-catering, super king bed, TV, insect screens and is tastefully decorated to reflect the natural colours of the surroundings. Safe off-street parking, all within a 5 minute stroll to the waterfront, restaurants and town centre.

PAIHIA   *1km N of Paihia*

Bay of Islands Bed & Breakfast   *B&B Homestay*
Laraine & Sid Dyer
48 Tahuna Road, Paihia, Bay of Islands

Tel (09) 402 8551   Fax (09) 402 8551
bayofislandsbnb@slingshot.co.nz
www.bnb.co.nz/bayofislandsbedbreakfast.html

Double $80   Single $40
(Continental Breakfast)
1 Queen 1 Double 1 Single (3 bdrm)
Bathrooms: 1 Host share

We invite you to stay and relax in our home, only minutes from the beach, with bush walks and golf course nearby. On arrival a warm welcome awaits you, with tea or coffee and a chance to unwind. Assistance with your itinerary is offered should you need help. We look forward to the pleasure of your company and ensuring your stay is as comfortable and memorable as possible. Our courtesy car will meet you if travelling by bus. We have a dog named Katie.

PAIHIA   *Paihia Central*

Marlin House   *B&B Separate/Suite Self-contained*
Christopher & Angela Houry
15 Bayview Road, Paihia, Bay of Islands New Zealand

Tel (09) 402 8550   Fax (09) 402 6770
Mob 021 487 937   marlinhouse@xtra.co.nz
www.bnb.co.nz/marlinhouse.html

Double $150   Single $110   (Special Breakfast)
Child neg   Credit cards accepted
1 King/Twin 1 King 2 Queen (3 bdrm)
Bathrooms: 3 Ensuite

Marlin House is a large comfortable colonial-style house with spacious luxury accommodation in three self-contained ensuites with fridge, microwave and TV. All with separate entrances onto decks with seating overlooking the bay. Ample off-road parking is available. Situated in a quiet tree-clad spot above Paihia with beautiful sea views and only 4 minutes easy walk to the beach, shops and restaurants. Special breakfasts with home baking. Benny the cat is outside.(minimum 2 night stay)

PAIHIA   *0.5km NW of Paihia*

Windermere
B&B Separate/Suite Self-contained Private entrance
Richard & Jill Burrows
168 Marsden Road, Paihia, Bay of Islands

Tel (09) 402 8696   Fax (09) 402 5095
Mob 021 115 7436   windermere@igrin.co.nz
www.windermere.co.nz

Double $100-$175   Single $80-$150
(Continental Breakfast) Child $25   C/C accepted
2 Queen 2 Single (2 bdrm)
Bathrooms: 2 Ensuite

Windermere is a large modern family home set in a bush setting and yet located right on one of the best beaches in the Bay of Islands. Superior accommodation is provided with suites having their own ensuite and kitchen facilities. For longer stays one suite has its own laundry, dryer and fully equipped kitchen. The other suite has microwave and fridge only. Each suite has its own decks where you can sit and enjoy the view enhanced by spectacular sunsets. Sky TV. Jill and Richard would welcome your company to enjoy our own little part of paradise.

PAIHIA *6km W of Paihia*

Appledore Lodge   *B&B Homestay Separate/Suite*
Self Contained Riverside Cottage & Riverside Studio
Janet & Jim Pugh
Puketona Road, Paihia, Bay of Islands

Tel (09) 402 8007   Fax (09) 402 8007
Mob 021 179 5839   appledorelodge@xtra.co.nz
www.appledorelodge.co.nz

Double $100-$150 Single $100-$120   (Full Breakfast)
Self-contained cottage and studio $130-$225
Credit cards accepted
1 King/Twin 1 King 1 Queen 1 Double (4 bdrm) Bathrooms: 4 Ensuite

 Miniature waterfalls and rapids await your discovery as the Waitangi River gently tumbles by your bedroom window just 25 meters away. House guests in the Riverside Suite & Victoria Room with romantic 4 poster are served a special home made breakfast on our antique Kauri table or grand deck. Self-contained superior Riverside Cottage, sleep 4 adults. Take delight in a 'breakfast basket'. We enjoy classic cars, golf, travel and meeting new guests, Janet, Jim and our golden retriever look forward to making your stay truly memorable.

PAIHIA   *3km Paihia*

Fallsview *B&B Homestay*
Shirley & Clive Welch
4 Fallsview Road, RD 1, Haruru, Paihia

Tel (09) 402 7871   Fax (09) 402 7861
Mob 025 627 1652
www.bnb.co.nz/fallsview.html

Double $80-$100 Single $60   (Full Breakfast)
Child neg   Credit cards accepted
Children welcome
1 Queen 1 Twin 1 Single (3 bdrm)
Bathrooms: 1 Guests share

Our studio apartment has all the comforts of home, a beautiful sunny lounge with fridge, microwave, stereo, TV, tea/coffee facilities, laundry, barbecue and undercover parking. All surrounded by a sub-tropical garden. With breakfast upstairs you will enjoy the beautiful panoramic view of the surrounding countryside. Extra twin beds are available upstairs if in a group. We share our home with a small gregarious poodle and 3 reclusive cats. Situated only 3km from main tourist attractions. We offer you a warm welcome.

PAIHIA   *6km W of Paihia*

Blue Heron Country Lodge   *B&B Homestay*
Beverly and George Barke
621B Puketona Road,
RD 1 Paihia, Bay of Islands

Tel (09) 402 8195   Fax (09) 402 8194
george.barke@xtra.co.nz
www.bnb.co.nz/blueheron.html

Double $100-$120 Single $60-$90
(Continental Breakfast) Credit cards accepted
1 Queen 1 Twin (2 bdrm)
Bathrooms: 1 Ensuite 1 Guests share

Our home is set in a large garden on 15 acres of peaceful, rural land. We invite you to join with us and experience unequalled comfort, peace and tranquillity, delicious breakfasts on the patio, fascinating bird life, picturesque rural views, totally relaxed privacy and revitalising country living. Historic sights, fabulous beaches, dolphins, a fantastic golf course, interesting walks and a wide choice of restaurants are just minutes away. We offer a warm welcome with complimentary refreshments on arrival.

PAIHIA   *Paihia-Central*

Allegra House   *B&B Self-contained*
Heinz & Brita Marti
39 Bayview Road, Paihia, Bay of Islands

Tel (09) 402 7932   Fax (09) 402 7930
allegrahouse@xtra.co.nz
www.allegra.co.nz

Double $120-$170   Single $120-$170
(Continental Breakfast)   Child neg
Apartment $145-$220   Credit cards accepted
1 King/Twin 2 Queen (3 bdrm)
Bathrooms: 3 Ensuite

Allegra House is located in our own native bush setting,
just above central Paihia, with expansive views over the Bay of Islands from each room. Our spacious
home has modern furnishings enhancing the light, airy atmosphere, with plenty of balcony space to
relax on and enjoy the views. We have a self-catering 1 bedroom apartment as well as bed & breakfast
rooms. Outdoor spa. Telescope. We are happy to help you choose the best options for your time with us
and can book activities for you.

PAIHIA   *Paihia Central*

Admiral's View Lodge   *B&B Self-contained*
Deb & Mark Yarrall
2 MacMurray Road, Paihia, Bay of Islands

Tel (09) 402 6236   0800 247 234   Fax (09) 402 6237
admiralsviewlodge@ihug.co.nz
www.admiralsviewlodge.co.nz

Double $85-$195 (Continental Breakfast)
Spa suites $130-$350   Credit cards accepted
4 King 6 Queen 3 Double 9 Twin 11 Single (13 bdrm)
Bathrooms: 9 Ensuite 2 Private

Relax at our Qualmark rated five-star lodge. Quiet
location, seaviews (most units), sunny terraces. 2
spacious apartments, seven luxury studios plus our popular B&B studios. 3 bedroom holiday apartment
available. Meander along to the beach, restaurants/cafés and activities, take the ferry to romantic
Russell or soak up historic Waitangi. Meet our children - Guy & Anna - and our friendly cat, Eva.
Features and attractions: Sky TV; airconditioning (most units); business & internet facilities; activity
booking service; courtesy car; free bikes & tennis; guest BBQs; filtered water.

PAIHIA - OPUA   *5km S of Paihia*

Rose Cottage   *B&B Separate/Suite*
Pat & Don Jansen
37A Oromahoe Road, Opua 0290, Bay of Islands

Tel (09) 402 8099   Fax (09) 402 8096
rosecottageopua@paradise.net.nz
www.bnb.co.nz/rosecottageopua.html

Double $80-$100 (Continental Breakfast)
1 King/Twin 1 Double (2 bdrm)
Bathrooms: 1 Private 1 Guests share

Our home overlooks a native bush garden and
picturesque upper harbour and rural views. The guest wing is separate from host accommodation with
private entrance, fridge, microwave, tea/coffee facilities and TV. Private bathroom and separate toilet
for exclusive guest use with the option of one party or shared facilities. Comfortable rooms enjoy sea
views. We are both retired and have been hosting guests since 1987. Our interests include local history,
gardening fishing, sailing and walking. We look forward to helping you enjoy your stay. Inspections
welcome.

PAIHIA - OPUA   *300m E of Opua*

B&B Homestay Self-contained
Margaret Sinclair
7 Franklin Street, Opua

Tel (09) 402 8285   Fax (09) 402 8285
bbopua@xtra.co.nz
www.bnb.co.nz/sinclair.html

Double $80   Single $40   (Continental Breakfast)
S/C Flat 1 double 2 single Double $80-$100 Single $10
Children welcome
1 Double 2 Single (2 bdrm)
Bathrooms: 1 Guests share 1 Host share

Welcome to my lovely home above Opua harbour. Enjoy panoramic views of water and boat activities
- always something happening. Tourist activities are nearby. Relax in the spa after your day's outing.
You may like to wander in my garden - my big interest. Downstairs is a 2 roomed unit, separate shower,
toilet and private deck with stunning views. Take the Whangarei - Paihia road. Turn right for Opua
- Russell ferry. This is Franklin Street. My house is clearly visible on the seaward side.

PAIHIA - OPUA   *5km S of Paihia*

Seascape   *B&B Homestay Self-contained*
Vanessa & Frank Leadley
17 English Bay Road, Opua, Bay of Islands

Tel (09) 402 7650   Fax (09) 402 7650
Mob 027 475 6793
frankleadley@xtra.co.nz
www.bnb.co.nz/leadley.html

Double $110-$140 Single $80   (Continental Breakfast)
Self-contained flat $110-$140   Credit cards accepted
1 Queen 2 Single (2 bdrm)
Bathrooms: 1 Ensuite 1 Guests share 1 Host share

Seascape is on a tranquil bush-clad ridge. Enjoy spectacular views, stroll through bush to the coastal
walk-way, enjoy our beautifully landscaped garden, experience the many activities in the bay, or relax
on your deck. We are keen NZ and international travellers. Other interests include music, gardening,
fishing, boating, and Rotary. Our fully self-contained flat has queen-size bed, TV, laundry, kitchen,
BBQ, own entrance and deck. Join us for breakfast, or look after yourselves. Guest room with shared
facilities also available.

PAIHIA - OPUA   *5km S of Paihia*

Mako Lodge & Fishing Charters
B&B Self-contained Lodge
Graeme & Jean McIntosh
18 Pt Veronica Drive, Opua 0290, Bay of Islands

Tel (09) 402 7957   0800 625 669 (bookings only)
Fax (09) 402 5957   Mob 027 473 9787
info@makolodge.co.nz   www.makolodge.co.nz

Double $140   Single $140   (Full Breakfast)
Dinner by arrangement Garden Suite from $170
Credit cards accepted   Pets welcome
2 Queen 2 Single (3 bdrm)   Bathrooms: 2 Ensuite

Fabulous cliff top location in quiet cul-de-sac with breathtaking views over harbour, just five minutes
from Paihia. Choose from our B&B unit or the garden suite (newly completed September 2003).
Services include own ensuites, TV/video with extensive video library, CD player, fridges, tea & coffee
making, outdoor BBQ area and lookout. Pets and children by arrangement. Resident golden labrador
(Tessa). Optional light tackle, saltfly, game fishing or sightseeing trips on our modern fully equipped
charter vessel 'Mako' (see www.makocharters.co.nz).

PAIHIA - OPUA   *5km S of Paihia*

Pt. Veronica Lodge   *B&B Homestay*
Audrey & John McKiernan
Pt. Veronica Drive, Opua 0290, Bay of Islands

Tel (09) 402 5579   Fax (09) 402 5579
Mob 021 182 0697
stay@ptveronicalodge.co.nz
www.ptveronicalodge.co.nz

Double $120-$160   Single $80-$120
(Special Breakfast)   Credit cards accepted
3 Queen (3 bdrm)
Bathrooms: 2 Ensuite 1 Private

Qualmark 4 Star guest & hosted property at Veronica
Point between Paihia & Opua. Access to the coastal track and views of the bay towards Paihia and
Russell; this is our special place. Peaceful, romantic and restful with wonderful bush and coastal walks
from the house. Soak in our spa or rest on the decks. TV in your room and Sky channels in the lounge.
Golf, sailing, fishing & historic buildings within 10 minutes drive. Audrey, John and Bonnie & Clyde,
our friendly dogs welcome you.

PAIHIA - OPUA   *5km S of Paihia*

Waterview Lodge   *B&B Separate/Suite*
Self-contained 3 bedroom cottage & 2 bedroom unit
Antionette & Jess Cherrington
14 Franklin Street, Opua, Bay of Islands 0290

Tel (09) 402 7595   Fax (09) 402 7596
Mob 021 102 3950   waterviewlodge@hotmail.com
www.waterviewlodge.com

Double $140-$230   Single $90-$120
(Continental Breakfast)   Child $20   Dinner $30-$40
Studio apartment & cottage $120-$180 & $150-$250   Credit cards accepted Children welcome
7 Queen 1 Twin 5 Single (8 bdrm) Bathrooms: 3 Ensuite 2 Private 2 Guests share

Overlooking the picturesque Port of Opua, Waterview Lodge is a quality accommodation establishment.
The Harbour and River Suites, with private balconies, have expansive sea views of Opua and the upper
harbour. Our 3 bedroom cottage also has beautiful sea views. Our 2 bedroom garden unit is located
downstairs next to the Garden Suite, with access to a private garden and native bush backdrop. Both my
husband and I are originally from the Bay of Islands. We enjoy living at Waterview Lodge with our 2
sons, Ben 17 and Oliver 10, and our little dog, Amy.

RUSSELL   *Russell Central*

Te Manaaki   *B&B Self-contained*
Sharyn & Dudley Smith
2 Robertson Road, Russell

Tel (09) 403 7200   Fax (09) 403 7537
Mob 027 424 4391
triple.b@xtra.co.nz
www.bay-of-islands.co.nz/accomm/tmanaaki.html

Double $150-$250   Single $150-$250   (Full Breakfast)
Child $20   Credit cards accepted
2 King/Twin (2 bdrm)
Bathrooms: 2 Ensuite

Te Manaaki overlooks the picturesque harbour and village of historic Russell with its delightful seaside
restaurants, shops and wharf a gentle stroll away. Magnificent harbour, bush and village views are a
feature of guests private accommodation. The Villa is an attractively appointed sunny spacious deluxe
unit set in its own grounds (with garden spa) adjacent to the main house. The Studio is a self-contained
suite-styled apartment on the ground floor of our new modern home. Both units have mini-kitchen
facilities and off-street parking.

RUSSELL - MATAUWHI BAY   *1km E of Russell*

Ounuwhao B&B
B&B Self-contained Cottage Detached garden suite
Marilyn & Allan Nicklin
Matauwhi Bay, Russell

Tel (09) 403 7310   Fax (09) 403 8310
thenicklins@xtra.co.nz
www.bnb.co.nz/ounuwhaobb.html

Double $185-$225 Single $135-$170
(Full Breakfast) Child $45 under 12 years
Detached garden-suite $200-250 double
Credit cards accepted
1 King/Twin 4 Queen 2 Twin 2 Single (6 bdrm)
Bathrooms: 4 Ensuite 1 Private

Welcome to historic Russell, the Heart of the Bay Of Islands and the first settled area of NZ. Take a step-back into a bygone era and spend some time with us in our delightful, nostalgic, immaculately restored Victorian Villa (circa 1894).

Enjoy your own large guest lounge; tea/coffee and biscuits always available, with open fire in the cooler months, and wrap-around verandahs for you to relax and take in the warm sea breezes. Each of our 4 queen rooms have traditional wallpapers and paintwork, with handmade patchwork quilts and fresh flowers to create a lovingly detailed, traditional romantic interior.

Breakfast is served in our farmhouse kitchen around the large kauri dining table or alfresco on the verandah if you wish. It is an all homemade affair; from the freshly baked fruit and nut bread, to the yummy daily special and the jam conserves.

Our self-contained cottage is set in park-like grounds for your privacy and enjoyment: with 2 double bedrooms, it is ideal for a family or 2 couples travelling together. It has a large lounge overlooking the reserve and out into the bay, a sun-room and fully self-contained kitchen. Wonderful for people looking for that special place for peace and time-out. Max 4 persons. Breakfast is available if required. Complimentary afternoon tea on arrival. Laundry service available.

We look forward to meeting you soon. Our homes are *smoke-free*. We are closed June and July.

Experience our historic B&B. Enjoy a world of difference.

RUSSELL *5km S of Russell*

Treetops *B&B Homestay Self-contained*
Vivienne & Andy Nathan
6 Pinetree Lane, Te Wahapu, Russell

Tel (09) 403 7475 Fax (09) 403 7459
Mob 027 272 8881
vnathan@xtra.co.nz
www.bnb.co.nz/treetopsrussell.html

Double $110 Single $100 (Full Breakfast)
Self-contained cottage $120 Credit cards accepted
1 King 1 Double (2 bdrm)
Bathrooms: 1 Guests share

Our home is situated at the end of Te Wahapu Peninsula. We are surrounded by native bush and tuis & fantails are our constant companions. Kiwis are sometimes heard during the night. Both upstairs bedrooms have beautiful sea views from your bed. Guests are welcome to sit in the spa pool and watch the sun set over Paihia across the Bay. A track through the bush leads down to the beach and the self-contained historic cottage, where you are welcome to use the dinghy and barbecue.

RUSSELL - OKIATO *9km S of Russell*

Aimeo Cottage
B&B Self-contained three bedroom holiday house
Annie & Helmuth Hormann
26 Okiato Point Road, RD 1, Russell-Okiato

Tel (09) 403 7494 Fax (09) 403 7494
Mob 027 272 2393 aimeo@xtra.co.nz
www.bnb.co.nz/aimeocottage.html

Double $120-$145 Single $110-$135
(Special Breakfast) Child $25
3 bedroom holiday home on request
Credit cards accepted Children welcome
4 King/Twin 1 Single (2 bdrm) Bathrooms: 1 Ensuite 1 Private

A quiet place to relax. We have sailed half way around the world to find this beautiful quiet place in the heart of the Bay of Islands and would be happy to share this with you for a while. Aimeo Cottage is built on the hill of Okiato Point, a secluded peninsula overlooking the bay. In 10 minutes you are in New Zealand's first capital, Russell, the site of many historic buildings, an interesting museum and art galleries. For golfers, a complimentary complete set of clubs available (men's and women's).

RUSSELL *1km E of Russell*

Lesleys *B&B*
Lesley Coleman
1 Pomare Road, Russell, Northland

Tel (09) 403 7099 Mob 021 108 0369
three.gs@xtra.co.nz
www.bay-of-islands.co.nz/accomm/lesley.html

Double $130 Single $95 (Special Breakfast)
Child $30 Dinner $25 Credit cards accepted
Children welcome
1 Double 1 Single (1 bdrm)
Bathrooms: 1 Private

Walk beside a palm cluster to our secluded home inspired by living in Greece. See Matauwhi Bay and overseas yachts from the deck. Enjoy breakfast (with organic emphasis) and eggs from our hens in the cosy guest conservatory. Our guest room has its own entrance and tea/coffee making facilities. Lesley's original artwork is on the walls and the private bathroom features a clawfoot bath. Guestbook comments; " We came exhausted and left refreshed!" "Awesome waffles." Billy the terrier lives here too. Welcome.

RUSSELL - TE WAHAPU   *7km S of Russell*

Brisa Cottages   *B&B Self-contained*
Jenny & Peter Sharpe
92B Te Wahapu Road, RD 1, Russell

Tel (09) 403 7757   Fax (09) 403 7758
brisa@xtra.co.nz
www.bay-of-islands.co.nz/accomm/brisa.html

Double $160-$180   Single $140   (Special Breakfast)
Dinner by arrangement $40pp   Credit cards accepted
1 King/Twin 3 Queen 1 Single (4 bdrm)
Bathrooms: 4 Ensuite

Our cottages and garden are hidden among the trees at the water's edge. We offer warm hospitality and quiet, clean, high quality accommodation with safe off street parking. Our guests can enjoy total privacy within a self contained cottage which has a kitchenette, a spacious bedroom/lounge area and ensuite bathroom.

Each cottage has its own area of flowers shrubs and trees, a separate entrance and large deck that overlooks the bay. The emphasis is on tasteful, comfortable surroundings with all the essential extras such as fresh flowers, home-baking, toiletries and bathrobes. Top quality beds and bedding, cotton sheets and soft absorbent towels ensure a feeling of luxury. In each suite a television, books and magazines are provided for your enjoyment.

Our breakfast table is set with white linen, silver and fine china and features fresh baking, home-grown fruit, our own preserves and eggs from our free-range hens. The menu changes daily. Picnic hampers and dinners are also available by arrangement.

A dinghy is at hand for a leisurely paddle from our beach and historic Russell's museum, restaurants and galleries are just seven minutes away by car. Come and enjoy this private and tranquil place with us.

*In the morning wake to the sound of the birds
and the sunrise over Orongo Bay.*

RUSSELL   *0.5km N of Russell*

La Veduta   *Homestay*
Danielle & Dino Fossi
11 Gould Street, Russell, Bay of Islands

Tel (09) 403 8299   Fax (09) 403 8299
laveduta@xtra.co.nz
www.laveduta.co.nz

Double $150-$200   Single $110-$130   (Full Breakfast)
Dinner by arrangement   Credit cards accepted
1 King 1 Queen 2 Double 1 Single (4 bdrm)
Bathrooms: 2 Ensuite 2 Private 1 Guests share

La Veduta. Enjoy our mix of traditional European culture in the midst of the beautiful Bay of Islands. Historic heartland of New Zealand. La Veduta is the perfect pied a terre for your Northland holiday. We offer our guests a warm welcome and personalised service. A delicious breakfast is served on the balcony. Enjoy refreshments watching the sunset over the bay. We can arrange tours and activities. Restaurants, beach, ferries handy, transport available. French and Italian spoken. Laundry facility. Complimentary afternoon tea.

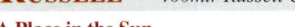

RUSSELL   *400mtr Russell Central*

A Place in the Sun
B&B Separate/Suite Self-contained Studio
Pip & Oliver Campbell
57 Upper Wellington Street, Russell, Bay of Islands

Tel (09) 403 7615   Fax (09) 403 7610
Mob 025 777 942   sailing@paradise.net.nz
www.aplaceinthesun.co.nz

Double $110-$160   Single $90   (Continental Breakfast)
Group of 4 $250   Credit cards accepted
2 Queen 1 Single (3 bdrm)
Bathrooms: 2 Ensuite

Romantic Russell is this retired Kiwi sailing couple's perfect anchorage. For memorable holidays or honeymoons, our home (and your separate private accommodation) is ideal. Overlooking Russell Village, great views across the bay. Convenient departure for all cruises. 2 ensuite apartments, (1 self-contained). Comfortable queen beds, TV, BBQ, fishing rods. Ranchsliders open to patio and garden (no stairs). A sunny peaceful setting bordering bush reserves (kiwi zone). Uncrowded beaches, heritage trails, rock or game fishing, cruise/sail/kayak or just unwind. It's Paradise.

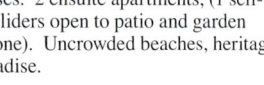

RUSSELL   *Russell Central*

Villa Russell   *B&B*
Sue & Steve Western
2 Little Queen Street, Russell, Bay of Islands

Tel (09) 403 8845   0800 546 434
Fax (09) 403 8845   Mob 027 492 8912
info@kingfishercharters.co.nz
www.kingfishercharters.co.nz

Double $135   Single $110   (Full Breakfast)
1 Queen (1 bdrm)
Bathrooms: 1 Ensuite

Enjoy a welcoming visit to Villa Russell, two minutes from the beach and Russell's restaurants. Relax with magnificent views of the bay and wharf from the deck of our beautifully restored 1910 Villa or from your spacious guest room, with own ensuite. A short walk takes you to Long Bay surf beach or up to historic Flagstaff Hill and native bush. Off-street parking provided. Charters on our 11.6 metre yacht Kingfisher may also be arranged to sail the Bay Of Islands. Friendly family dog.

KOHUKOHU   *80km S of Kaitaia*

Harbour Views Guest House
B&B Homestay Guesthouse
Jacky Kelly & Bill Thomson
32B Rakautapu Road,
Kohukohu, Northland

Tel (09) 405 5815   Fax (09) 405 5865
www.bnb.co.nz/harbourviewsguesthouse.html

Double $90   Single $45
(Full Breakfast) Dinner $20
1 Queen 2 Single (2 bdrm)
Bathrooms: 1 Private

Historic Kohukohu, now a friendly and charming village, is situated on the north side of the Hokianga Harbour. Our beautifully restored kauri home is set in 2 acres of gardens and trees and commands a spectacular view of the harbour. The guest rooms, opening on to a sunny verandah, are in a private wing of the house. Meals are prepared using home-grown produce in season. We are interested in and knowledgeable about the history and geography of the area. We have 2 cats.

RAWENE   *43km W of Kaikohe*

Searell's   *B&B Homestay*
Nellie & Wally Searell
11 Nimmo Street West, Rawene

Tel (09) 405 7835   Fax (09) 405 7835
searell3@hotmail.com
www.bnb.co.nz/searells.html

Double $80   Single $45   (Continental Breakfast)
Child $15-$20   Dinner $20   Triple $120
Full breakfast $5
1 Queen 1 Single (2 bdrm)
Bathrooms: 1 Private

The view of harbour and hills beautiful - sunsets breathtaking. Our 1 acre garden includes tropical flowers and fruit trees. Fresh fruit picked almost everyday. We are retired, Wally an ex-naval man. Interests: meeting people, gardening, wine making, photography, exploring New Zealand. Zola, friendly 3 year old german shepherd bitch. 1km to shops, hotel, ferry, petrol, hospital. Turn off main road, motor camp sign over hill veer left. At Nimmo Street West turn left to top of hill, flat parking area, easy access. Warm welcome.

OPONONI   *50km W of Kaikohe*

Koutu Lodge   *B&B Homestay*
Tony and Sylvia Stockman
Koutu Loop Road, Opononi, RD 3, Kaikohe

Tel (09) 405 8882   Fax (09) 405 8893
koutulodgebnb@xtra.co.nz
www.wairereboulders.co.nz/koutulodge

Double $100   Single $65   (Full Breakfast)
Dinner $35 by arrangement
Credit cards accepted
1 King 1 Queen 1 Double (3 bdrm)
Bathrooms: 2 Ensuite 1 Private

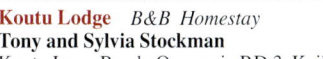

Situated on Koutu Point overlooking the beautiful Hokianga Harbour, our home has views both rural and sea. 2 rooms have private entrances, decks, and ensuites, and are very comfortable. We are a friendly, relaxed Kiwi couple, and our aim is to provide a memorable stay in the true B&B tradition. Stay a while and enjoy everything the historic Hokianga has to offer.Koutu Loop Road is 4.3km north of Opononi then left 2.3km on tar seal to Lodge on right.

OPONONI   *57km W of Kaikohe*

Opononi Dolphin Lodge   *B&B Homestay*
Sue & John Reynard (Resident Manager Pam)
Corner SH12 and Fairlie Crescent, Opononi

Tel (09) 405 8451   Fax (09) 405 8451
www.bnb.co.nz/opononidolphinlodge.html

Double $75-$85 Single $65
(Continental Breakfast)
Credit cards accepted
1 Queen 1 Double 1 Twin 1 Single (3 bdrm)
Bathrooms: 2 Ensuite 1 Private

Situated on the corner of Fairlie Crescent and SH12,
opposite a beach reserve on the edge of the pristine Hokianga Harbour. Our sunsets are breathtaking.
20 minutes from "Tane Mahuta" the largest kauri tree in the world. Step outside for picture postcard
views of beautiful blue beckoning waters and huge sand dunes. Visit the boulders, sand board, walking
tracks, boating, great fishing, local crafts. Come, enjoy the friendly hospitality. The west coast diamond
in the north awaits you.

OMAPERE   *55km W of Kaikohe*

Harbourside Bed & Breakfast   *B&B*
Joy & Garth Coulter
State Highway 12, 1 Pioneer Walk, Omapere

Tel (09) 405 8246
harboursidebnb@xtra.co.nz
www.bnb.co.nz/harboursidebedbreakfast.html

Double $90   Single $60   (Continental Breakfast)
Credit cards accepted
1 Queen 2 Single (2 bdrm)
Bathrooms: 2 Ensuite

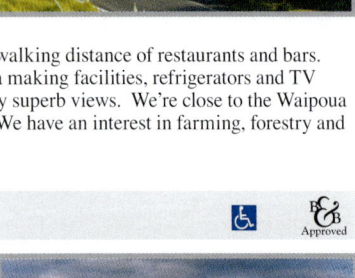

Our beachfront home on corner State Highway 12 and
Pioneer Walk overlooking the Hokianga Harbour is within walking distance of restaurants and bars.
The beach is 50 metres away. Both rooms have ensuites, tea making facilities, refrigerators and TV
with separate entrances onto private decks to relax and enjoy superb views. We're close to the Waipoua
Forest, west coast beaches, sand hills and historic Rawene. We have an interest in farming, forestry and
education. Stay and share our home and cat.

OMAPERE   *60km W of Kaikohe*

Hokianga Haven Omapere Beachfront   *B&B*
Heather Randerson
226 State Highway 12,
Omapere, Hokianga

Tel (09) 405 8285   Fax (09) 405 8215
Mob 021 393 973
tikanga2000@xtra.co.nz
www.hokiangahaven.co.nz

Double $130-$180   (Full Breakfast)
1 Queen (1 bdrm)
Bathrooms: 1 Private

Snuggled into this peaceful private, beachfront location, our comfortable home embraces the
continuously inspiring sea scape of the dramatic harbour entrance and magnificent dune. Simply
relaxing in this harbourside haven is revitalizing. Bush and forest walks, horse riding, harbour cruising,
fishing, river and coastal swimming are some of the natural delights to be enjoyed in this historic area.
Our dog will be a willing walking companion. Star gazing in the warmth of the hot tub is a wonderful
way to finish the day. Range of healing therapies available.

OMAPERE   *55km W of Kaikohe*

McKenzie's Accommodation   *B&B*
Leonie & Doug McKenzie
4 Pioneer Walk, Omapere,
South Hokianga

Tel (09) 405 8068   Fax (09) 405 8068
dlmk@xtra.co.nz   www.bnb.co.nz/mckenzie.html

Double $90   Single $60   (Continental Breakfast)
Child $15   Credit cards accepted   Children welcome
1 Queen 1 Single (1 bdrm)
Bathrooms: 1 Private

Our home is right on the beach of the scenic Hokianga Harbour. This photo is taken from just outside the house. The B&B room has separate outside entrance, queen and single beds, TV, fridge and jug. Separate bathroom and toilet exclusively for guests. We also have a separate 2 bedroom self-contained unit, this can be self-catering or B&B. Stop a night before or after visiting the Waipoua Kauri Forest or stay a few days and enjoy this unique environment. Your friendly hosts have extensive local knowledge.

DARGAVILLE   *2km Dargaville*

Awakino Point Boutique Motel   *Self contained suites*
June & Mick
State Highway 14, Dargaville, PO Box 168 Dargaville

Tel (09) 439 7870   Fax (09) 439 7580
Mob 027 451 9474   awakinopoint@xtra.co.nz
www.awakinopoint.co.nz

Double $85-$100   (Continental Breakfast)
Dinner by arrangement
2 bedroom unit, 4 persons $145 - $160
Rates seasonal   Credit cards accepted
3 Queen 4 Twin (5 bdrm)   Bathrooms: 3 Ensuite

This unique property set on its own acreage surrounded by attractive gardens is just 2km drive from Dargaville on SH14 (The road to Whangarei). The best features of a New Zealand motel and bed & breakfast have been amalgamated to produce something a little different. You will enjoy your own self-contained suite with private bathroom, friendly service and a good breakfast. 3 well appointed one & two bedroom self-contained ground floor units. One has a kitchen, bath and log fire. Guest laundry and BBQ available. Smokefree indoors

DARGAVILLE - BAYLY'S BEACH   *12km W of Dargaville*

Ocean View   *Separate/Suite*
Paula & John Powell
7 Ocean View Terrace, Bayly's Beach,
RD 7, Dargaville

Tel (09) 439 6256   Mob 021 0400 511
baylys@win.co.nz
www.bnb.co.nz/oceanview.html

Double $80   Single $45   (Continental Breakfast)
Child $10 under 12 years Credit cards accepted
Children welcome
1 Double 1 Single (1 bdrm) Bathrooms: 1 Ensuite

Just off the trail, this sometimes wild, always wonderful, expansive west coast beach is a fine place to relax. With a glimpse of the sea, your cottage is 2 minutes walk to the beach and clifftop walkways. We have 2 great cafés and 18 hole golf locally, with Kai Iwi Lakes and forests an easy day trip. Enjoy your sunny, comfortable cottage (great shower!) and breakfast at your leisure - provided in cottage for you. With our 2 children and Ruby the cat we look forward to welcoming you. Directions: Drive through the village, you will see our sign at the foot of the big hill.

DARGAVILLE   *1.5km S of Dargaville*

Approved

Kauri House Lodge
Farmstay B&B Luxury accomodation
Doug Blaxall
PO Box 382, Bowen Street, Dargaville

Tel (09) 439 8082   Fax (09) 439 8082
Mob 025 547 769
kaurihouse@xtra.co.nz
www.bnb.co.nz/kaurihouselodge.html

Double $200-$275 Single $200
(Full Breakfast) Credit cards accepted
1 King/Twin 2 King (3 bdrm)
Bathrooms: 3 Ensuite

Kauri House Lodge sits high above Dargaville amongst
mature trees. The 1880's villa retains all it's charm,
style and grace with original kauri panelling and period
antiques in all rooms.

Start your day woken by native birds, walk through
extensive landscaped grounds or read in our library. In
summer enjoy a dip in the large swimming pool. In
winter our billiard room log fire is a cosy spot to relax
for the evening.

Join us to explore beautiful mature native bush on our
nearby farm overlooking the Wairoa River and Kaipara
Harbour. The area offers many activities including
deserted beaches, lakes, river tours, horse treks, walks
and restaurants. We have been hosting bed and breakfast
for 30 years.

*The most common comment in our visitor
book: "Save the best to last!"*

DARGAVILLE   *2km S of Dargaville*

Turiwiri B&B   *B&B*
Bruce & Jennifer Crawford
Turiwiri RAPID 6775,
State Highway 12, Dargaville

Tel (09) 439 6003   Fax (09) 439 6003
crawford@igrin.co.nz
www.bnb.co.nz/turiwiribb.html

Double $80   Single $40
(Continental Breakfast)
2 Queen (2 bdrm)
Bathrooms: 1 Guests share

We enjoy sharing our local knowledge with guests in our modern, one level home 2km south from Dargaville on SH12, minutes from quality restaurants. Excellent parking for vehicles and an expansive garden in the midst of our 37 acre farmlet. Our family of three grown children all live away from home, interests include family, farming, Rotary International, gardening and big game fishing. We have 2 friendly cats.

DARGAVILLE

Birch's B&B   *B&B Self-contained*
Anson & Pat Clapcott
18 Kauri Street, Dargaville

Tel (09) 439 7565   Fax (09) 439 7520
Mob 027 252 2564 birch@kauricoast.co.nz
www.bnb.co.nz/birchs.html

Double $75-$90 Single $45-$60
(Continental Breakfast)   Child neg   Dinner b/a
S/C 2 bedroom cottage $85-$125   Credit cards accepted
3 Queen 3 Twin (6 bdrm)
Bathrooms: 1 Private 2 Guests share

You will need several days in the Dargaville area to fully appreciate the beauty of the Kauri Coast. We have two queen and two twin rooms. There is a large family lounge with fireplace and a modern kitchen with dining area. Enjoy a complimentary beverage from the balcony overlooking beautiful gardens and native trees or stay in our cute self-contained cottage with its own kauri trees. We're a walkable distance to the town, with excellent dining or dinner by arrangement. 1 dog, 1 Kiwi and 1 American to greet you.

MATAKOHE   *9km S of Matakohe*

Petite Provence   *B&B Homestay*
Linda & Guy Bucchi
703C Tinopai Road, RD 1, Matakohe

Tel (09) 431 7552   Fax (09) 431 7552
petite-provence@clear.net.nz
www.bnb.co.nz/petiteprovince.html

Double $115   Single $90   (Continental Breakfast)
Dinner $35 by arrangement   Credit cards accepted
2 Queen 1 Twin (3 bdrm)
Bathrooms: 2 Ensuite 1 Private

Bienvenue to our new home set on rolling farmland (distant Kaipara harbour views) 9km south of Matakohe Kauri museum. Guy is French, Linda a New Zealander, our family home in the South of France was also a homestay. Mediterranean/vegetarian/local cuisine (home grown produce, local seafood) Smoking outdoors. Pets: Loopy our outside dog. Bookings preferred. Directions: from Matakohe Museum travel 2km south, take Tinopai Road, drive approx. 7km. We are at end (500 metres) of private road on left. Sign on street frontage.

PAPAROA   *1km S of Paparoa Township*

Pioneer B&B   *B&B Separate/Suite*
Rowie & Pete Panhuis
The Pines Road, Paparoa

Tel (09) 431 6033   Fax (09) 431 6677
officeworkshop@xtra.co.nz
www.bnb.co.nz/pioneer.html

Double $115   Single $85   (Full Breakfast)
Child $25   Dinner $30 by arrangement
Children welcome Smoking area inside
1 Queen 1 Twin (2 bdrm)
Bathrooms: 1 Ensuite 1 Guests share

Pete and Rowie welcome you to their historic homestead.
Step back in time and relax in our charmingly restored cottage with ensuite and open fireplace.
Enhanced by surrounding native bush and cottage gardens, this is a delightful place to enjoy some
country hospitality. Evening meals are cooked on our coal range using fresh local produce if you care
to join us, or local restaurants are nearby. We have a passion for local history and memorabilia with the
famous Kauri Museum close by. Pets on property.

PAPAROA   *0.5km E of Paparoa*

The Old Post Office Guesthouse   *B&B Separate/Suite*
Janice Booth
Corner State Highway 12 & Oakleigh Road,
PO Box 79, Paparoa

Tel (09) 431 6444   Fax (09) 431 6444
Mob 021 975 314   paparoa.jan@xtra.co.nz
www.bnb.co.nz/postoffice.html

Double $75   Single $50   (Continental Breakfast)
Dinner $25   2 bedroom suite $125
Credit cards accepted
2 Queen 1 Twin 2 Single (5 bdrm)
Bathrooms: 1 Private 1 Guests share

From the moment you step inside you will succumb to the character & charm of this lovely old historic
building (circa 1903), with delightful cottage garden & rural backdrop. Enjoy our true Kiwi hospitality,
cuisine and homely atmosphere with separate guests lounge & free tea/coffee. Local restaurants nearby.
Spend a day at the world famous Matakohe Kauri Museum only 8km away or if, like us, you enjoy the
outdoors, our kayaks are available to explore the nearby Kaipara Harbour. Two cats on property.

PAPAROA   *7km W of Paparoa*

Palm House   *B&B Self-contained*
Jenny & Hector MacKinnon
Pahi, RD 1, Paparoa

Tel (09) 431 6689
palmhouse@paradise.net.nz
www.bnb.co.nz/palmhousebb.html

Double $100   Single $70   (Full Breakfast)
Dinner $35   Garden Cottage $80
Credit cards accepted
2 King/Twin 2 Queen (3 bdrm)
Bathrooms: 1 Ensuite 1 Guests share

Get off the beaten track for a night or two and enjoy
staying at peaceful Pahi. Stroll along the tideline or stand
on the wharf and watch the fish jump. Visit the largest
morton bay fig tree in the Southern Hemisphere. Tasty home-cooked meals served with fine NZ wines.
Just 13km from Matakohe Museum and enroute to the spectacular Kauri Forest. Signposted on the main
State Highway 12, travel 7km down Pahi Road and reach Palm House.

Maungaturoto
10km W of Maungaturoto

Conrads Retreat *B&B Country Retreat*
Brett & Jan Taylor
Whakapirau Road, RD 386, Maungaturoto

Tel (09) 431 9115 Fax (09) 431 9110
Mob 021 554 664 Jan.taylor@xtra.co.nz
www.bnb.co.nz/conrads.html

Double $100-$160 Single $80 (Full Breakfast)
Child neg Dinner neg Credit cards accepted
Smoking area inside
2 King 2 Queen 1 Double 1 Twin 1 Single (7 bdrm) Bathrooms: 2 Ensuite 2 Guests share

For a charming and relaxing break enjoy our Tudor Style kauri farm house set in beautiful subtropical gardens including water features offering a choice of indoor or outdoor dining with spectacular views. Food any time, just speak to our chef. We are on 10 acres and surrounded by 1000 acres of farmland. Unwind in our sauna or hotspring spa pool. We offer warm hospitality and quiet, clean, high quality accommodation, cosy lounge, farm house dining room, sunroom and all rooms lead to balconies or courtyard. Rooms served daily.

Oakura Bay
45km NE of Whangarei

Robin's Nest *Homestay Self-contained Studio*
Robin & Peter Cusdin
32 Ohawini Road, Oakura Bay, Whangaruru South

Tel (09) 433 6035 Fax (09) 433 6039
Mob 021 188 9000 robin@robinsnest.co.nz
www.robinsnest.co.nz

Double $90-$130 (Breakfast b/a)
Dinner $35pp by arrangement
Self-contained studio $130-$190
Credit cards accepted
1 King/Twin 1 Queen (2 bdrm) Bathrooms: 2 Ensuite

Our studio is self-contained with superb sea views, TV, CD player, underfloor heating, private decks & gas barbecue. Breakfast available if required at extra cost. The queen room in our home has tea making facilities, ensuite, heated towel-rail, TV, with breakfast included, plus glorious sea views. Enjoy scenic coastal and native forest drives to the Bay of Islands, fishing trips, boat & kayak hire, horse trekking. The Gallery enroute displays fine NZ artwork also. Guests are greeted by Cagney our old golden retriever.

Whangarei
16km W of Whangarei

Taraire Grove *B&B Homestay*
Jan & Brian Newman
Tatton Road, RD 9, Whangarei

Tel (09) 434 7279 Fax (09) 434 7279
www.bnb.co.nz/tarairegrove.html

Double $80 Single $50 (Full Breakfast)
Child 1/2 price Dinner $12-$20pp
Credit cards accepted Children welcome
1 Queen 2 Single (2 bdrm)
Bathrooms: 1 Guests share

We welcome you to our charming country residence at Maungatapere, within easy driving distances to east and west coast beaches. We are a semi-retired couple, and welcome the opportunity to return hospitality experienced overseas. Our home overlooks a stream and we are gradually developing the 3 1/2 acres into lawns, gardens and ponds. 2 resident pets. The guest wing is private - TV room - tea/coffee making facilities. Whangarei, 15 minutes away, has excellent restaurants or you can choose to dine with us and enjoy hospitality.

WHANGAREI *17km E of Whangarei*

Parua House *Farmstay Homestay*
Pat & Peter Heaslip
Parua Bay, RD 4, Whangarei

Tel (09) 436 5855 Mob 021 186 5002
paruahomestay@clear.net.nz
www.paruahomestay.homestead.com

Double $150 Single $90
(Full Breakfast) Child ¹/₂ price Dinner $35
Credit cards accepted
2 Queen 2 Twin 1 Single (4 bdrm)
Bathrooms: 2 Ensuite 1 Private

Parua House is a classical colonial house, built
in 1883, comfortably restored and occupying an
elevated site with panoramic views of Parua Bay
and the Whangarei Harbour.

The property covers 29 hectares of farmland
including 2 protected reserves, which are rich in
native trees (including kauri) and birds.

Guests are welcome to explore the farm and
bush, milk the jersey cow, explore the olive
grove and subtropical orchard, or just relax in the
spa-pool or on the veranda. A safe swimming
beach adjoins the farm, with a short walk to the
fishing jetty; two marinas and a golf course are
nearby.

Our wide interests include photography,
patchwork quilting and horticulture. The house
is attractively appointed with antique furniture
and a rare collection of spinning wheels.

Awake to home-baked bread and freshly
squeezed orange juice. Dine in elegant
surroundings with generous helpings of home
produce with our own meat, milk, eggs, home
grown vegetables, olive and subtropical fruit
(home-made ice cream a speciality). Pre-meal
drinks and wine are provided to add to the
bonhomie of an evening around a large french
oak refectory table.

As featured on TV's "Ansett NZ Time of Your Life" and "Corban's Taste NZ".

WHANGAREI *4.5km NE of Whangarei*

Graelyn Villa *B&B*
Joanie Guy
166 Kiripaka Road, Whangarei

Tel (09) 437 7532 Fax (09) 437 7533
graelyn@xtra.co.nz
www.bnb.co.nz/graelynvillla.html

Double $95 Single $65 (Continental Breakfast)
Child by arrangement Credit cards accepted
Children welcome Pets welcome Smoking area inside
2 Queen 2 Single (3 bdrm)
Bathrooms: 3 Ensuite

Welcome to my turn of the century villa, which has been lovingly restored to offer comfort and luxury. My rooms offer superbly comfortable beds, TV, tea/coffee, heaters and electric blankets. For your privacy, all rooms are separate to owners accommodation and all have ensuites. 5 minutes to city centre with a wide variety of top class restaurants, 25 minutes drive to Tutukaka Coast, handy to spectacular Whangarei Falls. I have 2 quiet dogs and a cat named Koko. Your pets welcome. Laundry facilities available.

WHANGAREI *10km NE of Whangarei CBD*

Country Garden Tearooms *Self-contained*
Margaret & John Pool
526 Ngunguru Road,
RD 3, Whangarei

Tel (09) 437 5127 Mob 025 519 476
www.countrygarden.co.nz

Double $70-$80 Single $55 (Full Breakfast)
Dinner $20 by arrangement Credit cards accepted
2 Queen (2 bdrm)
Bathrooms: 2 Ensuite

Enjoy a warm friendly welcome. We have over 3 acres
of beautiful trees, shrubs, bulbs, perennials, succulents and a large variety of bird life. Feel at home in a spacious self-contained unit with fridge, microwave and tea making facilities. Enjoy cooked or continental breakfast in our dining room overlooking the garden. We are 10km from central Whangarei on Ngunguru-Tutukaka Highway. 5km from Whangarei Falls. Beautiful beaches, restaurants, diving, fishing and golfing within 10km.

WHANGAREI *12km SW of Whangarei*

Owaitokamotu *B&B Homestay*
M & G Whitehead
727 Otaika Valley Road, Otaika, Whangarei

Tel (09) 434 7554 Fax (09) 4347554
minniegeorge@xtra.co.nz
www.bnb.co.nz/owaitokamotu.html

Double $75 Single $55
(Full Breakfast) Dinner $20
Children welcome Pets welcome
2 King/Twin 2 Queen (3 bdrm)
Bathrooms: 2 Guests share

Come and enjoy the absolute tranquillity of Owaitokamotu which is a place of water, magnificent rocks of all shapes and sizes, and pristine native bush awaiting your rambling walks, all set on 10 acres of easy contour and newly created gardens. Our home is newly built and is wheelchair friendly. Bedrooms have private access from exterior. TV, tea, coffee and cookies. A wide verandah offers pleasant relaxation. Smoking outside only please. Laundry facilities available.

WHANGAREI - GLENBERVIE   *12km NE of Whangarei*

Lupton House Homestay B&B   *B&B Homestay*
Marie & John Dennistoun-Wood
555 Ngunguru Road, Glenbervie, RD 3, Whangarei

Tel (09) 437 2989   Fax (09) 437 2989
Mob 025 203 9805   dennistoun-wood@xtra.co.nz
www.truenz.co.nz/luptonhouse

Double $125   Single $115
(Full Breakfast)   Dinner by arrangement
Smoking area inside
2 Queen (2 bdrm)
Bathrooms: 2 Ensuite

Welcome to our home which is located in the dry-stone
walled farmland of Glenbervie, between Whangarei and the beautiful beaches of Tutukaka coast.
Lovingly restored and furnished and with extensive gardens, swimming pool and games room, our
colonial villa offers guests comfort and relaxation in a friendly old-world country atmosphere which
we share with our grandson, golden retriever dogs and 2 donkeys. We offer a full breakfast and by
arrangement, dinner. Diving, fishing, golf, watersports and country walks within a 15km radius.

WHANGAREI   *25km SE of Whangarei*

Vealbrook B & B   *B&B Homestay Self-contained*
Bob and Pre Sturge
2013 McLeod Bay, Whangarei Heads, RD 4
Whangarei Heads Road, Whangarei

Tel (09) 434 0098   Fax (09) 434 0098
pretoria@clear.net.nz
www.bnb.co.nz/vealbrook.html

Double $100   Single $95   (Special Breakfast)
Child $15   Dinner $25   Self-contained unit $120
Children welcome
1 Queen 1 Double 1 Twin 3 Single (3 bdrm) Bathrooms: 1 Guests share

Stunning harbour views. Coastal scenic walks. Mountains to climb. 20 metres to the beach. Safe
swimming, snorkelling, kayaking, good fishing at jetty. Local dairy nearby. Pine Golf Course 15
minutes away. Surfing ocean beach. Pleasant drive round beautiful ocean bays. The house is arranged
with antique furniture. Antique lace garments on display. For breakfast enjoy Bob's homemade
marmalades jellies. Freshly picked fruit and fruit juice. Vegetables, subtropical fruits. Dinner supplied
on request. Pre-meal drinks. Enjoy warmth and friendliness of your hosts.

WHANGAREI - ONERAHI   *9km SE of Whangarei*

Channel Vista   *B&B Self-contained*
Braia & Paul Larsen
254 Beach Road, Onerahi, Whangarei

Tel (09) 436 5529   Fax (09) 436 5529
Mob 027 448 8507
channelvista@igrin.co.nz
www.bnb.co.nz/channelvistabb.html

Double $170   Single $100
(Full Breakfast)   Credit cards accepted
2 Queen (2 bdrm)
Bathrooms: 2 Ensuite

Channel Vista is situated on the shores of Whangarei
Harbour. We have 2 self-contained units each with
their own private decks where you can relax and watch boats go by. Laundry, fax and email facilities
available. Local shopping centre only 3 minutes away, 5 minute walk along waterfront to top restaurant.
Sports facilities, eg golf, diving, game fishing, bowls etc nearby. We are 1 hour from the Bay of Islands,
so it is a good place to base yourself for your Northland holiday.

WHANGAREI *20km E of Whangarei*

Juniper House *B&B Homestay*
Diane & Mike James
49 Proctor Road, RD 9, Whangarei

Tel **(09) 434 6399** Fax (09) 434 6399
Mob 0274 224 498
diane.james@xtra.co.nz
www.bnb.co.nz/juniperhouse.html

Double **$120-$135** Single $60-$70
(Full Breakfast) Credit cards accepted
1 Queen 1 Double 1 Twin (3 bdrm)
Bathrooms: 1 Ensuite 1 Guests share

Juniper House is a comfortable welcoming home set in a young Avocado orchard. Relax in our extensive gardens, enjoy a game of tennis or swim in our salt water pool and spa. For the snooker enthusiast we have a full size billiard table. We are an easy 15 minute drive from the Museum and Kiwi House, golf courses, cafés, galleries and Whangarei yacht basin. We offer full breakfast, dinner and drinks by arrangement. Our interests include sailing, fishing and decorative art. Orchard cat.

WHANGAREI - TAIHARURU *25km E of Whangarei*

Tidesong
B&B Homestay Separate/Suite Self-contained
Ros & Hugh Cole-Baker
Beasley Road, RD 1, Onerahi, Whangarei

Tel **(09) 436 1959** stay@tidesong.co.nz
www.bnb.co.nz/tidesong.html

Double **$95-$110** Single $70-$80
(Full Breakfast) Dinner $25-$30
2 Queen 1 Single (2 bdrm)
Bathrooms: 1 Ensuite 1 Guests share

From Whangarei drive east for 25 minutes to Taiharuru Estuary. Comfortable secluded accommodation in a separate upstairs flat. Full breakfast, with extra home-cooked meals available. Safe kayaking and other boating from our jetty. Large garden with bush tracks and outdoor games. Close to fishing, shellfish, varied birdlife,and great walks on surf beaches and spectacular ridges. Relax afterwards in the gas-fired outdoor garden bath. We look forward to showing you warm and friendly Northland hospitality.

WHANGAREI *4.5 km NE of Whangarei*

Luxury At The Lake *B&B Self-contained*
Individual retreat for couples Private Lake
Diane & Jim Watson
18 Takahe Street, Tikipunga, Whangarei

Tel **(09) 437 1989** Fax (09) 437 1989
Mob 027 444 11 74 relax@lakeluxuryretreat.co.nz
www.lakeluxuryretreat.co.nz

Double **$195-$250** (Special Breakfast)
Breakfast is self catering with ingredients supplied
Credit cards accepted
1 Queen (1 bdrm) Bathrooms: 1 Ensuite

Luxury At The Lake has one romantic boutique retreat, a hidden gem, nestled in 2 acres of native bush at a private lake. Unique, and exclusively yours, we will style your visit to meet your needs, making it perfect for that romantic interlude, or just the place to unwind. Tasteful, comfortable furnishings, kitchen, TV, DVD, barbeque, your own patio, kayaks plus many extras, ensuring your stay is memorable. Our late noon checkout, (subject to availability) provides ample time to relax. Sorry, not suitable children/pets.

WHANGAREI *15km E of Whangarei*

B&B
Approved

Headland Homestay

B&B   Homestay   2 Separate Units
Anthea Hawkins
36 Headland Farm Park, RD 4, Whangarei

Tel (09) 436 3202   Fax (09) 436 3202
Mob 021 436 320   anthea.hawkins@clear.net.nz
www.bnb.co.nz/headland.html

Double $125-$160   (Continental Breakfast)
Child ¹/₂ price   2 sofa beds in units
Credit cards accepted   Children welcome

1 Queen 1 Double (4 bdrm)
Bathrooms: 2 Private 2 Host share

Have a relaxing enjoyable stay in the beautiful setting
of the Headland Farm Park comprising of 120 hectares,
with elevated views over the sea, harbour, golf course,
hills and beyond.

Anthea and Brandon offer accommodation in two self
contained units, each facilitating up to 4 persons.
A private swimming pool and barbeque are available
in season.

The private Farm Park has lovely walks, and enjoy the sights of grazing sheep, cattle and deer, with
breathtaking water views on either side of the peninsular. A four hectare orchard provides fruit in
season. Guests also have access to a private sandy beach on the Farm Park, set in a safe swimming
bay. Or why not take a stroll across to the island at low tide. There is a jetty for the keen fisherman too.
Only 15 minutes drive to Whangarei City centre. And just 5 minutes drive to local shops, supermarket,
restaurants, pubs and airport.

WHANGAREI HEADS *31km SE of Whangarei*

Manaia Gardens
Self-contained Breakfast not provided
Audrey & Colin Arnold
2487 Whangarei Heads Road, Taurikura, Whangarei

Tel (09) 434 0797 arnoldac@igrin.co.nz
www.bnb.co.nz/manaiagardens.html

Double $60-$80 Single $60
Child under 5 free Credit cards accepted
Children welcome Smoking area inside
2 Queen 1 Double (3 bdrm)
Bathrooms: 2 Private

We have a small farm and a large garden, with 2 quaint old self-contained cabins in the garden.
They have comfortable beds and basic cooking facilities, 2 burner gas cooker or electric frypan,
microwave,toaster etc.There are nearby shops and galleries,laundry available. This is a beautiful area
with rocky bush clad hills, harbour and ocean beaches, lots of Conservation land for walks. Or just relax
in private. We are the only buildings in the bay. Mailbox 2487 on the Whangarei Heads Road.

WHANGAREI HEADS *28km SE of Whangarei*

Bantry *Homestay*
Karel & Robin Lieffering
Little Munro Bay, RD 4, Whangarei Heads

Tel (09) 434 0751 Fax (09) 434 0754
robinl@igrin.co.nz www.bnb.co.nz/bantry.html

Double $110 Single $55 (Full Breakfast) Child ¹/₂ price
Dinner $30 Children welcome Pets welcome
1 Queen 2 Single (2 bdrm)
Bathrooms: 1 Private 1 Guests share

We are a semi-retired couple with dog. We speak Dutch,
French, German, Japanese and we like to laugh. Our unusual
home with some natural rock interior walls is on the edge of a
safe swimming beach, and bush reserve with walking tracks and
several good fishing spots. A photographically fascinating area
with wonderful views of coastal mountains. Guests have own entrance and sitting room all
with sea views. Enjoyable food and NZ wine. Phone, fax or email us for reservations and directions.
One party bookings only.

WHANGAREI HEADS *24km E of Whangarei*

Cinque Terre Homestay *Homestay*
Desley & Graeme Howden
388/176 Taraunui Road, Parua Bay, Whangarei

Tel (09) 436 4060 Fax (09) 436 4060
Mob 025 285 7039 cinque_terre@ihug.co.nz
www.cinque-terre.co.nz

Double $110-$125 Single $80-$90 (Full Breakfast)
Child $35 (under 12) Day lounge sofa bed
Dinner $25 (Child $12) Wine optional
Credit cards accepted Children welcome
1 King/Twin 2 Queen (3 bdrm) Bathrooms: 1 Private 1 Guests share

Come stay with us and explore Whangarei Heads: the raw beauty of rugged mountains and wild white
sand surf beaches; the thrill of deep water diving and deep-sea fishing; the tranquillity of sheltered
waterways and native bush walks; the intrigue of local history. It's all here waiting for you to enjoy.
You'll find us slightly off the beaten track on 14 acres providing absolute peace and privacy. Our
beautiful Mediterranean home offers quality accommodation and warm and friendly Kiwi hospitality. 2
pets. 20 minutes to airport. Courtesy transport.

RUAKAKA   *30km S of Whangarei*

Waterview Bream Bay
B&B Farmstay Self-contained
Gayle Tilly & Rodney McPhee
34 Doctors Hill Road, Waipu, Ruakaka

Tel (09) 433 0050   Fax (09) 433 0050
Mob 027 273 0417   rodneyandgaylesb.b@xtra.co.nz
www.bnb.co.nz/waterviewbb.html

Double $80   Single $50
(Full Breakfast)   Child $20   Dinner $25
Credit cards accepted   Children welcome   Pets welcome
2 Queen   2 Single   (3 bdrm)
Bathrooms: 1 Private   1 Host share

Waterview Bream Bay offers a self-contained unit with panoramic sea and rural views. Beautiful beaches, golf course, race track fishing, horse treks and restaurants are all within a few minutes drive away. Our property has large gardens and children are welcome. Cot available. Wildlife appearing at our home includes moreporks, pheasants, duck and the rare brown bitton. Wonderful for people looking for that special place for peace and time out. We look forward to meeting you soon.

WAIPU   *10km S of Waipu*

Farmstay Self-contained
Andre & Robin La Bonte
PO Box 60, Waipu, Northland

Tel (09) 432 0645   Fax (09) 432 0645
labonte@xtra.co.nz
www.bnb.co.nz/labonte.html

Double $80   Single $50   (Continental Breakfast)
Dinner $20 by arrangement
Credit cards accepted
1 King   1 Queen   2 Double   2 Single   (3 bdrm)
Bathrooms: 2 Private

Sleep to the sound of the ocean in a separate studio apartment or in guest bedrooms on our 36 acre seaside farm. Explore our limestone rock formations or just sit and relax under the mature trees that grace our shoreline. The beach at Waipu Cove is a 10 minute walk along the sea. We are a licensed fish farm, graze cattle and have flea free cats. Glowworm caves, deep-sea fishing, scuba diving and golf available locally. No smoking please. American spoken. Bookings recommended.

WAIPU   *6km SE of Waipu*

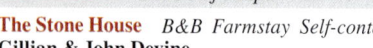 

The Stone House   *B&B Farmstay Self-contained*
Gillian & John Devine
Cove Road, Waipu

Tel (09) 432 0432   0800 007 358   Fax (09) 432 0432
stonehousewaipu@xtra.co.nz
www.bnb.co.nz/thestonehouse.html

Double $80-$120   Single $60-$70   (Full Breakfast)
Child $20   Dinner $25   Credit cards accepted
Children welcome   Pets welcome
1 King/Twin   2 Queen   1 Double   3 Single   (4 bdrm)
Bathrooms: 1 Ensuite   3 Private

Relax in a charming seaside cottage or with your hosts Gillian and John in their unique solid Stonehouse. Either way you will enjoy the green pastures of our farm, fringed with mature pohutakawa trees and the sound of surf on our magnificent ocean beach. Picturesque rock gardens, croquet lawn and sheltered patios complete the setting. Canoes and dinghys are available for exploring the adjacent lagoon and bird sanctuary. A touch of Cornwall with warm company around a log fire. German spoken.

WAIPU COVE *8km SE of Waipu*

Flower Haven *B&B Self-contained Downstairs Flat*
Shirley & Brian Flower
53 St Anne Road, Waipu Cove, RD 2, Waipu 0254

Tel (09) 432 0421
bnb@flowerhaven.com
www.flowerhaven.com

Double $95-$115 (Continental Breakfast)
Credit cards accepted
2 Double (2 bdrm)
Bathrooms: 1 Private

Flower Haven is elevated with panoramic coastal views, being developed as a garden retreat. The accommodation is a self-contained downstairs flat with separate access; kitchen includes stove, microwave, fridge/freezer. Washing machine, radio, TV, linen, duvets, blankets and bath towels provided. Reduced tariff if continental breakfast not required. Our interests are gardening, genealogy and meeting people. Near to restaurants, museums, golf, horse treks, fishing, walking tracks, oil refinery. 5 minutes to shop, sandy surf beach, rocks. Whangarei 35 minutes, Auckland 1^{1}/2 hours.

WAIPU COVE *10 km S of Waipu*

Melody Lodge *B&B Homestay*
Melody Gard
996 Cove Road, Waipu, Northland

Tel **(09) 432 0939** Fax (09) 432 0939
melody@melodylodge.co.nz
www.melodylodge.co.nz

Double $85-$110 Single $65
(Continental Breakfast)
1 Queen 1 Double 2 Twin (3 bdrm)
Bathrooms: 1 Ensuite 1 Guests share

Situated between the popular beaches of Waipu Cove and Langs Beach, Melody Lodge overlooks the whole of Bream Bay. Stunning sea views from all rooms. New cedar house with garden and spectacular stand of native bush adjacent. Resident artist and cat. Attached art gallery features local artworks and exclusive screenprinted souvenirs. Swim at Waipu, stroll Langs Beach, study birdlife, experience the bush, a round of golf, horse riding, kayaking, fishing. Bush, sea, music, art and good conversation... relax and enjoy it all from Melody Lodge.

LANGS BEACH *12km SE of Waipu*

Lochalsh Bed & Breakfast *B&B*
Graham & Billie Long
Cove Road, Langs Beach, Waipu

Tel **(09) 432 0053** Fax (09) 432 0053
Mob 025 203 1660 lochalsh@clear.net.nz
www.lochalsh.co.nz

Double $95-$125 Single $60-$95 (Full Breakfast)
Child price on application Dinner $25 by arrangement
Credit cards accepted Children welcome
1 King/Twin 1 King (2 bdrm)
Bathrooms: 2 Ensuite

Our great-grandfather settled this area in 1853. Our home is right beside this most beautiful of white surf beaches, lined by Pohutukawa trees. There is modern facilities, sunny guest lounge with Sky TV, kitchen and dining area running right along the front of the house, looking over the beach and Hen and Chicken Islands. Comfortable rooms with ensuites make this a delightful place for rest and relaxation. Billie & Graham provide friendly but unobtrusive hosting. From our visitors book: 'Our best stay in New Zealand!'

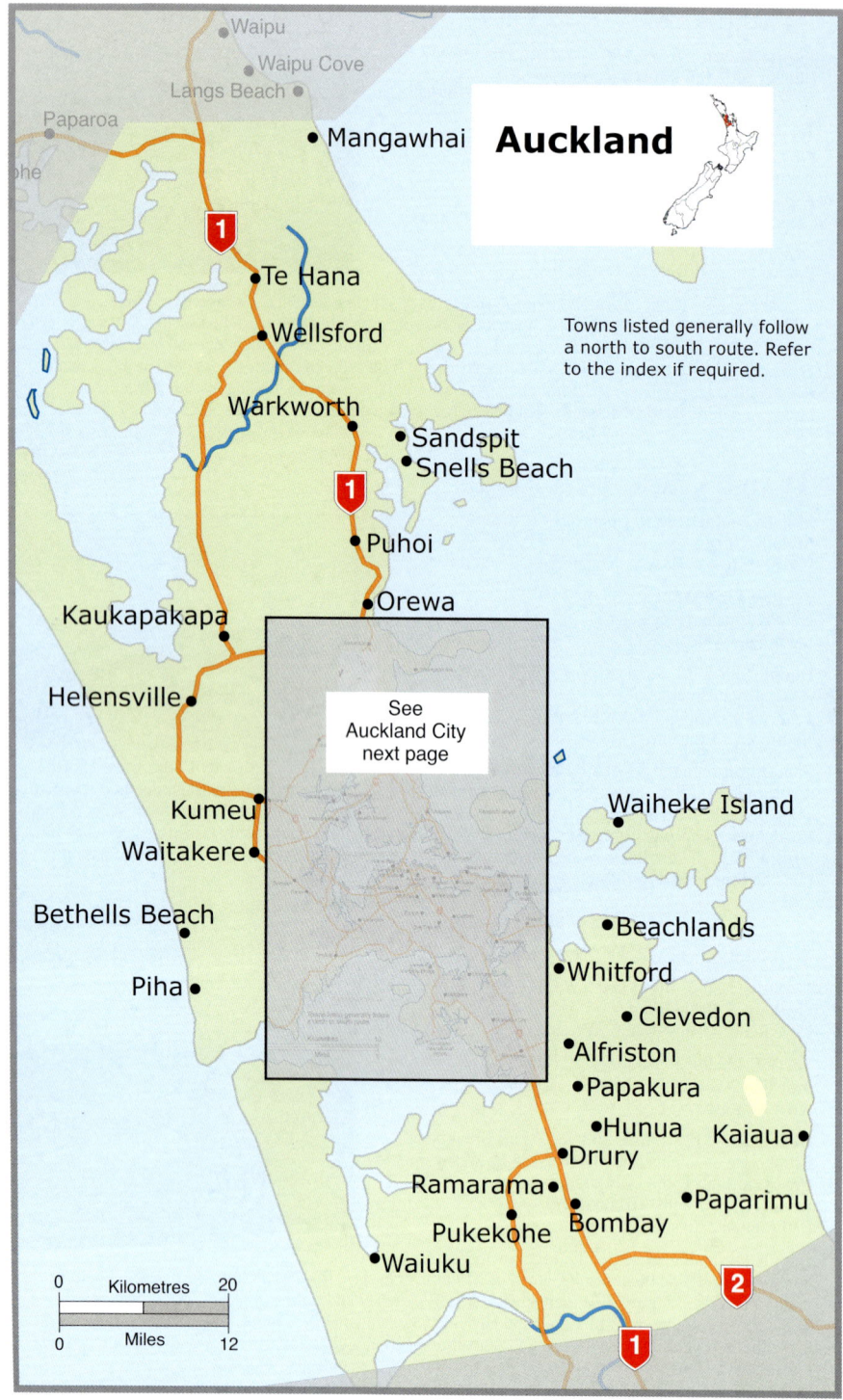

Auckland

Towns listed generally follow a north to south route. Refer to the index if required.

Waipu
Waipu Cove
Langs Beach
Paparoa
Mangawhai
Te Hana
Wellsford
Warkworth
Sandspit
Snells Beach
Puhoi
Orewa
Kaukapakapa
See Auckland City next page
Helensville
Waiheke Island
Kumeu
Waitakere
Beachlands
Bethells Beach
Whitford
Piha
Clevedon
Alfriston
Papakura
Hunua
Kaiaua
Drury
Ramarama
Paparimu
Pukekohe
Bombay
Waiuku

Kilometres 0 — 20
Miles 0 — 12

AUCKLAND

Auckland City

Red Beach
Silverdale
Whangaparaoa
Okura
Torbay
Browns Bay
Coatesville
Albany
28
Greenhithe
16
Hobsonville
Takapuna
Rangitoto Island
Bayswater
Devonport
Freemans Bay
Ponsonby
Herne Bay
Auckland Central
Mission Bay
St Heliers
Parnell
Orakei
Swanson
Ranui
Western Springs
Bucklands Beach
Henserson
Mt Eden
Remuera
Oratia
Epsom
Avondale
One Tree Hill
Howick
Pakuranga
Titirangi
Hillsborough
Mangere Bridge
Otahuhu
Mangere
1
Towns listed generally follow
a north to south route. Refer
to the index if required.
Manukau City
Auckland
International
Airport
Manurewa

0 Kilometres 5
0 Miles 3

WELLSFORD - TE HANA   *6km N of Wellsford*

The Retreat Historic Farmhouse   *Farmstay*
Colleen & Tony Moore
Te Hana, RD 5, Wellsford

Tel (09) 423 8547
booking@sheepfarmstay.com
www.sheepfarmstay.com

Double $95   (Full Breakfast)
Dinner $25pp by arrangement
Self-contained cottage $95
Credit cards accepted
2 Queen 1 Double 1 Single (3 bdrm)
Bathrooms: 1 Ensuite 1 Private

Tony and Colleen welcome you to The Retreat, a
spacious 1860's farmhouse built for a family with
12 children. Set well back from the road, the house is surrounded by an extensive landscaped garden,
including a productive vegetable garden and orchard. Fresh produce from the garden is a feature in our
home-cooking.

Colleen is a spinner and weaver and our flock of sheep provides the raw material for the woollen goods
that are hand-made and for sale from the studio. If you haven't got close up to a sheep this is your
chance, as we always have friendly sheep to hand feed. We have hosted guests at The Retreat since 1988
and appreciate what you require.

We know New Zealand well, our families have lived in NZ for several generations and we have visited
most places in our beautiful country, so if you have any questions on what to see or do, we are well
equipped to provide the answers. We host only one group at a time, so you won't have to share a
bathroom with someone you don't know.

The Retreat is very easy to find. Travelling North on SH1, we are 6km North of Wellsford, look
for the Weaving Studio sign on your left. You will pass through Te Hana before arriving at The
Retreat. Kaiwaka is 13km north of The Retreat.

MANGAWHAI HEADS *1km SE of Mangawhai Heads*

Mangawhai Lodge - A Room with a View Boutique B&B Inn *Boutique Bed and Breakfast Inn*
Jeannette Forde
4 Heather Street, Mangawhai Heads

Tel (09) 431 5311 Fax (09) 431 5312
mlodge@xtra.co.nz
www.seaviewlodge.co.nz

Double $150-$165 Single $120-$140 (Full Breakfast)
Credit cards accepted
3 King/Twin 2 Queen 8 Single (5 bdrm)
Bathrooms: 3 Ensuite 2 Private

Nestled above the seaside town of Mangawhai Heads, midway between the Bay of Islands and Auckland International Airport. Mangawhai Lodge offers spectacular sea and island views of the Hauraki Gulf and white sandy beaches of Mangawhai. 5 stylish guest rooms open onto wrap-around verandahs. Spend your days on the adjacent championship golf course, exploring the beaches and walkways or enjoying the tranquil environment. Ideal for couples, social & golfing groups. Walking distance to cafes and harbour beach. Guest kitchenette and lounges.

WELLSFORD *7km N of Wellsford*

Rosandra Homestay *B&B Farmstay*
Ross & Sandra Williams
557 SH1, RD 5, Wellsford

Tel (09) 423 9343 Fax (09) 423 9343
Mob 021 179 9311 rosandra@xtra.co.nz
www.bnb.co.nz/rosandrahomestay.html

Double $100 Single $80 (Full Breakfast)
Credit cards accepted
3 Queen 1 Twin (4 bdrm)
Bathrooms: 1 Ensuite 1 Guests share

Welcome to our 90 acre lifestyle farm. Beautifully covered with mature trees, where our sheep and beef cattle graze. Privately set in landscaped gardens our modern home offers you warm spacious guest rooms with ensuite, private lounge, opening on to a sunny outdoor deck area. Swim all year round in the indoor 15 metre heated pool or watch the big screen TV while relaxing in the spa pool. Situated close to golf courses and East Coast beaches, find us easily on SH1, 7km north of Wellsford and opposite Mangawhai turn-off. 2 cats.

WARKWORTH *0.5km N of Warkworth*

Homewood Cottage *B&B*
Ina & Trevor Shaw
17 View Road, Warkworth

Tel (09) 425 8667 Fax (09) 425 9610
Mob 025 235 7469 or 021 117 6457
ina.homewoodcottage@xtra.co.nz
www.bnb.co.nz/homewoodcottage.html

Double $90 (Continental Breakfast)
Credit cards accepted
1 Queen 1 Twin (2 bdrm)
Bathrooms: 2 Ensuite

Our home is in a peaceful, quiet garden with views of Warkworth and the hills. The bed-sitter style rooms are a good size. Each has own entrance, tea making, TV and patio with car parking. No cooking. The rooms are private but feel free to come in and chat. Breakfast is substantial continental with choice. We enjoy walking and golf. Ina is an artist. Close to town and a selection of restaurants. Our home is smoke-free. Please phone. View Road is off Hill Street.

WARKWORTH - SANDSPIT

7km E of Warkworth

Belvedere Homestay   *Homestay*
M & R Everett
38 Kanuka Road, RD 2,
Warkworth

Tel (09) 425 7201   Fax (09) 425 7201
Mob 027 284 4771
belvederehomestay@xtra.co.nz
www.belvederehomestay.co.nz

Double $130-$140 Single $90
(Special Breakfast) Dinner $40pp
Credit cards accepted
2 Queen 1 Twin (3 bdrm)
Bathrooms: 1 Ensuite 2 Private

*'Belvedere' has 360-degree views, sea to
countryside; it's 'awesome'.*

Relaxing decks, barbecue, garden,
orchards, native birds and bush, peace
and tranquillity with good parking. Air-
conditioned, spa, games room, comfortable
beds are all here for your comfort.

Many attractions are within 7km and
Margaret's flair with cooking is a great
way to relax after an adventurous day
with pre-drinks, two course meal and
wine. Have a warm and relaxing stay
with Margaret & Ron.

*'Sandspit' the perfect stop
to & from the Bay of Islands*

WARKWORTH *13km E of Warkworth*

Homestay Self-contained
Barbara & John Maltby
Omaha Orchards, 282 Point Wells Road,
RD 6, Warkworth

Tel (09) 422 7415   Fax (09) 422 7419
jandbmaltby@value.net.nz   www.bnb.co.nz/maltby.html

Double $60-$85 Single $60-$75 (Continental Breakfast)
Dinner $15-$25 by arrangement. Extra persons $12
In-house accommodation available if required.
1 Queen 1 Double (1 bdrm)
Bathrooms: 1 Ensuite

Our home and self-contained unit (built 1999) is set on 11 acres nestled beside the Whangateau Harbour. Relax in the extensive gardens and swim in the beautifully appointed pool. Nearby is Omaha Beach, golf course, tennis courts, restaurants, art and craft studios, pottery works, museum, Sheep World, Honey Centre and Kawau Island. This is some of the prettiest coastline in New Zealand. John and Barbara look forward to sharing their little slice of paradise with you.

WARKWORTH *9km E of Warkworth*

Island Bay Retreat
Self-contained studio loft apartment
Joyce & Bill Malofy
105 Ridge Road, Scotts Landing, RD 2, Warkworth

Tel (09) 425 4269   Fax (09) 425 4265
Mob 025 262 8358
www.bnb.co.nz/islandbayretreat.html

Double $115
1 Queen (1 bdrm)
Bathrooms: 1 Ensuite

Secluded intimate retreat on the beautiful Mahurangi
Peninsula. Set amongst 2 acres of lovely gardens right on Mahurangi Harbour's foreshore. Idyllic magical place to relax in total privacy, captivating panoramic sea and rural views from our cosy open plan accommodation. Facilities for weekend or longer stays (self-catering). Sundecks, reclining chairs, BBQ, kitchen, TV, ensuite (own entrance). Stroll along the bays to historic Scott's Landing, bush trails, swimming, boating, fishing (rods provided). Friendly village atmosphere, licensed restaurants, shopping and attractions. (Auckland 1 hour)

WARKWORTH - SANDSPIT *10km E of Warkworth*

Sea Breeze *B&B Self-contained*
Di & Robin Grant
14 Puriri Place, RD 2, Sandspit Heights, Warkworth

Tel (09) 425 7220   Fax (09) 425 7220
Mob 021 657 220
robindi.grant@xtra.co.nz
www.bnb.co.nz/seabreeze.html

Double $120 Single $100 (Continental Breakfast)
Credit cards accepted
1 Queen (1 bdrm)
Bathrooms: 1 Ensuite

Sea Breeze is a self-contained luxury apartment with magnificent sea views and surrounding bush. Breakfast is provided in the kitchenette to be enjoyed at your leisure and a bedsettee in the lounge doubles for extra guests. There are lovely bush walks to the beaches immediately below the property. Take a cruise to Kawau Island or visit the many vineyards, galleries and cafés. Your hosts have travelled extensively and now enjoy gardening and boating in their spare time. Phone/fax for directions.

WARKWORTH *2.5km S of Warkworth*

Warkworth Country House
B&B Private entrance/patio
Alan & Pauline Waddington
18 Wilson Road, RD 1, Warkworth

Tel **(09) 422 2485** Fax (09) 422 2485
Mob 027 660 3996 paulalan@xtra.co.nz
www.bnb.co.nz/warkworthcountry.html

Double $110-$130 Single $80-$100 (Full Breakfast)
Child price on application Credit cards accepted
1 Queen 1 Twin (2 bdrm)
Bathrooms: 2 Ensuite

Situated in 2 peaceful acres with country and estuary views, just 45 minutes north of Auckland. Each tasteful room has ensuite, private entrance and patio, TV, tea/coffee making facilities, heater, electric blankets, radio alarm and toiletries. Enjoy a delicious full breakfast in our country-style dining room then visit one of many local places of interest in this lovely part of New Zealand. Warkworth township with its variety of shops and restaurants is just 3 minutes drive away. A warm welcome awaits you.

WARKWORTH - SANDSPIT *7km E of Warkworth*

Shoalwater *B&B Self-contained Studio room*
Don & Jocelyn Adolph
1 Kanuka Road (entrance down right of way to 9A
Kanuka Road), Sandspit, RD2, Warkworth

Tel **(09) 425 0566** 0800 110 925 Fax (09) 425 0567
Mob 021 126 0081 shoalwater@xtra.co.nz
www.shoalwater.co.nz

Double $130-$170 Single $120-$160
(Continental Breakfast) Credit cards accepted
2 Queen (2 bdrm)
Bathrooms: 2 Ensuite 2 Private

Situated on the waterfront with breathtaking views of tidal movements and moored boats at Sandspit. 2 new luxurious studios with magical water views, own entrances to give maximum privacy, fresh cut flowers, candles for a touch of romance. Each studio has a large tiled ensuite, lounge chairs, dining table, tea/coffee, fridge, microwave, stereo, TV, video, home comforts to ensure you have a memorable stay. Visit boutique vineyards, restaurants, cafes, potteries, art galleries, beaches, short walk to Kawau ferry or just relax and listen to the sounds of native birds in a truly tranquil setting.

WARKWORTH - SANDSPIT *6km E of Warkworth*

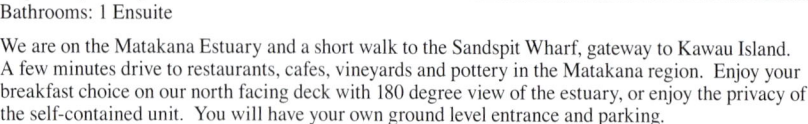

Jacaranda House B&B *B&B Self-contained*
Gillian Irons & Richard Bray
1186 Sandspit Road,
RD 2 Ext, Warkworth

Tel **(09) 422 2394** Fax (09) 422 2395
Mob 027 283 7772 or 027 497 6314
jacarandahouse@xtra.co.nz
www.bnb.co.nz/jacaranda.html

Double $100-$120 Single $80-$90 (Full Breakfast)
1 Queen (1 bdrm)
Bathrooms: 1 Ensuite

We are on the Matakana Estuary and a short walk to the Sandspit Wharf, gateway to Kawau Island. A few minutes drive to restaurants, cafes, vineyards and pottery in the Matakana region. Enjoy your breakfast choice on our north facing deck with 180 degree view of the estuary, or enjoy the privacy of the self-contained unit. You will have your own ground level entrance and parking.

WARKWORTH - RURAL   *8km SE of Warkworth*

The Cedar House   *B&B Homestay*
Shona & Julian Huxtable
60 Cowan Bay Road,
RD 3, Warkworth 1241

Tel (09) 422 2579   Mob 0212 383850
thecedarhouse@xtra.co.nz
www.bnb.co.nz/thecedarhouse.html

Double $120-$150   (Full Breakfast)
Dinner by prior arrangement $35
2 Queen (2 bdrm)
Bathrooms: 2 Ensuite

Set in 7 acres, The Cedar House commands magnificent views over rolling pasture and native bush to Kawau, Little and Great Barrier Islands. You are invited to share our home and perhaps swim in the pool or stroll around the gardens with our pet collies, Frank and Bonnie. Enjoy a relaxing breakfast, often served outside. We also offer a three course dinner, enhanced by the use of fresh produce from the garden and a complimentary glass of wine.

SNELLS BEACH   *8km SE of Warkworth*

Amble In   *B&B*
Trish & Chris Percival
25 Fidelis Avenue, Snells Beach

Tel (09) 425 6399   Fax (09) 425 6399
Mob 025 403 299   pinkperil@xtra.co.nz
www.bnb.co.nz/amblein.html

Double $80-$110   Single $50-$60   (Full Breakfast)
Child neg   Children welcome
1 Queen 1 Double (2 bdrm)
Bathrooms: 2 Ensuite

Trish and Chris warmly welcome you to Amble In. Your room has a lovely seaview with warm comfortable beds. Melodious birdsong to add to peaceful surroundings. Walk to adjoining nature reserve for panoramic views to Kawau Island or just amble along our beaches & walking paths. The friendly Jerusalem donkeys are always happy to see you! Attractions include many beautiful beaches and scenic walks. Ferry rides to Kawau Island, wineries, snorkelling & diving at Goat Island Marine Reserve. Rooms have TV and tea/coffee making facilities. Relax Unwind Enjoy!!

PUHOI   *20km N of Orewa*

Our Farm-Park   *Farmstay*
Nichola(s) & Peter Rodgers
Our Farm-Park, Krippner Road,
RD 3, Kaukapakapa, Auckland 1250

Tel (09) 422 0626   Fax (09) 422 0626 Mob 021 215 5165
ofp@friends.co.nz   www.ustay2.com

Double from $125   Single from $115 (Special Breakfast)
Children with parents no charge   All meals available
Credit cards accepted   Children welcome
1 Queen 2 Twin (2 bdrm)   Bathrooms: 1 Private

Farmstay, the gentle, organic way. Your family only guests. Tariff includes taste-filled organic meals; fruit and vegetables; fresh baking ... very comfortable beds. Come relax (no charge for your welcomed children); sleep off jet-lag. Panoramic views, fresh air, clean water; share experiences, ideas and knowledge over dinner. Walk through trees, streams, bird life, flora & fauna, secluded places. Use library, business facilities. We farm (with kindness) sheep, belted galloway cows, horses, ducks, poultry running free, providing milk, butter, yoghurt, ice-cream, cheeses ... more information at www.ustay2.com.

PUHOI   *9km N of Orewa*

Westwell Ho   *Homestay*
Fae & David England
34 Saleyards Road, Puhoi 1240

Tel (09) 422 0064   Fax (09) 422 0064
Mob 027 280 5795   dhengland@xtra.co.nz
www.bnb.co.nz/westwellho.html

Double $95   Single $75   (Full Breakfast) Child $35
Credit cards accepted   Children welcome
1 Queen 1 Double 1 Single (2 bdrm)
Bathrooms: 1 Ensuite 1 Private

We welcome you to our sunny colonial style home in the lovely Puhoi Valley. We are only 2 minutes by car west of Main North Highway up a small road behind the old pub in this historic Puhoi Village. The homestead has wide verandahs around 3 sides where you can relax as you view the gardens and beautiful trees. Nearby are the fantastic Waiwera Thermal Pools, or you could hire a canoe and paddle down the Puhoi River to Wenderholm Beach and Park. Sky TV available.

OREWA   *20min N of Auckland Central*

Villa Orewa   *B&B Homestay Self-contained*
Sandra & Ian Burrow
264 Hibiscus Coast Highway,
Orewa, Auckland

Tel (09) 426 3073   Fax (09) 426 3053
Mob 021 626 760   rooms@villaorewa.co.nz
www.villaorewa.co.nz

Double $150-$225 (Special Breakfast)
Dinner by arrangement Credit cards accepted
1 King/Twin 2 Queen (3 bdrm)
Bathrooms: 3 Ensuite

Welcome to our beautifully appointed unique new Mediterranean style home, with white-washed walls and blue vaulted roofs, - a taste of the Greek Isles here on beautiful Orewa Beach, just 25 minutes drive north of downtown Auckland. Stay in one of our self-contained rooms, each with private balcony, and enjoy the panoramic beach and sea views, or socialise with us in our spacious living areas as you wish. Orewa offers a great range of activities and amenities, and the cafés, reataurants, and shopping are all within a few metres walk. We are sure your stay will be enjoyable and memorable.

OREWA BEACH   *Orewa*

Orewa Bach   *B&B*
Lesley & Grahame Gilbertson
309A Hibiscus Coast Highway,
Orewa Beach, Auckland 1461

Tel (09) 426 3510   Fax (09) 426 3509
Mob 025 237 9567
grahame.g@xtra.co.nz   www.orewabach.co.nz

Double $150-$200 Single $130-$180
(Special Breakfast) Credit cards accepted
2 Queen (2 bdrm)   Bathrooms: 2 Ensuite

Welcome to Orewa Bach, situated on the picturesque Hibiscus Coast, with absolute beach frontage to popular Orewa Beach. The central shopping area with a variety of cafés, restaurants and bars is immediately adjacent. 2 luxurious bedrooms feature ensuites, heated towel rail, hairdryer, toiletries and quality bed linen. The guest lounge has modern furniture, Sky TV, complimentary refreshments are provided. Enjoy delicious breakfasts served in the dining alcove or outdoors on the patio. Local attractions include golf courses, hot pools, factory and craft shops and wineries.

OREWA   *3.5km SE of Orewa*

Red Beach Homestay   *Homestay*
Loretta Austin
13A William Bayes Place,
Red Beach, Orewa

Tel (09) 426 7204   Fax (09) 426 7204
Mob 025 619 5659   l.austin@xtra.co.nz
www.bnb.co.nz/redbeachhomestay.html

Double $85   Single $45   (Continental Breakfast)
1 Double 1 Single (2 bdrm)
Bathrooms: 1 Ensuite 1 Guests share

Escape the city. Relax by the park! Walk to our safe surf beach (body boards available). Red Beach is 30 minutes north of the harbour bridge, 1 hour from Auckland Airport and has easy access to highways north. It is a casual, relaxed seaside suburb, with 3 golf courses, yacht marina, hot pools, and beach and bush walks. My house is light and sunny, casual and comfortable, and the double ensuite room has tea and coffee facilities and TV. Off-season discount. Some German spoken.

OREWA - RED BEACH   *5km S of Orewa*

Hibiscus House   *B&B*
Judy & Brian Marsden
13A Marellen Drive, Red Beach,
Whangaparaoa - Hibiscus Coast

Tel (09) 427 6303   Fax (09) 427 6303
Mob 025 492 025 or 025 472 056
jb.marsden@xtra.co.nz
www.bnb.co.nz/hibiscushouse.html

Double $95   Single $75   (Full Breakfast)   Dinner $25
2 Queen 2 Twin (3 bdrm)
Bathrooms: 2 Ensuite 1 Private

We offer quality bed & breakfast opposite a beach for the relaxing break you deserve, en route to Northland. Judy and Brian give friendly, personal hospitality in a very convenient location. Handy to shops, markets, cinema, beaches, golf courses and a Leisure Centre complex with heated swimming pool. Easy walks to surf, tennis and squash clubs. RSA 5 minutes away. Gulf Harbour Marina for ferries, fishing and sailing. Restaurants/bars/cafés for all tastes and occasions 5-15 minutes away. Sorry no pets. Children over 12 welcome.

WHANGAPARAOA   *4km E of Orewa*

Duncansby by the Sea   *B&B*
Kathy & Ken Grieve
72 Duncansby Road, Whale Cove,
Red Beach, Whangaparaoa

Tel (09) 424 0025   Fax (09) 424 3607
Mob 025 200 9688 or 027 442 2278
duncansby@xtra.co.nz   www.duncansby-bnb.co.nz

Double $105   Single $70   (Full Breakfast)
Credit cards accepted
2 Queen (2 bdrm)
Bathrooms: 1 Ensuite 1 Private

Duncansby, our brand new home, offers relaxing panoramic sea views of the Hibiscus Coast. Located at Whale Cove between Red Beach and Stanmore Bay, our modern sunny well appointed rooms have own entrances, TV, decks, white linen, tea/coffee facilities. Paradise for golfers with 3 local golf courses including International Gulf Harbour Course with its boating and fishing marina. Visit Tiritiri Bird Sanctuary, walk Shakespeare Park. Enjoy 9 superb beaches, excellent local restaurants and cafés. Only 35 minutes north of Auckland City, we welcome you.

WHANGAPARAOA   *14km S of Orewa*

The Palms on Tindalls   *B&B Self-contained*
Colleen & Graham Davies
75 Deluen Ave, Tindalls Bay

Tel **(09) 424 1930**   Fax (09) 424 1930
Mob 025 293 4929   davies@palmsretreat.co.nz
www.palmsretreat.co.nz

Double $145-$225 Single $145-$225
(Continental Breakfast)
Extra adult $50 per night   Credit cards accepted
1 Queen 1 Double (2 bdrm)
Bathrooms: 1 Private

Enjoy the magic of this beachfront, luxury 2 bedroom cabana style villa. The Palms on Tindalls Beach: one of 12 fabulous beaches on the incredible Whangaparaoa Peninsula. Savour the private, romantic atmosphere with the lounge and other rooms providing indoor/outdoor living to the tropical garden and views across the bay. The Palms is close to many local activities and facilities, including boat ramps, amazing regional parks, geothermal hot pools, Gulf Harbour Marina, golf courses, shopping centres and a variety of quality restaurants.

KAUKAPAKAPA   *14km N of Kaukapakapa*

Kereru Lodge   *Homestay*
Mrs B Headford
Arone Farm, RD 3, Kaukapakapa

Tel **(09) 420 5223**   Fax (09) 420 5223
Mob 021 420 522   Bheadford@xtra.co.nz
www.bnb.co.nz/kererulodgekaukapakapa.html

Double $80   Single $45   (Full Breakfast)
Dinner $20   Credit cards accepted
1 Queen 1 Double 2 Single (3 bdrm)
Bathrooms: 1 Ensuite 1 Guests share

Relax in comfort and enjoy the warm hospitality of our large Kiwi country home. Set in a large much loved garden, in a quiet rural valley our home has lots of indoor/outdoor living. You may wish to play petanque or darts or pool, or just relax with a drink in the Summerhouse. Locally there are bushwalks, golf and tennis. We have many interests from shell collecting to geology and fossils. We enjoy sharing the delights of country living and meeting people from around the world.

SILVERDALE - WAINUI   *8km SW of Silverdale*

Whitehills Country Stay   *B&B Self-contained*
Maureen & Dennis Evans
224 Whitehills Road, Wainui, RD 1, Kaukapakapa

Tel **(09) 420 5666**   Fax (09) 420 5666
Mob 021 042 7958   d-mevans@xtra.co.nz
www.bnb.co.nz/whitehillscountrystay.html

Double $120 Single $75   (Continental Breakfast)
Child neg   Dinner $30 by arrangement
Self-contained studio $130
Credit cards accepted   Children welcome
1 Queen 4 Single (3 bdrm)   Bathrooms: 2 Private

Relax and unwind at Whitehills situated 25 minutes from Auckland and 7 minutes from the Silverdale motorway exit. Enjoy quality B&B accommodation in the main house with a choice of twin or queen room. The comfortable self-contained studio has its own entrance and deck. Breakfast provisions will be provided. You are most welcome to wander around our garden, walk in the 6 acres of native bush or simply relax on the covered verandah. We, and our friendly border collie, look forward to meeting you.

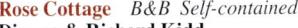

HELENSVILLE   *4km SW of Helensville*

Rose Cottage   *B&B Self-contained*
Dianne & Richard Kidd
2191 State Highway 16, RD 2, Helensville

Tel (09) 420 8007   0800 755 433   Fax (09) 420 7966
Mob 025 599 135   kidds@xtra.co.nz
www.bnb.co.nz/rosecottagehelensville.html

Double $110   Single $80   (Full Breakfast)
Credit cards accepted
1 Queen (1 bdrm)
Bathrooms: 1 Ensuite

Rose Cottage offers comfort and privacy set within peaceful gardens. Whenuanui is a 350 hectare Helensville sheep and beef farm providing magnificent farm walks. The family homestead and gardens have panoramic views over Helensville and the Kaipara Valley. Tasteful accommodation includes ensuite, TV and kitchenette. All-weather tennis court available for guests to use. Just 35 minutes from downtown Auckland on State Highway 16. A base to explore the Kaipara region or a great start or end to your Northland tour. Smoking outdoors appreciated.

KUMEU   *26km NW of Auckland*

Calico Lodge   *B&B Homestay Countrystay*
Kay & Kerry Hamilton
250 Matua Road, RD 1, Kumeu

Tel (09) 412 8167   0800 50 18 50   Mob 025 286 6064
bed@calicolodge.co.nz
www.calicolodge.co.nz

Double $110-$160 Single $95   (Full Breakfast)
Credit cards accepted
3 Queen 2 Single (4 bdrm)
Bathrooms: 2 Ensuite 2 Private

Kerry and Kay, Zippy our little dog, 3 cats and tame sheep welcome you to Calico Lodge. Amidst the wineries, wedding venues, and cafés, near west coast beaches, 25 minutes NW of Auckland our modern home on 4 acres has beautiful trees and gardens. Hand made teddy bears and patchwork quilting (for sale) adorn the bedrooms and lounge in separate guest wing. 2 minutes SH16, peace and beautiful bush views complete the picture. We love to share our little piece of paradise.

HOBSONVILLE   *15mins NW of Auckland*

Eastview   *B&B Homestay Separate/Suite*
Joane & Don Clarke
2 Parkside Road, Hobsonville, Auckland

Tel (09) 416 9254   Fax (09) 416 9254
eastview@xtra.co.nz
www.bnb.co.nz/eastview.html

Double $100-$120 Single $80-$100 (Full Breakfast)
Child $30 Dinner by arrangement   Exta adult discount
Credit cards accepted   Children welcome
2 Queen 2 Single (3 bdrm)
Bathrooms: 2 Private

Our easy to find location is well situated for exploring Auckland. Stunning panoramic water/city views. 2 sun-drenched spacious guest areas. Marina Suite, offers your own lounge opening into a colourful garden, studio kitchen, 2 bedrooms, (queen, twin) private bathroom. Upstairs 1 bedroom, (queen) private bathroom. Relax in comfort after your trip or sightseeing day with a tea/coffee and home-baked cookies. Be pampered with crisp linen, fluffy towels, robes, Sky TV, flowers, fruit, complimentary port. Enjoy Rosie (cat) and Pebbles (small dog). Welcome.

BETHELLS BEACH *15km W of Swanson*

Bethell's Beach Cottages *Self-contained Cottages & 100 Seater Summer Pavilion*
Trude & John Bethell-Paice
PO Box 95057, Swanson, Auckland

Tel (09) 810 9581 Fax (09) 810 8677
info@bethellsbeach.com www.bethellsbeach.com

Double $195-$295 (Special Breakfast)
Child under 12 years $1/2$ price
Dinner 2 course $35pp 3 course $45pp
Breakfast extra $25pp + GST
Credit cards accepted Children welcome
2 Queen 2 Double 3 Single (3 bdrm)
Bathrooms: 2 Private

"To Give is to Love & To Love is to Live"
Trude Bethell-Paice

Drive 30 minutes from Auckland city to one of the most unique parts of the west coast. The Bethell's settled this area 6 generations ago and Trude and John continue the long family tradition of hospitality.

They have created two magic cottages and venue in this spectacular place where the best sunsets and seaviews are to be experienced - as seen in: *Next (NZ), Cuisine NZ, Elle (UK), Fodors (USA), Turquiose Holiday (UK) 2003*. Both cottages have a sunny north facing aspect and are surrounded by 200 year old pohutukawa's (NZ Christmas tree). Each one is totally separate, private and has a large brick barbecue. The vast front lawn is ideal for games and the gardens are thoughtfully designed for relaxation.

The cottages are made up with your holiday in mind - not only are beds made and towels/linen put out, but Trude and John have attended to too many details to mention and laundry facilities are available. Even the cats will welcome you. As seen in Vogue Australia 1998. Life/The Observer (Great Britain 1998) - *'one of twenty great world wide destinations'*. British TV Travel Show 1998. She magazine (February 1999) - *'one of the 10 most romantic places to stay in NZ'*. North and South magazine (January 1999) - *'one of the 14 best Bed and Breakfasts in NZ'* Oct 2002 - USA Fodors travel guide.

'Turehu' Cottage has a studio atmosphere with double bi-folding doors from the conservatory. For outdoor dining sit under a pohutukawa tree at your own bench and table on the hillside with views over the beach and Bethell's valley. Cork floor in the kitchen, TV and bedroom area, gentle cream walls and white trim. Warm slate floors in the conservatory with lounge, dining table and bathroom (shower and toilet). Kitchen has microwave, large fridge/freezer, stove and coffee plunger, with all kitchen and dining amenities. Suitable for a couple and one child or two friends.

'Te Koinga' Cottage, this superb home away from home is 80 square metres and has two bi-folding doors onto a 35sqm wooden deck for outdoor dining and relaxation in this sun trap. Set under the shade of a magnificent spralling pohutukawa tree and surrounded by garden. A fireplace for winter warmth and sixteen seater dining table. The two bedrooms have carpet and terracotta tiles expand to the dining, kitchen, bathroom and toilet. Wood panelled and cream/tan rag rolled walls for a relaxing atmosphere. The bathroom offers a bath and shower. Open planned kitchen has microwave, large fridge/freezer, stove, dishwasher and coffee maker. Suitable for a family, two couples or a small function. Trude is a marriage celebrant and Trude and John specialise in weddings, private functions and company workshops. A local professional chef is available for these occasions.

Local adventures - Bethell's beach is a short drive or walk. Pack a picnic lunch and discover Lake Wainamu for fresh water swimming and expansive sand dunes or go on a bush walk with excellent examples of New Zealand native flora. If you head in the direction of the beach you may enjoy exploring the caves (at night the magic of glowworms and phosphorescence in the shallows), or go surfing or fishing. You are close to many world class vineyards and restaurants/cafés. You may fancy a game of golf - two courses within 10-20 minutes drive from your cottage. Many more activities in a short driving distance. No pets please. Children under 12 half price.

BETHELLS VALLEY - WEST AUCKLAND *15km W of Henderson*

Greenmead Farm *Separate/Suite Self-contained*
Averil & Jon Bateman
115 Bethells Road, RD 1, Henderson

Tel **(09) 810 9363** Fax (09) 810 8363
jabat@greenmead.co.nz
www.greenmead.co.nz

Double $110 Breakfast additional charge
Extra guests $20 each Children welcome
4 Single (2 bdrm)
Bathrooms: 1 Private

 (AUCKLAND side tab)

Guests have sole use of comfortable holiday home - 2 bedrooms, bathroom, lounge (TV) and large kitchen/dining room with excellent cooking facilities. Additional guests $20 each. Breakfast extra. The main house and guest cottage are surrounded by a large country garden - swings for children. Cattle, 2 border collie working dogs. Peaceful location in rural valley in the Waitakere Ranges. Good walking tracks in the area - rainforest, beach and lake. 30 minutes drive west of central Auckland. Beach 6 minutes.

WAITAKERE RANGES - SWANSON *4km W of Swanson*

Panorama Heights *B&B*
Allison & Paul Ingram
42 Kitewaho Road, Swanson,
Waitakere City, Auckland

Tel **(09) 832 4777** 0800 NZBNB4U Fax (09) 833 7773
Mob 025 272 8811 nzbnb4u@clear.net.nz
www.panoramaheights.co.nz

Double $125 Single $85 (Full Breakfast)
Dinner by request Credit cards accepted
2 Queen 1 Twin 1 Single (4 bdrm)
Bathrooms: 3 Ensuite 1 Private

Private and peaceful breathtaking panoramic views located high in the Waitakere Ranges on the "Twin Coast Discovery Route". Watch the sun rise across native kauri trees, bush and Auckland City beyond. Within easy access to over 250km of walking tracks through 17,000 hectares of native rainforest. 10-15 minutes from West Coast beaches (Piha, Bethells, Karekare, Muriwai), West Auckland wineries, 2 scenic golf courses, art trails, shopping centers. We offer you excellent quality accommodation at a very affordable price. Please phone for bookings/directions.

RANUI *15mins W of Auckland*

The Garrett *B&B Homestay Detached*
Alma & Rod Mackay
295 Swanson Road, Waitakere City, Auckland 8

Tel **(09) 833 6018** Fax (09) 833 6018
www.bnb.co.nz/mackay.html

Double $80 Single $50 (Continental Breakfast)
Child $22
2 King/Twin 1 King 2 Single (2 bdrm)
Bathrooms: 1 Ensuite

Just 15 minutes from Auckland City and 5 minutes from historical Henderson, The Garrett offers villa style accommodation with ensuite and private terrace. Twin beds or king-size if you prefer. We can accommodate extra guests with folding beds on request. High ceilings and period furniture and décor create an atmosphere of old in this delightful homestay, just minutes away from Waitakere City. Leading attractions include wine trails, Art Out West Trail - including Lopdell House Gallery. Waitake Ranges, bush walks, Aratiki Heritage & Environment Centre, golf courses. West City Shopping Centre, Lynn Mall and St Lukes. No pets; no campervans.

ORATIA *14km W of Auckland City*

Approved

The Shaw *B&B*
Eva Knausenberger
72 Shaw Road, Oratia, Auckland

Tel (09) 813 6652 or 813 6662 Fax (09) 813 6664
eva2@wave.co.nz www.bnb.co.nz/theshaw.html

Double $250 (Continental Breakfast)
Child free Credit cards accepted
Children welcome Pets welcome
1 Queen 1 Double (1 bdrm)
Bathrooms: 1 Ensuite

The Shaw is situated in a stunning area of gardens with a panorama of kauri bush as part of the property.

Enjoy our large, enclosed, non chlorinated heated swimming pool and its tropical garden.

Whether you are single, on honeymoon or with family members, you are welcome to our retreat.

Peace, fragrance and birdsong all grace visitors

56

RANUI *15mins W of Auckland*

The Brushmakers Cottage
B&B Separate/Suite Self-contained
Jeanette & Roger Brown
20 Clearview Heights, Ranui, Waitakere City, Auckland

Tel (09) 833 8476 Mob 027 459 6334
r.g.brown@xtra.co.nz
www.bnb.co.nz/brushmakers.html

Double $85-$150 Single $70-$100 (Full Breakfast)
Extra adults $20 Dinner by arrangement
2 Queen 1 Double 1 Twin (4 bdrm)
Bathrooms: 1 Ensuite 2 Private 1 Host share

Choose between luxury self-contained apartment, featuring full kitchen, dishwasher, dining/lounge, TV/DVD, laundry, or traditional B&B. Backing onto a vineyard this peaceful location has views of both the Waitakere ranges and central Auckland. 10 minutes walk from train and bus stations and only 15 minutes drive from downtown Auckland. Close to both east and west coast beaches, gannet colony, golf courses, winery, cafés, restaurants and shopping malls. A great base for exploring Auckland. Ask about discounts. Some gluten free food available.

PIHA *20km W of Henderson*

Piha Cottage *Separate/Suite Self-contained Cottage*
Tracey & Steve Skidmore
PO Box 48, Piha, Waitakere City, Auckland

Tel (09) 812 8514 Fax (09) 812 8514
info@pihacottage.co.nz
www.pihacottage.co.nz

Double $95-$120 Single $95-$120
(Continental Breakfast) Child $20 Children welcome
1 Double 1 Single (1 bdrm)
Bathrooms: 1 Private

Beautiful Piha Cottage is secluded in a quiet bush setting within easy walking distance of beach and tracks. This open plan home has a well-equipped kitchen and spacious dining, living and sleeping areas. We have 2 young children and a friendly cat. Piha Cottage is on the rugged west coast, nestled into native bush. So leave the city behind. Go surfing, swimming or choose from a network of outstanding walking tracks, through lush rainforest or spectacular coastline. We welcome you warmly and then leave you in peace to enjoy the tranquility.

PIHA *40mins W of Auckland*

Piha Lodge *Self-contained*
Shirley Bond
117 Piha Road, Piha

Tel (09) 812 8595 Fax (09) 812 8583
Mob 021 639 529   pihalodge@xtra.co.nz
www.pihalodge.co.nz

Double $140 (Continental Breakfast) Child $20
Additional adults $30 Credit cards accepted
Children welcome
2 Queen 3 Double 1 Single (5 bdrm)
Bathrooms: 2 Private

Awarded Best Accommodation. Our two quality self-contained units have satellite TV, own BBQ's, stunning panoramic sea and bush views, all the comforts of home plus privacy and security. Situated in the subtropical rainforest of the Waitakere Ranges and on the wild west coast, Piha is a world famous surfing beach with legendary sunsets. Enjoy the bush walks, climb Lion Rock, visit the fairytale Kitekite Falls or relax in the swimming pool, hot spa or games room. Internet access, laundry. Our 2 friendly little bichon dogs are kept separately.

PIHA   *25km W of Henderson*

Westwood Cottage   *Separate/Suite Self-contained*
Dianne & Don Sparrow
95 Glenesk Road, Piha, Auckland

Tel (09) 812 8205   Fax (09) 812 8203
Mob 021 278 8110   westwoodcottage.piha@clear.net.nz
www.bnb.co.nz/westwoodcottage.html

Double $120-$140   (Continental Breakfast)
Child $20   Credit cards accepted   Children welcome
1 Queen 1 Single (2 bdrm)
Bathrooms: 1 Private

Westwood Cottage offers a unique experience. Nestled in a secluded corner of our property, amongst beautiful bush overlooking Piha Valley. The Cottage is self-contained, open plan design, flowing on to a private deck. Full kitchen facilities with continental breakfast supplied. A cozy log fire for your enjoyment on cooler evenings. Off-road parking provided. Children 5 and over welcome. A short walk leads to Piha Surf Beach and bush walks include Kitekite Waterfall and Black Rock Dam.

OKURA   *20km N of Auckland Central*

Okura B&B   *B&B Own lounge*
Judie & Ian Greig
20 Valerie Crescent, Okura,
North Shore City, Auckland

Tel (09) 473 0792   Fax (09) 473 1072
ibgreig@clear.net.nz
www.bnb.co.nz/okurabb.html

Double $95   Single $75   (Full Breakfast)
Credit cards accepted
1 Queen 1 Single (2 bdrm)
Bathrooms: 1 Private

Situated on Auckland's North Shore, Okura is a small settlement bounded by farmland and the Okura River, an estuary edged with native forest. If you like peace, quiet, with only bird song nearby, estuary and forest views, then this is for you. Accommodation includes your own, not shared, TV lounge, tea making facilities, fridge, shower and toilet. Nearby is a wide variety of cafés, shops, beaches, walks, North Shore Stadium, Massey University and golf courses. Okura - one of Auckland's best kept secrets.

OKURA   *20km NE of Auckland Central*

Okura River Cottage   *B&B Self-contained*
Elizabeth & David Keay
12 Deborah Place, Okura, North Shore City

Tel (09) 473 6298   Fax (09) 478 3233
Mob 021 142 6699   nscd@xtra.co.nz
www.bnb.co.nz/okurarivercottage.html

Double $150-$175   (Special Breakfast)   Dinner $30pp
$100-$120 for double room in hosts house
Credit cards accepted
1 Queen 1 Double (2 bdrm)
Bathrooms: 1 Ensuite 1 Private

Okura River Cottage is nestled alongside Auckland's prettiest river. The view from the cottage is stunning. Imagine waking up to sun streaming on calm waters and bush clad hills. Bird life is amazing. Swimming beaches minutes away with bush walks at your doorstep. Self contained top quality detached cottage. Scrumptuous Kiwi home baking awaits your arrival. Ideally situated for a first or last stop from the airport. We and our 2 scottish terriers extend a warm welcome to you at this beautiful tranquil place.

COATESVILLE - ALBANY *7km N of Albany*

Camperdown *Farmstay*
Chris & David Hempleman
455 Coatesville/Riverhead Highway,
RD 3, Albany, Auckland

Tel (09) 415 9009 0800 921 479 Fax (09) 415 9023
chris@camperdown.co.nz www.camperdown.co.nz

Double $130 Single $90 (Full Breakfast) Child $45
Dinner $40 Children welcome
1 King/Twin 1 King 2 Queen 2 Single (4 bdrm)
Bathrooms: 2 Private 1 Guests share

We are only 20 minutes from Auckland City, relax in secluded tranquillity. Our home opens into beautiful gardens, native bush and stream offering the best of hospitality in a friendly relaxed atmosphere. On the farm we have sheep, cattle and pet lambs Our spacious guest areas consist of the entire upstairs. Guests may use our games room, play tennis on our new court, row a boat on the lake, or just stroll by the stream. Camperdown is easy travelling on the main tourist route north. Directions. travel North to Albany, onto Highway 17, turn left at BP into Coatesville/Riverhead Highway (28).

ALBANY - COATESVILLE *3km N of Albany*

Te Harinui Country Homestay
B&B Country Homestay
Mike & Sue Blanchard
102 Coatesville/Riverhead Highway,
RD 3, Albany, Auckland

Tel (09) 415 9295 sue@teharinui.co.nz
www.teharinui.co.nz

Double $95 Single $75 (Full Breakfast)
Child by arrangement Dinner $30 by arrangement
Credit cards accepted Children welcome
1 Queen 2 Single (2 bdrm)
Bathrooms: 1 Guests share

A home from home in the country only 20 minutes from the city. Stroll in the bush and paddocks; feed our pet coloured sheep, our dog and cats are very friendly. Learn to spin and browse our craft shop. We can arrange outings to local attractions including gardens, orchards and beaches. Close to stadium and Massey University. Generous breakfasts; coffee and teas are always available. Sue speaks French and is learning Mandarin.

TORBAY *5km N of Browns Bay*

The Bosun's Locker *B&B Self-contained*
Mandy & Clive Gumbley
11 Waiake Street, Torbay, Auckland

Tel (09) 473 3713 Fax (09) 473 3713
gums@xtra.co.nz www.bnb.co.nz/bosun.html

Double $150-$180 (Special Breakfast)
Child $20 Credit cards accepted
Children welcome Pets welcome
1 King/Twin 1 Double (1 bdrm)
Bathrooms: 1 Private

Welcome to our newly restored cottage, surrounded by a large garden only 80 metres from beautiful Waiake Beach, where a boat mooring is avaliable. Torbay is just 15km north of Auckland, a short walk to local shops, restaurants, cafés and other beautiful beaches. The cottage is self-contained with off-street parking, laundry, fully equiped kitchen. Spend some time relaxing in this tranquil part of NZ. Come and enjoy these wonderful surroundings of our 1933 family home and meet our 2 young children.

GREENHITHE *15km N of Auckland*

Waiata Tui Lodge (The Song of the Tui)
B&B Homestay Rural Homestay
Therese & Ned Jujnovich
177 Upper Harbour Drive, Greenhithe, Auckland

Tel (09) 413 9270 Fax (09) 413 9217
theresewa@xtra.co.nz   www.bnb.co.nz/waiata.html

Double $100-$115 Single $70 (Special Breakfast)
Child neg Dinner $25 Credit cards accepted
2 Queen 1 Twin 2 Single (3 bdrm)
Bathrooms: 3 Private

A warm welcome to our Haven – 8 acres of native forest and
pasture only 15 minutes from NZ's largest city yet so peaceful
you could be in the heart of the countryside. A handy relaxing
stay before your journey north.

Spectacular views from over the kauri trees to the tranquil water
below: with the distant Waitakere Ranges beyond.

A delicious healthy breakfast will be served: home-grown or
local in season fruit, various cereals, home-made yoghurt and
spreads as well as a cooked breakfast, fruit juice, tea or coffee.
From our large kauri breakfast table you can look out to the west
and see the changing patterns of trees, water and tide. Perhaps
a tui or a kereru (NZ's largest colourful pigeon) will stop for a
drink at the birdbath on the adjoining deck.

You may like to walk in our lush rain forest with tree ferns and
massive trees down to the waters edge or you can relax in the
bush hammock with a book. Do some bird watching or wander
around our large garden usually bright with seasonal flowers.
Swim in the pool in summer. Meet Harry our friendly goat.

Therese is a keen wine maker. Ned farmed in the far north.
Both have travelled extensively overseas and within NZ and will
be pleased to help you with you travel plans.

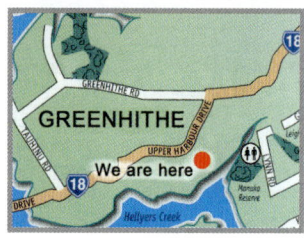

A Lockwood (solid-timber) home built for our family 30 years ago has been a homestay since 1987.
Only 5km to Albany & Glenfield. 5 minutes to Greenhithe Village and restaurants.

Waken to tui-song and the smell of freshly baked bread

BROWNS BAY   *1.5km W of Browns Bay*

Amoritz House   *B&B*
Carol & Gary Moffatt
730 East Coast Road, Browns Bay, Auckland

Tel (09) 479 6338   0800 936 338   Fax (09) 479 6338
Mob 025 806 958   amoritz@ihug.co.nz
www.aucklandaccommodation.co.nz

Double $90-$200 Single $70-$90 (Full Breakfast)
Dinner $10-$30pp Credit cards accepted
2 King/Twin 1 Double 1 Single (3 bdrm)
Bathrooms: 2 Ensuite 1 Private

Spend some peaceful nights in our quiet guest bedrooms with Sky TV, garden and rural outlooks.
Separate guest entrance leads into kitchenette with fridge, microwave, washing machine, dryer etc.
Adjoining dining room. Internet, email, fax etc available. Minutes from North Harbour Stadium,
Millennium Stadium, Massey University, a variety of cafés, restaurants, beaches, shopping and
Auckland City Centre with all its attractions. Bus stop at door. Barbeque. Off-street parking, 2 minutes
to motorway. Non smoking. Dinners $10, $20, $30 per person with prior notice.

BAYSWATER   *5km S of Takapuna*

Matuku Bed and Breakfast   *B&B*
Rhondda & Les Sweetman
39A Beresford Street, Bayswater, North Shore

Tel (09) 445 6649 0800 800 537 Fax (09) 445 6659
Mob 027 491 2281   rhondda@xtra.co.nz
www.bnb.co.nz/matukulodge.html

Double $150-$190 Single $110 (Full Breakfast)
Child $60 Dinner $30pp Credit cards accepted
Children welcome
1 King 2 Queen 1 Twin (3 bdrm)
Bathrooms: 2 Ensuite 1 Private

Tranquil Matuku Bed and Breakfast on the water's edge
of Shoal Bay, Bayswater Peninsula. Only 9 minutes by ferry to Downtown Auckland. Sail, row, canoe,
birdwatch, relax. Beautiful architect designed home complemented by original art (www.kiwiartz.co.nz).
Special concessions on our sailing catamaran (www.kowhaicat.co.nz). King bedroom with ensuite, and
queen bedroom with private bath, open onto deck to the sea. Third bedroom with ensuite has queen and
twin singles. Expect a warm welcome from our border collie, Jess.

DEVONPORT   *1.4km E of Devonport*

The Garden Room   *Self-contained garden cottage*
Perrine & Bryan Hall
23 Cheltenham Road, Devonport

Tel (09) 445 2472   Fax (09) 445 2472
Mob 021 989 642   perrinehall@xtra.co.nz
www.devonportgardenroom.co.nz

Double $160-$180   Single $130-$140
(Special Breakfast) Child $50
Longstay and winter rates available
Independent breakfast enquire Credit cards accepted
2 Queen 2 Single (2 bdrm) Bathrms: 1 Ensuite 1 Private

Private sunny self-contained garden cottage/studio with newly designed kitchen, bathroom, TV lounge.
Queen and large single beds. Crisp cotton sheets, bathrobes. Own entrance and parking. Spa pool.
Few steps from Cheltenham beach, short stroll to Devonport Village, cafés, 10 minute ferry ride to city.
McHughs, Duders receptions restaurants nearby. French doors open onto tranquil garden where breakfast
may be served - fresh juices, fruits, muesli, yoghurt, warm homemade breads, croissants, muffins, free range
eggs. Or you may prefer to be independent (check tariff). Fax/email, laundry in villa, where one queen
bedroom offered. Extra rollaway available. Both travelled widely, knowledge French/Spanish.

DEVONPORT *4km N of Auckland Central*

Karin's Garden Villa *B&B Self-contained Self-contained cottage*
Karin Loesch & Family
14 Sinclair Street, Devonport, Auckland 1309

Tel (09) 445 8689 Fax (09) 445 8689
stay@karinsvilla.com www.karinsvilla.com

Double $145-$175 Single $90-$135
(Continental Breakfast) Child $25
Dinner by arrangement Self-contained cottage $185
Credit cards accepted Children welcome Cot available
1 King/Twin 2 Double 3 Single (4 bdrm)
Bathrooms: 1 Ensuite 1 Private 1 Guests share

Karin's Garden Villa

Tucked away at the end of a quiet cul-de-sac, Karin's Garden Villa - a **Devonport Dream** - offers real home comfort with its light cosy rooms, easy relaxed atmosphere and the warmest of welcome from Karin and her family.

A beautifully restored spacious Victorian villa surrounded by large lawns and old fruit trees. Karin's Garden Villa has also been featured on NZ and Australian television advertising for its relaxed, peaceful setting. Just 5 minutes stroll from tree-lined Cheltenham Beach, sailing, golf, tennis, shops and restaurants and only a short drive or pleasant 10 minute walk past extinct volcanoes to the picturesque Devonport centre with its many attractions.

Your comfortable room offers separate private access through french doors, opening onto a wide verandah and cottage garden. And for those visitors wanting ultimate comfort and privacy, there is even a self-contained studio cottage with balcony and full kitchen facilities to rent (minimum 3 days).

Sit down to a nutritious breakfast in the sunny dining room with its large bay windows overlooking everflowering purple lavender and native gardens. Guests are welcome to join the family barbecue and relax on our large lawn. We welcome longer stays and can arrange favourable discounts accordingly. Help yourself to tea and German-style coffee and biscuits anytime, check your email and feel free to use the kitchen and laundry.

Karin comes from Germany and she and her family have lived in Indonesia for a number of years. We have seen a lot of the world and enjoy meeting other travellers. Always happy to help you arrange island cruises, rental cars, bikes and tours. From the airport take a shuttle bus to our doorstep or to downtown ferry terminal. Courtesy pick-up from Devonport Wharf. By Car: After crossing Harbour Bridge, take Takapuna-Devonport turn-off. Right at T-junction, follow Lake Road to end, left into Albert, Vauxhall Road and then first left into Sinclair Street.

Come As Guests - Leave As Friends

DEVONPORT   *1km Devonport*

Rainbow Villa   *B&B*
Judy McGrath
17 Rattray Street, Devonport, Auckland

Tel (09) 445 3597   Fax (09) 445 4597
rainbowvilla@xtra.co.nz
www.bnb.co.nz/rainbowvilla.html

Double $130-$160   Single $100-$130   (Full Breakfast)
Credit cards accepted
1 King 1 Queen 2 Twin 2 Single (3 bdrm)
Bathrooms: 3 Ensuite

Welcome to our Victorian Villa (1885) nestled in a quiet cul-de-sac on the lower slopes of Mt Victoria. 3 elegant spacious rooms with ensuites, Sky TV. Spa Pool in the garden. We serve a delicious full breakfast, coffee and tea available at all times. Situated just 100 metres from Historic Devonport Village, 5 minute walk to ferry, only 10 minute 'cruise' to downtown Auckland. Directions: Rattray Street is first on left past picture theatre. Shuttles available at airport. Not suitable for children or pets. www.rainbowvilla.co.nz, e-mail rainbowvilla@xtra.co.nz.

DEVONPORT   *1.5km N of Devonport*

Ducks Crossing Cottage   *B&B Homestay*
Gwenda & Peter Mark-Woods
58 Seabreeze Road, Devonport, Auckland

Tel (09) 445 8102   Fax (09) 445 8102
duckxing@splurge.net.nz
www.bnb.co.nz/duckscrossingcottage.html

Double $90-$120   Single $65-$85   (Full Breakfast)
Child $30
1 King/Twin 1 Queen 1 Single (3 bdrm)
Bathrooms: 1 Ensuite 2 Private

Welcome to our charming modern home, built in 1994, surrounded by trees and gardens. Peaceful, spacious and sunny bedrooms with attractive country décor. All rooms have TV and clock radios. Tea and coffee facilities available with delicious home-cooking. we are adjacent Waitemata Golf course and 5 minutes from Narrow Neck Beach. Swim, sail and explore. Devonport village is 2 minutes by car and has a variety of restaurants, cafés and antique shops. Hosts are well travelled, informative and enjoy hospitality. Directions: from airport shuttle direct (door to door). If driving take Route 26, into Seabreeze Road, first house on left. Off-street parking. Courtesy pickup to/from ferry upon request.

DEVONPORT   *75m N of Ferry Terminal*

The Jasmine Cottage   *B&B Self-contained Cottage*
Joan & John Lewis
20 Buchanan Street,
Devonport, Auckland

Tel (09) 445 8825   Fax (09) 445 8605
Mob 021 120 9532 joanjohnlewis@xtra.co.nz
www.photoalbum.co.nz/jasmine/

Double $100   (Full Breakfast)
1 Queen (1 bdrm)
Bathrooms: 1 Ensuite

Welcome to our cosy smoke-free quiet and private guest cottage. We are right in the heart of historic Devonport Village with all its attractions, cafés, beaches, golf course, scenic walks. The ferry to Auckland City and the Hauraki Gulf is 3 minutes walk away. A breakfast basket is delivered to your door and provides fruit juice, cereals, home made muesli and yoghurt, a platter of seasonal fruits, breads, English muffins, jams, spreads, cheeses, free range eggs, breakfast teas and freshly brewed coffee. TV, fax.

DEVONPORT *1km NE of Devonport*

The Devon
Gayle & Tom Kalaugher
41 Tainui Road, Devonport, Auckland

Tel (09) 445 7304 Fax (09) 445 7394
Mob 027 656 0784 devonportcouple@hotmail.com
www.bnb.co.nz/thedevon.html

Double $120 Single $100 (Continental Breakfast)
1 Queen (1 bdrm)
Bathrooms: 1 Private

Welcome to our comfortable and friendly home which is situated within minutes of all Devonport's desirable amenities; Cheltenham Beach, North Head, and for golfers, Waitemata Golf Course. A short pleasant stroll along the waterfront takes you to Devonport village with it's many cafés restaurants, shops and ferry to Auckland City. Continental breakfast with freshly baked muffins or cooked breakfast by arrangement. Spacious sunny room with very comfortable bed, electric blanket, heating, TV and bathrobes. Tea and coffee available. Off-street parking.

WAIHEKE ISLAND *0.3km Oneroa Village*

Apartment 57 *Self-contained*
Cheryl & Maurie Keeling
57 Church Bay Road, Oneroa, Waiheke Island

Tel (09) 372 8897 Fax (09) 372 8897
Mob 027 255 8897 stay@apartment57.co.nz
www.apartment57.co.nz

Double $210 Single $210 (Special Breakfast)
1 King/Twin (1 bdrm)
Bathrooms: 1 Ensuite

Luxury spacious studio apartment with sea and vineyard views and only a 10 minute easy walk into Oneroa
Village restaurants and wineries. Full breakfast includes home-grown fruits and vegetables, home-made breads, jams, yoghurts and treats; served on your terrace overlooking the village and Oneroa Bay. Spa pool, email and off-street parking. We have travelled extensively, enjoy the outdoors, garden, beach and arts. Builder and ESL teacher and Digby (the Jack Russell dog) welcome you to our part of this beautiful island. Free transfers from ferry.

WAIHEKE ISLAND

Blue Horizon *B&B*
David & Marion Aim
41 Coromandel Road, Sandy Bay,
Waiheke Island

Tel (09) 372 5632
www.bnb.co.nz/bluehorizon.html

Double $80-$95 Single $55-$70
(Continental Breakfast)
2 Queen (2 bdrm)
Bathrooms: 1 Ensuite 1 Guests share 1 Host share

We live above Sandy Bay which is 2-3 minutes walk away with spectacular sea views. All the rooms of our modest home face due north catching the sun all day. Waiheke caters for adventuring, dining out, sandy beaches, rock pools, which we enjoy after farming and owning a garden centre which our 4 children helped with. We really enjoy our B&B and look forward to sharing our beautiful island with you. Directions: ferry from Auckland. Car ferry from Howick. Complimentary ferry transfers.

AUCKLAND - HERNE BAY *2.5km W of Auckland central*

Moana Vista *B&B Homestay*
Tim Kennedy & Matthew Moran
60 Hamilton Road, Herne Bay, Auckland

Tel (09) 376 5028 0800 213 761 Mob 021 376 150
info@moanavista.co.nz   www.moanavista.co.nz

Double $140-$220 Single $120 (Continental Breakfast)
Credit cards accepted   Children welcome
2 Queen 1 Twin (3 bdrm)   Bathrooms: 2 Ensuite 1 Private

Just minutes stroll from the Waitemata Harbour, nestled in the
exclusive enclave of Herne Bay in Auckland, sits Moana Vista.
This charming, renovated 2 storey villa is owned and operated
by your friendly and well-travelled hosts, Tim and Matthew.
Moana Vista has 3 double bedrooms, 2 ensuites and 1 private bathroom. 2 of the upper rooms have lovely
harbour views. The bathrooms feature high-pressure showers and monogrammed Moana Vista toiletries.
We also offer complimentary use of multi-channel TV, high-speed internet/email services, mineral water,
tea, coffee and even a glass of wine. Stroll to shops and restaurants on Ponsonby Road. City, 10 minutes
away.

AUCKLAND - PONSONBY *3km W of Auckland Central*

The Big Blue House *B&B Homestay*
Kate Prebble & Lynne Giddings
103 Garnet Road, Westmere, Auckland

Tel (09) 360 6384 0800 360 638
Mob 021 884 662
kate-lynne@xtra.co.nz   www.thebigbluehouse.co.nz

Double $110-$140 Single $60-$120
(Continental Breakfast) Child $10   Children welcome
Dinner $25 by arrangement
Visa, Mastercard and EFT-POS available
2 King 3 Single (3 bdrm)
Bathrooms: 1 Ensuite 2 Host share

Kate and Lynne warmly invite you to enjoy our unique homestay environment close to Auckland's
central city and harbour. Be greeted by our friendly cat and dog. Enjoy the luxury of spacious rooms
with sea/hill views, TV, tea/coffee facilities, writing desk, heated towels and bathrobes. Luxuriate in
our spa, splash in the pool. Take an easy stroll to the Auckland Zoo, Western Springs Stadium, cafés or
seashore. Children welcome. Make yourself at home!

AUCKLAND - PONSONBY *1km W of Inner City*

Amitee's on Ponsonby *B&B*
Ian Stewart & Jill Slee
237 Ponsonby Road, Ponsonby, Auckland

Tel (09) 378 6325 Fax (09) 378 6329
info@amitees.co.nz   www.amitees.com

Double $180 (Continental Breakfast)
Twin $195 Queen $235 King $275 Penthouse $330
2 King 3 Queen 1 Double 1 Twin (7 bdrm)
Bathrooms: 7 Ensuite

Welcome to the only boutique Hotel on vibrant Ponsonby
Road. Choose from 6 spacious, comfortable and
beautifully appointed bedrooms all with ensuites; or the
penthouse suite with stunning city views. All rooms offer
sumptuous bedding, DVD players, Sky TV, DD phones, wireless internet access and luxurious robes.
Private garden & guest lounge with fireplace. Continental self-serve breakfast. Experience Auckland's
finest restaurants, cafés and boutique's right outside the door, or the city centre is only minutes away. For
business or pleasure, Amitee's is your perfect choice. Eftpos, Visa, MasterCard, Amex.

AUCKLAND - PONSONBY   *Auckland Central*

The Great Ponsonby   *Small hotel*
Sally James & Gerard Hill
30 Ponsonby Terrace, Ponsonby, Auckland

Tel (09) 376 5989   0800 766 792   Fax (09) 376 5527
info@greatpons.co.nz
www.bnb.co.nz/thegreatponsonby.html

Double **$180-$330** (Special Breakfast) Double Suites
6 King/Twin 5 Queen (11 bdrm)
Bathrooms: 11 Ensuite

Ponsonby is the liveliest area of Auckland, full of cafés, restaurants, boutiques, ceramics. The Great Ponsonby is in a cul-de-sac in the middle of all this. No traffic noises here as we are not on the main road.

Centrally located, close to all major attractions, walk or bus to the harbour and down town. Plenty of off-street parking. Link bus passes our corner every 10 minutes.

Large, restored 1898 villa tucked away in a quiet street. The white exterior is deceptive. Inside is a bold profusion of colour with art from the Pacific. There is a choice of accommodation from queen rooms to roomier courtyard studios courtyard or palm garden suites.

Colourful, understated modern design. They have their own bathroom with heated mirror and towel rails, hairdryer. Tea & coffee making facilities in all rooms, Sky TV, DDI phones, internet access, clock radio. Studios also have a fridge for the bubbly, king or twin beds, leather couch, CD player, video player. Suites have a bath tub.

Jason Cochrane, editor of Arthur Frommer's Budget travel magazine, November 2002 said in his article on Auckland *"my top choice is Great Ponsonby B&B"*. Leading English travel guide Footprint says *"one of the best B&Bs in the city"*. The Great Ponsonby topped the list of accommodation chosen by the NY Times 26/1/03. Resident cat and dog. Pets and children on application. Winter rates available.

Leisurely breakfasts served from our extensive menu in the dining room or alfresco on the verandah

AUCKLAND - PONSONBY   *Auckland Central*

Colonial Cottage   *B&B   Homestay*
Grae Glieu
35 Clarence Street
Ponsonby, Auckland 1034

Tel (09) 360 2820
Fax: (09) 360 3436

Double $100-$120   Single $80-$100
(Special Breakfast)   Dinner $25 by arrangement
www.bnb.co.nz/colonialcottage.html
1 king 1 queen 1 single (3 bedrooms)
Bathrooms: 1 shared

Delightful olde-world charm with modern amenities to assure your comfort - accent on quality. Hospitable and relaxing. Quiet with green outlook. Close to Herne Bay and Ponsonby Road cafés & quality restaurants. Airport shuttle service door-to-door. Handy to public transport, city attractions and motorways. Smoke-free indoors. Alternative health therapies and massage available. Special dietary requirements catered for. Organic emphasis. Single party bookings available.

AUCKLAND - FREEMANS BAY

Freemans B&B   *B&B*
Seema & Raj Chatly
65 Wellington Street,
Freemans Bay, Auckland

Tel (09) 376 5046   0800 437 336
Fax (09) 376 4052   Mob 021 677 544
freemansbb@xtra.co.nz
www.freemansbandb.co.nz
Double $85   Single $55   (Special Breakfast)
Dinner $10pp   Family room, sleeps 4 $119
Children welcome
1 King/Twin 2 King 3 Queen 1 Single (7 bdrm)
Bathrooms: 1 Private 3 Guests share

Hosts: Seema and Raj. Top location: walk to city centre, harbour, casino and markets. Near Ponsonby cafés and restaurants. Fully refurbished guest rooms with new beds and posturepaedic mattresses. Plus big TV, lounge, laundry, leafy garden, internet available. (1-4 persons).

Just as we have a variety of B&Bs you will also be offered a variety of breakfasts, and they will always be generous. **Continental breakfast** consists of fruit, cereal, toast and tea/coffee. A **Full breakfast** is the same with a cooked course and a **Special breakfast** is a full breakfast with something special.

AUCKLAND - PARNELL

1.5km E of Auckland Central

Approved

Ascot Parnell   *Small Hotel*
Therese & Bart Blommaert
St Stephens Avenue, Parnell, Auckland 1

Tel (09) 309 9012   Fax (09) 309 3729
info@ascotparnell.com
www.ascotparnell.com

Double $195-$325 Single $135-$295
(Full Breakfast)
$60 extra person ask about winter rates
1 King/Twin 2 Queen 3 Twin 2 Single
 (3 bdrm)
Bathrooms: 3 Ensuite

A moment's stroll from Parnell Village; with its numerous cafes, restaurants, art galleries and boutiques, and 1.5km to Auckland City centre. The Rose Gardens and Auckland Museum is an easy 5 minute walk.

The Airport Shuttle-Bus stops at the door. Bedrooms are bright and spacious, with large windows that open, some with balconies and have either garden or harbour views. Rooms are all non-smoking, have TV, air-conditioning, phone and internet connection. Breakfast is a five course feast with freshly squeezed juice, seasonal or tropical fruits, yoghurt, cereals and homemade muesli, gourmet omelettes, bacon and eggs, Belgian crepes, pancakes, French toast etc.

The cosy guest-lounge opens onto a large balcony with views on the harbour, city skyline and the Sky Tower, which is beautifully lit at night. A Mac-PC offers free internet. **Car parking is free and secure inside building.**

The hosts, Bart and Therese are well travelled and offer gracious yet down to earth friendly hospitality. They can help you book tours, rental cars and accommodations for your onward journey.
Reservations are essential.

The Ascot Parnell is a charming centrally located B&B in a tranquil garden setting.

AUCKLAND - CENTRAL *Auckland Central*

Redwood Vista Bed & Breakfast *B&B*
Dawn Feickert
4D Kingsbridge, 72 Wellesley Street, Auckland

Tel (09) 373 4903 0800 349 742 Fax (09) 373 4903
Mob 0274 758 996
kotuku@wave.co.nz www.redwood-bed-breakfast.ws

Double $135-$165 Single $100-$135
(Special Breakfast) Credit cards accepted
2 Queen 2 Twin (2 bdrm)
Bathrooms: 1 Ensuite 1 Host share

The Redwood Vista is a convenient central location
in the heart of Auckland City with stunning views day and night. Walk to all the city attractions
including art galleries, museums, theatres, cinemas, restaurants, shopping arcades, try your luck at Sky
City Casino. Go sailing, stroll around the Viaduct yacht basin, along the waterfront, and through the
renowned parks and reserves. Run down to the heated baths and gym.

Ideal for the business traveller where everything is close by in the CBD plus walk to the Auckland
University and Hospital. The Auckland Airport shuttles are available door to door on request 24 hours a
day. The ferry terminal is 15 minutes walk away. The link bus and city buses are close by to take you to
places like the Parnell Village the Rose Gardens, Ponsonby, Kelly Tartlton's Under Water World. We are
also close to motorways, north and south. You have several golf courses available, close to beaches.

From our fourth floor spacious and private apartment with views of the Harbour Bridge, Sky Tower
and Waitemata Harbour enjoy a gourmet breakfast with choices of fresh fruit, yoghurt, cereals daily
baked muffins, scones, breads and pastries as well as special dishes. This is served in the dining room
or you can wander onto the verandah. Our rooms are non-smoking, comfortable and have queen and
single beds with all the conveniences you would expect, including colour TV plus tea and coffee making
facilities.

We are well travelled with a great interest in wine and every effort has been made to ensure your stay
- be it business or pleasure is an enjoyable one. Email and office facilities available. Please phone for
directions to the apartment.

Ideal for the business traveller - everything is close by - CBD, university, hospital and ferry terminal

AUCKLAND - PARNELL *1.5km Auckland City*

Approved

St. Georges Bay Lodge *B&B*
Carol & Steven Quilliam
43 St. Georges Bay Road, Parnell, Auckland

Tel (09) 303 1050 Fax (09) 360 7392 Mob 021 214 1473
carol@stgeorge.co.nz   www.stgeorge.co.nz

Double $215-$255 Single $195-$215
(Full Breakfast) Without ensuite $135-$165
Credit cards accepted
4 King/Twin 1 Double (5 bdrm)
Bathrooms: 4 Ensuite 1 Host share

St Georges Bay Lodge is an elegant Victorian villa which has the charm of a by-gone era, with the comfort of modern amenities. There is no better location for your stay in Auckland City. We are minutes from: picturesque Parnell Village, designer boutiques and speciality stores, great cafés, restaurants, and night-club life, health centres, swimming pools, gardens, parks, and the museum in Auckland Domain and Holy Trinity Cathedral. Also within walking distance: Newmarket and the business district, the casino, more restaurants and city night life, the University of Auckland, Waitemata Harbour, watersports, island destinations, ferry tours, and beaches.

AUCKLAND - MT EDEN *Auckland Central*

Approved

811 Bed & Breakfast *B&B*
Bryan Condon & David Fitchew
811 Dominion Road, Mt Eden, Auckland 1003

Tel (09) 620 4284 Fax (09) 620 4286
Mob 021 260 4184 811bnb@quicksilver.net.nz
www.bnb.co.nz/bedbreakfast.html

Double $85 Single $55 (Full Breakfast)
2 Double 1 Twin (3 bdrm) Bathrooms: 2 Guests share

All are welcome at 811 Bed and Breakfast. Your hosts
Bryan and David, Pfeni and their Irish water spaniels welcome you to their turn of the century home. Our home reflects years of collecting and living overseas. Centrally located on Dominion Road (which is an extension of Queen Street city centre). The bus stop at the door, only 10 minutes to city and 20 minutes to airport, shuttle bus from airport. Easy walking to Balmoral shopping area (banks, excellent restaurants). We have operated a bed & breakfast on a farm in Digby County, Nova Scotia, Canada. The nicest compliment we can receive is when guests tell us it's like visiting friends when they stay with us. Our breakfast gives you a beaut start to your day in a laid back atmosphere. From north-south motorway, Greenlane off ramp, continue to Dominion Road. Turn left and we are 7 blocks on your right to 811.

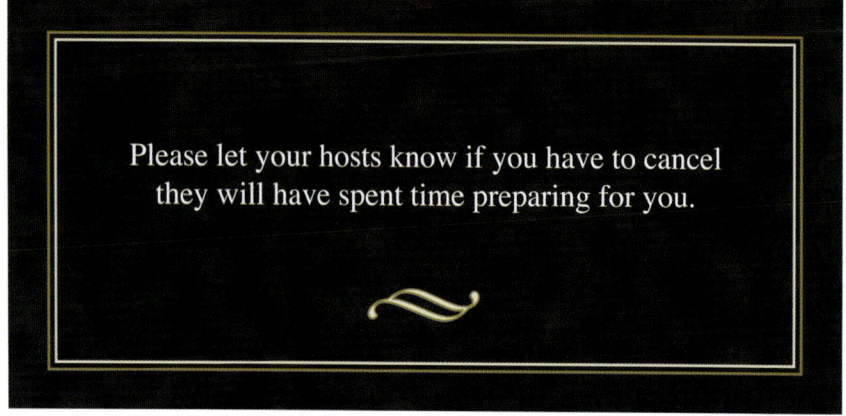

Please let your hosts know if you have to cancel
they will have spent time preparing for you.

AUCKLAND - MT EDEN

2km S of Auckland Central

Bavaria B&B Hotel   *B&B Small Hotel*
Ulrike & Rudolf
83 Valley Road, Mt Eden, Auckland 3

Tel (09) 638 9641   Fax (09) 638 9665
bavaria@xtra.co.nz   www.bavariabandbhotel.co.nz

Double $135   Single $95
(Full Breakfast)   Child $12 over 2 years
Reduced rates May-Sep   Credit cards accepted
Children welcome
1 King/Twin 4 Queen 2 Double 2 Twin 2 Single
(11 bdrm)
Bathrooms: 11 Ensuite

Our picturesque, colonial villa with its 11 guestrooms
is tastefully decorated with contemporary native timber
furniture. It is designed generously and maintained
immaculately. All rooms have ensuites, quality
commercial beds (extra length), telephones, suitcase
racks, desks, electric blankets and internet access for
your laptop computer.

Relax in our large sunny guest lounge which looks on
to a private sun deck and small exotic garden. Our
breakfast buffet is a house speciality offering a wide
selection of freshly prepared healthy foods with a touch
of German cuisine. Refreshments are offered during the day. There is plenty of off-street parking
available in the court yard. The city is only 2km away and can be easily reached by bus or car.

Within walking distance you will find excellent restaurants, cafés, banks, a modern supermarket,
internet cafes and many other shops. Despite the proximity to the city, you will enjoy the quiet
atmosphere of Mount Eden with its colonial villas, pretty gardens and Mount Eden summit lending
panoramic views over the city and harbour. Your hosts are always happy to give advice on rental cars,
tours or on any other topic about New Zealand.

*We invite you to stay at our charming small hotel offering quality B&B with all
modern facilities yet combined with a homely and welcoming atmosphere.*

AUCKLAND - WESTERN SPRINGS   *3mins W of Town*

Hastings Hall   *B&B*
Malcolm Martel
99 Western Springs Road, Western Springs
Tel (09) 845 8550   Fax (09) 845 8554
Mob 021 300 006   unique@hastingshall.co.nz
www.hastingshall.co.nz
Double $165-$375 Single $145-$295
Credit cards accepted Children welcome
2 King/Twin 1 King 4 Queen 1 Double (8 bdrm)
Bathrooms: 7 Ensuite 1 Private

Magnificently restored 1878 colonial mansion set in its own extensive grounds 5 minutes from the heart of Auckland City. Ideal for the tourist, businessman or a retreat away to unwind. Enjoy gourmet breakfasts in the conservatory, formal dining room, gazebo above the pool and spa pool. There are 8 themed guest rooms all with marble ensuites including one designed for disabled guests. Choose from the Grand Hastings suite with private lounge to the Moulin Rouge loft suite in the Stables. Upstairs areas are ideal for families with adjoining room. Tropically landscaped grounds, formal lounge & large pool lounge with library, home theatre & computer, email & fax facilities. Furnished with antiques from the period, fine linen & warm fluffy towels. Ideal for small conferences, functions, meetings or seminars.

AUCKLAND - EPSOM   *5km S of Auckland Central*

Auckland Homestay Bed & Breakfast
B&B Homestay
Isobel & Ian Thompson
37 Torrance Street, Epsom, Auckland

Tel (09) 624 3714 aucklandhomestay@xtra.co.nz
www.aucklandhomestay.co.nz

Double $125-$145 Single $85-$110 (Full Breakfast)
Child neg Dinner by arrangement
Credit cards accepted Children welcome
2 Queen 1 Single (3 bdrm)
Bathrooms: 1 Ensuite 1 Guests share

Experience warm, friendly hospitality in our large modern home in a quiet tree lined street. Just 5 minutes from motorway and 15 minutes from airport and CBD. Our central location is ideally positioned to explore the many attractions, whether by car or one of the nearby bus routes. Use of full laundry facilities. Telephone, email by request. Evening meals by prior arrangement. Off-street parking. We look forward to sharing our non-smoking home with you.

Ensuite or private bathroom is yours exclusively.
Guest share bathroom is shared with other guests.
Host share bathroom is shared with the family.

AUCKLAND - EPSOM   *5km S of Auckland City Centre*

Millars Epsom Homestay   *Homestay*
Janet & Jim Millar
10 Ngaroma Road, Epsom, Auckland 1003

Tel (09) 625 7336   Fax (09) 625 7336   Mob 027 251 3817
jmillar@xtra.co.nz
www.bnb.co.nz/millarsepsomhomestay.html

Double $90-$100   Single $60-$70
(Full Breakfast)   Child $10-$20   Dinner $30
Credit cards accepted   Children welcome
1 King/Twin 1 King 1 Queen 2 Single (3 bdrm)
Bathrooms: 1 Ensuite 2 Private

Our home, a spacious 1919 wooden bungalow, is surprisingly quiet and restful, set in a garden suburb in a tree-lined street, 200 metres from Greenwoods Corner Village with its bank, post office, reasonably priced non-tourist restaurants, and bus stop on direct route (15 minutes to the CBD).

There is a short walk to One Tree Hill, one of Auckland's loveliest parks with a playground, farm animals, groves of trees, the observatory, and a magnificent panorama of Auckland from the summit. A 15 minute walk through the park leads to the Expo Centre and Greenlane Hospital.

There are 2 accommodation areas - either the Garden Suite with its queen-sized double bedroom, large lounge with 3 single beds, patio, desk and TV, own bathroom, and which is the area we find really suitable for families, or the Upstairs Bedroom (king-size, can be converted to twin beds) with own ensuite, desk and TV.

We have travelled widely both in NZ and overseas (our son lives in Finland) and very much like conversing with guests and assisting in making their stay as pleasant as possible in our country and especially in this attractive suburb of Auckland. We are a smoke-free family. Jim and I were both born in NZ, and we belong to @ Home NZ.

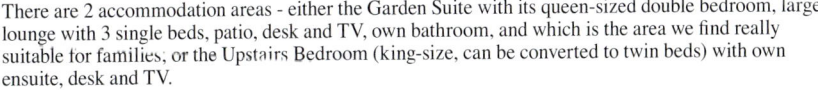

Surprisingly quiet and restful

AUCKLAND - ONE TREE HILL *3km S of Newmarket*

Approved

Greenlane Bed and Breakfast *Homestay*
Clare & Don Boyd and Winston
21 Atarangi Road, Greenlane

Tel (09) 523 3419   0800 25 4419
Fax (09) 524 8506   Mob 025 281 3222
Stay@Paradise.net.NZ
www.CityStay.net.NZ

Double $90   Single $60
(Full Breakfast)   Credit cards accepted
2 Queen 1 Twin 4 Single (4 bdrm)
Bathrooms: 1 Ensuite   2 Guests share

For tourists and business people alike, our one
hundred year old home has modern facilities
with a huge 400 acre treed park at the end of
our short street. We are close to Great South
Road and The NZ Expo Centre (Auckland
Showgrounds). Rooms have TV, phone, DSL,
and desk. Available: laundry, fax, computer, off-
street parking. Frequent buses to city centre.

Directions: Exit route 1 at Green Lane East, head west 300 metres,
free left turn at lights, then second street on right.

AUCKLAND - REMUERA *7km N of Auckland Central*

Woodlands *B&B Homestay*
Jude & Roger Harwood
18 Waiatarua Road, Remuera, Auckland 1005

Tel (09) 524 6990 Fax (09) 524 6993
jude.harwood@xtra.co.nz
www.bnb.co.nz/woodlands.html

Double $135-$145 Single $100 (Special Breakfast)
Child not suitable Dinner $65pp Credit cards accepted
1 King 1 Double 1 Twin 1 Single (3 bdrm)
Bathrooms: 1 Ensuite 1 Private

Guest book comments "Absolutely purr-fect"."Very comfortable with stunning food". "A lovely oasis of calm with wonderful breakfasts". "Peaceful retreat with excellent breakfasts". Our breakfasts ARE special using seasonal fruit and produce. Join us for a Cordon Bleu candlelit evening dinner - booking essential. "Woodlands" is very quiet, surrounded by native trees and palms and central to many places of interest. The three guest bedrooms have tea/coffee facilities, heated towel rails,swimming towels, and coloured TV's. Fridge. Safe off-street carparking. Arrive a guest - leave a friend.

AUCKLAND - REMUERA

Lillington Villa *B&B Self-contained*
Carol & Peter Dossor
24 Lillington Road, Remuera, Auckland

Tel (09) 523 2035 Fax (09) 523 2036
Mob 025 927 063 caropet@xtra.co.nz
www.babs.co.nz/lillington

Double $120 Single $100 (Full Breakfast)
Child $20 Dinner $40 Full week $550-$600
Credit cards accepted Children welcome
1 Queen 3 Single (2 bdrm)
Bathrooms: 1 Ensuite

Home away from home. Two large, sunny, welcoming flats in well-restored villa 10 minutes from central Auckland. Own entrances and courtyards. Lock-up garages. Security and fire alarm systems. Gas heating. Telephone and Sky TV. Full modern open-plan kitchens and well-equipped bathrooms. Dishwasher, microwave, fridge/freezer, stove, washing machine, dryer. Quality fittings and equipment. 1 bedroom flat has queen and single beds and double bed-settee in living area. 2 bedroom family flat has queen and 3 single beds.

AUCKLAND - REMUERA *1.5km E of Newmarket*

Green Oasis *B&B Homestay Self-contained*
James & Joy Foote
25A Portland Road, Remuera, Auckland 5

Tel (09) 520 1921 Fax (09) 522 9004
Mob 021 175 8291 footes1@xtra.co.nz
www.babs.co.nz/greenoasis

Double $100-$120 Single $75 (Full Breakfast)
Child $65 Credit cards accepted Children welcome
1 Queen 1 Single (2 bdrm)
Bathrooms: 1 Private 1 Host share

Green Oasis, a secluded, tranquil location in a much-loved garden of native trees, ferns - 10 minutes to city centre. Close to the museum, antique, specialty shops, restaurants, cafés of Remuera, Newmarket, Parnell. An informal home of natural timbers, sunny decks where you will find us relaxed and welcoming, sensitive to your needs, be it to withdraw and rest, or to engage with us. Your accommodation, entered from a private garden, is self-contained with fully equipped kitchen, tea/coffee making facilities, washing machine, TV. Special breakfast of seasonal and home-made taste sensations!

AUCKLAND - REMUERA *8km E of Auckland City*

Tenth Tee Lodge *B&B*
Dale & Dick Kirk
3 Charles Fox Place, St. John's Park, Auckland

Tel (09) 521 5228 0800 261 268 Mob 021 932 332
dick.kirk@xtra.co.nz
www.bnb.co.nz/tenthteelodge.html

Double $160 Single $140 (Full Breakfast)
Child $30 Dinner $40 Children welcome
1 Queen 1 Double (2 bdrm)
Bathrooms: 1 Guests share

Tenth Tee Lodge is situated in a quiet cul-de-sac with safe, off-street parking and adjoins the tenth tee of the Remuera Golf Course. Ellerslie racecourse is only 5 minutes away. Auckland's downtown and famous waterfront restaurants are 10-15 minutes drive. The lounge overlooks the golf course and caters for your comfort with Sky TV and tea/coffee making facilities. A sauna, full laundry, access to email, telephone, fax are all available. Guests have their own private access to the property.

AUCKLAND - ORAKEI - OKAHU BAY *5km E of Auckland Central*

Nautical Nook/Free Sailing *B&B Homestay*
Trish & Keith Janes & Irish Setter
23b Watene Crescent, Orakei, Auckland

Tel (09) 521 2544 0800 360 544
nauticalnook@bigfoot.com
www.nauticalnook.com

Double $110-$130 Single $85-$95 (Full Breakfast)
Credit cards accepted Children welcome
2 Queen 1 Single (2 bdrm)
Bathrooms: 1 Ensuite 1 Private

Friendly, relaxed beachside hospitality overlooking park/harbour, 4.8km from downtown. 100 metres from Okahu Bay, fringed by Pohutukawa trees. Gourmet breakfast. Stroll along picturesque promenade to Kelly Tarlton's Underwater World, Mission Bay Beach and cafés, Te Pa Cultural Visitors Centre. Bus at door to downtown, ferry terminal, museums. Unwind for 2-3 day stopover. Complimentary sailing on the sparkling harbour on our 34 foot yacht. We have a wealth of local knowledge and international travel experience and can assist with sightseeing, travel planning, rental-car. Take taxi or shuttle from airport. Welcome! Excellent website.

AUCKLAND - MISSION BAY *6km E of Auckland Central*

Homestay
Jean & Bryan Cockell
41 Nihill Cresent, Mission Bay,
Auckland

Tel (09) 528 3809
www.bnb.co.nz/cockell.html

Double $95 Single $70 (Full Breakfast)
Dinner $25 by arrangement
Credit cards accepted
1 Double (1 bdrm)
Bathrooms: 1 Private

We warmly welcome you to our modern split level home. The upper level is for your exclusive use including a private lounge. 5 minutes walk to Mission Bay beach, cafés and restaurants and 10 minutes scenic car or bus ride to down town Auckland and ferry terminal for harbour and islands in the gulf. We are retired and look forward to sharing our special part of Auckland with you. Please phone for directions or airport shuttle bus to our door. Please no smoking.

AUCKLAND - ST HELIERS   *10km E of Auckland*

B&B
Jill & Ron McPherson
102 Maskell Street, St Heliers, Auckland

Tel (09) 575 9738   Fax (09) 575 0051
Mob 021 752 034
ron&jill_mcpherson@xtra.co.nz
www.bnb.co.nz/mcpherson.html

Double $120   Single $85   (Continental Breakfast)
1 Queen 1 Twin (2 bdrm)
Bathrooms: 1 Private

Welcome to our modern home with off-street parking
in a smoke-free environment. One group of guests is accommodated at a time. Having travelled
extensively ourselves we are fully aware of tourists' needs. 8 minutes walk to St Heliers Bay beach,
shops, restaurants, cafés, banks and post office. Picturesque 12 minutes drive along the Auckland
waterfront past Kelly Tarlton's Antarctic and Underwater Encounter to Downtown Auckland.
Interests including all sports, gardening and Jill is a keen cross-stitch embroiderer. Not suitable for
children/pets.

AUCKLAND - ST HELIERS   *10km E of Auckland City*

Burnt Fig   *B&B*
Dianne & Alister Benvie
2/1 Walmsley Road, St. Heliers, Auckland

Tel (09) 575 4150   Mob 027 281 6893
benvie@xtra.co.nz
www.burntfig.co.nz

Double $130-$165   Single $115-$130   (Full Breakfast)
Credit cards accepted
1 Queen 1 Double 1 Twin 2 Single (3 bdrm)
Bathrooms: 1 Ensuite 1 Private

Welcome to Burnt Fig, a modern architect-designed house located in beautiful St. Heliers Bay. Only
minutes walk to local beaches and great cafés. A stunning waterfront drive takes you to downtown
Auckland. Among the facilities available are tea and coffee in a separate guest lounge, off-street parking
and use of laundry. Tia, the Belgian Shepherd is very popular with our guests. We both play golf at
Titirangi, one of New Zealand's finest championship courses where tee times can be arranged.

AUCKLAND - TITIRANGI   *20min W of Auckland City*

Kaurigrove   *B&B*
Gaby & Peter Wunderlich
120 Konini Road, Titirangi,
Auckland 7

Tel (09) 817 5608   Fax (09) 817 5608
Mob 025 275 0574
www.bnb.co.nz/kaurigrove.html

Double $95-$100   Single $60
Credit cards accepted
1 Queen 1 Single (2 bdrm)
Bathrooms: 1 Guests share

Welcome to our home! Kaurigrove offers a tranquil
location amidst kauri trees in a park-like setting, yet close to shops, cafés and restaurants. Situated at
Titirangi we are near Auckland's historic west coast with its magnificent beaches and vast native bush
with a wonder world of walking tracks. Gaby and Peter, your hosts of German background, are keen
trampers themselves and are happy to introduce you to the highlights of Auckland and its surrounding
areas. PS: We have a shy cat called Coco. Non-smoking inside residence.

AUCKLAND - AVONDALE   *10km W of Auckland Central*

B&B Approved

Kodesh Community   *Homestay Self-contained*
Kodesh Trust
31B Cradock Street,
Avondale, Auckland

Tel (09) 828 5672   Fax (09) 828 6495
Kodesh_Trust@free.net.nz
www.bnb.co.nz/kodeshcommunity.html

Double $60   Single $40   (Continental Breakfast)
Child $20   Dinner $8   Flat - 2 people $60-$80
2 Queen 1 Twin 2 Single (5 bdrm)
Bathrooms: 2 Private 1 Host share

Kodesh is an ecumenical, cross-cultural Christian community of around 25 residents, about 8 minutes by car from downtown Auckland. Guest rooms are in a large modern home. One self-contained flat sleeps 4, the other 7. An evening meal is available in the community dining room Monday-Friday. Bookings essential. The atmosphere is relaxed and guests can amalgamate into the life of the community as much or little as desired. No smoking, no pets, children under 12 welcome in self-contained unit

AUCKLAND - HILLSBOROUGH   *10km SW of Auckland*

B&B Approved

Hillsborough Heights Homestay
B&B Homestay Separate/Suite Self-contained
Sarah & Sean Ryu
434A Hillsborough Road, Waikowhai, Auckland

Tel (09) 626 0115   Fax (09) 626 0115   Mob 025 686 7129
hillsboroughhomestay@hotmail.com
www.bnb.co.nz/hillsborough.html

Double $120   Single $90   (Continental Breakfast)
Child $30   Children welcome
2 Queen 2 Double (4 bdrm)
Bathrooms: 2 Ensuite 1 Guests share

A warm welcome to our beautifully appointed mediterranean-style home and garden overlooking the manukau harbour, just 15 minutes from Auckland Airport and city. Stay in our delightful spacious upstairs room with ensuite, TV; or in our self-contained apartment (bedroom, bathroom, kitchen, lounge with extra sofa-bed, TV). Enjoy bush and coastal walks nearby and golfing, or just relax on your own. Breakfast alfresco in the garden or sunny kitchen conservatory. We look forward to sharing our tranquil surroundings and hospitality. Japanese is well understood.

AUCKLAND AIRPORT - MANGERE BRIDGE   *14km S of Auckland Central*

B&B Approved

Mangere Bridge Homestay   *Homestay*
Carol & Brian
1 Boyd Ave, Mangere Bridge,
Auckland

Tel (09) 636 6346   Fax (09) 636 6345
www.bnb.co.nz/mangerebridgehomestay.html

Double $80   Single $60   (Full Breakfast)
Child $20 under 12
Dinner $25 by prior arrangement
2 King/Twin 1 Double (3 bdrm)
Bathrooms: 3 Ensuite

We invite you to share our home, which is within 10 minutes of Auckland Airport, an ideal location for your arrival or departure of New Zealand. We enjoy meeting people and look forward to making your stay an enjoyable one. We welcome you to join us for dinner by prior arrangement. Courtesy car to or from airport, bus and rail. Off-street parking available. Handy to public transport. Short stroll to the waterfront. Please no smoking indoors. Our cat requests no pets. Inspection welcome.

AUCKLAND - MANGERE *4km Airport*

Airport Bed and Breakfast *B&B*
Laurel Blakey
1 Westney Road, Corner Kirkbride Road,
Mangere

Tel (09) 275 0533   Fax (09) 275 0968
Mob 027 270 5810   airportbnb@xtra.co.nz
airportbnb.co.nz

Double $80-$110 Single $65-$95
(Continental Breakfast)   Credit cards accepted
1 King 2 Queen 6 Double 1 Twin (10 bdrm)
Bathrooms: 2 Ensuite 3 Guests share

Just 5 minutes drive from Auckland Airport a friendly Kiwi welcome and great value accommodation await. 10 quality rooms, 2 ensuites, central heating, large TV/Sky/dining room. Internet access. 2 minutes walk to city bus stop - see Auckland by bus and ferry on the $8 day pass. Restaurants/ takeaways nearby. Car, cycle and luggage storage. Rental cars and NZ wide sightseeing tours booked. Courtesy airport transfer (not 24 hour), free phone at airport, dial 28. Buffet breakfast, complimentary tea/coffee.

AUCKLAND AIRPORT - MANGERE *2km Mangere*

Airport Homestay/B&B *B&B Homestay*
May Pepperell
288 Kirkbride Road, Mangere, Auckland

Tel (09) 275 6777   Fax (09) 275 6728
Mob 025 289 8200
www.bnb.co.nz/airporthomestay.html

Double $65 Single $40   (Continental Breakfast)
Child $20
3 Single (2 bdrm)
Bathrooms: 1 Guests share

Clean comfortable home 5 minutes from airport but not on flight path. Easy walk to shops and restaurants. 10 minutes from shopping centres and Rainbows End amusement park. Aviation golf course near airport, winery and Lakeside Convention Centre nearby. My interests are golf, travel, Ladies' Probus and voluntary work. Beds have woollen underlays and electric blankets. There is a sunny terrace and fenced swimming pool. Courtesy car to/from airport at reasonable hour. Vehicles minded while you're away from $1 per day. Bus stop very close.

AUCKLAND AIRPORT - MANGERE BRIDGE *7.5km N of Auckland Airport*

Mountain View B&B *B&B Homestay*
Ian & Jenny (and cat Oscar) Davis
85A Wallace Road, Mangere Bridge, Auckland

Tel (09) 636 6535   Fax (09) 636 6126
mtviewbb@xtra.co.nz
www.bnb.co.nz/mountainviewbb.html

Double $95-$140 Single $75-$95 (Full Breakfast)
Child $20 Dinner by arrangement
Credit cards accepted Children welcome
2 King/Twin 2 King 1 Queen 3 Twin 1 Single
(6 bdrm)   Bathrooms: 4 Ensuite 1 Guests share

Spacious villa with quality décor in quiet locality. Auckland Airport 8 minutes. Exit on George Bolt Drive, left into Kirkbride Road, follow through to Wallace Road, we're 1.2km on right from roundabout. Convenient off-street parking, public transport at gate. Friendly, hospitable NZ hosts are aircraft builders/enthusiasts. Enjoy superb harbour views whilst eating delicious breakfast. Typed navigational sheet gives assistance to north, south or city. Central to many attractions, golf courses and sports stadiums. Guests state: "Outstanding B&B", Owens, USA.

AUCKLAND - OTAHUHU　　*17km S of Auckland*

Oasis in Otahuhu　*B&B*
Jerrine & Gerard Fecteau
70 Mangere Road, Otahuhu, Auckland

Tel (09) 276 9335 Fax (09) 276 9235
oasisbb@xtra.co.nz
www.bnb.co.nz/fecteau.html

Double $70 Single $50 (Continental Breakfast)
Child neg Dinner $20 Credit cards accepted
Children welcome Pets welcome
1 Queen 1 Double 1 Twin (3 bdrm)
Bathrooms: 2 Guests share

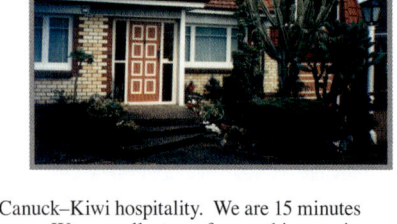

We welcome you to the Oasis in Otahuhu with the best Canuck–Kiwi hospitality. We are 15 minutes from the airport and 5 minutes from the train and motorway. We are collectors of many things: coins of the world, brass, Canadian Indian art. Cactus garden. We can help you plan your holiday and get a rental car. In addition to breakfast you can join us for dinner by arrangement or dine at one of the many restaurants in Otahuhu. Please phone, fax or email and our courtesy van will pick you up.

AUCKLAND - MANUKAU　　*6.5km NE of Manukau City*

Tanglewood　*Homestay*
Roseanne & Ian Devereux
5 Inchinnam Road, Flat Bush, Auckland

Tel (09) 274 8280 Fax (09) 634 6896
tanglewood@clear.net.nz
www.bnb.co.nz/tanglewoodmanukau.html

Double $95 Single $60 (Full Breakfast) Child $10
Credit cards accepted Children welcome
1 Queen 1 Double 2 Single (3 bdrm)
Bathrooms: 1 Ensuite 1 Guests share

Our homely country cottage, set in 2 acres is close to the international airport. The garden loft is separate from the house with ensuite, TV, fridge, deck overlooking large peaceful gardens and ponds. Accommodation inside the house has its own bathroom. We are 30 minutes from downtown Auckland, close to bush walks, Regional Botanic Gardens and restaurants. Delicious home cooked breakfast includes eggs from our free range hens. We have a swimming pool and a friendly dog Daisy. We are non-smoking. Booking is essential.

AUCKLAND - MANUKAU　　*6.5km NE of Manukau*

Calico Cottage　*B&B*
Patty & Murray Glenie
7 Inchinnam Road,
Flat Bush, Auckland

Tel (09) 274 8527 Fax (09) 274 8528
Mob 021 303 402 MG-PT@xtra.co.nz
www.bnb.co.nz/calico.html

Double $95 Single $60 (Full Breakfast) Child $10
Credit cards accepted Children welcome Pets welcome
1 Queen 1 Single (2 bdrm)
Bathrooms: 1 Ensuite

Welcome to Calico Cottage. We are on 2 acres with garden, paddocks, sheep, chickens - free-range eggs, and two dogs who live outdoors. Peaceful and yet only 10 minutes from both Manukau City centre and Botany town centre and 20 minutes from Auckland Airport. Transport to and from airport arranged if required. We have a double bedroom with new ensuite and a TV room adjoining for your own use. We look forward to your visit.

AUCKLAND - MANUREWA *2km S of Manukau City*

Hillpark Homestay *Homestay*
Katrine & Graham Paton
16 Collie Street, Manurewa, Auckland 1702

Tel (09) 267 6847 Fax (09) 267 8718
Mob 021 215 7974 hillpark.homestay@xtra.co.nz
www.bnb.co.nz/hillparkhomestay.html

Double $90-$100 Single $50-$60 (Full Breakfast)
Child $20 Dinner $20 by arrangement
Credit cards accepted Children welcome
1 Double 4 Single (3 bdrm)
Bathrooms: 1 Ensuite 1 Guests share

Welcome to our sunny, spacious home and meet our friendly tonkinese cat. We are 15 minutes from Auckland Airport, 20 minutes from Auckland City centre, by motorway, gateway to the route south and Pacific Coast Highway. Nearby are Manukau City Shopping Centre, Rainbow's End Adventure Park, restaurants, cinemas, souvenir shops, Community Arts Centre, Regional Botanic Gardens (Ellerslie Flowershow), and bush walks. Our interests include teaching, classical music, painting, gardening, photography, Christian interests, reading and travel. We're a smoke-free home. Directions: please phone.

AUCKLAND - BUCKLANDS BEACH *2km N of Howick*

Bucklands Beach Bed & Breakfast *B&B*
Jo & David Woolford
45B The Parade, Bucklands Beach, Auckland

Tel (09) 535 6092 Fax (09) 535 6092
Mob 027 287 5015
woolford@bucklandsbeachbedandbreakfast.co.nz
www.bucklandsbeachbedandbreakfast.co.nz

Double $150 Single $120 (Full Breakfast)
Credit cards accepted
1 Queen (1 bdrm)
Bathrooms: 1 Private

A warm welcome awaits you as our sole guests at our modern beachfront home. A queen-size bedroom, separate private bathroom and own lounge with TV, stereo and library are provided for your comfort. Complimentary tea and coffee are available as are an iron, ironing board and hair dryer. Metres to restaurants and convenience store. Close to golf courses, bowling green and boat ramp. 30 minutes from airport and 30 minutes to downtown Auckland. A 16 year old tibetan spaniel owns us.

AUCKLAND - HOWICK *Howick*

The Old Bakehouse *B&B*
Rosemary & Clive Cockle
23 Selwyn Road, Howick, Auckland

Tel (09) 533 3514 Fax (09) 534 1502
Mob 021 234 3372 cp.r.cockle@xtra.co.nz
www.bnb.co.nz/bakehouse.html

Double $125-$140 Single $100 (Full Breakfast)
Credit cards accepted
1 King 1 Queen 1 Double (3 bdrm)
Bathrooms: 1 Ensuite 1 Guests share

Opening in October 2004. Rosemary and Clive have converted their home on the site of the old Howick Bakehouse (circa 1880) into a charming bed & breakfast establishment where they offer warm, relaxed hospitality in a beautiful setting with excellent facilities. Guestrooms are private spacious and comfortable and all have french doors onto private verandah or patio. Enjoy a continental or cooked breakfast overlooking the pool and garden in the summer time or in the dining room in winter. There is a private guest lounge with tea and coffee facilities.

BEACHLANDS   *25km E of Howick*

B&B Homestay
Enid & Terry Cripps
51 Wakelin Road,
Beachlands 1705

Tel (09) 536 5546 etcripps@xtra.co.nz
www.bnb.co.nz/cripps.html

Double $90 Single $60 (Full Breakfast)
Dinner $30 by arrangement
1 Queen (1 bdrm)
Bathrooms: 1 Private

Enid and Terry offer you a warm welcome to the Marine
Garden suburb of Beachlands which is situated on the East Coast, 40km South East of Auckland City.
Our converted cottage is only 3 minutes walk from the beach at Sunkist Bay, local shops and licensed
restaurant. The Formosa Auckland Golf Course and Pine Harbour marina are 5 minutes drive away.
We are both in our 60's, have travelled widely. Guest accommodation is a large upstairs bedroom
with sitting area, TV and a shaded balcony facing the sea. Shuttle bus from the Airport or phone for
directions.

WHITFORD   *25km SE of Auckland*

Springhill Country Homestay *Farmstay*
Judy & Derek Stubbs
Polo Lane, Whitford, RD, Manurewa, Auckland

Tel (09) 530 8674 Fax (09) 530 8274
Mob 021 251 2518 djstubbs@ihug.co.nz
www.bnb.co.nz/springhillfarmstay.html

Double $120 Single $80 (Full Breakfast) Child $40
Dinner $30pp by arrangement
One room suitable for children
Credit cards accepted Children welcome
1 Queen (1 bdrm)   Bathrooms: 1 Ensuite

Springhill is an 8 hectare farm in Whitford, an attractive rural area approximately 25km south-east of
Auckland. We are close to a beautiful golf course, beaches and Auckland Airport. We farm angora
goats, sheep and free range hens, pets include a cat and a dog. Guest accommodation is one detached
double room with ensuite, but children can be accommodated. TV, tea & coffee making facilities, and a
private spa pool are available. Directions: left off Whitford Park Road. 1km past Golf Course.

WHITFORD   *12km Howick*

Albertine *Homestay*
Averill & Bart Allsopp - Smith
298 Clifton Road, Whitford, RD 1,
Howick, Auckland

Tel (09) 530 9441 Fax (09) 530 9441
Mob 021 974 119 albertinestay@xtra.co.nz
www.bnb.co.nz/albertine.html

Double $90 Single $65 (Full Breakfast)
Credit cards accepted
1 Double (1 bdrm)
Bathrooms: 1 Ensuite 1 Private

Enjoy a game of tennis on our peaceful rural 5 acre block. Wake up in your separate self-contained loft
to the sound of the birds. We are 30 minutes from Auckland City and within 15 minutes of cinemas,
shopping, restaurants, cafés and craft shops. Nearby is a Marina where sailing/boating and fishing are
available by arrangement. We are close to beaches, golf courses and polo ground, or you may prefer a
quiet country walk. Unsuitable for children or animals.

CLEVEDON *3km S of Clevedon Village*

The Gables *B&B Self-contained*
Phil & Cathy Foulkes
122 Tourist Road, Clevedon, RD 2 Papakura

Tel (09) 292 8373 Fax (09) 292 8629
Mob 027 494 1249 foulkes@xtra.co.nz
www.the-gables.co.nz

Double $100-$120 Single $90 (Full Breakfast)
Children welcome Dinner by arrangement
Additional person $20 Credit cards accepted
2 Queen 2 Double (2 bdrm)
Bathrooms: 2 Ensuite

In 1988 Phil and Cathy Foulkes set out to create a dream country home and garden for themselves and their family. Tucked away in their garden are 2 self-contained spacious cottage units where they invite guests to share their hospitality. Set on 10 acres, handy to Clevedon Village, each cottage unit offers a queen-size bedroom with ensuite, lounge/dining room with double bed settee, laundry and cooking facilities. Clevedon features green pastures, friendly people and old fashioned hospitality within 30 minutes drive from Auckland CBD and International Airport.

MANUKAU CITY - ALFRISTON *2km from Manukau City*

Thistlefern *B&B*
Evelyn & Patrick Scanlon
36 Cairnsvale Rise, Alfriston/Manurewa,
Manukau City

Tel (09) 267 6787 Fax (09) 267 6781
Mob 027 602 6677 pateve@clear.net.nz
www.thistlefern.co.nz

Double $90 Single $80 (Full Breakfast)
Child neg Dinner as arranged, wine if requested
Queen $100 Children welcome
1 Queen 2 Double 1 Single (3 bdrm)
Bathrooms: 2 Guests share

Ceud-mile-failte (A Hundred Thousand Welcomes). Off Pacific Coast Highway, walking distance Botanic Gardens/Flowershow. 20 minutes to Auckland Airport, Auckland City, Sky City/Viaduct. 10 minutes to Manukau, Botany Down Shopping Centre, Rainbow's End, bus, trains. 25 minutes to beach. Quiet and comfortable, an ideal stopover or base to tour central region. Stay 3 or more nights - free bottle of wine, full week at discount. Excellent BBQ area & spa. Our cat is called Robyn.

KAIAUA *85km SE of Auckland*

Kaiaua Seaside Lodge *B&B Lodge*
Fran Joseph & Denis Martinovich
1336 Pacific Coast Highway, Kaiaua

Tel (09) 232 2696 Fax (09) 232 2699
Mob 025 274 0534 kaiaua_lodge@xtra.co.nz
www.bnb.co.nz/kaiauaseasidelodge.html

Double $100-$120 Single $75 (Full Breakfast)
Children welcome
2 Queen 1 Double 2 Single (5 bdrm)
Bathrooms: 2 Ensuite 1 Guests share

Situated on the water's edge, 4km north of Kaiaua Township, the Lodge features attractive beach gardens and panoramic views of the Coromandel. It is ideally positioned for leisurely seashore strolls or more active tramps in the Hunua Ranges. Boating and fishing facilities are available and breakfast includes flounder or snapper, in season. Ensuite rooms are spacious and the separate guest lounge has a refrigerator and television. The Seabird Coast is renowned for its birdlife, thermal hot pools, nearby Regional Parks and fish 'n chips.

PAPAKURA *5km E of Papakura*

Hunua Gorge Country House *B&B Country stay*
Ben, Amy & Joy Calway
482 Hunua Road, Papakura, South Auckland

Tel **(09) 299 7926** Fax (09) 299 7926
Mob 021 669 922 hunuagorge@xtra.co.nz
www.friars.co.nz/hosts/hunua.html

Double $90-$150 Single $90 (Full Breakfast)
Child depending on age Dinner $25-$35
Credit cards accepted Children welcome
1 King 2 Queen 1 Double 2 Single (5 bdrm)
Bathrooms: 1 Ensuite 1 Private 1 Guests share 1 Host share

Welcome to our rural wilderness on the doorstep of Auckland City. A great place to start or end your NZ holiday. Great food, magic sunsets, wild scenery, leafy greenery, starry skies, and views from all rooms. Large comfortable newly decorated home, verandahs, lawns, garden, bush and rural setting on 50 acres with cattle and birdlife. Stay a few days and discover the wonders of Auckland. Fresh food, fresh air, comfortable beds guaranteed. Please phone. Dinner from $25 or $35, three courses, by prior arrangement. Children welcome.

PAPAKURA *1.5km W of Papakura*

Campbell Clan House *Homestay*
Colin & Anna Mieke Campbell
57 Rushgreen Ave, Papakura

Tel **(09) 298 8231** Fax (09) 298 7792
Mob 027 496 7754 colam@pl.net
www.campbellclan.co.nz

Double $100-$120 Single $65-$75 (Full Breakfast)
Child neg Dinner $25/$35 by arrangement
Credit cards accepted Children welcome
2 Queen 2 Single (3 bdrm)
Bathrooms: 2 Ensuite 1 Private

Our peaceful location is close enough to Auckland to visit downtown attractions (25minutes) as well as being close to the motorway system (2minutes) for speedy access north, south or to the airport. Our separate upstairs guest accomodation includes 3 double bedrooms, large comfortable lounge with tea/ coffee facilities, TV, tourist information and private balcony with estuary views. We can assist you with holiday arrangements, hire vehicles & airport transfers and offer fax, internet & laundry facilities. We offer a discounted rate for 3+ nights bookings.

HUNUA - PAPARIMU *20mins S of Papakura*

Erathcree Countrystay
B&B Self-contained Separate cottage
Rob & Gillian Wakelin
10 Wilson Road, Paparimu, RD 3, Papakura, Auckland

Tel **(09) 292 5062** Fax (09) 292 5064
Mob 021 128 1547 gillrob@xtra.co.nz
www.bnb.co.nz/erathcree.html

Double $110-$125 Single $80 (Full Breakfast)
Child under 12 years reduced rate, cot available
Dinner $35-$40pp by arrangement Queen upstairs
Double bed settee in lounge Additional person: $20pp
Credit cards accepted Children welcome
1 Queen 1 Double (2 bdrm) Bathrooms: 1 Private

An easy drive to Auckland Airport/City (40 minutes), quick access to State Highway 2 for travel south... but in its own tranquil world of green countryside, tree filled garden and Hunua Ranges backdrop. Well travelled hosts offer a warm, helpful welcome, the pets are friendly and the atmosphere relaxed. The cottage is a short garden stroll away from the house. Wheelchairs; ground floor access.

DRURY *5km S of Drury*

Tuhimata Park *B&B*
Susan & Pat Baker
697B Runciman Road, Runciman, RD 2, Drury

Tel (09) 294 8748   Fax (09) 294 8749
tuhimata@iprolink.co.nz
www.bnb.co.nz/tuhimatapark.html

Double $90-$120   Single $60-$80   (Full Breakfast)
Child neg   Dinner $35-$40   Credit cards accepted
Children welcome
2 Queen 2 Single (3 bdrm)
Bathrooms: 2 Ensuite 1 Guests share

Our spacious, comfortable, and relaxing home is an ideal place to start or finish a NZ holiday. Only 20 minutes from Auckland Airport and 30 minutes from the city centre. Set in expansive lawns and giant oak trees, with wide verandahs, overlooking rolling green farmland, indoor garden and BBQ in a large conservatory, tennis court, swimming pool, spa pool, and games room. Two or three course dinners, including pre-dinner drinks and nibbles, wine, and liqueurs with coffee. Laundry facilities. Pets - a family cat.

DRURY *3km E of Drury*

The Drury Homestead   *B&B*
Carolyn & Ron Booker
349 Drury Hills Road, Drury,
South Auckland

Tel (09) 294 9030   Fax (09) 294 9035
Mob 021 158 5061   druryhome@paradise.net.nz
www.bnb.co.nz/thedruryhomestead.html

Double $100-$130   Single $70   (Special Breakfast)
Child neg   Dinner $30
3 Queen 1 Twin (4 bdrm)
Bathrooms: 3 Ensuite 1 Private

Hosts Carolyn and Ron, have undertaken a labour of love in restoring an early colonial New Zealand home to its former glory. The Drury Homestead was originally built c. 1879 and is set in majestic rolling farmland, bordered by native bush and a glorious tumbling stream. Choose from 4 character filled rooms, all with their own special views. Refurbished with an emphasis on comfort and style. Your comfort our style! Dine with us, enjoying the best of fresh local produce or choose from nearby restaurants. Family cat and dog.

RAMARAMA *1km N of Bombay*

Thistledown Lodge   *B&B Homestay*
Sue & Archie McPherson
1810 Great South Road, Ramarama, Drury, RD 3

Tel (09) 236 0044   Mob 0274 736313
inquiries@thistledownlodge.co.nz
www.thistledownlodge.co.nz

Double $100-$120   Single $60   (Full Breakfast)
Child neg   Dinner by arrangement
Credit cards accepted   Children welcome
1 King 2 Queen 3 Single (4 bdrm)
Bathrooms: 2 Ensuite 2 Private

Warm hospitality in a peaceful country setting - it's the perfect start or end to your holiday. The English colonial style home's large second floor bedrooms have TV and welcoming extras. Guest activities include swimming and spa pools, infrared sauna, lawn games or a walk through private bush to a secluded pond. Find out why guests remember Archie's breakfasts and keep returning for more! Easy to find from Ramarama or Bombay motorway exits, secure off-street parking and just 40 minutes from Auckland airport.

WAIUKU   *5km E of Waiuku*

Totara Downs   *Homestay*
Janet & Christopher de Tracy-Gould
Baldhill Road, RD 1, Waiuku,
South Auckland

Tel (09) 235 8505   Fax (09) 235 8504
Mob 021 154 8713   totaradw@ihug.co.nz
www.totaradowns.co.nz

Double $150   Single $100   (Full Breakfast)
Credit cards accepted
1 King/Twin 1 Queen (2 bdrm)
Bathrooms: 1 Ensuite 1 Private

Just 50 minutes drive from Auckland's International Airport and city, Totara Downs is found on a quiet country road. Set in large country house gardens with breath taking rural views. We offer feather and downs pillows and duvets, sitting room with open fire, swimming pool, lawn croquet. Historic Waiuku boasts wonderful peninsula beaches and country garden tours. With Flora our westie and 2 cats we look forward to meeting you. Not suitable for children under 12. Smoke-free home.

BOMBAY   *50km S of Auckland*

Pinnacle Farm Countrystay
B&B Self-contained Countrystay
Robin & Alton Ross
438 Pinnacle Hill Road, RD Bombay 1850, Auckland

Tel (09) 236 0956   Fax (09) 236 0957
Mob 021 250 5651   nzgolfing@clear.net.nz
www.bnb.co.nz/pinnaclefarm.html

Double $150   Single $140   (Continental Breakfast)
Child $30   Credit cards accepted   Children welcome
2 King/Twin 1 Queen (2 bdrm)
Bathrooms: 1 Private

Self-catering, 2 bedroom guesthouse on 10 acres, 6km from Southern Motorway and 4km from SH2 to Coromandel and Bay of Plenty, 15 minutes from Pukekohe Racetrack. Exclusive use, with private entrance, own balcony with views, sitting room, TV, kitchenette and electric blankets on each bed. Continental breakfast tray delivered, other meals available in Bombay (6km), Pukekohe (12km) or self-catering. Heated salt water swimming pool and tennis court available. A quiet place for your first or last nights in New Zealand as we are 40 minutes south of Auckland Airport.

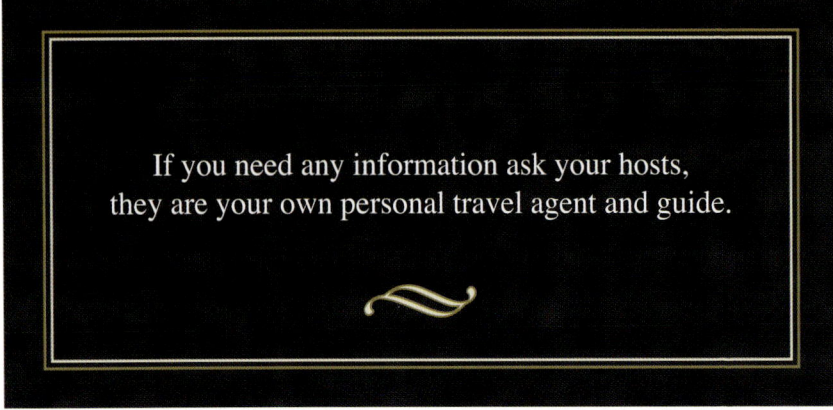

If you need any information ask your hosts,
they are your own personal travel agent and guide.

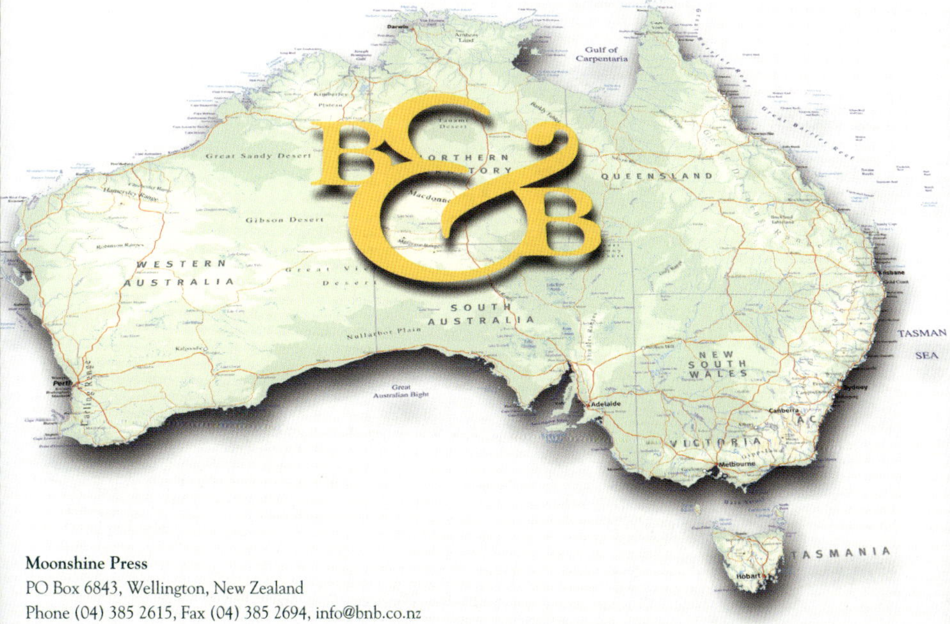

Waikato, King Country

Towns listed generally follow a north to south route. Refer to the index if required.

Kopu

Mangatarata

Te Kauwhata

Glen Murray

Huntly

Ngaruawahia

Hamilton

Tamahere

Raglan

Cambridge

Ohaupo

Tirau

Te Awamutu

Otorohanga

Waitomo

0 Kilometres 20

0 Miles 12

Te Kuiti

Piopio

Mangatarata   *13km W of Ngatea*

Clark's Country Touch   *Farmstay*
Betty & Murray Clark
209 Highway 27,
Mangatarata, RD 6, Thames

Tel (07) 867 3070   Fax (07) 867 3070
Mob 021 808 992   bmclark@xtra.co.nz
www.bnb.co.nz/clarkscountrytouch.html

Double $70   Single $45   (Continental Breakfast)
Child Discount   Dinner $20
Credit cards accepted   Children welcome
1 King/Twin (1 bdrm)   Bathrooms: 1 Host share

Welcome to our beef farm with views of rolling pasture, bush and Coromandel Ranges. Our sunny guestroom with TV, tea, coffee & cookies is opposite the bathroom. We are handy to the Hauraki Golf Course, bowling club, Seabird Coast, Miranda Hot Pools, Ngatea Gemstone Factory, water gardens and Thames Coromandel Coast. Our friendly dog Becky lives outside and our cat Watson shares our home. We enjoy handcrafts, gardening, four wheel driving and vintage machinery. Warm country hospitality awaits you. Non-smoking indoors.

Te Kauwhata   *7km E of Te Kauwhata*

Herons Ridge   *Farmstay Self-contained*
David Sharland
1131 Lake Waikare Scenic Drive,
RD 1, Te Kauwhata

Tel (07) 826 4646   Fax (07) 826 4646
Mob 027 259 5662   herons.ridge@xtra.co.nz
www.huntly.net.nz/herons.html

Double $100-$140   Single $60-$80   (Full Breakfast)
Child Discount   Dinner by arrangement
S/C studio $140   Children welcome Pets welcome
1 King 2 Queen 1 Double 1 Twin 1 Single (4 bdrm)
Bathrooms: 2 Ensuite 1 Private

Welcome to your home in the Waikato. Our quality inhouse family suite and superb garden studio overlooking the pool and garden are the perfect setting for your stay. The horse stud, set amongst ponds and pinewoods, enhance our rural location close to Lake Waikare. Meals are served in-house. Horse riding, country walks, golf and hot springs - the choice is yours. From SH1 go through Te Kauwhata village, 6km east along Waerenga Road, 1km on right - Welcome.

Te Kauwhata   *7.5km E of Te Kauwhata*

Puriri Grove   *B&B Farmstay Separate/Suite*
Linda & John Morris
784 Waerenga Road, Te Kauwhata, RD 1

Tel (07) 826 7714   Fax (07) 826 7714
Mob 021 157 9138   puririgrove@paradise.net.nz
www.huntly.net.nz/puririgrove.html

Double $120   Single $75   (Full Breakfast) Dinner $30
Studio self-contained $140   Credit cards accepted
Children welcome   Pets welcome
1 Queen 2 Double 1 Twin (4 bdrm) Bathrooms: 1 Private 1 Guests share

On a hilltop overlooking Lake Waikare, Puriri Grove is an architect designed property with a self-contained studio, giving outstanding views to the Coromandel peninsula and Karioi in the west. The house has a spa, 9 hole pitch & putt course, croquet lawn, petanque court and table tennis, 10 acres of native bush with guided walks. We cater for vegetarians and provide evening meals with local wine and produce for sale. Several excellent golf courses. John runs a recording studio (See our website link)

Glen Murray - Te Kauwhata 22km W of Te Kauwhata

Awaroa Vineyard Cottage
B&B Farmstay Self-contained separate cottage
Jan and Brian White
121 Insoll Road, Glen Murray

Tel **(09) 233 3289** Fax (09) 233 3290
Mob 021 773 327 jan_white@xtra.co.nz
www.bnb.co.nz/awaroa.html

Double $100-$120 (Full Breakfast) Dinner $35
Credit cards accepted
1 Queen 1 Twin (2 bdrm)
Bathrooms: 1 Private

Awaroa Cottage offers attractive self contained accommodation set in tranquil surroundings with panoramic rural views. Guests can relax in the lounge, around the barbecue in the private garden setting or stroll around the boutique vineyard on the property. Our hamper breakfast ensures you wake and dine at your leisure. We share the historic homestead with our 2 cats. Centrally located less than 1 hour from Auckland and Hamilton and within easy reach of Te Kauwhata cafés and wineries, excellent golf courses and other attractions.

Huntly 4km NW of Huntly

Parnassus Farm & Garden
B&B Farmstay Self-contained
Sharon & David Payne
Te Ohaki Road, RD 1, Huntly

Tel **(07) 828 8781** Fax (07) 828 8781
Mob 021 458 525 parnassus@xtra.co.nz
www.parnassus.co.nz

Double $120-$140 Single $70-$100 (Full Breakfast)
Child according to age Dinner by arrangement
Credit cards accepted Children welcome
2 King/Twin 2 Double 2 Single (3 bdrm)
Bathrooms: 3 Private

B&B on working farm 1 hour south of Auckland and only 4km off SH1. Enjoy the opportunity to experience farm life or simply have time out in the rural tranquility. All bedrooms are beautifully appointed & have private facilities. Our extensive gardens supply an abundance of produce & preserves for farmhouse meals & feature many species native to New Zealand. Leave SH1 at traffic lights by Huntly KFC. Cross river, right into Harris Street, after 2km right into Te Ohaki Road, 1.9km on left.

Raglan 20km S of Raglan

Matawha *Farmstay Separate/ Suite/ Studio*
Jenny & Peter Thomson
61 Matawha Road,
RD 2, Raglan

Tel **(07) 825 6709** Fax (07) 825 6715
jennyt@wave.co.nz
www.bnb.co.nz/matawha.html

Double $90 Single $45 (Full Breakfast)
Dinner $20 Cash or cheque only please
1 King 1 Double 4 Single (3 bdrm)
Bathrooms: 1 Private 1 Guests share 1 Host share

We live on the west coast and our family has farmed this land for 100 years. Come and enjoy our private beach, expansive garden, home-grown vegetables, spa, 2 cats and the peace of no other buildings or people for miles. Take bush or mountain walks, a scenic drive, go surfing or fishing, or maybe find the hot water beach! Directions: take Hamilton/Raglan route 23, turn left at Bridal Veil Falls sign, right at Te Mata onto Ruapuke Road, left onto Tuturimu Road and follow to T-junction, straight ahead across cattlestop – 61 Matawha Road. Auckland 2.5 hours, Hamilton 1 hour, Raglan 30 minutes.

HAMILTON *3km N of Hamilton*

Kantara *Homestay*
Mrs Esther Kelly
7 Delamare Road,
Bryant Park, Hamilton

Tel (07) 849 2070 Mob 025 263 9442
esther@slingshot.co.nz
www.bnb.co.nz/kelly.html

Double $100-$125 Single $60 (Full Breakfast)
Dinner $25 Credit cards accepted
1 Double 1 Twin (2 bdrm)
Bathrooms: 1 Ensuite 1 Private

I have travelled extensively throughout New Zealand and overseas and welcome tourists to my comfortable home. I live close to the Waikato River with its tranquil river walks and St Andrews Golf Course. My interests are travel, golf, tramping, Mah Jong and gardening. A member of NZ Association Farm & Home Hosts and Probus. I look forward to offering you friendly hospitality. Directions: from Auckland - leave main Highway north of Hamilton at second round intersection into Bryant Road. Turn left into Sandwich Road and second street on right.

HAMILTON *1.5km E of Hamilton Central*

Matthews B&B *B&B Homestay*
Maureen & Graeme Matthews
24 Pearson Avenue,
Claudelands, Hamilton

Tel (07) 855 4269 Fax (07) 855 4269
Mob 027 474 7758 mgm@xtra.co.nz
www.matthewsbnb.co.nz

Double $75-$85 Single $50-$55 (Full Breakfast)
Child ¹/₂ price Dinner $20 Credit cards accepted
1 Double 1 Twin (2 bdrm)
Bathrooms: 2 Guests share 1 Host share

Welcome to our home 2 seconds off the city bypass on Routes 7 and 9 at Five Crossroads. We are adjacent to the Waikato Events Centre, Ruakura Research Station and handy to the university and only 3 minutes from central city. Our home is a lived-in comfortable home, warm in winter and cool in summer, with a pool available. We enjoy spending time with visitors from NZ and overseas . We have travelled extensively and enjoy helping to plan your holiday. Dinner by arrangement.

HAMILTON *Hamilton Central*

Ebbett Homestay *B&B Homestay*
Glenys & John Ebbett
162 Beerescourt Road,
Hamilton

Tel (07) 849 2005 johnebbett@xtra.co.nz
www.bnb.co.nz/ebbett.html

Double $90 Single $60 (Full Breakfast)
Dinner $25
2 Single (1 bdrm)
Bathrooms: 1 Private

Only minutes from town centre, our 13 year old home has a spectacular view of the Waikato River (New Zealand's longest) and access to Hamilton's popular river walk. We enjoy sharing travel anecdotes, but also respect our guests' wish for privacy. Your room has its own tea/coffee facility and private bathroom. 85 minutes from Auckland International Airport appeals to tourists arriving or departing New Zealand. Our interests include people, music, sport, travel, gardening and community. We have had 11 years of happy hosting. No pets or children.

HAMILTON   *Hamilton Central*

Homestay
Judy & Brian Dixon
50A Queenwood Avenue,
Chartwell,
Hamilton

Tel (07) 855 7324 ju.dixon@xtra.co.nz
www.opotiki2.co.nz/waiotahi

Double $65 Single $45 (Continental Breakfast)
1 Queen 1 Single (1 bdrm)
Bathrooms: 1 Private

Haere mai - Welcome to our comfortable smoke-
free, homely Lockwood nestled within a quiet garden. Guests have sole access to their bathroom and
bedroom. Our aim is to provide a warm environment where guests relax and enjoy themselves. Within
walking distance are popular "Café en Q", "The Platter Place". Chartwell Square and Waikato River
walks. We also have a beach home with magnificent sea views near Opotiki if requested. We share our
home with a friendly cat named Zapper. Directions: please phone.

HAMILTON - OHAUPO   *4km SW of Hamilton*

Green Gables of Rukuhia *B&B Homestay*
Earl & Judi McWhirter
35 Rukuhia Road, RD 2, Ohaupo

Tel (07) 843 8511   Fax (07) 843 8514
Mob 021 583 462   judi.earl@clear.net.nz
www.bnb.co.nz/greengablesofrukuhia.html

Double $80-$90 Single $40-$50
(Continental Breakfast) Dinner by arrangement
Credit cards accepted
2 Double 3 Single (3 bdrm)
Bathrooms: 1 Guests share

Warm, comfortable smoke-free family home in a quiet
rural setting, close to Hamilton, airport and Field Days (Mystery Creek). Free pick up/delivery airport,
bus, train terminal all part of the friendly service. 5km to Vilagrad Winery; 2 minutes walk to Gostiona
Restaurant. 2 storey house with guest rooms, lounge downstairs; dining, hosts upstairs. Fresh home-
baked bread and selection of coffees to suit. Judi lectures statistics at University of Waikato. Earl is a
"retired" school teacher. One teenage daughter still lives at home. Non-smokers preferred.

HAMILTON   *4km S of Hamilton*

The Poplars *Home & Garden*
Lesley & Peter Ramsay
402 Matangi Road,
RD 4, Hamilton

Tel (07) 829 5551   Mob 025 668 0985
pramsay@ihug.co.nz

Double $95 Single $70 (Full Breakfast)
Dinner $30pp by arrangement
Children welcome Pets welcome
1 King 1 Twin (2 bdrm)   Bathrooms: 1 Private

Just minutes from Hamilton, Mystery Creek and Cambridge, The Poplars offers a haven of peace and
quiet. Set in a majestic 3 acre garden with internationally acclaimed daffodils, 500 roses and many
water features. Each guest room has tea and coffee making facilities, electric blankets and TV. Solar
heated swimming pool and spa are adjacent to guest rooms. Hosts Peter and Lesley, themselves
seasoned travellers, offer you the charms of country living. A warm welcome shared with family pets
awaits you. A unique and special place to stay. Directions: please phone.

HAMILTON   *28km S of Hamilton*

Country Quarters Homestay   *B&B Homestay*
Ngaere & Jack Waite
No 11 Corcoran Road,
Te Pahu, Hamilton

Tel (07) 825 9727   graeme.waite@xtra.co.nz
www.bnb.co.nz/countryquartershomestay.html

Double $80   Single $40   (Full Breakfast)
Child $10   Dinner $25   Caravan $15
Children welcome   Pets welcome
1 Queen 1 Twin 3 Single (5 bdrm)
Bathrooms: 1 Guests share

We welcome you to the peace and tranquillity of country life. Our place is central from Te Awamutu and Hamilton and are located in the little farming community of Te Pahu, right under Mount Pirongia. We are in the middle of a block of chestnut trees and are quite secluded. We have our small dog and 2 fat cats. Our home is very large and roomy and we have special facilities for the elderly person. Comfort and nice meals is what we offer you.

HAMILTON - TAMAHERE   *10km S of Hamilton*

Lenvor B&B   *B&B*
Lenora & Trevor Shelley
540E Oaklea Lane,
RD 3, Tamahere, Hamilton

Tel (07) 856 2027   Fax (07) 856 4173
lenvor@clear.net.nz
www.bnb.co.nz/lenvorbb.html

Double $110   Single $65   (Full Breakfast) Child $25
Dinner by arrangement Children welcome
3 Queen 3 Single (4 bdrm)
Bathrooms: 1 Ensuite 2 Guests share 1 Host share

Lenora and Trevor warmly invite you to relax and to share the comfort of our home Lenvor, which is set in a rural area, down a country lane. Our 2 storey home has guest rooms, small lounge upstairs; dining, lounge, hosts, downstairs. 10 minutes to Hamilton or Cambridge; 5 minutes to Mystery Creek or airport. Lenora's interests are floral art and cake icing. Trevor enjoys vintage cars. Centrally situated for day trips to Coromandel, Tauranga, Rotorua, Taupo and Waitomo Caves.

HAMILTON   *10km E of Hamilton*

A&A Country Stay   *Self-contained Country Cottage*
Ann & Alan Marsh
275 Vaile Road, RD 4, Hamilton

Tel (07) 824 1908 or (07) 8241909   Fax (07) 824 1908
Mob 027 476 3014 aacountrystay@callplus.net.nz
www.bnb.co.nz/aacountrystay.html

Double $100   Single $60   (Continental Breakfast)
Child ncg   Breakfast supplied for first morning
Credit cards accepted Children welcome Pets welcome
1 Queen 2 Single (2 bdrm)
Bathrooms: 1 Private

Enter down our driveway treelined with London Planes to our country cottage. The Cottage is 2 bedrooms, self-contained including laundry and Sky Digital. Enjoy our peaceful surroundings set in 2 acres of garden with pond, short distance from our home. Sit, relax in privacy out on the veranda, have our ducks and doves visit you while overlooking our 47 acres with sheep and cattle. Portacot and highchair available. We have two Jack Russells who will also welcome you.
Longterm stayers are welcome.

OHAUPO   *15km S of Hamilton*

Ridge House   *B&B*
Margaret Birtles & Matthew Harris
15 Main Road, Ohaupo

Tel (07) 823 6555   Fax (07) 823 6550
Mob 021 156 9582   m.a.birtles@xtra.co.nz
www.bnb.co.nz/ridgehousenz.html

Double $80   Single $65   (Continental Breakfast)
Child $15   Dinner $20 by arrangement
Credit cards accepted   Children welcome   Pets welcome
1 Queen 2 Double 1 Twin (3 bdrm)
Bathrooms: 1 Guests share 1 Host share

We welcome you to come and visit our home with its wonderful lake and pastoral views. Our home is shared with our dog, Zoe, who loves to welcome visitors. We are just 6 minutes to Hamilton International Airport and can arrange pick up from there and car storage ($10). This is an ideal base for trips to Hamilton, Te Awamutu, Waitomo Caves, Cambridge, Rotorua and Tauranga. Mystery Creek (home of the Field Days) and popular golf courses are close by. Travel well.

CAMBRIDGE   *Cambridge Central*

Park House   *B&B*
Pat & Bill Hargreaves
70 Queen Street, Cambridge

Tel (07) 827 6368   Fax (07) 827 4094
Park.House@xtra.co.nz   www.parkhouse.co.nz

Double $130-$160 Single $120 (Full Breakfast) C/C accepted
1 King/Twin 1 Queen (2 bdrm)
Bathrooms: 1 Ensuite 1 Private

Park House, circa 1920, is for guests of discernment who appreciate quality and comfort. For 15 years we have offered this superb setting for guests. Throughout this large home are antiques, traditional furniture, patchworks and stained glass windows creating an elegant and restful ambience. The guest lounge features an elaborately carved fireplace, fine art, library, TV and complimentary sherry. Bedrooms in separate wing upstairs ensues privacy. Unbeatable quiet location overlooking village green, 2 minutes walk to restaurants, antique and craft shops. Member of Heritage Inns.

CAMBRIDGE   *5km SW of Cambridge*

Birches   *B&B Farmstay Separate/Suite*
Sheri Mitchell & Hugh Jellie
263 Maungatautari Road,
PO Box 194, Cambridge

Tel (07) 827 6556   Fax (07) 827 3552   Mob 021 882 216
birches@ihug.co.nz   www.birches.co.nz

Double $95 Single $65   (Full Breakfast)
Child by arrangement Dinner by arrangement
Credit cards accepted Children welcome
1 Queen 1 Double 1 Single (2 bdrm)
Bathrooms: 1 Ensuite 1 Private

Our 1930's character farmhouse offers open fires in guests' sitting room, tennis and swimming pool set in country garden amongst picturesque horse studs. Proximity to Cambridge and Lake Karapiro makes Birches an ideal base for lake users. Hugh, a veterinarian, and I are widely travelled. Olivia, 12, is happy to show her farm pets and cat. Little Cherry Tree Cottage (queen/ensuite) is ideal for couples wanting privacy. The twin room in farmhouse has private bathroom with spabath. We serve delicious farmhouse breakfasts alfresco or in dining room.

CAMBRIDGE *5min w Cambridge*

Hansel & Gretels B&B *B&B*
Debbie Worth
58 Hamilton Road, Cambridge
(On the corner of Hamilton Road & Bryce Street)

Tel (07) 827 8476 Fax (07) 827 8476
Mob 027 453 7928 gretels@xtra.co.nz
www.bnb.co.nz/hanselgretelsbb.html

Double $90 Single $75 (Continental Breakfast)
Credit cards accepted Children welcome
Pets welcome Smoking area inside
1 Queen 1 Double 2 Single (3 bdrm) Bathrooms: 2 Private

Wanting home comfort and privacy or want to chat you will find it here. Located 5 minutes from the town centre, restaurants, antique and gift shops, harness racing and golf club. This is the centre of the thoroughbred horse industry (horse studs 5 minutes drive). Daily leisurely drives to Waitomo Caves 40 minutes, Rotorua 55 minutes, Hamilton Field Days 10 minutes, Lake Karapiro 10 minutes and a host of other interesting drives and walks. Children and pets welcome. We're happy to pick you up from the bus stop or Hamilton Airport. Bookings recommended. Look forward to meeting you.

CAMBRIDGE *2km S of Cambridge*

Glenelg *B&B Homestay*
Shirley & Ken Geary
6 Curnow Place, Cambridge

Tel (07) 823 0084 Fax (07) 823 4279
glenelgbnb@ihug.co.nz www.bnb.co.nz/glenelg.html

Double $100 Single $65 (Full Breakfast)
Child $20 Dinner $20 by arrangement
Credit cards accepted Children welcome Pets welcome
3 Queen 1 Twin (4 bdrm)
Bathrooms: 3 Ensuite 1 Private

Glenelg welcomes you to Cambridge to a new home with quality spacious accommodation - warm quiet and private overlooking Waikato farmland, with plenty of off-street parking. Beds have electric blankets and woolrests. 200 rose bushes in the garden. 5 minutes to Lake Karapiro. Mystery Creek, where NZ National Field Days and many other functions are held, is only 15 minutes away. Laundry facilities available. No smoking indoors please. "Home away from Home." For a brochure and directions please phone. Evening dinner by arrangement. Pets and children are welcome.

CAMBRIDGE *6km S of Cambridge*

Hydro Road Gallery & Homestay
Homestay Gallery
Judy & Gavin Smith
53 Hydro Road, RD 2, Cambridge

Tel (07) 823 2044 Fax (07) 823 2047
Mob 0274 386 502 studioart@clear.net.nz
www.bnb.co.nz/hydroroad.html

Double $100 Single $60 (Continental Breakfast)
Child $25 Dinner $40pp Gallery
Credit cards accepted
1 Queen 3 Single (2 bdrm)
Bathrooms: 1 Ensuite 1 Guests share

Welcome to our new home & garden at Karapiro set amongst old English trees just 6km from Cambridge. We are within 1 hours drive to Hamilton, Rotorua, Tauranga/Mt.Manganui, Tirau and Waitomo Caves. Enjoy a relaxed rural retreat just a few minutes walk to Lake Karapiro. Watch the water sports, have a game of golf or just go shopping in Cambridge, the town of arts, crafts and antiques. Gavin is a well known watercolour artist and we have our own gallery on site.

CAMBRIDGE   *2km S of Cambridge*

Pamade B&B   *B&B Self-contained*
Paul & Marion Derikx
229 Shakespeare Street, Cambridge -Leamington
(Opposite turn-off to Karapiro Lake)

Tel (07) 827 4916   Fax (07) 827 4988
Mob 021 261 7122 pamades@slingshot.co.nz
www.bnb.co.nz/pamade.html

Double $80-$90   Single $55-$65   (Special Breakfast)
Dinner by arrangement
1 King 1 Queen 1 Twin 4 Single (3 bdrm)
Bathrooms: 2 Ensuite 1 Host share

Pamade is a character home, very comfortable with beautiful gardens. We are situated 2 minutes from central Cambridge with its wonderful selection of fascinating art, craft, boutique and antique shops, restaurants, stud farms and golf course. Just around the corner from Lake Karapiro (5 minutes drive), with its water-skiing, rowing and other aquatic sports. Mystery Creek (Field Days) is only 10 minutes drive away. Self-contained unit plus large double room (ensuite and coffee and tea arrangements) with private exit. Ideal for longer stays. Great breakfast guaranteed. Dinner by prior arrangement.

CAMBRIDGE   *5km NE of Cambridge*

Gainsborough House   *B&B Self-contained*
Lisa & Scott Avery
1/103 Maungakawa Road,
RD 4, Cambridge

Tel (07) 823 2473   Fax (07) 823 1678
gainsboroughhouse@xtra.co.nz
www.gainsboroughhouse.co.nz

Double $120-$150 Single $90   (Full Breakfast)
Child $15 Dinner by arrangement
Cottage on application   Children welcome
1 King 1 Queen 2 Double 4 Single (6 bdrm)
Bathrooms: 4 Ensuite

Our restored historic home offers a peaceful retreat only minutes from Cambridge. Come and ramble in the gardens or relax in the library, with our book and magazine selection. Enjoy a lavish breakfast - cooked or continental. Gainsborough cottage, our self-contained accomodation is perfect for those wanting privacy or for family groups, as it sleeps up to 6. We are within easy reach of many of NZ's major tourist attractions.

CAMBRIDGE   *1km S of Cambridge*

Cambridge Handi Homestay   *B&B Homestay*
Isobel & Harry Hopkins
7 Marlowe Drive,
Cambridge

Tel (07) 823 2142   Fax (07) 823 2143
Mob 025 290 5477   handi.homestay@xtra.co.nz
www.handi-homestay.co.nz

Double $85 Single $55 (Full Breakfast) Child $20
Children welcome   Infants no charge
Credit cards accepted
1 Queen 1 Double 1 Twin (3 bdrm)
Bathrooms: 1 Ensuite 1 Guests share

A warm welcome awaits you at our home close to the Waikato River. Spacious guestrooms have TV, tea and coffee facilities. Superb breakfast. Easily located with tranquil gardens, a pleasant stroll to town centre - close to childrens playgrounds.   Drive to south end of Victoria Street (Main Street), cross bridge and turn right at roundabout onto Pope Street - Highway to Te Awamutu. Marlowe Drive is first on the right.

CAMBRIDGE *10km S of Cambridge*

Hilltop Haven *B&B Homestay*
Marie & Warwick Price
55 Gorton Road, RD 2, Cambridge

Tel (07) 823 2246 Fax (07) 823 2248
wmprice@xtra.co.nz
www.bnb.co.nz/hilltophaven.html

Double $100 Single $60 (Full Breakfast) Child $25
Dinner by arrangement Credit cards accepted
1 Queen 1 Double 4 Single (3 bdrm)
Bathrooms: 1 Ensuite 1 Guests share

We offer you a warm welcome to our country home which is just off State Highway 1. We have a commanding view of the Waikato country side from our 20 acres. We graze cattle (pet cows which can be patted and hand milked), 2 donkeys Simon and Jenny, and several breeds of poultry. There is an in-ground swimming pool, flood lit tennis court, table tennis and a pool table. Lake Karapiro is 5 minutes away, 20 minutes to Mystery Creek Field Days and Hamilton Airport. Rotorua, Tauranga and Waitomo Caves are within an hour away. Separate, we have a queen room, with ensuite, tea/coffee facility and carport adjacent. Ideal for as long as you like.

CAMBRIDGE *1km NE of Cambridge*

Bacton House *B&B*
Mary & John Cubitt
46 Williams Street, Cambridge,

Tel (07) 827 3353 Fax (07) 827 3353
Mob 027 696 7594 mjcubitt@wave.co.nz
www.bactonhouse.co.nz

Double $90 Single $60 (Full Breakfast)
Dinner $30 by prior arrangement Credit cards accepted
2 Queen (2 bdrm)
Bathrooms: 1 Ensuite 1 Private power showers

Welcome to Bacton House. Centrally situated, Bacton House offers large rooms with complete quiet and privacy. Enjoy the large garden and swimming pool. Bedrooms have been completely refurbished using quality materials and with your comfort in mind. Queen-size beds, electric blankets, comfortable lounge chairs, television, tea/coffee making facilities, private bathroom or ensuite. A delicious cooked breakfast is offered in the guest's dining room. Dinner is offered. Lady Grey is our resident cat.

CAMBRIDGE - TIRAU *20 S of Cambridge*

Emanuel's *B&B*
Eddie & Ann Rompelberg
Karapiro Heights, State Highway 1
(20kms south of Cambridge), RD 1 Tirau

Tel (07) 823 7414 Fax (07) 823 7219
info@emanuels.co.nz www.emanuels.co.nz

Double $250-$600 Single $200 (Full Breakfast)
Credit cards accepted
6 King 3 Twin (6 bdrm)
Bathrooms: 6 Ensuite

Emanuel's is a superbly located, new, purpose-built B&B, offering luxury accommodation for discerning travellers, or for those seeking a sophisticated, peaceful retreat. Small conferences and intimate weddings are also our speciality. Our guestrooms offer twin or king-size beds, ensuite bathrooms with power-showers, air-conditioning, elegant décor and private patio. All capture stunning views of Lake Karapiro. We are an easy drive to Hamilton, Tauranga, Cambridge, Rotorua, Tirau and Waitomo. Our friendly hospitality includes full, cooked breakfast and we are happy to provide other meals by arrangement.

TE AWAMUTU 4.5km N of Te Awamutu

Farmstay Guesthouse
Mrs R Bleskie & C Bleskie
Storey Road, Te Awamutu

Tel (07) 871 3301 sophy@ihug.co.nz
www.bnb.co.nz/bleskie.html

Double $115 Single $60 (Full Breakfast)
Child $25 Dinner $25
Children welcome Pets welcome
1 Double 8 Single (5 bdrm)
Bathrooms: 1 Ensuite 2 Guests share 1 Host share

The 85 acre farm, situated in beautiful country side with cattle, horses, pigs, poultry, sheep, goats and pets. A spacious home welcomes you with swimming pool and tennis court. Large guest rooms with doors to garden. Specials: Horseback riding and gig rides for children and adults for $10 a ride. Raspberry picking in season and access to the milking of 500 dairy cows.

TE AWAMUTU 2km S of Te Awamutu

Leger Farm *B&B Farmstay*
Beverley & Peter Bryant
114 St Leger Road,
Te Awamutu

Tel (07) 871 6676 Fax (07) 871 6679
www.bnb.co.nz/legerfarm.html

Double $125-$140 Single $85-$100 (Full Breakfast)
Dinner $35
1 Queen 1 Double 1 Twin 3 Single (4 bdrm)
Bathrooms: 1 Ensuite 1 Private 1 Guests share

Leger Farm is a private residence with country living at its finest. The discerning leisure traveller seeking quality accommodation, in peaceful, relaxing surroundings, will find warm hospitality and every comfort here. Spacious bedrooms share stunning panoramic views of surrounding countryside. Each bedroom has its own balcony with beautiful garden vistas. We farm cattle and sheep, and are centrally based for visiting Waitomo Caves and black water rafting, Rotorua with its thermal activity and NZ's dramatic west coast and ironstone sands. Golf course nearby for relaxation. Smoke-free home.

TE AWAMUTU 4km S of Te Awamutu

Morton Homestay *B&B Homestay*
Marg and Dick Morton
10 Brill Road, RD 5, Te Awamutu

Tel (07) 871 8814 Fax (07) 871 8865
www.bnb.co.nz/mortonhomestay.html

Double $80 Single $50 (Full Breakfast)
Dinner $25 by arrangement
Rates neg for more than 3 people
Credit cards accepted
1 Double 4 Single (3 bdrm)
Bathrooms: 1 Private

We welcome visitors to enjoy our hospitality and the peacefulness of our home 5 minutes from the centre of New Zealand's "Rosetown". Waitomo, Rotorua and Lake Taupo are within easy driving distance from us. Hamilton airport and Mystery Creek are 20 minutes away. Te Awamutu is an excellent base for bushwalking, golfing, fishing and garden visits. Gardening, philately and woodturning are among our interests. We also have an interest in classic cars. Please phone or fax for reservations and directions.

Otorohanga - Waitomo District *8km NW of Otorohanga*

Meadowland *B&B Farmstay Self-contained*
Jill & Tony Webber
746 State Highway 31, RD 3, Otorohanga

Tel (07) 873 7729   0800 687 262   Fax (07) 873 7719
meadowland@xtra.co.nz
www.bnb.co.nz/meadowland.html

Double $85 Single $60 (Full Breakfast) Child $20
Credit cards accepted   Children welcome
2 Queen 1 Double 1 Twin 2 Single (5 bdrm)
Bathrooms: 1 Private 1 Guests share

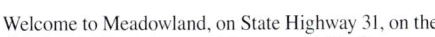

Welcome to Meadowland, on State Highway 31, on the
right hand side at the top of the second hill. Our accommodation is: a self-contained unit which can
sleep up to 6. 1 twin and 2 double bedrooms in homestead with guest shared bathroom and separate
toilet. All beds have woolrests and electric blankets. We have a tennis court, swimming pool and spa
pool on site. We are 5 minutes from the Otorohanga Kiwi House and Aviary, 20 minutes from Waitomo
Caves area. We have 3 outside cats. Non-smokers preferred.

Otorohanga - Waitomo District *1km N of town centre*

Angus House *B&B Homestay*
Pauline & Michael Masters
63 Mountain View Road, Otorohanga

Tel (07) 873 8955 Fax (07) 873 8954
Mob 025 58 2227 ppf@clear.net.nz
www.angushouse.co.nz

Double $75 Single $50 (Full Breakfast)
Child $20 Dinner $20
Credit cards accepted Children welcome
1 Double 2 Single (2 bdrm) Bathrooms: 1 Guests share

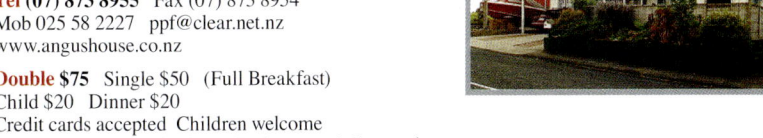

Angus House is on the outskirts of Otorohanga, less than a kilometre from town centre and the Kiwi
House. We invite you to stay at our comfortable home, relax and enjoy our hospitality, the pool and
the 2 cats. Local activities beyond Otorohanga include Waitomo Caves 20km away where there is
adventure caving, blackwater rafting, abseiling, and horse trekking. Trout fishing, bush walks, farm
and garden visits are amongst the other attractions the region provides. We are able to assist you with
places of interest

Waitomo Caves *9.7km w of Waitomo Village*

Te Tiro *B&B Self-contained*
Rachel & Angus Stubbs
970 Caves Te Anga Road, RD 8 Te Kuiti

Tel (07) 878 6328 Fax (07) 878 6328
Mob 027 226 7681 stubbs.a_r@xtra.co.nz
www.waitomocavesnz.com

Double $80-$95 Single $60 (Continental Breakfast)
Child $15 Credit cards accepted Children welcome
Pets welcome
2 Queen 4 Single (2 bdrm)
Bathrooms: 2 Private

Te Tiro (The View) welcomes you. Enjoy fantastic panoramic views of the central North Island and
mountains. At night enjoy glowworms nestled in lush NZ bush only metres from your cottage. Situated
on an established sheep farm with 350 acres of reserve bush. Our self-contained pioneer style cottages
can accommodate up to 5 people in a cosy open plan room. Hosts Rachel and Angus have 30 years of
tourism experience between them and would be happy to advise you on the wonders of Waitomo.

WAITOMO CAVES *16km S of Otorohanga*

Waitomo Caves Guest Lodge *B&B detached units*
Janet & Colin Beeston
PO Box 16, Waitomo Caves

Tel (07) 878 7641 Fax (07) 878 7466
jancolbeeston@xtra.co.nz
www.bnb.co.nz/waitomo.html

Double $70-$80 Single $60 (Continental Breakfast)
Child $10 Credit cards accepted
Children welcome
6 Queen 7 Single (7 bdrm)
Bathrooms: 7 Ensuite

We are located right in the centre of Waitomo Caves Village, an easy walking distance to the Waitomo Caves Information Centre and Museum, the glowworm caves and a variety of eating places. Our quality ensuite units are in a beautiful peaceful garden setting, overlooking the Waitomo Domain and surrounding bush. You can expect a warm welcome from Janet, Colin and Gypsy, our australian kelpie. We have travelled widely in New Zealand and can advise you knowledgeably on your itinerary.

TE KUITI - WAITOMO DISTRICT *1km S of Te Kuiti*

Te Kuiti B&B *B&B Homestay*
Pauline Blackmore
5 Grey St,
Te Kuiti

Tel (07) 878 6686
pauline.blackmore@xtra.co.nz
www.bnb.co.nz/tekuitibb.html

Double $80 Single $50 (Full Breakfast)
Credit cards accepted
2 Queen 2 Single (3 bdrm)
Bathrooms: 2 Ensuite 1 Private

We live only 50 metres off Highway 3. Expect a warm welcome, peace and relaxation in our 1920's bungalow. The bedrooms have tea and coffee making facilities, quality beds and bedding and heaters. Breakfast timed to suit you and includes cereals, fruit, juice and toast followed by cooked English breakfast and brewed coffee or tea. Feel free to use the TV in one of the lounges. We can help you with advice about local attractions including great places to walk or tramp.

TE KUITI - WAITOMO DISTRICT *20km NW of Te Kuiti*

Tapanui Country Home *B&B Farmstay Homestay*
Sue & Mark Perry
1714 Oparure Rd, Te Kuiti

Tel (07) 877 8549 Fax (07) 877 8541
Mob 025 949 873 tapanuibnb@ihug.co.nz
www.tapanui.co.nz

Double $165-$180 Single $155-$170 (Full Breakfast)
Dinner by arrangement Credit cards accepted
3 King/Twin (3 bdrm)
Bathrooms: 1 Ensuite 1 Private

Luxury farmstay bed and breakfast accommodation near the famous Waitomo Glowworm Caves. Enjoy elegance, peace and uninterrupted views of hill country pasture. Relax and recharge with comfortable king/twin-size beds, cotton bathrobes, hair dryers, heated towel rails, spacious ensuite and private bathrooms. Experience New Zealand farming hospitality and delicious cooked meals while recharging from Waitomo adventures and activities. Meet the family of hand-reared sheep, pig, goat and donkey on our 1900 acre sheep and cattle farm. Guests welcome after 4pm. Unsuitable for children.

TE KUITI - WAITOMO DISTRICT *6km E of Te Kuiti*

Panorama Farm *B&B Farmstay Homestay*
Raema & Michael Warriner
65 Carter Road, RD 2, Te Kuiti

Tel (07) 878 5104   Fax (07) 878 8104
panoramab.b@xtra.co.nz
www.bnb.co.nz/panoramafarm.html

Double $72 Single $36 (Full Breakfast) Child $18
Dinner $20 Credit cards accepted Children welcome
1 Double 3 Single (2 bdrm)
Bathrooms: 1 Guests share

Raema, Michael and the cat welcome you to our hill top home, overlooking bush clad hills, fertile valleys and distant peaks with golden dawns and spectacular sunsets. We offer comfortable beds and the quiet surroundings of a 30 hectare farm plus 40 years experience of the district and its attractions. Waitomo is 25 minutes away, Rotorua, Taupo 2 hours so come and enjoy the company, the scenery and a good night's rest. Arriving or departing from Auckland - we are 2 1/2 hours to the airport.

TE KUITI - WAITOMO DISTRICT *1km S of Te Kuiti Post Office*

Sanaig House *B&B Homestay*
Sue & Mike Wagstaff
35 Awakino Road, Te Kuiti

Tel (07) 878 7128
Fax (07) 878 7128
sanaig@xtra.co.nz
www.bnb.co.nz/sanaighouse.html

Double $100 Single $70 (Continental Breakfast)
2 Queen 1 Double (3 bdrm)
Bathrooms: 1 Ensuite 1 Private

Sanaig House built in 1903 is one of Te Kuiti's gracious homesteads. Our guest bedrooms are attractive, spacious and overlook a garden with lovely mature trees. The Waitomo area, famous for its glowworm caves, has a variety of other exciting outdoor adventures – blackwater rafting, abseiling, quad bike riding and horse riding. Relaxing bush walks, fishing, bird watching and garden visits can all be arranged. Sanaig House is only 500 metres from a good restaurant and there is a selection of cafés and other restaurants in Te Kuiti.

TE KUITI - WAITOMO DISTRICT *2km N of Te Kuiti*

B&B Farmstay
Margaret & Graeme Churstain
129 Gadsby Road, RD 5, Te Kuiti

Tel (07) 878 8191   Fax (07) 878 5949
www.bnb.co.nz/churstain.html

Double $70 Single $40 (Continental Breakfast)
Dinner $15pp by arrangement Children welcome
1 Queen 1 Double 1 Twin (3 bdrm)
Bathrooms: 1 Ensuite 1 Private 1 Guests share

Welcome to the peace and tranquility of our hilltop farmlet, signposted on SH3, northern end of Te Kuiti.
Having welcomed travellers for many years, come and enjoy our wonderful rural views and Kiwi hospitality. Being the sheep shearing capital of the world, Te Kuiti and surrounding areas offer many leisure activities, Waitomo Caves 10 minutes away. Comfortable double rooms are available with private bathrooms. Within 1 hour (Hamilton) and 2 1/2 hours (Auckland) of international airports this is the place to begin or end your New Zealand journey. ...simply the best...

TE KUITI - WAITOMO DISTRICT *2km N of Te Kuiti*

Gadsby Heights   *B&B Farmstay Homestay*
Janis & Ross MacDonald
137 Gadsby Road, RD 5, Te Kuiti

Tel (07) 878 3361   Fax (07) 878 3361
Mob 027 696 7122   info@gadsbyheights.co.nz
www.gadsbyheights.co.nz

Double $80-$90 Single $50-$60 (Full Breakfast)
Child $10   Dinner $25 per person by arrangement
Credit cards accepted   Children welcome   Pets welcome
1 Queen 1 Double 2 Single (2 bdrm)
Bathrooms: 1 Ensuite 1 Private

Fantastic views, farm animals, lovely gardens, just 2
minutes from Te Kuiti and 10 minutes to Waitomo. Ross, Janis, Sophie (5) and Sox the cat welcome you
to Gadsby Heights. Warm and friendly accommodation, conveniently located for you to take advantage
of all that the Waitomo area and the central North Island have to offer. We have sheep shearing, dog
demonstration, farm visits by appointment and a tour service available to take you off the beaten track,
to out of the way places and beyond. We look forward to meeting you.

PIO PIO - WAITOMO DISTRICT *24km SW of Te Kuiti*

Bracken Ridge   *B&B Country Homestay*
Susan & Rob Hallam
Aria Road, Piopio 2555

Tel (07) 877 8384   www.bnb.co.nz/hallam.html

Double $85 Single $50 (Continental Breakfast)
Dinner $20 per person by arrangement
1 Queen 1 Twin 1 Single (2 bdrm)
Bathrooms: 1 Private

Enjoy a peaceful, quiet relaxing time at our large,
modern home set in landscaped gardens on a small
sheep and cattle farmlet. Our elevated site provides panoramic views of green pastures, trees and
limestone. All rooms have a garden or rural outlook. Spacious heated bedrooms have comfortable
beds and electric blankets. Just 1km off SH3 at Piopio, we are the perfect base for exploring the scenic
northern King Country. Waitomo Caves just 35 minutes away. Please phone ahead for reservations and
directions.

PIO PIO - WAITOMO DISTRICT   *19km S of Te Kuiti*

Approved

Carmel Farm   *B&B Farmstay Homestay*
Barbara & Leo Anselmi
Main Road, PO Box 93, Pio Pio

Tel (07) 877 8130   Fax (07) 877 8130
Carmelfarms@xtra.co.nz
www.bnb.co.nz/carmelfarm.html

Double $100   Single $50
(Continental Breakfast) Dinner $25pp Children welcome Pets welcome
2 King/Twin 4 Single (4 bdrm)
Bathrooms: 1 Ensuite 1 Guests share 1 Host share

Barbara and Leo Anselmi own and operate a 1200 acre sheep, beef and dairy farm. You will be welcomed into a 3000 square feet modern home set in picturesque gardens, in a lovely limestone valley.

Whether enjoying the excitement of mustering mobs of cattle and sheep, viewing the milking of 550 cows, driving around the rolling hills on the four wheeled farm bike, relaxing as you bask in the sun by the pool or wandering through the gardens, you will experience unforgettable memories of breathtaking scenery, a clean green environment.

We have farm pets who love the attention of our guests. The donkeys are waiting to be fed. We look over a beautiful 18 hole golf course which welcomes visitors.

The property is a short distance from Black Water Rafting and canoeing activities, The Lost World Cavern, and the famous Waitomo Caves. Nearby are bush walks and the home of the rare kokako bird. We can help to arrange activities for people of all ages and interests including garden visits and horse riding. Please let us know your preference. We are 140km from Rotorua/Taupo.

Directions: Travel 19km south of Te Kuiti on SH3 towards Piopio. Carmel Farm is on the right. We can arrange to pick up from Otorohanga, Te Kuiti or Waitomo, if required.

You will be treated to delicious home cooked meals
and the warmth of our friendship

Coromandel Peninsula

Coromandel

Kuaotunu

Whitianga

Hahei

Cooks Beach

Hot Water Beach

Coroglen

Tairua

Te Puru

Thames

25

Whangamata

2

Paeroa

Waihi

Waihi Beach

Waiheke Island

Beachlands

Whitford

Clevedon

Papakura

Kaiaua

rury

Bombay

Mercer

Towns listed generally follow
a north to south route. Refer
to the index if required.

0   Kilometres   20

0   Miles   12

PAEROA *2km S of Paeroa*

Hillsdale at Paeroa *B&B Separate/Suite*
Nancy & Peter Anderson
37 Keepa Avenue, Paeroa

Tel (07) 862 8452 Fax (07) 862 8452
hillsdale@paradise.net.nz
www.homepages.paradise.net.nz/hillsdale/

Double $110 Single $85 (Full Breakfast)
Credit cards accepted
1 Queen 2 Twin (2 bdrm)
Bathrooms: 1 Private

Our modern home overlooks Paeroa, farmland and hills. Accommodation is in a private wing of the house comprising 1 queen room and 1 twin room. Facilities include shower and bath, separate toilet. We are minutes from the Karangahake Gorge, rivers and old gold mine workings. Paeroa is the gateway to Coromandel Peninsula. Close to Miranda Seabird Coast and hot pools. Activities include abseiling, rockclimbing, kayaking in the Gorge. Approx 1 hour from Auckland, Hamilton, Tauranga. We have 2 friendly cats. Smoke-free property.

THAMES *8km SE of Thames*

Wharfedale Farmstay *Farmstay Self-contained*
Rosemary Burks
RD 1, Kopu, Thames

Tel (07) 868 8929 Fax (07) 868 8926
wharfedale@xtra.co.nz
www.bnb.co.nz/wharfedalefarmstay.html

Double $100-$125 Single $85 (Full Breakfast)
Child not suitable Credit cards accepted
1 Double 2 Single (2 bdrm)
Bathrooms: 2 Private

For 13 years our guests have enjoyed the beauty of Wharfedale which has featured in Air NZ "Airwaves" and Japan's "My Country" magazines. We invite you to share our idyllic lifestyle set in 9 acres of park like paddocks and gardens surrounded by native bush. Delight in private river swimming, abundant bird life, our dairy goats. We enjoy wholefood and organically grown produce. There are cooking facilities in the studio apartment. We have no children or indoor animals. Cool shade in summer and cozy log fires and electric blankets in winter. We look forward to meeting you.

THAMES *6.4km E of Thames*

Mountain Top B&B *Homestay*
Elizabeth McCracken & Allan Berry
452 Kauaeranga Valley Road, RD 2, Thames

Tel (07) 868 9662 Fax (07) 868 9662
nzh_mountain.top@xtra.co.nz
www.bnb.co.nz/mountaintopbb.html

Double $95-$100 Single $50 (Full Breakfast)
Child 1/2 price Dinner $20-$30 Credit cards accepted
Children welcome Pets welcome
1 Queen 1 Double 1 Single (2 bdrm)
Bathrooms: 1 Guests share

Allan and I grow mandarins, olives, native trees & raise coloured sheep on a small organic farm. Our guest wing with lounge, fridge, TV and extensive library has bedrooms with decks overlooking river and mountains. Coromandel Forest Park has superb walking tracks or nearby you can amble over neighbouring farmland or swim in forest pools. We have a relaxed garden, Jack Russell Roly and cat Priscilla. We love meeting people, often cooking for guests mostly from farm produce. Come and let us look after you.

THAMES *4km E of Thames*

Acorn Lodge *B&B*
Dennis & Pat
161 Kauaeranga Valley,
RD 2, Thames

Tel (07) 868 8723 Fax (07) 868 8713
AcornLodge@xtra.co.nz
www.bnb.co.nz/acornlodge.html

Double $110 Single $70 (Full Breakfast) Child neg
Dinner $40 by arrangement Credit cards accepted
1 Queen 1 Double 1 Single (3 bdrm)
Bathrooms: 2 Private

Relax and enjoy the tranquil views from our spacious home set in 2 acres of park-like grounds. Enjoy a pot of tea or coffee and home-baking on your sunny patio or relax in your comfortable lounge featuring an atrium and waterfall. At night marvel at the glowworms - only 2 minutes walk. Our interests include tramping in the nearby Forest Park, fishing and gardening. Dennis and Pat, along with Penny our cat and Coco our friendly German Shepherd, assure you of a warm welcome.

THAMES COAST - TE PURU *12km N of Thames*

Te Puru Coast Bed & Breakfast
B&B Homestay Self-contained
Bill and Paula Olsen
2A Tatahi Street, Te Puru, Thames Coast, Coromandel

Tel (07) 868 2866 Fax (07) 868 2866
Mob 027 656 6058 tepurucoastbnb@xtra.co.nz
www.tepurucoastbnb.co.nz
Double $110 Single $70 (Full Breakfast)
Self-contained unit $125 per night for 2 people
Child $25 Dinner $30pp Children welcome
1 Queen 2 Double 1 Twin 1 Single (4 bdrm)
Bathrooms: 1 Ensuite 2 Private

Welcome to the beautiful Thames Coast. Our modern comfortable home is 80 metres off the main coast road with off-street parking. Guest lounge has TV and tea/coffee facilities. You may choose a continental or cooked breakfast and evening meals are on request with a complimentary glass of New Zealand wine or beer. Our large deck is yours to enjoy or take a short 2 minute walk to the beach. Fishermen welcome. The separate self-contained unit has own laundry, kitchen/dining, bathroom, BBQ.

COROMANDEL *11km S of Coromandel*

Coromandel Homestay *Homestay*
Hilary & Vic Matthews
74 Kowhai Drive, Te Kouma Bay, Coromandel

Tel (07) 866 8046 Fax (07) 866 8046 Mob 021 123 7341
vc.hm.matthews@xtra.co.nz
www.bnb.co.nz/coromandelhomestay.html

Double $95-$120 Single $75 (Continental Breakfast)
Dinner $40 by arrangement Credit cards accepted
2 Queen 1 Single (2 bdrm)
Bathrooms: 2 Ensuite

Our homestay is near an attractive safe beach. We have a bush setting and beautiful views of Coromandel Harbour. The area is very quiet and peaceful. Vic is a professional furniture/designer maker. Hilary enjoys gardening, spinning and woodturning. We have a cat. The house is unsuitable for young children. Take SH25 for 50km travelling north from Thames. Turn sharp left into Te Kouma Road. After 3km turn left into Kowhai Drive. We are 15 minutes drive south of Coromandel town. Dinner by prior arrangement.

COROMANDEL   *0.5 E of Coromandel*

Country Touch   *B&B Self-contained*
Colleen & Geoff Innis
39 Whangapoua Road, Coromandel

Tel (07) 866 8310   Fax (07) 866 8310
Mob 027 497 1196   countrytouch@xtra.co.nz
www.bnb.co.nz/countrytouch.html

Double $95   Single $65   (Continental Breakfast)
Child $10   Credit cards accepted   Children welcome
2 Queen 2 Twin (4 bdrm)
Bathrooms: 4 Ensuite

Geoff and I are a retired couple who enjoy meeting people, and invite you to a restful holiday in a country setting. With newly established trees and gardens, roses a speciality. You have the independence of 4 units situated apart from our home, all with fold out sofas, TV, fridge, tea and coffee making facilities. You have a country touch feeling with only a 10 minute stroll to Coromandel township, where you can enjoy our local arts, crafts and restaurants. Come and enjoy.

COROMANDEL   *10km S of Coromandel*

AJ's Homestay   *Homestay*
Annette & Ray Hintz
24 Kowhai Drive, Te Kouma, RD, Coromandel

Tel (07) 866 7057   Fax (07) 866 7057
Mob 027 458 1624   rm.aj.hintz@actrix.gen.nz
www.bnb.co.nz/ajshomestay.html

Double $95-$125   Single $80   (Continental Breakfast)
Dinner $30- $40 Credit cards accepted
Children welcome
3 Queen 1 Twin (3 bdrm)
Bathrooms: 1 Ensuite 1 Guests share 1 Host share

AJ's Homestay with panoramic sea views overlooking the Coromandel Harbour, spectacular sunsets. Five minute walk to a safe swimming beach. Most mornings breakfast is served on the terrace. Our games room has a billiard and table tennis table. Dinner can be arranged. Directions, Thames coast main road (SH25), approx 50 minutes. At the bottom of the last hill overlooking the Coromandel Harbour. Turn sharp left, at the Te Kouma Road sign. Travel past the boat ramp, next turn left. Kowhai Drive, we are number 24.

COROMANDEL   *0.5km S of Coromandel*

The Green House   *B&B*
Gwen Whitmore
505 Tiki Road, Coromandel

Tel (07) 866 7303   0800 473 364
whitmore@wave.co.nz
www.greenhousebandb.co.nz

Double $110-$150   Single $80-$100
(Continental Breakfast)   Child negotiable
Credit cards accepted
1 King/Twin 2 Queen (3 bdrm)
Bathrooms: 3 Ensuite

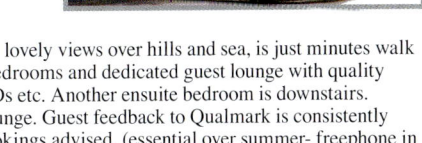

This relaxed home with very comfortable facilities, lovely views over hills and sea, is just minutes walk from excellent restaurants etc. Upstairs 2 ensuite bedrooms and dedicated guest lounge with quality furnishings, tea/coffee, refrigerator, TV, videos, CDs etc. Another ensuite bedroom is downstairs. Guests are welcome to use the host's downstairs lounge. Guest feedback to Qualmark is consistently "Excellent and exceeds expectations". Advance bookings advised, (essential over summer- freephone in NZ) for this very clean, friendly great place to stay. Pet on property.

COROMANDEL   *3km S of Coromandel*

Jacaranda Lodge   *B&B*
Robin Münch
3195 Tiki Road, Coromandel RD 1

Tel (07) 866 8002   Fax (07) 866 8002
Mob 021 252 6892   info@jacarandalodge.co.nz
www.jacarandalodge.co.nz

Double $100-$145   Single $50-$110
(Continental Breakfast)   Credit cards accepted
Children welcome
2 Queen 2 Double 1 Twin 1 Single (6 bdrm)
Bathrooms: 2 Ensuite 1 Private 1 Guests share

Robin invites you to share her spacious home set on 6 acres of tranquil country paradise. Located 3km south of Coromandel town, Jacaranda Lodge provides the perfect escape: relax in one of the guest lounges; stroll around the gorgeous gardens; or experience Coromandel's walks, galleries, unique attractions and spectacular coastline. Delicious continental breakfasts include fresh organic produce from Jacaranda's orchard. Large, comfortable bedrooms. Ensuite, private or shared bathrooms. Fully equipped guest kitchen. Special dietary needs catered for, including kosher. Sleep, eat, enjoy.

KUAOTUNU   *17km N of Whitianga*

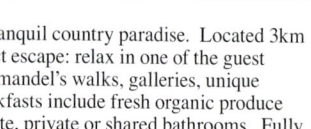

Kaeppeli's   *B&B Country Stay*
Jill & Robert Kaeppeli
Grays Avenue, Kuaotunu,   RD 2, Whitianga

Tel (07) 866 2445   Mob 025 656 3442
kaeppeli.kuaotunu@paradise.net.nz
www.kaeppeli.co.nz

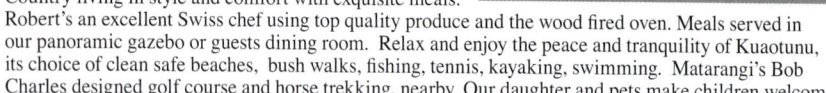

Double $110-$140   Single $85-$120 (Full Breakfast)
Child neg   Dinner by arrangement $35
Credit cards accepted   Children welcome   Pets welcome
2 King 4 Single (4 bdrm)
Bathrooms: 4 Ensuite

Country living in style and comfort with exquisite meals.
Robert's an excellent Swiss chef using top quality produce and the wood fired oven. Meals served in our panoramic gazebo or guests dining room. Relax and enjoy the peace and tranquility of Kuaotunu, its choice of clean safe beaches, bush walks, fishing, tennis, kayaking, swimming. Matarangi's Bob Charles designed golf course and horse trekking, nearby. Our daughter and pets make children welcome. Ideal for exploring the Coromandel Peninsula.   And our view?? Just the best!

KUAOTUNU   *16km N of Whitianga*

@ The Peacheys   *B&B Homestay*
Yvonne & Dale Peachey
15 Kawhero Drive, Kuaotunu RD 2, Whitianga

Tel (07) 866 5290   Fax (07) 866 5290
DYPeachey@xtra.co.nz
www.thepeacheys.co.nz

Double $100-$130   Single $90   (Special Breakfast)
Dinner $30pp   Credit cards accepted
1 King 1 Queen 2 Single (2 bdrm)
Bathrooms: 2 Ensuite

Located 2 1/2 hours from Auckland International Airport, Kuaotunu is a world away from the urban sprawl. Its unique landscape and relaxed lifestyle make it an ideal destination for NZ and international visitors. Pristine beaches, misty rainforests, wonderful walks. Your spacious room has bathrobes, beach towels, refrigerator, tea/coffee. Treat yourself to a relaxing massage with our resident massage therapist. Dine out at Whitianga (15 minutes) Matarangi (7 minutes) or with us, prior arrangement required. Take a few days out to enjoy this exceptional part of NZ - it is too good to miss.

KUAOTUNU   *18km N of Whitianga*

Kuaotunu Bay Lodge   *B&B Self-contained*
Lorraine and Bill Muir
State Highway 25, Kuaotunu, RD 2, Whitianga

Tel (07) 866 4396   Fax (07) 866 4396
Mob 025 601 3665   muir@kuaotunubay.co.nz
www.kuaotunubay.co.nz

Double $150-$180 Single $120   (Special Breakfast)
Dinner $45pp Credit cards accepted
2 Queen 2 Single (3 bdrm)
Bathrooms: 2 Ensuite 1 Private

An elegant beach house situated 18km north of
Whitianga on a 4 hectare property overlooking Kuaotunu Bay, panoramic views of the peninsula and
Mercury Island. Our home has been purpose built for guest with ensuites, decks, private entrances and
underfloor heating. Watch the waves from your bed or enjoy a morning swim before a hearty breakfast
on the deck. Walks, kayaking, horse riding all within easy reach. Savour some of the fine restaurants in
Whitianga or dine at the Lodge with prior arrangement. Spending two or three days with us gives you
time to explore the whole peninsula.

KUAOTUNU   *17km N of Whitianga*

Blue Penguin   *B&B Self-contained*
Glenda Mawhinney & Barbara Meredith
11 Cuvier Crescent, Kuaotunu, RD 2,
Whitianga, Coromandel Peninsula

Tel (07) 866 2222   Fax (07) 866 0228
holidayhomes@bluepenguin.co.nz
www.bluepenguin.co.nz
Double $110-$125 Single $65   (Continental Breakfast)
Child $30   Dinner $25 by arrangement
Full house available Dec-Feb Credit cards accepted
Children welcome   Pets welcome
1 King/Twin 1 Double 4 Single (2 bdrm) Bathrooms: 1 Guests share

We welcome you to our architecturally designed home with spectacular views over the beach and
pohutukawa trees to the Mercury Islands and Great Barrier. The master guestroom has king bed,
window seats and small private balcony. Children love the family guestroom, double, 2 singles, bunks,
cot, TV/video, toys & games. We have a retriever, poodle and little foxy. We are 2 professional women
who also manage 300 private beach houses which are available for holiday rental - see our website for
full descriptions, colour photographs, seasonal rates and availability calendars.

KUAOTUNU   *17km N of Whitianga*

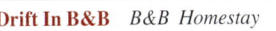

Drift In B&B   *B&B Homestay*
Yvonne & Peppe Thompson
16 Grays Avenue, Kuaotunu, RD 2, Whitianga

Tel (07) 866 4321   Fax (07) 866 4321
Mob 025 245 3632   driftin@paradise.net.nz
www.coromandelfun.co.nz/driftin

Double $95-$105 Single $55   (Full Breakfast)
Child $30 (5-12 years)   Dinner $28 by arrangement
Credit cards accepted   Children welcome
1 Queen 2 Single (2 bdrm)
Bathrooms: 1 Guests share

Welcome is assured. This tranquil comfortable modern cedar home is designed to take full advantage
of the sun and breathtaking island views by day and moonlit night. An unique beach theme pervades
house and garden with small dog in residence. Just a minute stroll to white sand beaches for safe
swimming and fossicking. Breakfast is a memorable occasion with sight and sounds of birds and
sea complementing an excellent range of home cooking. Delicious evening meals available by prior
arrangement. Drift in, relax and enjoy this unique and special part of New Zealand.

COROMANDEL

WHITIANGA *1km S of Whitianga*

Cosy Cat Cottage *B&B Self-contained cottage*
Gordon Pearce
41 South Highway, Whitianga

Tel (07) 866 4488 Fax (07) 866 4488
Mob 025 798 745 cosycat@xtra.co.nz
www.cosycat.co.nz

Double $85-$105 Single $55-$75 (Full Breakfast)
Cottage $90-$160 Credit cards accepted
2 Queen 1 Double 1 Single (3 bdrm)
Bathrooms: 2 Ensuite 1 Private

Welcome to our picturesque two storied cottage filled with feline memorabilia! Relax with complimentary tea or coffee served on the veranda or in the guest lounge. Enjoy a good nights rest in comfortable beds and choose a variety of treats from our breakfast blackboard menu. You will probably like to meet Sylvie, the cat, or perhaps visit the cat hotel in the garden. A separate cottage is available with queen beds, bathrooms and kitchen. Friendly helpful service is assured - hope to see you soon!

WHITIANGA *Whitianga Central*

Anne's Haven *B&B Homestay*
Anne & Bob
119 Albert Street, Whitianga

Tel (07) 866 5550 anneshaven@paradise.net.nz
www.bnb.co.nz/anneshaven.html

Double $70 Single $45 (Full Breakfast)
Child $20 Dinner $20
1 Double 2 Single (2 bdrm)
Bathrooms: 1 Guests share 1 Host share

Welcome to our comfortable modern home and the tranquillity of the garden. Guests share the lounge/TV room. The shower, toilet and bathroom are each separate rooms for easy access. Breakfast includes homemade bread and jams. We are 400 metres from shops and restaurants and within walking distance to 6 lovely beaches. Bob enjoys building and flying radio controlled model planes. Anne makes pottery, dabbles with watercolours and gardens. Let us make your stay a memorable one. Our moggie Gordon Bennett is also friendly.

WHITIANGA *3.5km S of Whitianga*

Camellia Lodge *B&B Homestay*
Pat & John Lilley
South Highway, RD 1, Whitianga

Tel (07) 866 2253 Fax (07) 866 2253
Mob 021 217 6612 camellia@wave.co.nz
www.whitianga.co.nz/camellia-lodge

Double $95-$120 Single $65 (Full Breakfast)
Child ¹/2 price Dinner $30 Double share bathroom $95
Double ensuite $120 Credit cards accepted

1 Queen 2 Double 2 Twin (4 bdrm)
Bathrooms: 2 Ensuite 2 Guests share

Welcome to our friendly home, which is nestled in a secluded park-like garden, which includes native, and many mature trees. We also offer you a spa and swimming pool and lots of lovely gardens to relax in. You would normally be woken up to the tune of bellbirds, then you settle into a hearty breakfast which will set you up for the whole day. We have a guest lounge and tea and coffee making facilities. We can assure you of a warm friendly welcome and a comfortable stay.

WHITIANGA - COOKS BEACH   *17km N of Tairua*

Mercury Orchard *Homestay Rural*
Heather and Barry Scott
141 Purangi Road, Cooks Beach, Whitianga

Tel **(07) 866 3119** Fax (07) 866 3115
mercorchard@xtra.co.nz
www.mercuryorchard.co.nz

Double $120 Single $100 (Full Breakfast)
Child $15 Dinner $25
Self-contained cottage or self-contained bach $140
Credit cards accepted Children welcome
1 King/Twin 3 Queen 1 Single (4 bdrm)
Bathrooms: 3 Ensuite

Mercury Orchard is 5 acres of peaceful country garden and orchard close to Cooks, Hahei and Hot Water Beaches. As well as our large guest room with ensuite and private entry we have Fig Tree Cottage and Paua Bach. Both are self-contained country style comfort,with french doors opening into orchard, crisp cotton bed linen, fresh fruit and flowers, breakfast hamper. We share our smoke-free home with 2 small dogs and a cat. We look forward to making your Coromandel experience a memorable one.

WHITIANGA   *4km N of Whitianga*

At Parkland Place *B&B Hotel style*
Maria & Guy Clark
14 Parkland Place, Brophys Beach, Whitianga

Tel **(07) 866 4987** Fax (07) 866 4946
Mob 025 291 7495 parklandplace@wave.co.nz
www.atparklandplace.co.nz

Double $135-$200 Single $100-$150
(Special Breakfast) Child neg Dinner by arrangement
Credit cards accepted Children welcome
1 King/Twin 3 King 2 Queen 3 Single (5 bdrm)
Bathrooms: 4 Ensuite 1 Private

Enjoy European hospitality in Whitianga's most luxurious boutique accommodation. Maria, a ship's chef from Poland and New Zealand husband Guy, a master mariner, will make your stay a memorable experience. Large luxuriously appointed rooms. Magnificent breakfasts. Superb candle-lit dinners or BBQ by arrangement. Sunny picturesque outdoor area with spa pool. Large guest lounge with TV, library, music and refreshments. Situated near the beach and next to reserves and farmland ensures absolute peace and quiet. Privacy and discretion assured. You will not regret coming.

WHITIANGA - COROGLEN   *14km S of Whitianga*

Coroglen Lodge *B&B Farmstay Self-contained*
Wendy & Nigel Davidson
2221 State Highway 25, RD 1, Whitianga 2856

Tel **(07) 866 3225** Fax (07) 866 3235
clover@wave.co.nz
www.mercurybay.co.nz/coroglen.html

Double $85-$100 Single $60-$80
(Continental Breakfast) Child $40
Credit cards accepted Children welcome
2 Queen 2 Single (3 bdrm)
Bathrooms: 2 Guests share

Coroglen Lodge is situated on 17 acres of farmland with cattle, sheep and alpacas. Nestled in the hills with views of the Coromandel Ranges, this is rural tranquillity. Halfway between Whitianga Township and Hot Water Beach there is easy access to both areas and all attractions. Guest area is separate, relaxed, and spacious with a large sunny lounge area for your comfort. Wendy spins and knits with wool from her sheep and alpacas, and Nigel has a collection of vintage tractors.

WHITIANGA   *22 km S of Whitianga*

Coppers Creek Farmstay   *B&B Farmstay*
Self-contained studio apartment & childrens bedroom
Graham & Pamela Caddy
1587 State Highway 25, Coroglen,
RD 1 Whitianga 2856

Tel (07) 866 3960   Fax (07) 866 3960
Mob 025 526 151   caddy.copperscreek@xtra.co.nz
www.copperscreekfarmstay.co.nz

Double $90-$75 Single $65   (Full Breakfast)
Child $20-$15 Credit cards accepted Children welcome
1 Queen 3 Single (2 bdrm)
Bathrooms: 1 Ensuite 1 Private

Coppers Creek is a small working beef breeding farm comprising of 120 acres of pasture, bush and streams. We have the usual assortment of farm animals including the odd teenager. Enjoy the freedom of our self-contained studio apartment and adjacent childrens bedroom, with private entrance and BBQ area, with fresh produce available from the farm garden in season. We are only 15 minute drive from Hot Water Beach, Hahei, Cooks Beach and Whitianga. We enjoy boating, kayaking, fishing, diving and bush walks.

WHITIANGA   *4km N of Whitianga*

Centennial Heights B and B   *B&B*
Paul   and Johanna Blackman
141 Centennial Drive, Whitianga,

Tel (07) 866 0279   Fax (07) 866 0276
Mob 027 237 9086   Blackmanmathis@xtra.co.nz
www.centennialheights.unitrental.com/

Double $130   (Special Breakfast) Child $20
2 Queen 1 Single (3 bdrm)
Bathrooms: 2 Ensuite 1 Private

Centennial Heights overlooks the sparkling waters of Whitianga Harbour. Paul and Johanna (who speaks fluent German & French) and Mollie (our border collie) offer warm hospitality in elegant surroundings. Over complimentary pre-dinner drinks we can assist you with information on the areas attractions including fishing, kayaking, tramping, scuba diving, snorkelling, boat cruises and dining out etc. We offer a delicious cooked breakfast which can be enjoyed with spectacular sea views. We look forward to welcoming you and making your stay a pleasant and memorable one.

WHITIANGA   *3kms S of Whitianga*

A Hi-Way Haven   *B&B*
Vicky & Tony Heyblom
1 Golf Road, Whitianga

Tel (07) 866 2427   Fax (07) 866 2424
Mob 025 659 0841
a-haven@paradise.net.nz
www.bnb.co.nz/ahi-wayhaven.html

Double $75-$90 Single $60   (Continental Breakfast)
Children welcome
2 Queen 2 Single (3 bdrm)
Bathrooms: 1 Ensuite 1 Guests share

Looking for comfortable affordable accommodation then look no further. We are situated 3km south of Whitianga, just a short stroll to Whitianga's 18 hole golf course. We are a friendly, no hassle place to stay. Come and enjoy our home grown hospitality. We are family friendly, with 2 children and of course the house cat. You will come as a visitor and depart as a friend.

HAHEI *38km S of Whitianga*

The Church *B&B Self-contained*
Richard Agnew & Karen Blair
87 Beach Road, Hahei, RD 1, Whitianga

Tel (07) 866 3533 Fax (07) 866 3055
Mob 025 596 877 hahei4ch@xtra.co.nz
www.thechurchhahei.co.nz

Double $95-$150 (Continental Breakfast)
Child $10-$15 Dinner menu
Credit cards accepted Children welcome
11 Queen 1 Double 11 Twin 13 Single (11 bdrm)
Bathrooms: 11 Ensuite

The Church is Hahei's most unique accommodation and dining experience. The Church building provides a character dining room/licensed restaurant for wholesome breakfasts and delicious evening meals. 11 cosy wooden cottages scattered through delightful bush and gardens offer a range of accommodation and tariffs, with ensuites, fridges and tea and coffee facilities. Some cottages fully self-contained with woodstoves for winter. Enjoy the wonders of Cathedral Cove, Hot Water Beach, and the Coromandel Peninsula. Seasonal rates. Smoking outside.

HAHEI BEACH *28km N of Tairua*

Cedar Lodge *Homestay*
Jenny & John Graham
36 Beach Road, Hahei, RD 1, Whitianga

Tel (07) 866 3789 Fax (07) 866 3978
cedarlodge@wave.co.nz
www.cedarlodge.gen.nz

Double $100 Single $75 (Full Breakfast)
Credit cards accepted
1 Queen 1 Single (1 bdrm)
Bathrooms: 1 Private

Come and unwind in our comfortable private upstairs studio apartment with its own entrance. Enjoy the sea views and relaxing atmosphere. Take a 200 metre stroll to the beautiful beach and experience the magic of Hahei. Cathedral Cove walkway and Hot Water beach are nearby. Scenic boat/dive trips are easily arranged with local operators. We have an adult family scattered around the world. We thank you for not smoking indoors. We enjoy an active retired lifestyle, so please phone ahead for bookings and directions.

HAHEI BEACH *200m NE of Hahei shops and cafes*

Hawleys Bed and Breakfast Hahei *B&B*
Peter and Rhonda Hawley
19 Hahei Beach Road,
RD 1, Whitianga

Tel (07) 8663272 0800 2 78783 Fax (07) 8663273
Mob 025 971090 hawleysb&b@haheibeach.co.nz
www.haheibeach.co.nz

Double $120 Single $110 (Full Breakfast)
Credit cards accepted Children welcome
1 Queen 2 Single (2 bdrm)
Bathrooms: 1 Private

Situated on the flat, half-way (200 metres) between the beach and the shops and cafés. Ideal for those who enjoy extra space and comfort. The purpose built 2 double bedrooms (house completed mid 2000) and spacious bathroom and take up all of the second storey at the rear of the house. The larger room has a balcony and a queen size bed and the smaller room 2 single beds. A cot is available. There is secure garaging. No children at home and no pets.

COROMANDEL

HAHEI *36km NW of Whitianga*

Hahei-Haven B&B   *B&B Homestay*
Valerie Thomson
8 Robyn Crescent, Hahei,
RD 1, Whitianga

Tel (07) 866 3136   Fax (07) 866 3137
Mob 025 622 1700
info@hahei-haven.co.nz
www.hahei-haven.co.nz

Double $100-$160 Single $100   (Full Breakfast)
1 King/Twin 1 Queen (2 bdrm)
Bathrooms: 2 Ensuite

Hahei-Haven, newly purpose built for Bed & Breakfast is superbly located in the heart of Hahei.
A few minutes walk to the beach and cafés. We offer upstairs guest rooms with their own ensuites.
Guest fridge, tea & coffee making facilities provided. Cooked breakfast served in our dining room.
Walk to Cathedral Cove. Relax in our secluded garden, or sit by our large outside fireplace after a days
activities, before going to the café for dinner. Looking forward to welcoming you with our 12 year old,
blind labrador.

HOT WATER BEACH   *24km N of Tairua*

Auntie Dawns Place   *Self-contained apartments*
Dawn & Joe Nelmes
15 Radar Road, Hot Water Beach, Whitianga, RD 1

Tel (07) 866 3707 Fax (07) 866 3701
enquiries@auntiedawn.co.nz   www.auntiedawn.co.nz

Double $90-$120 Single $50   (Continental Breakfast)
Credit cards accepted
2 Queen 1 Double 1 Single (2 bdrm)
Bathrooms: 2 Private

Hot Water Beach is a surf beach. At low tide hot water
bubbles up in the sand and you dig yourself a hot pool.
Our house is surrounded by huge Pohutukawa trees, 3
minutes walk from the hot springs. We have a terrier
and Joe makes home-brew beer. Each apartment is comfortably furnished with a queen bedroom, and
a spare bed in the living room. We provide tea, coffee, bread, butter, jam, milk and cereals. Guests
prepare breakfast at preferred time. Nearest restaurant at Hahei. Directions: turn right into Radar Road
200 metres before shop.

HOT WATER BEACH   *32km S of Whitianga*

Hot Water Beach B&B   *B&B Homestay*
Gail & Trevor Knight
48 Pye Place, Hot Water Beach, RD 1,
Coromandel Peninsula

Tel (07) 866 3991   0800 146 889   Fax (07) 866 3291
Mob 025 799 620   TKnight@xtra.co.nz
www.hotwaterbedandbreakfast.co.nz

Double $160-$200 Single $140-$180 (Full Breakfast)
Credit cards accepted
2 Queen (2 bdrm)
Bathrooms: 2 Ensuite

We have a spacious elevated home with extensive decks, on which you can have fresh coffee or juice,
while enjoying sweeping panoramic sea/beach views. Sit under the brilliant southern stars in our spa
pool or play on our full sized billiard table. You can swim, surf, dive, fish, kayak, play golf, bushwalk,
horse trek or visit spectacular Cathedral Cove or alternatively just dig a hole and soak in the natural hot
springs on our beach. We have a cat and a sociable boxer.

TAIRUA   *30km E of Thames*

On the Edge - Tairua   *Homestay*
Andrea Patten
219 Paku Drive, Tairua, Coromandel Peninsula

Tel (07) 864 8285 Fax (07) 864 8232
Mob 025 736 176 ontheedge717@hotmail.com
www.bnb.co.nz/ontheedgetairua.html

Double $140-$180 Single $100-$130 (Full Breakfast)
Child $50 Dinner $30 Credit cards accepted
Children welcome
2 Queen 2 Double (2 bdrm) Bathrooms: 2 Ensuite

'On The Edge' of Paku Hill, panoramic views of the
Pacific Ocean and islands. Ideally situated for walks to Paku Hill with spectacular views of Pauanui and
Tairua. 20 minutes north - Hot Water Beach and Cathedral Cove. Close to 18 hole golf course and good
restaurants. Andrea and James have travelled extensively, spending their leisure time diving, fishing
and skiing. With their intimate knowledge of the Coromandel Peninsula they can provide a tour of the
Coromandel in their green coach. While having breakfast enjoy the sound of the sea below the deck.
Double and ensuite bedrooms with spectacular sea and island views.

TAIRUA   *45km E of Thames*

Harbour View Lodge   *B&B*
Sheryl Allan & John Goldstone
179 Main Road, Tairua

Tel (07) 864 7040 Fax (07) 864 7042
Mob (021) 303 982 info@harbourviewlodge.co.nz
www.harbourviewlodge.co.nz

Double $120-$180 Single $110-$140 (Full Breakfast)
Credit cards accepted Smoking area inside
1 King/Twin 2 Queen (3 bdrm)
Bathrooms: 3 Ensuite

Situated on the foothills of Tairua. Our B&B has been
recently refurbished with the finest of linens and interior design. All rooms have their own ensuite,
hair dryers, electric blankets, tea/coffee facilities. Guest lounge, swimming pool, off-street parking.
Continental/full cooked breakfast is served in the dining room with its ever-changing views of Tairua
Harbour and Paku Mountain. Enjoy our beaches, bush walks,18 hole golf course. 5 minutes level walk
to local restaurants. Close to Cathedral Cove and Hot Water Beach.

TAIRUA   *40km E of Thames*

Dell Cote Homestay   *B&B*
Barry & Trish Oldham
37 Rewarewa Valley Road, Tairua

Tel (07) 864 8142 Fax (07) 864 8142
homestay@dellcote.com
www.dellcote.co.nz

Double $160-$180 Single $140-$160
(Generous continental/cooked options)
Child by arrangement Credit cards accepted
3 Queen 1 Single (3 bdrm)
Bathrooms: 2 Ensuite 1 Private

A welcoming eco friendly home, set in an acre of garden
and orchard in the bush clad Rewarewa Valley. Rooms have private access, quality cotton bed linen,
electric blankets, toiletries, hair dryer, heated towel rails, fresh flowers. Generous continental breakfast
choices/cooked options, with home-grown seasonal produce and preserves. Guest lounge. Off-street
parking. Pleasant walking to Tairua Village, art galleries, cafés and restaurants. Enjoy the beach, bush
walks, golf, fishing and diving. Just 20 minutes to Hot Water Beach, Catherdral Cove, and Pauanui.

COROMANDEL

Planning a trip around Australia?

Ask for …

The Bed & Breakfast Book
Australia 2005
Accommodation with Character

- Small Hotels
- Romantic Hideaways
- Pet Friendly Getaways
- Self-Contained Cottages
- Short Breaks for the less able
- Farmstays and Retreats for Families and Children

Available on-line at **www.bnb.co.nz** and good book shops

$19.95

Moonshine Press
PO Box 6843, Wellington, New Zealand
Phone (04) 385 2615, Fax (04) 385 2694, info@bnb.co.nz

WHANGAMATA (RURAL) *8km N of Whangamata*

Copsefield B&B *B&B*
Trish & Richard Davison
1055 State Highway 25, RD 1, Whangamata

Tel **(07) 865 9555** Fax (07) 865 9555
Mob 027 289 0131 copsefield@xtra.co.nz
www.copsefield.co.nz

Double $180 Single $130 (Full Breakfast)
Self-contained rustic cottage, sleeps 4 $100
Credit cards accepted
2 Queen 2 Single (3 bdrm)
Bathrooms: 3 Ensuite

Character country home situated on 3 acres, at the southern end of the stunning Coromandel Peninsula. Copsefield is purpose built for your comfort, with 3 ensuite rooms. 2 beaches close by. Canoes, bikes, walks, spa pool, 6 hole pitch & putt golf. Peace and tranquility beside native bush and river. Guest lounge with TV, tea and coffee . Complimentary wine. Full breakfast including locally grown eggs and fresh fruit. Your hosts Trish & Richard and Mia, our burmese cat, offer you a warm and friendly welcome, and personal attention.

WHANGAMATA *200m N of town centre*

Sandy Rose Bed & Breakfast *B&B Homestay*
Shirley & Murray Calman
Corner Hetherington & Rutherford Roads,
Whangamata

Tel **(07) 865 6911** Fax (07) 865 6911
Mob 027 420 4296 sandyrose@whangamata.co.nz
sandyrose.whangamata.co.nz

Double $120 Single $90 (Special Breakfast)
Credit cards accepted
1 Queen 1 Double 1 Twin (3 bdrm)
Bathrooms: 3 Ensuite

A charming B&B in the Coromandel Peninsula's popular holiday destination, we have 3 tastefully decorated guest bedrooms, all with ensuite bathrooms, comfortable beds and in-room TVs. Complimentary tea and coffee is available in the guest lounge. We are ideally located, close to Whangamata's shops, cafés and restaurants, and an easy stroll to the surf beach, harbour and wharf. Enjoy our extensive continental breakfast and use our home as a base to relax and enjoy the natural attractions that Whangamata and area has to offer.

WHANGAMATA *2km S of town centre*

Kotuku *B&B*
Linda & Peter Bigge
422 Otahu Road, Whangamata

Tel **(07) 865 6128** Fax (07) 865 6128
Mob 021 149 1584 lindapeter@internet.co.nz
www.bnb.co.nz/kotuku.html

Double $80-$120 (Full Breakfast)
Credit cards accepted
3 Queen (3 bdrm)
Bathrooms: 3 Ensuite

We offer comfortable accommodation in a purpose built home. Rosie, our friendly huntaway/labrador and Elizabeth, the cat will welcome you. Relax in the spacious lounge or private patio, enjoy the Coromandel sunset from our deluxe outdoor spa. Kotuku is situated at the quieter end of Whangamata, just a 2 minute stroll to the lovely Otahu Estuary and Reserve; ideal for walking, swimming, kayaking or just take a picnic lunch and watch the fascinating shorebirds. Bikes, kayaks and surfboards are available for your use.

WAIHI *5km N of Waihi*

The French Provincial Country House *B&B Country House*
Margaret van Duyvenbooden
Golden Valley - Trig Road North, RD 1, Waihi

Tel (07) 863 7339 Fax (07) 863 7330 Mob 021 130 8081
www.bnb.co.nz/thefrench.html

Double $165-$195 Single $140
(Continental Breakfast)
1 King (1 bdrm)
Bathrooms: 1 Ensuite

A warm welcome awaits you at The French Provincial Country House, with fine accommodation. Sited on farmland in a picturesque valley only 5km from an historic township, close to all attractions.

Upstairs is a private, large luxurious suite with lovely rural views, two private balconies, super king bed, ensuite bathroom, TV, fresh flowers, crisp white bed linen, electric blanket, hairdryer, toiletries and big soft bath towels. Serviced daily.

A generous continental breakfast is served at a time to suit. Fresh fruit salad, yogurt, assortment of cereals and homemade muesli. Croissants or muffins, fresh orange juice, tea and coffee. This home is not suitable for children and is smoke free.

In summer there are colourful gardens with large shade trees and front door parking for guests. Close to beautiful beaches for swimming and fishing, gold mining tours, cafés and restaurants. A day trip to the beautiful Coromandel Peninsula is recommended. Please make an early reservation to save disappointment.

One night in this beautiful area is not long enough.

WAIHI   *1km S of Waihi*

West Wind Gardens   *B&B Homestay*
Josie French & Merv Scott
58 Adams Street, Waihi

Tel (07) 863 7208   westwindgarden@xtra.co.nz
www.bnb.co.nz/westwind.html

Double $75   Single $40   (Continental Breakfast)
Child $20   Dinner $20   Credit cards accepted
Children welcome
1 Double 2 Single (2 bdrm)
Bathrooms: 1 Guests share

We offer a friendly restful smoke-free stay in our modern home and garden. Waihi is the gate way to both the Coromandel with its beautiful beaches and the Bay of Plenty. Waihi is a historic town with vintage railway running to Waikino, a working gold mine discovered 1878 closed 1952. Reopened in 1989 as a open-cast mine. Free mine tours available. Beach 10 minutes away, beautiful bush walks, golf courses, trout fishing. Enjoy a home-cooked meal or sample our restaurants. Our interests are gardening, dancing and travel.

WAIHI BEACH   *11km E of Waihi*

Waterfront Homestay   *Self-contained*
Kay & John Morgan
17 The Esplanade (Off Hinemoa Street), Waihi Beach

Tel (07) 863 4342   Fax (07) 863 4342
Mob 025 287 1104   k.morgan@xtra.co.nz
www.bnb.co.nz/waterfronthomestay.html

Double $100   Single $75   (Continental Breakfast)
Credit cards accepted Children welcome
1 King 1 Double 1 Single (2 bdrm)
Bathrooms: 1 Private

Waterfront Homestay. Fully self-contained 2 double bedrooms plus single bed. Suitable for 2 couples or small family group. Unit is lower floor of family home on waterfront of beautiful uncrowded ocean beach. Walk from front door directly onto sandy beach. Safe ocean swimming, surfcasting, surfing and coastal walks. 9 hole golf course with club hire at beach township. Restaurant within walking distance of accommodation or use facilities provided with accommodation. Tariff $100 per couple bed and continental breakfast, $10 per extra persons. Hosts John & Kay Morgan.

WAIHI   *2km W of Waihi*

Trout & Chicken at Drift House
B&B Homestay Studio
Michael & Adrienne Muir
9137 State Highway 2, RD 2, Waihi

Tel (07) 863 6964   Fax (07) 863 6966
Mob 027 206 4080   troutandchicken@paradise.net.nz
www.troutandchicken.co.nz

Double $110-$150   Single $100   (Special Breakfast)
Dinner by arrangement   Studio $50pp
Credit cards accepted
2 King/Twin 1 Queen (2 bdrm)
Bathrooms: 2 Ensuite

On an organic blueberry orchard, our home is 300 metres off the main highway. Quiet, peaceful and designed for your comfort. Enjoy a spacious bedroom, lounge and deck: a special breakfast in the dining room or alfresco. Blueberry muffins and coffee on arrival then relax or walk by the Waitete Stream or in the orchard. Visit the spectacular gorge, gold mine, antique shops, art gallery and museum. Plan on at least two nights, there is a lot to see in the Waihi area. We have pets at home.

WAIHI *2km N of Waihi*

Ashtree House *B&B Separate/Suite*
Anne & Bill Ashdown
20 Riflerange Road, Waihi

Tel (07) 863 6448 Fax (07) 863 6443
Mob 021 2924 987 www.bnb.co.nz/waihi.html

Double $80 Single $50 (Full Breakfast)
Child $10 under 10 Dinner $20pp Garden unit $35pp
Children welcome Smoking area inside
1 Queen 1 Double 2 Single (3 bdrm)
Bathrooms: 2 Private

Modern brick home set on the side of a hill with
extensive views and access to trout river. Private guest wing comprising 2 double bedrooms, large
private bathroom with shower and bath. Guest lounge with TV, stereo and large selection of New
Zealand books. Laundry and separate toilet. 8 acres, large attractive garden and pond area. 1 house
dog. Situated 2 minutes to centre of Waihi, complete privacy and quiet guaranteed. Self-contained unit
with wheelchair facilities. 5 minutes to beautiful Karangahake Gorge.

WAIHI *0.5km W of Waihi*

Chez Nous *B&B Homestay*
Sara Parish
41 Seddon Avenue, Waihi

Tel (07) 863 7538 Mob 027 644 5562
Sara.P@xtra.co.nz
www.bnb.co.nz/cheznous.html

Double $65 Single $45 (Continental Breakfast)
Child $20 Dinner $20pp by arrangement
Credit cards accepted Children welcome
1 Queen 1 Twin (2 bdrm)
Bathrooms: 1 Guests share

Enjoy a relaxed and friendly atmosphere in a spacious, modern home in an attractive garden setting.
Shops and restaurants are within easy walking distance. Discover past and present gold mining activities
(tours available), sandy surf beaches, bush walks, 9 and 18 hole golf courses, art, craft and wine trails.
Waihi is an ideal stopover for the traveller who wants to explore the Coromandel Peninsula, Bay of
Plenty and Waikato.

WAIHI BEACH *11km E of Waihi*

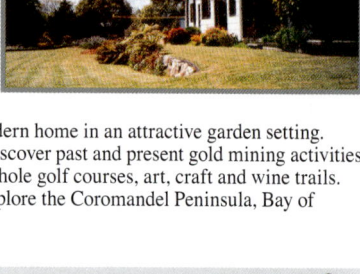

Seagulls Bed & Breakfast *B&B*
Marie & Steve Quinlan
8 West Street (Off Pacific Road),
Waihi Beach

Tel (07) 863 4633 Fax (07) 863 4634
seagullsquinlan@clear.net.nz
www.bnb.co.nz/seagullsbb.html

Double $100-$125 Single $85-$95 (Full Breakfast)
1 Queen 1 Double (2 bdrm)
Bathrooms: 1 Guests share

Relax and unwind at beautiful Waihi Beach - gateway to Coromandel Peninsular and the sunny Bay of
Plenty. Enjoy the spectacular panoramic views of beach (3 minutes walk) and Mayor Island. Listen to
tuis sing in bush on our boundary. See the sunrise. Modern spacious luxury home with your own double
bedroom, lounge and bathroom. Excellent outdoor areas. Cafés, restaurant, fishing, golf, tennis, beach
and bush walks nearby. Breakfast include fresh seasonal fruits and organic produce when available. Our
foxy, Jacky, will meet you.

WAIHI BEACH   *11km E of Waihi*

Approved

Coq on Fyfe   *B&B*
Robyn & Dave Smith
33 Fyfe Road, Waihi Beach

Tel (07) 863 4627   Fax (07) 863 4627
Mob 027 495 7663   daverobynsmith@xtra.co.nz
www.bnb.co.nz/coqonfyfe.html

Double $100   (Continental Breakfast)
1 Queen (1 bdrm)
Bathrooms: 1 Ensuite

At Coq on Fyfe we can offer you peace and quiet. Awake
to the sound of tuis and be lulled to sleep by the sound
of the ocean. Waihi Beach has lovely bush walks with safe swimming and good fishing spots. There are
several cafés close at hand. Our unit has its own heated bathroom, tea and coffee making facilities and
room to relax. We have a lush tropical garden with panoramic sea and bush views.

---

visit... **www.bnb.co.nz**

For the most up-to-date information from our hosts,
and links to our other web sites around the world.

Search New Zealand for a Bed & Breakfast

Back Forward Stop Refresh Home AutoFill Print Mail

Address: http://www.bnb.co.nz   go

New Zealand Bed & Breakfast Book Online

Bed & Breakfast
Bed And Breakfast Book - New Zealand Online

Favorites History Search Scrapbook Page Holder

Main Menu
Home / Map Search
Database Search
About The B&B Book
Buy the Book
FAQ
Contact Us
Australian B&B

B&B Owners
New Listing
- Application Form
- About Joining
- Services for Hosts
Members Area

Search New Zealand for a Bed & Breakfast
B&B Home > New Zealand

Click on a name

Northland
Auckland
Coromandel
Bay of Plenty
Waikato, King Country
Gisborne
Taranaki, Wanganui,
Ruapehu, Rangitikei
Hawkes Bay
Manawatu, Horowhenua
Wairarapa
Nelson, Golden Bay
Wellington
Marlborough
West Coast
Canterbury &
Christchurch
South Canterbury,
North Otago
Chatham
Islands
Otago, North Catlins
Southland, South Catlins
Stewart Island

DATABASE SEARCH

Find a B&B
MAP SEARCH Use this map to find
B&Bs by clicking on a region.
DATABASE SEARCH Use the
database to find B&Bs.

**The New Zealand Bed &
Breakfast Book**
The Bed & Breakfast Book lists more
Homestays, Farmstays, B&B Inns and
Boutique B&Bs than any other
publication in New Zealand. First
established in 1987 it is by far the most
comprehensive home hosted
accommodation guide for New
Zealand. Every property has been
visted by our team of inspectors.

© Bed and Breakfast Book 2003

Internet zone

Bay of Plenty

Towns listed generally follow
a north to south route. Refer
to the index if required.

Kilometres
0   40
0   Miles   24

Katikati
Omokoroa
Mt. Maunganui
Papamoa
Tauranga
Maketu
Te Puke
Pukehina
Matata
Whakatane
Ohope
Waihau Bay
Te Kaha
Opotiki
Ngongotaha
Rotorua
Ngakuru
Taupo
Motuoapa
Turangi

aotunu
Hahei
Coroglen
Tairua
Whangamata
Waihi

Whatatutu
Waipaoa
Ormond
Gisborne
Waikaremoana
Mahanga
Beach
Wairoa

KATIKATI   *30km N of Tauranga*

Jacaranda Cottage *B&B Farmstay Self-catering chalet*
Lynlie & Rick Watson
230 Thompson's Track, RD 2, Katikati

Tel (07) 549 0616 Fax (07) 549 0616
Mob 025 272 8710   relax@jacaranda-cottage.co.nz
www.jacaranda-cottage.co.nz

Double $90-$95 Single $55-$60 (Full Breakfast)
S/C Chalet (2 night minimum stay) $95 double
Extra adult $25pp   Children welcome, discount by age
House: 1 Queen 1 Twin (2 bdrm) Bathrooms: 1 Private
S/C: 1 Double 1 Single (1bdrm)   Bathrooms: 1 Ensuite

Spectacular 360 degree views, from forests and farmlands to mountains and the sea - the backdrop for your stay on our five acre farmlet 8km south of Katikati Mural Town. Enjoy true Kiwi friendliness and generous hospitality with B&B in our clean and comfy family home, or opt for more independence in our fully equipped, self-catering hillside chalet. We enjoy children 'helping' us with our quiet smallfarm animals. Pool, glowworm trails. Near beaches, tramping, golf, horse rides, hot pools, bird gardens, winery, restaurants, arts/crafts.

KATIKATI   *20km S of Katikati*

Jones Lifestyle   *Self-contained*
Thora & Trevor Jones
Pahoia Road, RD 2, Tauranga

Tel (07) 548 0661 Fax (07) 548 0661
joneslifestyle@clear.net.nz
www.bnb.co.nz/joneslifestyle.html

Double $90 Single $60 (Continental Breakfast)
Child $20   Credit cards accepted
1 Queen (1 bdrm)
Bathrooms: 1 Private

This modern apartment has all amenities including fully equipped kitchen, bathroom, laundry, games rooms (billiards etc), BBQ. The bedroom has a queen bed. The lounge has a convertible sofa providing an extra bed. Extra bedrooms and private bathroom are also available in the main house. Deluxe continental breakfast is provided for self-service. We share our peaceful horticultural lifestyle property on Pahoia peninsula with many birds. There are spectacular views of Tauranga harbour (water's edge 200 metres away) and sunset over the Kaimai Ranges.

KATIKATI   *3km N of Katikati*

Aberfeldy *B&B Farmstay*
Mary Anne & Rod Calver
164 Lindemann Road,
RD 1, Katikati

Tel (07) 549 0363 0800 309 064
Fax (07) 549 0363 Mob 021 909 710
aberfeldy@xtra.co.nz   www.aberfeldy.co.nz

Double $100 Single $60 (Full Breakfast) Child $30
Dinner by arrangement Credit cards accepted Children welcome Pets welcome
1 Queen 1 Twin 1 Single (2 bdrm)   Bathrooms: 1 Private

Large attractive home set in extensive gardens with private sunny guest accommodation. The private lounge opens onto a patio, and has TV and coffee making facilities. One party at a time in guest accommodation. We farm sheep and cattle. Rod's associated with kiwifruit and is a Rotarian. Panoramic views of bush-clad hills, farmland and harbour. Activities include bush and farm walks, meeting tame animals especially Sue & Lucy, the kune kune pigs. Golf course, horse riding, and beaches nearby. Jax, our australian terrier will welcome you.

KATIKATI   *1km N of Katikati*

Waterford House (katikati.8k.com)   *B&B*
Alan & Helen Cook
15 Crossley Street, Katikati 3063

Tel (07) 549 0757 www.katikati.8k.com
www.bnb.co.nz/waterfordhouse.html

Double $70   Single $45   (Full Breakfast)
Child discounted Dinner $20 by arrangement
Credit cards accepted Children welcome
1 Queen 1 Double 2 Twin 1 Single (5 bdrm)
Bathrooms: 3 Guests share

Waterford House, situated in a quiet semi-rural area,
provides spacious accommodation with wheelchair access throughout. A large comfortable lounge with
television, stereo-radio, fridge-freezer, microwave and tea/coffee making facilities. Cot and highchair
are available. Local attractions include Twickenham Homestead Café, Morton Estate Winery, bird
gardens, Ballantyne Golf Course, Sapphire Springs Hot Pools, Kaimai bush walks, Uretara River
Walkway and craft workshops. 32 murals and sculptures depict the history of Katikati "Mural Town",
located on Pacific Coast Highway. Our cat is called Matilda.

KATIKATI   *7km N of Katikati*

Cotswold Lodge Countrystay   *B&B Countrystay*
Alison & Des Belsham
183 Ongare Point Road, RD 1, Katikati

Tel (07) 549 2110   Fax (07) 549 2109
cotswold@ihug.co.nz
www.cotswold.co.nz

Double $120-$140 Single $95-$100 (Special Breakfast)
Dinner by arrangement Credit cards accepted
2 Queen 2 Single (3 bdrm)
Bathrooms: 3 Ensuite

We offer warm Kiwi hospitality, a little luxury and a relaxed peaceful environment in our rural home,
Cotswold Lodge. Gourmet breakfasts. Evening meals by prior arrangement. Wander through the
gardens, kiwifruit orchard or down to the harbour. Sit on the deck and watch the sunset over the Kaimai
Ranges or relax in the hot spa and listen to the birds. All rooms have ensuite bathrooms, bathrobes,
toiletries, hairdryers etc. Guest refrigerator, tea and coffee making facilities. We have a friendly
labrador. Restaurants, golf etc nearby.

KATIKATI   *9km N of Katikati*

Panorama Country Lodge   *B&B Private suites*
Barbara & Phil McKernon
901 Pacific Coast Highway (SH2), RD1, Katikati

Tel (07) 549 1882   Fax (07) 549 1882
Mob 021 165 5875 mckernon@xtra.co.nz
www.panoramalodge.co.nz
Double $120-$145 Single $100-$120
(Special Breakfast) Credit cards accepted
1 King 1 Queen 2 Single (3 bdrm)
Bathrooms: 1 Ensuite 1 Private

Perfectly situated between beautiful Waihi Beach and
Katikati. Nestling in the foothills of the Kaimai Ranges and
commanding magnificent Pacific and island views from every
room! Relax in splendid & peaceful private guest suites,
with ensuite & private facilities, quality furnishings, french doors to swimming pool and terrace. TV &
CD, slippers & robes, coffee & tea. Delicious breakfasts, served: in-suite, terrace or dining room. Explore
the grounds, orchards, paddocks and meet 'our boys' the alpacas, not forgetting our very friendly dog,
Kaimai. Nearby: cafés, beaches, golf, boating, walks, etc. 'We love it here...so will you!'

KATIKATI   *15km S of Waihi*

Paradiso   *B&B Self-contained*
Theo & Gerda Blok
101 Athenree Road, RD 1, Katikati

Tel (07) 863 5350   Fax (07) 863 5678
paradijs@xtra.co.nz
www.paradisobb.co.nz

Double $100   Single $50   (Continental Breakfast)
Child $10 under 5 Children welcome
1 Queen 2 Single (1 bdrm)
Bathrooms: 1 Private

Paradiso, 5 acres of park-like gardens, with children's
playground, nestled on the edge of Tauranga harbour. A double seated kayak is available to explore the
harbour, native bush walks nearby. 5km from Waihi beach. We offer friendly B&B in clean, comfortable
studio-style accommodation, or you can self-cater, be as private as you wish. We came from Holland
36 years ago and lived on a dairy farm for 30 years, and we have found paradise. For more information,
look on our website.

KATIKATI   *12km N of Katikati*

The Candy's B&B   *B&B*
Gloria & Neil Candy
Athenree Road, RD 1,
Katikati

Tel (07) 863 1159   Fax (07) 863 1196
Mob 025 233 8116 neilcandy@ihug.co.nz
www.bnb.co.nz/athenree.html

Double $90   Single $70-$80 (Continental Breakfast)
Dinner $28pp
1 King 1 Queen 2 Twin (2 bdrm)
Bathrooms: 1 Ensuite 1 Guests share

Take time out: relax. Our new home is on 3 acres, with beautiful harbour views: each room has a
patio. Walk to Athenree Hotpools, drive 3 minutes to Waihi Surf Beach, 10 minutes south to Katikati,
Ballantynes Golf Course, Morton Winery, Lavender Farm. 10 minutes north to Waihi Goldmine, walks
and excellent restaurants. Neil loves fishing, and is an ex-chef, Gloria loves crafts. Meals on request.
This is paradise and our city pets agree.

OMOKOROA   *15km N of Tauranga*

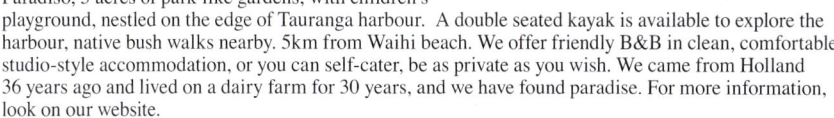

Walnut Cottage   *B&B Self-contained Cottage*
Ken & Betty Curreen
309 Plummers Point Road, Omokoroa,
RD 2, Tauranga

Tel (07) 548 0692   Fax (07) 548 1764
walnuthomestay@actrix.co.nz
www.cybersurf.co.nz/curreen

Double $80-$95   Single $50-$80
(Continental Breakfast) Dinner $20
1 Queen 1 Double (2 bdrm)
Bathrooms: 1 Ensuite 1 Private

Situated on scenic Plummers Point Peninsula overlooking Tauranga Harbour we invite our guests to
enjoy the tranquility our little corner of the world has to offer. Stroll along the peninsula with its superb
views, boat jetty and reserve. In the vicinity we have mineral hot pools, golf course, fountain and quarry
gardens,tramping tracks, wineries and eating houses. Walnut Cottage is self contained. Kowhai Suite
has own entrance, conservatory with tea/coffee, TV. Directions: Plummers Point Road is opposite
Caltex Service Station on SH2.

BAY OF PLENTY

OMOKOROA   *20K N of Tauranga*

Serendipity   *B&B Homestay*
Sarath & Linda Vidanage
77 Harbour View Road, Omokoroa, Tauranga

Tel (07) 548 2044   Mob 021 999 815
sarathv@yahoo.com
www.bnb.co.nz/vidanage.html

Double $120   Single $85   (Full Breakfast)
Child $30   Dinner $40   Credit cards accepted
Children welcome
4 Double (2 bdrm)
Bathrooms: 2 Private

Welcome to our home and garden nestled above
spectacular Omokoroa Beach. The beach is a short walk down the steps. Leisurely walking treks take
you through the groves and gardens of the peninsula. A beautiful golf course and local hot pools are
minutes away. We are a well-traveled couple who have found our paradise. We love to cook and offer a
varied cuisine from traditional to exotic. In one stop you will experience the best of the Bay of Plenty.

OMOKOROA   *17km N of Tauranga*

Seascape   *B&B*
Sue & Geoff Gripton
5 Waterview Terrace, Omokoroa

Tel (07) 548 1027   Mob 021 171 1936
grippos@xtra.co.nz
www.geocities.com/seascapebb

Double $90-$100   Single $65   (Full Breakfast)
Credit cards accepted
1 Double 2 Single (2 bdrm)
Bathrooms: 1 Ensuite 1 Guests share

Come share our stunning views of Tauranga Harbour and Kaimais. On our doorstep are beaches,
walkways, golf, hot pools, boat ramps etc. Just halfway (15 minutes) between Tauranga and Katikati, we
offer a double room with ensuite and TV, twin room with shared bathroom, both with tea/coffee. Enjoy a
cooked or continental breakfast with homemade bread and jams while gazing at the ever-changing view.
Only 3.5km from SH2, left at roundabout, first right, first left into Waterview Terrace. Geoff, Sue and
our cat will welcome you.

TAURANGA   *2km W of Tauranga*

B&B Homestay
Christine Ross
8A Vale Street, Bureta,
Tauranga

Tel (07) 576 8895
rossvale@xtra.co.nz
www.bnb.co.nz/ross.html

Double $80   Single $50   (Full Breakfast)
1 Twin 1 Single (2 bdrm)
Bathrooms: 2 Private

Welcome. We are located close to town, with a golf course and licensed restaurants nearby and a
park opposite. Twin room has every comfort and large private bathroom. The single guest room has
own facilities and TV. You can enjoy our spacious lounge and sunny balcony, or take a short stroll to
harbour edge. Your hostess Christine, is a miniaturist and doll maker and has travelled extensively
and is enjoying retirement. Breakfast of your choice. Off-street parking plus a garage. Will meet
public transport.

TAURANGA - MATUA *6km N of Tauranga*

Christiansen's B&B *B&B*
John Christiansen
210 Levers Road, Matua, Tauranga

Tel (07) 576 6835 Fax (07) 576 6464
Mob 021 766 835 relax@christiansensbnb.co.nz
www.christiansensbnb.co.nz

Double $100 Single $70 (Full Breakfast)
Credit cards accepted
1 Queen 2 Single (2 bdrm)
Bathrooms: 1 Guests share

Relax at Matua, Tauranga in quiet, private accommodation within a garden of NZ native plants. The bedrooms look out on to a private patio You are welcome to use the home lounge, browse the books, listen to music, or engage in the art of conversation with your host. Matua is central to all of Tauranga's many attractions. Guests regularly comment on the quality of their breakfasts, referring to them as "sumptuous, spectacular, yummy". My interests include the visual and performing arts, and motorcycling.

TAURANGA - OROPI *9km S of Tauranga*

home

Grenofen
Jennie & Norm Reeve
85 Castles Road, Oropi, RD 3, Tauranga

Tel (07) 543 3953
Fax (07) 543 3951
n.reeve@wave.co.nz
www.bnb.co.nz/grenofen.html

Double $120 Single $80 Child by age Dinner $35
1 King 2 Single (2 bdrm)
Bathrooms: 2 Ensuite

We invite you to stay with us in our spacious home overlooking the countryside, sea, Tauranga city and Mt Maunganui. Our property is a sheltered 3 1/2 acres with trees, gardens and lawns. You may relax in quiet and privacy, enjoy the spa, or swim in our pool. both rooms have ensuite, electric blankets, TV, and comfortable chairs. Tea facility in guest area, laundry done overnight if required. We love to share our home and travel experiences with guests. Be sure of a warm welcome.

TAURANGA - BETHLEHEM *6km NW of Tauranga*

The Hollies *B&B*
Shirley & Michael Creak
Westridge Drive, Bethlehem,
Tauranga 3001

Tel (07) 577 9678 Fax (07) 579 1678
stay@hollies.co.nz www.hollies.co.nz

Double $120-$250 Single $95-$165 (Full Breakfast)
Dinner $40pp Credit cards accepted
2 King/Twin 1 Queen 2 Single (3 bdrm)
Bathrooms: 1 Ensuite 2 Private

Hollies, an elegant sophisticated modern country house, acre of gardens. Large luxuriously appointed rooms, panoramic views of gardens and rolling hills. The spacious suite has super king (or twin) bed, ensuite, lounge & TV, kitchenette, alternative private entrance and balcony. Hairdryers, bathrobes and toiletries. Fresh flowers, chocolates and crisp linen and every attention to detail combine to ensure your stay is truly memorable. Complimentary tea/coffee. Landscaped gardens, swimming pool. Breakfast: home made bread, muffins, fresh fruit and tempting cooked dishes. Muffee our cat. Children by arrangement.

TAURANGA   *6km N of Tauranga*

Matua Bed and Breakfast   *B&B*
Anne & Peter Seaton
34 Tainui Street, Matua, Tauranga

Tel (07) 576 8083   Fax (07) 576 8086
Mob 027 491 5566   pa_seaton@clear.net.nz
www.bnb.co.nz/matuahomestay.html

Double $80   Single $50   (Continental Breakfast)
Child $25   Children welcome
1 Queen 1 Twin (2 bdrm)
Bathrooms: 1 Guests share

Welcome to our quality one level well appointed home set in a peaceful garden, only 200 metres to the estuary beach. Enjoy a generous continental breakfast overlooking our picturesque garden. Tea, coffee, home-baking, laundry facilities are available anytime. We have travelled extensively. Let us help you plan your sightseeing visits to local and regional places of interest . We look forward to offering you friendly Kiwi hospitality making your stay very special. Please phone for directions or the free pick up service from public transport.

TAURANGA   *3km N of Tauranga Central*

Harbinger House   *B&B Homestay*
Helen & Doug Fisher
209 Fraser Street, Tauranga

Tel (07) 578 8801   Fax (07) 579 4101
Mob 025 583 049   d-h.fisher@xtra.co.nz
www.harbinger.co.nz

Double $80-$95   Single $60-$75   (Special Breakfast)
Child ¹/2 price Dinner $25   Credit cards accepted
2 Queen 2 Single (3 bdrm)
Bathrooms: 1 Guests share

Harbinger House provides 'affordable luxury in the heart of Tauranga', being close to hospital, conference facilities, downtown and a new shopping mall 100 metres away. Our upstairs has been renovated with your comfort in mind, using quality furnishings, linen, bathrobes, fresh flowers, tea and coffee. A guest phone and laundry facilities are available. The queen rooms have separate vanities and private balconies. Breakfast is a gourmet event. We offer complimentary pick up from public transport depots and off-street parking is available.

TAURANGA   *10km E of Tauranga*

Birch Haven   *B&B Homestay*
Judy & George McConnell
R403 Welcome Bay Road,
RD 5, Tauranga

Tel (07) 544 2499   Mob 025 414 289
george.mcconnell@paradise.net.nz
www.bnb.co.nz/birchhaven.html

Double $100   Single $60   (Full Breakfast)
Child $25   Dinner $30
1 King/Twin 1 Queen (2 bdrm)
Bathrooms: 1 Private

Luxurious, comfortable 1 level home away from home on 3 acres growing tamarillos and avocados. We enjoy meeting people, have travelled extensively and our interests include Blackie our cat, sport, reading, gardening, good food and wine. We offer a three course dinner option, swimming and spa pools, tour information and local courtesy pickup. Tauranga, Mt Maunganui, cafés and restaurants are a 10 minute drive. Make us your base for day trips to Lake Taupo, Rotorua, Waitomo Caves or Coromandel Peninsula. Go sightseeing - have fun - return and relax!

TAURANGA   *10km SW of Tauranga*

Redwood Villa   *B&B*
Mike & Dee Forsman
17 Redwood Lane, Tauriko
RD 1, Tauranga

Tel (07) 543 4303   Fax (07) 543 4303
Mob 025 296 5565   redwoodvilla@ihug.co.nz
redwoodvilla.co.nz

Double $100   Single $75   (Continental Breakfast)
Dinner $30   Full breakfast by arrangement
1 Queen (1 bdrm)
Bathrooms: 1 Ensuite 1 Private

Relax in a completely refurbished 100 year old villa. This historic dwelling was originally the Tauriko
Post Office and serviced river traders during the saw-milling era early last century. Rural property
comprising 3 acres with house situated amongst giant redwood and oak trees. Your own lounge,
bathroom (claw foot bath), verandahs and outdoor areas. Only 12 minutes to downtown Tauranga and
over Harbour bridge to Mt Maunganui. Attractions: stroll to river, tramping, parks, wineries, beaches,
restaurants. We have 2 cats and a dog. Smoking outside only.

TAURANGA   *10km W of Tauranga*

The Lavender Patch Countrystay B & B   *B&B*
Separate/Suite Self-contained
Mike & Pamela Mail
136 Kennedy Road, Pyes Pa RD 3, Tauranga

Tel (07) 543 2113   Fax (07) 543 2731
Mob 025 974 259   mikemail@xtra.co.nz
www.bnb.co.nz/user131.html

Double $120   Single $105   (Continental Breakfast)
Child $15, free under 10   Dinner $30pp
Credit cards accepted Children welcome
1 Queen 1 Single (1 bdrm) Bathrooms: 1 Ensuite 1 Private

Idyllic "country-style" apartment overlooking peaceful lavender gardens - a hint of the Provence. Your
own private patio to relax outdoors. Separate entrance, sole occupancy, quiet location. Queen bed
with fresh cotton linen scented with lavender. Shower with our own lovely lavender-scented shower
gel and use our home-made lavender soap. Friendly but unobtrusive hosting guaranteed. Generous
healthy breakfast with home-made preserves. Phone, fax, email and laundry services available. Visa/
Mastercard. Children welcome. Pets - Winnie cat.

TAURANGA - TAURIKO   *11km SW of Tauranga*

Wairoa Lodge   *Separate/Suite Self-contained*
Wendy Broome
48 Redwood Lane, Tauriko
RD 1, Tauranga

Tel (07) 543 4018   Mob 021 048 4520
broomes@clear.net.nz   www.bnb.co.nz/wairoa.html

Double $80   Single $50 (Breakfast provisions supplied)
Child $15   Dinner $25 by arrangement
Children welcome
1 Double 1 Twin (2 bdrm)
Bathrooms: 1 Private

Nestled on the banks of the Wairoa River, Wairoa Lodge offers you 33 acres of peaceful seclusion just
12 minutes drive from downtown Tauranga. Enjoy local beaches, bush walks and sports facilities:
swim, canoe, fish or simply relax and enjoy the view. We offer a self-contained unit with shower room
and complimentary tea and coffee. Dinner by prior arrangement. Double bed is a foldout. We have 2
daughters and some curious beefies. Sorry no smokers.

TAURANGA   *3km W of Tauranga City centre*

Be Our Guest   *B&B Self-contained units*
Aileen and Lang Pringle
160 Waihi Road, Tauranga City

Tel **(07) 571 8862**   Fax (07) 571 8862
Mob 021 030 9627   beourguest@xtra.co.nz
www.beourguest.co.nz

Double $80-$100 Single $60   (Full Breakfast)
Child $20   Dinner $25   Self-contained unit $70-$85
Credit cards accepted
2 Queen 1 Twin 1 Single (2 bdrm)
Bathrooms: 1 Ensuite 1 Guests share

Welcome to warm Kiwi hospitality, with itinerary help. Our rooms all have, TV, electric blankets, internet and laundry facilities available. Just a few minutes away is shopping in the city, wonderful cafés, hot mineral pools, bush walks, waterfalls, surf beaches, fishing, golf, horse riding, boating, plus more. Lang is a therapeutic masseur, Aileen loves to cook. Complimentary pick up within city. Fresh coffee/tea and homemade biscuits are always available. Aileen & Lang would love to share some time with you. Contact us today

TAURANGA - TAURIKO   *10km SW of Tauranga*

Redwood Heights   *B&B Farmstay*
Chrissy & Errol Jefferson
50 Redwood Lane, Tauriko RD1, Tauranga

Tel **(07) 543 1116** Fax (07) 543 1742
Mob 027 417 2891   redwoodheights@value.net.nz
www.bnb.co.nz/redwoodheights.html

Double $95 Single $70   (Full Breakfast)   Child $30
Dinner $25 by arrangement   Cot available
Credit cards accepted   Children welcome
1 King 2 Single (2 bdrm)
Bathrooms: 1 Private

Welcome to our 30 acre farm overlooking the Wairoa River and home of our belted galloway cattle, various animals and outside pets. We have a swimming pool, spa pool, extensive gardens with ponds and waterfall, kayaking, fishing on the river and walks. Only 5 minutes to winery and restaurants, 12 minutes to downtown Tauranga. Guest lounge with tea/coffee, TV/video or join us and exchange travel experiences. Relax and unwind with nothing to disturb you but the sounds of nature.

TAURANGA   *10km SW of Tauranga*

Redwood Villa   *B&B*
Bridget & Rod Hill
17 Redwood Lane,
Tauriko RD 1, Tauranga

Tel **(07) 543 2880**   Fax (07) 543 4780
Mob 021 779 589   redwoodvilla@xtra.co.nz
www.redwoodvilla.co.nz

Redwood Suite $125   Walnut Room $95
(Continental Breakfast)   Full breakfast b/a $15pp
Candle light dinner $35pp   Credit cards accepted
2 Queen (2 bdrm)
Bathrooms: 1 Ensuite 1 Guests share

Relax, enjoy, recharge amongst the ambience of the giant Redwood/Oak trees in our 100 year old villa. As the original Tauriko Trading Post (10km from Tauranga) servicing the district at the turn of the last century, much of the yesteryear charm remains. If you are looking for a home away from home, want to be treated to something special, enjoy your own space, or simply looking for a place to stay for a night or two, give us a call. Steffe our schnauser will welcome you.

TAURANGA   *8km NW of Tauranga*

Oakridge Views   *B&B*
Diane & Trevor Hinton
557 Cambridge Road,
Tauriko, Tauranga

Tel (07) 543 0292   Fax (07) 543 0294
Mob 025 285 2189   www.bnb.co.nz/oakridge.html

Double $85-$95 Single $50-$55 (Full Breakfast)
Child $30   Dinner $35 by arrangement
Children welcome
1 Queen 1 Twin (2 bdrm)
Bathrooms: 1 Ensuite 1 Private

Welcome to Oakridge Views, where your comfort is our concern. Enjoy our panoramic views of gardens and rolling hills. Relax in our comfortable 1 level home away from home, an acre of gardens. Handy to some of the top restaurants in the bay. Only 10 minutes to downtown Tauranga and over the harbour bridge to Mt Maunganui. Attractions include garden walks, tramping, parks, wineries, beaches, golf courses. Spa pool available. We love our small pooch Molly.

MT MAUNGANUI   *4km N of Mt Maunganui*

Homestay on the Beach   *Homestay Self-contained*
Bernie & Lolly Cotter
85C Oceanbeach Road, Mt Maunganui

Tel (07) 575 4879   Fax (07) 575 4828
Mob 025 766 799   bernie.cotter@xtra.co.nz
www.bnb.co.nz/homestayonthebeachcotter.html

Double $130   Single $90   (Continental Breakfast)
Child neg   Suite double $160, extra guests $25pp
Credit cards accepted   Children welcome
2 Queen 1 Single (2 bdrm)
Bathrooms: 1 Ensuite 1 Private

Welcome to our magnificent home by the sea. Choose from our self-contained suite, sleeping 2 couples and 1 single (suitable for children) with private deck. 1 minute to beach for those casual walks. Upstairs is our Queen ensuite with TV. Your continental breakfast includes eggs any style. International golf course 500 metres. The famous Mount walk up or around with 360 degree views is breathtaking. 4km to shops, hot salt water pools, and restaurants for your enjoyment. Sorry no pets. Off-street parking. Look forward to having you stay.

MT MAUNGANUI   *8km S of Mt Maunganui*

Bermuda Homestay   *Homestay*
Barbara Marsh
19 Bermuda Drive, Papamoa,
Mount Maunganui

Tel (07) 575 5592   Fax (07) 575 5592
Mob 021 707 243   barbmarsh1@hotmail.com
www.bnb.co.nz/bermuda.html

Double $100 Single $70 (Continental Breakfast)
Credit cards accepted
1 Queen 2 Single (2 bdrm)
Bathrooms: 1 Guests share

Welcome to our modern, quiet home, a short walk from one of New Zealand's finest beaches. Excellent shopping available at both Bayfair Mall or Palm Beach Shopping Plaza, only minutes away. Local activities include golf courses, hot salt pools, great restaurants and cafés, fishing, swimming, surfing and walks around and up the glorious Mount. Relax in our private outdoor garden and make yourself at your home away from home. Your well travelled hostess looks forward to having you stay and assures unique hospitality.

Mt Maunganui
3km S of Mt Maunganui

Fairways   *Homestay Self-contained*
Philippa & John Davies
170 Ocean Beach Road, Mt Maunganui

Tel (07) 575 5325   Fax (07) 578 2362
pipjohn@clear.net.nz
www.bnb.co.nz/fairways.html

Double $95   Single $75   (Full Breakfast)
Dinner including wine $35pp by arrangement
1 Queen 1 Double (2 bdrm)
Bathrooms: 1 Ensuite 1 Host share

A golfer's paradise. Our comfortable, timbered, character home adjoins the 8th fairway of the Mount golf course, and is across the road from the wonderful ocean beach. Enjoy with us interesting food, wine, art, music, conversation, and a bonus golf lesson. John is a retired solicitor, teacher and former scratch golfer, and Pippa a registered nurse involved in natural health. Our leisurely dinners are fun occasions, and John's desserts legendary. We are well travelled both in New Zealand and abroad, and look forward to meeting you.

Mt Maunganui
9km S of Mt Maunganui

Pembroke House   *B&B*
Cathy & Graham Burgess
12 Santa Fe Key, Royal Palm Beach,
Papamoa/ Mt Maunganui

Tel (07) 572 1000   PembrokeHouse@xtra.co.nz
www.bnb.co.nz/pembrokehouse.html

Double $90-$95 Single $70-$75 (Full Breakfast)
Child $35   Credit cards accepted
2 Queen 2 Single (3 bdrm)
Bathrooms: 2 Ensuite 1 Private

A modern home. Cross the road to the Ocean Beach, where you can enjoy swimming, surfing and beach walks. Enjoy stunning sea views while dining at breakfast. Near Palm Beach Shopping Plaza, restaurants and golf courses. Close proximity to Mount Maunganui, Tauranga, Rotorua and Whakatane. Separate guest lounge with TV and tea making facilities. Cathy, a schoolteacher, and Graham, semi-retired are your hosts. We are widely travelled and both enjoy meeting people. Our home is shared with our persian cat, Crystal. Unsuitable for pre-schoolers.

Mt Maunganui
3km S of Mt. Maunganui

Beachside   *B&B Homestay*
Lorraine & Jim Robertson
21B Oceanbeach Road, Mt Maunganui

Tel (07) 574 0960   Fax (07) 574 0960
Mob 021 238 0598   jim.lorraine@ihug.co.nz
www.bnb.co.nz/beachsideocean.html

Double $90-$125 Single $75   (Full Breakfast)
Credit cards accepted
1 King/Twin 2 Queen (3 bdrm)
Bathrooms: 1 Ensuite 2 Private

We are close to the action but far enough away to be quiet and only 30 seconds to NZ's most popular beach. Off-street parking and laundry facilities available. Courtesy transport from local airport, buses & information centre. Relax or indulge with Jim's cappuccinos and enjoy great sea views from our third storey guest lounge. Our generous breakfast includes a seasonal fresh fruit salad and home-baked bread. We are widely travelled and enjoy meeting people. We would love to help you to have a memorable stay in our beautiful locality.

Mt Maunganui - Papamoa   *9km SE of Mt Maunganui*

Hesford House   *B&B Homestay*
Sally & Derek Hesford
45 Gravatt Road, Royal Palm Beach,
Papamoa/Mt Maunganui

Tel **(07) 572 2825**   derek.sally@clear.net.nz
www.hesfordhouse.co.nz

Double $85-$110   Single $45-$60 (Full Breakfast)
Child $25   Credit cards accepted Children welcome
2 Queen 1 Twin (3 bdrm)
Bathrooms: 1 Ensuite 1 Guests share

We invite you to stay in our tastefully decorated modern, architecturally designed character home. Enjoy panoramic views of the Papamoa Hills together with exquisite sunsets. A short stroll to the shopping plaza or through the lakes to the beach. Close to restaurants, cafés and popular tourist attractions. Relax in a beautiful outdoor garden setting. Complimentary tea/coffee facilities and TVs in each room. Our unique location offers you magnificent beaches and only 50 minutes drive to Rotorua and Whakatane. Courtesy pick up from public transport.

Papamoa   *11km SE of Mt Maunganui*

Alraes   *B&B Homestay*
Raema & Alf Owen
1 Santa Cruz Drive, Palm Springs, Papamoa 3003

Tel **(07) 542 3818**   0800 RAEMAS   Fax (07) 542 3818
Mob 021 119 0071   relax@alraes.co.nz
www.alraes.co.nz

Double $95-$140 (Special Breakfast)
Credit cards accepted
1 King/Twin 1 Queen (2 bdrm)
Bathrooms: 1 Ensuite 1 Guests share

A warm welcome awaits you at Alraes B&B. A home away from home. This new home has won the National Show Home of the Year 2003 and is luxuriously appointed with guest lounge leading into a conservatory and the family room where you are welcome to join us. Lovely outdoor area. Laundry, email. Complimentary tea/coffee. This beautiful home is well located, and an ideal base for golf, fishing and exploring the beautiful Bay of Plenty. Beach, restaurant, bar, medical centre and shops, 2 minutes walk. We look forward to meeting you.

Te Puke   *2km NW of Te Puke*

Lindenhof Homestay   *Homestay Separate/Suite*
Beth & Murray Allen
58 Dunlop Road, Te Puke

Tel **(07) 573 4592**   Fax (07) 573 9392
Mob 025 339 405   lindenhofhomestay@wave.co.nz
www.bnb.co.nz/lindenhofhomestay.html

Double $120   Single $75   (Full Breakfast)
Dinner $25   Credit cards accepted
1 Queen 2 Single (2 bdrm)
Bathrooms: 1 Ensuite 1 Private

Lindenhof is an imposing building in the style of a Georgian country home. You are able to indulge in affordable luxury. Te Puke is the heart of kiwifruit country. Close to town, semi-rural. Tennis court, swimming pool, spa pool, billiard room, formal lounge and dining room. No smoking in house. Not suitable for children. SH2 from Tauranga, Dunlop Road turns right by Gas Centre (international B/B sign) 1km. Up Dunlop Road on left.

BAY OF PLENTY

MAKETU BEACH - TE PUKE   *8km E of Te Puke*

Blue Tides Beachfront B&B/Homestay
plus Self-contained sea view unit
Patricia Haine
7 Te Awhe Road, Maketu Beach, Bay of Plenty

Tel (07) 533 2023   0800 359 191
Fax (07) 533 2023   Mob 025 261 3077
info@bluetides.co.nz   www.bluetides.co.nz

Double $120-$145 Single $100-$110   (Full Breakfast)
Self-contained unit $120 double   Credit cards accepted
2 King/Twin 2 Queen (4 bdrm)
Bathrooms: 4 Ensuite 1 Private

Qualmarked 3+. Stay in an historic seaside village, white sand beach and café across the road. Regional Award Winner 02-03 quality accommodation with many thoughtful extras. delicious full breakfasts with home made local produce. Awesome coastal views, romantic sunsets and stunning starry night skies. Easy drive to Rotorua, Tauranga, Whakatane and the 'Junction'. Home of kiwifruit. Recommended at least a 2 night stay.Also a self-catering sea view unit, full kitchen, separate entrance and garage. A special place I'd love to share with you.

PUKEHINA BEACH   *21km E of Te Puke*

Homestay on the Beach   *Homestay*
Alison & Paul Carter
217 Pukehina Parade, Pukehina Beach,
RD 9, Te Puke

Tel (07) 533 3988   Fax (07) 533 3988
Mob 025 276 7305   p.a.carter@pukehina-beach.co.nz
www.homestays.net.nz/pukehina.htm

Double $110 Single $70   (Full Breakfast)
Child ¹/₂ price   Dinner $30   Unit $140
Credit cards accepted   Children welcome
2 Double (2 bdrm)   Bathrooms: 1 Guests share

Welcome to our absolute beachfront home situated on the Pacific Ocean. Your accommodation situated downstairs, allowing complete privacy, if you so wish, includes, TV lounge with coffee/tea, fridge, microwave and laundry facilities, also available at separate rate. Enjoy magnificent views from your own sundeck, including White Island volcano and occasional visits from friendly dolphins. A golf course 13km. 30-40 minute drive from Tauranga, Mount Maunganui, Whakatane and Rotorua. A licensed restaurant 2km, surf casting, swimming walks or relax and enjoy our unique paradise.

MATATA   *34km W of Whakatane*

Pohutukawa Beach B&B & Cottage
B&B Self-contained 2 bedroom cottage
Jorg Prinz
693 State Highway 2, RD 4, Whakatane

Tel (07) 322 2182 Fax (07) 322 2186
joe@prinztours.co.nz   www.prinztours.co.nz/bube.html

Double $110 Single $90   (Continental Breakfast)
Self-contained cottage (sleeps 4) $150-$180
Dinner $35 Credit cards accepted Children welcome
1 King/Twin 1 King 2 Queen 1 Double 1 Twin (4 bdrm)
Bathrooms: 2 Ensuite 1 Private

Pohutukawa Beach B&B and Cottage are set in a picturesque location at the beach of the Pacific Ocean with views to active volcano White Island. Sometimes dolphins and whales pass by. We offer warm hospitality, sharing our home and cottage with travellers. The B&B is base for our tour company Prinz Tours, specialised in guided day tours and personalised itineraries New Zealand-wide. Dinners with ingredients from the organic garden and cattle farm on request. We speak German.

MATATA - PIKOWAI *30km NW of Whakatane*

Fothergills on Mimiha *B&B Separate/Suite Self-contained*
Bev & Hilton Fothergill
84 Mimiha Road, Pikowai/Matata, Whakatane

Tel (07) 322 2224 Fax (07) 322 2224 Mob 021 131 5171
beverlyf@xtra.co.nz   www.fothergills.co.nz
Double $100-$110 Single $80-$90 (Continental Breakfast)
Extra person $20 each Dinner by arrangement

'Mimiha Cottage' holiday home $150-170pn $650-750pw
Credit cards accepted Children welcome

2 Queen 1 Twin 1 Single (4 bdrm)
Bathrooms: 1 Ensuite 2 Private

Our modern, high-standard B&B unit, upstairs to maximise
farm and coast views, is situated on a quiet country road yet
only 1km from the sea. Self-contained with 2 bedrooms,
1 queen, the other king-single plus fold-down, private
bathroom, kitchenette with fridge and microwave, TV,
this has lots of little extras! A full continental breakfast
is offered with treats from the home garden and delicious
preserves.

Mimiha Cottage, our Holiday Home, is built on its own site
amongst natives beside Mimiha Stream, at the bottom of our garden. A 2 bedroomed cottage, catering
for up to 6, this is fully equipped, sunny and warm, wheelchair accessible throughout, comfortably and
tastefully furnished. An outdoor area provides respite in hot weather. Basic provisions are included,
including your first breakfast.

Surrounding our house is 1 hectare of beautiful garden featuring 230 roses, with areas to relax in and a
petanque court. Our organic vegetable garden and fruit trees provide the ingredients for the preserves
we offer at meals and for sale. Many facets of horticulture are represented, providing interest and
fascination. Mo, our fox terrier puppy, will entertain you! The whole is set in the beautiful, peaceful
Mimiha Valley, behind the towering Pikowai cliffs on the seaside halfway between Te Puke and
Whakatane just off the Pacific Coast highway.   Trips to take: Rotorua and Tauranga (1 hour), White
Island, Diving with Dolphins, Awakeri Hot Springs, Kiwifruit Country and many more. Or just go for
walks on surrounding farmland, up Mimiha Road or down to the beach.

Hilton and Bev, your hosts, are newly retired and committed to offering a unique experience, taking
a great deal of pleasure in sharing our wonderful location and delights of the area. Visitors regularly
comment on the friendliness and caring we offer, plus the wonderful location. **Come and enjoy!**

WHAKATANE   *7km W of Whakatane*

Whakatane Homestay- Leaburn Farm   *Homestay*
Kathleen & Jim Law
237 Thornton Road, RD 4, Whakatane

Tel (07) 308 7487 or 308 7955 Fax (07) 308 7487
kath.law@theredbarn.co.nz
www.bnb.co.nz/leaburnhomestay.html

Double $80-$90 Single $50-$60
(Full Breakfast) Dinner $25
Credit cards accepted
1 Queen 2 Single (2 bdrm)
Bathrooms: 1 Guests share

Whakatane is off the beaten tourist track, yet it is the centre for a wide range of activities. We can arrange sightseeing trips, including White Island and jet boat rides. We are handy to the Golf Links. Relax in peaceful surroundings in the homestead on our dairy farms, which are managed by our 50/50 sharemilker.

No longer actively involved in dairy farming activities, we have a small citrus orchard and breed black and coloured sheep as well as managing the Red Barn Craftshop on our property. This is run in conjunction with the Tio Tio Café/Restaurant. As 'young oldies', we enjoy bowls, Lions Club, genealogy and organic gardening. We no longer have domestic pets and as our family has fled we enjoy company.

Our queen bedroom is adjacent to a separate shower room and bathroom/toilet facilities. These facilities are only shared if other guests occupy the other twin bedroom. Guest's comments: *'A wonderful warm bed and a yummy breakfast.'* Jay, Auckland. *'Nice place, nice weather, great hosts.'* Uli, Germany. *'We struck a winner, grateful thanks.'* Pat and Ray, Cornwall, England. *'A wonderful stay and stimulating conversation.'* Judi, California, USA.

Be as busy or as quiet as you like

WHAKATANE *18km S of Whakatane*

Omataroa Deer Farm *Farmstay*
Jill & John Needham
Paul Road, RD 2, Whakatane

Tel **(07) 322 8399** Fax (07) 322 8399
Mob 025 449 250 jill-needham@xtra.co.nz
www.bnb.co.nz/needham.html

Double $90 Single $60 (Full Breakfast)
Child $40 Dinner $25
1 King 1 Queen (2 bdrm)
Bathrooms: 1 Ensuite 1 Private

We invite you to stay with us in our contemporary home which sits high on a hill commanding panoramic views. We farm deer organically and grow hydrangeas for export. You will be the only guest so you have sole use of a quiet private wing. Your evening meal will be 'special', venison, lamb or fresh seafood with home-grown vegetables. We dive, fish, tramp, ski, golf and love to travel. We have a friendly chocolate labrador and a burmese cat. Laundry available.

WHAKATANE *Whakatane Central*

Travellers Rest *Homestay*
Karen & Jeff Winterson
28 Henderson Street, Whakatane 3080

Tel **(07) 307 1015** Mob 027 276 6449
travrest@wave.co.nz
www.bnb.co.nz/travellersrest.html

Double $70-$80 Single $35-$40
(Continental Breakfast) Modern undercover caravan
Credit cards accepted Children welcome Pets welcome
1 King/Twin 1 Twin (2 bdrm)
Bathrooms: 1 Guests share

Needing time out? Join Jeff and Karen in their quiet home and garden beside the Whakatane River. Enjoy scenic river walks, rest in their garden, or visit the vibrant local, art, craft, or garden trail. Take a short drive to Ohope Beach, hot pools, river or sea activities. Our interests are: family, caravaning, gardening, photography, model cars, and stamp collecting. We look forward to sharing time with our guests, as does our friendly cat. Internet facility available.

WHAKATANE *10km S of Whakatane*

Baker's *B&B Homestay Private Cottage*
Lynne & Bruce Baker
40 Butler Road, RD 2, Whakatane

Tel **(07) 307 0368** Fax (07) 307 0368
Mob 027 284 6996 bakers@world-net.co.nz
www.bakershomestay.co.nz

Double $100-$130 Single $80 (Full Breakfast)
Dinner $25 by arrangement
Self-contained private cottage Credit cards accepted
1 King/Twin 2 Queen 2 Single (4 bdrm)
Bathrooms: 2 Ensuite 1 Private

You will be sure of a friendly welcome to our lovely country home nestled amongst mature gardens, croquet lawn, swimming and spa pool to enjoy and relax in. Choose between our delightful fully self-contained 2 bedroom cottage or be pampered with bed & breakfast in our warm spacious home. Guest lounge has Sky TV, tea/coffee and treats. Lynne and Bruce are keen outdoor hosts enjoying fishing, surfing, gardening and travel. White Island tours, dolphin watching, deep-sea fishing and diving activities can be arranged for your memorable stay.

BAY OF PLENTY

WHAKATANE *1.5km S of Whakatane Central*

Crestwood Homestay
B&B Homestay Separate/Suite Self-contained
Janet & Peter McKechnie
2 Crestwood Rise, Whakatane, Bay of Plenty

Tel (07) 308 7554 0800 111 449 Fax (07) 308 7551
Mob 025 624 6248 pandjmckechnie@xtra.co.nz
www.crestwood-homestay.co.nz

Double $90-$120 Single $70-$90
(Continental Breakfast) Dinner $30 by arrangement
Credit cards accepted
1 Queen 2 Single (2 bdrm) Bathrooms: 1 Private

So close to town, information centre, wharf and coastal walkway. Quiet scenic surroundings with superb sea views from all rooms. Entire upstairs area for guests with private entrance way, sunny spacious rooms, lounge, kitchenette and balcony. Home comforts include electric blankets, bathrobes, hairdryer, toiletries, writing desk, internet, home-baking and refreshments. We enjoy company, fishing, picnics, have travelled extensively and Janet learns German. We will be happy to advise you on places of interest around our area. Safe off-road parking. Option of single party booking or shared facilities.

WHAKATANE *13 W of Whakatane*

Kanuka Cottage *B&B Farmstay*
Carol & Ian Boyd
880 Thornton Road, RD 4, Whakatane

Tel (07) 304 6001 Fax (07) 304 6001
Mob 021 883 684 kanuka1@xtra.co.nz
www.bnb.co.nz/kanukacottage.html

Double $80-$100 (Full Breakfast) Child $15
Dinner $25 by arrangement Credit cards accepted
1 King/Twin 1 Queen 3 Single (2 bdrm)
Bathrooms: 2 Ensuite

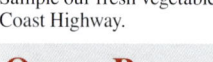
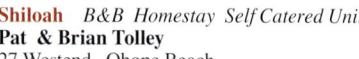

Enjoy expansive sea and active volcano views from our B&B and self-contained units. Set in 23 secluded acres of coastal kanuka with private access to sandy surf beach. Good surfcasting and kontiki fishing. White Island tours, deep-sea fishing, and other recreational activities arranged. Handy to golf courses. Large and interesting succulent, cacti and bromeliad gardens with plants for sale. Feed our friendly alpaca, boer goats, ducks and chickens. Sample our fresh vegetables, fruit and eggs organically produced on our property. We are on the Pacific Coast Highway.

OHOPE BEACH *6km E of Whakatane*

Shiloah *B&B Homestay Self Catered Unit*
Pat & Brian Tolley
27 Westend, Ohope Beach

Tel (07) 312 4401 Fax (07) 312 4401
www.bnb.co.nz/shiloah.html

Double $66-$90 Single $35-$45 (Full Breakfast)
Child ½ price Dinner $18-$25 by arrangement
Self-catered unit also available.

1 Queen 1 Twin 4 Single (2 bdrm)
Bathrooms: 2 Private 1 Guests share

Homestay: Paradise on the beach - view White Island and enjoy our hospitality. Facilities available for disabled guests. Classic car enthusiasts - well travelled. Also available is a self-catered unit, separate from our B&B, with 1 twin bedroom, 1 single bed and 2 bed settees if required, complete with shower and kitchenette. Tariff; $30-$50 own bedding, extra if supplied. Access to beach across road. Fishing, swimming, surfing, and bush walks.

OHOPE BEACH   *8km Whakatane*

B&B
Approved

The Rafters   *Self-contained*
Pat Rafter
261A Pohutukawa Ave, Ohope Beach

Tel (07) 312 4856   Fax (07) 312 4856
The_Rafters_Ohope@xtra.co.nz
www.wave.co.nz/pages/macaulay/The_Rafters.htm

Double $80-$90   Single $75-$80
(Continental Breakfast)   Child $10
Dinner $30-$45   Children welcome
Pets welcome   Smoking area inside
1 King 1 Single (2 bdrm)
Bathrooms: 1 Ensuite 1 Private

Rafter

Panoramic sea views of White Island, Whale Island and the East Coast. Safe swimming nearby. Many interesting walks. Golf, tennis, bowls are all within minutes. Licensed Chartered Club Restaurant is opposite. Trips to volcanic White Island, fishing, jet boating, diving and swimming with dolphins can be arranged.

Full cooking facilities; private entrance, sunken garden and BBQ. Complimentary tea, coffee, biscuits, fruit, newspaper and personal laundry service. By special arrangement dine with host and his friendly weimaraner dog, Gazelle, in the library - dining room, this includes pre-dinner drinks and wines.

Pat's interests are: philosophy, theology, history, English literature, the making of grape wines and all spirits, golf, bowls, music and tramping. Courtesy car is available. House trained animals are also welcomed.

3 restaurants and an oyster farm are within 5 minutes drive. I look forward to your company and assure you unique hospitality.

Directions: on reaching Ohope Beach turn right, proceed 2km to 261A (beach-side), name *Rafters* on a brick letterbox with an illuminated B&B sign.

Panoramic sea views - safe swimming nearby - golf, tennis, bowls - unique hospitality

OHOPE BEACH   *8km SE of Whakatane*

Oceanspray Homestay
B&B Homestay Self-contained Separate cottage
Frances & John Galbraith
283A Pohutukawa Avenue, Ohope, Bay of Plenty

Tel (07) 312 4112   Fax (07) 312 4192
Mob 027 286 6824   frances@oceanspray.co.nz
www.oceanspray.co.nz

Double $100-$120 Single $60-$80
(Continental Breakfast)   Child neg
Credit cards accepted   Children welcome
3 Queen 2 Twin (5 bdrm)   Bathrooms: 2 Private

Panoramic views and a warm welcome greet you at Oceanspray Homestay - a beachfront property with upstairs views to White Island, also East Cape. Our downstairs separate unit within our home has 3 attractively furnished bedrooms, lounge/kitchen. Adjacent to our house, a 2 bedroom, modern, self-contained cosy cottage. Home comforts - Sky TV, videos/toys for children. Special breakfasts - home-made bread, preserved fruits. John's pursuits are kayaking/longline fishing; Frances enjoys entertaining, providing excellent cuisine. Our cat and labrador dog also make you welcome.

OHOPE BEACH   *10km NE of Whakatane*

Tawai House   *B&B Self-contained*
Audrey & Ray Butler
13 Tawai Street,
Ohope Beach 3085

Tel (07) 312 4332
www.bnb.co.nz/tawai.html

Double $85 Single $60   (Continental Breakfast)
1 Double 2 Single (2 bdrm)
Bathrooms: 1 Private

Our home is situated 100 metres from the ocean beach, swimming and surfing. Ray an experienced fisherman will enjoy taking you fishing. You may enjoy a game of snooker with us and enjoy our views. Only minutes from the Chartered Club, restaurants, golf, bowls and bush walks.
Directions: Tawai Street left off Harbour Road.

OHOPE   *10km SE of Whakatane*

Moanarua Beach Cottage   *Self contained cottage*
Miria & Taroi Black
2 Hoterini Street, Ohope

Tel (07) 312 5924
Mob 021 255 6192
info@moanarua.co.nz
www.moanarua.co.nz

Double $95-$115 Single $70   (Continental Breakfast)
Dinner by arrangement
1 King   (1 bedroom cottage)
Bathrooms: 1 Ensuite

Naumai, haeremai - Ohope the place of fun, surf, sand and sunshine! Miria and Taroi of Moanarua Beach Cottage offer you a romantic hideaway nestled between the Ocean and the Harbour. Feel free to use our kayaks, BBQ, expansive decks with sea views of both sides and luxury spa. Chat with us about local history and the displays of contemporary Maori art works that adorn our home, cottage and garden. Kick back and relax in your private fully self-contained cottage or enjoy some of the many local activities.

OHOPE BEACH   *6km E of Whakatane*

Memorymakers   *B&B Self-contained*
Lionel Korach & Hilary Kearns
186 Ocean Road, Ohope

Tel (07) 312 5404   Mob 0274 545 597
memorymakers@xtra.co.nz
www.memorymakers.co.nz

Double $100-$150   Single $100   (Special Breakfast)
Child neg   Dinner by arrangement
Children welcome   Pets welcome
1 King 2 Single (2 bdrm)
Bathrooms: 1 Ensuite

Hi from your hosts, Hilary & Lionel, we have a modern
2 bedroom self-contained apartment with sundeck especially for you. We are perfectly situated with the beach across the road, handy access to cafés, restaurants or try our cusine. We have stacks of off-road parking for car and boat. We have options available for fishing or scenic trips on our boat. Bush walks, trout fishing beach walks, or guided trips around the bay. Use us, or on your own or a bit of both.

OPOTIKI   *18km E of Opotiki*

Coral's B&B   *B&B Farmstay Self-contained*
Coral Parkinson
Morice's Bay, Highway 35, RD 1, Opotiki

Tel (07) 315 8052   Fax (07) 315 8052
Mob 021 299 9757   coralsb.b@wxc.net.nz
www.bnb.co.nz/coralsbb.html

Double $75-$115   Single $52-$65   Child $10
Breakfast provided on request $15 double   Dinner $25
Children welcome   Pets welcome
2 Queen 1 Double 2 Single (3 bdrm)
Bathrooms: 2 Private

We provide 2 self-contained accommodation options located on our hobby farm. As well as pets and farm animals we collect varied memorabilia. Enjoy the beach and bird life; swim at nearby sandy beach. Fish, ramble over the rocks, explore caves. The 2 storied cottage features lead-light windows, native timbers, large decks look out across the bay and native bush. The mews has separate bedroom, large lounge, all on one level. 3 golf courses within an hours drive; covered parking, home-made bread and preserves.

OPOTIKI - OHIWA HARBOUR   *16kms W of Opotiki*

Rivendell   *B&B Self-contained*
Bev & Kev Hamlin
255 Ruatuna Road, RD 2, Opotiki

Tel (07) 315 8599   Fax (07) 315 8599
r.dell@value.net.nz
www.bnb.co.nz/rivendell-bnb.html

Double $100-$110   Single $75-$110
(Continental Breakfast)   Dinner $25
S/C double $110 $15 extra person   C/C accepted
2 King/Twin 1 Queen (3 bdrm)   Bathrooms: 2 Ensuite

Rivendell Cottage is situated on the waters edge of the upper Ohiwa Harbour. The private fully self-contained cottage sleeps up to 5 guests. Indoor/outdoor living is a speciality here. Amid native bird song, a tranquil aura and spectacular views. Rivendell House offers private B&B for 1 couple with own bathroom and guest lounge with TV, tea/coffee facilities. On art and craft and garden trails. Handy to surf beaches, boat ramp, kayaking and harbour tours. Rivendell is 15 minutes to Opotiki and Ohope, 25 minutes to Whakatane. B&B $100 double, self-contained $110 double $15 each extra person per night.

BAY OF PLENTY

OPOTIKI - TIROHANGA *7km E of Opotiki*

Tirohanga Beach Holiday Home *Two self-contained units*
Natalie & Jeff Jaffarian
787 State Highway 35E, Opotiki

Tel (07) 315 8899   Fax (07) 315 8896
Mob 027 412 6411   jaffarian@xtra.co.nz

Double $90   Additional person $45 each
(Continental Breakfast)   Dinner by arrangement
Weekly and monthly specials during winter

Upstairs: 1 Double, 1 Twin
Downstairs: 1 Queen, 1 Twin, 1 Double foldout

Each unit has a private bathroom, living room with TV and
VCR, full kitchen with fridge, stove, microwave, kettle, and
utensils. Barbecue, washing machine, Internet access and
telephone may be available.

Tirohanga Beach Holiday Home is an ideal get-away for
all seasons. Upstairs has a magnificent ocean view right
from your bed! The downstairs unit has a wood fire. The
beautiful beach extends
for miles in each direction.
Swimming, surfing, fishing
and beach walking are at
your doorstep.

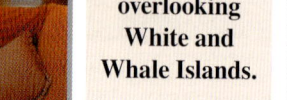

**Enjoy
breathtaking
sunrises and
sunsets from
the large deck
overlooking
White and
Whale Islands.**

www.beachholidayhomenewzealand.com

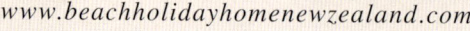

OPOTIKI - TE KAHA *66km E of Opotiki*

B&B Approved

Tui Lodge *B&B*
Joyce, Rex & Peter Carpenter
200 Copenhagen Road, Te Kaha, BOP 3093

Tel (07) 325 2922 Fax (07) 325 2922
jorex@xtra.co.nz www.tuilodge.co.nz

Double $115-$140 Single $95-$110
Child price on application Dinner $30pp
3 Queen 2 Twin 1 Single (6 bdrm)
Bathrooms: 4 Ensuite 1 Private

Set in 3 acres of gardens Tui Lodge offers comfort and tranquility without equal on 'the coast'. Purpose built in 1998 the lodge is in complete harmony with out native bush surrounds while affording views of volcanic White Island and the Pacific Ocean.

Joyce's meals exclusively feature naturally grown fruit and vegetables from our own gardens. We are situated a short walk from Maungaroa Beach and can arrange fishing, horse treks, tramping, jet boating or four wheel drive excursions.

From our visitor's book:
The lodge is a dream, I could stay for life.
Horst Kersten, Germany.
Wonderful, the best hosts we have ever had.
Shirley & Stan Kind, Auckland.
We'll never forget your warm hospitality; we'll be back again one day. Balleraud family, Noumea.
We were so lucky to find you, a wonderful stay in a glorious setting. Pat & Jim Roy Bucks, UK.
The best example of Kiwi hospitality ever. Derek Henderson, Sydney.
Beautiful gardens, even better food and great hosts. Kitty & Paul Brennan, Ireland.
What a paradise, how wonderful our time here has been. Karen & Bill Lillibridge, USA.
Absolutely unique, great food and great people. Marie & Jakob Lundberg, Sweden.
We'll come back again, hospitality you can only dream about. Corry & Peter van Meggelen, Holland.

Can we stay forever in this little bit of paradise? Nell & Ron Reid, Rotorua

OPOTIKI *11km W of Opotiki*

Fantail Cottage *Homestay*
Meg & Mike Collins
318 Ohiwa Harbour Road,
RD 2, Opotiki

Tel (07) 315 4981 0800 153 553 Fax (07) 315 4981
wendylyn@wave.co.nz
www.bnb.co.nz/fantailcottage.html

Double $85 Single $50 (Full Breakfast)
Dinner $25 pp
1 Twin (1 bdrm)
Bathrooms: 1 Ensuite

Set on a bush-clad spur, your cosy room and hot spa have expansive views of the tidal Ohiwa Harbour. A birdwatcher's paradise, on one of the best coastal birding sites in the North Island. Meg and Mike have travelled widely overseas and offer a classic NZ experience. Enjoy organic home-grown produce, fishing, swimming or walking on the beach. 34km from Whakatane, 15km from Opotiki. From SH2 turn at Waiotahi Bridge. Follow signs to Ohiwa Holiday Park and Fantail Cottage.

OPOTIKI - WAIHAU BAY *112km N of Opotiki*

Waihau Bay Homestay *B&B Self-contained*
Noelene & Merv Topia
RD 3, Opotiki

Tel (07) 325 3674 0800 240 170 Fax (07) 325 3679
Mob 025 784 762   n.topia@clear.net.nz
www.nzhomestay.co.nz/topia.html

Double $85-$100 Single $55-$75 (Full Breakfast)
Child 1/2 price Dinner $25 Credit cards accepted
Pets welcome
1 King/Twin 1 King 1 Queen 2 Twin (4 bdrm)
Bathrooms: 2 Ensuite 2 Private 1 Guests share

Surrounded by unspoiled beauty we invite you to come and enjoy magnificent views, stunning sunsets, swim, go diving, kayaking (we have kayaks) or just walk along the sandy beach. You are most welcome to join Merv when he checks his craypots each morning and his catches are our cuisine specialty. Fishing trips, horse treks and guided cultural walks are also available. We have 2 self-contained units with disabled facilities, and a double room with ensuite. Our cat Whiskey, and dog Meg enjoy making new friends.

Please let us know
how you enjoyed your B&B experience.
Ask your host for a comment form,
or leave a comment on www.bnb.co.nz

ROTORUA - NGONGOTAHA *17km N of Rotorua*

B&B Approved

Deer Pine Lodge *Farmstay Self-contained*
John Insch
255 Jackson Road, Ngongotaha, Rotorua

Tel (07) 332 3458 Fax (07) 332 3458 Mob 025 261 9965
deerpine@clear.net.nz www.bnb.co.nz/deerpinelodge.html

Double $60-$100 Single $70-$85
(Continental Breakfast) Child $20-$25
Dinner $30 by arrangement Credit cards accepted
3 King 1 Queen 4 Single (5 bdrm)
Bathrooms: 5 Ensuite

We farm deer, our property surrounded with trees planted by the New Zealand Forest Research as experimental shelter belts on our accredited deer farm.

The nearby city of Rotorua is fast becoming New Zealand's most popular tourist destination offering all sorts of entertainment. We have a cat and a boxer (Jake), very gentle. Our 4 children have grown up and left the nest.

Our bed & breakfast units/rooms are private with ensuites, TV, radio, fridge, microwave, electric blankets all beds, tea/coffee making facilities, heaters. Heaters and hair dryers also in bathrooms. Our 2 bedroom fully self-contained units, designed by prominent Rotorua architect Gerald Stock, each having private balcony, carport, sundeck, ensuite, spacious lounge, kitchen, TV, radio, heater etc. Cot and highchair available, also laundry facilities. Security arms fitted on all windows, smoke detectors installed in all bedrooms and lounges, fire extinguisher installed in all kitchens.

Holding NZ certificate in food hygiene ensuring high standards of food preparation and serving. Guests are free to do the conducted tour and observe the different species of deer and get first hand knowledge of all aspects of deer farming after breakfast. If interested please inform host on arrival. Three course meal of beef, lamb, or venison by prior arrangement, pre-dinner drinks.

Hosts John and Betty, originally from Scotland have travelled extensively overseas and have many years experience in hosting look forward to your stay with us. Prefer guests to smoke outside.

Welcome to Deer Pine Lodge

ROTORUA   *2km from Rotorua centre*

Rotorua Lakeside Homestay
Homestay
Ursula & Lindsay Prince
3 Raukura Place, Rotorua

Tel (07) 347 0140
Freephone 0800 223 624
Fax (07) 347 0107
the-princes@xtra.co.nz
www.bnb.co.nz/
rotorualakesidehomestay.html

Double $90-$100 Single $70-$80
Minimum stay 2 nights
Discount for 3 or more nights

PLEASE TELEPHONE TO
CONFIRM VACANCY.

(Special Breakfast)
1 King/Twin 1 Queen (2 bdrm)
Bathrooms: 1 Ensuite 1 Private

You can be sure of a warm welcome when you decide to stay with us at our spacious modern home right at the lakefront in Rotorua. Quiet and secluded, yet only five minutes by car from the city centre, our house is ideally situated for easy access to visitor's activities.

You will find both guestrooms spacious and well appointed; with electric blankets at the cooler time of the year. While staying with us, take time to relax on the deck, as you view the tranquil lake and mountain scene; watch the waterbirds. Have fun as you make free use of our Canadian canoe.

We have enjoyed sharing our home with guests from all over the world since 1988, we hope the informal atmosphere will give you too the feeling of being with friends.

Your breakfast, consisting of a platter of fresh fruit, orange juice, home-made jams and preserves and a variety of cereals, is followed by toast and home-made muffins with tea or coffee. Conversations over breakfast often prove to be a highlight for both guests and hosts.

We will help you make the most of your stay in Rotorua, feel free to use our extensive range of maps and guide books. We will be happy to arrange your local bookings. The highlight of your stay could be an evening spent learning about Maori culture and customs, as well as being treated to a delicious meal – the HANGI. If at all possible, allow yourself two full days to explore New Zealand's volcanic wonderland.

We are an active, retired couple, enjoying life with all its challenges. We take an interest in local and international affairs, have travelled and lived overseas and are very concerned about environmental issues. We love the outdoors and are still active in canoeing, swimming, fishing, cycling, walking and camping. Being non-smokers, we thank you for not smoking in the house.

HOW TO FIND US
From Lake Road turn into Bennetts Road, then first left into Koutu Road, then first right into Karenga Street. Turn RIGHT into Haumona Street, a left turn at the end brings you down Raukura Place to our door.

ROTORUA   *4km SW of Rotorua*

Hunts Farm   *Farmstay*
Maureen and John Hunt
363 Pukehangi Road,
Rotorua

Tel (07) 348 1352
www.bnb.co.nz/hunt.html

Double $100   Single $70   (Full Breakfast)
Child $25
1 King/Twin 1 Queen 2 Single (2 bdrm)
Bathrooms: 2 Ensuite

Come rest in our new home as we help you plan your itinerary and book your local tours. Explore by foot or farm vehicle our 150 acre farm running beef and deer. Now children have flown, Tigger, our trusty farm dog, who lives in the garden, is chief helper. Views are magical, 360 degrees of lake, island, forest, city and farm. Guest area has private entrance, includes lounge tea coffee facilities, TV, fridge. 2 triple rooms, each with ensuite lead out to sunny private terraces.

ROTORUA - NGAKURU   *32km S of Rotorua*

Te Ana Farmstay   *Farmstay Cottage & Homestead*
The Oberer Residence: Heather Oberer
Poutakataka Road, Ngakuru, RD 1, Rotorua

Tel (07) 333 2720   Fax (07) 333 2720
Mob 027 482 8151   teanafarmstay@xtra.co.nz
www.teanafarmstay.co.nz

Double $95-$150 Single $75   (Special Breakfast)
Child $35   Dinner by arrangement
Credit cards accepted   Children welcome
2 Queen 4 Single (4 bdrm)
Bathrooms: 2 Ensuite 1 Guests share 1 Host share

Te Ana, a 569 acre dairy beef and sheep property, offers peace and tranquility in a spacious rural garden setting affording magnificent views of lake, volcanically-formed hills and lush farmland. Enjoy a leisurely stroll before joining host for a very generous country breakfast. Ideal base from which to explore the Rotorua and Taupo attractions, Waiotapu and Waimungu Thermal Reserves, Waikite thermal mineral swimming pool and Tamaki Tours Hangi. Families welcomed by Sam, our loyal Jack Russell. Farm tour, canoe and fishing rod available.

ROTORUA   *4km S of Rotorua*

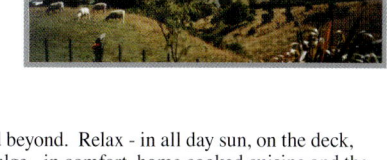

Serendipity Homestay   *B&B Homestay*
Kate & Brian Gore
3 Kerswell Terrace, Tihi-o-Tonga,
Rotorua

Tel (07) 347 9385   Mob 025 609 3268
b.gore@clear.net.nz
www.bnb.co.nz/serendipityrotorua.html

Double $100-$110 Single $65   (Full Breakfast)
Child $30 Dinner $30 by arrangement
Credit cards accepted Children welcome
1 Double 2 Twin (2 bdrm)   Bathrooms: 1 Private

Marvel - at unsurpassed views of geysers, city, lakes and beyond. Relax - in all day sun, on the deck, in the conservatory or in the privacy of our garden. Indulge - in comfort, home cooked cuisine and the friendly folk who have been enjoying hosting for many years. Our interests are, golf, tramping, travel, antiques and sharing our extensive local and national knowledge with you. Let us advise you on the 'must see' list while in Rotorua and other highlights of our beautiful country. Welcome!

ROTORUA - NGONGOTAHA *10km N of Rotorua*

Waiteti Lakeside Lodge   *Homestay Lakestay*
Val & Brian Blewett
2 Arnold Street, Ngongotaha, Rotorua

Tel (07) 357 2311 Fax (07) 357 2311
Local UK Call Phone 0871 474 1575
Mob 025 615 6923
waitetilodge@xtra.co.nz
www.waitetilodge.co.nz

Double $150-$250 Single $140-$240
(Full Breakfast) Child $40 10 & over
Multiple-night rates available
Credit cards accepted
4 Queen 2 Single (5 bdrm)
Bathrooms: 3 Ensuite 1 Private 2 Guests share

Waiteti Lakeside Lodge is situated on the shores of Lake Rotorua at the mouth of the picturesque Waiteti trout stream, away from the sulphur fumes and traffic noise of Rotorua City but close to all of Rotorua's attractions, fine restaurants, and Maori culture.

Brian and Val will arrange bookings for all local attractions and activities including:

- Rotorua's best cafes and restaurants
- Maori culture and entertainment
- Six golf courses
- Back country/wilderness trout fishing
- White water rafting
- Canoeing
- Forest walks
- Mountain biking
- Float plane trips from the lodge

The timber and natural stone lodge offers luxury private accommodation in traditional style and an extremely quiet and tranquil setting. There are five supremely comfortable bedrooms, three with ensuites, one private or two sharing a bathroom. The ensuite rooms have TVs and open on to balconies overlooking the lake, and in addition there is a private guests' lounge with satellite TV, video, library, pool table, and tea and coffee facilities. All rooms enjoy spectacular views of the lake and stream mouth, and the lodge's gardens extend to the water's edge, home to numerous native birds and waterfowl.

Enjoy trout fishing (with or without professional guide) from the lodge's grounds, on the lake in the lodge's own charter boat, or on one of the many productive local trout streams - your catch can be fresh smoked for a superb breakfast or lunch treat.

Alternatively you may prefer to take a guided boat trip to historic Mokoia Island, a sacred Maori site and wildlife sanctuary, where native flora and birdlife, including several rare and endangered species, abound. Your experienced hosts Brian and Val Blewett are available to advise and/or guide you at all times to ensure that your stay is highly enjoyable. Brian is a professional fishing guide with more than 30 years experience, so success is virtually guaranteed.

Directions: take Highway 5 from Rotorua to Ngongotaha, through town centre, over the railway line, turn second right into Waiteti Road. At the end turn right into Arnold Street and the lodge is at the end of the street next to the footbridge.

ROTORUA   *1.5km S of Rotorua*

Heather's Homestay   *B&B Homestay*
Heather Radford
5A Marguerita Street,
Rotorua

Tel (07) 349 4303   Mob 027 289 3059
heathermr@xtra.co.nz
www.bnb.co.nz/heathershomestay.html

Double $80   Single $50   (Full Breakfast)
Credit cards accepted Children welcome
2 Queen 1 Twin (2 bdrm)
Bathrooms: 2 Private

Haeremai - Welcome to my comfortable home in the heart of the thermal area, minutes from the city centre yet quiet and private. Rotorua born and bred, I am proud of my city and enjoy sharing what knowledge I have with guests. A keen tramper/walker, I also enjoy showing off the lovely walks in the area. For 10 years I have been a B&B host and look forward to many more visitors to my home and unique city. Directions: off Fenton Street.

ROTORUA   *5km SE of Rotorua*

Walker Homestay and B&B   *Self-contained*
Colleen & Isaac Walker
13 Glenfield Road, Owhata, Rotorua

Tel (07) 345 3882   Fax (07) 345 3856
Mob 025 289 5003   colleen.walker@clear.net.nz
www.bnb.co.nz/walkerhomestay.html

Double $80-$85 Single $50-$55
(Continental Breakfast)   Child ¹/2 price Dinner b/a
Extra adult $15   C/C accepted   Children welcome
2 Double 1 Twin 1 Single (3 bdrm)
Bathrooms: 1 Ensuite 1 Private

The cottage, situated in its own garden area has one double and one twin bedroom, lounge, kitchen, bathroom and laundry. Room in the house has one double; one single bed; ensuite; tea/coffee facilities; microwave; separate entrance as well as access to hosts living area. Have complete privacy or be one of the family. Hosts are both Lions. Colleen is a Technical Institute tutor and Ike is a NZ Maori, fisherman, golfer and tour bus driver with a background of farming and the paper industry. 2 small dogs will welcome you. Off-road parking. 24 hours notice if meal required. Caravan power available

ROTORUA   *14km NE of Rotorua*

Homestay
Joy & Lin Cathcart
99 Brunswick Drive, RD 4, Rotorua 3221

Tel (07) 350 1472   Fax (07) 350 1472
joylin@clear.net.nz
www.bnb.co.nz/cathcart.html

Double $95   Single $60   (Full Breakfast)
Dinner by arrangement   Credit cards accepted
1 King (1 bdrm)
Bathrooms: 1 Private

Having retired from dairy farming, we once again welcome guests to our new home on a 2 acre section in a quiet life-style subdivision overlooking Lake Rotorua. We are 15 minutes from Rotorua City centre and 5 minutes from Rotorua Airport. Our interests include gardening, golf, bridge and family. The guest room has TV and tea making facilities. We are non-smoking and have no pets. Sorry no children under 12 years. We look forward to your stay.

ROTORUA   *3km W of Rotorua*

West Brook   *B&B Homestay*
Judy & Brian Bain
378 Malfroy Road, Rotorua

Tel **(07) 347 8073**   Fax (07) 347 8073
www.bnb.co.nz/westbrook.html

Double $80   Single $50   (Continental Breakfast)
Child under 12 ¹/2 price   Dinner $25
Credit cards accepted   Children welcome
4 Single (2 bdrm)
Bathrooms: 1 Host share

Retired farmers with years of hospitality involvement, live 3km from city on western outskirts. Interests include meeting people, farming, international current affairs. Brian a Rotorua Host Lions member, Judy's interest extend to all aspects of homemaking and gardening. Both well appointed comfy guest rooms are equipped with electric blankets. The friendly front door welcome and chatter over the meal table add up to our motto "home away from home". Assistance with sightseeing planning and transport to and from tourist centre available.

ROTORUA CITY   *200m N of Tourism Centre*

Inner City Homestay   *B&B Homestay*
Susan & Irvine Munro
1126 Whakaue Street, Rotorua

Tel **(07) 348 8594**   Fax (07) 348 8594
Mob 025 359 923   innercityhomestay@clear.net.nz
www.bnb.co.nz/innercityhomestay.html

Double $85   Single $50   (Full Breakfast)
Child $30   Children welcome
1 Double 2 Single (2 bdrm)
Bathrooms: 1 Guests share

Innercity Homestay, 1126 Whakaue Street is 200 metres north of the Tourism Centre. We are centrally situated and close to many tourist attractions, thermal areas and spas. Overlooking Lake Rotorua. Comfortable thermally heated home with 2 guest bedrooms. Full or continental breakfasts included, with special diets catered for. Most restaurants, cafés and entertainment are within short walking distance. Buses met at Tourism Centre. We will make reservations and recommendations for tours and cultural performances. Laundry service available. Cat on property. We welcome your enquiries.

ROTORUA   *3km S of Rotorua*

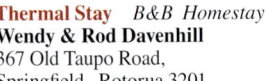

Thermal Stay   *B&B Homestay*
Wendy & Rod Davenhill
367 Old Taupo Road,
Springfield, Rotorua 3201

Tel **(07) 349 1605**   Fax (07) 349 1641
Mob 025 377 122   davenhill@clear.net.nz
www.bnb.co.nz/thermalstay.html

Double $95-$120   Single $65-$80   (Full Breakfast)
Dinner $30pp by arrangement   Credit cards accepted
1 King 2 Queen 2 Single (3 bdrm)
Bathrooms: 1 Private 2 Guests share 1 Host share

An oasis in the city. Quiet location, central, private. Thermally heated home and swimming pool, spa in winter. Tranquil gardens featuring waterfall, fish and native birdlife. Half hour walk to city centre. Nearby thermal activities, forests and golf courses. Well travelled hosts who enjoy good food, wine and conversation. Our company, or time in the guest lounge with private patio, your choice. Dine with us or sample a local restaurant or Maori hangi/concert. Off road parking, table tennis. Laundry, email and fax available. Pet - Candy, a very friendly tabby cat. Discounts for multiple nights.

ROTORUA - NGONGOTAHA   *17km N of Rotorua*

Clover Downs Estate   *B&B Farmstay Homestay Countrystay*
Lyn & Lloyd Ferris
175 Jackson Road, RD 2, Ngongotaha, Rotorua

Tel (07) 332 2366   0800 3687 5323
Fax (07) 332 2367   Mob 021 712 866
Reservations@clov erdowns.co.nz
www.accommodationinrotorua.co.nz

Double $195-$275 Single $180-$260
(Special Breakfast) Credit cards accepted
Child neg Children welcome
3 King/Twin 1 King (4 bdrm)
Bathrooms: 4 Ensuite

Welcome to our fine country Bed and Breaskfast
accommodation on a deer and ostrich farm, nestled in a
peaceful country setting just 15 minutes drive north of
Rotorua city.

We can offer a choice of 4 individually decorated
spacious king-size suites each comprising ensuite
bathroom, tea/coffee making facilities, refrigerator,
telephone, ironing facilities, hairdryer, TV, VCR, stereo
and individual outdoor decks. We serve a leisurely
breakfast each morning which, if you desire, is followed
by our popular free deer & ostrich farm tour.

Visit our awesome cultural and scenic attractions. Minutes drive from our property you will discover
a myriad of things to do and see: stand on active volcanoes, peer into craters, see boiling mud or just
soak in a mineral pool. We can advise you on trout fishing at one of the many lakes and rivers in the
area, walk cool forest glades or maybe play a round of golf. If you wish to go out, Rotorua has some
wonderful restaurants and cafés. or you may like to enjoy a Maori hangi and concert. We strive to
exceed our guests' expectations through an ineffable blend of warmth, generosity and detail.

Directions: take State Highway 5 to roundabout. Travel through Ngongotaha village on Hamurana Road
- go over railway line then take third left into Central Road. Turn first right into Jackson Road - Clover
Downs Estate is number 175 on left hand side.

With days as busy as this you'll be glad to come home to our gracious haven of relaxation

ROTORUA *4km W of Rotorua City Centre*

The Towers Homestay Rotorua *B&B Homestay*
Doreen & Des Towers
373 Malfroy Road, Rotorua

Tel (07) 347 6254   0800 261 040   Fax (07) 347 6254
ddtowers@clear.net.nz   www.mist.co.uk/homestaynz/

Double $95 Single $55 (Continental Breakfast)
Child $25 under 12 Dinner $25 by arrangement
One party at a time   Credit cards accepted
Children welcome
1 Double 1 Twin (2 bdrm)
Bathrooms: 1 Private

Welcome to our elevated home with views over Rotorua. We have been enjoying home hosting since 1998 and are able to spend time, as required, with our guests. Guest bedrooms/bathroom downstairs. Breakfast is served upstairs in our spacious lounge. Public transport pick up. Off-street parking and laundry available. Des has many years experience with a national organisation providing both local and NZ touring information. Doreen, originally from South Wales, likes gardening, reading, and enjoys meeting people. We host only one party at a time.

ROTORUA *12km NE of Rotorua*

Eucalyptus Tree Country Homestay
B&B Farmstay Country Homestay
Manfred & Is Fischer
66 State Highway 33, RD 4, Rotorua

Tel (07) 345 5325   Fax (07) 345 5325
Mob 025 261 6142   euc.countryhome@actrix.co.nz
users.actrix.co.nz/euc.countryhome

Double $90 Single $60 (Full Breakfast) Dinner $30
1 King/Twin 2 Queen 1 Double (3 bdrm)
Bathrooms: 2 Guests share 1 Host share

Welcome to our quiet, smokefree, high quality country home. On our small farm near Lake Rotorua, close to Lake Rotoiti and Okataina, we have a donkey, calves, sheep, chickens, rabbits, bees, organic vegetables and fruit trees. Native bush drive to clear trophy trout fishing lakes and bush walks, thermal area, Maori culture, hotpools, horseriding, skydiving, whitewater rafting. Our hobbies are trout fishing from boat, and fly fishing in lakes and rivers, hunting and shooting. We lived in the USA, Canada, Indonesia, Mexico and Germany and speak their languages.

ROTORUA *20km E of Rotorua*

Lakeside B & B *B&B Homestay*
Laurice & Bill Unwin
155G Okere Road, RD 4, Rotorua

Tel (07) 362 4288   Fax (07) 362 4288
Mob 027 452 1483   laurice.bill@xtra.co.nz
www.lakesidebnb.co.nz

Double $120-$130 Single $90 (Full Breakfast)
Child $10-22 Dinner $35pp Credit cards accepted
Children welcome
1 King/Twin 2 Queen 1 Single (3 bdrm)
Bathrooms: 2 Ensuite 1 Private

We have a new home in a beautiful setting beside Lake Rotoiti. Bird life abounds and within short walking distance there are bush walks, glow worms, waterfalls, river and lake fishing. Maori concerts, hangis, plus thermal activity are nearby. Each B&B is centrally heated with ensuite, comfortable beds, TV, refrigerator, tea/coffee making facilities. We share convivial meals with many guests. Small friendly outdoor dog. We are easy to find just one minute from Highway 33. Please ring for details. Laundry facilities available.

ROTORUA   *4km E of Rotorua*

Honfleur *B&B Homestay*
Bryan & Erica Jew
31 Walford Drive, Lynmore, Rotorua

Tel (07) 345 6170   Fax (07) 345 6170
Mob 021 256 5463   honfleurmaison@xtra.co.nz
www.bnb.co.nz/honfleur.html

Double $100-$110 Single $50-$75 (Full Breakfast)
Dinner $40   Credit cards accepted
1 Double 2 Twin (2 bdrm)
Bathrooms: 1 Ensuite 1 Guests share 1 Host share

Honfleur is a French country-style home in quiet, semi-rural surroundings close to lakes and forest. We offer generous hospitality amid antique furnishings and a beautiful garden featuring roses and perennials. Downstairs double bedroom with ensuite bathroom has a private entrance. Upstairs a twin bedroom has lake views and shares family bathroom (separate toilet). We are long-term Rotorua residents with sound local knowledge - retired medical professionals with friendly labrador dog. We offer a three course dinner (with wine) by arrangement. Not suitable for young children

ROTORUA   *4km E of Rotorua*

Aroden B&B Homestay *B&B Homestay*
Leonie & Paul Kibblewhite
2 Hilton Road, Lynmore, Rotorua

Tel (07) 345 6303 Fax (07) 345 6353
aroden@xtra.co.nz
www.bnb.co.nz/lynmorebbhomestay.html

Double $100-$120 Single $70-$90 (Special Breakfast)
Credit cards accepted
2 Queen (2 bdrm)
Bathrooms: 1 Ensuite 1 Private

Discover real character and warmth just 4km from the city, nestled beside beautiful Whakarewarewa Forest. Leonie, ex-teacher, and Paul, scientist, delight in being New Zealanders - share our love of this remarkable area over refreshments or a wine on the patio. Meet Taupo, Paul's engaging guide dog. Enjoy well-appointed rooms (quality linen and great showers); winter central heating; a lovely garden featuring native trees. You also have the choice of 2 living areas to relax in. Delicious breakfast - this couple enjoys food! Leonie parle francais.

ROTORUA - LAKE TARAWERA   *15 SE of Rotorua*

Boatshed Bay Lodge *B&B Homestay Self-contained*
Lorraine & Steve Jones
95 Spencer Road,   Lake Tarawera, RD 5,   Rotorua

Tel (07) 362 8441 Fax (07) 362 8441
Mob 027 279 9269   boatshedbay@xtra.co.nz
www.bnb.co.nz/boatshedbaylodge.html

Double $120 Single $90 (Full Breakfast)
Child $25 Dinner $40pp Self-contained $95
Credit cards accepted
2 Queen 1 Double 2 Single (2 bdrm)
Bathrooms: 2 Ensuite

Boatshed Bay is located on the shore of scenic Lake Tarawera with its sparkling waters fringed by native bush at the foot of majestic Mount Tarawera. We offer boat charter, world renowned trout fishing, tramping (mountain trek), bushwalks or just relax in peace and tranquillity only 15km from Rotorua. All facilities are available, including laundry, kitchen and nearby licensed restaurant The Landing Café. We provide home-style breakfast and meals on request. Your hosts Lorraine and Steve are well travelled and enjoy meeting people. Our place is your place.

ROTORUA - LAKE TARAWERA   *20km SE of Rotorua*

Lake Tarawera Rheinland Lodge   *B&B Homestay*
Gunter & Maria
484 Spencer Road,
RD 5, Rotorua

Tel (07) 362 8838   Fax (07) 362 8838
Mob 025 234 3024   tarawera@ihug.co.nz
www.bnb.co.nz/rheinlandlodge.html

Double $100-$130   Single $75-$95   (Special Breakfast)
Child ½ price Dinner $30
1 King/Twin 1 Queen (2 bdrm)
Bathrooms: 1 Private 1 Guests share 1 Host share

Located at the magic Lake Tarawera renowned for its scenery and history we offer warm hospitality with a personal touch. Expect total privacy, magnificent lake views, luxurious and relaxing outdoor whirlpool, spacious bathroom with shower and bath, fitness area, stereo, TV, internet connection, lake beach 5 minutes on foot, sea 45 minutes by car, bush walks, fishing and hunting trips by arrangement, home-made bread, German cuisine on request, organic garden, German/English spoken, free pick up from airport or city.

ROTORUA - LAKE TARAWERA   *23km SE of Rotorua*

Bush Haven   *Self-contained Tourist flat / Suite*
Marie & Rob Dollimore
588 Spencer Road,
Lake Tarawera,
Rotorua

Tel (07) 362 8447   Fax (07) 362 8447
www.bnb.co.nz/bushhaven.html

Double $145   Single $115
1 Queen 1 Double (2 bdrm)
Bathrooms: 1 Private

Bush Haven is a self-contained/self-catering tourist suite. There is a fully equipped kitchen, bathroom, 2 bedrooms (1 queen and 1 double), dining area and a large living area with 2 couches/beds: so the unit can sleep 4-8. The suite is the ground floor of a 2 story dwelling. Hosts Rob and Marie, with their friendly pet spaniels, live in the upper level. Bush Haven is secluded, quiet and peaceful with bush walks. There is ample safe car and boat parking.

ROTORUA   *10km W of Rotorua*

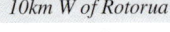

Rhodohill   *B&B Self-contained*
Ailsa & Dave Stewart
569 Paradise Valley Road,
Rotorua

Tel (07) 348 9010   Fax (07) 348 9041
Mob 025 672 4009   rhodohill@xtra.co.nz
www.bnb.co.nz/rhodohill.html

Double $80-$90   Single $60   (Continental Breakfast)
Child $20   Credit cards accepted Children welcome
1 Queen (1 bdrm)
Bathrooms: 1 Ensuite

Rhodohill is set in a mature 4 acre garden in picturesque Paradise Valley, 10km west of Rotorua. Its hillside setting, large trees and hundreds of rhododendrons, camellias etc. and many native birds offer a relaxing retreat within easy distance of major tourist attractions, golf courses and cafés and restaurants. The renowned Ngongotaha trout stream flows through the valley. Modern, self-contained accommodation with own entrance, ensuite bathroom, fully equipped kitchen, dining room-lounge. Smoke-free indoors. We also operate a specialist plant nursery.

ROTORUA - CENTRAL *Rotorua Central*

Tresco *B&B*
Gwyn & John Hanson
3 Toko Street, Rotorua

Tel (07) 348 9611 0800 TRESCO (873 726)
Fax (07) 3489611 trescorotorua@xtra.co.nz
www.trescorotorua.co.nz

Double $90 Single $50 (Full Breakfast)
Single ensuite $75 Triple $120 Credit cards accepted
1 King/Twin 3 Queen 2 Twin 2 Single (6 bdrm)
Bathrooms: 3 Ensuite 1 Private 2 Guests share

Central location - A warm welcome awaits you at our comfortable friendly home, situated on a tree-lined street only 150 metres from central Rotorua with its many attractions and excellent restaurants. Established for over 30 years and recently renovated, Tresco offers all the comforts of home. We serve a substantial breakfast and 24 hour complimentary refreshments. Genuine hot mineral pool. Free pick up from airport or bus terminal. Off-street parking. Laundry/drying facility. Guest survey gives us top marks for friendliness, cleanliness and location.

ROTORUA *2km N of Rotorua*

Ferntree Cottage *B&B Homestay Separate/Suite*
Val & Geoff Brannan
1 Tatai Street, Rotorua

Tel (07) 348 0000 0800 398 633
Mob 021 104 7203 or 021 049 1910
v.g.brannan@xtra.co.nz
www.bnb.co.nz/ferntreecottage.html

Double $80-$120 Single $70-$80 (Special Breakfast)
Child neg Credit cards accepted
1 Queen 1 Double (2 bdrm)
Bathrooms: 1 Ensuite 1 Host share

Welcome to our home and your suite with log fire for cold nights and garden deck for sunny days. Relax, explore or use our kayak on Lake Rotorua. Walk to town and local attractions. Soak in the jacuzzi. Pick up from local transport terminals. Meet Josiedog and Snappercat. We enjoy travel, travellers tales and sharing our knowledge of Rotorua and New Zealand. Stay longer than 2 nights and enjoy discounted rates. Begin your day with waffles, fresh fruit, brewed coffee and other tasty breakfast treats.

ROTORUA - NGONGOTAHA *8km N of Rotorua*

Bayadere Lodge *B&B Homestay*
Cynthia and Neil Clark
38 Hall Road, Ngongotaha, Rotorua

Tel 07 357 5965 Fax 07 357 5965
Mob 027 292 8520 c.clark@clear.net.nz
www.bnb.co.nz/bayaderelodge.html

Double $120-$150 Single $90-$100 (Full Breakfast)
Child neg Dinner $40pp
Credit cards accepted Children welcome
2 King 1 Twin (3 bdrm)
Bathrooms: 1 Ensuite 1 Private 1 Guests share

Bayadere Lodge, a modern spacious home which is 8km from Rotorua and 400 metres from Ngongotaha village and stream. We are close to the world famous attractions. Rainbow Springs, Skyline Rides, horse trekking and the Agrodome Sheep Show. The lake front and Waiteti stream are within walking distance. Our home has king and twin rooms with a guest lounge that has garden lake and rural views. Full breakfast is served. Tea/coffee complimentary, laundry service and ample parking. You will be welcomed as special guests in our home.

BAY OF PLENTY

ROTORUA   *2km N of Rotorua*

Moana Rose Lakeside Bed and Breakfast
B&B Homestay
Pauline and Bruce Kingston
23 Haumoana Street, Koutu, Rotorua

Tel (07) 349 2980 Fax (07) 349 2997
Mob 027 273 2008 moanarose@bktours.co.nz
www.bnb.co.nz/moanarose.html

Double $120 Single $80 (Full Breakfast)
Child $35 Credit cards accepted Children welcome
1 Queen 1 Twin (2 bdrm)
Bathrooms: 1 Private

Situated on the lake edge, 2km from the city centre, we offer a quiet relaxed atmosphere, including separate entrance, comfortable spacious bedrooms, electric blankets, own bathroom and a delightful garden spa. Enjoy our company or the privacy of your own sitting room, including Sky TV, fridge, tea/coffee facilities. From our sun deck walk down to the lake and watch the bird life grazing on the reserve with Lizzie our cat in hot pursuit. Bruce is a licensed tour operator and will gladly assist with your tour options. Welcome, Kia Ora.

ROTORUA - LAKE ROTOITI   *20km NE of Rotorua*

Kamahi Cottage *B&B Separate/Suite*
Sheryl & Kevin Jensen
137 Okere Road,
RD 4, Lake Rotoiti, Rotorua

Tel (07) 362 4244 Fax (07) 362 4244
Mob 027 4570 496 S&KJensen@xtra.co.nz
www.bnb.co.nz/jensen.html

Double $95-$105 Single $70 (Continental Breakfast)
Child $15 Credit cards accepted Children welcome
1 Queen 1 Twin (2 bdrm)
Bathrooms: 1 Private

Kamahi (ka-ma-he)is a cottage, separate from our home,
with beautiful views of Lake Rotoiti - a few steps to the water edge. Kayaks and bicylces are available. Handy to Okere Falls, whitewater rafting, bush walks, fishing, golf course. One room with queen bed, TV, radio, microwave, fridge, table/chairs, tea/coffee, breakfast provisions in cottage. Separate bathroom. Another room with twin beds. Fish smoker and BBQ available. We are friendly NZers and love meeting with you on the shared deck. 2 friendly small dogs.

ROTORUA   *10km E of Rotorua*

Peppertree Farm *B&B Farmstay*
Robyn Panther & Barry Morris
25 Cookson Road, RD 4, Rotorua

Tel (07) 345 3718 Fax (07) 345 3718
peppertree.farm@xtra.co.nz
www.bnb.co.nz/peppertree.html

Double $95-$105 Single $65 (Full Breakfast)
Child half price Credit cards accepted
Children welcome
1 Double 2 Twin (3 bdrm)
Bathrooms: 1 Ensuite 1 Guests share

Handy to the airport our quiet rural retreat overlooking Lake Rotorua provides a picturesque and homely welcome. Farm animals are horses, cows, sheep, a young donkey and chickens. Lucy, our cavalier king charles spaniel, is a house pet, and Ben, our very friendly labrador lives outside. We are knowledgable locals who enjoy horse-racing, rugby, most sports and meeting interesting people! If you wish to attend a Maori concert and hangi, we can arrange pick up and delivery back to the farm.

ROTORUA *30km S of Rotorua*

Caradoc Farm *B&B Farmstay*
Robyn & Bunny Stunell
466 Galatos Road, Ngakuru, RD 1, Rotorua

Tel (07) 333 2779   Fax (07) 333 2779
Mob 021 347 934   stunell@wave.co.nz
www.caradocfarm.co.nz

Double $95-$120 Single $70-$90 (Full Breakfast)
Child $25-$35   Dinner by arrangement
Credit cards accepted   Children welcome
2 Queen 1 Single (2 bdrm)
Bathrooms: 1 Private

Bunny and Robyn, our dog Mac and Cairo the cat extend a very warm welcome to our deer and beef farm. Take a break at Caradoc Farm, Bed & Breakfast/Farmstay accommodation. Our quiet and comfortable guest wing has 2 queen bedrooms with private bathroom and toilet facilities. We are a short drive to trout fishing lakes and Rotorua's cultural, thermal and adventure activities. Enjoy spectacular views overlooking Lake Ohakuri and Ngakuru. Complimentary farm tour offered : full breakfast : evening meals by arrangement.

ROTORUA *10km N of Rotorua*

Ngongotaha Lakeside Lodge *Lakestay B&B*
Lyndsay & Graham Butcher
41 Operiana Street, Ngongotaha, Rotorua

Tel (07) 357 4020 0800 144 020   Fax (07) 357 4020
Mob 021 266 1341   lake.edge@xtra.co.nz
www.bnb.co.nz/ngongotahalodge.html

Double $130-$190 Single $110-$170 (Full Breakfast)
Child neg over 12   Dinner by arrangement $40-$45pp
Credit cards accepted
1 King/Twin 1 King 2 Twin (3 bdrm)
Bathrooms: 3 Ensuite

Absolute lake edge, amazing, panaramic views, fishing, bird watching, great food and warm hospitality are what you will find at our spacious comfortable home. The upper level is exclusively for guests with fully equipped lounge/conservatory overlooking the lake. All bedrooms have ensuite facilities with everything provided. The famous Waiteti Stream is only metres away, with Rainbow and Brown Trout waiting to be caught. Free use of fishing gear and canoe ... You catch and we'll cook. Smoke-free inside. Safe parking and sulphur free.

ROTORUA *10km NE of Rotorua centre*

Lake Okareka B&B *Homestay Self-contained*
Patricia & Ken Scott
10 Okareka Loop Road, RD 5, Rotorua

Tel (07) 362 8245 0800 652 735
patricia.scott@xtra.co.nz
www.bnb.co.nz/lakeokarekabnb.html

Double $95-$120 Single $65   (Full Breakfast)
Dinner by arrangement Credit cards accepted
Children welcome
2 Double 1 Single (3 bdrm)
Bathrooms: 1 Private 1 Host share

Welcome to our modern home set in tranquil surroundings with stunning views. Take a stroll along the waters edge, enjoy the native bush, ferns and bird life. We are 10 minutes drive from city centre; conveniently situated for all tourist attractions and activities. Downstairs 1 self-contained unit, upstairs are 2 guest bedrooms. To find us turn off Te Ngae Road at the roundabout into Tarawera Road, travel to the Blue Lake then turn left into Okareka Loop Road. See you at number 10.

ROTORUA

Robertson House *B&B*
Patrice Legrande & John Ballard
70 Pererika Street, Rotorua

Tel (07) 343 7559 info@robertsonhouse.com
www.bnb.co.nz/robertson.html

Double $150 Single $120 (Full Breakfast) Child $80
1 King/Twin 2 Queen 1 Double 2 Twin (4 bdrm)
Bathrooms: 3 Ensuite 1 Private

Our historic home, only 2 minutes drive from the city centre, was built by one of Rotorua's forefathers, in 1905. Under the auspices of the Historic Places Trust it has been carefully renovated, retaining its colonial charm. Relax in its warm comfortable atmosphere, or take time out on the verandah and enjoy our old English cottage garden resplendent with colour and fragrance, citrus trees and grape vines. Our friendly hosts are happy to asssist with information and bookings for Rotorua's many Maori cultural, and sightseeing attractions.

TAUPO   *2km E of Taupo*

Yeoman's Lakeview Homestay   *B&B Homestay*
Colleen & Bob Yeoman
23 Rokino Road, Taupo 2730

Tel (07) 377 0283   Fax (07) 377 4683
www.bnb.co.nz/yeomans.html

Double $100   Single $50 (Full Breakfast)
Child $25   Dinner $30 by arrangement
Children welcome
1 Queen 3 Single (3 bdrm)
Bathrooms: 1 Ensuite 1 Guests share

Bob and I have enjoyed hosting for many years, our Lakeview Homestay with beautiful mountains backdrop makes our guests' stay in Taupo very special. Our home is spacious, comfortable and relaxing. All Taupo's attractions are nearby, golf courses, thermal pools, Huka Falls and fishing. We are retired sheep and cattle farmers, Bob excels at golf and is in charge of cooked breakfasts. Home-made jams and marmalade are my specialty. Turn into Huia Street from lakefront, take fourth turn on the rigth into Rokino Road. Off-street parking.

TAUPO   *3km S of Taupo*

Hawai Homestay   *Homestay Self-contained*
Jeanette Jones
18 Hawai Street, 2 Mile Bay, Taupo

Tel (07) 377 3242   Mob 025 234 0558
jeanettej@xtra.co.nz
www.beds-n-leisure.com/hawai.htm

Double $90   Single $60   (Full Breakfast) Child $20
Dinner $20   Marmite Cottage $65 double
Credit cards accepted Children welcome
1 Queen 1 Twin (2 bdrm)
Bathrooms: 1 Guests share

Come and relax and unwind in our comfortable modern warm home. Befriend our adorable shitzu who just loves visitors. Enjoy our hearty breakfasts, which include homemade muesli, muffins, bread and preserves. We are close to hot pools, good walking paths, the lake and restaurants. The self-contained cottage is ideal for families. A typical Kiwi bach, sleeps 7 - linen, firewood, books and games provided. Interests include church, travel, roses and crafts. Hawai Street comes off SH1.

TAUPO - ACACIA BAY   *5km W of Taupo*

Pariroa Homestay   *Homestay*
Joan & Eric Leersnijder
77A Wakeman Road,
Acacia Bay, Taupo

Tel (07) 378 3861 pariroa@xtra.co.nz
www.bnb.co.nz/pariroahomestay.html

Double $80   Single $65   (Full Breakfast)
Credit cards accepted
1 Queen 2 Single (2 bdrm)
Bathrooms: 1 Guests share

Views views! Our home is Scandinavian style with
wooden interior. Situated in a very quiet area and minutes from the beach, we have magnificent,
uninterrupted views of Lake Taupo and The Ranges from bedrooms and living room. We have travelled
extensively and Eric was previously a tea planter in Indonesia, having lived in The Netherlands, Spain
and Italy. Directions: turn down between 95 and 99 Wakeman Road. We are the last house on this short
road (200 metres).

TAUPO - ACACIA BAY   *6km W of Taupo*

Leece's Homestay   *Homestay*
Marlene and Bob Leece
98 Wakeman Road,
Acacia Bay, Taupo 2736

Tel (07) 378 6099
Fax (07) 378 6092
www.bnb.co.nz/leeceshomestay.html

Double $90   Single $60   (Continental Breakfast)
Credit cards accepted
1 King 1 Double 2 Single (2 bdrm)
Bathrooms: 1 Guests share

Your hosts Bob and Marlene extend a warm welcome to our large wood interior home with woodfire
for winter and north facing sunny deck from guest bedroom. Also magnificent view of Lake Taupo
from lounge and front deck. There are bush walks and steps down to lake to swim in summer. We are
awaiting your arrival with anticipation of making friends. Please phone for directions. Jaspa has arrived,
he is a birman cat.

TAUPO   *1km S of Taupo*

Pataka House   *Homestay Separate/Suite*
Raewyn & Neil Alexander
8 Pataka Road, Taupo

Tel (07) 378 5481   Fax (07) 378 5461
Mob 025 473 881 pataka@beds-n-leisure.com
www.patakahouse.co.nz

Double $100   Single $70   (Full Breakfast)
Child $30   Separate suite $120   Children welcome
2 Queen 4 Twin (4 bdrm)
Bathrooms: 1 Ensuite 1 Private 1 Guests share

Pataka House is highly recommended for its hospitality.
We assure guests that their stay lives up to New Zealand's reputation as being a home away from
home. We are easily located just one turn-off the lake front and up a tree-lined driveway. Our garden
room is privately situated, has an appealing décor and extremely popular to young and old alike. Stay
for one night or stay for more as Lake Taupo will truly be the highlight of your holiday. Toddy the cat
enjoys visitors.

TAUPO - ACACIA BAY   *5km W of Taupo*

Paeroa Lakeside Homestay   *B&B Homestay Separate/Suite*
Barbara & John Bibby
21 Te Kopua Street, Acacia Bay, Taupo

Tel (07) 378 8449   Fax (07) 378 8446   Mob 027 481 8829
bibby@reap.org.nz   www.taupohomestay.com

Double $200-$350 Single $200-$350 (Full Breakfast)
Child $75   Dinner $45   Triple (2 Rooms) $400
Credit cards accepted
2 King 1 Queen (3 bdrm)   Bathrooms: 3 Ensuite

Unique genuine lake front location. Paeroa's hosts Barbara and
John welcome you to their spacious modern quality homestay
at sheltered Acacia Bay, developed on 3 levels to capture the
magnificent uninterrupted, panoramic views of world famous
Lake Taupo and beyond. Catch a fishing charter with John in
his 30 foot cruiser. The house is large, comfortable and well
appointed for your comfort and privacy. Laundry service. A
large guest lounge, tea and coffee facilities. Close to all attractions. Central, stay several days.

TAUPO   *15km W of Taupo*

Ben Lomond   *Homestay Self-contained*
Mary & Jack Weston
1434 Poihipi Road,
RD 1, Taupo

Tel (07) 377 6033   Fax (07) 377 6033
Mob 025 774 080   benlomond@xtra.co.nz
www.bnb.co.nz/benlomond.html

(Full Breakfast) $100 per night for cottage
Credit cards accepted Children welcome Pets welcome
1 Queen 1 Twin (2 bdrm)
Bathrooms: 1 Private

Welcome to Ben Lomond. Jack and I have farmed here for 40 years and our comfortable family home is
set in a mature garden. There is a self-contained cottage in the garden where you can do your own thing,
or pop to the house for breakfast. We have interests in fishing, golf and the equestrian world and are
familiar with the attractions on the Central Plateau. Our pets include dogs and cats who wander in and
out. Taupo restaurants are 15 minutes away.

TAUPO   *Taupo Central*

Lakeland Homestay   *Homestay*
Lesley, Chris & Pussycats
11 Williams Street,
Taupo

Tel (07) 378 1952   Fax (07) 378 1912
Mob 025 877 971   lakeland.bb@xtra.co.nz
www.bnb.co.nz/lakelandhomestay.html

Double $100-$120 Single $60 (Continental Breakfast)
Credit cards accepted
1 Queen 2 Twin (2 bdrm)
Bathrooms: 1 Ensuite 1 Host share

Nestled in a restful tree-lined street, a mere 5 minutes
stroll from the Lake's edge and shopping centre, Lakeland Homestay is a cheerful and cosy home that
enjoys views of the lake and mountains. Keen gardeners, anglers and golfers Chris and Lesley work
and play in an adventure oasis. For extra warmth on winter nights all beds have electric blankets, and
laundry facilities are available. A courtesy car is available for coach travellers and there is off-street
parking. Please phone for directions.

TAUPO   *3km SE of Taupo*

Homestay
Ann & Dan Hennebry
28 Greenwich Street, Taupo

Tel (07) 378 9483   Mob 025 297 4283
brie@xtra.co.nz
www.bnb.co.nz/hennebry.html

Double $90   Single $60   (Full Breakfast)
Dinner $35
1 King 1 Single (2 bdrm)
Bathrooms: 1 Guests share

We enjoy having guests in our spacious home overlooking farmland and bordering Taupo's Botanical Gardens. We hope you will join us for dinner (maybe a barbecue in the summer) and complimentary wine in our pleasant dining room. There are many good restaurants in Taupo should you prefer that. Our launch, Bonita, is available for fishing or sightseeing on the beautiful lake - Dan is an excellent skipper. We look forward to welcoming you to our warm, comfortable, home.

TAUPO - COUNTRYSIDE   *35km NW of Taupo*

South Claragh & Bird Cottage
B&B Homestay Self-contained
Lesley & Paul Hill
South Claragh, 3245 Poihipi Road,
RD Mangakino, Taupo Region
Tel (07) 372 8848   Fax (07) 372 8047
welcome@countryaccommodation.co.nz
www.countryaccommodation.co.nz
Double $100-$140   Single $80-$90   (Full Breakfast)
Child $10-$45   Dinner $45pp   Credit card accepted
Bird Cottage   Double $100-$110   Child $10
1 Queen 1 Double 1 Single (3 bdrm)   Bathrooms: 2 Private

Turn into our leafy driveway and relax in tranquil, rambling gardens with donkeys, coloured sheep, outdoor dog. Accommodation options: 1. Enjoy bed & breakfast in our comfortable, centrally heated farmhouse. Delicious farm breakfasts. Home-grown produce and excellent cooking make dining recommended.
2. Settle into Bird Cottage which is self-contained and cosy, with delightful views. Perfect for 2, will sleep 3-4. Firewood and linen provided, cot available. No meals included, but breakfast/dinner happily prepared by arrangement. Children welcome. Details and pictures on our website.

TAUPO   *2km S of Taupo*

Bramham   *B&B Homestay*
Julia & John Bates
7 Waipahihi Avenue,
Taupo,

Tel (07) 378 0064   Fax (07) 378 0065
Mob 025 240 9643 & 021 240 9643
info@bramham.co.nz
www.bramham.co.nz

Double $100-$110 Single $60-$80 (Full Breakfast)
1 Double 2 Twin 1 Single (3 bdrm)
Bathrooms: 3 Ensuite

Bramham is situated just 2 minutes walk form the Hot Beach of Lake Taupo and offers tremendous views of the lake and mountains to the south.   John and Julia, having spent 24 years in the RNZAF, including service with the USAF in Tucson Arizona, welcome you to our quiet, homely and peaceful atmosphere. Hearty breakfasts are our specialty. Local knowledge is our business. Bus terminal and airport service complimentary. Being non-smokers our dogs, Koko and Daisy, ask you not to smoke in our home.

TAUPO   *14km NW of Taupo*

Minarapa   *Homestay Rural Homestay*
Barbara & Dermot Grainger
620 Oruanui Road, RD 1, Taupo

Tel (07) 378 1931   Mob 025 272 2367
info@minarapa.co.nz
www.minarapa.co.nz

Double $110-$130 Single $90-$100   (Full Breakfast)
Child price on application   Dinner by arrangement
Credit cards accepted
1 King/Twin 2 Queen 2 Single (4 bdrm)
Bathrooms: 2 Ensuite 1 Private

Wend your way along a wonderful tree-lined drive into rural tranquillity. Minarapa, our 11 acre country retreat, 12 minutes from Taupo, 45 minutes from Rotorua and central to the region's main tourist attractions, is a great place to unwind. Here you may wander among colourful tree-sheltered gardens, play tennis, billiards, or ball with Toby the dog, or relax in our guest lounge/games room. Retire to spacious guest rooms, 2 with balcony, appointed with your comfort in mind. Barbara speaks fluent German.

TAUPO   *2km S of Taupo*

Mountain Views Homestay   *Homestay*
Bridget & Jack Grice
17B Puriri Street, Taupo

Tel (07) 378 6136   Fax (07) 378 6134
Mob 021 268 0711 & 021 122 7248
mtviews@reap.org.nz
www.bnb.co.nz/mountainviewshomestay.html

Double $80 Single $50   (Continental Breakfast)
Child neg   Dinner by arrangement
Credit cards accepted
2 Queen 1 Single (2 bdrm)
Bathrooms: 1 Guests share

Enjoy a warm welcome and a nice cuppa on arrival. Our spacious home is cool in summer and warm in winter. Breakfast is served in the main living room and includes Bridget's home-made bread and jams. We recommend 2 restaurants just around the corner. We're just a short walk to the lake. With over 10 years in tourism, Jack and Bridget are very knowlegeable about this area. We enjoy many local walks. Off-street parking. Phone for directions.

TAUPO   *2km S of Info Centre*

Gillies of Taupo - Gillies Lodge
Margi Martin & Alan Malpas
77 Gillies Ave, Box 1924,
Taupo

Tel (07) 377 2377
Fax (07) 377 2377
info@gilliesoftaupo.co.nz
www.bnb.co.nz/gilliesoftaupo.html

Double $95-$115 Single $75
4 Double 8 Single (9 bdrm)
Bathrooms: 9 Ensuite

Taupo's original licensed guest house, minutes from Lake Taupo and town. A perfect base for groups to explore and enjoy Taupo and the region's many attractions. Warm, peaceful, sunny and quiet with ample off-street parking. With a pot of good coffee or tea, relax and enjoy the views or sunsets from the lounge with log fire and library or sit outside on the lounge deck. Breakfast with your hosts Alan and Margi and share their intimate local knowledge and sense of history. Children by arrangement. Extra facilities available. Discuss jet boat rides.

TAUPO   *10km NW of Taupo*

Whitiora Farm   *Farmstay*
Judith & Jim McGrath
1281 Mapara Road, RD 1, West Taupo

Tel (07) 378 6491   Fax (07) 378 6491
mcg.whitiora@xtra.co.nz
www.bnb.co.nz/whitiorafarm.html

Double **$100**   Single $60   (Full Breakfast)
Child $25   Dinner $30   Lunch $15 by arrangement
Children welcome
1 Queen 3 Single (3 bdrm)
Bathrooms: 1 Private 1 Host share

Three course dinner, booking essential. Breakfast: your choice of cereal, home-grown fruit, eggs, bacon, sausages, home-made bread and conserves, coffee, English/herb tea. Our 461 acre farm grazes sheep, cattle, deer, thoroughbred horses, which we breed and Jim trains and races. Judith enjoys gardening, and serving home grown produce. We enjoy sharing our large comfortable home, garden, farm, welcome children (5-12 $25, under 5 negotiable). We appreciate you not smoking in our home. Booking advisable to avoid disappointment.

TAUPO   *13km N of Taupo*

Bellbird Ridge Alpaca Farm
B&B Farmstay Self-contained
Mike & Lorraine Harrison
68 Tangye Road, RD 1, Taupo

Tel (07) 377 1996   Fax (07) 377 1992
Mob 025 668 7754   lharrison@xtra.co.nz
www.bnb.co.nz/bellbirdridge.html

Double **$100-$130**   Single $90   (Full Breakfast)
Child $30   Dinner $40pp by arrangement
Credit cards accepted   Children welcome Pets welcome
2 Queen 1 Twin 1 Single (4 bdrm)
Bathrooms: 1 Ensuite 1 Private

Our 1 bedroom self-contained cottage is the perfect retreat to relax, unwind and enjoy the serenity of country life. The cottage has quality fittings and nestles into our extensive garden with deck overlooking the pond. We also have available in the main house a twin bedroom, a single bedroom and a large double bedroom, where you would be our only guests. Situated on 10 acres, the cottage and homestead have sweeping rural views and 15 minutes easy drive from Taupo and 1.5 hours from the snowfields.

TAUPO   *5km S of Taupo centre*

Beside Lake Taupo   *B&B Homestay*
Irene & Roger Foote
8 Chad Street, Taupo

Tel (07) 378 5847   Fax (07) 378 5847
Mob 025 804 683   besidelaketaupo@xtra.co.nz
www.besidelaketaupo.co.nz

Double $220-$250   (Full Breakfast)
Credit cards accepted
2 King/Twin 1 Queen (3 bdrm)
Bathrooms: 1 Ensuite 2 Private

Our luxury, shoreline, eco-friendly home has garaging with internal access to house and elevator. Rooms have lake views, balcony or terrace, Sky TV, guest controlled air-conditioning/heating and tea/coffee. Organic ingredients for the breakfast of your choice. Laundry, email/fax, hairdryers and robes for guest use. Enjoy the lakeshore bird life. Kayaks and dinghy provided. Walks, boating, fishing and swimming from site. Explore the volcanic countryside and experience the numerous adventure and leisure activities available locally. Enjoy your break beside the lake.

TAUPO   *2.5km S of Taupo*

Fairviews   *Homestay Boutique Accommodation*
Brenda Watson & Mike Hughes
8 Fairview Terrace, Taupo

Tel (07) 377 0773 fairviews@reap.org.nz
www.reap.org.nz/~fairviews

Double $115-$145 Single $95-$110 (Full Breakfast)
Credit cards accepted
1 Queen 1 Twin (2 bdrm)
Bathrooms: 1 Ensuite 1 Private

You are invited to stay at our modern smoke-free homestay situated in a tranquil neighbourhood within walking distance of hot Pools and lake. Relax and enjoy Fairview's gardens. Be as private as you wish or socialise with hosts. Rooms are tastefully decorated and comfortable. Double room is large with private entrance, TV, fridge, tea/coffee facilities, robe and hairdryer. Generous breakfasts provided. Email facilities and laundry are available at small charge. Our regional knowledge is extensive. Interests include theatre, travel, cycling, tramping, antiques/collectables.

TAUPO   *2km SE of Taupo*

Finial House   *B&B Homestay*
Jan & Neil Fleming
51 Ngauruhoe Street, Taupo

Tel (07) 377 4347   Fax (07) 377 4348
Mob 025 685 8255   n.j.fleming@xtra.co.nz
www.finial-homestay.co.nz

Double $120-$150 Single $90-$125 (Full Breakfast)
Dinner $25-35 Credit cards accepted
2 King/Twin 2 Queen (3 bdrm)
Bathrooms: 2 Ensuite 1 Host share

Finial House is a spacious home in a peaceful setting. Enjoy the magnificent views of the lake and volcanic mountains from our extensive lounge, or deck with a relaxing spa pool. Close to town and lake with their many attractions. We are ex-dairy farmers who enjoy talking with you about your travels and interests. Our interests are: sports, travel, music, walking, running and gardening. Our 3 children have families of their own and we are left with our 2 timid cats.

TAUPO   *16km N of Taupo*

Brackenhurst
B&B Homestay Separate/Suite Self-contained
Barbara & Ray Graham
801 Oruanui Road, RD1, Taupo

Tel (07) 377 6451 Fax (07) 377 6451
Mob 0274 456 217   rgbg@xtra.co.nz
www.bnb.co.nz/brackenhurst2.html

Double $100   Single $60   (Full Breakfast) Child $30
Dinner $35   C/C accepted Children and Pets welcome
1 Queen 1 Double 4 Single (3 bdrm)
Bathrooms: 2 Ensuite 2 Private

Brackenhurst is a warm modern Lockwood design home on 14 acres of peaceful countryside with fantails, tuis, & bellbirds in the large garden.We have friendly highland cattle and lovely donkeys. We offer a warm welcome with peace and tranquility. You can also practise your chipping and putting. We are half a kilometre from SH1 and close to Huka Falls, geothermal activities, golf courses and a day's outing to Rotorua, Waitomo Caves or Napier. Private guests wing in the house or a separate annex offer away from home comforts. Breakfast to suit, continental style or full English. Dinner is available by arrangement.

TAUPO - ACACIA BAY   *7km W of Taupo*

Hazeldene Lodge   *B&B Homestay*
Judy & Tony Pratt
119 Acacia Heights Drive, Acacia Bay, Taupo

Tel (07) 377 0560   Fax (07) 377 0560   Mob 025 609 2647
hazeldene@xtra.co.nz   www.hazeldenelodge.co.nz

Double $150-$195 Single $140-$195 (Full Breakfast) Child POA
Dinner by arrangement Credit cards accepted Children welcome
1 Super King/Twin 3 Queen 1 Double (5 bdrm)
Bathrooms: 5 Ensuite

We warmly invite you to come and stay with us at Hazeldene Lodge which has been architecturally designed, which is set in 2 acres of landscaped gardens planted with many native shrubs and bushes, but also lots of English plants. We have stunning views of Mount Tauhara and Lake Taupo, from here you can easily access the nearby attractions of the town, Huka Falls, international golf courses, geothermal activity, and some excellent restaurants all of which are only 7km away.

We ran a very successful Bed & Breakfast in Devon England for 3 years before coming to New Zealand and we are offering the same high standard of 'Home from Home' accommodation.

All our bedrooms have been very tastefully furnished and fitted out with all the luxuries in life, such as TV, electric blankets, hair dryers, iron and ironing board, coffee and tea making facilities. Also from your rooms you have spectacular views during the day, and by night twinkling lights of Taupo township are gorgeous. We assure you of a very relaxing time and a comfortable stay.

Please phone, fax or email for bookings, or visit our website. Hazeldene Lodge is a stunning architectually designed up-market home planned specifically for the comfort of guests.

TAUPO - ACACIA BAY   *5km W of Taupo*

Bay View Homestay   *Homestay*
Marion & Guy Whitehouse
50/1 Wakeman Road, Acacia Bay, Taupo

Tel (07) 378 7873   Fax (07) 378 7893
Mob 021 211 2904
www.bnb.co.nz/bayviewhomestay.html

Double $100   Single $60   (Continental Breakfast)
Dinner by arrangement
1 Queen 1 Twin (2 bdrm)
Bathrooms: 1 Guests share

Enjoy the warm hospitality with your hosts Marion and Guy, retired deer farmers and friendly cat Kita. Our quiet, relaxing, modern, contemporary home of native timbers offers open-plan living, air-conditioning, double glazing, off-road parking. Spectacular panoramic views of Lake Taupo and mountains. Taupo's shimmering lights by night. Minutes from lake, fishing, tennis, native walks, restaurant. 5km to Taupo township and local attracions, thermal pools, Huka Falls, Huka jet, chartered fishing, bungy, golf. Bookings can be arranged. Please phone for directions.

TAUPO   *3km S of Taupo*

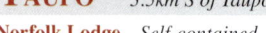

Moorhill   *B&B Boutique Accommodation*
Liz & Peter Sharland
27 Korimako Road, Taupo

Tel (07) 377 1069   Fax (07) 377 1069
Mob 021 300 455   petenlizr@xtra.co.nz
www.moorhill.co.nz

Double $125-$160   Single $110-$130
(Special Breakfast) Dinner b/a   Credit cards accepted
1 King/Twin 1 Queen (2 bdrm)
Bathrooms: 2 Ensuite

A warm welcome awaits you at Moorhill. Set in a
peaceful, mature garden our home is ideally situated
for relaxing weekends or experiencing Taupo's adventurous activities. Downstairs queen room with luxury ensuite has sitting area and garden access. Upstairs room has super king or twin bed(s), ensuite, sitting area with lake view. Rooms have hairdryer, electric blankets, fridge, tea/coffee making, ironing facilities. Guest lounge opens onto sunny decks. Choose breakfast style at your leisure. Ample parking. Discounts for extended stays and winter weekend specials.

TAUPO   *3.5km S of Taupo*

Norfolk Lodge   *Self-contained*
Elizabeth Lomas
1 Norfolk Road,
Taupo

Tel (07) 377 4318   Mob 025 605 0724
liz@norfolk-lodge.co.nz
www.norfolk-lodge.co.nz

Self-contained $175 per night for 4
Credit cards accepted   Children welcome
3 Double 2 Single (2 bdrm)
Bathrooms: 2 Guests share

Discover Norfolk Lodge situated in a tranquil tree setting
with stunning lake views. Enjoy space and style in your private self-contained apartment with fully equipped kitchen and laundry. What could be better than watching the sunset over the lake from your secluded garden patio? Short stroll to scenic lakeside walks. 4 minutes drive to Taupo's many top class restaurants and shops. Located in a quiet cul-de-sac with ample off-street parking. Sorry, the apartment is not suitable for children under 9.

TAUPO - ACACIA BAY *5km W of Taupo*

The Loft *B&B*
Grace Andrews & Peter Rosieur
3 Wakeman Road, Acacia Bay, Taupo

Tel (07) 377 1040 Fax (07) 377 1049 Mob 027 485 1347
book@theloftnz.com www.theloftnz.com

Double $125-$175 Single $90-$120 (Full Breakfast)
Child $50-$75 Dinner $30-$45 Credit cards accepted
3 Queen 2 Single (3 bdrm)
Bathrooms: 3 Ensuite

Situated five minutes from Taupo township and a few minutes walk to Lake Taupo *The Loft* is set in a small cottage garden adjacent to a native bush reserve.

Your hosts, Peter & Grace are friendly people who delight in the best things in life. Both have travelled extensively throughout New Zealand and the rest of the world. Their passions vary from food and fine wine to tramping and gardening. Enjoy their scrumptious breakfast of fresh fruit salad, freshly squeezed orange juice, freshly baked muffins and croissants; wonderful scrambled eggs with mushrooms, bacon and home-grown tomatoes – an experience not to be missed. Arrange an evening meal at *The Loft* and be treated to a pleasurable three course dinner that will leave you with a lasting memory of New Zealand hospitality. After dinner, join your hosts for a complimentary port before retiring for a good nights sleep.

The upstairs guest accommodation comprises 3 private bedrooms with queen-size beds and ensuite bathrooms. The guest lounge, with an open fire welcomes you to relax and enjoy afternoon tea whilst chatting about the Taupo region and your sight seeing plans. Trout fishing trips and adventure treks can be arranged by your hosts along with a myriad of other more relaxing activities.

Grace and Peter look forward to sharing their home and their company with you, assuring you of a warm welcome and a luxurious stay. Turtle the red-eared turtle and Sweetie, the cat complete the family. **Directions:** www.theloftnz.com

Rustic, romantic and warm where attention to detail shows that your comfort takes top priority

TAUPO   *15km N of Taupo*

Maimoa House   *B&B Farmstay Homestay*
Margaret & Godfrey Ellis
41 Oak Drive, Taupo
(Off Palmer Mill Road)

Tel (07) 376 9000   mewestview@xtra.co.nz
www.maimoahomestay.co.nz

Double $95-$110 **Single $65**   (Special Breakfast)
Child $30   Dinner by arrangement $30
Credit cards accepted
Children welcome Pets welcome
1 Queen 1 Double 1 Twin (3 bdrm)
Bathrooms: 1 Guests share

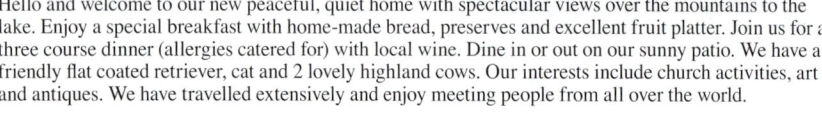

Hello and welcome to our new peaceful, quiet home with spectacular views over the mountains to the lake. Enjoy a special breakfast with home-made bread, preserves and excellent fruit platter. Join us for a three course dinner (allergies catered for) with local wine. Dine in or out on our sunny patio. We have a friendly flat coated retriever, cat and 2 lovely highland cows. Our interests include church activities, art and antiques. We have travelled extensively and enjoy meeting people from all over the world.

TAUPO   *1km N of Town Centre*

Magnifique   *B&B Homestay*
Gay & Rex Eden
52 Woodward Street,
Taupo

Tel (07) 378 4915   Fax (07) 378 4915
Mob 021 388 498   info@magnifique.co.nz
www.magnifique.co.nz

Double $125-$135 **Single $85-$100**
(Special Breakfast) Credit cards accepted
2 Queen 1 Twin (3 bdrm)
Bathrooms: 2 Private

Leave your car and walk to dinner. We are just 6 minutes walk from Taupo's lovely restaurants and shops. But before you do, enjoy refreshments with home-baking while taking in the magnificent panoramic views of town, lake and mountains. Our life's focus is people, so be assured of a warm welcome and the highest standards of comfort and hospitality. Each room has tea making facilities, fridge, TV. We will treat you with our special breakfasts which have not yet failed to delight our guests.

TURANGI   *1.5km E of Turangi Central*

The Andersons'
B&B Homestay Self-contained cottage
Betty & Jack Anderson
3 Poto Street, Turangi

Tel (07) 386 8272   Fax (07) 386 8272
Mob 025 628 0810   jbanderson@xtra.co.nz
www.bnb.co.nz/anderson.html

Double $100 **Single $80**   (Full Breakfast)
Self-contained cottage $80-$150
Child in cottage only Credit cards accepted
2 Queen 1 Twin (3 bdrm)   Bathrooms: 3 Ensuite

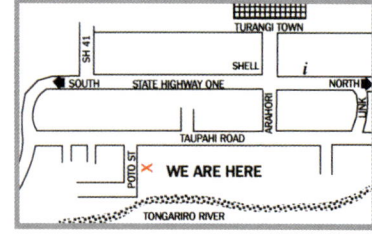

Welcome to our smoke-free home, with ensuite bathrooms for your comfort. Situated in a quiet street, beside Tongariro River walkway, handy to restaurants and town and fishing. Arranged transport to Tongariro National Park at your door. Lake Taupo and thermal baths 5 minutes drive. Upstairs queen rooms with balconies, separated for privacy by tea/coffee making area. Downstairs has twin suite, laundry and lounge where we'll share interests in flying, skiing, fishing, tramping, and maps of our volcanic area. Guest-shy cat. Cottage is suitable for families.

TURANGI   *53km S of Taupo*

Akepiro Cottage   *B&B Self-contained*
Jenny & John Wilcox
PO Box 256, Turangi

Tel **(07) 386 7384**   Fax (07) 386 6838
jennywilcox@xtra.co.nz
www.bnb.co.nz/akepirocottage.html

Double $100   Single $60   Twin $100
(Continental Breakfast on request $10)
Credit cards accepted   Children welcome
2 Queen 2 Single (2 bdrm)
Bathrooms: 1 Private

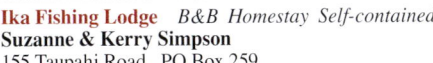

Half-acre woodland garden, featuring rhododendrons and native plants, attracting many species of birds. Access through garden gate to Tongariro River, major fishing pools. Perfect retreat for restful break. Close to excellent 18 hole golf course, ¹/₂ hour to the mountains, the Tongariro Crossing. Many walking tracks and World Heritage park. Our home and garden are adjacent, but utmost privacy maintained. Full kitchen, laundry, linen & power including TV, BBQ. Breakfast must be requested if required. Come, share this corner of nature's paradise.

TURANGI   *1km E of Turangi*

Ika Fishing Lodge   *B&B Homestay Self-contained*
Suzanne & Kerry Simpson
155 Taupahi Road, PO Box 259,
Turangi

Tel **(07) 386 5538**   Fax (07) 386 5538
ikalodge@xtra.co.nz
www.ika.co.nz

Double $140-$160   Single $120-$140   (Full Breakfast)
Dinner $50pp Self-contained apartment $160-$250
Credit cards accepted
2 King/Twin 3 Queen (4 bdrm)
Bathrooms: 3 Ensuite

You open the back gate and there is the Island Pool. We can now offer 1 self-contained unit with 2 bedrooms, kitchen, lounge and sun deck. 2 double rooms inside the lodge with ensuites. A spacious lounge with open fire is available along with Sky TV. Kerry, your guide has fished the area for 50 years and has been a guide for some 30 years. Suzanne, the other Simpson partner is your resident chef and is renowned for her trout sashimi. Please come and enjoy.

TURANGI - MOTUOAPA   *10km N of Turangi*

Meredith House   *B&B Self-contained*
Frances & Ian Meredith
45 Kahotea Place, Motuoapa, RD2, Turangi

Tel **(07) 386 5266**   Fax (07) 386 5270
meredith.house@xtra.co.nz
www.bnb.co.nz/meredithhouse.html

Double $90   Single $60   (Continental Breakfast)
Self-contained (breakfast extra) $100-$120
Credit cards accepted Children welcome
1 Queen 3 Single (2 bdrm)
Bathrooms: 1 Private

Stop and enjoy this outdoor paradise. Just off SH1 (B&B Sign). Overlooking Lake Taupo, our 2 storey home offers ground floor self-contained accommodation with own entrance. Full breakfast on request. Fully equipped kitchen, dining room, lounge. 2 cosy bedrooms (each with TV). Vehicle/boat off-street parking. Minutes to marina and world-renowned lake/river fishing. Beautiful bush walks. 45 minutes to ski fields and Tongariro National Park. Our association with Tongariro/Taupo area spans over 30 years, through work and outdoor pursuits. Welcome to our retreat.

BAY OF PLENTY

TURANGI *54km S of Taupo*

Founders at Turangi *B&B Homestay*
Peter & Chris Stewart
253 Taupahi Road, Turangi

Tel **(07) 386 8539**   0800 FOUNDERS
Fax (07) 386 8534   Mob 025 854 000
founders@ihug.co.nz   www.founders.co.nz

Double $170   Single $100   (Full Breakfast)
Whole lodge, sleeps 12-13 persons neg
Credit cards accepted
1 King/Twin 1 King 3 Queen (4 bdrm)
Bathrooms: 4 Private

Welcome to Turangi and to our New Zealand colonial-style home. Relax and enjoy the unique beauty of the "trout fishing capital of the world". Many outdoor activities are available at this "place for all seasons", with the Tongariro river, mountains and magnificent Lake Taupo on our doorstep. 4 ensuite bedrooms open on to the veranda. Enjoy breakfast outside in the summer or pre-dinner drinks by the fire après-ski in the winter! Our friendly dog has her own kennel. Whole lodge available - sleeps 13 self-catered.

TURANGI *52km S of Taupo*

The Birches *B&B*
Tineke & Peter Baldwin
13 Koura Street,
Turangi

Tel **(07) 386 5140**   Fax (07) 386 5149
Mob 021 149 6594   tineke.peter@xtra.co.nz
www.bnb.co.nz/thebirches.html

Double $120   Single $100   (Special Breakfast)
Dinner by arrangement   Credit cards accepted
1 Queen (1 bdrm)
Bathrooms: 1 Ensuite

Close to the world renowned Tongariro River we offer a charming and gracious residence in a quiet street. This unique setting has exceptional access to tramping, fly fishing, skiing, rafting or purely a retreat from life's hustle and bustle. Enjoy superior and spacious ensuite accommodation with TV and coffee/tea making facilities in a separate part of the house. Your Dutch/Canadian hosts have considerable international experience and can speak Dutch and French. Dinner by arrangement.

TURANGI *16km NW of Turangi*

Wills' Place *B&B*
Jill & Brian Wills
145 Omori Road, Omori

Tel **(07) 386 7339**   Fax (07) 386 7339
Mob 027 228 8960   willsplace@wave.co.nz
www.laketaupo.co.nz/turangi/motels/willsplace/

Double $110   Single $80   (Full Breakfast) Child neg
Dinner by arrangement
Credit cards accepted   Children welcome
2 Queen 3 Single (2 bdrm)
Bathrooms: 1 Private

Our home is lakeside in the beautiful southwest corner of Lake Taupo with wonderful views, excellent fishing, boating, swimming, walks. Just off the beaten track, yet only 10-15 minutes to shops, restaurants, thermal pools, Tongariro River, rafting, kayaking, etc. 40 minutes to Tongariro National Park and ski fields. We offer a comfortable 2 bedroom suite with separate entry and complete privacy. Private bathroom with bath and shower. Tea making facilities, fridge, microwave, television, laundry. A special place we'd love to share with you.

TURANGI   *16km NW of Turangi*

Inukshuk Homestay   *B&B Homestay*
Peter and Sharon Simpson
56 Te Waaka Terrace, Kuratau, RD 1, Turangi

Tel (07) 386 5686   Fax (07) 386 5683
Mob 021 272 9464 or 021 811 182
inukshukhomestay@attglobal.net
www.inukshukhomestay.co.nz

Double $125-$150 Single $100-$125   Child negotiable
Dinner by arrangement   Credit cards accepted
1 King 1 Queen (2 bdrm)
Bathrooms: 1 Ensuite 1 Private

At Inukshuk Homestay we warmly welcome guests
to our new home with panoramic views of Lake Taupo. Our beautifully appointed guest rooms are
furnished with your comfort in mind and include many extras. We are centrally located 10 minutes
from restaurants and 40 minutes from the ski fields and National Park. Your day begins with a
sumptuous special breakfast before enjoying local adventure activities, thermal pools, bush walks, and
trout fishing.

TURANGI   *2km N of Turangi*

Dyden Cottage   *B&B Separate/Suite Self-contained*
Sarah & Graeme Henshaw
Old Mill Lane, 134 Grace Road RD 2, Turangi

Tel (07) 386 6050   Fax (07) 386 6052
Mob 021 402 278   dydencottage@xtra.co.nz
www.bnb.co.nz/dydencottage.html

Double $90   Single $60 (Breakfast provisions supplied)
Child $10   Dinner $35 by arrangement
Credit cards accepted   Children welcome
1 Queen 1 Single (1 bdrm)
Bathrooms: 1 Ensuite

Dyden Cottage offers self-contained accommodation set in five acres of mature gardens and farmland.
It has a separate entrance and private outdoor area. The cottage sleeps three and includes an ensuite
bathroom and living area with television. The kitchen is stocked with everything you need for breakfast,
including fresh eggs from the property. Enjoy the peace and tranquility of your surroundings or take
advantage of the world class fly fishing, bush walks, golf, boating, river rafting and skiing all within easy
reach of Turangi.

BAY OF PLENTY

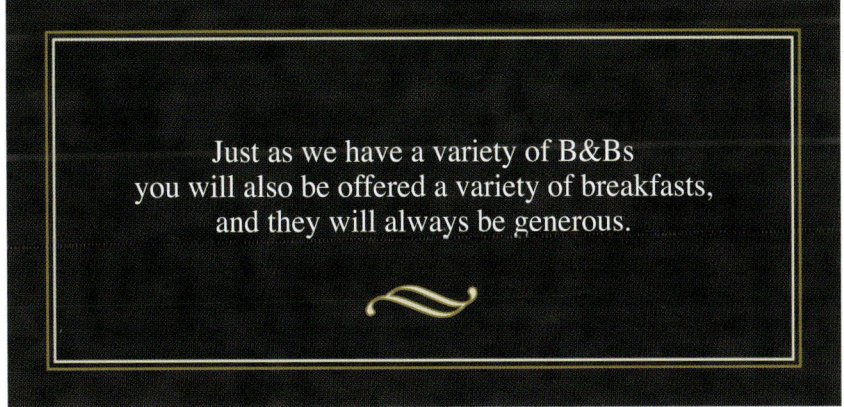

Just as we have a variety of B&Bs
you will also be offered a variety of breakfasts,
and they will always be generous.

Gisborne

Waihau Bay

Te Kaha

Maraenui

35

Anaura Bay

Tolaga Bay

2

Waipaoa

Ormond

Gisborne

Tiniroto

2

Towns listed generally follow
a north to south route. Refer
to the index if required.

0   Kilometres   20

0   Miles   12

ANAURA BAY   *23km N of Tolaga Bay*

Anaura Beachstay or Willowflat Farmstay B&B
B&B Farmstay Self-contained Beachstay
June & Allan Hall
Anaura Bay, Tolaga Bay East Cape 3854, Gisborne

Tel (06) 862 6341   Fax (06) 862 6371
Mob 021 039 1136   willowflat@xtra.co.nz
www.anaurabeachstay.com

Double $100   Single $70   (Full Breakfast)
Child ¹/2 price   Dinner $25
Self-contained beachfront cottage $120-$200
1 Queen 1 Double (2 bdrm)   Bathrooms: 2 Host share

Paradise – the best of both worlds – Breakfast in tranquility on our deck in picturesque Anaura Bay, glorious sunrises, white sand and backdrop of beautiful native bush, fishing, walkways..... or soak in the spa at our spacious home Willowflat, our sheep, cattle and cropping farm. Tolaga Bay Village, medical centre, takeaways, Cashmere Company, fishing charters, hunting, golf, within 12km of Willowflat or 23km of Beachstay. Self-contained option available - both venues $120-$180 per night for 2 couples, plus $20 per extra adult, minimum 2 nights stay.

TOLAGA BAY   *3km N of "Tolaga Bay, Gisborne 55km"*

Papatahi   *Homestay Self-contained*
Nicki & Bruce Jefferd
427 Main Road North, Tolaga Bay

Tel (06) 862 6623   Fax (06) 862 6623
Mob 021 283 7178   nickibrucej@xtra.co.nz
www.bnb.co.nz/papatahi.html

Double $95   Single $60   (Full Breakfast)
Child ¹/2 price   Dinner $25   Children welcome
1 Queen 1 Double (2 bdrm)
Bathrooms: 1 Ensuite 1 Guests share

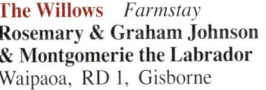

Papatahi Homestay is very easy to find being just 3km north of the Tolaga Bay township, on the Pacific Coast Highway. We have a comfortable, modern, sunny home set in a wonderful garden. Papatahi offers separate accommodation with ensuite. A golf course, fishing charters, the Tolaga Bay Cashmere Co and several magnificent beaches are all just minutes away. Daily farm activities are often of interest to our guests. Friendly farm pets and 3 children add to the experience! Great country meals and good wine are a speciality. Inspection will impress!

WAIPAOA   *20km N of Gisborne*

The Willows   *Farmstay*
**Rosemary & Graham Johnson
& Montgomerie the Labrador**
Waipaoa, RD 1, Gisborne

Tel (06) 862 5605   Fax (06) 862 5601
Mob 0274 837 365
www.bnb.co.nz/thewillows.html

Double $80   Single $50   (Full Breakfast)
Child 10% discount   Dinner $30 by arrangement
2 Queen 2 Single (3 bdrm)
Bathrooms: 1 Private 1 Guests share

Our home is situated on a hill amid a park like garden with some wonderful trees planted by our forefathers. We enjoy the amenities available in the city and also the country life on our 440 acre property involving deer, cattle, sheep, grapes and cropping. We now offer a double bedroom with a private bathroom. The bedroom has its own access so you can enjoy privacy if you so desire. We are situated 20km north of Gisborne on SH2 through the scenic Waioeka Gorge.

GISBORNE

ORMOND   *18km N of Gisborne*

Kiwifruit Orchard Stay
B&B Orchard Stay Large self-contained villa
Jenny & Greig Foster
37 Bond Road, RD 1, Gisborne

Tel (06) 862 5688   Fax (06) 862 5688
Mob 027 441 2876   jdfoster@ihug.co.nz
www.bnb.co.nz/kiwifruitorchardstay.html

Double $95-$120 Single $85-$95
(Continental Breakfast) Child $25
Dinner $35 Children welcome
3 Queen 3 Single (3 bdrm)   Bathrooms: 2 Private

Set amongst the chardonnay capital of NZ. Country living with style and comfort. Stay in our Villa Moderna, self-contained or our home with private lounge and bathroom. Spend lazy afternoons in the sun sampling wine from our local wineries. During the chillier winter nights take a long soak in our indoor spa and watch the stars set amongst the chardonnay capital of NZ. Come relax with us and our cats and dogs on our kiwifruit orchard and sample the fruit. 5 minutes to restaurant bar/grill. Fax, internet, email, spa, swimming pool available.

GISBORNE   *5km NE of Gisborne*

Beach Stay   *B&B Beachstay*
Peter & Dorothy Rouse
111 Wairere Road, Wainui Beach, Gisborne

Tel (06) 868 8111   Fax (06) 868 8162
Mob 027 479 4929
pete.dot@xtra.co.nz
www.bnb.co.nz/beachstaygisborne.html

Double $85   Single $50   (Full Breakfast)
Child $10   Dinner $25
1 Queen 2 Double 2 Single (2 bdrm)
Bathrooms: 1 Ensuite 1 Private

We welcome you to our home which is situated right on the beach front at Wainui. The steps from the lawn lead down to the beach, which is renowned for its lovely clean sand, surf, pleasant walking and good swimming. Gisborne can also offer a host of entertainment, including golf on one of the finest golf courses, charter fishing trips, wine trails, Eastwood Hill Arboretum, horse trekking etc, or you may wish to relax on the beach for the day with a light luncheon provided.

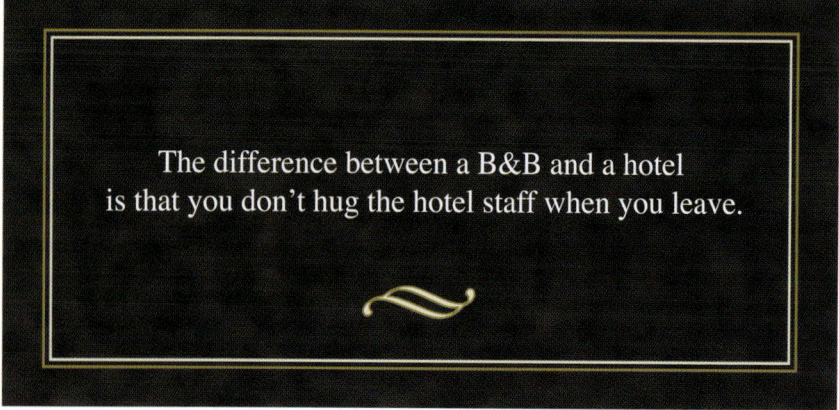

The difference between a B&B and a hotel
is that you don't hug the hotel staff when you leave.

GISBORNE   *8km N of Gisborne*

Makorori Heights   *Homestay*
Roger & Morag Shanks
36 Sirrah Street, Wainui Beach, Gisborne

Tel (06) 867 0806   Fax (06) 868 7706
Mob 021 250 4918
www.bnb.co.nz/makororiheights.html

Double $80   Single $45   (Full Breakfast)
Dinner $25   Credit cards accepted
1 Double 2 Single (2 bdrm)
Bathrooms: 1 Guests share

Our home is ¹/2 km off Highway 35 at the northern end of Wainui Beach. With beautiful sea and sunrise views, surrounded by farmland and our own young olive grove. Handy to bush and coastal walkways. We have travelled overseas and enjoy the company of others. Roger is a water colour artist with examples of his overseas and local works available for viewing or purchase. Horse trekking, fishing trips, country excursions by arrangements. We have one friendly small dog not allowed indoors.

GISBORNE   *1km E of Gisborne*

Fox Street Retreat   *B&B Homestay*
Jan Saunders
103 Fox Street, Gisborne

Tel (06) 868 8702   0800 868 8702
Fax (06) 868 8702   Mob 025 907 777
jan.saunders@clear.net.nz
www.geocities.com/fox_street_retreat

Double $70   Single $50   (Continental Breakfast)
Child $25   Dinner by arrangement
1 Queen 1 Twin (2 bdrm)
Bathrooms: 1 Guests share 1 Host share

Welcome to our tasteful retreat situated in our delightful gardens in a quiet location within easy walking distance of city. Relax around our pool and enjoy use of our BBQ. Sky TV in bedrooms. We play bowls and bridge and will gladly arrange games for guests. We are tuberous begonia enthusiasts with lovely display in gardens, pots and baskets in season. We will gladly arrange tours. Cut lunches on request. Off-street parking available.

GISBORNE   *Gisborne*

Riverbank Homestay   *B&B*
Judy, David and Marney Newell
100 Oak Street, Gisborne

Tel 021 633 372   Fax (06) 868 9340   Mob 021 633 372
riverbank@xtra.co.nz
www.anaura-stay.co.nz

Double $75-$85   Single $55-$65   (Full Breakfast)
Child $20   Dinner $25   Credit cards accepted
Children welcome
2 Queen 1 Double 1 Twin (4 bdrm)
Bathrooms: 1 Ensuite 1 Private 1 Guests share

We are a retired couple used to travel during working lives - our guests now keep us (and daughter Marney) in touch with the outside world and are a welcome source of new friendships. Our home is on a quiet riverbank section 5 minutes by car from city centre. We offer either a large, airy, private studio with ensuite, TV, and deck or rooms, with private bathroom, in the family living area. We also have a beachfront homestay Rangimarie at beautiful Anaura Bay on SH35.

GISBORNE

GISBORNE   *2km NE of Gisborne*

Herons Mead Lodge   *B&B Homestay*
Avril & Brian Jackson
5 Island Road, Gisborne

Tel **(06) 868 1224**   Fax (06) 868 1224
Mob 021 189 2486   heronsmead@xtra.co.nz
www.roan.co.nz/heronsmead

Double $80-$90   Single $55-$65   Family $100-110
(Full Breakfast)   Child $20 sharing family room
Dinner $25pp by prior arrangement   Children welcome
2 Double 1 Single (2 bdrm)
Bathrooms: 2 Ensuite 1 Private

Herons Mead Lodge is situated on the outer boundary of Gisborne City, in a semi-rural setting. Avril and Brian offer comfortable, home from home, accommodation, where guests are welcomed as part of the family. Gisborne is New Zealand's best kept secret, with miles of clean golden beaches, and beautiful scenery. Enjoy our restaurants and cafés, where good food and a wide choice is the norm. Soak up the sunshine, the atmosphere, the history of the region, and visit local wineries and other places of interest in the area.

GISBORNE - WAINUI   *5km NE of Gisborne*

Best Beach View   *B&B*
Annabel Reynolds
8 Tuahine Cresent, Wainui, Gisborne

Tel **(06) 868 9757**   Fax (06) 867 9003
mahara_hara@family.net.nz
www.bnb.co.nz/reynolds.html

Double $95   Single $60   (Full Breakfast)
Children welcome
1 Queen (1 bdrm)
Bathrooms: 1 Ensuite 1 Private

Best Beach View sits on Tuahine Point at the southern end of Wainui Beach. Because of its elevated position it has spectacular and panoramic views overlooking all of Wainui, and seeing the early morning sunrise is fantastic. The double room and ensuite has outside access opening onto a private garden with a barbeque for your use. Tuahine Crescent is very peaceful and quiet with plenty of off-street parking. Walking on the beach is a great way to unwind after travelling and you can get a wonderful meal at the Sandbar Restaurant (5 minutes walk away).

GISBORNE   *40km W of Gisborne*

Awawhenua   *Farmstay*
Sally & Andrew Jefferd
RD 2, Ngatapa, Gisborne

Tel **(06) 867 1313**   0800 469 4401313
Fax (06) 867 6311   jefferd@xtra.co.nz
www.bnb.co.nz/jefferd.html

Double $100   Single $60   (Full Breakfast)   Child $1/2 price
Dinner $25   Children welcome   Pets welcome
1 Double 1 Twin (2 bdrm)
Bathrooms: 1 Ensuite 1 Private 2 shared

We live 5 minutes drive from the famous Eastwood Hill Arboretum. Eastwood Hill is internationally recognized comprising 65 hectares of numerous varieties of trees and shrubs. We have a 1400 acre hill country property, farming sheep, cattle and deer. Farm tours and walks easily arranged. In a tranquil setting we offer our guests separate accommodation with ensuite just a few metres from the main house, giving them the privacy they may desire. Tea, coffee making facilities provided in room. Complimentary drink and a good Gisborne chardonnay, together with farm fresh food and good company make your dinner a memorable experience. Reservations: free phone 0800 469 4401313. Please phone for directions.

GISBORNE *6km from Gisborne*

Cameron Cottage *B&B Self-contained*
Bev & Warwick Willson
21 Cameron Road,
RD 1, Gisborne

Tel (06) 863 1430 Fax (06) 863 1432
Mob 027 417 9876
www.bnb.co.nz/cameroncottage.html

Double $125 Single $110 (Continental Breakfast)
1 Queen (1 bdrm)
Bathrooms: 1 Ensuite

Our tastefully decorated self-contained cottage is situated on 1 hectare just 6km from Gisborne City. We offer luxurious cotton linen and bedding, also robes for your use. Toiletries, hairdryer, iron, heated towel rail and a complimentry bottle of wine for you to enjoy. Fishing and helicopter tours can be arranged. Our cottage with deck gets full all day sun. We have room for boat parking. Tasty continental breakfast in our cottage. Come and enjoy a restful visit in our gorgeous cottage. Inspection welcome.

---

visit... **www.bnb.co.nz**

For the most up-to-date information from our hosts,
and links to our other web sites around the world.

GISBORNE

Taranaki, Wanganui, Ruapehu, Rangitikei

Te Awamutu

Otorohanga

Waitomo

Te Kuiti

Piopio

Taumarunui

Piriaka

Owhango

Inglewood

Waitara

New Plymouth

Raurimu

National Park

Stratford

Hawera

Raetihi

Ohakune

Waitotara

Taihape

Mangaweka

Wanganui

Hunterville

Marton

Towns listed generally follow
a north to south route. Refer
to the index if required.

0   Kilometres   40

0   Miles   24

Fielding

Colyton

Newbury

Woodville

Oroua Downs

Palmerston North

Tokomaru

Pahia

Foxton

Eketahuna

Levin

Otaki
Te Horo

WAITARA   *15kms N of New Plymouth*

Trenowth Gardens
B&B Homestay Separate/Suite Self-contained
Sherril George
2 Armstrong Avenue, Waitara, Taranaki

Tel (06) 754 7674 Fax (06) 754 8884
Mob 027 473 6055 sherril@trenowth.co.nz
www.trenowth.com

Double $90 Single $70 (Full Breakfast) Child $15
Dinner $25pp Children welcome Pets welcome
2 Double 1 Single (2 bdrm)
Bathrooms: 1 Ensuite 1 Private

Garden homestay plus self-contained B&B cottage situated right on the main north-south Auckland/ New Plymouth/Wellington highway at historic Waitara. Large family house with guest homestay (ensuite) plus additional B&B cottage with separate bedroom, lounge/dining/kitchen area with separate bathroom/laundry/toilet. Fully equipped with TV/music/library; all set in 18 acres of landscaped gardens, private lake and orchards. Close to 4 golf courses, local fishing, bush and mountain walks. 10 minutes from New Plymouth restaurants, 20 minutes from the mountain.

NEW PLYMOUTH   *6km SE of New Plymouth*

Blacksmiths Rest   *Homestay*
Evelyn & Laurie Cockerill
481 Mangorei Road,
New Plymouth

Tel (06) 758 6090   Fax (06) 758 6078
Mob 025 678 8641   laurev@xtra.co.nz
www.bnb.co.nz/blacksmithsrest.html

Double $90 Single $50 (Full Breakfast)
Dinner $25 by arrangement Credit cards accepted
2 Queen 1 Twin 2 Single (3 bdrm)
Bathrooms: 1 Ensuite 1 Private 1 Host share

Relax and enjoy our rural views although we are only five minutes drive from city centre while the well known Tupare Gardens are just next door. Each guest room has a queen and a single bed with an ensuite in the upstairs bedroom. We have a large garden, some sheep and a friendly dog, called Bill, who lives outside. Interests: equestrian, sport, gardening. There is plenty of off-street parking. Mangorei Road can be easily found when approaching New Plymouth from either north or south.

NEW PLYMOUTH - OMATA   *5km S of New Plymouth*

Rangitui   *B&B*
Therese & Tony Waghorn
Waireka Road, RD 4, New Plymouth

Tel (06) 751 2979 Fax (06) 751 2985
twaghorn@clear.net.nz
www.accommodationtaranaki.co.nz

Double $75-$95 Single $65-$85 (Full Breakfast)
Portacot available Dinner $40
Credit cards accepted
1 Queen 2 Single (2 bdrm)
Bathrooms: 1 Ensuite 1 Private

10 minutes from New Plymouth. Separate chalet with ensuite, queen bed, TV, and balcony overlooking bush and sea. Twin room with guest facilities in house. Your choice of breakfast (except kippers!) Dinner with wine, $40 per head, by arrangement. Enjoy bush or orchard walks, relax by our pool, or visit some of the nearby attractions: beautiful Mt Taranaki, some of the best surf in the world, famous gardens, art gallery, museum, historic sites and golf courses. Bookings: please phone for reservations/directions.

New Plymouth — New Plymouth Central

Kirkstall House *Homestay*
Ian Hay & Lindy MacDiarmid
8 Baring Terrace, New Plymouth

Tel (06) 758 3222 Fax (06) 758 3224
Mob 025 973 908 kirkstall@xtra.co.nz
www.bnb.co.nz/kirkstallhouse.html

Double $85 Single $65 (Continental Breakfast)
Ensuite room $95/$75 Credit cards accepted
1 Queen 1 Double 1 Twin (3 bdrm)
Bathrooms: 1 Ensuite 2 Private

Kirkstall House invites you to experience its old world beauty and comfort, in an atmosphere of easy hospitality and relaxed surroundings. Kirkstall House is one of surprise. Enjoy our superb mountain views, cosy open fire, and delightful garden leading down to the river. The sea, beaches, and walkways, restaurants and shops are all within easy walking distance. Lindy, a practising physiotherapist, and Ian, involved with tourism, are here to help you enjoy Taranakai to the utmost. We are smoke-free, have 2 cats and a dog named Eva.

New Plymouth — 3km S of New Plymouth

Oak Valley Manor
B&B Farmstay Separate/Suite Self-contained
Pat & Paul Ekdahl
248 Junction Road, RD 1, New Plymouth

Tel (06) 758 1501 Fax (06) 758 1052
Mob 027 442 0325 kauri.holdings@xtra.co.nz
www.bnb.co.nz/oakvalleymanor.html

Double $105-$125 Single $75 (Continental Breakfast)
Child $1 per year up to 12 years Backpackers
Credit cards accepted Children welcome Pets welcome
2 Queen 1 Single (2 bdrm) Bathrooms: 2 Ensuite

Your hosts, Pat and Paul, 2 friendly people with experience in the hospitality industry, invite you to a unique bed & breakfast in their beautifully home with views of Mount Taranaki from all rooms. These beautiful views make an everlasting impression. Guests can choose their own privacy or socialise with us. We have a variety of animals, donkey, peacocks, pigs, ducks, geese and an ex-guide dog. Tours available in our family owned brewery. Golf course 5 minute drive. Tariff reduces $125-$105 pending nights stayed.

New Plymouth — 25km N of New Plymouth

Cottage by the Sea/Seacliff Villa *Self-contained*
Nancy & Hugh Mills
66 Lower Turangi Road, RD 43, Waitara

Tel (06) 754 4548 or (06) 754 7915
cottagebythesea@clear.net.nz
www.cottagebythesea.co.nz

Double $120-$160 Single $110-$140
(Breakfast by arrangement) Child neg Extra Adults $25
Credit cards accepted Children welcome Pets welcome
1 King/Twin 1 Queen 1 Double 1 Single (1 bdrm)
Bathrooms: 1 Ensuite

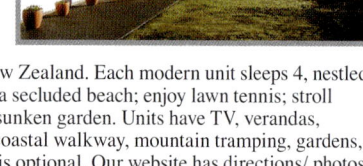

Spectacular seaviews, peace and quiet, in this unique, self-contained or B&B cottage near New Plymouth in New Zealand. Each modern unit sleeps 4, nestled in its own private garden. Descend steps through bush to a secluded beach; enjoy lawn tennis; stroll through 10 acres of avocado and fruit trees; discover the sunken garden. Units have TV, verandas, access to BBQ. 20 minutes from New Plymouth's cafés, coastal walkway, mountain tramping, gardens, adventure sports. Folding bed or cot available. Breakfast is optional. Our website has directions/ photos. Seasonal rates. Discounts for longer stays. Our gentle dog may greet you.

NEW PLYMOUTH

The Grange *Homestay*
Cathy Thurston & John Smith
The Grange, 44B Victoria Road,
New Plymouth Central

Tel (06) 758 1540 Fax (06) 758 1539
Mob 027 433 3497 cathyt@clear.net.nz
www.bnb.co.nz/thegrange.html

Double $110 Single $85 (Full Breakfast)
Credit cards accepted
1 King/Twin 1 Queen 2 Single (2 bdrm)
Bathrooms: 2 Ensuite

Come and stay in our modern architecturally designed award-winning home built with the privacy and comfort of our guests in mind. With unique bush views and a house designed to take full advantage of the sun our guests can enjoy relaxing in the lounge or the extensive tiled courtyards. The Grange is centrally heated, security controlled and located adjacent to the renowned Pukekura Park and Bowl of Brooklands. The city is within a short 5 minute walk.

NEW PLYMOUTH *New Plymouth Central*

93 By the Sea *B&B Separate/Suite Separate suite*
Patricia & Bruce Robinson
93 Buller Street, New Plymouth

Tel (06) 758 6555 Mob 025 230 3887
pat@93bythesea.co.nz   www.93bythesea.co.nz

Double $120-$100 Single $100-$80
(Special Breakfast) Child by arrangement
Dinner by arrangement Credit cards accepted
Children welcome
1 King/Twin 1 Queen (2 bdrm)
Bathrooms: 1 Private

Park beside your own front door; enjoy a 2 minute wander down to sandy surf beaches; follow the mountain-fed Te Henui stream through parks and native bush; stroll the popular coastal walkway to many excellent city restaurants/attractions, (15-20 minutes); share a sumptious breakfast while enjoying the view over gardens, to the ever-changing Tasman sea; relax in a private B&B suite (2 bedrooms, lounge, spabath) that our guests say is warm, comfortable, spacious, and well-appointed. We look forward to meeting and greeting you.

NEW PLYMOUTH

Vineyard Holiday Flat *B&B Self-contained*
Shirley & Trevor Knuckey
12 Scott Street,
Moturoa, New Plymouth

Tel (06) 751 2992 Fax (06) 751 2995
shirley12vineyard@xtra.co.nz
www.bnb.co.nz/vineyardholidayflat.html

Double $80 Triple $100 Single $55 (Full Breakfast)
Child $20 Credit cards accepted Children welcome
1 Double 1 Twin (1 bdrm)
Bathrooms: 1 Ensuite

Situated in New Plymouth's port-view Moturoa suburb. Enter through hobby vines to the spacious upstairs open-plan studio, maximising 320 degree views of harbour, mountains, city; coast north and south. Near surf and shoreline pleasures. Guests may be as self-contained as wished - with lock-up garage, separate entrance, mini-kitchen. Lounge has private balcony, dining-table, Sky TV, phone. Extra bed(s) by arrangement. Ideally situated for exploring Taranaki's attractions, or the perfect R&R retreat. There is a pet cat.

NEW PLYMOUTH *New Plymouth central*

Issey Manor *Self-contained Boutique Guest House*
Carol & Lewis
32 Carrington Street, New Plymouth

Tel (06) 758 2375 Fax (06) 758 2375
Mob 027 248 6686 issey.manor@actrix.co.nz
www.isseymanor.co.nz

Double $100-$150 (Full Breakfast)
Child by arrangement   Corporate rates available
Credit cards accepted   Pets welcome
1 King/Twin 3 Queen (4 bdrm)
Bathrooms: 4 Ensuite

A stylish blend of old architecture and modern living. Issey offers 4 contemporary suites all with designer bathrooms, 2 having spa baths. Well appointed for tourists, holiday makers and business guests. Free internet, DD phones, refreshments, a separate guest's lounge with DVD and Sky TV plus a fully equipped kitchen. Just minutes stroll to wonderful restaurants, cafés, parks, Pukeariki Museum, Govett Brewster Art Gallery and awesome coastal walkway. Off-street parking is available. If you enjoy comfort and privacy, stylish décor, NZ artwork, reading and relaxing, try Issey.

NEW PLYMOUTH *8km N of New Plymouth*

Rockvale Lodge Homestay *B&B Homestay*
Jeannette & Neil Cowley
97 Manutahi Road, RD 2, New Plymouth

Tel (06) 755 0750 Fax (06) 755 0750
Mob 027 682 1236 jeannette.neil@xtra.co.nz
www.bnb.co.nz/user200.html

Double $90 Single $65 (Full Breakfast)
Child $35 Dinner $25 by arrangement
Credit cards accepted Children welcome
1 Queen 2 Single (2 bdrm)
Bathrooms: 1 Private

We welcome you to our large, country-style home,
surrounded by deer farm, with Mt. Egmont as a backdrop. Guests' double room and lounge open onto a balcony, with rural views. Your comfort is our concern. We will book one guest party at a time. Relax in your private spabath, and join us for dinner, on the deck in summer, or by the fire in winter. We are close to airport, city, beaches, parks and the mountain. Six 18 hole golf courses are within 15 minutes drive. We look forward to sharing our home with you. Families welcome.

NEW PLYMOUTH *New Plymouth Central*

Kawaroa-by-the-Sea *B&B Separate/Suite*
Jan & Bruce Meachen
3A Kawaroa Close, New Plymouth 4601

Tel (06) 759 1943   Fax (06) 759 1947
Mob 027 699 1890 or 021 292 7791
b.meachen@xtra.co.nz
www.bnb.co.nz/kawaroa.html

Double $110 Single $85 (Special Breakfast)
Credit cards accepted   Children welcome
1 Queen 1 Twin (2 bdrm)
Bathrooms: 1 Private

Sleep to the sound of the sea. New, spacious, peaceful and luxurious, ground level accommodation - sleeps 4 (one party only) either queen or twin, heating, electric blankets, quality cotton bedlinen, fresh, modern décor. Guests own lounge/office (TV, fax, email) opens onto pretty walled garden - coastal walkway, the port, CBD, restaurants, art gallery, new museum & theatres just a pleasant stroll away. Guests own tea/coffee making facility. Ask about special winter, weekend & family rates.

NEW PLYMOUTH   *8km New Plymouth*

Churchwood Manor   *B&B Homestay*
Jo-Anne & Warren Boys
1148 Devon Road, RD 3, New Plymouth

Tel (06) 755 1947   Fax (06) 755 1947
Mob 027 471 8660   churchwoodmanor@xtra.co.nz
www.churchwoodmanor.co.nz

Double $110-$150 Single $85-$110 (Special Breakfast)
Child $30, under 5 free of charge
Dinner by arrangement Children welcome Pets welcome
3 Queen 1 Twin 1 Single (3 bdrm)
Bathrooms: 2 Ensuite 1 Host share

Churchwood is a 1920's style bungalow set back off
the main road, off-street parking and a 2 minute drive from the airport. Secret rose gardens with rural
surroundings ensure you relax and take in the country ambiance that is only minutes into the CBD of
New Plymouth. Dinners by arrangement, full breakfast included in tariffs. The family cats (a moggy and
a ragdoll) add character to this family homestead. Spoil yourselves with luxury affordable hospitality
only at Churchwood Manor, Taranaki's best kept secret!

NEW PLYMOUTH   *5km W of New Plymouth centre*

Whaler's Rest   *B&B*
Maureen & Denis Whiting
86A Barrett Road,
New Plymouth

Tel 06 751 4 272   Mob 025 245 0246
whalersrest@clear.net.nz
www.whalersrest.co.nz

Double $100 Single $80   (Full Breakfast)
Child $20 Children welcome Pets welcome
1 Double 1 Twin (2 bdrm)
Bathrooms: 1 Ensuite 1 Private

Large double bedroom with ensuite, with your own deck for drinks, plus twin room with private
bathroom. Breakfast, continental or cooked. We are on the gateway to Surf Highway, 10 minutes
to Oakura Beach and 5 minutes to New Plymouth City centre featuring the Wind Wand, coastal
walkway, Puke Ariki Museum and Pukekura Park. Your hosts Maureen and Denis who love their
tennis and garden welcome you. Children and pets by arrangement. We have a Jack Russell, Angus,
and two fat cats, Tuffy and Biscuit.

NEW PLYMOUTH   *500m W of New Plymouth*

Airlie House   *B&B Separate/Suite Self-contained*
Gabrielle Masters
161 Powderham Street,
New Pymouth

Tel (06) 757 8866   Fax (06) 757 8866
Mob 021 472 072   email@airliehouse.co.nz
www.airliehouse.co.nz

Double $125-$140 Single $95-$110 (Full Breakfast)
Child neg Credit cards accepted
1 King/Twin 2 Queen 2 Single (3 bdrm)
Bathrooms: 1 Ensuite 2 Private

Airlie House is a 110 year old character home nestled among mature trees and garden. This home has
been beautifully renovated to provide 2 large guest bedrooms with ensuites, plus a studio apartment
with its own kitchen and private bathroom. Located in central New Plymouth, Airlie House is an easy
5 minute walk from shops, restaurants, the sea front, parks and many other local attractions. All rooms
have many features and amenities available for your comfort, including Sky TV and broadband internet
access.

New Plymouth - Inglewood   *12km SE of New Plymouth*

Araheke Cottage   *B&B Self-contained*
John Apps
Egmont Road, RD 6, Inglewood

Tel (06) 752 2722   Mob 025 609 1173
arahekecottage@xtra.co.nz
www.bnb.co.nz/arahekecottage.html

Double $130   Single $100   (Full Breakfast)
1 Queen (1 bdrm), plus 1 Double sofa bed in lounge
Bathrooms: 1 Private

Nestling amidst lush pasture, mature trees, and overlooking a bubbling stream, Araheke Cottage enjoys an idyllic rural setting, which includes spectacular views of Mount Taranaki. Having traditional board and batten cladding, but enjoying all the benefits of modern building insulation, Araheke Cottage is a contemporary interpretation of an early settler's cottage. Chooks, sheep and calves will be your neighbours when you visit our 5 acre hobby farm. Allow yourselves to escape to this beautifully warm, comfortable and cosy haven, just minutes from New Plymouth.

Stratford   On edge of town

Stallard B&B   *B&B Farmstay Homestay*
Billieanne & Corb Stallard
3514 State Highway 3, Stratford Northern Boundary

Tel (06) 765 8324   Fax (06) 765 8324
stallardbb@infogen.net.nz
www.bnb.co.nz/stallardbb.html

Double $70   Single $45   (Full Breakfast)
Child $20   Family (4) $85   Credit cards accepted
Children welcome
2 Double 2 Twin 2 Single (4 bdrm)
Bathrooms: 4 Ensuite 1 Guests share

1900 "Upstairs Downstairs" comfort. Cooked or continental breakfast included. Free self-catering kitchen, tea, coffee, biscuits. Homely or private. Own key. Optional separate lounge. Restaurants, taverns, shops nearby. Rooms are antique, romantic with TV, heaters, electric blankets, serviced daily. Gardens, BBQ, row boat, bush bath, river walks. 15 minutes Mt Egmont ski fields, climbing, tramping. Centrally located on edge of Stratford, easy distance to New Plymouth, museums, famous gardens, tourist attractions. We are semi-retired farmers. Interests include gemstones travel, art. Welcome.

Egmont National Park   *9km W of Stratford*

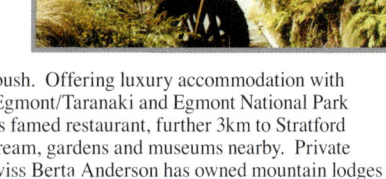

Anderson's Alpine Lodge   *Farmstay Homestay*
Berta Anderson
PO Box 303, Stratford, Taranaki

Tel (06) 765 6620   0800 668 682   Fax (06) 765 6100
Mob 025 412 372   mountainhouse@xtra.co.nz
www.mountainhouse.co.nz

Double $155-$195   Single $155   (Full Breakfast)
Dinner a la carte Mountain House Motor Lodge $155
Credit cards accepted Pets welcome
1 King/Twin 1 Queen 1 Double 2 Single (3 bdrm)
Bathrooms: 3 Ensuite

Swiss style chalet surrounded with native gardens and bush. Offering luxury accommodation with special alpine ambiance. Spectacular views of Mount Egmont/Taranaki and Egmont National Park opposite our front gate. 5km to Mountain House and its famed restaurant, further 3km to Stratford Plateau and ski fields. Tramps, summit climbs, trout stream, gardens and museums nearby. Private helicopter summit flights. Pet sheep, pig, ducks etc. Swiss Berta Anderson has owned mountain lodges since 1976, winning many awards. Beautiful paintings from Keith, her husband (Died 1.Feb.03) are on display.

STRATFORD   *15km NE of Stratford*

Sarsen House   *Country Retreat*
Bruce & Lorri Ellis
Te Popo Gardens, 636 Stanley Road,
RD 24, Stratford

Tel (06) 762 8775   Fax (06) 762 8776
tepopo@clear.net.nz   www.tepopo.co.nz

Double $130-$150   Single $110-$130
(Special Breakfast)   Dinner $30-$40 by arrangement
Credit cards accepted
1 King 2 Queen 1 Single (3 bdrm)
Bathrooms: 3 Ensuite

We have a special place which we love to share. Sarsen House is set in Te Popo Gardens (34 acres), a charming woodland garden of regional significance encircled by a deep river gorge and native forest. Each of the 3 spacious guestrooms opens to the garden and has private access, ensuite, woodfire, sound system, and superior bed and linen for your comfort. Special breakfast is served in the sunny conservatory or beside the fire. Fine food and wine for dinner (by arrangement). Self-catering available. Wonderful dogs.

HAWERA   *1.5km S of Hawera Central*

Tairoa Lodge   *B&B Self-contained*
Linda & Steve Morrison
3 Puawai Street, PO Box 117, Hawera

Tel (06) 278 8603   Fax (06) 278 8603
Mob 027 243 5782   tairoa.lodge@xtra.co.nz
www.tairoa-lodge.co.nz

Double $140-$185   Single $120   (Full Breakfast)
Dinner by arrangement
Self-contained cottage, sleeps 6 $195-$355
Credit cards accepted   Children welcome
2 Queen 1 Single (2 bdrm)   Bathrooms: 2 Ensuite

TAIROA LODGE
❧ BED & BREAKFAST ❧

Originally built in 1875 our Kauri villa has been renovated to its former Victorian glory and is nestled amongst established grounds. Polished kauri floors add a golden glow to the tastefully decorated guest rooms. Enjoy; private garden setting, swimming pool, sumptuous breakfasts, afternoon tea or aperitif on arrival, robes, hairdryers, toiletries and fresh flowers. For peace, privacy and retreats our self-contained Tairoa Cottage is perfect for honeymooners, families or special occasions. Sleeps 6. Linda, Steve, Hannah, & Caitlyn assure you a memorable stay.

WAITOTARA - WANGANUI   *29km W of Wanganui*

Ashley Park   *Farmstay Self-contained*
Wendy & Barry Pearce
State Highway 3,
Box 36,
Waitotara, Wanganui

Tel (06) 346 5917   Fax (06) 346 5861
ashley_park@xtra.co.nz
www.bnb.co.nz/ashleypark.html

Double $80-$115   Single $60   (Full Breakfast)
Dinner $25   Credit cards accepted
1 Queen 4 Single (3 bdrm)
Bathrooms: 1 Ensuite 1 Guests share

We have a 500 acre sheep and cattle farm and live in a comfortable home, set in an attractive garden with a swimming pool and tennis court. Also in the garden is an antique shop selling Devonshire teas. 100 metres from the house is a 4 acre park and lake, aviaries and a collection hand fed pet farm animals. We welcome guests to have dinner with us. Self-contained accommodation is available in the park.

TARANAKI, WANGANUI RUAPEHU, RANGITIKEI

WANGANUI   *45km N of Wanganui*

Operiki Farmstay   *Farmstay*
Trissa & Peter McIntyre
3302 River Road,
Operiki, RD 6,
Wanganui

Tel (06) 342 8159
www.bnb.co.nz/operikifarmstay.html

Double $70   Single $35   (Full Breakfast)
Child $15   Dinner $20
1 Queen 2 Single (2 bdrm)
Bathrooms: 1 Guests share 1 Host share

Farmstay overlooking the Whanganui River - en route to the Bridge to Nowhere - sheep, cattle and deer farming. Pottery and macadamia nuts and cat. Enjoy a country picnic and/or walk. Other activities along the river can be arranged: canoeing, jet boat rides, mountain bike riding, Marae visit and farm activities according to season.

WANGANUI   *5min w Wanganui Centre*

Bradgate   *B&B Homestay*
Frances
7 Somme Parade, Wanganui

Tel (06) 345 3634   Fax (06) 345 3634
vige@value.net.nz
www.bnb.co.nz/bradgate.html

Double $75-$80   Single $40-$50 (Full Breakfast)
Dinner $25
1 Queen 1 Twin 1 Single (3 bdrm)
Bathrooms: 1 Guests share

Welcome to Bradgate, a gracious 2 storey home. With its
beautiful entrance hall and carved rimu staircase which reflects the original character and gracefulness of the house. My husband and I came to New Zealand 28 years ago. We owned Shangri-La Restaurant by Virginia Lake. 20 years later the family have flown the nest. We decided to welcome guests into our home. My Mum and I share an energetic young labrador named Crunchy. I enjoy playing golf, gardening and meeting people. Non-smoking house, Dinner by arrangement.

WANGANUI   *2km NW of Wanganui*

Kembali   *B&B Homestay*
Marylyn & Wes Palmer
26 Taranaki Street,
St Johns Hill, Wanganui

Tel (06) 347 1727   Mob 025 244 4347
wespalmer@xtra.co.nz
www.bnb.co.nz/kembali.html

Double $90   Single $60   (Full Breakfast)
Credit cards accepted
1 Queen 1 Twin (2 bdrm)
Bathrooms: 1 Private

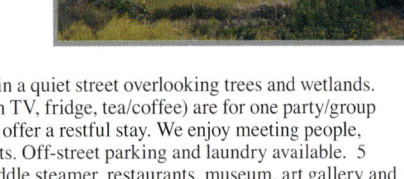

Kembali is a modern, centrally heated, sunny home in a quiet street overlooking trees and wetlands. Upstairs guest bedrooms, bathroom and lounge (with TV, fridge, tea/coffee) are for one party/group exclusive use. Retired, no pets, children married, we offer a restful stay. We enjoy meeting people, gardening, travel, reading and have Christian interests. Off-street parking and laundry available. 5 minutes drive to city, heritage buildings, restored paddle steamer, restaurants, museum, art gallery and walks. We look forward to welcoming you.

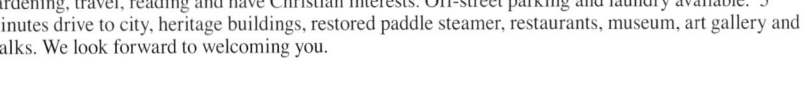

WANGANUI   *20km NE of Wanganui*

Misty Valley Farmstay   *Farmstay*
Linda & Garry Wadsworth
RD 5, 97 Parihauhau Road,
Wanganui

Tel **(06) 342 5767**   linda.garry.wadsworth@xtra.co.nz
www.bnb.co.nz/mistyvalley.html

Double $80   Single $50   (Full Breakfast)
Child $20   Dinner $30 by arrangement
Credit cards accepted   Children welcome
2 Double 2 Twin (2 bdrm)
Bathrooms: 1 Guests share

Misty Valley is a small organic farm at 4 hectares. We prefer to use our own produce whenever possible.
There are farm animals for you to meet including our brittany, George and cats, Alice and Calico, who
all live outside. Our 2 grandchildren visit us regularly and children will be made very welcome. We are
non-smoking, but have pleasant deck areas for those who do. Our famous river and historical city offer
plenty of activities for the whole family to enjoy.

WANGANUI   *2 min Wanganui centre*

Braemar House   *B&B*
Clive Rivers & Rob Gooch
2 Plymouth Street, Wanganui

Tel **(06) 347 2529**   Fax (06) 347 2529
Mob 021 159 7690   contact@braemarhouse.co.nz
www.braemarhouse.co.nz

Double $70-$85 Single $45-$55
(Continental and Full breakfast - optional)
Child $10   Dinner $25 by arrangement
Credit cards accepted   Children welcome
1 Queen 3 Double 4 Twin (8 bdrm)   Bathrooms: 3 Guests share

Welcome to 'olde worlde charm'. This restored historic homestead circa 1895, nestled alongside the
Wanganui River, has a homely ambience that makes your stay restful and enjoyable. The graceful
entrance leads to centrally heated, comfortable period designed bedrooms, guest lounge and dining
room. Laundry facilities and fully equipped kitchen available. Off-street parking surrounded by lovely
gardens. The Homestead is close to the city and tourist attractions. We look forward to you visiting.
Clive, Rob, the hens and Pippin, the resident cat, all welcome you.

TAUMARUNUI   *5km NE of Taumarunui*

Farmstay
Shirley & Allan Jones
213 Taringamotu Road,
Taumarunui

Tel **(07) 896 7722**   costleyj@xtra.co.nz
www.bnb.co.nz/taumarunui.html

Double $100   Single $70   (Full Breakfast)
Child half price   Dinner by arrangement
Children welcome
1 King 1 Twin (2 bdrm)
Bathrooms: 1 Private

Our spacious home is situated 5km from the centre of
Taumarunui surrounded by a peaceful one-acre garden with a native bush backdrop filled with NZ
native birds. The bedrooms open on to a large verandah. Laundry available. A stream runs along
one boundary of the 80 acre property suitable for walks and summertime swimming. A golf course
is located within 2km, along with guided mountain walks, canoeing, hot pools, scenic flights, skiing,
trout fishing and whitewater rafting are all within an hours drive.

TAUMARUNUI   *3km N of Taumarunui*

Le Cornu Farms Bed & Breakfast
B&B Farmstay Self-contained
Rosemary & John Filleul
31 Simmons Road, Taumarunui

Tel (07) 896 8901   Mob 025 6519431
filleul.family@xtra.co.nz
www.bnb.co.nz/lecornu.html

Double $80   Single $40   (Continental Breakfast)
Child $20   Children welcome Pets welcome
1 Queen 1 Single (1 bdrm)
Bathrooms: 1 Private

A self-contained farmstay B&B on 700 acres of farmland only 3 minutes from town. So if you feel like wandering across our hills with breathtaking views of the mountains and valleys, fishing or swimming in a private part of the river, chatting with the livestock or family pets or just having a wine on the sundeck you can. But you can also cross the road to the golf course, shoot into town for a coffee, canoe the Wanganui, or go skiing, all in the same day. Cooked breakfast, evening meals and packed lunches available by arrangement. Child minders and pet sitters on call.

TAUMARUNUI - PIRIAKA   *10km S of Taumarunui*

Awarua Lodge   *B&B Self-contained*
Raewyn & Jack Vernon
1063 State Highway 4,
Piriaka, Taumarunui

Tel (07) 896 8100   0800 5000 42   Fax (07) 896 8102
info@awarualodge.co.nz
www.awarualodge.co.nz

Double $200   (Full Breakfast) Suite $350
Credit cards accepted
1 King/Twin 1 King (2 bdrm)
Bathrooms: 1 Private

Awarua Lodge, set in parkland grounds overlooking the Whanganui River, is self contained guest accommodation offering a suite that sleeps 4. The décor simply commands you to relax. Visit the Whanganui and Tongariro National Parks. Try your hand golfing on Taumarunui's premiere golf course, rated in the top NZ 50. Plan your adventures ie tramping, fishing, canoeing, skiing, mountain biking. Watch sheep shearing and the milking of a large NZ dairy herd. Beau, the retired sheep dog, could be on hand to met you!

OWHANGO - TAUMARUNUI   *8km N of Owhango*

Fernleaf   *B&B Self-contained Cottage*
Carolyn & Melvin Forlong
58 Tunanui Road, RD 1, Owhango

Tel (07) 895 4847   0800 FERNLEAF
Fax (07) 895 4837   Mob 027 285 1441 or 027 415 3179
fernleaf.farm@xtra.co.nz   www.bnb.co.nz/fernleaf.html

Double $100   Single $60   (Full Breakfast)   Child $40
Dinner $20   Outside Cottage $75
Credit cards accepted   Children welcome
2 Queen 1 Double 1 Single (3 bdrm)
Bathrooms: 1 Guests share

Relax in the tranquil Tunanui Valley just 500 metres from SH4. Close for convenience, far enough away for peace and quiet. We are the third generation to farm "Fernleaf" and our Romney flock has been recorded every year since the First World War. The views from various vantage point on the farm are awesome, taking in the mountains: Ruapehu, Ngaruahoe, Tongariro and Taranaki. Enjoy our generous country hospitality, wonderful breakfast, 2 beautiful dalmatians and friendly cats. Other meals by arrangement.

RAETIHI   *0.5km N of Raetihi*

Log Lodge *B&B Homestay Self-contained*
Jan & Bob Lamb
5 Ranfurly Terrace,
Raetihi

Tel (06) 385 4135   Fax (06) 385 4835
Lamb.Log-Lodge@Xtra.co.nz
www.bnb.co.nz/loglodge.html

Double **$105**   Single $55   (Full Breakfast)
Child $40   Credit cards accepted
2 Double 4 Single (2 bdrm)
Bathrooms: 2 Private

A unique opportunity to stay in a modern authentic log home sited high on 7 acres on the edge of town. Completely private accommodation, with own bathroom. All sleeping on mezzanine, your own lounge with wood fire, snooker table, TV/video, stereo and dining area, opening onto large verandah, with swimming pool and spa available. Panoramic views of Mts. Ruapehu, Ngauruhoe and Tongariro. Tongariro National Park and Turoa Ski Field is half hour scenic drive.

OHAKUNE   *6km W of Ohakune*

Mitredale *Farmstay Homestay*
Audrey & Diane Pritt
Smiths Road, RD, Ohakune

Tel (06) 385 8016   Fax (06) 385 8016   Mob 025 531 916
www.bnb.co.nz/mitredale.html

Double **$90**   Single $50   (Continental Breakfast)
Dinner $25pp by arrangement
Credit cards accepted   Pets welcome
1 Double 2 Single (2 bdrm)
Bathrooms: 1 Guests share 1 Host share

We farm sheep, bull beef and run a boarding kennel in a beautiful peaceful valley with magnificent views of Mt Ruapehu. Tongariro National Park for skiing, walking, photography. Excellent 18 hole golf course, great fishing locally. We are members of Ducks Unlimited a conservation group and our local wine club. Have 2 labradors. We offer dinner traditional farm house (Diane, a cook book author,) or breakfast with excellent home-made jams. Take Raetihi Road, at Hotel/BP Service Station Corner. 4km to Smiths Road. Last house 2km.

OHAKUNE   *1km SW of Ohakune*

Kohinoor *Homestay*
Nita & Bruce Wilde
1011 Raetihi Road, Ohakune

Tel (06) 385 8026   Fax (06) 385 8026
Mob 021 253 3415   kohinoor@xtra.co.nz
www.bnb.co.nz/kohinoor.html

Double **$120**   Single $65   (Full Breakfast)
Child $40   Dinner $35   Credit cards accepted
1 King/Twin 1 Double 1 Twin (3 bdrm)
Bathrooms: 1 Ensuite 1 Private 1 Host share

Enjoy spectacular views of volcanic Mt Ruapehu while relaxing in our tranquil 3 acre garden. Kohinoor (a gem of rare beauty) is an ideal base from where you can ski Turoa or Whakapapa Ski Fields. Do the Tongariro Crossing and other mountain walks, visit "The Bridge to Nowhere" enjoy trout fishing, bird watching and golf. We are just 1km from Ohakune with its cafés and restaurants. Our interests include tramping, trout fishing, photography, skiing and giving genuine Kiwi hospitality. Room rates apply in the ski season.

TARANAKI, WANGANUI
RUAPEHU, RANGITIKEI

TAIHAPE   *1km on hill above Taihape*

Korirata Homestay   *B&B Homestay*
Patricia & Noel Gilbert
25 Pukeko Street, Taihape

Tel (06) 388 0315   Fax (06) 388 0315
korirata@xtra.co.nz
www.bnb.co.nz/koriratahomestay.html

Double $80   Single $50   (Full Breakfast)
Child 1/2 price under 10yrs
Dinner By arrangement   Credit cards accepted
4 Single (2 bdrm)
Bathrooms: 1 Guests share

A warm welcome awaits you at the top of the hill in Taihape, where panoramic views of the mountains, ranges and surrounding countryside, add to the tranquil surroundings. 3/4 acre has been landscaped with shrubs, hydroponics, home grown vegetables and   chrysanthemums in season. Meals, if desired, are with hosts, using produce from the garden where possible. Comfortable beds with electric blankets. Rafting, bungy jumping and farm visits can be arranged. One hour to Ruapehu, Lake Taupo and 2 $^{1}/_{2}$ - 3 hours to Wellington and Rotorua.

visit... www.bnb.co.nz

For the most up-to-date information from our hosts, and links to our other web sites around the world.

TAIHAPE/RANGITIKEI   *26km Taihape*

Tarata Fishaway   *B&B Farmstay Homestay
Self-contained Fishingstay/Retreat*
Stephen & Trudi Mattock
Mokai Road, RD 3, Taihape

Tel (06) 388 0354   Fax (06) 388 0954
Mob 025 227 4986
fishaway@xtra.co.nz   www.tarata.co.nz

Double $100-$160 Single $50-$85
(Continental Breakfast)
Child half price under 12 years Dinner $30pp
Visa and Mastercard accepted
4 King/Twin 4 Queen 1 Double 6 Single (9 bdrm)
Bathrooms: 3 Ensuite 1 Private 1 Guests share

We are very lucky to have a piece of New Zealand's natural beauty. Tarata is nestled in bush in the remote Mokai Valley where the picturesque Rangitikei River meets the rugged Ruahine Ranges. With the wilderness and unique trout fishing right at our doorstep, it is the perfect environment to bring up our 3 children.

Stephen offers guided fishing and rafting trips for all ages. Raft through the gentle crystal clear waters of the magnificent Rangitikei River, visit Middle Earth and a secret waterfall, stunning scenery you will never forget. Our spacious home and our large garden allow guests private space to relax and unwind. Whether it is by the pool on a hot summers day with a good book, soaking in the spa pool after a day on the river or enjoying a cosy winters night in front of our open fire with a glass of wine.

Come on a farm tour meeting our many friendly farm pets, experience our 'nightlife' on our free spotlight safari and Tarata is only 6km past the new flying fox and bungy jump. Stay in our Homestead or in Tarata's fully self-contained River Retreats where you can enjoy a spa bath with 'million dollar views' of the river and relax on the large decking amidst native birds and trees. Peace, privacy and tranquillity at its best! We will even deliver a candle light dinner to your door. We think Tarata is truly a magic place and we would love sharing it with you Approved pets welcome.

Features & Attractions
*   Trout Fishing and Scenic Rafting
*   Visit LOTR, Anduin, Middle Earth
*   6km past Bungy & Flying Fox
*   'Mini' golf (with a difference)
*   Swimming & spa pool
*   Bush walks/spotlight safaris
*   Camp outs
*   Clay Bird shooting

Directions: Tarata Fishaway is 26 scenic kilometres from Taihape. Turn off SH1, 6km south of Taihape at the Gravity Cannon Bungy and Ohotu signs. Follow the signs (14km) to the Bungy bridge. We are 6km past here on Mokai Road.

MANGAWEKA *12km E of Mangaweka*

Mairenui Rural Retreat *B&B Farmstay*
Sue & David Sweet
Ruahine Road, Mangaweka 5456

Tel (06) 382 5564 Fax (06) 382 5564 Mob (025) 517 545
info@mairenui.co.nz www.mairenui.co.nz www.nzstay.co.nz

> *Mairenui Rural Retreat offers three accommodation options and meals are available at the Homestead for guests in the self contained houses.*

On the farm there is a concrete tennis court, a full size petanque court, a croquet lawn and river swimming. There is also a trout stream for catch and release fishing only. Locally there are the renowned Rangitikei gardens, river adventure, historic home tours, 4 scenic golf courses.

Sue & David, Bess the terrier cross dog, and Norman the cat welcome guests of all nationalities. French and German are spoken. We also accept EFTPOS payment.

Mairenui Rural Retreat - The Homestead

Double $130-$280 Single $95-$140
(Special Breakfast) Dinner $40 Credit cards accepted
1 Queen 1 Twin (2 bdrm)
Bathrooms: 2 Ensuite

The Homestead offers quality in house accommodation for up to 4 people. 1 heritage-style double room with a small sitting area and a slate floored ensuite bathroom with sunken bath, toiletries, hairdryer and its own verandah. The twin room is larger with shower/toilet and also its own verandah.

Mairenui Rural Retreat - The Retreat

Double $150 Single $50
Dinner $40 min $150 - max $300 Breakfast $10-$15
Credit cards accepted Children welcome Pets welcome
1 Queen 1 Double 1 Twin (3 bdrm)
Bathrooms: 1 Guests share

A 1977 Comeskey designed open plan, three and a half storey building set in a stand of 700 year old native trees. A semi-circular living room leads up to a brick paved kitchen which is fully equipped with electric oven, microwave and a wood burning stove. Double-hung doors lead through to a tiled breakfast conservatory. Also on this level are the glass-roofed toilet and bathroom. The bricked central circular stair tower leads to 2 first storey double bedrooms, with another toilet off the landing, and the twin room which is up a vertical ladder. A *seventies* experience! $150 double if a single night booking, otherwise $120 double per night. Meals available at Homestead.

Mairenui Rural Retreat - The Colonial Villa

Double $70 Single $35
Dinner $40 min $70 - max $250 Breakfast $10-$15
Credit cards accepted Children welcome
Pets welcome
3 Double 2 Twin (5 bdrm)
Bathrooms: 2 Guests share

A restored hundred year old dwelling with polished wooden floors, a wind up gramophone, a small pool table, two open fires and a wood stove. There's a refrigerator, stove, microwave, some electric blankets and heaters. The beds have duvets and blankets, there is a separate shower and the bath is an original claw foot beauty! Verandahs on 2 sides of the house provide plenty of room for relaxing on the comfortable seats in the sun. Meals available at Homestead

HUNTERVILLE *10km NE of Hunterville*

Richmond Station - Vennell's Farmstay *Farmstay*
Oriel & Phil Vennell
Mangapipi Road, Rewa, RD 10

Tel **(06) 328 6780** 0800 220 172
Fax (06) 328 6780 Mob 025 407 164
www.bnb.co.nz/vennellsfarmstay.html

Double $120 Single $60 (Full Breakfast)
Child neg Dinner $30
1 King/Twin 1 Queen 1 Twin 4 Single (3 bdrm)
Bathrooms: 2 Private

We are fifth generation farmers on Richmond Station, a 1200 acre sheep/cattle hill country farm. Our spacious home is in a tranquil setting of 100 year old trees and garden with swimming pool. You will enjoy our large family room, cosy lounge with open fire, great farm walks and beautiful views. Central to private gardens and river activities. We are midway Rotorua/Wellington, just off SH1 near Hunterville on scenic SH54. We are featured in "50 Great New Zealand Farmstays". Group lunches a specialty. 2 outdoor cats.

HUNTERVILLE *10km S of Hunterville*

Maungaraupi *Separate/Suite Heritage*
Elizabeth Robertson
Maungaraupi Country Estate,
Leedstown Road,
RD 1, Marton

Tel **(06) 327 7820** Fax (06) 327 8619
mcestate@xtra.co.nz www.bnb.co.nz/maungaraupi.html

Double $150-$190 Single $100 (Full Breakfast)
Child $50 Dinner $40
Credit cards accepted Children welcome
5 Double 2 Twin 4 Single (9 bdrm)
Bathrooms: 3 Ensuite 1 Guests share

Situated just off SH1 this historic home is set in bush and gardens with expansive views from the Ruahine Ranges to Kapiti. The 9 bedrooms are furnished with antiques, 3 rooms have open fireplaces and there are 2 large old baths. You can play billiards, tennis or read in the library. Whether you spend a night to break your journey or a couple of days to relax in the heartland of the Rangitikei, Maungaraupi will be a unique experience.

MARTON *45km N of Palmerston North*

Rea's Inn *B&B Homestay*
Keith and Lorraine Rea
12 Dunallen Avenue, Marton

Tel **(06) 327 4442** Fax (06) 327 4442
Mob 025 799 589 keithandlorraine@xtra.co.nz
www.bnb.co.nz/reasinn.html

Double $80 Single $45 (Continental Breakfast)
Child half price Dinner $20 Credit cards accepted
Children welcome
1 Queen 1 Twin (2 bdrm)
Bathrooms: 1 Guests share

We have a warm comfortable home offering hospitality, peace and tranquility. Situated in quiet cul-de-sac with a private garden setting. Guests stay in separate wing of home. Close to Nga Tawa and Huntley Schools. Ideal for weekend retreat or stopover. (Only 2 hours from Wellington Ferry). Organic farm tour available by arrangement. Your comfort and pleasure are important to us. Our 2 cats like people too, and we all welcome you to come, relax and enjoy the friendly atmosphere at Rea's Inn.

Hawkes Bay

Tiniroto

Wairoa

Mahanga Beach

Mahia Beach

Waiwhenua

Bay View

Taradale · Napier

Hastings

Havelock North

Waimarama

Waipawa

Waipukurau

Dannevirke

0 Kilometres 40

0 Miles 24

Mahia Peninsula - Mahanga Beach   *50km N of Wairoa*

Reomoana   *Farmstay   Self-contained cottage*
Louise Schick
RD 8, Nuhaka, Hawkes Bay

Tel (06) 837 5898   Fax (06) 837 5990
reomoana@paradise.net.nz
www.bnb.co.nz/reomoana.html

Double $120-$150   Single $60   (Continental Breakfast)
Child $20   Dinner $30   Cottage $100
Credit cards accepted   Children welcome   Pets welcome
2 Queen 1 Twin 1 Single (4 bdrm)
Bathrooms: 1 Ensuite 1 Private

Reomoana - The voice of the sea. Pacific Ocean front farm at beautiful Mahia Peninsula. The spacious, rustic home with cathedral ceilings, hand-crafted furniture overlooks the Pacific with breathtaking views. Enjoy the miles of white sandy beaches, go swimming, surfing or fishing. A painter's paradise. Attractions in the area include: Morere Hot Springs, Mahia Reserve, golf course and fishing charters by arrangement. 6km to 'Sunset Point Restaurant'. Outside pets: golden labrador and cat. Also self-contained cottage in avocado orchard, ideal for families, 3 minutes walk to beach.

Just as we have a variety of B&Bs you will also be offered a variety of breakfasts, and they will always be generous. **Continental breakfast** consists of fruit, cereal, toast and tea/coffee. A **Full breakfast** is the same with a cooked course and a **Special breakfast** is a full breakfast with something special.

Bay View   *12km N of Napier*

Beachfront Homestay *B&B Homestay Self-contained*
Christine & Jim Howard
20A Le Quesne Road, Bay View, Napier

Tel (06) 836 6530   Fax (06) 836 6531
Mob 021 159 0162   j-howard@clear.net.nz
www.beachfronthb.co.nz

Double $100   Single $60   (Full Breakfast)   Child $20
Dinner $25   4 person apartment $175
Credit cards accepted   Children welcome
1 Queen 1 Twin (2 bdrm)   Bathrooms: 1 Private

Jim, Christine and Sarcha (Jack Russell) will welcome you to their beachfront home with breathtaking views of Hawkes Bay and walking distance to local wineries. Guests are offered self-contained accommodation and own entrance on ground floor. Jim a local transport operator and Christine works at a local winery both enjoy meeting people and their interests are fishing and the outdoor life. surfcasting and kontiki fishing available. Beachfront homestay is just 5 minutes from the Napier Taupo turn-off and 12 minutes from Napier's Marine Parade and cafés. Personalised wine and sightseeing tours available.

HAWKES BAY

BAY VIEW - NAPIER   *12km N of Napier*

Kilbirnie   *Homestay Beach*
Jill & John Grant
84 Le Quesne Road, Bay View, Napier

Tel (06) 836 6929   Mob 025 234 7363
jill.johng@xtra.co.nz   www.bnb.co.nz/kilbirnie.html

Double $70-$90   (Special Breakfast)   Child not suitable
Dinner $30pp by arrangement   Credit cards accepted
1 King 1 Queen (2 bdrm)
Bathrooms: 1 Ensuite 1 Private

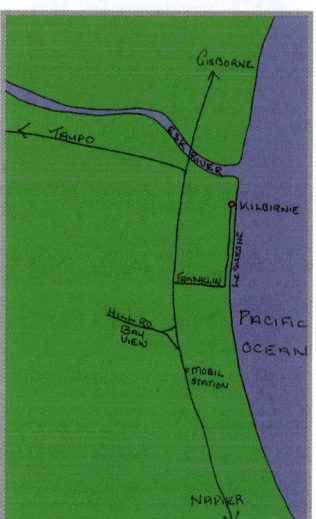

We moved with our dog in 1996 to the quiet end of an unspoiled fishing beach by the Esk river, attracted by the beauty and position away from the traffic, while only 15 minutes from the main attractions. Nearby are vineyards, gardens, walks and a full range of harbourside restaurants north of Napier.

Kilbirnie is near the Taupo Road intersection with the Pacific Highway to Gisborne, with off-road parking. Upstairs, air-conditioned guest rooms have restful views of the Pacific Ocean one side or vineyards on the other, private bathrooms, excellent showers, abundant hot water, comfortable firm beds and guest lounge.

We are retired farmers with time to share good company, fresh imaginative food and juice, real coffee, an eclectic range of books, who invite you to enjoy our hospitality in modern surroundings. We have 14 years home hosting experience and are non-smokers.

Directions: from Taupo first left after intersection Highways 2 & 5. Franklin Road to Le Quesne, proceed to far end beachfront. From Napier first right after Mobil Station. Prior contact appreciated.

A special breakfast overlooking the ocean is an experience which makes lunch seem superfluous

The View

BAY VIEW - NAPIER   *12km N of Napier*

home

The Grange   *B&B Farmstay*
Winery and Self-contained lodge
Roslyn & Don Bird
263 Hill Road, Eskdale, Hawkes Bay

Tel (06) 836 6666   Fax (06) 836 6456
Mob 025 281 5738
thefarmstay@xtra.co.nz   www.thegrangelodge.com

Double $100   Single $85   (Full Breakfast)
Dinner $35
Self-contained Lodge $120-$140 double $100 single
$25 extra person Optional breakfast provided $9pp
Credit cards accepted   Children welcome
2 King/Twin 1 Double 2 Single (2 bdrm + loft)
Bathrooms: 2 Private

The Winery

Inside the Lodge

In the heart of a thriving *wine region* overlooking the picturesque Esk Valley nestles *The Grange* our delightfully modern farmstay and superior self-contained lodge. Private, spacious accommodation in relaxing peaceful surrounds with spectacular rural, coastal and city *views.*

Feel the comforts of home as we tempt you with our farm produce, baking, and preserves. We're an outgoing family who really enjoy the company of guests. Hospitality is guaranteed! Experience our *farm* life with Roslyn, Zac (our weimaraner farm pup), and Sparkie (our resident cat). Feed the sheep, cows, pigs, chickens and dairy goats. Try milking Nancy the goat or bottle-feeding a lamb (seasonal).

Don a passionate third generation *winemaker* combines 28 years knowledge with tasting over dinner or at our *Wishart Estate Winery.* You might like to try hand plunging the reds at vintage or a barrel sample of future releases.

The Farm

Explore the world's *Art Deco capital Napier only 12 minutes drive* away and Hawkes Bay's many regional attractions within 30 minutes. Unwind on the deck to the soothing chorus of native birds in the surrounding gardens and trees and at day's end spend time romancing over our wonderful night sky. Taupo (Kinloch) holiday home and email access available. 1km off SH5 at Eskdale or 3km off SH2 at Bay View.

Share our home or retreat in the Lodge - "Our Place Is Your Place"

HAWKES BAY

BAY VIEW - NAPIER   *10km N of Napier*

Bev's on the Bay   *B&B*
Beverley White
32 Ferguson Street North, Bay View, Napier

Tel (06) 836 7637 bevann@paradise.net.nz
www.bnb.co.nz/bevs.html

Double $100-$120 Single $80   (Full Breakfast)
Child $30   Credit cards accepted
Children welcome   Pets welcome
1 King 1 Queen (2 bdrm)
Bathrooms: 1 Ensuite 1 Private

This stylish beach-front property offers large, modern rooms, each with bathroom, TV, sitting area, tea and coffee facilities and private entrances. The king room has its own balcony and sea views. The queen room has near-level access and doors to the courtyard. Step off the front lawn for swimming or surf casting. Wineries in walking distance. 5 minutes drive from the airport and 10 minutes from Napier City. Undercover parking is provided. Your host, Beverley White, is an amateur artist and former business woman. Elderly poodle on property.

NAPIER - WESTSHORE   *3km NW of Napier*

A Bed At The Beach   *Self-contained*
Averil & Bayne Smart
88 Charles Street, Westshore, Napier

Tel (06) 833 6566   Fax (06) 833 6569
Mob 025 275 9759
averilbayne@xtra.co.nz
www.bed-at-the-beach.co.nz

Double $105 Single $95   (Continental Breakfast)
Credit cards accepted
1 Queen (1 bdrm)
Bathrooms: 1 Private

Just 100 metres from the beach, Averil, Bayne and Chelsea our Sheltie, welcome you to stay in our charming self-catering studio suite situated upstairs with private entrance and off-street parking. A continental breakfast tray will be delivered to you each morning to enjoy at your leisure. We are central to Hawkes Bay wineries, art deco and tourist attractions well known to the bay as well as being walking distance to cafés and restaurants.   We are Smoke-free and regret not suitable for children.

NAPIER   *1km N of Napier*

Spence Homestay   *B&B Homestay*
Kay & Stewart Spence
17 Cobden Road, Napier

Tel (06) 835 9454   0800 117 890   Fax (06) 835 9454
Mob 025 235 9828   ksspence@actrix.gen.nz
www.bnb.co.nz/spence.html

Double $125 Single $90   (Full Breakfast)
Credit cards accepted
1 Queen 1 Single (1 bdrm)
Bathrooms: 1 Ensuite

Welcome to our comfortable near new home.   Quiet area 10-15 minutes walk from art deco city centre. Guest suite opens outside to patio, petanque court and colourful garden.   Lounge includes double bed settee, TV, kitchenette with tea making facilities, fridge and microwave. Bedroom has queen and single beds, ensuite bathroom. We have hosted for over 10 years and enjoy overseas travel. Able to meet public transport. Directions: port end of Marine Parade, Coote Road, right into Thompson Road, left into Cobden Road opposite water tower.

NAPIER   *1.5km N of Post Office*

Approved

A Room with a View   *B&B Homestay*
Robert McGregor
9 Milton Terrace, Napier

Tel (06) 835 7434   Fax (06) 835 1912
Mob 027 249 2040
roomwithview@xtra.co.nz
www.bnb.co.nz/mcgregor.html

Double $100   Single $65   (Continental Breakfast)
Credit cards accepted
1 Queen (1 bdrm)
Bathrooms: 1 Private bath & shower

Having hosted for 10 years with my late wife, I'm continuing to enjoy companionship, conversation and laughter with guests. Spacious room with 180 degree sea view, large garden and sunny hill location. Only a 15 minute walk to restaurants at historic Port Ahuriri or our world-famous art deco city centre. Private bathroom with bath and shower. Laundry facilities available. Free pick up service. No smoking inside please. I'm interested in travel, gardening, the arts, and especially local history, as I'm Executive Director of the Art Deco Trust.

NAPIER   *1.2km N of Napier Central*

home
NEW ZEALAND

Hillcrest   *B&B Homestay*
Nancy & Noel Lyons
4 George Street, Hospital Hill, Napier

Tel (06) 835 1812   lyons@inhb.co.nz
www.hillcrestnapier.co.nz

Double $90-$95   Single $65   (Continental Breakfast)
Credit cards accepted
1 Double 2 Single (2 bdrm)
Bathrooms: 1 Guests share

If you require quiet accommodation just minutes from
the city centre, our comfortable home provides peace in restful surroundings. Relax on wide decks overlooking our garden, or enjoy the spectacular sea views. Explore nearby historic places and the Botanical Gardens. Your own lounge with tea/coffee making; laundry and off-street parking available. We have travelled extensively and welcome the opportunity of meeting visitors. Our interests are travel, music, bowls and embroidery. We will happily meet you at the travel depots.
Holiday home at Mahia Beach available.

NAPIER   *5km S of Napier*

home
NEW ZEALAND

Snug Harbour   *Homestay Separate/Suite*
Ruth & Don McLeod
147 Harold Holt Avenue, Napier

Tel (06) 843 2521   Fax (06) 843 2520
donmcld@clear.net.nz
www.bnb.co.nz/snugharbour.html

Double $80-$95   Single $55   (Full Breakfast)
Dinner $30 by arrangement   Credit cards accepted
1 Queen 1 Twin 1 Single (3 bdrm)
Bathrooms: 1 Ensuite 1 Guests share

Ruth & Don welcome you to their comfortable home with its rural outlook and sunny attractive patio. The garden studio with ensuite and tea making facilities has its own entrance. We are situated on the outskirts of Napier City, the art deco city of the world, and in close proximity to wineries and many other tourist attractions. We both have a background in teaching, with interests in travel, gardening and photography.

NAPIER - TARADALE   *18km W of Napier*

Silverford   *Homestay*
Chris & William Orme-Wright
Puketapu, Hawkes Bay

Tel (06) 844 5600   Fax (06) 844 4423
homestay@paradise.net.nz   www.silverford.co.nz

Double $145-$165 Single $115
(Full Breakfast) Credit cards accepted
1 King 1 Queen 1 Double (3 bdrm)
Bathrooms: 1 Ensuite 1 Guests share

Situated on the Wine Trail, Silverford - one of Hawkes Bay's most gracious homesteads - is spaciously set in 17 acres of farmland, established trees and gardens. Drive through our half a kilometre long gorgeous oak lined avenue to the sweeping lawns, bright flower gardens and ponds surrounding our elegant home designed by Natusch at the turn of the century.

We are relaxed and friendly and offer a warm ambience in private, comfortable and tranquil surroundings - a romantic haven with tastefully furnished bedrooms, charming guest sitting room and a courtyard to dream in.

Friendly deer, cow, pigeons, ducks and dogs. Central heating. Swimming pool. Good restaurants close by. We are smoke-free and regret the property is unsuitable for children. Some French and German spoken.

Silverford is an idyllic welcoming haven for a private, peaceful and cosy stay whilst at the same time being close to all the amenities and attractions that Hawkes Bay has to offer.

NAPIER - TARADALE   *8km W of Napier*

Kerry Lodge   *B&B*
Jenny & Bill Hoffman
7 Forward Street, Greenmeadows, Napier

Tel **(06) 844 9630**   Fax (06) 844 1450
Mob 0274 932 874   kerrylodge@xtra.co.nz
www.kerrylodge.co.nz

Double $100   Single $70   (Full Breakfast)
Child $45   Credit cards accepted   Children welcome
1 King 1 Queen 2 Twin (3 bdrm)
Bathrooms: 1 Ensuite 1 Private

Set in tranquil gardens, we invite guests to share the
warmth and comfort of our home. Our large rooms offer heating, refreshment facilities and colour
television. A mobility ensuite and wheelchair access is available for guests convenience. Also a
laundry. Your day with us begins with a scrumptious breakfast and a chat to help plan your day's
activities. Relax in our sparkling pool or indoor spa. Situated near Church Road and Mission wineries.
Our dog Hogan and cat Tabitha wait to welcome you.

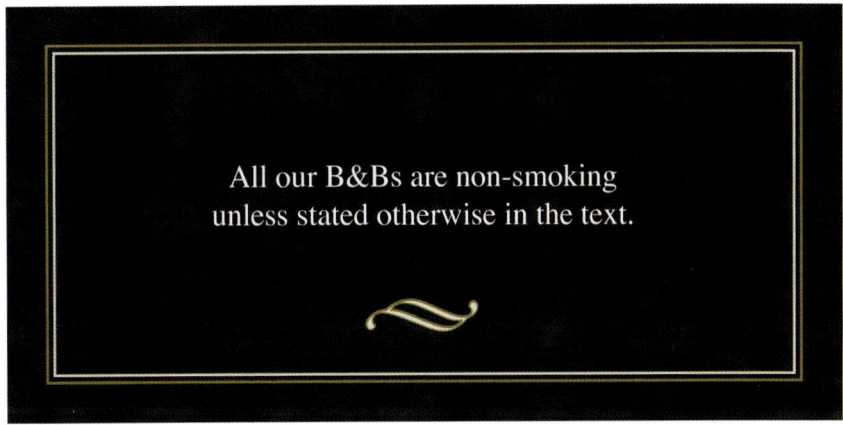

All our B&Bs are non-smoking
unless stated otherwise in the text.

NAPIER

Blue Water Lodge Ltd   *B&B Guesthouse*
471 Marine Parade,
Napier

Tel *(06) 835 8929*
Fax (06) 835 8929
bobbrown2@xtra.co.nz
www.bnb.co.nz/bluewaterlodgeltd.html

Double $70-$80   Single $40   (Continental Breakfast)
Child $10 under 14 years
Credit cards accepted
6 Double 9 Single (9 bdrm)
Bathrooms: 1 Ensuite 2 Guests share

Blue Water Lodge is on the beach front opposite the Aquarium on Napier's popular Marine Parade.
Close to all local tourist attractions and within walking distance to the city centre, information centre,
family restaurants, RSA and Cosmopolitan Club. Owner operated.

HAWKES BAY

NAPIER   *1km N of Napier*

The Coach House   *Self-contained*
Jan Chalmers
9 Gladstone Road,
Napier

Tel (06) 835 6126   Mob 025 657 3263
www.bnb.co.nz/thecoachhouse.html

Double $100   Single $80   (Full Breakfast)
Child $25, babies free   4 people $160
Children welcome   Pets welcome
1 Queen 2 Single (2 bdrm)
Bathrooms: 1 Private

On the hill overlooking a gorgeous Mediterranean garden and sea views, the historic Coach House is tastefully renovated and totally self-contained. It contains 2 bedrooms , open plan kitchen, dining, living rooms, bathroom and separate loo. The fridge will be full of a variety of breakfast supplies. TV and radio included and fresh flowers in all rooms. The sunny deck has a table and chairs and gas barbecue. Off-street parking and easy access plus peace and privacy complete the picture.

NAPIER - TARADALE   *8km SW of Napier*

Greenwood Bed and Breakfast   *B&B*
Ann & Peter Green
62 Avondale Road, Taradale, Napier

Tel (06) 845 1246   Fax (06) 845 1247
Mob 025 795 403
info@greenwoodbnb.co.nz
www.greenwoodbnb.co.nz

Double $100-$120 Single $70   (Full Breakfast)
Dinner $35   Credit cards accepted
2 Queen 1 Twin (3 bdrm)
Bathrooms: 3 Ensuite

Relax in our guest lounge or on the deck as trees filter the afternoon sun. Put the world to rights as we discuss the follies of presidents and kings. Laugh as Peter tries to converse in German and French. Our loves are family and entertaining. Our interests are history, language, art, computers and golf. A short walk takes you to Taradale shops, restaurants and wineries. Tourist attractions and golf courses within easy driving distance. Dinner by arrangement.

NAPIER - TARADALE   *10km W of Napier*

Otatara Heights   *B&B Self-contained*
Sandra & Roy Holderness
57 Churchill Drive,
Taradale, Napier

Tel (06) 844 8855   Fax (06) 844 8855
sandroy@xtra.co.nz
www.bnb.co.nz/otataraheights.html

Double $90   Single $65   (Continental Breakfast)
Extra person $30pp   Credit cards accepted
1 Queen 1 Double (1 bdrm)
Bathrooms: 1 Private

Comfortable, quiet apartment in the heart of our foremost wine producing area. Superb day and night views over Napier and local rural scenes. 10 minutes drive to the art deco capital of the world. 2km to Taradale village. Safe off-street parking. Top quality restaurants and wineries nearby. We are a friendly couple who have enjoyed B&B overseas and like meeting people. Our interests are travel, theatre, good food and wine. Bella, our cat, keeps to herself. Handy to EIT and golf course.

NAPIER - TARADALE   *7.5km SW of Napier*

'279' Church Road   *B&B Homestay*
Sandy Edginton
279 Church Road, Taradale, Napier

Tel **(06) 844 7814**   Fax (06) 844 7814
Mob 021 447 814   sandy.279@homestaynapier.co.nz
www.homestaynapier.co.nz

Double $120   Single $70-$80 (Full Breakfast)
Dinner by arrangement Smoking area available
Credit cards accepted
1 Queen 1 Double 1 Single (2 bdrm)
Bathrooms: 1 Guests share

279, an elegant and spacious home set amongst mature trees and gardens, offers excellent hospitality in a relaxed, friendly atmosphere to domestic and international visitors. Located adjacent to Mission Estate and Church Road wineries, restaurants and craft galleries, 279 is within a short drive of art deco Napier, Hastings, golf courses, and tourist activities. I welcome you to 279 and will help make your visit the highlight of your travels.

NAPIER   *500m N of Post Office*

Cameron Close   *Homestay*
Joy & Graeme Thomas
33 Cameron Road,
Napier

Tel **(06) 835 5180**   Fax (06) 835 4115
Mob 021 683 551
besco@xtra.co.nz
www.bnb.co.nz/cameronclose.html

Double $100   Single $80   (Special Breakfast)
1 Queen 1 Double 1 Single (3 bdrm)
Bathrooms: 1 Guests share

Come and share our 1920's home, garden and pool situated above the lovely art deco city of Napier. A 5 minute stroll will have you amongst the art deco buildings, town, cafés and restaurants, or relax poolside and enjoy our garden. Offering home cooked goodies using fresh produce from Hawkes Bay. Our interests include food, wine, classic cars, art deco and good company. Let us share our knowldge of NZ with you. Shiraz our cat lives here too. Laundry facilities/parking available. Phone for easy directions.

NAPIER   *1km N of Napier*

Cobden Garden Homestay   *B&B Homestay*
Rayma and Phillip Jenkins
1 Cobden Crescent, Bluff Hill, Napier

Tel **(06) 834 2090**   0800 426 233
Fax (06) 834 1977 Mob 025 540 062
info@cobden.co.nz
www.cobden.co.nz

Double $110-$170 Single $90-$150 (Full Breakfast)
Credit cards accepted
2 King/Twin 1 King 5 Single (3 bdrm)
Bathrooms: 2 Ensuite 1 Private

We invite you to stay in our quiet and sunny colonial villa on Bluff Hill. Each bedroom is spacious with lounge furniture, TV, tea and coffee facilities, electric blankets and hairdryers. There is a beautiful garden for your enjoyment. Each evening join us for complimentary tastings of local wine and hors d'oeuvres. Choose your gourmet breakfast from the menu of local foods and homemade delights. We make sure your stay will be extra special and memorable. We have 2 unobtrusive cats in residence.

HAWKES BAY

NAPIER - MARINE PARADE *Napier*

Mon Logis *B&B Boutique hotel*
Gerard Averous
415 Marine Parade, PO Box 871, Napier

Tel (06) 835 2125 Fax (06) 835 8811 Mob 025 725 332
monlogis@xtra.co.nz   www.babs.co.nz/monlogis

Double $140-$200 Single $120
(Special Breakfast) Credit cards accepted
2 King/Twin (4 bdrm)
Bathrooms: 3 Ensuite 1 Private

Built as private hotel in 1915, this grand colonial
building overlooking the Pacific's breakers is only a few minutes
walk from the city centre. Now lovingly renovated Mon Logis
will cater to a maximum of 8 guests and is modelled on the small
privately owned French hotel. Charm, personal service and French
cuisine are the specialities.

Of the upstairs individually furnished rooms, 2 have queen beds
and 2 have twin beds, all have their own private facilities. Owner,
Frenchman Gerard Averous, has decorated each guest room
differently but in a style in keeping with the original charm of the
building. Iron bedsteads, feather duvets, lace covers and fine cotton
linen all create a special elegance and one room is totally furnished
with pieces bought from France.

Downstairs, an informal guest lounge invites relaxation, television
viewing, a quiet time reading or perhaps a game of chess or bridge.
Guests can help themselves to coffee or tea and home-made biscuits
any time of the day. Breakfast, served in the privacy of your own
room or in the downstairs dining room, could be a basket of freshly
baked breads, croissants, or brioche, with a compote of locally grown
fruits or a wonderful herb omelette, with crispy bacon and grilled tomatoes. Should you want to dine out,
Gerard is happy to give recommendations and can help with insight into Napier's unique architecture.

All perfectly designed for comfort and relaxation, Mon Logis is a non-smoking establishment and does
not cater for children. French and Spanish spoken. Exclusive customised vineyard tours with host by
arrangement. Casual elegance at a price you can afford.

A little piece of France nestled in the heart of the beautiful wine-growing region of Hawke's Bay

Napier Hill   *1km N of Napier*

Maison Béarnaise   *B&B*
Christine Grouden & Graham Storer
25 France Road, Bluff Hill,
Napier 4001

Tel (06) 835 4693   0800 624 766
Fax (06) 835 4694   chrisgraham@xtra.co.nz
www.hawkesbaynz.com/pages/maisonbearnaise

Double $140   Single $95   (Full Breakfast)
Credit cards accepted
2 Queen (2 bdrm)
Bathrooms: 2 Ensuite

Christine, Graham and Brewster (shy cat), welcome you to our attractive, peaceful oasis. Walk to city centre, restaurants, Bluff Hill lookout. Off-street parking, internet, laundry services available. Each bedroom has TV, electric blankets, heating, and ensuite for complete privacy. Relax with tea or coffee in your room or guest lounge, to read or perhaps play cards, backgammon. Delicious breakfasts served in dining room or colourful courtyard. Warm and friendly atmosphere. Christine, Napier born, is happy to assist with helpful local, national sightseeing suggestions.

Napier   *500m N of Town Centre*

The Green House On The Hill   *B&B*
Ruth Buss & Jeremy Hutt
18B Milton Oaks, Milton Road, Napier

Tel (06) 835 4475   Mob 021 187 3827
ruth@the-green-house.co.nz
www.the-green-house.co.nz

Double $88-$120 Single $60-$75 (Special Breakfast)
Child neg Dinner $25   Credit cards accepted
2 Queen 1 Twin (3 bdrm)
Bathrooms: 1 Ensuite 1 Guests share

The Green House On The Hill is a vegetarian Bed & Breakfast, 5 minutes walk from the heart of art deco Napier, yet surrounded by woodland, with plenty of native birds ... and sea views! We aim to provide a peaceful, smoke-free environment for our guests. Home-made breads and preserves for breakfast! Our hillside home is built on several levels and unsuitable for wheelchairs or small children, although babies or older chidren would be very welcome. We have ample parking, or can pick up from airport, buses etc. Internet access available.

Napier - Taradale   *7km W of Napier*

Dudley's Bed & Breakfast/Home Stay
B&B Homestay
Marie & Colin Dudley
12 Weathers Place, Taradale, Napier

Tel (06) 844 6580   Fax (06) 844 6580
Mob 027 280 6610   c.dudley@clear.net.nz
www.bnb.co.nz/dudleys.html

Double $100-$115 Single $75   (Full Breakfast)
Dinner $30pp by arrangement   Credit cards accepted
1 Twin (1 bdrm)
Bathrooms: 1 Private

Peaceful retreat to recharge your batteries. Located in a quiet cul-de-sac with attractive private gardens, in ground pool, barbecue area. Bright sunny twin bedroom with tea/coffee making facilities. Private bathroom with luxury spa bath, shower. Separate guests toilet. Guests lounge, TV, or join us for coffee and chat or watch Sky Digital TV. Laundry facilities available. Continental/full breakfast provided. Off-street parking. Handy to shops, restaurants. 2 famous wineries and a top New Zealand golf course are nearby. Tours to numerous wineries can be arranged.

NAPIER *5 min walk to Napier City centre*

Inglenook *B&B*
Mieko S. & Chieko O.
3 Cameron Terrace,
Napier Hill, Napier

Tel (06) 834 2922 Fax (06) 835 9538
Mob 025 276 1221
napierin@hotmail.com
www.bnb.co.nz/inglenook.html

Double $105 Single $75 (Full Breakfast)
1 Queen 1 Twin (2 bdrm)
Bathrooms: 2 Ensuite

Inglenook is situated on the hill in a peaceful garden
setting overlooking city and sea, and only five minutes stroll to get there. Inglenook offers privacy (own
separate entrances & keys) and a quiet restful atmosphere. It is immaculately presented and serviced.
Guests are asked to remove their shoes inside the house. Cooked breakfast is delivered to guest rooms.
TV, telephone line, hair dryer, refrigerator and tea/coffee making facilities are available in each suite.
Laundry service is provided if necessary. No pets or children please.

NAPIER *1km N of Napier*

East Towers *Homestay*
Dale & Alan East
121 Thompson Road, Napier

Tel (06) 834 0821 Fax (06) 834 0824
Mob 025 661 2806
alandales.easttowers@xtra.co.nz
www.bnb.co.nz/easttowers.html

Double $120 Single $70-$90 (Full Breakfast)
King single beds
1 Queen 2 Single (2 bdrm)
Bathrooms: 1 Private

Dale and Alan welcome you to East Towers. Quality accommodation for a couple or group of up to 4
people. 2 bedrooms with queen, double or 2 king singles. Own lounge, tea making facilities, TV. Quiet
area, stunning views, native birds, rambling gardens. Off-street parking. 15 minutes walk to Napier
City. 10 minutes walk to Bluff Hill lookout. Arrive as guests, leave as friends.

NAPIER *Napier Central*

Seaview Lodge *B&B Homestay*
Catherine & Evert Van Florenstein
5 Seaview Terrace, Napier

Tel (06) 835 0202 Fax (06) 835 0202
Mob 021 180 2101
cvulodge@xtra.co.nz
www.bnb.co.nz/seaviewlodge.html

Double $100-$140 Single $80-$90
(Continental Breakfast) Credit cards accepted
1 King/Twin 1 King 1 Queen (3 bdrm)
Bathrooms: 1 Ensuite 2 Private

Seaview Lodge is a lovingly renovated, spacious late
Victorian home. This inner city, beachside bed & breakfast offers a warm welcome and spectacular
views over the city and ocean. Enjoy breakfast on the lower verandah while watching the waves break
on the shore. In the evening relax in the spacious guest lounge or on the upstairs balcony. Seaview Lodge
has an ideal location, it is situated above Marine Parade, across the road from the hot pools and a 3
minute stroll to the city centre.

NAPIER   *1 N of Napier Central*

Villa Vista   *B&B Apartment*
Susana Lustig
22A France Road, Bluff Hill, Napier

Tel (06) 8358770   Fax (06) 8358770   Mob 027 435 7179
accommodation@villavista.net   www.villavista.net

Double $145   Single $110   (Continental Breakfast)
Self-contained $165   Credit cards accepted
Children welcome Smoking area inside
3 Queen 1 Double 3 Single (5 bdrm)
Bathrooms: 4 Ensuite

A Villa with a view and much more. 3 beautifully
appointed bedrooms with fantastic views over Cape Kidnnapers and a 2 bedroom fully self-contained
apartment. Each room with ensuite, a special one with a lovely balcony, tea/coffee making facilities,
air-conditioning, TV, bathrobes and hair dryer. Car park, internet and guest laundry available. Breakfast
is scrumptious and is served in the main dining room at your leisure. Whatever your plans, Susana your
host will be happy to assist to meet your requirements. Winter rates apply beetween May and end of
September. 2 children at home and 3 cats outside in the garden. Spanish also spoken.

NAPIER - HASTINGS   *15km E of Napier/Hastings*

Farmstay Homestay
Heather and Bill Shaw
Charlton Road,
RD 2, Hastings

Tel (06) 875 0177   Fax (06) 875 0525
www.bnb.co.nz/shaw.html

Double $150   Single $100   (Full Breakfast)
Dinner by arrangement
4 Single (2 bdrm)
Bathrooms: 1 Ensuite 1 Guests share 1 Host share

Our home is situated in Charlton Road, Te Awanga,
which is approximately 20 minutes from both Napier and Hastings and right next door to the gannets
at Cape Kidnappers and one of Hawkes Bay leading winery restaurants. With us you can enjoy space,
tranquillity, and fine hospitality while receiving every assistance to make your stay in our area as
interesting and enjoyable as possible. We have 2 Jack Russell dogs. Directions: Charlton Road is the
first road on your right after passing through Te Awanga village.

NAPIER - HASTINGS   *btw Napier/ Hastings*

Copperfields   *B&B Separate/Suite Self-contained*
Pam & Richard Marshall
Pakowhai Road, Napier

Tel (06) 876 9710   Fax (06) 876 9710
Mob 021 21 29 631   rich.pam@clear.net.nz
www.copperfields.co.nz

Double $100-$120   Single $80   (Full Breakfast)
Child under 12 $15   Dinner $35pp by arrangement
Separate S/C flat in old church, Weekly rates neg
Credit cards accepted   Children welcome
1 Double 3 Single (2 bdrm)
Bathrooms: 1 Private

Welcome to Copperfields lifestyle orchard within 10 minutes of Napier, Hastings, Havelock North
and Taradale - central for all tourist attractions. Guests stay in Glen Cottage, spacious self-contained
cottage attached to our house with private entrance. Large lounge with log fire, fully equipped kitchen/
dining. Also on property an historic church converted into self-contained accommodation and a craft
and antiques gallery. Family rates negotiable. Children love our pet pig! Dogs welcome (conditions
apply). Special dinner available by prior arrangement.

HAWKES BAY

NAPIER - HASTINGS   *12km E of Hastings & Napier*

Merriwee Homestay   *Homestay Self-contained*
Jeanne Richards
29 Gordon Road, Te Awanga, Hawkes Bay

Tel (06) 875 0111   Fax (06) 875 0111   Mob 021 214 5023
merriwee@xtra.co.nz   www.merriwee.co.nz

Double $110-$220   Single $100-$150
(Full Breakfast) Dinner by arrangement
Extra person $30   Credit cards accepted
1 King/Twin 1 King 3 Queen (5 bdrm)
Bathrooms: 2 Ensuite 1 Private

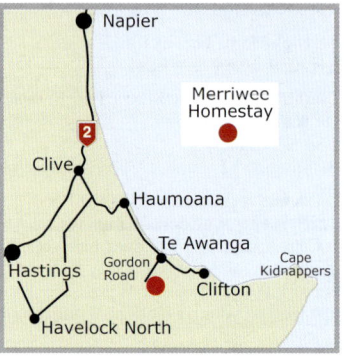

Merriwee was built in 1908 and is set in an apricot
orchard, just a stroll from Te Awanga Beach. The
secluded 10 acre property lies on the stretch of coastline
between Napier and Hastings, a short distance from the
famous Cape Kidnappers Gannet Colony and golf course.

The homestead is elevated and spacious, with quality furnishings, open fires and french doors leading
to verandahs and gardens. There is a large guest sitting room. The main accommodation area is self-
contained, with private entrance, sitting room, open fire and tiny kitchen.

The large grounds include a swimming pool, pètanque court and sea views. Mags, the terrier and cat
Poppy will greet you. There are many local attractions and wineries nearby. Merriwee is 15 minutes
from Napier, Hastings and Havelock North.

Merriwee offers guests peace, comfort, relaxation and good food

Waiwhenua homestead

Hastings - Waiwhenua   *50km W of Napier/Hastings*

B&B Approved

Waiwhenua Homestead and Farmstay
B&B Farmstay Self-contained
Gary Holden, Kirsty Hill and family
808 River Road, RD 9, Hastings

Tel (06) 874 2435 Fax (06) 874 2465 Mob 027 479 4094
kirsty.hill@xtra.co.nz   www.waiwhenua.co.nz

Double $120-$150 Single $60-$100
Annie's Cottage $120-$200 double
(Continental Breakfast) Child $50-$60 Dinner $25
Credit cards accepted Children welcome Pets welcome
1 King 1 Queen 2 Twin 4 Single (bedrooms: 2 homestead and 3 cottage) Bathrooms: 1 Private 1 Host share

Waiwhenua - The perfect place to experience a genuine farmstay and friendly rural hospitality at our 120 year old historic homestead or cottage. Come and join us on our extensive 440 hectare sheep, beef & deer farm and apple & pear orchard in heartland Hawkes Bay. Enjoy informative guided farm tours and join in farm activities on the day. Try fishing our boundary trout-filled Tutaekuri River (in the season October-April - rental equipment avaiable). Relax with a book on our cool verandahs, beside our swimming pool or in the garden. Watch and listen to the many native birds visiting our garden. Our home and family offer guests a friendly environment catering for individuals or families interested in the outdoor life. (Two night stay recommended). Enjoy specialty farm-cooked meals of home-grown beef, lamb or venison complemented with fresh garden vegetables and fruit.

Annie's Cottage - For those seeking total privacy and a longer stay at Waiwhenua, our recently renovated, fully self contained, cozy, 3 bedroom, historic rural retreat awaits families and visitors wanting a holiday away from the hassle and bustles of every day life. Relax and unwind at The Annie Cottage and enjoy the extensive views over farm land and to the cliffs of the river beyond. Self-catering continental breakfast available. All guests welcome to join us for dinner at the homestead. Sleeps up to 6 people @ $120 $200 per night. Extended stay options available.   Enrich your stay by including other outdoor activities at our backdoor; hunting, fishing,  bush and farm walks, garden tours, jet boating and extensive mountain hikes plus many attractions in the greater sunny Hawkes Bay area. To avoid disappointment please book ahead.

Directions: turn off SH50 between Napier and Hastings into Taihape Road at Omahu/Fernhill. Travel 35km to River Road on right, then along River Road for 8km. Waiwhenua #808. Main drive, 100 metres from mail box on right. Cottage #746 on right.

HASTINGS - HAVELOCK NORTH   *16km S of Havelock North*

Wharehau   *Farmstay Homestay*
Ros Phillips
RD 11, Hastings

Tel (06) 877 4111   Fax (06) 877 4111
ros.phillips@xtra.co.nz
www.bnb.co.nz/wharehau.html

Double $90-$100   Single $50   (Full Breakfast)
Child ¹/2 price   Dinner $25   Beach bach
Children welcome
1 Queen 2 Twin 1 Single (4 bdrm)
Bathrooms: 2 Guests share 1 Host share

Wharehau is in the beautiful Tuki Tuki valley -a great base for Hawkes Bay experience. 15 minutes travel from Hastings or Havelock North in the midst of wine country. Close to golf courses, Splash Planet, gannets and art deco. Or enjoy the peace and space on the farm. Weather permitting a farm 4WD tour is available. Walks available locally. Trout fishing (Local guide can be hired) in the Tuki Tuki River. Comfortable beach bach at Kairakau Beach is available for rent.

HASTINGS CITY   *Hastings Central*

McConchie Homestay   *Homestay*
Barbara & Keta McConchie
115A Frederick Street, Hastings

Tel (06) 878 4576   Mob 021 109 2707
barbaramcconchie@xtra.co.nz
www.bnb.co.nz/mcconchie.html

Double $90   Single $55   (Full Breakfast)
Child $25   Dinner $25 by arrangement
Credit cards accepted   Children welcome
1 Queen 2 Single (2 bdrm)
Bathrooms: 1 Guests share

Enjoy our peaceful garden back section, no traffic noises, yet central to Hastings City. My Siamese cat says "Hi". Nearby are parks, golf courses, wineries, orchards and the best icecream ever. Short trips take you to spectacular views, Cape Kidnapper's Gannet Colony, or Napier's art deco, hot pools, or just relaxing and enjoying great hospitality. Directions: From Wellington, arriving Hastings City, turn left into Eastbourne Street, right into Nelson Street, right into Frederick Street, cross Caroline Road. Driveway on right. 115A first house off driveway.

HASTINGS   *2.5km Hastings*

Woodbine Cottage   *Homestay*
Ngaire & Jim Shand
1279 Louie Street, Hastings

Tel (06) 876 9388   Fax (06) 876 9666
Mob 025 529 522 or 029 876 9388
nshand@xtra.co.nz
www.bnb.co.nz/woodbinecottage.html

Double $100   Single $70   (Continental Breakfast)
Dinner $25pp by arrangement
Credit cards accepted
1 Queen 1 Twin (2 bdrm)
Bathrooms: 1 Guests share

Our home is set in half acre of cottage garden on the Hastings boundary close to Havelock North. A tennis court for the energetic, and a spa bath to relax in at night. Hastings city centre is 5 minutes by car and Havelock North 2 minutes. Splash Planet, with its many water features and hot pools is only 2 minutes away. We look forward to your company and can assure you of a comfortable and relaxing stay. Not suitable for small children or pets.

HASTINGS   *3km S of Hastings*

Raureka   *B&B Separate/Suite Self-contained*
Rosemary & Tim Ormond
26 Wellwood Road,
RD 5, Hastings

Tel (06) 878 9715   Fax (06) 878 9728
Mob 021 104 5124   r.t.ormond@xtra.co.nz
www.bnb.co.nz/raureka.html

Double $100   Single $80   (Continental Breakfast)
Credit cards accepted
1 Queen (1 bdrm)
Bathrooms: 1 Ensuite

'One of Hawkes Bay's best kept secrets.' This is one of many wonderful comments written in our visitor's book. 'Raureka' is an apple orchard. You will enjoy all the special surprises to be found here. Fresh flowers, superior linen, home baking are among the many treats to be enjoyed here. A quiet attractive double room with ensuite, fridge, microwave, TV and separate from the house. Relax by the pool with views of our unique property where a dozen 100 year old trees grow.

HASTINGS   *12km W of Hastings, 12km S of Taradale*

Stitch-Hill Farm   *B&B Homestay*
Charles Trask
170 Taihape Road,
RD 9, Hastings

Tel (06) 879 9456   Fax (06) 879 9806
cjtrask@xtra.co.nz
www.bnb.co.nz/stitchhill.html

Double $85   Single $50   (Continental Breakfast)
Dinner $30 by arrangement
1 Queen 1 Twin (2 bdrm)
Bathrooms: 2 Ensuite

Welcome to Hawkes Bay, the premier food and wine region of New Zealand. Stitch-Hill invites you to relax in the quiet countryside surrounded with panoramic views. Our prime location is just minutes from the city centres, wineries, attractions, fishing and tramping. In our comfortable smoke-free home we offer the very best hospitality. Your requirements our challenge. Your choice of room, twin with ensuite, queen bed with ensuite. Stroll in our gardens or around our acres. Unsuitable for children and pets.

HASTINGS   *3km S of Hastings*

Primefruit Orchard   *B&B Self-contained*
Elly & Dick Spiekerman
74 Longlands Road East,
Hastings

Tel (06) 876 4163   Fax (06) 876 4163
Mob 027 444 8798
info@holidaynewzealand.co.nz
www.holidaynewzealand.co.nz

Double $90   Single $70   (Continental Breakfast)
Cottage $120   Children welcome Pets welcome
2 Queen 1 Double 2 Single (4 bdrm)
Bathrooms: 3 Private

We like to be your host on our orchard where we have an abundance of fruit and guided tour in season. We offer a double bedroom with continental breakfast. Explore our indoor games room or gazebo. If you like privacy we have a self-contained cottage with two bedrooms, barbecue on deck, enjoy swimming pool, spa, table tennis, petanque and lawn croquet. All welcome.

HASTINGS - NGATARAWA *7km NW of Hastings*

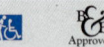

Cardoness Lodge *B&B Luxury Lodge accommodation*
Sarah & Neil Smith
2543 SH50, Roys Hill Road, Ngatarawa (Near Hastings)

Tel (06) 879 8869   Fax (06) 879 8666
Mob 021 047 8229   bookings@cardoness.co.nz
www.bnb.co.nz/cardonesslodge.html

Double $200-$245 (Full Breakfast)
$35 dinner by arrangement
Credit cards accepted Children welcome
2 King/Twin 1 Queen (3 bdrm)   Bathrooms: 3 Ensuite

Having lived in some exciting countries around the world, we are delighted to have found and settled in Hawkes Bay. Turning off Roys Hill Road on State Highway 50 into Cardoness Estate, guests will drive along a line of Paulonia trees and through the olive grove to approach the Lodge.

Surrounded by vineyards, this well-designed property, set in 32 acres of land in the Ngatarawa triangle will provide peace and privacy for our guests. Magnificent views of the surrounding hills can be seen from every room, and quality beds, linen and furnishings will ensure our guests have a comfortable stay. Climate control throughout the house plus an open log fire in the lounge will allow comfort at all times of the year.

All rooms have a private deck area, television and tea/coffee making facilities.

A heated swimming pool, petanque court and badminton net are all on site, and there are 2 golf courses within 5 minutes drive of the property. Also available in the area are cycle rides, scenic flights, heritage trails and many more activities. For the wine enthusiast 5 award winning wineries are within minutes drive, plus many others in the locality, and guided wine tours are available. A

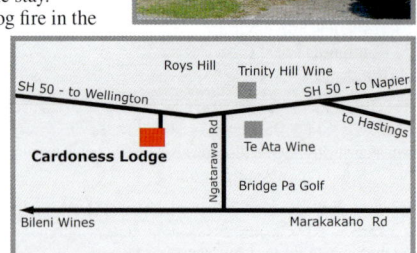

20 minute drive will take you to the art deco city of Napier, 10 minutes to visit the farmers market in Hastings, 17 minutes to find boutique shopping in Havelock North, and 30 minutes to beaches. A visit to the gannet colony, or golf on the superb course at Cape Kidnappers is also within easy reach.

In Hawkes Bay we have a wonderful climate, marvellous countryside, great activities and excellent wine. Our home will provide comfort, luxury and privacy, and as you sip your drinks on the veranda and watch the sunset you can reflect on a memorable stay in the Bay.

HAVELOCK NORTH *1km S of Havelock North*

PeakView Farm *Farmstay Homestay*
Dianne & Keith Taylor
92 Middle Road, Havelock North

Tel (06) 877 7408 Mob 025 668 0252
homestays@xtra.co.nz
www.bnb.co.nz/peakviewfarm.html

Double $75 Single $50 (Full Breakfast)
Child neg Dinner $25 Credit cards accepted
Children welcome
1 Double 2 Single (2 bdrm)
Bathrooms: 1 Host share

 Relax in our 1900 built home admidst large gardens and lawns. Enjoy our friendly, personal and caring hospitality, Comfortable beds with firm mattresses and electric blankets. Wholesome dinners on request.After nearly 17 years hosting we have made many new friends - with many returning. Interests include tramping, bushwalks, gardening and genealogy - Dianne has a Certificate in Homestay Management. Lovely boutique shops and cafés in Havelock North. Napier 25 minute drive. Look forward to meeting you, and aim to make your stay a memorable one. No smoking inside please.

HAVELOCK NORTH *1km N of Havelock North*

Weldon Boutique Bed & Breakfast
B&B Homestay Boutique
Pracilla Hay
98 Te Mata Road, Havelock North, Hawkes Bay

Tel (06) 877 7551 0800 206 499 Fax (06) 877 7051
pracilla@weldon.co.nz www.weldon.co.nz

Double $130-$140 Single $90-$110 (Full Breakfast)
Queen $130-$150 Twin $120 Dinner $45
Credit cards accepted
1 Queen 2 Double 1 Twin 1 Single (5 bdrm)
Bathrooms: 2 Private 1 Guests share

Nearly 100 years old, Weldon offers quality, comfort and peace with a romantic olde worlde charm and a French Provincial ambience. Accommodation is in spacious, elegantly appointed bedrooms, furnished with period and antique furniture. TV and tea/coffee are provided in each room. Fresh flowers, fine linen and fluffy towels reflect the luxury of fine accommodation. Breakfast of fresh local fruits and gourmet cooked options is served alfresco in summer or in the dining room during winter. 2 toy poodles (James and Thomas) will greet you enthusiastically!

HAVELOCK NORTH *5km N of Havelock North*

Totara Stables *B&B Homestay*
Sharon A. Bellaart & John W. Hayes
324 Te Mata - Mangateretere Road,
Havelock North, RD 2, Hastings

Tel (06) 877 8882 Fax (06) 877 8891
Mob 025 863 910 totarastables@xtra.co.nz
www.geocities.com/totarastables

Double $120-$140 Single $100
(Continental Breakfast) Credit cards accepted
1 King/Twin 1 Queen 1 Twin (3 bdrm)
Bathrooms: 1 Ensuite 1 Private

Offering a unique Bed & Breakfast experience in a lovingly restored 1910 villa. Take a peek into the museum of early pioneer farming displayed in the century old stables or marvel at the simplicity of early stationary motors. Feed the hand reared deer or arrange a ride in a classic 1951 Sunbeam Talbot motor car. We are located in the heart of the Te Mata wine region only minutes from the pictureque village of Havelock North. Non-smoking and not suitable for children under 12 years.

HAWKES BAY

HAVELOCK NORTH   *5km N of Havelock North*

Peak Place   *B&B Self-contained*
Diane & Blaine Stride
236 Durham Drive,
Havelock North

Tel (06) 877 1402   Fax (06) 877 1403
Mob 0274 743 757   stride@maxnet.co.nz
www.hawkesbaynz.com/pages/peakplace

Double $70-$130 (Continental Breakfast)
Child POA Children welcome Pets welcome
1 King 1 Queen 2 Twin 1 Single (2 bdrm)
Bathrooms: 1 Ensuite

Nestled high on Te Mata Peak with sweeping views, set on 2 acres, lies Peak Place. Our self-contained guest wing accommodating 5 people, consists of lounge, kitchen/dining, 2 bedrooms, ensuite bathroom. 2 decks are for guests sole use. Single party bookings only ensures privacy. BBQ and laundry facilities are available. Only 5 minutes from the village we are well situated for all the activities that make Hawkes Bay desirable. Your hosts, Diane & Blaine, and our 2 children and labradors would love to welcome you (children welcome).

HAVELOCK NORTH   *6km E of Havelock North*

Borak B&B   *B&B Homestay*
Doris & Mike Curkovic
433 Te Matamangateretere Road,
RD 12, Havelock North

Tel (06) 877 6699   Fax (06) 877 6615
Mob 027 408 2575 dcurkovic@clear.net.nz
www.borakbed-breakfast.co.nz

Double $120   Single $100   (Full Breakfast)
2 Queen 1 Single (2 bdrm)
Bathrooms: 1 Guests share

Experience relaxing hospitality on a producing apple orchard. We are located in the heart of Te Mata wine region nestled amongst 7 wineries with Craggy Range along the road. 5 minutes to the Havelock North Village centre, 7 minutes to Hastings and 15 minutes to Napier. Waimarama, Ocean Beach and Te Awanga within easy reach. For the trout-fisher there is paradise at the back of our orchard. Play petanque, relax. We speak English, German and Croatian. Not suitable for children under 12. Pet cat.

WAIMARAMA BEACH   *34km SE of Hastings*

Waimarama Bed & Breakfast   *Homestay*
Rita & Murray Webb
68 Harper Road,
Waimarama, Hawkes Bay

Tel (06) 874 6795
rwebb@xtra.co.nz
www.bnb.co.nz/webb.html

Double $100   Single $55   (Full Breakfast)
Dinner $25 pp   Credit cards accepted
2 Double (2 bdrm)
Bathrooms: 1 Guests share

Lovely beach for surfing, swimming, diving, boating, fishing etc. Bushwalks and golf course nearby. Situated only 5 minutes walk from beach with lovely views of sea, local park and farmland. Nearest town is Havelock North - 20 minutes drive, with Napier 40 minutes. We have 2 double rooms available, a spa pool and separate toilet and bathroom for guests. Cooked breakfast is offered and dinner is available if required. Please phone for reservations (06) 874 6795.
No smoking inside please. Pets: 1 cat, 1 dog.

WAIPAWA   *2km E of Waipawa*

Haowhenua *Farmstay Country Home*
Caroline & David Jefferd
77 Pourerere Road, RD 1, Waipawa 4170

Tel (06) 857 8241 Fax (06) 857 8261
Mob 027 268 4854 d.jefferd@xtra.co.nz
www.bnb.co.nz/haowhenua.html

Double $100 Single $75 (Full Breakfast)
Child ½ price Dinner $25pp Credit cards accepted
Children welcome
1 Queen (1 bdrm)
Bathrooms: 1 Ensuite

Come and enjoy an evening or two at Haowhenua with a farming family in a spacious and comfortable old country home set in park like surrounds with lovely gardens and swimming pool, and share your adventures with us. We have a cat, a labrador and numerous other farm animals and are only 2km off State Highway 2 and in close proximity to all of Hawkes Bay's attractions.   Please phone for directions.

WAIPAWA   *1km NE of Waipawa*

Abbot Heights *B&B*
Jacqui & Charlie Hutchison
47 Abbot Avenue, Waipawa

Tel (06) 857 8585   Fax (06) 857 8580
Mob 027 433 0146   chipper@paradise.net.nz
www.bnb.co.nz/abbotheights.html

Double $130 Single $80 (Continental Breakfast)
2 Queen (2 bdrm)
Bathrooms: 1 Ensuite 1 Private

Abbot Heights is a comfortable colonial style home set
in 14 tranquil acres of park. Spacious private lounge with logfire and television. Our 2 guest bedrooms have goose down duvets, bathrobes, electric blankets and percale linen. One bathroom with spa bath. Indoor heated pool, tennis courts closeby. Hunting or fishing guide available; bookings essential. Local golf courses, restaurants, wineries, beaches within 30 minutes drive. Our friendly cat is Myrtle. Directions: from north turn right on Abbotsford Road just past the 50km sign, left onto Domain Road, then left onto Abbot Avenue. From south turn left over town bridge onto Kenilworth Street, straight ahead onto Domain Road, right onto Abbot Avenue. Our home is at the top of the hill.

WAIPAWA   *1km W of Waipawa*

B&B
Christl & Christopher Boys
17 Domain Road, Waipawa 4170

Tel (06) 857 8737 Fax (06) 857 8386
chmboys@clear.net.nz
www.bnb.co.nz/waipawa.html

Double $100 Single $75 (Special Breakfast)
Dinner $25 by arrangement   Smoking area inside
1 King 2 Single (2 bdrm)
Bathrooms: 1 Private

Gorgeous, centrally heated John Scott designed home one minute from State Highway 2 on Abbots Hill. Your home away from home has stunning views and beautiful rolling gardens. Enjoy European or NZ breakfast on the balcony nestled amongst the trees. Separate living, bathroom and entrance for privacy. 20 minutes drive to Hawkes Bay wine country. Optional stay close by at our spacious beach house for the ultimate getaway. Long, secluded beach and panoramic views. Wake up to the sun streaming through french doors in your separate double bedroom. German and English spoken. We have 2 dogs.

HAWKES BAY

WAIPAWA *40km S of Hastings*

Abbotsford Oaks *B&B*
Nicolette Brasell & Chris Davis
85 Abbotsford Road, Waipawa, Central Hawke's Bay

Tel (06) 857 8960 Fax (06) 857 8961
Mob 025 296 1160
nicolette@abbotsfordoaks.co.nz
www.abbotsfordoaks.co.nz

Double $135-$225 Single $100-$190 (Full Breakfast)
Dinner by arrangement Credit cards accepted
1 King 3 Queen (4 bdrm)
Bathrooms: 1 Ensuite 3 Private

Nicolette and Chris warmly welcome you to Abbotsford
Oaks. Nestled in picturesque central Hawke's Bay and
surrounded by 3.5 acres of gardens and orchard. Ideal for
that restful getaway (as our 2 cats have found), corporate
retreat, or as a base to explore the many attractions
Hawke's Bay has to offer. Beaches, wineries and art
deco/Spanish mission architecture are only 30 minutes
away. Golf courses and trout fishing are close by.

Our property was purpose built as a children's home in
the 1920s and has been extensively renovated to provide
quality boutique Bed & Breakfast accommodation. It
has spacious rooms most with their own sitting/sun room and private bathroom, with wonderful views
of the grounds and countryside. There is also a substantial and elegantly furnished guest lounge with
open fire where you can watch TV or just relax. The large dining room also has a comfortable lounge
area in which to relax, listen to music or read a book.

Breakfast either cooked or continental can be served in the dining room, the garden or your private
lounge. Complimentary coffee, tea and biscuits are available throughout the day. Dinner is available by
arrangement. Visit our website www.abbotsfordoaks.co.nz for more details.

Abbotsford Oaks offers a special venue for those wanting a break from their busy lifestyle

WAIPUKURAU *7km E of Waipukurau*

Approved

Mangatarata Country Estate   *Farmstay*
Judy & Donald Macdonald
415 Mangatarata Road, RD 5, Waipukurau

Tel (06) 858 8275   0800 858 857
Fax (06) 858 8270   Mob 021 480 769
mangatarata@xtra.co.nz
www.hawkesbaynz.com/pages/mangataratacountryestate

Double $150-$170 Single $85
(Full Breakfast) Dinner $35pp
2 Queen 1 Double 3 Single (4 bdrm)
Bathrooms: 1 Private 1 Guests share

Retreat to a beautiful historic homestead nestled in the heart of Hawkes Bay, Wine Country.

Unwind with uninterrupted farm views from the gracious Victorian verandah. Experience beef and sheep farming first hand or wander through the extensive gardens with swimming pool, pathways and a pond where birdlife prevails.

Enjoy a generous breakfast and good coffee in the private dining room or on the verandah, weather providing. Other sumptuous meals may be arranged by request. Gourmet lamb is Judy's speciality, complimented with fresh produce from the kitchen garden or grown locally

Donald is a pilot, fixed wing and helicopter and instructs in the local club's Tiger Moth. Donald and Judy have been hosting since 1985 and enjoy travelling.

Mangatarata is one of Hawkes Bay's most historic sheep stations and is still a working farm of 2500 acres. The perfect location for a memorable getaway with truly New Zealand uniqueness.

HAWKES BAY

WAIPUKURAU · *20km S of Waipukurau*

Hinerangi Station *Farmstay Self-contained*
Caroline & Dan von Dadelszen
615 Hinerangi Road, RD 1, Waipukurau

Tel (06) 855 8273 Fax (06) 855 8273
caroline@hinerangi.co.nz
www.hinerangi.co.nz

Double $110-$130 Single $80 (Full Breakfast)
Child $30 Dinner $35pp
Self Contained Cottage $120 Double, $40 per extra person
Children welcome Pets welcome
1 King/Twin 2 Queen 3 Single (4 bdrm)
Bathrooms: 2 Private

Hinerangi Station is an 1800 acre sheep, cattle and deer farm set in the rolling hills of central Hawkes Bay. Our spacious 1920 homestead was designed by Louis Hay of Napier art deco fame. It has a full size billiard table and there is a tennis court and swimming pool in the garden. Guests have their own private entrance. The Cookhouse, a recently renovated 100 year old cottage, offers self-contained accommodation for couples and families. We have one terrier and a cat.

WAIPUKURAU · *9km W of Waipukurau*

Mynthurst *Farmstay*
Annabelle & David Hamilton
912 Lindsay Road, RD 3, Waipukurau

Tel (06) 857 8093 Fax (06) 857 8093
Mob 027 232 2458 mynthurst@xtra.co.nz
www.bnb.co.nz/mynthurst.html

Double $150 Single $85 (Full Breakfast) Child $35
Dinner $35pp Extra space available for families
Children welcome
1 King/Twin 1 Double 1 Twin 1 Single (4 bdrm) Bathrooms: 1 Ensuite 1 Private

Mynthurst, genuine working sheep and cattle farm 560 hectares. Guests from NZ and overseas welcomed for 20 years. The homestead is large, warm and comfortable. Observe farm activities, enjoy swimming, trout fishing, golf, tennis, wineries. Dinner available on request, using finest local produce. Whether travelling north or south, visiting beautiful Hawkes Bay, you'll find Mynthurst the perfect retreat. 30 minutes from Hastings SH2. Booking avoids disappointment. Phone for directions. No smoking. Children welcome. 2 cats. Expect excellence. Farm tour included. Superb environment.

WAIPUKURAU · *4.5km S of Waipukurau*

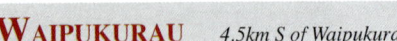

Pukeora Vineyard Cottage
Self-contained (Exclusive)
Kate Norman
Pukeora Estate, 208 Pukeora Scenic Road, RD 1
(off SH2 south of Waipukurau)

Tel (06) 858 9339 Fax (06) 858 6070
Mob 021 701 606 cottage@pukeora.com
www.pukeora.com

Double $100 Single $80 (Continental Breakfast)
Child $25 Children welcome
1 Queen 1 Double 2 Twin 1 Single (3 bdrm) Bathrooms: 1 Private

Our charming, hilltop country cottage boasts stunning views over the vineyard, river, plains and beyond. The spacious cottage built circa 1920, with character wooden floors, sunny verandah, and open plan lounge/kitchen with log fire, is a private annex to our house. Pukeora Estate, set on 86 acres, is a working 12 acre vineyard, boutique winery and a conventions venue. Your hosts Kate and Max, with daughters Jessica (age 2) and baby Marika, and 3 cats, welcome you. Wine tasting and sales available. Exclusive hire for each booking.

DANNEVIRKE   *1km N of Dannevirke*

B&B
Approved

Wahi Pai Cottage   *B&B Farmstay Homestay*
Nadeem & Peter
14 Wahi Pai Reserve,
Dannevirke

Tel (06) 374 6357   Fax (06) 374 6357
Mob 025 448 011
wahipai@yahoo.co.nz
www.bnb.co.nz/wahipai.html

Double $85   Single $55   (Continental Breakfast)
Dinner $25 per person Credit cards accepted
2 Queen (2 bdrm)
Bathrooms: 2 Ensuite

Wecome to Wahi Pai. A treasure to behold that should not be overlooked by the discerning traveller. Tranquility and ambience and the feeling of belonging to a different era quickly envelops you. Set on 10 acres with all the modern conveniences. Relax on the verandah and enjoy the sun and the sounds of the tuis and bellbirds. No smoking inside. Please phone for directions.

visit... **www.bnb.co.nz**

For the most up-to-date information from our hosts,
and links to our other web sites around the world.

HAWKES BAY

Manawatu and Horowhenua

Towns listed generally follow a north to south route. Refer to the index if required.

Feilding
Colyton

Oroua Downs

Palmerston North

Foxton

Waitarere Beach

Levin

Manakau

Otaki

0 Kilometres 10

0 Miles 6

COLYTON - FEILDING *16km E of Feilding*

Hiamoe *Farmstay*
Toos & John Cousins
Waiata, Colyton, Feilding

Tel (06) 328 7713 Fax (06) 328 7787
Mob 027 410 0931 johnhiamoe@clear.net.nz
www.bnb.co.nz/hiamoe.html

Double $80 Single $50 (Full Breakfast)
Child $20, preschool free Dinner $15
Children welcome Pets welcome
1 Queen 1 Double 1 Single (2 bdrm)
Bathrooms: 1 Ensuite

Toos, John, Edmund (10 years), Julius (9 years) and Guido (9 years) look forward to giving you a warm welcome to Hiamoe and during your stay, it is our aim that you experience a home away from home. We are the third generation, farming our deer, cattle, sheep and forestry property and live in a restored 100 year old colonial home. We have many interests, enjoy visitors and as Holland is Toos original homeland, we are accustomed to travel. Central heating, open fires, fenced pool.

FEILDING *Feilding Central*

Avoca Homestay *Homestay*
Margaret Hickmott
12 Freyberg Street, Feilding

Tel (06) 323 4699 margh-avoca@inspire.net.nz
www.bnb.co.nz/avocahomestay.html

Double $85 Single $50-$70 (Full Breakfast)
Dinner $25 by arrangement
1 Queen 2 Twin (2 bdrm)
Bathrooms: 1 Ensuite 1 Guests share 1 Host share

Enjoy a break in friendly Feilding, 12 times winner of
New Zealand's Most Beautiful Town Award. You are assured of a warm welcome and an enjoyable stay in a comfortable smoke free home set in an attractive garden with mature trees and a spectacular shrubbery. Off-street parking is provided for your vehicle. The main bedroom has a queen-size bed, ensuite and an outside entrance for your convenience. We are within easy walking distance of the town centre and well situated for the Manfield Park complex.

PALMERSTON NORTH - HOKOWHITU *Palmerston North Central*

Glenfyne *Homestay*
Jillian & Alex McRobert
413 Albert Street, Hokowhitu, Palmerston North

Tel (06) 358 1626 Fax (06) 358 1626
glenfyne@inspire.net.nz
www.bnb.co.nz/glenfyne.html

Double $80 Single $50 (Full Breakfast)
Credit cards accepted
1 Double 2 Single (2 bdrm)
Bathrooms: 1 Guests share

Welcome to Glenfyne. Our home is spacious and comfortable. We are a retired, non-smoking couple with many interests, including, meeting people, travel, cooking and golf. Our home is situated close to Massey University, the Manawatu Golf Club and 2 minutes walk will take you to the Hokowhitu Village (post office, pharmacy, restaurants etc). Jillian is a Kiwi Host, assuring you of excellent hospitality. Laundry, tea/coffee making facilities and covered off-street parking are available. We are happy to meet public transport.

MANAWATU HOROWHENUA

PALMERSTON NORTH *3.5km E of City Centre*

Clairemont *B&B*
Joy & Dick Archer
10 James Line, RD 10,
Palmerston North

Tel (06) 357 5508 Fax (06) 357 5501
clairemont@inspire.net.nz
www.bnb.co.nz/clairemont.html

Double $80 Single $50 (Full Breakfast)
1 Double 1 Twin (2 bdrm)
Bathrooms: 1 Guests share

Welcome to Clairemont. We are a rural spot within
the city boundary, plenty of trees and a quite extensive garden. On our 1 1/4 acres we keep a few sheep,
silky bantams, and our little dog Toby. We are handy to river walks, golf course, and shops are a few
minutes away. We have a cosy, spacious family home we would like to share with you. Our interests are
walking, gardening, model engineering and barbershop singing. Good off-street parking. Home-baked
suppers provided.

PALMERSTON NORTH *4km E of Palmerston North*

Panorama B&B *B&B*
Claire & Bill Sawers
30 Moonshine Valley Road,
RD 1, Aokautere, Palmerston North

Tel (06) 354 8816 Fax (06) 356 2757
panorama.bb@paradise.net.nz
www.homepages.paradise.net.nz/sawers/

Double $90 Single $60 (Full Breakfast) Child $20
Credit cards accepted Children welcome
1 Double 1 Twin (2 bdrm)
Bathrooms: 1 Private

A warm welcome awaits you at our home in Moonshine Valley. We offer a private and peaceful stay in
a rural-residential area. Situated only 8 minutes drive to the Square, 4 minutes to Massey University
and closer to the International Pacific College. Guests lounge/dining room with fridge and refreshments
always available. The bathroom includes a bath and shower. Interesting walkways are nearby, or just
relax on the terrace and enjoy the panoramic city, rural and mountain views with our cat, Sophie and
collie, Coby.

PALMERSTON NORTH *13km E of Palmerston North*

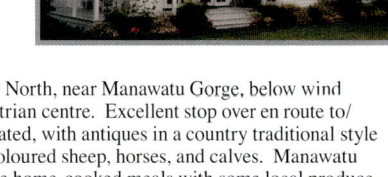

Country Lane Homestay *B&B Homestay*
Fay and Allan Hutchinson
52 Orrs Road, RD 1, Aokautere, Palmerston North

Tel (06) 326 8529 Fax (06) 326 9216
Mob 027 448 5833 countrylane@xtra.co.nz
www.bnb.co.nz/user82.html

Double $90-$120 Single $50-$75 (Full Breakfast)
Dinner $25-$30
1 King/Twin 1 Queen 1 Double 1 Single (3 bdrm)
Bathrooms: 1 Ensuite 2 Private
1 Guests share 1 Host share

Luxury country living, short distance from Palmerston North, near Manawatu Gorge, below wind
farm. 10km from Pacific College and 2km from equestrian centre. Excellent stop over en route to/
from Wellington, east coast. Our home is newly decorated, with antiques in a country traditional style
surrounded by our garden. Sawmill on the property, coloured sheep, horses, and calves. Manawatu
River borders our property. It is our pleasure to provide home-cooked meals with some local produce.
Directions: please phone. A brochure with map is available.

PALMERSTON NORTH   *5km SW of Central Palmerston North*

Udys on Anders   *B&B Self-contained*
Glenda & Tim Udy
52 Anders Road, Palmerston North

Tel **(06) 354 1722**   0800 157 981   Fax (06) 354 1711
Mob 027 440 9299   kiwitim@clear.net.nz
www.udysonanders.co.nz

Double $120   Single $90   (Full Breakfast)   Child $20
Dinner neg   Credit cards accepted   Children welcome
1 Queen 1 Double (1 bdrm)
Bathrooms: 1 Ensuite

We offer superior accommodation. An elegantly furnished self-contained apartment, own lounge and full kitchen. Quiet country location, huge lawn, edge of town, 7 minutes to CBD. Plexipave tennis court, beautiful mediterranean courtyard and large games room for our guests to make use of. Cleanliness, attention to detail and great hospitality are our priorities. We are well travelled and love meeting people. Enjoy your own space or get to know us. So...come, relax, enjoy. Tariff includes full breakfast. Apartment is smoke-free. Dinner by arrangement.

PALMERSTON NORTH   *5km E of Palmerston North*

Weltevreden B&B   *B&B*
Diann & Harry Vyver
11 The Bush Track, RD 1,
Aokautere, Palmerston North

Tel **(06) 357 6346**   Mob 025 411 803
d.vyver@xtra.co.nz
www.bnb.co.nz/weltevreden.html

Double $90   Single $60   (Full Breakfast)
Family $120   Separate Lounge
Credit cards accepted   Children welcome
1 Queen 1 Twin (2 bdrm)
Bathrooms: 1 Guests share

Shadowed beneath the undulating landscape of the Tararua Ranges and only 5 minutes (5km) drive from Palmerston North's city centre. Weltevreden offers guests a warm welcome and comfortable stay. Nestled amongst 20 acres of native NZ bush with 2.5 acres of spacious landscaped gardens. The bush is frequently visited by native bird life, namely the tui, fantail and wood pigeon. Guests share separate bathroom and lounge with TV, log fire, tea and coffee facilities.

OROUA DOWNS   *14km N of Foxton*

Oroua Downs Country Hideaway Bed & Breakfast
Farmstay
Bev & Ian Wilson
Omanuka Road,
RD 11, Foxton

Tel **(06) 329 9859**   Fax (06) 329 9859
Mob 027 249 2369   getwilsons@xtra.co.nz
www.bnb.co.nz/orouadownsfarmstay.html

Double $80   Single $40   (Full Breakfast)
Child $20   Dinner $25pp by arrangement
1 Queen 1 Double 1 Twin (3 bdrm)
Bathrooms: 1 Guests share

Bev and Ian invite you to share their spacious 2 storey, smoke-free home nestled amongst 1.5 acres of tree-lined gardens. Enjoy the opportunity to relax and leisurely walk amongst the garden listening to the bird song. We also operate a building and wooden toy manufacturing business. Directions: turn off at Bed & Breakfast sign on State Highway 1, 14km north of Foxton and 16km south of Sanson. Travel 2km down Omanuka Road.

LEVIN   *5min Levin*

Fantails *B&B Self-contained*
Heather Watson
40 MacArthur Street, Levin

Tel (06) 368 9011   Fax (06) 368 9279
fantails@xtra.co.nz   www.fantails.co.nz

Double $100-$130   Single $70-$90   (Special Breakfast)
Child neg   Dinner $45   Self-contained cottages $110-$150
Credit cards accepted   Pets welcome   Smoking area inside
1 King 2 Queen 1 Twin 4 Single (4 bdrm)
Bathrooms: 3 Ensuite 1 Private

Welcome to Fantails, set in 2 acres of park-like gardens only
minutes from the town centre by car. Experience our garden
where you can pick fruit of the season from our trees, view our
raised vegetable garden made of ponga logs. Learn about worm
farming and companion planting plus a little humour tossed in.

Our breakfasts are quite a treat with a lovely view of fantails,
native pigeons and other bird life. Different diets are catered for
and all our meals are certified organic.

We also have a treat for you with milking our goat (Mayling) or
you can have afternoon tea with our giant flemish bunnies (Anna
& Bella), excellent with children.

If you require timeout for a few days take one of our two cottages;
they sleep 2-4 people. They are very private and have everything
you require. In the evening why not try our sauna and whirlpool
spa and then rest in our quiet and secure environment and very
comfortable beds. Bikes for hire .

We are also only 1 hour away from the Wellington Ferry
Terminal and are smoke-free.

*A hidden oasis of native bush, mature trees,
native birds and other species*

WAITARERE BEACH *14km NW of Levin*

Dunes *Homestay Separate/Suite*
Robyn & Grant Powell
10 Ngati Huia Place, Waitarere Beach

Tel **(06) 368 6246** Mob 027 285 3643
sand.dunes@xtra.co.nz
www.bnb.co.nz/sand.dunes.html

Double $115 Single $75 (Continental Breakfast)
Dinner $30 Credit cards accepted
2 Queen (2 bdrm)
Bathrooms: 2 Ensuite

Robyn & Grant Powell welcome you to our new absolute beachfront retreat. Enjoy beach walks and magnificent views of Kapiti and Mounts Taranaki and Ruapehu. We offer 2 queen-size bedrooms with own private entrance and deck areas, ensuites, own living areas with TV, tea/coffee making facilities - continental breakfast provided. Situated 14km north west of Levin, approximately 1 $\frac{1}{2}$ from Wellington and 35 minutes from Palmerston North. Laundry facilities, off-street parking, non-smoking. Dinner by arrangement.

LEVIN *1 km N of Levin*

Greenacres *B&B Farmstay Homestay*
Derek & Dorothy Burt
88 Avenue North, Levin

Tel **(06) 368 7062** Fax (06) 368 7062
info@levinbb.com www.levinbb.com

Double $100 Single $70 (Full Breakfast)
Child neg Dinner $25 Credit cards accepted
Children welcome
2 Queen (2 bdrm)
Bathrooms: 2 Ensuite

Quality accommodation in peaceful, relaxing rural surrounds, warm hospitality and every comfort considered. Spacious bedrooms with ensuite, TV, coffee and tea in room. Laundry, computer, fax/ phone. Derek & Dorothy Burt your hosts, Somerset & Edward their cats. New house on 10 acres 1km north of Levin. Cattle in paddocks. Dinner available on request, full English or continental breakfast. 100 metres off SH1 on Avenue North. Horses and floats accommodated. Camper vans.

MANAKAU *6.5km N of Otaki*

Serendipity Country Homestay *Homestay*
Chris Lloyd & Barbara Lucas
1236 State Highway 1,
Manakau, RD 31, Levin

Tel **(06) 362 6031** Fax (06) 362 6331
Mob 027 413 1504 relax@serendipitynz.co.nz
www.serendipitynz.co.nz

Double $95-$130 Single $95-$130 (Full Breakfast)
Dinner $35-$50 Credit cards accepted Pets welcome
1 King/Twin 1 Queen 1 Double (3 bdrm)
Bathrooms: 2 Ensuite 1 Private

Experience Serendipity, a quality homestay, one hour from Wellington. Our home is not suitable for children. 3 comfortable bedrooms (2 air-conditioned) with all facilities. We have a large, varied home orchard and garden for fresh foods in season and make all of our delicious jams & jellies. Our bees provide honey. Please feel free to wander around the gardens - our elderly dog, Kariba, may keep you company. The native plantings and nearby bush encourage visits by tui, kereru and fantails.

MANAWATU
HOROWHENUA

Wairarapa

Colyton

Woodville

Pahiatua

Mangamaire

Oroua Downs

Palmerston North

Tokomaru

Foxton

Levin

Otaki

Te Horo

Waikanae

Masterton

Carterton

Featherston

Greytown

Upper Hutt

Martinborough

Kahutara

Towns listed generally follow
a north to south route. Refer
to the index if required.

0   Kilometres   20

0   Miles   12

PAHIATUA - MANGAMAIRE   *8km S of Pahiatua*

Lizzie's Country Bed & Breakfast
B&B Separate/Suite Self-contained
Lizzie & Craig Udy
86 Mangamaire Road, Mangamaire, Pahiatua

Tel (06) 376 7367   Fax (06) 376 7367
Mob 025 204 2648   craigandlizudy@inspire.net.nz
www.bnb.co.nz/lizzies.html

Double $100   Single $70   (Full Breakfast)   Child $20
Extra adult $30   C/C accepted   Children welcome
1 King 2 Single (2 bdrm)   Bathrooms: 1 Private

Lizzie and Craig welcome you to our friendly home and
mini-farm. Your tastefully decorated, self-contained, private accommodation is the entire lower storey
of our spacious home and includes a private lounge and dining with log fire. Relax and watch a movie
in our luxurious home cinema, take a swim in the pool or soak under the stars in our outdoor hot water
bath in an intimate bush setting. Enjoy our farm animals, tour the wind farm, go trout fishing, visit the
wildlife centre or go horse trekking. You can dine out at our award winning local restaurant or relax and
have the cuisine delivered to your dining table.

PAHIATUA   *19km E of Palmerson North*

Borderlands B&B   *B&B Separate/Suite*
Rural self-contained cottage
Tania & Mark McBride
933 Makomako Road, RD 3, Pahiatua

Tel (06) 376 6064   M-TM@xtra.co.nz
www.bnb.co.nz/borderlands.html

Double $100   Single $70   (Continental Breakfast)   Child neg
Credit cards accepted   Children welcome
1 Queen (1 bdrm)   Bathrooms: 1 Private

Experience a unique slice of rural life. Your bedroom/deck offers
views of the Tararua foothills and farmland. Ramble along the
7 acre woodland garden, play tennis or visit the farm animals.
Explore the Tararua, Wairarapa, Manawatu and Hawke's Bay
regions. Bathe in the antique clawfoot bath or relax by the logfire
in the spacious lounge. Full kitchen, television, seperate shower.
Small creek beside cottage, laundry facilities available.
20 minutes to Palmerston North or Pahiatua. We have 3 children, 2 friendly dogs and 2 cats.

MASTERTON   *3km W of Masterton*

Harefield   *B&B Farmstay Self-contained*
Marion Ahearn
147 Upper Plain Road, Masterton

Tel (06) 377 4070   Fax (06) 377 4070
www.bnb.co.nz/harefield.html

Double $80   Single $45   (Full Breakfast)
Child ¹/2 price   Dinner $20 by arrangement
Self-contained flat for 2 $55   Children welcome
1 Double 1 Single (1 bdrm)
Bathrooms: 1 Private

A warm welcome awaits you at Harefield, a small farmlet on the edge of town. A quiet country
garden surrounds the cedar house and self-contained flat. The flat has 1 bedroom with double and
single beds. 2 divan beds in living area. Self-cater or have breakfast in our warm dining room.
Convenient for restaurants, showgrounds, vineyards, schools, tramping. 1 ¹/2 hour drive to Picton
Ferry. We enjoy meeting people, aviation, travel, reading, art, farming and tramping.
Baby facilities available. Smoke-free.

MASTERTON *10km W of Masterton*

Tidsfordriv *B&B Rural Homestay*
Glenys Hansen
4 Cootes Road, Matahiwi
RD 8, Masterton

Tel (06) 378 9967 Fax (06) 378 9957
ghansen@contact.net.nz
www.bnb.co.nz/tidsfordriv.html

Double $80-$85 Single $50 (Full Breakfast)
Child ¹/₂ price Dinner $20 by arrangement
Credit cards accepted Children welcome
1 Queen 2 Single (2 bdrm) Bathrooms: 1 Private

A warm welcome awaits you at 'Tidsfordriv' - a 64 acre farmlet - 7km off the main bypass route. A comfortable modern home set in park like surroundings with large gardens, ponds and many species of wetland birds. Enjoy bird watching with ease. Glenys has home-hosted for 17 years and invites you to join her for dinner. Conservation, gardening and travel are her interests. A labrador dog is the family pet. Local Wairarapa attractions - National Wildlife Centre, gardens, vineyards, Tararua Forest Park.

MASTERTON *1km E of Masterton*

Mas des Saules *Homestay*
Mary & Steve Blakemore
9A Pokohiwi Road, Homebush, Masterton

Tel (06) 377 2577   Fax (06) 377 2578
Mob 027 620 8728   mas-des-saules@wise.net.nz
www.bnb.co.nz/masdessaules.html

Double $110 Single $65 (Full Breakfast)
Child $40 Dinner $35 Credit cards accepted
Children welcome Pets welcome
2 Queen (2 bdrm) Bathrooms: 1 Guests Share

Down a country lane, amongst apple orchards, discover our tranquil French Provencal farmhouse with its stream, water fowl, and petanque court. Our children have departed, leaving us with a cat, small dog, and cattle on our small farm. Guest lounge and bathroom with bath and shower. Open fire and central heating. Enjoy farmhouse cooking with fresh vegetables from our large country garden. We can also provide barbecues and picnic lunches. We are a well travelled couple who enjoy helping guests discover the unspoilt Wairarapa.

MASTERTON *2km E of Masterton*

Apple Source Orchard Stay *Farmstay*
Niel & Raewyn Groombridge
Te Ore Ore,
RD 6, Masterton

Tel (06) 377 0820   Fax (06) 370 9401
Mob 021 667 092   racg@wise.net.nz
www.bnb.co.nz/applesource.html

Double $100 Single $75 (Continental Breakfast)
Child ¹/₂ price Dinner $30   Credit cards accepted
2 Queen 1 Single (2 bdrm)
Bathrooms: 2 Ensuite

Try an experience that's a little different! Our colonial style homestead is set in an operating apple orchard and has a separate guest wing with lounge and two bedrooms with ensuites. You are welcome to share dinner (special diets catered for) with us and enjoy the ambience of Stanley range-based cooking along with relaxing by the open fire or on the deck. There are orchard walks and a garden haven. Watch the daily orchard activities and pick some fruit in season. Ask us about the Model A Tourer courtesy car.

MASTERTON *Central Masterton*

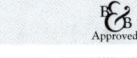

Victoria House *B&B Guesthouse*
Marion and Sara Monks and Mike Parker
15 Victoria Street,
Masterton

Tel (06) 377 0186   Fax (06) 377 0186
parker.monks@xtra.co.nz
www.bnb.co.nz/victoriahouse.html

Double $80   Single $50 Twin $80
(Continental Breakfast)   Credit cards accepted
3 Double 1 Twin 2 Single (6 bdrm)
Bathrooms: 2 Guests share

Victoria House is a 2 storey house built pre-1886, renovated to retain the character of the period. The peaceful nature of the furnishings and outdoor area create a quiet, relaxing atmosphere, great for a "get away from it" weekend. We are also only a 3 minute walk from the town centre and Masterton's excellent restaurants. Being "wine friendly" hosts we enjoy discussing wines and freely offer advice on the Wairarapa's growing wine industry.

MASTERTON *Masterton Central*

Natusch Town House *B&B Self-contained*
Anne Bohm
55 Lincoln Road, Masterton

Tel (06) 378 9252   Fax (06) 378 9330
Mob 021 617 398   anne@natusch.co.nz
www.natusch.co.nz

Double $160   Single $100   (Continental Breakfast)
Credit cards accepted
4 Queen 1 Single (4 bdrm)
Bathrooms: 1 Ensuite 1 Private

Self contained, hosts live off-site. Booking is for the
whole house. You choose who, if any, are to share with you. A marvellous old 2 storied self-contained home built in 1893. Right in the centre of town within easy reach of great dining, bars, parks etc. 4 double bedrooms each with a queen-sized bed, 2 bathrooms, parlour, dining room and well appointed modern kitchen, off-street parking for up to 4 cars. Old style with luxury appointments. This is an Historic Places Trust listed home - a delight to stay in. A delicious breakfast is included on a self help basis.

MASTERTON *7km E of Masterton*

Grapeview *B&B Homestay*
Carol & Quenten Hansen
17 Te Ore Ore Settlement Rd, RD 6, Masterton

Tel (06) 370 8919   Mob 021 292 6062
cqhansen@xtra.co.nz
www.bnb.co.nz/grapeview.html

Double $80-$85 Single $50   (Continental Breakfast)
Child $30   Dinner $20 by arrangement
Credit cards accepted   Children welcome
1 Double 2 Single (2 bdrm)
Bathrooms: 1 Private

Grapeview provides the perfect relaxing stop over. It is situated in a tranquil environment overlooking a vineyard with stunning views of the Tararaua Ranges. Our home garden and pond with its own jetty and wildlife are for you to enjoy. You will be welcomed by the smell of fresh flowers, home-baking and brewed coffee, perhaps even Pollyana the cat. Breakfast will be served at your leisure and we invite you to join us for dinner or we can drive you to a local restaurant or function.

CARTERTON   *1km N of Carterton*

Homecroft   *B&B Separate/Suite*
Christine & Neil Stewart
Somerset Road,
RD 2, Carterton

Tel (06) 379 5959 homecroft@xtra.co.nz
www.bnb.co.nz/homecroft.html

Double $85-$95 Single $50   (Full Breakfast)
Dinner $25pp by arrangement
1 Queen 1 Double 1 Twin (3 bdrm)
Bathrooms: 1 Ensuite 1 Private

Homecroft is surrounded by our country garden and farmland yet handy to the vineyards, crafts, antiques, and golf courses of the Wairarapa. Wellington and the Interisland Ferry 90 minutes away. Guests accommodation, with own entrance, in a separate wing of the house with small lounge, the sunny bedrooms open onto a deck. The double room with ensuite, The Croft is separate from the house. All bedrooms overlook the garden. A leisurely breakfast at Homecroft is an enjoyable experience. We look forward to making your stay with us happy and relaxing.

CARTERTON   *3km S of Carterton*

Portland House   *B&B*
Judy Betts
Portland Road, State Highway 2,
Carterton

Tel (06) 379 8809   Mob 025 602 8358
portlandhouse@paradise.net.nz
www.bnb.co.nz/portlandhouse.html

Double $80 Single $50   (Full Breakfast)
Dinner by prior arrangement   Credit cards accepted
1 Queen 1 Twin (2 bdrm)
Bathrooms: 1 Private 1 Guests share 1 Host share

A warm and friendly welcome awaits you at Portland House, a 130 year old refurbished villa and home to birmans, Missy and George. You can rest, relax and enjoy the country air of the Wairarapa in our peaceful surroundings and comfortable home. We are just off the main highway (SH2) and within 5-10 minutes drive to Masterton, the cafés in Greytown, the vineyards in Martinborough, the scenic Waiohine Gorge, the Tararua Forest Park and many wonderful Wairarapa gardens.

GREYTOWN   *Greytown Central*

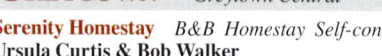

Serenity Homestay   *B&B Homestay Self-contained*
Ursula Curtis & Bob Walker
37 Jellicoe Street,
Greytown

Tel (06) 304 8666   Mob 025 465 535 or 021 211 7165
serenity.homestay@ihug.co.nz
www.bnb.co.nz/serenityhomestay.html

Double $100-$120 Single $80   (Full Breakfast)
Credit cards accepted
2 Queen 1 Single (3 bdrm)
Bathrooms: 1 Ensuite 1 Guests share

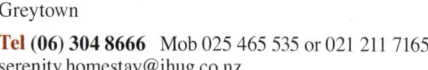

Set in an acre of grounds, we offer a private or romantic getaway in The Cottage; a fully self-contained 1 bedroom home with its own facilities for cooking, washing and relaxing. Or you can stay in our home. Either way you will enjoy the serenity and beauty of our landscaped gardens and can relax in the separate spa pool. Non-smokers preferred. We are situated within easy walking distance of the Greytown shops and restaurants and the wine fields of Martinborough are just 12 minutes away by car. Weekly rates available.

GREYTOWN   *80km N of Wellington*

The Ambers
B&B Homestay Self contained serviced apartment
Marilla Rankin
58A McMaster Street, Greytown

Tel (06) 304 8588 Fax (06) 304 8590
Mob 025 994 394
ambershomestay@xtra.co.nz
www.ambershomestay.co.nz

Double $100-$120 Single $75-$100
(Continental Breakfast) Child $25
Self-contained cottage
Credit cards accepted   Children welcome
1 King 1 Queen 2 Double 1 Single (4 bdrm)
Bathrooms: 3 Ensuite 1 Host share

The Ambers is now in a 1920's two storey home originally from Lowry Bay in Wellington, moved over the Rimutaka Ranges and set on a lovely private section with mature trees. We offer spacious accommodation in this new home. **The Cherub Room** has a large ensuite bathroom, queen bed, TV and coffee making facilities, french doors opening onto deck. **The Vintage Suite** provides a large ensuite bathroom, king bed, private lounge with TV and coffee making facilities, a single bed for extra guests or children in the same group. **The Oak-Aged Room** has a shared bathroom, double bed. This room is ideal for any overflow or big groups wishing to stay together.

The Ambers now offers a serviced apartment **The Garden Suite** with french doors to own outdoor area.(see Photo) Great for romantic weekends. Facilities include a mini kitchen with microwave and fridge, lounge area with TV and sofa bed for the kids, a double bed and bathroom.

If you desire the ultimate privacy or a 'romantic getaway' we offer a "Blissful" cottage set in its own private garden featuring lovely old trees. Country Bliss Cottage has two double bedrooms, with own amenities including fire and bath. For tariff please contact Marilla Rankin at above numbers.

GREYTOWN *2km W of Greytown*

Totara Manoir *Homestay*
Lyn & Peter Besseling
RD 1 Woodside Road, Greytown

Tel (06) 304 7972 Fax (06) 304 7960
Mob 025 579 130
p.besseling@xtra.co.nz
www.bnb.co.nz/totara.html

Double $110 Single $60 (Continental Breakfast)
1 Queen 1 Double (2 bdrm)
Bathrooms: 2 Ensuite

Totara Manoir, is a rural homestay situated 2km from
the heart of Greytown. Enjoy expansive rural views while meandering on the wrap around verandahs.
Relax in the internal courtyard, read a book or two. Wander around the property or explore the small
totara forest. Play petanque, feed the alpacas and gotland sheep. A pleasant 30 minute walk sees you
in the heart of Greytown with its many shops and cafés.

FEATHERSTON

Woodland Holt Bed & Breakfast *B&B*
Judi Adams
47 Watt Street, Featherston

Tel (06) 308 9927 Mob 025 291 2774
woodland-holt@xtra.co.nz
www.bnb.co.nz/woodlandholtbedbreakfast.html

Double $100-$120 Single $65 (Continental Breakfast)
Dinner $35
1 Double 1 Twin 1 Single (3 bdrm)
Bathrooms: 1 Guests share

Providing friendly hospitality. Interests include
travelling, gardening, books, music, cross-stitch and collecting. Secluded gardens contain native, exotic
and rare plants. Warm, luxury accommodation with off-street parking. Breakfast includes home-made
treats and preserves. Explore beautiful Wairarapa or relax in comfort. View Meakin-at-Woodland, an
extensive private collection of china by Alfred Meakin and J&G Meakin. Dine at a local restaurant
or arrange to join me for an evening meal. Picnic hampers are available (additional charge). We look
forward to your company and making your stay enjoyable.

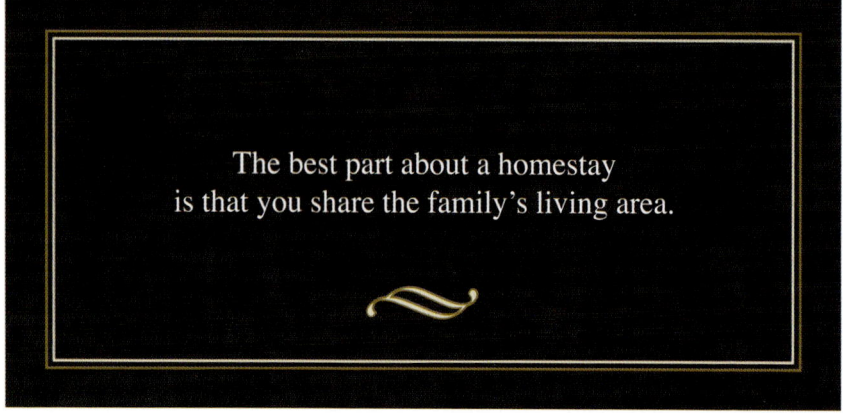

The best part about a homestay
is that you share the family's living area.

SOUTH WAIRARAPA - KAHUTARA   *13km SW of Martinborough*

B&B Separate/Suite
Jane and Sam Cooke
2298 Kahutara Road,
Near Featherston, South Wairarapa

Tel (06) 308 8881   Mob 021 476 989
jane@reddeckchair.co.nz
www.reddeckchair.co.nz

Double $100-$130   Single $70   (Full Breakfast)
Child $30   Dinner by arrangement
Extra bed in king room $30   Children welcome
2 King/Twin 2 Queen (4 bdrm)
Bathrooms: 1 Ensuite 1 Private 1 Guests share

Stay and Play - you won't want to leave! Escape and delight in our spacious rural home. Snooze in the garden. Swim. Pitch golf balls in the paddock - but mind the deer and ostrich over the fence! BYO wine to enjoy with a delicious home-cooked evening meal and perhaps encourage Sam to play his guitar! Close to vineyards, walks, golf, fishing and canoes.   Visit www.reddeckchair.co.nz for details of our creative workshops and celebrations with a twist.

MARTINBOROUGH   *0.5km NW of Martinborough*

Oak House   *B&B Homestay*
Polly & Chris Buring
45 Kitchener Street, Martinborough

Tel (06) 306 9198   Fax (06) 306 8198
chrispolly.oakhouse@xtra.co.nz
www.bnb.co.nz/oakhouse.html

Double $100-$120   Single $55   (Special Breakfast)
Child by arrangement   Dinner by arrangement
2 Queen 2 Single (3 bdrm)
Bathrooms: 1 Ensuite 1 Guests share

Our characterful 80 year old Californian bungalow offers gracious accommodation. Our spacious lounge provides a relaxed setting for sampling winemaker Chris's wonderful products. Our guest wing has its own entrance, bathroom (large bath and shower) and separate wc. Our new bedroom has ensuite facilities. Bedrooms enjoy afternoon sun and garden views. Breakfast features fresh croissants, home preserved local fruits and conserves. Creative cook Polly matches delicious dishes (often local game) with Chris's great wines. Tour our onsite winery with Chris. Meet our multi-talented cats.

MARTINBOROUGH   *1km SW of Martinborough*

Ross Glyn   *Homestay*
Kenneth & Odette Trigg
1 Grey Street, Martinborough

Tel (06) 306 9967   Fax (06) 306 8267
Mob 021 217 6337   rossglyn1@hotmail.com
www.bnb.co.nz/rossglyn.html

Double $95   Single $65   (Full Breakfast)
Dinner $25+   Credit cards accepted
Children welcome
1 Double 2 Single (2 bdrm)
Bathrooms: 1 Private 1 Guests share

Our home nestles in over 2 acres of landscaped gardens which includes a rose garden, orchard, Japanese garden and we are surrounded by vineyards. Both our guestrooms have french doors opening onto a sunny deck with private access. Guests are welcome to relax with us and our small spoilt dog and cat in our large cosy (woodburner heated) lounge. Breakfast includes fresh croissants, home-made jams, jellies and preserved fruit. Cooked breakfast on request and dinner by arrangement.

MARTINBOROUGH   *Martinborough Central*

Beatson's of Martinborough   *B&B Self-contained*
Karin Beatson & John Cooper
9A Cologne Street,
Martinborough, Wairarapa

Tel (06) 306 8242   Fax (06) 306 8243
Mob 0274 499 827   beatsons@wise.net.nz
www.beatsons.co.nz

Double $120-$150 Single $100   (Full Breakfast)
Dinner by arrangement   Credit cards accepted
4 King/Twin 5 Queen (9 bdrm)
Bathrooms: 9 Ensuite

Beatson's offer a friendly and relaxed stay. Harrington and Cologne are restored villas operated as hosted guest houses for your year round comfort. Individually decorated spacious bedrooms with ensuites feature. In the living rooms french doors open onto verandahs overlooking the gardens. Full country breakfasts use local produce, home made breads and preserves. Dinner and functions by arrangement. Beatson's are just 5 minutes walk from Martinborough Square with its cafés and restaurants. Close to great wineries.

MARTINBOROUGH   *1km Martinborough*

The Old Manse   *B&B Homestay*
Sandra & John Hargrave
Corner Grey & Roberts Streets, Martinborough

Tel (06) 306 8599   0800 399 229
Fax (06) 306 8540   Mob 025 399 229
info@oldmanse.co.nz
www.bnb.co.nz/theoldmanse.html

Double $150-$170 (Full Breakfast)
Credit cards accepted
5 Queen 1 Twin (6 bdrm)
Bathrooms: 6 Ensuite

In the heart of the wine district, a beautifully restored Presbyterian Manse, built 1876, has been transformed into a boutique homestay. Spacious, relaxed accommodation in a quiet, peaceful setting. One twin, 5 queen size bedrooms all with their own ensuites. All day sun. Off-street parking, open fireplace. Amenities include spa pool, petanque, billiards. Enjoy breakfast or wine overlooking vineyard. Walking distance to Martinborough Square with selection of excellent restaurants. Close to vineyards, antique and craft shops, adventure quad bikes and golf courses. Qualmark 4+

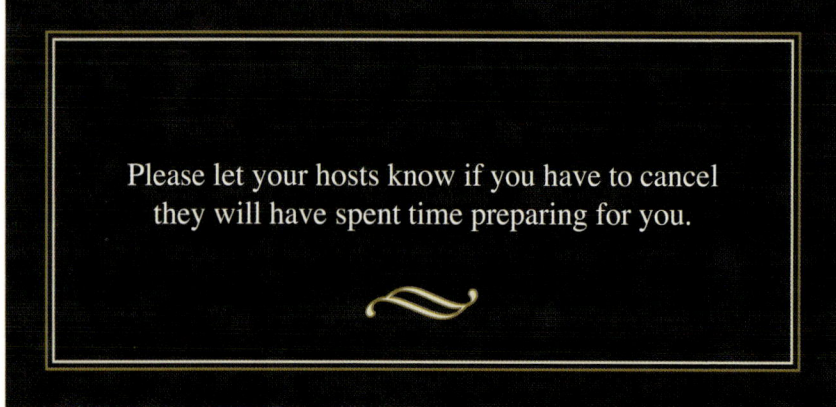

Please let your hosts know if you have to cancel
they will have spent time preparing for you.

Planning a trip around Australia?

Ask for …

The Bed & Breakfast Book
Australia 2005

Accommodation with Character

- Small Hotels
- Romantic Hideaways
- Pet Friendly Getaways
- Self-Contained Cottages
- Short Breaks for the less able
- Farmstays and Retreats for Families and Children

Available on-line at www.bnb.co.nz and good book shops

$19.95

Moonshine Press
PO Box 6843, Wellington, New Zealand
Phone (04) 385 2615, Fax (04) 385 2694, info@bnb.co.nz

Wellington

Towns listed generally follow
a north to south route. Refer
to the index if required.

Kapiti Island

Manaka

Otaki

Te Horo

Waikanae

Paraparaumu

Paekakariki

Pukerua Bay

Plimmerton

Pauatahanui

Whitby

Upper Hutt

Tawa

Stokes Valley

Lower Hutt

Korokoro

Petone

Wainuiomata

Eastbourne

Ohariu Valley   Johnsonville

See
Wellington City
next page

Aro Valley   Mt Victoria
Brooklyn   Hataitai
Vogeltown   Mt Cook
Mornington   Karaka Bay
Melrose   Seatoun
Island Bay   Breaker Bay
Palmer Head
Wellington
International
Airport

0   Kilometres   10

0   Miles   6

Wellington City

Towns listed generally follow a north to south route. Refer to the index if required.

Khandallah

Ngaio

Wadestown
Thorndon

Interisland ferry terminal

Karori

Kelburn

Aro Valley

Brooklyn

Vogeltown

Mornington

Melrose

Island Bay

Wellington Central

Oriental Bay
Roseneath

Mt Victoria

Mt. Cook

Hataitai

Seatoun

Wellington International Airport

TE HORO   *3km S of Otaki*

Cottle Bush   *B&B Homestay*
Roz White & Jon Allan
990a State Highway 1,
Te Horo 5560

Tel (06) 364 3566   Mob 021 254 3501
jonandroz@msn.com
www.bnb.co.nz/cottlebush.html

Double $90-$120   Single $65-$80   (Full Breakfast)
Dinner $30
2 Queen 1 Twin (3 bdrm)
Bathrooms: 1 Ensuite 1 Guests share

Roz and Jon invite you to share their spacious 2 storey, smoke-free home, nestled among the mature native totara, matai and titoki trees of Cottle Bush. Join us and our friendly dogs for a relaxing stay in a secluded rural atmosphere, not far from local attractions and amenities and only an hour from Wellington. When you wake, enjoy your choice of cooked or continental breakfast. In the evening dine at a local restaurant or join us for dinner. Please make contact prior to arrival by letter, phone or email.

TE HORO   *7 km N of Waikanae*

Pateke Lagoons Wetlands   *B&B Farmstay Homestay*
Peter & Adrienne Dale
152 Te Hapua Road, Te Horo, RD 1, Otaki

Tel (06) 364 2222   Fax (06) 364 2214
Mob 021 439 661   peter@pateke-lagoons.co.nz
www.pateke-lagoons.co.nz

Double $195   Single $175   (Special Breakfast)
Dinner $65 including wine   Credit cards accepted
2 Queen 1 Single (2 bdrm)
Bathrooms: 2 Ensuite 1 Private

Pateke Lagoons is a purpose built lodge overlooking a private 50 acre wetland and wildfowl refuge. It offers peace and quiet in tranquil rural surroundings. 2 guest rooms, each with private courtyard. Large lounge with wildfowl and wetland ecology library. Beautiful views of farmland, sea and wetland. Easy 30 minute walking tracks through native bush and wetland, with golf cart available. Fresh seafood is our specialty with garden fresh vegetables. Full breakfast using local products. Feed the horses and pet the cat. Open wetlands are unsuitable for children.

WAIKANAE   *59 N of Wellington*

Shepreth Homestay   *B&B Homestay*
Lorraine & Warren Birch
12 Major Durie Place, Waikanae Beach 6010

Tel 04 905 2130   Fax 04 905 2139
Mob 0274 441 088
shepreth@paradise.net.nz
www.bnb.co.nz/shepreth.html

Double $100-$120   Single $70-$80 (Full Breakfast)
Credit cards accepted
1 Queen 2 Twin (2 bdrm)
Bathrooms: 1 Private

You will find it easy to relax and enjoy your surroundings in our comfortable modern home overlooking Kapiti Island and the beach. The spacious guest rooms have their own lounge and kitchenette. Breakfasts are delicious! We only take one party of guests at a time, and enjoy spending time with both New Zealand and overseas guests. We're 50 minutes from Wellington, easy to find, with several cafés and restaurants close by. Our cat lives here too. You are assured of a warm welcome.

WAIKANAE BEACH   *5km W of Waikanae*

Konini Cottage and Homestead
Separate/Suite Self-contained
Maggie & Bob Smith
26 Konini Crescent, Waikanae Beach, Kapiti Coast

Tel (04) 904 6610 Fax (04) 904 6610
konini@paradise.net.nz www.konini.co.nz

Double $130 Single $115 (Full Breakfast)
Child $25 Extra person $45
Less $15 per head if self catering.
Credit cards accepted Children welcome
2 Queen 2 Single (3 bdrm)
Bathrooms: 2 Private

Set in an acre of tranquil grounds, both the Lockwood Cottage and Homestead offer a restful haven just 300 metres from the beach and bordering the golf links. For the independent traveller the Cottage is your choice with full self-catering facilities. Deduct $15 per head if breakfast not required. The Homesteads guest wing offers a traditional B&B. Directions: turn off SH1 at traffic lights to beach, 4km to old service station, take right fork, then first right, 1km to Konini Crescent.

WAIKANAE   *1km E of Waikanae*

Country Patch *Self-contained*
Sue & Brian Wilson
18 Kea Street, Waikanae

Tel (04) 293 5165 Fax (04) 293 5164
Mob 027 457 8421 booking@countrypatch.co.nz
www.countrypatch.co.nz

Double $110-$185 Single $85-$130
(Continental Breakfast) Child $25
Dinner by arrangement
Credit cards accepted Children welcome
2 King/Twin 1 Queen 2 Single (3 bdrm)
Bathrooms: 3 Ensuite

2 delightful self-contained accommodation sites. Country patch studio with its own entrance and deck has a queen bed with ensuite and twin beds on the mezzanine floor of the kitchen lounge. Country patch villa has an open fire and a large verandah with magic views. It is wheelchair accessible and the 2 bedrooms (each with ensuite) have king beds that unzip to twin. We warmly invite you to share our patch of the country with Kate (16), Simon (14) and Holly, our labrador.

WAIKANAE   *6km E of Waikanae*

RiverStone *B&B Self-contained Rural Cottage*
Paul & Eppie Murton
111 Ngatiawa Road,
Waikanae

Tel (04) 293 1936 Fax (04) 293 1936
riverstone@paradise.net.nz
www.bnb.co.nz/riverstone.html

Double $100-$120 Single $70 (Full Breakfast)
Child $45 Credit cards accepted
1 Queen 1 Twin (2 bdrm)
Bathrooms: 1 Private

Birdsong, the sound of the river and complete privacy.
Peace and quiet with a scrumptious breakfast and
comfortable accommodation. Riverstone has 5 hectares of paddocks and garden with river walks and local pottery and café. Waikanae, Raumati and Paraparaumu have a variety of cafés, shops, boutiques, Lindale Farm Park, the Southward Car Museum, Nga Manu Bird Sanctuary, golf courses and beautiful beaches. Pick up from train or bus. Laundry facilities. Smoke-free. No pets.

WAIKANAE *Waikanae*

Camellia Cottage @ Sudbury Estate *B&B*
Homestay Boutique Cottage
Glenys and Brian Daw
39 Manu Grove, Waikanae 6010, Kapiti Coast

Tel (04) 902 8530 Fax (04) 902 8531
Mob 021 129 6970 stay@sudbury.co.nz
www.sudbury.co.nz

Double $150-$195 Single $120-$195
(Special Breakfast) Dinner by arrangement
Credit cards accepted
2 Queen (2 bdrm) Bathrooms: 1 Private 1 Guests share

'The place to stay in Kapiti' 50 minutes from Wellington.
Sincere Kiwi hospitality in a superb location. Charming fully equipped self-contained cottage tastefully furnished and nestled in a beautiful 2 $^1/_2$ acre garden with large lily pond. We also offer traditional B&B in our residence. Handy to SH1 - 4 golf courses - galleries and museum - bush walks and beach nearby - Excellent local restaurants - Off-street parking - TV/DVD/Hi-Fi. Guest email/fax/phone - A relaxing and peaceful environment where your comfort is our priority.

WAIKANAE BEACH *5km N of Paraparaumu*

Waikanae Beach B&B/Homestay *B&B Homestay*
Helen Anderson
115 Tutere Street, Waikanae Beach 6010

Tel (04) 902 5829 Fax (04) 902 5840
Mob 021 259 3396 helenanderson@xtra.co.nz
www.bnb.co.nz/waikanaebeach.html

Double $110-$130 Single $90-$110 (Full Breakfast)
Child $40 under 12 years Credit cards accepted
2 Queen 1 Single (2 bdrm)
Bathrooms: 1 Ensuite 1 Private

Need to unwind? Then look no further! Come and experience warm and friendly hospitality by the sea. Count stars, not sheep and fall asleep to the soothing sound of the ocean. Direct access to a sandy swimming beach where you can enjoy long leisurely walks, beautiful sunsets, spectacular views of Kapiti Island, and the Tararua Ranges. Tea making facilities. Generous breakfasts. Dinner by prior arrangement. Guest laundry. Off-street parking. Good restaurants nearby. Please request directions when booking. Looking forward to meeting you soon.

WAIKANAE *6km N of Paraparaumu*

Broadeaves Bed & Breakfast *B&B*
Liz Kirkland
24 Ngarara Road, Waikanae

Tel (04) 293 1483 Fax (04) 293 1583
Mob 021 545 175 stay@broadeaves.co.nz
www.broadeaves.co.nz

Double $120-$200 Single $100 (Special Breakfast)
Child $25-50 Dinner by arrangement
Credit cards accepted Children welcome Pets welcome
1 King/Twin 2 Queen (3 bdrm)
Bathrooms: 1 Ensuite 1 Private 1 Guests share

Elegant accommodation for the entire family. Whether its just a night away or your honeymoon, join us for a drink, relax and wander around our garden. The separate guest wing includes large luxurious bedroom, ensuite and private spa pool. After a great night's sleep you'll enjoy a freshly prepared breakfast. Visit local tourist attractions, dine in great restaurants or just sleep in. We invite you to share our paradise with Thomas and Rebecca (the kids) and our 2 dogs. We can also provide childcare.

PARAPARAUMU   *55kms N of Wellington*

Homestay
Jude & Vic Young
72 Bluegum Road, Paraparaumu

Tel (04) 902 0199   Fax (04) 902 0199
judeandvicyoung@paradise.net.nz
www.bnb.co.nz/youngparaparaumu.html

Double $80   Single $50   (Full Breakfast)
Child ¹/2 price   Dinner $20   Children welcome
1 Queen 1 Twin (2 bdrm)
Bathrooms: 1 Private 1 Guests share 1 Host share

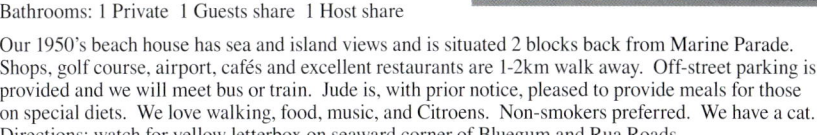

Our 1950's beach house has sea and island views and is situated 2 blocks back from Marine Parade. Shops, golf course, airport, cafés and excellent restaurants are 1-2km walk away. Off-street parking is provided and we will meet bus or train. Jude is, with prior notice, pleased to provide meals for those on special diets. We love walking, food, music, and Citroens. Non-smokers preferred. We have a cat. Directions: watch for yellow letterbox on seaward corner of Bluegum and Rua Roads.

PARAPARAUMU   *55km N of Wellington*

M & S Homestay   *Self-contained*
Sytske & Marius Kruiniger
60A Ratanui Road, Paraparaumu

Tel (04) 299 8098   (after hours) (04) 297 3447
Fax (04) 297 3447   mskapiti@xtra.co.nz
www.bnb.co.nz/mshomestay.html

Double $75   Single $60   (Continental Breakfast)
Child $5 under 5 years   Extra persons $10
Credit cards accepted   Children welcome
1 Queen 2 Single (2 bdrm)   Bathrooms: 1 Private

Our self-contained accommodation is peaceful and sunny. A view across small lake, full with wildlife. Beach, shopping centre and excellent restaurants close by. Sunny lounge with TV, books and games; well equipped kitchen, bathroom and laundry facilities. Information about indoor and outdoor attractions available. No dogs please and guests are asked not to smoke indoors. Please phone or fax for bookings and directions. We look forward meeting you. Breakfast is optional and is $7.50 per person.

PARAPARAUMU BEACH   *5.km NW of Paraparaumu*

Beachstay   *Homestay*
Ernie & Rhoda Stevenson
17 Takahe Drive, Kotuku Park,
Paraparaumu Beach 6010

Tel (04) 902 6466   Fax (04) 902 6466
Mob 025 232 5106   ernandrho@paradise.net.nz
www.bnb.co.nz/beachstayparaparaumu.html

Double $80   Single $55   (Continental Breakfast)
Dinner $25 by arrangement   Credit cards accepted
1 Double 2 Single (2 bdrm)
Bathrooms: 1 Private

Enjoy warm friendly hospitality in the relaxing atmosphere of our modern new home. Peaceful surroundings next to river estuary and beach. Wonderful views of sea, lake and hills. Lovely coastal and river walks. Close to Paraparaumu Beach world ranking golf course and Southward's Car Museum. Trips to Kapiti Island Bird Sanctuary can be arranged with prior notice. South Island Ferry Terminal 45 minutes away. We enjoy meeting people and sharing our love of NZ scenery and bush walking. Ernie paints landscapes. Enquiries welcome.

PARAPARAUMU   *45km N of Wellington*

On The 10th   *B&B   Self-contained*
Deirdre & Dene Power
24 Golf Road, Paraparaumu

Tel (04) 902 2499   Mob 021 1822 694
dd.pow@xtra.co.nz
www.bnb.co.nz/the10th.html

Double $100 - $150   (Continental Breakfast)
1 Queen 1 Double (1 bdrm)
Bathrooms: 1 Private

Golfers paradise: Overlooking the 10th green of New
Zealand's number one golf course, Paraparaumu Beach.
Walk out the back gate and you are there. 100 metres
walk to beach, local restaurants and cafés. New self-contained apartment with fully equiped kitchen,
bathroom and laundry facilities. Sky TV, DVD player and sound system.   Private outdoor living, caddie
cart and golf clubs available for hire. Local golf tours (including transport) and trips to Kapiti Island can
be arranged in advance. Seasonal and long term rates negotiable.

PARAPARAUMU   *45km N of Wellington*

Rosetta House B&B   *B&B   Self-contained*
Delightful garden suite for 3-4 people
Lorraine & Michael Sherlock
349 Rosetta Road, Raumati, Paraparaumu, Kapiti Coast

Tel (04) 905 9055   Fax (04) 905 9055
Mob 021 122 0939   rosettahouse@paradise.net.nz
www.rosetta.co.nz

Double $95-$125   Single $75-$95   (Special Breakfast)
Unsuitable for young children   Credit cards accepted
1 King/Twin 2 Queen 1 Double (4 bdrm)
Bathrooms: 2 Ensuite 1 Private 1 Guests share

Discover our coastal paradise on Kapiti Coast. Beach, restaurants and village are just around the corner.
Our home is elegant and charming with lovely gardens(a restful retreat). Enjoy walks on the beach
returning to gracious crystal and silver settings, enhancing our gourmet/cooked breakfast. Homemade
bread and cooking: our breakfasts are exceptional. Travellers speak highly of our friendly hospitality.
Allow two days/nights to enjoy the unique setting of our coastal paradise. Winter tariff less 15%,
Laundry/internet available. Excellent ferry stopover. We have cat, dog (outside).

PAEKAKARIKI   *40km N of Wellington*

Killara Homestay   *B&B   Separate/Suite*
Carole & Don Boddie
70 Ames Street, Paekakariki

Tel (04) 905 5544   Fax (04) 905 5533
Mob 027 494 4551
killara@paradise.net.nz
www.killarahomestay.co.nz

Double $120-$140 Single $100-$120
(Continental Breakfast) Credit cards accepted
1 Queen 1 Twin (2 bdrm)
Bathrooms: 1 Private

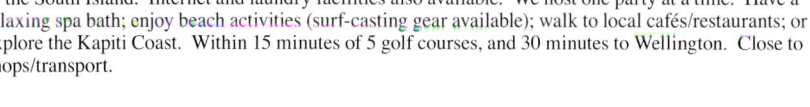

Relax, enjoy the sound of the sea, fabulous views and beach access from our absolute beachfront home.
Spacious accommodation upstairs includes a guest lounge, with outstanding views from Kapiti Island
to the South Island. Internet and laundry facilities also available. We host one party at a time. Have a
relaxing spa bath; enjoy beach activities (surf-casting gear available); walk to local cafés/restaurants; or
explore the Kapiti Coast. Within 15 minutes of 5 golf courses, and 30 minutes to Wellington. Close to
shops/transport.

PAEKAKARIKI

Seaside Getaway *Self-contained*
Marion & Eddie Clark
27/8 Beach Road, Paekakariki

Tel 0274 421 111 Mob 027 284 1002
marion.clark@harcourts.co.nz
www.bnb.co.nz/beachfront.html

Double $130-$160 Single $120
(Continental Breakfast)
2 Queen 1 Double (2 bdrm)
Bathrooms: 1 Private

Unwind and get away to this slice of paradise - watch the sea roll in, revel in the glorious sunsets and the panoramic views of Kapiti and the South Island from this superbly refurbished self contained seaside retreat. New kitchen, bathroom. Garage, plus extra car parking. Private decking for outdoor relaxation, barbeques. Enjoy the quaint village with 4 great restaurants. Easy access to Wellington (30 minutes). Swim, fish or walk the sandy beach. Golf courses and scenic QE2 park (walking/biking), are nearby. Kayaks available.

PUKERUA BAY

Sheena's Homestay *Homestay*
Sheena Taylor
2 Gray Street, Pukerua Bay 6010,
Kapiti Coast

Tel (04) 239 9947 Fax (04) 239 9942
Mob 025 602 1503 homestay@sheenas.co.nz
www.bnb.co.nz/sheenashomestay.html

Double $85 Single $45 (Full Breakfast) Child $20
Dinner by arrangement Credit cards accepted Children welcome
1 Double 1 Twin 1 Single (2 bdrm) Bathrooms: 1 Host share

Come share our warm, sunny refurbished smokefree home. Relax in the conservatory - enjoy the views. We have 2 friendly cats, Tabitha & Sienna. Pukerua Bay, home of creative people, has an interesting beach about 15 minutes walk. Railway station closeby. Sheena is a keen spinner - spinning wheel/fibre available to use. Restaurants and cafes 5-15 minutes drive. Most special diets catered for, lunches arranged. Smokers seating undercover; off-street parking; laundry facilities; garaging for bikes; powerpoint small campervans; cot & highchair. Personal care for people with disabilities.

PLIMMERTON

Southridge Farm *Farmstay Self-contained*
Katrina and Andrew Smith
Southridge, 96 The Track, Plimmerton, Wellington

Tel (04) 233 1104 Mob 021 1436 404
aksmith@paradise.net.nz
www.bnb.co.nz/southrigefarm.html

Double $95-$115 Single $75-$90
(Continental Breakfast) Child free
Children welcome Pets welcome
1 Queen 1 Single (1 bdrm)
Bathrooms: 1 Ensuite

Looking for something special away from the city noise? Southridge Farm has it. Rural in a residential area. We have a lovely modern self-contained cottage with full kitchen including washing machine if self-catering is preferred. Couch has a sofabed. Cot and foldaway bed also available. Beach, trains and restaurants 1km away. Major shopping centre 7km. Our pets: ponies, sheep & goats are waiting to greet you. Andrew & Katrina, children Lachlan & Ella, farm dog Penny warmly invite you to share in our relaxing rural experience.

WHITBY   *10km NE of Porirua*

Oldfields   *Homestay*
Elaine & John Oldfield
22 Musket Lane,
Whitby, Wellington

Tel **(04) 234 1002**   Mob 021 254 0869
oldfields@paradise.net.nz
www.oldfieldshomestay.co.nz

Double $105   Single $85   (Full Breakfast)
Dinner $25 by arrangement   Credit cards accepted
2 Queen (2 bdrm)
Bathrooms: 1 Guests share

Would you enjoy a stay in a tranquil home with bush views and overlooking a mature and well-tended garden? Oldfields is situated in a quiet cul-de-sac in the suburb of Whitby, 10 minutes by car from Paremata Station and 25 minutes from central Wellington. Having travelled and lived overseas we are always interested in meeting people, whether they are from just up the road in New Zealand or further afield. We welcome you to stay with us and our cats Tinker & Roxy.

PAUATAHANUI   *5km E of Plimmerton*

Ration Point Country Cottage   *B&B Self-contained*
Leigh Tuohy
485 Grays Road, Pauatahanui

Tel **(04) 237 8349**   Fax (04) 237 4797
Mob 021 427 629   rationpointbb@xtra.co.nz
www.rationpoint.com

Double $150   Single $110   (Full Breakfast)
Child $25   Credit cards accepted   Children welcome
1 Queen 1 Double 2 Single (1 bdrm)
Bathrooms: 1 Private

Our rural homestead and cottage is sited on 10 acres overlooking the picturesque Pauatahanui Inlet and surrounding countryside. The cottage features open-plan living, dining and kitchenette. Fully equipped bathroom includes hairdryer, bathrobes, toiletries, washing machine and clothes dryer. Full breakfast provisions are included plus many extra features to enjoy. Young children will enjoy riding our friendly shetland pony Lulu or mini quad bike. Our house pets are 2 german shepherds and a cat. Handy to excellent cafés, shopping, beaches and walking tracks.

TAWA   *15km N of Wellington*

Tawa Homestay   *Homestay*
Jeannette & Alf Levick
17 Mascot Street,
Tawa, Wellington

Tel **(04) 232 5989**   Fax (04) 232 5987
milsom.family@xtra.co.nz
www.bnb.co.nz/tawahomestay.html

Double $90   Single $50
3 course candlelit dinner $20pp
1 Queen 1 Single (2 bdrm)
Bathrooms: 1 Host share

Our comfortable family home is in a quiet street in Tawa. We have a separate toilet, shower and spa bath. Freshly ground coffee a speciality, with breakfast of your choice. Jeannette's interests are: Japanese language, porcelain painting, knitting, dressmaking, playing tennis, learning to play golf and the piano and gardening. Alf's interests are: amateur radio, woodwork, Toastmasters International - and being allowed to help in the garden. We are both members of Lions International.

TAWA   *15km N of Wellington*

Chaplin Homestay   *Homestay*
Joy & Bill Chaplin
3 Kiwi Place,
Tawa, Wellington

Tel (04) 232 5547   Fax (04) 232 5547
Mob 025 680 3599   chapta@xtra.co.nz
www.bnb.co.nz/chaplin.html

Double $90   Single $45   (Continental Breakfast)
Dinner by arrangement
1 King 1 Double 1 Single (3 bdrm)
Bathrooms: 1 Guests share 1 Host share

Number 3 is situated in a quiet cul-de-sac with safe off-street parking 7 minutes by car and rail
to Porirua City and 15 minutes from Wellington and the Interisland Ferry Terminal. Our house is
wheelchair friendly and comfortable with laundry facilities available. Tawa is close to beaches,
ten-pin bowling, swimming pool and fine walks.We offer dinner by arrangement. Please phone for
directions.

TAWA   *15km NW of Wellington CBD*

B&B Homestay
Jocelyn & David Perry
5 Fyvie Avenue,
Tawa, Wellington 6006

Tel (04) 232 7664   djperry@actrix.co.nz
www.bnb.co.nz/perry.html

Double $80   Single $50   (Continental Breakfast)
Child $20   Dinner By arrangement
Credit cards accepted Children welcome
1 Double 1 Twin 1 Single (3 bdrm)
Bathrooms: 1 Guests share 1 Host share

We are a retired couple. Together we welcome you to stay with us. There is a 5 minute walk to the
suburban railway station with a half hourly service into the city (15 minutes) and north to the Kapiti
Coast. Alternatively you can drive north to the coast, enjoying sea and rural views before sampling
tourist attractions in this area. We are happy to provide transport to and from the Interisland Ferry.
Laundry facilities available.

UPPER HUTT - TE MARUA   *7.4km N of Upper Hutt*

Te Marua Homestay   *Homestay*
Sheryl & Lloyd Homer
108A Plateau Road,
Te Marua, Upper Hutt

Tel (04) 526 7851   0800 110 851
Fax (04) 526 7866 Mob 025 501 679
sheryl.lloyd@clear.net.nz
www.bnb.co.nz/homer.html

Double $90   Single $60   (Continental Breakfast)
Dinner $25pp by arrangement Credit cards accepted
1 Queen 1 Double (2 bdrm)
Bathrooms: 1 Private

Our home is situated in a secluded bush setting. Guests may relax on one of our private decks or read
books from our extensive library. For the more energetic there are bush walks, bike trails, trout fishing,
swimming and a golf course within walking distance. The guest wing has a kitchenette and television.
Lloyd is a landscape photographer with over 30 years experience photographing New Zealand. Sheryl is
a teacher. Travel, tramping, skiing, photography, music and meeting people are interests we enjoy.

UPPER HUTT   *30 min Wellington*

Tranquility Homestay   *B&B Homestay*
Elaine & Alan
136 Akatarawa Road, Birchville, Upper Hutt

Tel (04) 526 6948   0800 270 787   Fax (04) 526 6968
Mob 0274 405 962   tranquility@xtra.co.nz
www.bnb.co.nz/tranquility1.html

Double $100   Single $50-$90   (Continental Breakfast)
Child neg   Dinner $20 by prior arrangement
Credit cards accepted   Children welcome   Pets welcome
1 Queen 1 Twin 1 Single (3 bdrm)
Bathrooms: 1 Ensuite 2 Guests share 2 Host share

Tranquility Homestay. The name says it all. Escape from the stress of city life approx 30 minutes from Wellington off SH2. Close to Upper Hutt - restaurants, cinema, golf, racecourse, leisure centre (swimming), bush walks. We are near the confluence of the Hutt and Akatarawa Rivers which is noted for its fishing. 13km to Staglands. Country setting, relax, listen to NZ tuis, watch the fantails or wood pigeons, or simply relax and read. Comfortable, warm and friendly hospitality. Close by locations used for The Lord of the Rings.

LOWER HUTT

Judy & Bob's Place   *Homestay*
Judy & Bob Vine
11 Ngaio Crescent, Lower Hutt

Tel (04) 971 1192   Fax (04) 971 6192
Mob 021 510 682   bob.vine@paradise.net.nz
www.bnb.co.nz/judybobsplace.html

Double $100   Single $50   (Full Breakfast)   Dinner $30
Credit cards accepted
1 Queen 2 Single (2 bdrm)
Bathrooms: 1 Private

Located in Woburn, a picturesque and quiet central city suburb of Lower Hutt, known for its generous sized houses and beautiful gardens. Within walking distance of the Lower Hutt downtown, 15 minutes drive from central Wellington, its railway station and ferry terminals; airport 25 minutes; 3 minutes walk to Woburn Rail Station. Private lounge and TV. Love to entertain and share hearty Kiwi style cooking with good New Zealand wine. Laundry facilities. Transfer transport available. High speed and dial up Internet connections.

LOWER HUTT   *12km N of Wellington*

Casa Bianca   *B&B Self-contained*
Jo & Dave Comparini
10 Damian Grove, Lower Hutt

Tel (04) 569 7859   Fax (04) 569 7859
dcompo@xtra.co.nz
www.bnb.co.nz/casabianca.html

Double $95   Single $65   (Continental Breakfast)
1 King 1 Single (1 bdrm)
Bathrooms: 1 Private

Our comfortable house is situated in the peaceful eastern hills of Lower Hutt. We are within easy reach of the city centre, the Open Polytech, Waterloo Railway Station. Wellington is 20 minutes by train or car. We have a self contained apartment with bedroom (double), bathroom, large lounge, fully equipped kitchen, extra single bed in lounge. Breakfast provisions provided in apartment. We specialise in long or short term stays. Come and enjoy our special hospitality. Computer line if required. Off-street parking. No smoking please.

LOWER HUTT   *2km SE of Lower Hutt*

Dungarvin   *B&B Homestay*
Beryl & Trevor Cudby
25 Hinau Street,
Woburn, Lower Hutt

Tel **(04) 569 2125**   Fax (04) 569 2126
t.b.cudby@clear.net.nz
www.bnb.co.nz/dungarvin.html

Double $100-$115 Single $80-$100 (Full Breakfast)
Dinner $30 by arrangement   Credit cards accepted
1 Queen (1 bdrm)
Bathrooms: 1 Private

Our 70 year old cottage has been fully refurbished while retaining its original charm. It is 15 minutes from the ferry terminal and the stadium, and 20 minutes from Te Papa - the Museum of NZ. Our home is centrally heated and the sunny guest bedroom looks over our secluded garden. The bed has an electric blanket and wool duvet. Vegetarians are catered for, laundry facilities are available and we have ample off-street parking. Our main interests are travel, music, gardening, shows and NZ wines.

LOWER HUTT   *0.5km SE of Lower Hutt Central*

Rose Cottage   *B&B Homestay*
Maureen & Gordon Gellen
70A Hautana Street, Lower Hutt, Wellington

Tel **(04) 566 7755**   Fax (04) 566 0777
Mob 021 481 732   gellen@xtra.co.nz
www.bnb.co.nz/rosecottagelowerhutt.html

Double $105-$115 Single $75-$85 (Full Breakfast)
Dinner $30 by arrangement Credit cards accepted
1 King/Twin 1 Queen (2 bdrm)
Bathrooms: 1 Ensuite 1 Host share

Relax in the comfort of our cosy home which is just a 5 minute walk to the Hutt City centre. Originally built in 1910 the house has been fully renovated. We have travelled extensively overseas and in NZ. Interests include travel, gardening, sports and live theatre. As well as TV in guest room there's coffee and tea making facilities. Breakfast will be served in our dining room at your convenience. Unsuitable for children. We look forward to welcoming you into our smoke-free home which we share with Scuffin our cat.

LOWER HUTT

Park Avenue B&B   *Homestay*
Pam & Ray Ward
788 High Street, Lower Hutt

Tel **(04) 567 4788**   Mob 025 285 8709
pam.ray.ward@xtra.co.nz
www.bnb.co.nz/parkave.html

Double $90-$130 Single $60-$90
(Continental Breakfast) Dinner by arrangement
Credit cards accepted
1 Queen 1 Double 1 Twin (3 bdrm)
Bathrooms: 1 Ensuite 2 Private

A warm, friendly welcome awaits guests in this gracious home. Conveniently situated 1500 metres off SH2 (Avalon exit). 15km to ferry terminal and Westpac Stadium. Short walk to trains or Airport Flyer bus stop. All essential services and facilities available at nearby Park Avenue shops. 1km to hospitals and golf courses, short stroll to Avalon Park and Hutt Riverbank Walkway. Indoor pool (heated, spring-autumn). Centrally heated home with secluded garden and off-street parking. Full English breakfast and/or dinner, by prior arrangement.

LOWER HUTT   *2km E of Lower Hutt*

Tyndall House   *Homestay*
Paulene & Nigel Lyne
6/2 Tyndall Street,
Lower Hutt, Wellington 6009

Tel (04) 569 1958   Fax (04) 569 1952
Mob 025 851 901   tyndallhouse@xtra.co.nz
www.bnb.co.nz/tyndallhouse.html

Double $110-$115   Single $80-$95   (Full Breakfast)
Dinner $30
2 Queen (2 bdrm)
Bathrooms: 2 Ensuite

Nigel and Paulene warmly invite you to share their home which is situated beneath a bush reserve in a tranquil haven. We offer a high standard of accomodation, secure parking, sunny elegant bedrooms with garden views, Sky TV and tea/coffee making facilities, electric blankets and a heat pump. We are 15 minutes from the ferry terminal and 20 minutes from Te Papa – the Museum of New Zealand. Come and relax in our peaceful surroundings. We look forward to welcoming you into our home.

LOWER HUTT - STOKES VALLEY   *8km NE of Lower Hutt*

Kowhai B&B   *B&B Homestay*
Glenys & Peter Lockett
88a Manuka Street,
Stokes Valley, Lower Hutt

Tel (04) 563 6671   Mob 027 443 3341
p_g.lockett@xtra.co.nz
www.bnb.co.nz/kowhaibb.html

Double $95   Single $70   (Full Breakfast)
Credit cards accepted
1 Queen 1 Double (2 bdrm)
Bathrooms: 1 Private

We are surrounded by bush and gardens in a quiet street.
Your rooms and large guest lounge are upstairs with private deck, Sky TV, stereo, tea/coffee facilities. We want you to feel relaxed, so take only one booking at a time.   Nearby: golf, boutique cinema, race course, swimming pool, bush walks and restaurants. Wellington CBD/Picton Ferry 25 minutes. Lower/ Upper Hutt, 15 minutes. We have travelled extensively and enjoy meeting people.
Not suitable for children.

LOWER HUTT   *500 metres W of Lower Hutt*

Bridge Lodge B&B   *B&B*
Rita & David Graves
101 Pharazyn St,
Lower Hutt

Tel (04) 977 0623   Fax (04) 977 8269
Mob 027 4432 897   davidgraves@clear.net.nz
www.bnb.co.nz/bridgelodge.html

Double $90   Single $70   (Full Breakfast)
Credit cards accepted
2 Queen 2 Single (3 bdrm)
Bathrooms: 1 Guests share 1 Host share

Easy to find and handy to everything • Excellent
facilities and modest rates • Ideal for tourists, visitors and business people • Short walk to Hutt CBD, shops and cafés • Easy access (road or rail) to Wellington City, Interisland Ferries and airport • Off-street parking, safe and secure location • Friendly hosts who appreciate some guests require privacy and discretion • Just minutes to golf, trout fishing, bush and riverbank walks • Comprehensive tourist and travel advice and assistance • Breakfast in bed on request.

PETONE   *3km S of Lower Hutt*

Homestay
Anne & Reg Cotter
1 Bolton Street,
Petone, Wellington

Tel (04) 568 6960   Fax (04) 568 6956
www.bnb.co.nz/cotter.html

Double $80   Single $40   (Full Breakfast)
Child ¹/2 price over 10 years   Dinner $15
Children welcome
1 Double 2 Single (2 bdrm)
Bathrooms: 1 Guests share

We have a 100 year old home by the beach. We are 2 minutes from a museum on beach, shop and bus route to the city. A restaurant is nearby. We are 10 minutes from Picton Ferries. Off-street parking available. Children are very welcome. Reg is a keen amateur ornithologist and goes to the Chatham Islands with an expedition trying to find the nestling place of the Taiko - a rare sea bird, on endangered list. Other interests are genealogy and conservation. Laundry facilities are available.

PETONE - KOROKORO   *2km W of Petone*

Korokoro Homestay   *Homestay*
Bridget & Jim Austin
100 Korokoro Road,
Korokoro, Petone

Tel (04) 589 1678   0800 116 575
Fax (04) 589 2678   jaustin@clear.net.nz
www.bnb.co.nz/korokorohomestay.html

Double $100-$120 Single $70-$80
(Continental Breakfast) Child by arrangement
Dinner by arrangement Credit cards accepted
1 King/Twin (1 bdrm)
Bathrooms: 1 Ensuite

Our one acre property is secluded and quiet but only 12 minutes to ferries and central Wellington. Easy to find. We came from England to NZ in 1957 and enjoy travel. Jim is a desultory woodworker with a machinery background. Bridget teaches art and is a weaver/feltmaker. We enjoy visual arts, theatre, cinema, music, books, gardening, and the outdoors. Your food will be mainly organic as we prefer an environmentally friendly lifestyle. The new house reflects our interests and skills.

PETONE - KOROKORO   *2km W of Petone*

Matairangi
Kate & Barry Malcolm
29 Singers Road,
Korokoro, Petone

Tel (04) 566 6010   barrym@actrix.co.nz
www.bnb.co.nz/malcolm.html

Double $90   Single $60   (Full Breakfast)
Child $30
1 Twin (1 bdrm)
Bathrooms: 1 Private

Welcome to our hectare of peaceful natural bush and native birds, a hilltop perch with amazing views over Wellington Harbour and surrounding hills. Here you can enjoy your own private ground floor space including sitting room with tea/coffee facilities. Upstairs, Kate and Barry look forward to your company. Our interests are forest restoration, beekeeping, gardening and local history. New laid eggs and freshly baked bread are on the breakfast menu. The ferry terminal is a 15 minute drive away. Also email, laundry, parking.

LOWER HUTT - KOROKORO   *12km N of Wellington*

Approved

Devenport Estate   *B&B Vineyard Accommodation*
Alasdair, Christopher, Marlene
1 Korokoro Road, Korokoro, Petone, Wellington 6008

Tel (04) 586 6868   Fax (04) 586 6869
devenport_estate@hotmail.com
homepages.paradise.net.nz/devenport

Double $100-$135 Single $80-$100
(Continental Breakfast) Credit cards accepted
Children welcome
3 Queen 2 Single (3 bdrm)
Bathrooms: 2 Ensuite 1 Private

Stay at the closest hobby vineyard to the capital. Only 15 minutes to ferry, city & stadium yet with the privacy and quietness of a country retreat. Devenport Estate is an Edwardian- styled homestead overlooking Wellington Harbour, built at the turn of the century (2000!) based upon the MacDonald family home in Scotland.

Nestled amongst native bush we have carved out a colourful garden around the homestead and planted over 400 Pinot Gris/Pinot Noir grapevines in our hobby vineyard.

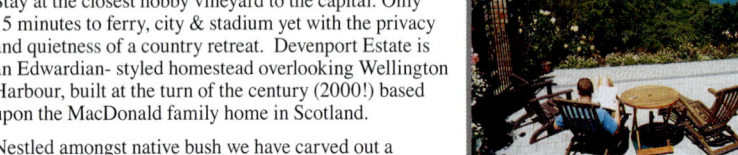

Guests enjoy stunning sea, bush and garden views. Bedrooms contain queen-sized bed, writing desk, chairs, TV, tea making services, hair dryer, electric blanket with either an ensuite or private bathroom. Relax in the guest living room or outside in the sun on the titanic deck chairs. Play petanque or deck quoits, admire the vines and water features or watch the yachts sail past on the harbour.

Avoid city stress and leave your car here, we are only a 15 minute train ride to central Wellington. We offer free arrival/departure transfers from Petone Station. Devenport provides; free internet, free laundry service for stays of 2 or more nights. Some limits apply. We have plenty of off-street parking. Breakfast in the formal Dining Room or alfresco, overlooking Somes Island. At night, enjoy the vast variety of restaurants of Petone's Jackson Street - only a 5 minute drive from Devenport.

Alasdair, Christopher, Marlene and two cocker spaniels, welcome you to a comfortable stay in Wellington on our vineyard estate.

Devenport was built for views, comfort and peacefulness

WAINUIOMATA   *6km E of Lower Hutt*

Kaponga House   *B&B Homestay Self-contained*
Hilary and Neville
22 Kaponga Street,
Wainuiomata

Tel (04) 564 3495 after 5pm
Fax (04) 564 3495   hilwha@xtra.co.nz
www.bnb.co.nz/kaponga.html

Double $80   Single $50   (Continental Breakfast)
1 Queen (1 bdrm)
Bathrooms: 1 Private

Hilary and Neville offer you top quality accommodation
in a quiet bush setting just 20 minutes drive from Wellington City. Our ground floor apartment includes
1 double bedroom, private bathroom with heated towel rail, laundry, spacious lounge/living room with
gas heating, TV, tea/coffee making facilities and fridge. Nearby attractions include the Rimutaka Forest
Park, seal colony, and 18 hole golf course. We enjoy gardening, golf, tennis and travel, and meeting new
people. We look forward to welcoming you to our home. Genuine Kiwi hospitality guaranteed.

WAINUIOMATA   *12km E of Lower Hutt*

Moores Valley Homestay
B&B Farmstay Self-contained
Steve & Julie Galyer
107 Crowther Road, Wainuiomata

Tel (04) 564 7018   Fax (04) 564 2664
steve@mvscl.co.nz   www.mvscl.co.nz/homestay

Double $100-$120   Single $90-$110 (Full Breakfast)
Child $15   Dinner $30   Credit cards accepted
1 Double (1 bdrm)   Bathrooms: 1 Private

Set on a small rise in a stunning rural area you can find
Moores Valley Homestays. We offer a self-contained
unit with gorgeous views of our farm and surrounding
area. This unit has undercover parking, non-smoking
environment, double bed, own laundry and kitchen
facilities, Sky TV and free internet access. Daily
breakfasts are provided and evening meals available (at a

small charge) if desired. We have a friendly farm dog, and a little boy of 4 who all add to the atmosphere.

EASTBOURNE   *3km N of Eastbourne*

Bush House   *Homestay*
Belinda Cattermole
12 Waitohu Road, York Bay, Eastbourne, Wellington

Tel (04) 568 5250   Fax (04) 568 5250
Mob 027 408 9648   belindacat@paradise.net.nz
www.bnb.co.nz/bushhouse.html

Double $100   Single $70   (Full Breakfast)
Dinner by arrangement
1 Double 1 Single (2 bdrm)
Bathrooms: 1 Private 1 Guests share 1 Host share

Come and enjoy the peace and tranquility of the Eastern
Bays. You will be hosted in a restored 1920's settler
cottage nestled amongst native bush and looking towards
the Kaikoura mountains of the South Island. My love of
cordon-bleu cooking and the pleasures of the table are satisfied through the use of my country kitchen
and dining room. Other attractions: A Devon Rex cat. Eastbourne is a small seaside village across the
harbour from Wellington City with a range of attractions.

EASTBOURNE   *12km E of Wellington*

Treetops Hideaway   *B&B Self-contained*
Robyn & Roger Cooper
7 Huia Road, Days Bay, Eastbourne

Tel (04) 562 7692   Fax (04) 562 7690
Mob 025 616 9826   bnb@treetops.net.nz
www.treetops.net.nz

Double **$120-$150**   Single $110-$140
(Continental Breakfast)   Child $25
Sofabeds in lounge $30pp   Credit cards accepted
1 Queen (1 bdrm) plus 2 single divans in lounge
Bathrooms: 1 Private

Secluded, romantic retreat in stunning location above Wellington harbour. Ride our private cable car through native bush to the front door, or walk up through ferns and beeches. Sparkling sea views from bedroom and lounge, fully equipped kitchenette, bath/shower/toilet, phone, computer port, separate entrance. Wake to bellbird song; breakfast on your private garden patio; relax indoors with books, games, TV, radio. Portacot, highchair available. Laundry small charge. Picturesque swimming beach, cafés, galleries 200 metres. Central Wellington 20 minutes by local ferry, or car.

EASTBOURNE   *17km E of Wellington*

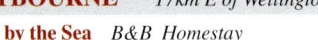

Lowry Bay Homestay   *B&B Homestay*
Pam & Forde Clarke
35 Cheviot Road, Lowry Bay,
Eastbourne, Wellington

Tel (04) 568 4407   0508 266 546
Fax (04) 568 4408   homestay@lowrybay.co.nz
www.lowrybay.co.nz

Double **$100-$130**   Single $80-$110 (Full Breakfast)
Child neg Credit cards accepted Children welcome
1 King 1 Queen 1 Single (2 bdrm)
Bathrooms: 1 Private

Enjoy our hospitality. Welcome to our special home. Warm, restful, peaceful, yet close to Wellington and Hutt Cities, transport, local restaurants and art galleries. Play tennis on our court, stroll to the beach, walk in the bush, sail on our 28 foot yacht, or relax under a sun umbrella on the deck. Native birds abound. Our sunny, elegant bedrooms have garden views, TV, tea/coffee and central heating. We have two daughters, Isabella 21 and Kirsty 15, a cat and many interests. Laundry. Non-smoking indoors. From SH2 follow Petone signs then Eastbourne.

EASTBOURNE   *17km E of Wellington*

Frinton by the Sea   *B&B Homestay*
Wendy & Doug Stephenson
55 Rona Street, Eastbourne, Wellington

Tel (04) 562 7540   Fax (04) 562 7860
Mob 027 441 7365   frinton@xtra.co.nz
www.frintonbythesea.co.nz

Double **$125-$145**   Single $100-$130 (Full Breakfast)
Child not suitable Dinner on request C/C accepted
Discounts mid year & extended stays
2 Queen (2 bdrm)
Bathrooms: 1 Ensuite 1 Private

You are invited to share in the peace and tranquillity of our bush clad home overlooking Wellington Harbour. We offer cosy well appointed bedrooms with doors opening out onto a balcony. Enjoy the unique village atmosphere of Eastbourne with its restaurants, galleries, gift shops and beach, or take the harbour ferry to Wellington. Our interests are the arts, theatre and music. Wendy, Doug, our golden lab Max, JR Missy and two cuddly cats look forward to greeting you. Be assured of a warm welcome in our smoke-free haven.

WELLINGTON - KHANDALLAH *7km N of Wellington*

Homestay
Sue & Ted Clothier
22 Lohia Street, Khandallah, Wellington

Tel **(04) 479 1180**   Fax (04) 479 2717
www.bnb.co.nz/clothier.html

Double **$100**   Single $70   (Full Breakfast)
Credit cards accepted
1 Twin (1 bdrm)
Bathrooms: 1 Ensuite

This is a lovely, sunny and warm open plan home with glorious harbour and city views. A quiet easily accessible street just 10 minutes from the city and 5 minutes from the ferry. Close to Khandallah village where you can make use of the excellent local restaurant, café or English country pub. We are a non-smoking household. Another family member is an aristocratic white cat called Dali. We enjoy sharing our home with our guests.

WELLINGTON - KHANDALLAH *6km N of Wellington*

The Loft in Wellington   *B&B Self-contained*
Phillippa & Simon Plimmer
6 Delhi Crescent,
Khandallah, Wellington

Tel **(04) 938 5015**   Mob 021 448 491
plimmers@paradise.net.nz
www.bnb.co.nz/theloft-wellington.html

Double **$120**   Single $90   (Full Breakfast)
Credit cards accepted
1 Queen (1 bdrm)
Bathrooms: 1 Ensuite

The Loft in Wellington offers the discerning traveller comfort and style in a beautifully appointed self-contained studio. Enjoy complete privacy with your own entrance and brand new ensuite bathroom. Sky TV, off-street parking, laundry, email/phone/internet access available. 10 minutes from downtown Wellington. 300 metres to local train and bus. 500 metres from Khandallah village and local restaurants. Not suitable for pets or children.

WELLINGTON - KHANDALLAH *7km N of Wellington Central*

Khandallah Villa B&B   *B&B*
Pamela Wilson
31 Izard Road,
Khandallah, Wellington

Tel **(04) 479 6581**   Mob 025 671 8864
pamelawilson@xtra.co.nz
www.bnb.co.nz/khandallah.html

Double **$110-$140**   Single $90-$130
(Continental Breakfast)
1 King/Twin 1 Queen (2 bdrm)
Bathrooms: 1 Private 1 Guests share

Welcome to quiet charming 1911 villa, premium area, 10 minutes from CBD, 5 minutes from ferry, 4-5 minutes walk excellent restaurant, English style pub and cafés. Bus stop at door to CBD and greater Wellington City area. Easy free parking. TV, tea/coffee, electric blankets in comfortable rooms, one with french doors opening to garden deck. Continental breakfast. Relax by log fire in lounge or in pretty garden. Two beautiful purring family members. Bushwalks nearby. Hosts keen travellers and passionate Wellingtonians.

WELLINGTON - NGAIO   *7km NW of Wellington*

Ngaio Homestay   *B&B Homestay & Self-contained*
Jennifer & Christopher Timmings
56 Fox Street, Ngaio, Wellington

Tel (04) 479 5325   Fax (04) 479 4325
jennifer.timmings@clear.net.nz
www.bnb.co.nz/ngaiohomestay.html

Double $120-$130 Single $90-$120   (Continental Breakfast)
Self-contained $130 per double   Extra person $45
Child neg   Dinner $35pp by arrangement
Visa and Mastercard accepted

B&B 1 Double 1 Single (2 bdrm)
Apartments 1 Queen bed 1 Twin (2 apartments)

Bathrooms: 3 Ensuite 1 Private

Welcome to Wonderful Wellington! Our unusual multi-level open
plan character home [built1960] is in the suburb of Ngaio. Guests
may leave their car here and take the 10 minute train journey to
CBD. We are 5 minutes by car from the Interisland ferry terminal.

Our double room has tea/coffee facilities, quality bedding,
tiled ensuite and french doors opening onto a deck and private
'jungle' garden. Breakfast is continental. Evening meals an
optional extra. Dinner with live music $40pp.

2 self-contained apartments, 1 queen, 1 twin, adjacent to our
property, are comfortable, convenient, tastefully furnished and
recently re decorated. Each apartment also has a couch with
a fold out bed in lounge, fully equipped kitchen, shower, bath,
laundry facilities, cable TV, phone and internet [small fee]
There is a large garden with trees, birds and views. Perfect for
business, holiday or relocating. Weekly rates on application.

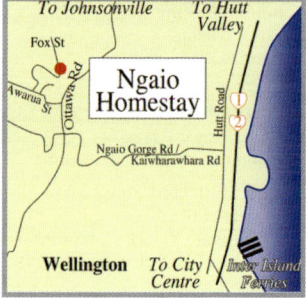

Jennifer plays harp at home and live piano music daily in NZ's
leading department store. Our adult son Christopher lives at home and is a computer whiz.

Compliment from guest 'This is a home where there is beautiful music, art and love'. Do come and
share! Please phone before 11am or after 3pm or fax or email. Bookings essential.

Share your visit with us and enjoy helpful personal hospitality!

WELLINGTON - KARORI
5km W of Wellington

Campbell Homestay *Homestay*
Murray & Elaine Campbell
83 Campbell Street, Karori, Wellington

Tel (04) 476 6110   Fax (04) 476 6593
Mob 025 535 080   ctool@ihug.co.nz
www.bnb.co.nz/campbellhomestay.html

Double $95   Single $60   (Continental Breakfast)
Child ¹/2 price   Dinner $30   Credit cards accepted
Children welcome   Pets welcome
1 Queen 2 Twin 4 Single (3 bdrm)
Bathrooms: 1 Guests share

Welcome to our home in the suburbs, easy to find from motorway or ferry terminal. We will meet you at ferry, train, bus or air terminals. Dine with us, or eat out at the local pub or cafés. We are within easy reach of the city and Westpac Stadium being on 3 bus routes. Make use of our laundry, large garden, spacious home, email/internet facilities. Meet Charlie our border collie dog. Close to Karori Wildlife Sanctuary, Botanic Gardens and Otari-Wilton's Bush.

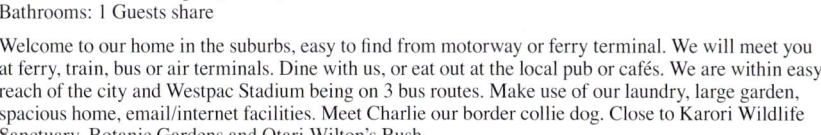

WELLINGTON - KARORI
4 km W of Wellington CBD

Bristow Place *B&B Self-contained*
Helen & Tony Thomson
8 Bristow Place, Karori, Wellington

Tel (04) 476 6291   Fax (04) 476 6293   Mob 021 656 825
h.t.thomson@xtra.co.nz
www.bnb.co.nz/bristowplace.html

Double $150-$180 Single $110   (Full Breakfast)
Dinner by arrangement
Long stay/self-catered by arrangement
Credit cards accepted
1 Queen 2 Double (2 bdrm)   Bathrooms: 2 Private

We offer a private apartment, able to sleep up to 4, that can be enjoyed either as a regular B&B facility or on a self-catered, self-serviced basis. In addition we have another guestroom with double bed and private bathroom. Enjoy Sky TV, electric blankets, bathrobes, heated towel rails, etc. Share coffee and conversation with us – we enjoy music, theatre, travel, sports and bridge – German spoken. Inner suburb location with ample parking, good transport and local shops and restaurants. Internet, fax and laundry service at small charges.

WELLINGTON - KARORI
5km W of Wellington

Karori Cottage *Self-contained*
Kaye & Peter Eady
11 Shirley Street,
Karori, Wellington

Tel (04) 977 5104   Mob 025 609 9003
eady1@paradise.net.nz
www.bnb.co.nz/karoricottage.html

Double $100-$120 (Continental Breakfast)
Child $10   Children welcome
1 Queen 1 Twin (2 bdrm)
Bathrooms: 1 Private

A cosy self-contained cottage at the rear of our section with drive on access. Queen and twin bedrooms and bathroom upstairs, lounge/dining area with open fire and kitchen downstairs opening onto a sunny courtyard. Children can play on the large front lawn, climb trees and share the trampoline with our three children (8, 11 and 14 years). Laundry facilities. Close to bus route and great local deli/café.

WELLINGTON - KARORI   *6km W of Wellington*

Norlan Homestay   *Homestay*
Dale Mansill
15 Cathie Place, Karori, Wellington

Tel (04) 476 4469   Fax (04) 476 4472
Mob 027 612 3605   dale.mansill@xtra.co.nz
www.bnb.co.nz/norlan.html

Double $95   Single $60 Twin $90
(Continental Breakfast)   Dinner by arrangement
Children welcome
1 Queen 1 Twin (2 bdrm)
Bathrooms: 1 Ensuite 1 Host share

Enjoy comfort and good company at Norlan Homestay in the suburb of Karori 15 minutes from the city centre. Close to transport, local shops, restaurants, and cable car. Relax in front of the log burner with Sox the cat or take advantage of Wellington's many sights and cultural activities. Continental breakfast provided. Laundry facilities, internet, Sky TV available. Plenty of parking. Happy to pick up from airport or ferry terminals. Choice of queen with ensuite / single or twin share bathroom. Dinner by arrangement.

WELLINGTON - WADESTOWN   *5km W of Wellingtom*

Ti Whanake   *Homestay*
Julie Foley
72 Wilton Road, Wadestown, Wellington

Tel (04) 499 6602   Fax (04) 473 7332
julie@prickle.co.nz
www.bnb.co.nz/foley.html

Double $120   Single $75   (Continental Breakfast)
Dinner by arrangement   Credit cards accepted
1 Twin 1 Single (2 bdrm)
Bathrooms: 1 Private

A short walk to Otari Native Botanic Gardens and bus from door to central city is only 10 minutes. Own bathroom, separate lounge if preferred, electric blankets and heaters. Share the fireside in the evening with the host and Persian cat or attend some of the varied activities in the 'Cultural Capital'. Gardening, embroidery, playing the cello and mahjong are some of the interests the host enjoys. Visitors can be collected from the ferry etc. Parking on the street. Phone for directions.

WELLINGTON - WADESTOWN   *2.5km NW of Wellington*

The Nikau Palms Bed & Breakfast   *B&B*
Diane & Bill Boyd
95 Sar Street, Wadestown, Wellington

Tel (04) 499 4513   Mob 025 674 0644
thenikaupalms@xtra.co.nz
www.thenikaupalms.co.nz

Double $120-$150   Single $90-$110   (Full Breakfast)
Child $30   Credit cards accepted
Children welcome   Pets welcome
2 Queen 1 Single (2 bdrm)
Bathrooms: 2 Ensuite

You are invited to share our spectacular views of Wellington Harbour overlooking the city, ferry and Westpac Stadium, all within walking distance. Our home is a few minutes drive from Wellington's attractions, historic Thorndon's restaurants, shops and Heritage Trail and Katherine Mansfield's birthplace. The bedrooms include ensuites, one with private sitting room. Full cooked or continental breakfast provided. The guests' dining room includes tea and coffee making facilities and refrigerator. Off-street parking provided.

www.bnb.co.nz

WELLINGTON - WADESTOWN   *2km N of Wellington*

Harbour Lodge Wellington   *B&B*
Lou & Chris Bradshaw
200 Barnard Street,
Wadestown, Wellington

Tel (04) 976 5677   Mob 021 032 6497
lou@harbourlodgewellington.com
www.harbourlodgewellington.com

Double $180-$230 (Continental Breakfast)
Children welcome
4 King (4 bdrm)
Bathrooms: 4 Ensuite

Let your stresses be gently lulled away in the luxurious comfort of this beautiful new lodge. Admire the fabulous views of Wellington Harbour from the large sunny deck. Swim in the 11 metre indoor heated pool or take a spa. Laze in the comfort of a large guest lounge with an open fire and stunning harbour views. All this is only a few minutes drive from central Wellington, ferry terminal or Wellington Stadium. Children of all ages welcome, no pets please.

WELLINGTON - WADESTOWN   *2.3km N of Central Wellington*

Annaday Homestay   *B&B*
Anne & David Denton
39 Wadestown Road, Wellington

Tel (04) 499 1827   Fax (04) 499 9561
Mob 027 444 7610   annaday@tavis.co.nz
www.tavis.co.nz/annaday

Double $110-$140 Single $90-$130 (Full Breakfast)
Child $20   Dinner $15-$35   Cot $5   Spa $5   Sauna $5
Credit cards accepted   Children welcome   Pets welcome
1 King 2 Queen 1 Twin (4 bdrm)
Bathrooms: 1 Ensuite 1 Guests share 2 Host share

For a comfortable, convenient and interesting stay in the capital city, try this lovely restored character home. There's music, book, art and technology inside, and glorious views outside. Hosts who take trouble to meet your needs. Guest lounge with kitchenette. Many extra services, including transport, available. Pets accommodated - none resident. Children welcome - one resident.

WELLINGTON - THORNDON   *0.5km W of Wellington Central*

Thorndon House   *B&B character cottage*
Gabriele & Markus Landvogt
17 Park Street, Thorndon, Wellington

Tel (04) 499 0503   Fax (04) 499 0504   Mob 021 030 3601
thorndon.house@x tra.co.nz   www.thorndonhouse.co.nz

Double $150-$200 Single $130-$170
(Special Breakfast) Child $30   Dinner $35 on request
Credit cards accepted   Children welcome
4 Queen 1 Single (3 bdrm)   Bathrooms: 3 Ensuite

Within walking distance to Wellington's main attractions and finest restaurants, Interislander Ferries and railway station, Thorndon House has been immaculately restored to enhance its character features to offer you an excellent standard of accommodation. Have a wonderful breakfast of your choice in the peaceful courtyard, relax in our elegant guest lounge and let yourself be inspired to enjoy your days in our favourite city. We recommend our charming cottage for a special occasion and if you want a little more privacy.

WELLINGTON - KELBURN *1km W of Wellington central*

Rawhiti *Boutique B&B*
Annabel Leask
40 Rawhiti Terrace, Kelburn, Wellington

Tel (04) 934 4859 Fax (04) 972 4859
Mob 027 276 8240 rawhiti@paradise.net.nz
www.rawhiti.co.nz

Double $185-$230 Single $150-$185
(Special Breakfast) Credit cards accepted
1 King/Twin 1 King (2 bdrm)
Bathrooms: 2 Ensuite

Rawhiti is located in the prime suburb of Kelburn and within walking distance of the city centre. Magnificent views of harbour and city are seen from all rooms including the small private garden at the rear. A charming 1903 two storeyed home furnished to create an elegant and tranquil ambience. Its historical features, wonderful outlook and quality chattels combine to offer guests a special stay in Wellington. A 2 minute walk to the Cable Car, Botanic Gardens and Victoria University.

WELLINGTON - KELBURN *2km W of Wellington*

Rangiora B&B *B&B Homestay*
Lesley and Malcolm Shaw
177 Glenmore Street,
Kelburn, Wellington 6005

Tel (04) 475 9888 rangiora.bnb@xtra.co.nz
www.rangiorabnb.co.nz

Double $120 Single $90 (Continental Breakfast)
Child neg Credit cards accepted Children welcome
1 Queen 1 Double (2 bdrm)
Bathrooms: 1 Guests share

Location, Location, Location!!! Our modern hillside home is very easy to find. From north, take the Hawkestone Street motorway exit, follow brown signs for 1km to Botanic Gardens. We are another 1km on the left past the Gardens entrance. 5 minutes drive from central city, stadium, ferry/bus/train terminals. Walking distance from 8 restaurants, Cable Car, Victoria University and Karori Sanctuary. Tea/coffee/TV in rooms. Free email access. On-street parking. Courtesy car to or from ferry/bus/train. On city bus route. We have a small dog named Patsy.

WELLINGTON - KELBURN *1km W of Wellington Central*

Glenlodge *B&B*
Brenda Leighs
5 Glen Road, Kelburn, Wellington

Tel (04) 973 7881 Fax (04) 499 5694 Mob 021 294 0747
glenlodge@paradise.net.nz www.bnb.co.nz/glenlodge.html

Double $140-$165 (Full Breakfast)
Weekly rate available on request Credit cards accepted
1 Queen (1 bdrm) Bathrooms: 1 Ensuite

There is no better location for your stay in Wellington than at Glenlodge. The Botanical Gardens and Cable Car, which will have you in downtown Wellington within minutes, are literally at our front door. There are excellent cafés, galleries and shops within walking distance. With your beautifully appointed bedroom, ensuite and private guest lounge a memorable visit is guaranteed. Start your day with a full breakfast before heading off for a days sightseeing. Meet and greet and laundry facilities available. Unsuitable for children. Smoke-free. We have a miniature schnauzer.

WELLINGTON - ARO VALLEY   *1km S of Wellington Centre*

206 Aro Self-Contained Cottage   *B&B Self-contained*
Shirley & Russell Martin
206 Aro St, Aro Valley

Tel (04) 973 7008   Mob 021 177 1957
info-206aro@paradise.net.nz   www.206aro.co.nz

Double $140   Single $140   (Continental Breakfast) Child $10
Credit cards accepted   Children welcome   Pets welcome
1 Queen 1 Double (1 bdrm)   Bathrooms: 1 Private

206 Aro is a self-contained cottage, with complete privacy in Aro
Valley. Fully fitted with quality accommodation touches - 100%
cotton sheets, new futon sofa, etc. Native bush behind cottage and
over the road. Wellington City downtown is a 5-10 minutes drive
(free parking), or a nice 20 minute walk. Complimentary breakfast
materials, drinks and daytime snacks, and free cable TV, range of
videos, and use of stereo. Kids/pets welcome. Discounts for stays
more than 2 nights. We live offsite for your privacy.

WELLINGTON - MT COOK   *Wellington*

Apartment One   *B&B Homestay*
Jim & Colleen Bargh
2 King Street, Mt Cook, Wellington

Tel (04) 385 1112   Mob Colleen 025 247 8145
Jim 027 275 0913   apartmentone@yahoo.co.nz
www.bnb.co.nz/apartmentone2.html

Double $130-$140 Single $90-$100 (Full Breakfast)
Credit cards accepted
2 Queen (2 bdrm)
Bathrooms: 2 Ensuite

Experience apartment living in the city. We moved off the farm into our converted warehouse to try
city life. We love its ever-changing beauty and the people are simply the best. Come try it for yourself.
Buses depart every few minutes. 2 minutes walk to the Basin Reserve and 10-15 minutes walk to
Courtenay Place (Wellington's restaurant, café and theatre district). Less than 10 minutes drive to the
ferry terminal and airport. We serve a deluxe breakfast to get you through your eventful day.

WELLINGTON - ORIENTAL BAY   *0.75km N of Wellington*

No 11   *B&B*
Virginia Barton-Chapple
11 Hay Street, Oriental Bay, Wellington

Tel (04) 801 9290   Fax (04) 801 9295
v.barton-chapple@xtra.co.nz
www.bnb.co.nz/noorientalbay.html

Double $130   Single $110   (Full Breakfast)
1 King/Twin (1 bdrm)
Bathrooms: 1 Host share

Step up to a bed & breakfast with stunning views
of Wellington harbour and the inner city. No 11 is an easy stroll to Te Papa - the Museum of New
Zealand, the City Art Gallery, all the major theatres and cinemas, great restaurants and cafés.
Virginia has extensive knowledge of what's going on, and where to go. The comfortable room has an
adjacent bathroom, electric blankets, and tea & coffee facilities. Breakfast will be an occasion. Cat in
residence.

WELLINGTON - ORIENTAL BAY   *1km E of Wellington CBD*

Oriental Bay Watch   *Self-contained*
Gill Porteous
3B Lindum Terrace,
Oriental Bay, Wellington

Tel 021 718 948   Fax (04) 479 3295
Mob 021 718 948
orientalbaywatch@yahoo.co.nz
www.orientalbaywatch.co.nz

Double $250
1 Queen (1 bdrm)
Bathrooms: 1 Private

Romantic seaside self-contained accommodation in
Oriental Bay. Santorini views from every room, including the bathroom! To complement the view,
there are heated travertine floors throughout, a dining table and fully equipped kitchen, a terrace with
BBQ and jade trees, a stereo and a washing machine. The large, separate bedroom has a queen-size
bed. Walk along the seaside promenade to Te Papa, Courtenay Place, and the CBD. Access is via a short
uphill walk. 10 minute harbourside drive direct from the airport.

WELLINGTON - MT VICTORIA   *Wellington Central*

Dream Catcher - Arts & Accommodation   *B&B*
Homestay
Taly & John Hoekman
56 Pirie Street, Mt Victoria, Wellington

Tel (04) 801 9363   Mob 021 210 6762
www.bnb.co.nz/dreamcatcher.html

Double $130-$150   Single $110-$130
(Continental Breakfast) Child $40, second child free
Credit cards accepted Children welcome
1 Queen 2 Double 2 Single (4 bdrm)
Bathrooms: 1 Ensuite 2 Private 1 Guests share

Dream Catcher is a spacious colonial house in historic Mount Victoria, only 5 minutes stroll from day/
night attractions in vibrant central Wellington. Guests may choose: (1) "VIP Suite" - separate lounge,
bedroom (queen-size futon bed), ensuite with a claw bathtub. (2) "Upstairs" - a self-contained apartment,
2 double bedrooms, childrens room, lounge, kitchen, guests shared bathrooms, sun and views. Taly,
John, their teenage daughter and 2 cats, keen travellers themselves, welcome the city visitor to enjoy the
relaxed comfort of home and the fresh generous breakfasts in the dining room or the sunny garden.

WELLINGTON - MT VICTORIA   *500m E of Courtenay Place*

Scarborough House   *B&B Homestay*
Sue Hiles & Miles Davidson
36 Scarborough Terrace,
Mt Victoria, Wellington

Tel (04) 801 8534   Fax (04) 801 8536
Mob 027 450 1346 info@scarborough-house.co.nz
www.scarborough-house.co.nz

Double $140-$160   Single $120 (Full Breakfast)
Child $50   Credit cards accepted
1 King/Twin 1 Queen (2 bdrm) Bathrooms: 2 Private

Enjoy a hassle-free visit to Wellington. Share our modern centrally-heated home in sunny Mt Victoria.
Walk to city centre, Te Papa Museum, Courtenay Place with its restaurants and nightlife, Oriental Bay
beach and the waterfront. 10 minutes drive from airport and ferry terminals. Option of king, queen or
twin accommodation. Private guest bathrooms. Breakfast of your choice with fresh seasonal fruits.
Tea/coffee facilities, hairdryer, bathrobes, Sky Digital TV, laundry and garaging available. Our interests
include promoting Wellington, travel, skiing, golf. Children over 12 welcome.
@home NEW ZEALAND approved

WELLINGTON - MT VICTORIA

0.5km E of Central Wellington

Villa Vittorio *B&B Homestay*
Annette & Logan Russell
6 Hawker Street, Mt Victoria, Wellington

Tel (04) 801 5761 Fax (04) 801 5762 Mob 0274 321 267
l&a@villavittorio.co.nz   www.villavittorio.co.nz

Double $150-$180 Single $115-$125
(Full Breakfast) Dinner from $50 Credit cards accepted
1 Double (1 bdrm) Bathrooms: 1 Private

WELCOME TO VILLA VITTORIO. Centrally located
close by Courtenay Place. A short walk to restaurants,
theatres, shopping, conference centres, Te Papa Museum,
Parliament and the stadium. Guest bedroom with TV,
tea and coffee facilities. Adjoining sitting room with
balcony overlooking city. Bathroom with shower and
bath.

Breakfast served in Italian styled dining room or outside
in courtyard. We enjoy having guests, having travelled
extensively ourselves. Transport and gourmet dinner by
arrangement. Garaging and laundry at small charge. No
children or pets.
Directions: please phone, fax, email or write to us.

WELLINGTON - MT VICTORIA *Wellington City*

Austinvilla *B&B Self-contained*
Averil & Ian
11 Austin Street, Mt Victoria, Wellington

Tel (04) 385 8334 Fax (04) 385 8336
Mob 027 273 7760 info@austinvilla.co.nz
www.austinvilla.co.nz

Double $120-$160 Single $100-$120
(Continental Breakfast) Credit cards accepted
Children welcome
2 Queen (2 bdrm) Bathrooms: 2 Ensuite

Austinvilla

Top location: A warm welcome to one of Mt Victoria's most elegant turn of the century villas. Set amongst beautiful gardens, and only a few minutes walk to theatres, restaurants, Oriental Bay and Te Papa. Close to public transport and short drive to airport, ferries, and Westpac Stadium. 2 spacious, elegant apartments offer sun, privacy, and include kitchen, queen bed, ensuite with bath and shower, lounge, Sky TV, and phone. Apartments have french doors to private courtyard and own entrance way. Laundry facilities and garaging available. Continental breakfast provided. Children welcome. Smoke-free.

WELLINGTON - ROSENEATH *3km E of Wellington*

Harbourview Homestay and B&B *B&B Homestay*
Hilda & Geoff Stedman
125 Te Anau Road, Roseneath, Wellington

Tel (04) 386 1043 0800 080 078 Mob 021 038 6351
hildastedman@clear.net.nz
www.bnb.co.nz/harbourviewbb.html

Double $120-$150 Single $95-$115 (Full Breakfast)
Dinner from $35 Credit cards accepted
Children welcome
1 Double 2 Single (2 bdrm) Bathrooms: 2 Private

This boutique guesthouse is 5 minutes drive from Wellington City, 10 minutes drive from the airport and on the number 14 bus route. The house offers comfortable hospitality and elegance. Each bedroom opens on to a wide deck, offering expansive views of Wellington harbour. Pleasantly decorated rooms feature quality beds and linen. There is a choice of a double bedroom and/or share twin room, separate guest's bathroom with shower and spa bath. Harbourview is situated in a peaceful setting close to the city, catering for businesspeople, tourists and honeymooners. A surcharge will be added if paying by credit card

WELLINGTON - ROSENEATH *2km N of Central city*

Panorama *B&B*
Peg Mackay
1 Robieson Lane,
Roseneath, Wellington

Tel (04) 801 8691
Fax (04) 801 8691
Mob 021 801 869
www.bnb.co.nz/panorama.html

Double $120-$150 (Special Breakfast)
1 King/Twin 1 Queen (2 bdrm)
Bathrooms: 1 Private 1 Guests share

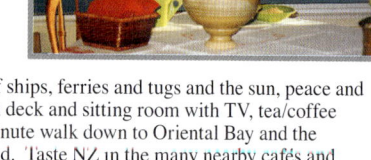

Above Oriental Bay lie in bed enjoying the panorama of ships, ferries and tugs and the sun, peace and privacy of our warm modern home. You have your own deck and sitting room with TV, tea/coffee etc. Take the 5 minute walk to Mt Victoria or the 20 minute walk down to Oriental Bay and the city, galleries and Te Papa - the Museum of New Zealand. Taste NZ in the many nearby cafés and restaurants. Ferry/airport 10 minutes, city 5 minutes drive.

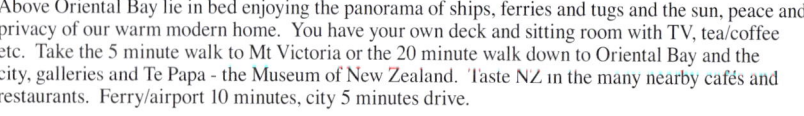

WELLINGTON - HATAITAI   *3km E of Wellington CBD*

Top O' T'ill   *B&B Homestay Self-contained*
Cathryn & Dennis Riley
2 Waitoa Road, Hataitai, Wellington 6003

Tel (04) 976 2718   Fax (04) 976 2719
Mob 025 716 482   top.o.hill@xtra.co.nz
www.bnb.co.nz/topotill.html

Double $100-$130 Single $65-$110 (Full Breakfast)
Credit cards accepted
Unsuitable for young children
2 Queen 1 Twin 1 Single (4 bdrm)
Bathrooms: 2 Ensuite 1 Private 1 Guests share

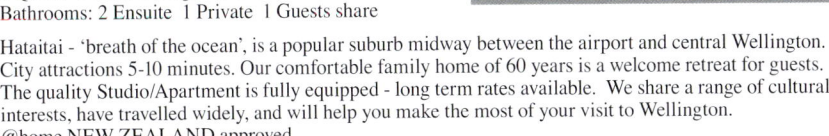

Hataitai - 'breath of the ocean', is a popular suburb midway between the airport and central Wellington. City attractions 5-10 minutes. Our comfortable family home of 60 years is a welcome retreat for guests. The quality Studio/Apartment is fully equipped - long term rates available. We share a range of cultural interests, have travelled widely, and will help you make the most of your visit to Wellington. @home NEW ZEALAND approved.
Directions: www.wellingtonmap.co.nz (Accommodation/Top O' T'ill Homestay)

WELLINGTON - HATAITAI *1km E of Wellington City Centre*

Matai House   *B&B Boutique*
Raema & Rex Collins
41 Matai Road, Hataitai, Wellington 6003

Tel (04) 934 6985 Fax (04) 934 6987
matai@paradise.net.nz   www.mataihouse.co.nz

Double $200-$250 Single $200-$250
(Special Breakfast)
C/C accepted: Visa MasterCard Amex JCB Diners
2 King (2 bdrm)
Bathrooms: 2 Ensuite

Frommers Guide: Special find- a place only insiders know about. Qualmark 4 star plus - Excellent, consistently achieves high quality levels and wide range of facilities/services. Panoramic sea views, purpose-built guest floor, lounge, private entrance. Suites have cable TV, laptop access, bi-fold doors decking. Hairdryers, toiletries, robes, heated towel rails, fresh flowers, tea/coffee making, fridge, laundry, ironing. Telephone/fax/email access. Off-street parking. Flexitime breakfast, espresso coffee. City 4 minutes, ferry 8. Friendly, helpful hosts. Instant confirmations on www.mataihouse.co.nz

WELLINGTON - BROOKLYN (CITY END) *3km SW of CBD*

Karepa   *Homestay*
Ann and Tom Hodgson
56 Karepa Street, Brooklyn, Wellington

Tel (04) 384 4193 Fax (04) 384 4180
Mob 025 KAREPA (025 527 372)   golf@xtra.co.nz
www.holidayletting.co.nz/karepa

Double $130-$165 Single $95-$125 (Full Breakfast)
Child by arrangement   Dinner $35 by arrangement
Extra person $35   Credit cards accepted
2 King 1 Double 1 Single (3 bdrm)
Bathrooms: 1 Ensuite 1 Guests share

Stay at Karepa our sunny, spacious home overlooking city, harbour and mountains. The secluded rear garden adjoins native bush. Private guest rooms have TV, and tea/coffee facilities. City 5 minutes, ferry 10 and airport 15. Residents of 22 years, ex-UK, we have travelled widely, play golf and tennis, and enjoy Wellington's many attractions. Ann gardens and Tom watches from his deckchair. On-site parking. Bus at door. Laundry facilities. Sorry, no smokers or pets. Please phone/fax for directions.

WELLINGTON - BROOKLYN (CITY END) *2km S of CBD*

Quintessential Wellington *B&B Homestay*
Georgie Jones
2A Coolidge Street, Brooklyn, Wellington

Tel (04) 380 1982   Fax (04) 380 1985
Mob 025 243 5674   georgie.jones@xtra.co.nz
www.bnb.co.nz/quintessentialwellington.html

Double $100-$120 Single $80-$100 (Full Breakfast)
Child neg Credit cards accepted
1 Queen 2 Single (2 bdrm)
Bathrooms: 1 Private 1 Host share

Experience Wellington as Wellingtonians do! Private hillside contemporary home, remarkable downtown, harbour, sky, bush views. Just minutes from city, airport, ferries, transport hubs. Peaceful spot, secure doorside parking; handy to local bus and walking tracks. Classy guest facilities -spacious double room, shower and double bath, secluded deck. Help yourself to tea/coffee - choose your time for healthy breakfast. Free laundry, email, TV. Plenty of reference material. Modest single room with family share facilities. Feel free to hibernate - or talk travel, arts, architecture, current affairs, family!

WELLINGTON - VOGELTOWN *3km S of Wellington CBD*

Finnimore House *B&B Homestay*
Willie & Kathleen Ryan
2 Dransfield Street,
Vogeltown, Wellington

Tel (04) 389 9894 Fax (04) 389 9894
w.f.ryan@xtra.co.nz
www.finnimorehouse.co.nz

Double $90-$115 Single $70-$85 (Full Breakfast)
Child $20   Credit cards accepted   Children welcome
2 Queen 2 Single (2 bdrm)
Bathrooms: 1 Guests share

Welcome to our Victorian manor 5 minutes drive from downtown Wellington. Your hosts, Willie and Kathleen Ryan, offer a warm welcome, good conversation, large comfortable rooms and a hearty breakfast. We guarantee hospitality, from a traditional B&B experience, to a welcoming family homestay with a genuine Irish flavour. Our great location is close to: airport, ferries, local cafés, Basin Reserve, hospital, Massey University, Hurricanes rugby training ground, National School of Dance and Drama. Secure parking, convenient public transport. Wellington is yours at Finnimore House.

WELLINGTON - MORNINGTON

Ngahere House *Homestay*
Hilary & David Capper
147 The Ridgeway,
Mornington, Wellington

Tel (04) 389 4501
h.capper@xtra.co.nz
www.bnb.co.nz/ngahere.html

Double $120-$132 (Full Breakfast)
1 Queen (1 bdrm)
Bathrooms: 1 Private

Relax in our private, modern, sunny home with panoramic views of the city, harbour and mountains. We overlook a grove of native trees from our sunroom and deck. Our private guestroom has tea and coffee facilties, a desk, coffee table and 2 lounge chairs. The bathroom is of a high standard. City 10 minutes. Ferry and airport 15 minutes. On bus route. Restaurants and art deco cinema nearby. We enjoy entertaining, travel, reading, films, walking and the arts.

WELLINGTON - SEATOUN *9km S of Wellington*

Francesca's *B&B Homestay*
Frances Drewell
10 Monro Street,
Seatoun, Wellington

Tel (04) 388 6719 Fax (04) 388 6719
francesdrewell@paradise.net.nz
www.bnb.co.nz/francescas.html

Double $100 Single $60 (Full Breakfast) Child $25
Dinner $25 by arrangement   Credit cards accepted
1 Double 2 Single (2 bdrm)
Bathrooms: 1 Guests share

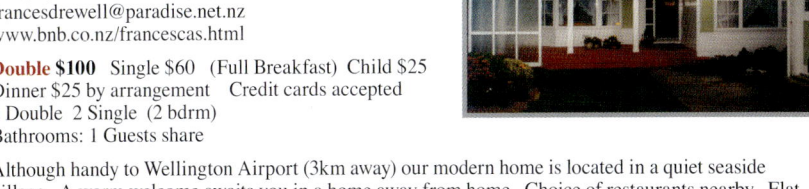

Although handy to Wellington Airport (3km away) our modern home is located in a quiet seaside village. A warm welcome awaits you in a home away from home. Choice of restaurants nearby. Flat off-street parking. Laundry facilities available. Directions: entering Wellington from the north follow the signs to the airport then the signs to Seatoun. Monro Street is the second street on the left after the shops. From the airport first turn right then as above. Bus stop 1 minute, frequent service.

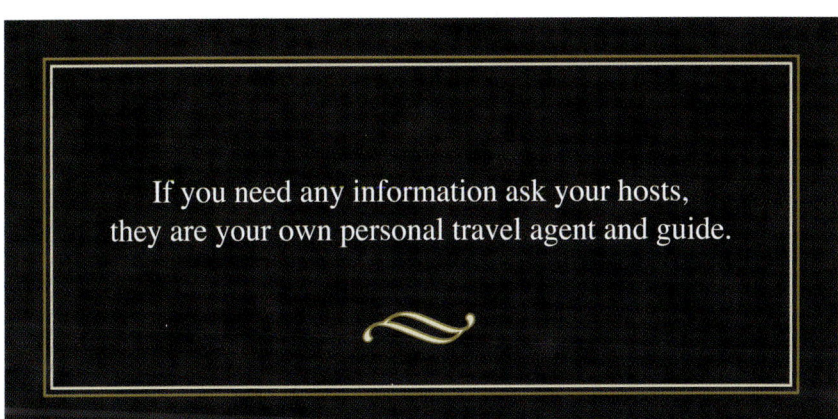

If you need any information ask your hosts,
they are your own personal travel agent and guide.

WELLINGTON - ISLAND BAY/MELROSE *4km S of Courtenay Place*

Buckley Homestay   *B&B Homestay Self-contained*
Mrs Wilhelmina Muller
51 Buckley Road, Melrose, Island Bay, Wellington

Tel (04) 934 7151 Fax (04) 934 7152
Mob 025 607 1853 kandwmuller@paradise.net.nz
www.buckleyhomestay.co.nz

Double $95-$130 (Full Breakfast) Child neg
Dinner b/a C/C accepted Children and Pets welcome
1 King/Twin 1 Double 2 Single (3 bdrm)
Bathrooms: 1 Private 1 Host share

Large 2 storey sunny home with spectacular scenery and beautiful views over Wellington, Cook Strait and mountains. New tastefully decorated, private entrance, 1 bedroom, self-contained, double flat with private balcony, TV, tiled conservatory, fridge and microwave. We are interested in food, wine, travel, relaxing and meeting people. Willy is a nurse, enjoys cooking, gardening and speaks Dutch. No pets or children at home. Off-street parking is provided. Complimentary tea, coffee & biscuits available as well as books to read. Laundry facilities are available and pickup arrangements can be made. Join Wilhelmina or have your own space. On bus route. Dinner by arrangement. Inspection invited. Plus separate double bedroom with super king-size bed.

WELLINGTON - ISLAND BAY   *6km S of Welington city central*

The Lighthouse and The Keep
Bruce Stokell
326 The Esplanade & 116 The
Esplanade, Island Bay, Wellington

Tel (04) 472 4177   Fax (04) 472 4177
Mob 027 442 5555
bruce@thelighthouse.net.nz
www.bnb.co.nz/thelighthouse.html

Double $180-$200
(Special Breakfast)
1 Double (1 bdrm)
Bathrooms: 1 Private

Island Bay - 10 minutes city centre,
10 minutes airport, 20 minutes ferry
terminal.

The Lighthouse is on the South
coast and has views of the island,
fishing boats in the bay, the beach
and rocks, the far coastline, the open
sea, the shipping and, on a clear day,
the South Island. There are local
shops and restaurants nearby.

The Lighthouse has a kitchen and bathroom on the first floor, the bedroom/sitting room on the middle
floor and the lookout/bedroom on the top. Romantic.

The Keep is a stone tower just 2 minutes from the lighthouse. It has a lounge/kitchen on one level and
a bed with ensuite on the next level. Also a spa bath in the bedroom. Stairs from the bedroom lead to a
hatch which opens on to the roof.

Very cosy with excellent views of the seas, especially during a storm

WELLINGTON - ISLAND BAY

Island Bay Homestay *Homestay*
Theresa & Jack Stokes
52 High Street,
Island Bay,
Wellington 6002

Tel (04) 970 3353
0800 335 383
Fax (04) 970 3353
tandjstokes@paradise.net.nz
www.wellingtonhomestay.com

Double $80 Single $50 (Full Breakfast)
2 Double (2 bdrm)
Bathrooms: 2 Private

We live in a Lockwood house, at the end of High Street in a very private section. Our land goes three quarters of the way up the hill and above that is Town Belt. Wonderful views, overlooking the Cook Strait with its ferries, cargo and fishing boats on the move day and night. We see planes landing or taking off (depending on wind direction) but the airport is round a corner and we get no noise from it.

We only let 2 of our rooms and each has its own private bathroom, just outside the bedroom door. TV in rooms. A warm, comfortable smoke-free home with warm clean comfortable beds and two warm owners who enjoy meeting people. We do our best to provide good, old fashioned Homestay, without charging the earth!
We have two lovely Moggies.

Full breakfast 7:30am onwards.
Regrets we cannot accept bookings from guests arriving from Australia on the midnight arrivals or guests leaving on the 6am departures. Not suitable for children under 14.

Directions:
From State Highway 1 or 2 take the Aotea Quay turn-off. (From the ferry take the city exit). Follow the main road which bears slightly to the left until you come to a T junction (Oriental Parade). Turn right in to Kent Terrace and get in the right hand lane before going round the Basin Reserve (cricket ground) and in to Adelaide Road. Keep going straight, up the hill and the road becomes The Parade. Keep going until you reach the sea and then turn SHARP right (new guests can easily miss this turn-off). into Beach Street. Left and left again in to High Street and up the private road at the end.

From Wellington Airport:
Take the rear exit (past the cargo warehouses) and turn right. Follow the coast road for 10 minutes and Beach Street is on the right.

For the navigator we live at -
Lat. S.41.20.54
Long. E.174.45.54

WELLINGTON - ISLAND BAY

B&B
Maurice Burnett
392 The Esplanade,
Island Bay, Wellington

Tel (04) 383 6128   Fax (04) 383 6128
mauriceburnett@paradise.net.nz
www.bnb.co.nz/islandbaybb.html

Double $120   Single $65   (Continental Breakfast)
1 Double 1 Twin (2 bdrm)
Bathrooms: 2 Ensuite

Comfortable home on the south coast offering extensive views of Cook Strait and the South Island, from Red Rocks to the harbour entrance. Sit back and relax, enjoy the magnificent sunsets and watch the Interislander ferries go past the front door. Both rooms are ensuite, have Sky TV, fridge, tea and coffee making facilities. Excellent restaurants and takeaway meals are available nearby. We are situated 10 minutes from the central city and 10 minutes from the airport. We will meet public transport by arrangement.

WELLINGTON - ISLAND BAY   *3km S of Courtenay Place*

Ma Maison   *B&B Homestay*
Margo Frost
9 Tamar Street, Island Bay, Wellington

Tel (04) 383 4018   Fax (04) 383 4018
Mob 025 242 9827
bedandbreakfast@paradise.net.nz
www.nzwellingtonhomestay.co.nz

Double $120   Single $100   (Full Breakfast)
2 Queen (2 bdrm)
Bathrooms: 1 Ensuite 1 Private

Comfort and quality, our 1920's boutique homestay is decorated with a French flavour. Drive to door, lovely garden. Romantic rooms, posturepaedic queen beds and everything to ensure your total comfort. One bedroom has ensuite and private entrance, the other a private bathroom with shower and bath. Easy walking to local restaurants, 8 minutes drive to city, very close to excellent bus service that will take you to Te Papa, theatres, shopping, stadium, ferries, airport, public and private hospitals. A sweet timid cat called Chloe.

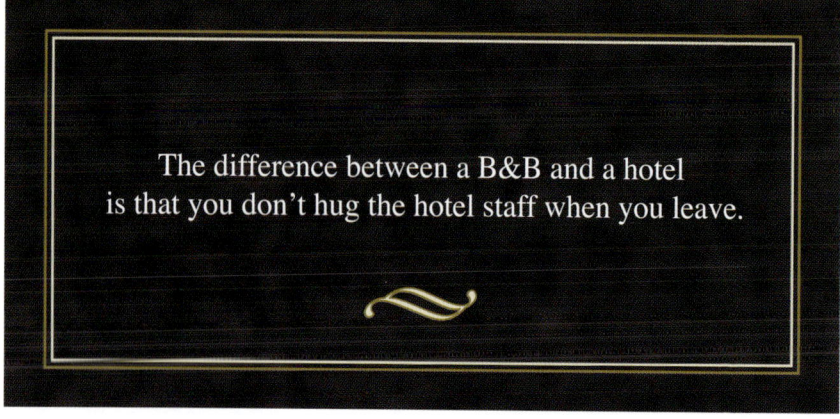

The difference between a B&B and a hotel
is that you don't hug the hotel staff when you leave.

CHATHAM ISLANDS

Te Matarae *Farmstay*
Wendy & Pat Smith
PO Box 63, Te Matarae, Chatham Islands

Tel (03) 305 0144 Fax (03) 305 0144
www.bnb.co.nz/smithchathamislands.html

Double $100 Single $85 (Special Breakfast)
Dinner $30 Children welcome
2 Queen 2 Single (3 bdrm)
Bathrooms: 2 Ensuite 1 Guests share 1 Host share

Chatham Islands

Relax in our natural wood home which is situated in 80 acres of bush on lagoon edge with mown walkways throughout. The lagoon is ideal for swimming and fishing and has nice sandy beaches. Farm activities and kayaks available. Farm is 1100 acres and includes 4 other bush reserves. Guests may meal with family or in separate dining room. Bedrooms are separated from main house by covered swimming pool. We are a non-smoking household; so request guests to refrain from doing so in our home. Most meal ingredients are home produced. We have 2 cats and a host of domestic farm animals. Air travel exit points are Christchurch and Wellington. Rental car with guide available. Pick up and deliver to airport. The Chatham Islands, situated 800km east of Mainland New Zealand, are Islands of Mystery. A place where volcanic cones rise from the mist and sea. Due to isolation and recent history of colonisation, many plants and animals are unique.

Marlborough

Towns listed generally follow
a north to south route. Refer
to the index if required.

French Pass

Pelorus Sound

6

Mahau Sound   Anakiwa   Queen Charlotte Sound

Canvastown   Havelock   Picton   Port Underwood

Koromiko

Rapaura

63   Renwick   Blenheim

1

Awatere Valley

able Bay

Kilometres
0   20

Miles
0   12

FRENCH PASS - PELORUS SOUNDS   *110km NE of Nelson*

Ngaio Bay Homestay, B&B, and Retreat
B&B Homestay Separate/Suite
Jude and Roger Sonneland
Ngaio Bay, French Pass Road, Pelorus Sounds

Tel **(03) 576 5287** homestay@ngaiobay.co.nz
www.ngaiobay.co.nz

Double $140 Single $95 (Full Breakfast)
Dinner $30pp/$15 child Lunch $15pp/$7 child
Child 3-12 years $55 Child under 2 $30 all inclusive
Credit cards accepted
2 Queen 3 Single (2 bdrm) Bathrooms: 2 Private

Ngaio Bay, 2 hours scenic drive from Nelson or Blenheim, in remote Pelorus Sounds wilderness with private beach, near awesome waters of French Pass. The Garden Cottage and Rose & Dolphin offer comfortable private accommodation overlooking beach, garden and bush. A honeymoon favourite. Guests linger at our table enjoying scrumptious food and good conversation, open fire for cool evenings. Organic vegetable garden and orchard, colourful flower garden. Swimming, walking, boating. Private fireheated bath on beach a speciality. Children welcome. 3 loveable labradors.

PICTON - ANAKIWA   *22km W of Picton*

Crafters *Self-contained Self-catering*
Leslie & Ross Close
Anakiwa Road, RD 1, Picton

Tel **(03) 574 2547** Fax (03) 574 2947
Mob 025 231 2245 crafters@actrix.gen.nz
www.bnb.co.nz/crafters.html

Double $100 (Continental Breakfast)
Credit cards accepted
1 King/Twin (1 bdrm)
Bathrooms: 1 Private

Perfect for a longer stay, as a base to explore the beautiful Marlborough Sounds. Peaceful, private surroundings at the head of Queen Charlotte Sound with bush walks (Queen Charlotte Walkway), bird life, boating and kayaking. Our self-catering warm and comfortable groundfloor apartment has king/twin bedroom, sunny lounge, private bathroom and fully equipped kitchen. Laundry facilities available. Not suitable for children. Ross is a woodturner, Leslie a potter, our on-site gallery is open every day. Friendly dog, Milly. Breakfast hamper provided.

PICTON   *1km E of Picton Central*

Retreat Inn *B&B Homestay*
Alison & Geoff
20 Lincoln Street, Picton

Tel **(03) 573 8160** Fax (03) 573 7799
Mob 021 143 2224
elliott.orchard@xtra.co.nz
www.retreat-inn.co.nz

Room rate $70-$130 (Special Breakfast)
Credit cards accepted
2 Queen 2 Single (3 bdrm)
Bathrooms: 1 Ensuite 1 Private 1 Guest share

'Retreat Inn' - 1km from Picton Village, yet quiet and relaxing, with beautiful tree-fern and bush surroundings. We have 3 lovely guest bedrooms - 2 upstairs, queen & twin (or single)- bright and cosy, facing the sun and 1 room downstairs - queen, ensuite - peaceful & spacious, with outside access to fern/seating area. Breakfast at Retreat Inn is special! Transport provided locally. Laundry facilities. Flat off-street parking. Sorry, no smoking indoors. We are a happy 2 person/2 cat household!

PICTON *200m S of Picton*

Rivenhall *B&B Homestay*
Nan & Malcolm Laurenson
118 Wellington Street, Picton

Tel (03) 573 7692 Fax (03) 573 7692
rivenhall.picton@xtra.co.nz
www.bnb.co.nz/rivenhall.html

Double $110 Single $70 (Full Breakfast)
Dinner $30pp by arrangement
Credit cards accepted Children welcome
1 Queen 1 Double (2 bdrm)
Bathrooms: 2 Private

Up the rise, on the left, at the top of Wellington Street, is Rivenhall. A gracious home with all the warmth, comfort and charm of days gone by, overlooking the town of Picton with its background of surrounding hills. Yet it is an easy walk to the centre of town or the ferries beyond. Evening meal on request, courtesy car pick up from the ferry, bus or train. Laundry facilities. The Marlborough Sounds start at the bottom of our street.

PICTON *Picton Central*

Grandvue *B&B Self-contained*
Rosalie & Russell Mathews
19 Otago Street, Picton

Tel (03) 573 8553 Fax (03) 573 8556
grandvue-mathews@clear.net.nz
www.nzhomestay.co.nz/mathews.htm

Double $100 Single $60 (Full Breakfast)
Child $25 Credit cards accepted
1 Queen (1 bdrm)
Bathrooms: 1 Ensuite

Situated on the hills overlooking Picton, Grandvue offers panoramic views of Queen Charlotte Sound and surrounding areas. At the end of a cul-de-sac Grandvue is a quiet haven in a secluded garden, 5 minutes walk to town and its assortment of restaurants. Accommodation is a quality, warm, self-contained apartment with TV, video and access to a barbecue. Feast on scenic views from our upstairs conservatory, while enjoying a delicious and satisfying breakfast. Courtesy transport and laundry facilities available.

PICTON *800m N of Picton*

Echo Lodge *B&B Homestay*
Lyn & Eddie Thoroughgood
5 Rutland Street,
Picton

Tel (03) 573 6367 Fax (03) 573 6387
echolodge@xtra.co.nz
www.bnb.co.nz/echolodge.html

Double $90 Single $60 (Full Breakfast)
1 Double 1 Twin 1 Single (2 bdrm)
Bathrooms: 2 Ensuite

Lyn and Eddie and our little dog, Osca, welcome you to a relaxed atmosphere at Echo Lodge. Breakfast is our speciality which includes home-made breads; jams and a smorgasbord. Comfortable bedrooms with ensuites. Also tea and coffee making facilities ensure a good nights sleep. We are 5 minutes walk to shops, restaurants, ferries, buses and bush walks. Make yourself comfortable in our large lounge with a cosy wood fire for those chilly nights. A courtesy car is available, as is off-street parking.

Picton - Kenepuru Sounds   *80km NE of Havelock*

The Nikaus   *B&B Farmstay*
Alison & Robin Bowron
86 Manaroa Road, Waitaria Bay, RD 2, Picton

Tel **(03) 573 4432**   Fax (03) 573 4432
Mob 025 544 712   info@thenikaus.co.nz
www.thenikaus.co.nz

Double $100   Single $50   (Full Breakfast)
Dinner $30   Credit cards accepted
1 Queen 2 Single (2 bdrm)   Bathrooms: 1 Guests share

The Nikaus is a Sounds sheep & cattle farm situated
in Waitaria Bay, Kenepuru Sound, 2 hours drive from Blenheim or Picton. We offer friendly personal
service in our comfortable spacious home. The large gardens (in AA Garden Book) contain many
rhododendrons, roses, camellias, lilies and perennials with big sloping lawns and views out to sea.
We have 3 adult children. A non-smoking household with interests in farming, boating, fishing and
gardening. We have a dog, Minny (Jack Russell cross). Other animals include the farm dogs, donkeys,
pet wild pigs, turkeys, hens and peacocks. Good hearty country meals, home grown produce. There are
local operators available for fishing trips, launch charters and water taxis, also golf and various walks.

Picton   *Picton Central*

The White House   *Homestay*
Gwen Stevenson
114 High Street,
Picton

Tel **(03) 573 6767**   Fax (03) 573 8871
thewhitehousepicton@xtra.co.nz
www.bnb.co.nz/thewhitehousepicton.html

Double $65-$140   Single $45   Twin $65
(Continental Breakfast)
2 Double 3 Single (4 bdrm)
Bathrooms: 2 Guests share

The White House in Picton's main street offers affordable luxury - just ask any previous guest - a
minute's walk to Picton's fabulous cafés and restaurants for your evening meal. Bedrooms and lounge
are upstairs and guests are welcome to make tea/coffee in the kitchen. Laundry available at small
charge. Non-smoking. Not suitable for children.

Picton   *Picton central*

Palm Haven   *B&B Homestay*
Dae & Peter Robertson
15A Otago Street, Picton

Tel **(03) 573 5644**   Fax (03) 573 5645
palmhaven@xtra.co.nz
www.bnb.co.nz/palmhaven.html

Double $80-$100   Single $55-$75
(Continental Breakfast)   Child $25
Dinner by arrangement
Children welcome   Pets welcome
2 Queen 2 Twin 2 Single (4 bdrm)
Bathrooms: 2 Ensuite 1 Guests share

Couples, families and singles are welcome in our modern, spacious home, designed for your comfort
and convenience. It's just a few minutes walk from the centre of town and all leisure activities. Our
guest rooms - 2 with full ensuite facilities and 2 with ensuite vanities and guest-only shared shower and
separate toilet - can be easily adapted to your needs. We provide cot, highchair, offer a laundry service
and courtesy pick up. We're keen lawn bowlers, and we share our home with Toby, the red tabby cat.

PICTON - QUEEN CHARLOTTE SOUNDS *11km Picton*

Ngakuta Bay Homestay *Homestay Self-contained*
Eve & Scott Dawson
Manuka Drive, Ngakuta Bay, Picton RD 1

Tel (03) 573 8853 Fax (03) 573 8353
Mob 025 237 3300 ngakutabayhouse@xtra.co.nz
www.picton.co.nz/ngakuta

Double $120-$150 Single $100
(Continental Breakfast)
Self-contained unit $120-$180
1 King 1 Double 2 Twin (4 bdrm)
Bathrooms: 2 Ensuite 2 Private

Ngakuta Bay Homestay is on the scenic Queen Charlotte Drive set in an acre of bush, the Homestay is built of NZ larch with large verandahs giving magnificent views over Ngakuta Bay. Each room has french doors onto the verandah with fridge and complimentary tea & coffee. Large lounge area with Sky TV. Also available from the Homestay are sailing dinghys, windsurfers and kayaks. The bay has landscaped recreational area with safe swimming and barbecue facilities making it an ideal holiday resort for water sports, walking and fishing.

PICTON - NGAKUTA BAY *11km W of Picton*

Bayswater *B&B Homestay Self-contained*
Paul & Judy Mann
25 Manuka Drive, Ngakuta Bay,
Queen Charlotte Drive, RD 1, Picton

Tel (03) 573 5966 Fax (03) 573 5966
www.bnb.co.nz/bayswater.html

Double $90 Single $50 (Continental Breakfast)
Self-contained unit 2 people $100, 4 people $150
1 Queen 1 Twin (2 bdrm)
Bathrooms: 1 Ensuite 1 Private

Welcome to Bayswater B&B in Ngakuta Bay, situated 11km from Picton and 24km from Havelock on Queen Charlotte Drive in the beautiful Marlborough Sounds. Your accommodation consists of a self-contained apartment with 2 double bedrooms, 2 bathrooms, kitchen, dining and lounge. Spectacular views over Ngakuta Bay and the surrounding bush. The bay has a picnic area and safe swimming; the Queen Charlotte Track is close by. Remember to bring food if self-catering. Suitable for longer stays. Come and relax in paradise. Complimentary transport available.

PICTON - QUEEN CHARLOTTE SOUNDS *16km W of Picton*

Tanglewood *B&B Homestay Separate/Suite*
Linda & Stephen Hearn
1744 Queen Charlotte Drive, The Grove, RD 1, Picton

Tel (03) 574 2080 Fax (03) 574 2044
Mob 027 481 4388 tanglewood.hearn@xtra.co.nz
www.bnb.co.nz/tanglewoodpicton.html

Double $105-$125 Single $90 (Special Breakfast)
Dinner $35 Self-contained unit $170
Credit cards accepted
2 King/Twin (2 bdrm)
Bathrooms: 2 Ensuite

Nestled amongst the native ferns overlooking Queen Charlotte Sounds. Our private guest wing includes spacious rooms with ensuites, lounge, kitchenette and barbeque area. Guests may choose to self-cater or home-cooked meal available by arrangement. Relax in our new spa surrounded by our beautiful native garden, listen to the birds or take a walk with us to view the glowworms. For privacy, swimming, fishing, kayaking or walking the Queen Charlotte Track. We look forward to making you welcome.

PICTON - WHATAMANGO BAY   *10km E of Picton*

Whatamango Lodge   *B&B Homestay Self-contained*
Ralph and Wendy Cass
17 McCormicks Road, Whatamango Bay, Picton

Tel (03) 573 5110   Fax (03) 573 5110
whatamango.lodge@paradise.net.nz   www.picton.co.nz/whatamango

Double $120-$150 Single $90   (Full Breakfast) Dinner $35
2 Queen (2 bdrm)
Bathrooms: 2 Ensuite

Welcome to Whatamango Lodge, situated at the head of Whatamango Bay, looking out towards Queen Charlotte Sound. We invite you to share our modern, waterfront home and enjoy total peace and tranquillity.

Relax on your own private balcony and watch the magnificent birdlife. Take a stroll around the beach or swim in the crystal clear water. There are also numerous bush walks. You may like to use our dinghy or fish off the rocks. Kayaks are available to paddle round the bay.

We are situated 10 minutes on a sealed road from Picton. Follow the Port Underwood Road from Waikawa to Whatamango Bay, turn left into McCormicks Road, waterfront location, no 17. A courtesy car is also available for transport to or from the ferry.

Guest accommodation comprises: 1. A self-contained unit (sleeps four), queen-sized bedroom, lounge (sofa bed), full kitchen facilities, large deck. 2. queen-sized bedroom with ensuite. Use of spacious lounge and balcony. Laundry facilities available.

Dinner is available by arrangement and features traditional New Zealand cuisine, served with complimentary wine. For breakfast choose either a full country style cooked breakfast, or a light continental breakfast, or if you prefer a delectable combination of both. We are a non-smoking household. Not suitable for children. We have a small dog, Sam

PICTON   *Picton Central*

Lincoln Cottage   *B&B Separate/Suite Self-contained*
Laurel & Bruce Sisson
19 Lincoln Street, Picton

Tel (03) 573 5285   Fax (03) 573 5286
Mob 021 658 140
lincolncottage@xtra.co.nz   pictonstay.com

Double $95-$120 Single $95   (Continental Breakfast)
Child $15   Credit cards accepted Children welcome
Smoking area inside
1 King/Twin 2 Queen 1 Twin 1 Single (4 bdrm)
Bathrooms: 2 Ensuite 1 Guests share

A warm welcome awaits you at our completely refurbished self-contained cottage, set in a peaceful location within walking distance of town. We are surrounded by beautiful bush and delightful walkways. Enjoy a delicious breakfast - panoramic views from the dining room, the ambience (including a cosy fire in the winter), or just relax on the sundeck. A fully equipped kitchen, off-street parking, laundry facilities and courtesy transport are available for your convenience. We look forward to meeting you.

PELORUS - MAHAU SOUND   *33km W of Picton*

Ramona   *B&B Homestay*
Phyl & Ken Illes
460 Moetapu Bay Road,
Mahau Sound, Marlborough

Tel (03) 574 2215   Fax (03) 574 2915
Mob 025 247 6668   illes@clear.net.nz
www.bnb.co.nz/ramona.html

Double $95   Single $75   (Continental Breakfast)
Lunch & dinner by arrangement   Credit cards accepted
2 Double 2 Twin (2 bdrm)
Bathrooms: 1 Private

Our new beachfront home on the beautiful Mahau Sound has been designed for you to share. Our guest floor has its own conservatory, here you can view the passing water traffic. Awake to the call of bellbirds and tuis, and after breakfast stroll around our rhododendron garden, or fossick on the beach. In the evening, see our glowworms. Phyl, a quilter and keen gardener, and Ken, a retired builder, will arrange visits to local art and craft studios, at your request. We host only one party at a time.

PICTON - MAHAU SOUND   *33km W of Picton*

The Rock Sound Stay™   *B&B Homestay*
Melvyn & Denyse Goodall
464 Moetapu Bay Road, RD2, Picton 7372

Tel (03) 574 2672   Fax (03) 574 2672   Mob 025 952 024
soundstay@therock.org.nz
www.therock.org.nz

Double $125-$150 Single $100   (Full Breakfast)
Dinner & lunch by arrangement Credit cards accepted
1 Queen 1 Double (2 bdrm)
Bathrooms: 2 Ensuite

The Rock Sound Stay is a unique accommodation experience where you can relax in a bygone era, with your hosts and their 3 dogs. Offering full ensuite facilities with claw footed baths and rooms overlooking the water or the garden. The original homestead built by a timber baron at the turn of the century, is set in almost 3 acres of native bush on the side of Mount Cawte only 20 metres from the sea, with gentle sloping paths to over 100 metres of sea frontage.

PICTON   *3km NE of Picton*

B&B
Approved

Michiru   *B&B*
Rosemary & Paul Royer
247B Waikawa Road, Waikawa, Picton

Tel (03) 573 6793   Fax (03) 573 6793
royer@xtra.co.nz   www.picton.co.nz/for/michiru

Double $110-$130   Single $75
(Special Breakfast) Dinner $35 by arrangement
Credit cards accepted Children welcome
1 King 1 Queen 2 Single (3 bdrm)
Bathrooms: 1 Ensuite 2 Private

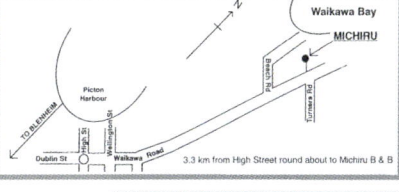

We only have one aim – to give you the finest and most memorable experience that we are able to provide.

We overlook Waikawa Bay and the beautiful Queen Charlotte Sounds so you can watch the ferries and cruise ships pass while enjoying breakfast: and all of this is only 3km from Picton town center.

The bright and sunny rooms are all located on the ground floor with a lovely private guest lounge and garden patio: probably shared with Puss the cat. Guests have the use of laundry facilities, bikes and kayaks around the bay.

We invite you to join us for Rosemary's delightful three course dinners with a glass of wine (by arrangement). We will of course meet or drop you at the ferry terminal, especially if you are walking the Queen Charlotte Track and don't have your own transport. There is a waterside restaurant and a café/bar within 5 minutes walk of the house. You'll love this location!

• Walk the Queen Charlotte Track • Kayak or sail the Queen Charlotte Sounds • Take half or whole day winery tours • Daily dolphin watch tours • Re-live 'The Edwin Fox' experience – she's the world's ninth oldest ship • Visit the fascinating 'Seahorse World' • Our favourite place – Karaka Point historical site • Superb accommodation for the discerning guests!

PICTON - WAIKAWA BAY   *4km Picton*

Sunny Corner   *B&B Homestay*
Dorothy & Joe Brewer
4 Whitby Close,
Waikawa Bay,
Picton

Tel (03) 573 8238
jodobrewer@xtra.co.nz
www.bnb.co.nz/sunnycorner.html

Double $90   Single $60   (Full Breakfast)
2 Double (2 bdrm)
Bathrooms: 1 Ensuite 1 Guests share

Our new home overlooks hills covered in native bush – a haven for bird life. We would love to make you welcome. A lounge with Sky TV and video is available for guests' use and also free internet access. Laundry available. Tea and coffee making facilities in rooms. Courtesy collection from ferries, train or bus and we offer lifts to local restaurants in the evenings. Enjoy the peaceful surrounding only 4km from the ferry and minutes from Waikawa Marina.

PICTON - LITTLE NGAKUTA BAY   *11km W of Picton*

Waterfront Bed & Breakfast   *B&B Homestay*
Vicki & David Bendell
Queen Charlotte Drive, 2383 Little Ngakuta Bay
RD 1, Picton

Tel (03) 573 8584   Mob 021 216 5955
bendell@xtra.co.nz
www.picton.co.nz/for/kotare

Double $145-$165   Single $125   (Full Breakfast)
Child $35   Dinner by arrangement Children welcome
1 Queen 1 Double 2 Single (2 bdrm)
Bathrooms: 1 Ensuite 1 Private 1 Host share

If staying on the waterfront is your accommodation requirement then our seaside cottage will exceed that expectation. It is as close to the water's edge as you can get. The aptly named 'Boatshed' and 'Pacific' rooms are separate from the cottage and offer ensuite private bathrooms, comfortable beds with Italian cotton linen, writing bureau, toiletries, tea/coffee (no TV in the room here). We consider accommodation an integral part of your holiday itinerary. Our young family (and dog) welcome you for a break from the ordinary.

PICTON - ANAKIWA   *22km W of Picton*

Tirimoana House   *Homestay Self-contained*
Jan & Brian Watts
257 Anakiwa Road, RD 1, Picton

Tel (03) 574 2627   Fax (03) 574 2647
Mob 025 277 5697   jan.w@xtra.co.nz
www.tirimoanahouse.com

Double $110-$150   Single $95   (Full Breakfast)
Dinner $35   Credit cards accepted
S/C flat (5 person) $110 + $20 per extra person
1 King/Twin 3 Queen 1 Double 1 Single (4 bdrm)
Bathrooms: 3 Ensuite 1 Private

Every room in our long-established homestay commands spectacular views down Queen Charlotte Sound. Our considerable reputation has been built on creating a warm and friendly environment for our guests. Dinners are available using local cuisine and wines. All bedrooms and our stunning Sunrise Suite have own ensuites and self-contained flat has own private deck. After kayaking,walking,mountain biking or visiting local wineries, relax in our swimming or hot spa pools. Jan and Brian and Pepsi, the poodle, would love to meet you. "Arrive as guests,leave as friends".

PICTON   *.5 km W of Picton*

Glengary   *B&B*
Glenys & Gary Riggs
5 Seaview Cres, Picton

Tel (03) 573 8317   Mob 027 498 6388
inquires@glengary.co.nz
www.bnb.co.nz/glengary.html

Double $100-$120 **Single** $50   (Continental Breakfast)
2 Queen 1 Twin (3 bdrm)
Bathrooms: 1 Ensuite 1 Guests share

Located a short drive from Picton ferry terminal and a
few minutes walk to the town centre. Whether you are
interested in visiting wineries, fishing, bush walking, cruising, sea kayaking or simply relaxing in idyllic
surroundings. Glengary Bed & Breakfast is ideally located to explore the Marlborough area. Your
friendly hosts will provide you with the best service to ensure your stay in the beautiful Marlborough
Sounds is relaxing and enjoyable. They will pick you up from ferry or airport, provide you with advice
on local trips, tours, travel and cruises. Family cat in residence.

PICTON - PORT UNDERWOOD SOUND   *20km E of Picton*

Oyster Bay Lodge   *B&B Homestay*
Raewyn & Rob Kirkwood
Oyster Bay, PO Box 146, Picton

Tel (03) 579 9644 Fax (03) 579 9645
Mob 025 363 363 or 021 763 753
r.kirkwood@xtra.co.nz
www.bnb.co.nz/oyster-bay.html

Double $95 **Single** $65   (Full Breakfast)
Dinner $30   Credit cards accepted
1 King/Twin 1 Queen 1 Twin (3 bdrm)
Bathrooms: 1 Ensuite 1 Guests share

Our lodge is set in picturesque Oyster bay. We have an uninterupted view over the bay in a charming
and historical part of Marlborough Sounds. We share an enjoyment of the outdoors. Our 8 metre boat
can offer access to a full range of marine activities in comfort and safety. Personally guided tours and
activities of your choosing also available at the Lodge.

PICTON   *25km N of Blenheim*

Noble House Bed & Breakfast   *B&B*
Susan & Jim Noble
5 Newgate Street,
Picton

Tel (03) 573 6414
Fax (03) 573 6414 noblehouse@xtra.co.nz
www.noblehouse.co.nz

Double $100 **Single** $50   (Continental Breakfast)
2 Queen 1 Twin 1 Single (4 bdrm)
Bathrooms: 2 Ensuite 1 Guests share

Kiwi hospitality awaits you at Noble House from your
hosts Susan and Jim - and Jock, the west highland terrier
- we aim to give you all the comforts of a home away from home. A 5 minute easy walk takes you to
the Picton foreshore, restaurants and information centre where you can choose boat tours, fishing trips,
dolphin and bird watching, kayaking, bushwalks, etc. We look forward to enjoying your company and
hope you will enjoy ours - you can't help but enjoy the beauty of the Marlborough Sounds.

PICTON - KOROMIKO *5km S of Picton*

Koromiko Valley Homestead *B&B*
Caryll & Vic Hewson
30 Freeths Road,
Koromiko, Picton

Tel (03) 573 5674 Fax (03) 573 7682
Mob 027 240 8632 hewson@clear.net.nz
www.koromikohomestead.co.nz

Double $120 (Full Breakfast)
Dinner prior notice Credit cards accepted
2 Queen (2 bdrm)
Bathrooms: 2 Private

Koromiko Valley Homestead is situated 5km south of
Picton, just off State Highway 1. We offer quality accommodation, evening meal, rural setting, ferry
& airport transfers with prior request. The home is situated on 10 acres with various animals. Stroll in
the large gardens, go for a game of golf on the nearby course. Relax in the spa or enjoy a glass of wine
by the fire or on the deck. Sky TV and internet available. Not suitable for children or pets. Friendly
resident dog.

BLENHEIM *3km S of Blenheim*

Hillsview *Homestay*
Adrienne & Rex Handley
Please Phone

Tel (03) 578 9562 Fax (03) 578 9562
Mob 025 627 6727 aidrex@xtra.co.nz
www.bnb.co.nz/hillsview.html

Double $80-$85 Single $60 (Full Breakfast)
Less 10% if pre-booked by the night before
1 King/Twin 1 Double 2 Twin (3 bdrm)
Bathrooms: 2 Private

Welcome to our warm, spacious, non-smoking home in a quiet suburb with outdoor pool, off-street
parking, and no pets. All beds have quality mattresses, electric blankets and wool underlays. Interests:
Rex's (retired airline pilot) - are aviation oriented - models, microlights, homebuilts and gliding. Builds
miniature steam locomotives, has 1930 Model A soft-top tourer vintage car and enjoys barbershop
singing. Adrienne's - cooking, spinning, woolcraft. Let us share these hobbies, plus our caring personal
attention, complimentary beverages and all the comforts of home with you.

BLENHEIM - RAPAURA *12km NW of Blenheim*

Thainstone *Self-contained Vineyard Homestay*
Vivienne & Jim Murray
120 Giffords Road,
RD 3, Rapaura

Tel (03) 572 8823 Fax (03) 572 8623
Mob 021 283 1484 thainstone@xtra.co.nz
www.marlborough.co.nz/thainstone

Double $120 Single $70 (Full Breakfast) Dinner $30
S/C House, 2-4 people $120-$180 breakfast not provided
Credit cards accepted
1 King 2 Queen 1 Double 1 Twin 1 Single (5 bdrm)
Bathrooms: 1 Ensuite 1 Private 1 Guests share

Our large home is surrounded by vineyards and within walking distance of the Wairau River and several
wineries. In our home there are 3 upstairs bedrooms and a guest lounge which opens onto an enclosed,
solar heated swimming pool. The self-catering house has 2 bedrooms and is fully equipped for longer
stays. We are widely travelled and some interests are bird watching, trout fishing, woodworking and
cards. Evening meals, by prior arrangement, are served with Marlborough wines. Unsuitable for
children.

BLENHEIM   *500m W of Blenheim Central*

Beaver B&B *Homestay Self-contained*
Jen & Russell Hopkins
60 Beaver Road,
Blenheim

Tel **(03) 578 8401**   Fax (03) 578 8401
Mob 021 626 151   rdhopkins@xtra.co.nz
www.bnb.co.nz/beaverbb.html

Double **$90**   Single $60   (Continental Breakfast)
Credit cards accepted
1 Queen (1 bdrm)   Bathrooms: 1 Ensuite

Our self-contained unit can accommodate one couple or a single. Features include your own entrance, queensize bed, mini kitchen, bathroom - large bath, shower and separate toilet. Use of our laundry can be made upon request. Two cats and a bird live with us. We have off-street parking and are within ten minutes walk from central Blenheim. Please phone before 8am or after 4:30pm during the working week. If no response, Jennie can be contacted via her cell-phone. Fax us anytime.

BLENHEIM   *2km N of Blenheim*

Philmar *B&B Homestay*
Wynnis & Lex Phillips
63 Colemans Road, Blenheim

Tel **(03) 577 7788**   Fax (03) 577 7788
www.bnb.co.nz/philmar.html

Double **$70**   Single $50   (Continental Breakfast)
Dinner $20pp
2 Queen 1 Twin (3 bdrm)
Bathrooms: 1 Guests share

Welcome to our home 2km from the town centre. Guests can join us in our spacious sunny living areas. We both enjoy all TV sports and our other interests include wood turning, handcrafts and the Lions organisation. Blenheim is an ideal place to visit Picton, Nelson, whale watch and the many wineries, parks and craft shops in the area . Smoking is not encouraged. Just phone to be picked up at airport, train or bus. Dinner on request.

BLENHEIM - AWATERE VALLEY   *63km S of Blenheim*

Duntroon *Farmstay*
Trish & Robert Oswald
Awatere Valley, Private Bag, Blenheim

Tel **(03) 575 7374**   Fax (03) 575 7281
Mob 027 486 5223   oswald@xtra.co.nz
www.bnb.co.nz/duntroon.html

Double **$130**   Single $90   (Full Breakfast)
Child $70   Dinner by arrangement
Backpacker accommodation $20
1 Double 4 Single (3 bdrm)
Bathrooms: 1 Guests share 1 Host share

Come and enjoy the peaceful surroundings of our 3500 acre high country Merino property in the beautiful Awatere Valley. The large homestead set in established grounds with tennis court and swimming pool offers warm spacious bedrooms with comfortable beds.   Lunch and dinner served with local wines by arrangement. Farm tours on request. Our interests include clay-target shooting, travel, flying, tennis, boating and handcrafts. Over the summer the Awatere Valley Road is open through Molesworth Station to Hamner Springs.

MARLBOROUGH

BLENHEIM

Baxter Homestay   *Homestay*
Kathy & Brian Baxter
28 Elisha Drive, Blenheim

Tel (03) 578 3753   Fax (03) 578 3796
Mob 021 129 2062   baxterart@clear.net.nz
www.baxterhomestay.com

Double $100-$130 (Continental Breakfast)
Credit cards accepted
1 King/Twin 1 King 1 Double (3 bdrm)
Bathrooms: 2 Ensuite 1 Guests share

Brian, a renowned NZ artist, and Kathy, a keen gardener, welcome you to their spacious, sunny, modern home and art gallery. TV in all bedrooms (smoke-free). Guests can enjoy magnificent panoramic views over Blenheim and nearby vineyards, or explore terraced gardens of roses, rhododendrons, camellias, perennials, deciduous trees etc. We can arrange tours to wineries, gardens, ski field, golf courses etc. Laundry facilities. Our interests include gardening, music, travel, fishing, skiing, art, video production, and meeting people from all over the world.

BLENHEIM   *12km W of Blenheim*

Black Birch Lodge   *B&B Vineyard Homestay*
Margaret & David Barnsley
Jeffries Road, RD 3, Blenheim

Tel (03) 572 8876   Fax (03) 572 8806
barnsley@ihug.co.nz
www.bnb.co.nz/blackbirchlodge.html

Double $140-$150 Single $85-$110 (Full Breakfast)
Child ¹/₂ price Dinner $40 by arrangement
Credit cards accepted Children welcome
2 Queen 3 Single (3 bdrm)   Bathrooms: 2 Ensuite

Black Birch Lodge is ideally situated for exploring Marlborough's wine trail. Your hosts have been involved in the wine industry since 1981 both as growers and David as editor of Winepress. Most Marlborough wineries are only a matter of minutes away, the closest being the prestigious Herzog Winery and Restaurant situated at the bottom of Black Birch's vineyard. Other features include tennis court, pool, bikes, library, laundry, wine trail advice, vineyard walks and trout fishing in nearby Wairau River. We have a small friendly dog, Perro.

BLENHEIM   *5km S of Blenheim*

The Willows   *B&B Homestay*
Millie Amos
6 The Willows,
Springlands,
Blenheim

Tel (03) 577 7853   Fax (03) 577 7853
www.bnb.co.nz/6thewillows.html

Double $80 Single $50 (Continental Breakfast)
1 Queen 2 Twin (2 bdrm)
Bathrooms: 1 Private

Only 5km from the centre of town. The Willows is a spacious and modern home in close proximity to shops, restaurants and wineries. Peaceful location surrounded by lovely gardens. I welcome you to my home, so please phone first.

BLENHEIM   *Blenheim Central*

Approved

Grove Bank   *B&B Homestay Family*
Pauline & Peter Pickering
2652 State Highway 1, Grovetown, Blenheim

Tel (03) 578 8407   0800 422 632   Fax (03) 578 8407
grovebank@xtra.co.nz   www.grovebank.co.nz

Double $70-$85 Single $50-$55
(Full Breakfast) Dinner $20-$35 Groups $75-$180
Credit cards accepted
3 King/Twin 4 Queen 2 Single (8 bdrm)
Bathrooms: 6 Ensuite 1 Private 1 Spa bath

Pauline and Peter invite you to stay at our 8 acre olive grove and vineyard, which is located conveniently on SH1 on the northern boundary of Blenheim.

We offer eight double bedrooms with ensuites plus bedroom and bathroom appliances. Our home is designed especially with homestay guests in mind. Spacious guest lounges (with televisions) opening onto large balconies, offer panoramic views of the plains ranges and river. After a day of sightseeing and enjoying the delights of the "Gourmet Province", cool off in the swimming pool, relax in the spa, take a stroll in Pauline's gardens the olive grove/vineyard. Some courtesy transport is available for evening dining.

We offer continental and cooked breakfast and meals as requested. A former restaurateur and butcher, Peter's breakfasts are legendary. Evening meals may consist of meats and fresh grown vegetables or fish caught by Peter from the Marlborough Sounds, rivers and lakes. If you feel like dining out, Marlborough's finest Italian restaurant (Best pasta in the world - "Cuisine"), the Whitehaven Winery & Café and local bar and bistro are within 5 minutes walking distance.

We are happy to share our extensive local knowledge and contacts which will enable you to personalise and optimise your stay in the "Gourmet Province"/ Free laundry facilities.

Directions: on Blenheim's north boundary definitely 100 metres north of narrow concrete bridge, on State Highway 1, turn into multi signed entrance shared by the Research Centre. Then immediately turn left into gravel drive and follow to house.

BLENHEIM *1.5km S of Blenheim*

Green Gables *B&B Country Homestay*
Jeannine & Benjamin Van Straaten
St Andrews, SH1, Gate 3011, Blenheim

Tel (03) 577 9205 0800 273 050   Fax (03) 577 9206
Mob 021 115 8811
green_gables_blenheim@xtra.co.nz
www.greengableshomestay.co.nz

Double $90-$130 Single $70
(Continental Breakfast) Dinner $40
Cooked breakfast $5 extra Credit cards accepted
2 Queen 2 Double (3 bdrm)
Bathrooms: 3 Ensuite

Enjoy your stay at our luxurious and exceptionally spacious
2 storey home located in rural Blenheim. Only 2km from
the town centre, Green Gables is set in a tranquil, 1 acre
landscaped garden and offers quiet, luxurious surroundings,
although close to State Highway 1 and to town.

Guest accommodation comprises of 3 large bedrooms, all
with ensuite bathrooms. 2 of our rooms have queen-sized
beds and the third has a double bed. All rooms are fully
equipped with electric blankets, radio clocks, hair dryers and
room heating and 2 rooms have glass doors that open onto
private balconies affording panoramic views of Blenheim.
An adjoining guest lounge has a small library and television
set and there are additional TV sets in the queen rooms.
Coffee and tea making facilities are available and you are
invited to use the laundry, fax and email facilities if required.

For breakfast choose either a full, country-style cooked breakfast or a light continental
breakfast or if you prefer a delectable combination of both, served with delicious home-made jams and
preserves. Dinner is available by arrangement and features traditional New Zealand cuisine served with a
complimentary drink.

We are horticulturists and grow cut flowers. Our ginger cat, Sharky, is visitor friendly and lives outside.
Green Gables backs onto the picturesque Opawa river. In season this gentle river offers trout fishing,
eeling and whitebaiting. A small rowing boat is available for your use at no extra charge. As an
additional courtesy we would be pleased to help you with the on-booking of your B&B accommodation.
Let us phone ahead for you and you'll make valuable savings on your phone card.

Directions: On SH1, ¹/₂ km south of Blenheim town, gate number 3011. 20 minutes from Picton
Ferry. Green Gables sign at drive entrance.

BLENHEIM   *Blenheim Central*

Maxwell House   *Homestay*
John and Barbara Ryan
82 Maxwell Road,
Blenheim

Tel **(03) 577 7545**   Fax (03) 577 7545
mt.olympus@xtra.co.nz
www.bnb.co.nz/maxwellhouse.html

Double $125   Single $100   (Full Breakfast)
Credit cards accepted Children welcome
1 Queen 1 Twin (2 bdrm)
Bathrooms: 2 Ensuite

Welcome to Marlborough. We invite you to stay at Maxwell House, a grand old Victorian residence. Built in 1880 our home has been elegantly restored and is classified with the Historic Places Trust. Our large guest rooms are individually appointed with ensuite, lounge area, television and tea and coffee making facilities. Breakfast will be a memorable experience, served around the original 1880's kauri table. Set on a large established property Maxwell House is an easy 10 minute walk to the town centre. Non-smoking.

BLENHEIM   *3km Blenheim Centre*

Richmond View   *B&B Homestay*
Allan & Jan Graham
25 Elmwood Avenue, Blenheim

Tel **(03) 578 8001**   Fax (03) 578 8001
Mob 025 458 074   a.w.graham@xtra.co.nz
http://nzhomestay/graham.html

Double $100   Single $100   (Continental Breakfast)
Child $70   Children welcome
1 Queen 1 Twin (2 bdrm)
Bathrooms: 1 Guests share

We welcome you to our new home built on the slopes of Wither Hills situated to the south side of Blenheim, having panoramic views of town, Richmond Ranges and Cook Strait in the distance. Offering queen and twin rooms with electric blankets and heating. Complimentary spa available. Bathroom and toilet are separate and private. Our interests comprise boating, four wheel driving, vintage cars, flying and enjoying Marlborough's fantastic waterways and wineries which you can share by arrangement. Local pickup available on request.

BLENHEIM   *6 min N of Blenheim*

Chardonnay Lodge   *B&B Homestay*
2 Self-contained villas / 1 bedroom with ensuite
George and Ellenor Mayo
1048 Rapaura Road, Rapaura, Blenheim

Tel **(03) 570 5194**   Fax (03) 570 5196
info@chardonnaylodge.co.nz
www.chardonnaylodge.co.nz

Double $115-$135   (Special Breakfast)
Child $30 (5 years and over) Dinner $60 by arrangement
Extra persons in villa $30pp   Credit cards accepted
3 Queen 3 Single (3 bdrm) Bathrooms: 3 Ensuite

We offer excellent accommodation and facilities, including secluded solar heated swimming pool, private spa, sun lounges, BBQ, a full sized tennis court. Central to the superb vineyards and restaurants, with Blenheim just 6 minutes away we provide homestay with own ensuite or high standard self-contained villas. You will find everything you and your family need for a comfortable and relaxing stay. Our fluffy persian cats will welcome you to the lawns and garden. We are 2.2km from the Spring Creek turn-off on SH1. Courtesy vehicle to ferry, bus and rail. Location map, pictures and information on web site.

BLENHEIM   *9km NW of Blenheim*

Stonehaven Vineyard Homestay   *B&B Homestay*
Paulette & John Hansen
414 Rapaura Road, RD 3, Blenheim

Tel (03) 572 9730   Fax (03) 572 9730
Mob 025 682 1120
stay@stonehavenhomestay.co.nz
www.stonehavenhomestay.co.nz

Double $180-$200 Single $90-$120
(Full Breakfast) Dinner $50pp wine included
Credit cards accepted
1 King 1 Queen 1 Twin (3 bdrm)
Bathrooms: 2 Ensuite 1 Private

The house, which reflects the warmth, space and comfort
to make your stay relaxing and memorable, commands
exquisite views over the vineyards to the craggy
Richmond Ranges beyond. Close by are some of New
Zealand's most outstanding wineries.

Start the day with a delicious breakfast served in the
summerhouse overlooking the swimming pool. Wines
are served to match the first two courses of the three
course evening meal which features our home-grown
vegetables and locally produced seasonal ingredients.
Occasionally game such as venison or wild pork may be
included - booking essential.

Marlborough offers many activities to occupy your day
and a picnic lunch can be provided.   You may like us to
organise and book some of these attractions or, if you
plan to stay with us for two or more nights, we can offer scenic tours, winery tours, four wheel drive
tours such as Pelorus to Nelson over old gold trails or we can take you to more out of the way locations
for trout fishing or tramping in our beautiful backcountry where we can introduce you to our native flora
and fauna.

We can meet you or drop you off at either the airport at Blenheim or the ferry terminal at Picton. We
look forward to making your stay with us as relaxing or as active as you choose. We are non-smokers
and our interests include native flora and fauna, hunting, fishing, tramping, cooking and New Zealand
history. We have two pets, Frisky the cat & Bess, a gentle black labrador. Check out room availability &
book on-line by visiting our website.

*Our stone and cedar house is surrounded by gardens and 18 acres of
Sauvignon Blanc vines in the premium grape growing area of Marlborough*

BLENHEIM *100m W of Blenheim*

Henry Maxwell's Central B&B *B&B*
Rae Woodman
28 Henry Street, Blenheim

Tel (03) 578 8086 0800 436 796 Fax (03) 578 8086
Mob 025 200 9862 stay@henrymaxwells.co.nz
www.henrymaxwells.co.nz

Double $90-$120 Single $65 (Full Breakfast)
3 Queen 4 Twin 3 Single (4 bdrm)
Bathrooms: 2 Ensuite 1 Private 1 Guests share

Welcome to 'Henry's', a gracious 75 year old home.
Guests have spacious quiet rooms, 2 with ensuites,
2 share bathroom. TV, tea, coffee, cookies and
complimentary port. Queen-size beds and large comfortable armchairs. All overlook gardens.
Breakfast in the unique dining room (maps and charts) is something to remember. 3 minutes stroll to
town, many excellent restaurants, shops, theatre, movies, etc. Find Henry's, corner of Henry and Munro
Streets between High Street and Maxwell Road. Off-street parking. Relax and enjoy the garden and
sun.

BLENHEIM *7km N of Blenheim*

Blue Ridge Estate *B&B Homestay*
Lesley & Brian Avery
50 O'Dwyers Road,
RD 3, Blenheim

Tel (03) 570 2198 Fax (03) 570 2199
lavery@clear.net.nz
www.blueridge.co.nz

Double $150-$195 Single $120-$165 (Full Breakfast)
Dinner by arrangement Credit cards accepted
2 Queen 2 Twin (3 bdrm)
Bathrooms: 1 Ensuite 2 Private

Set on a 20-acre purpose-designed homestay property, Blue Ridge Estate, 2002 Marlborough Master
Builders' "House of the Year", enjoys a rural setting with stunning views across vineyards to the
Richmond Range and is close to many of Marlborough's fine wineries, restaurants and gardens. Our
home has proven most popular with both international and New Zealand visitors. Come share our home
with Bella, our friendly young labrador, where comfort and privacy will ensure your Marlborough visit
is indeed a memorable one.

RENWICK *15km W of Blenheim*

LeGrys Vineyard
Homestay Self-contained Vineyard Lodge
Jennifer & John Joslin
Conders Bend Road, Renwick, Marlborough

Tel (03) 572 9490 Fax (03) 572 9491 Mob 021 313 208
stay@legrys.co.nz www.legrys.co.nz

Double $140 (Full Breakfast)
S/C double + max 4 $225 + $45 pp
Credit cards accepted
2 Queen 2 Single (3 bdrm) Bathrooms: 2 Private

Waterfall Lodge - self-contained, vineyard setting. 2 beds queen, 2 single. Kitchen facilities, dining,
lounge area, gas BBQ. Main house - queen room, private bathroom. Both offer unique mud-brick
construction, offering rustic charm combined with stylish furnishings. Breakfast hamper, full
provisions daily. Ideal base for winery visits, golf, Sounds cruising, walking, Trout fishing. Blenheim
town 10 minutes drive. Solar heated indoor pool. LeGrys & Mudhouse wines available, complimentary
tasting, tray of nibbles to welcome you. John and Jennifer cruised the world in their yacht. We have a
springer spaniel, Pippin and airedale Alice.

RENWICK *10km W of Blenheim*

Clovelly *Homestay*
Don & Sue Clifford
2A Nelson Place, Renwick,
Marlborough 7352

Tel **(03) 572 9593** Fax (03) 572 7293
Mob 025 986 917 clifford@actrix.co.nz
www.clovelly.co.nz

Double $110 Single $80 (Special Breakfast)
Credit cards accepted
1 Queen 1 Twin (2 bdrm)
Bathrooms: 2 Private

Our colonial style home is set in ¹/₂ an acre of lovely private grounds in the heart of vineyard country. We overlook orchards and out to the Richmond Range. Relax under the trees with refreshments or by a glowing fire in winter. Visit our quaint local English pub - dine in the village or vineyard restaurants. We are within 'stroll and taste' distance of a number of prestigious vineyards. Rest and unwind with Don and Sue and our 2 little scottish terriers, Chloe and Phoebe, who will welcome you warmly.

CANVASTOWN *10km W of Havelock*

Woodchester *B&B Homestay*
Judy & Ted Tomlinson
84 Te Hora Pa Road,
RD 1, Havlock, Marlborough

Tel **(03) 574 1123** Fax (03) 574 1123
woodchesterlodge@woodchesterlodge.co.nz
www.woodchesterlodge.co.nz

Double $110 Single $55 (Full Breakfast)
Child from $18 Dinner from $20
Single divan in queen room Children welcome
1 Queen 1 Twin (2 bdrm)
Bathrooms: 1 Guests share

We are a friendly retired couple and have a Jack Russell dog, called Mr Fox, to say hello. Our home is lodge style with country atmosphere. We look forward to enjoying your company and share meals and conversation in our dining room and lounge. BBQs in the summer available. Consider more than one nights stay, as fishing and sightseeing trips are only minutes away. Walking and tramping tracks are prolific or cruise the fabulous sounds in comfort. Welcome to Woodchester Lodge and enjoy.

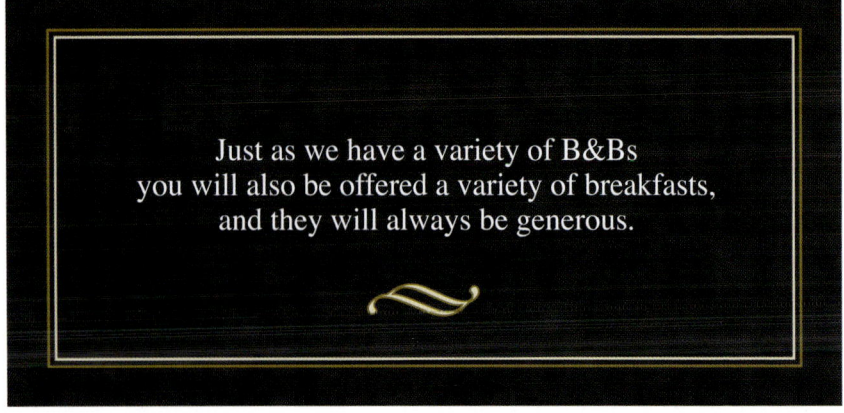

Just as we have a variety of B&Bs
you will also be offered a variety of breakfasts,
and they will always be generous.

Nelson, Golden Bay

- Pakawau
- Collingwood
- Parapara
- Patons Rock
- Tata Beach
- Takaka
- **60**
- Abel Tasman National Park
- Marahau
- Kaiteriteri
- Riwaka
- Motueka
- Tasman
- Thorpe
- Ruby Bay
- Cable Bay
- Atawhai
- Mapua
- Upper Moutere
- **6**
- Nelson
- Richmond
- Wakefield
- Golden Downs

Towns listed generally follow a north to south route. Refer to the index if required.

| 0 | Kilometres | 20 |
| 0 | Miles | 12 |

- **6**
- **63**
- Tophouse
- Murchison
- **65**
- Nelson Lakes
- St Arnaud

CABLE BAY   *20km N of Nelson*

Quail Ridge   *B&B*
Ken and Gerrie Young
Cable Bay Road, Hira, RD1, Nelson

Tel (03) 545 1899   Fax (03) 545 1890
quailridge@clear.net.nz
www.quailridge.co.nz

Double $150   Single $130   (Continental Breakfast)
Child $25   Dinner $40pp   Barbecue $25pp
Credit cards accepted
2 Queen 2 Single (2 bdrm)
Bathrooms: 2 Ensuite

Quail Ridge offers a very special, memorable experience. The Cable Bay location is quiet and beautiful with wonderful water, island and farmland views. The 2 attractive separately located guest studios are designed for privacy and relaxation. Terraces provide socialising, barbecuing and outdoor dining areas. A quiet swimming beach, walkway, and fishing spots are nearby with 4WD bikes, skywire, kayaking, and horse trekking locally. Restaurants and activities of Nelson City are 20 minutes away. Always a friendly welcome - our dog and cat enjoy sharing the moment.

NELSON - ATAWHAI   *6km NE of Nelson*

Mike's B&B   *B&B Homestay*
Mike Cooper & Lennane Cooper-Kent
4 Seaton Street, Nelson

Tel (03) 545 1671   Fax (03) 545 1671
cooperkent@actrix.gen.nz
www.bnb.co.nz/kent.html

Double $70-$80 (Full Breakfast)
Dinner $30 with prior notice
Credit cards accepted
2 Queen (2 bdrm)
Bathrooms: 2 Ensuite

5 minutes from Nelson City centre we give you a warm welcome to our comfortable home in a safe quiet neighbourhood with superb views over Tasman Bay and out to the Tasman mountains. Our guest accommodation is almost self-contained and is well equipped with a small lounge, fridge, TV, tea and coffee making facilities and a microwave. Laundry facilities are available for your use. Our interests include our large collection of books which you are welcome to use, sea fishing, education and our lively schnauzer dog.

NELSON   *2km SW of Nelson*

Harbour View Homestay
B&B Homestay OR Self Contained Apartment
Judy Black
11 Fifeshire Crescent, Nelson

Tel (03) 548 8567   Fax (03) 548 8667
Mob 027 247 4445   harbourview-homestay@xtra.co.nz
www.bnb.co.nz/harbourbb.html

Double $125-$145 Single $90-$125
(Continental Breakfast - Full breakfast $10pp extra)
Credit cards accepted
2 Queen 2 Single (3 bdrm)
Bathrooms: 2 Ensuite 1 Private

Harbour View Homestay
Nelson NZ

Our home is above the harbour entrance. Huge windows capture spectacular views of beautiful Tasman Bay, Haulashore Island, Tahunanui Beach, across the sea to Abel Tasman National Park and mountains. Observe from the bedrooms, dining room and decks, ships and pleasure craft cruising by as they enter and leave the harbour. If you can tear yourself away from our magnificent view, within walking distance along the waterfront there are excellent cafés and restaurants. Your hosts, Judy and David and Possum the cat, offer you a warm welcome and a memorable stay.

NELSON   *5km SW of Nelson*

Arapiki   *Homestay Units*
Kay & Geoff Gudsell
21 Arapiki Road,
Stoke, Nelson

Tel (03) 547 3741   Fax (03) 547 3742
bnb@nelsonparadise.co.nz
www.nelsonparadise.co.nz

Double $75-$110   Single $70-$90
(Continental Breakfast - optional $7.50pp)
1 Queen 1 Double 1 Single (2 bdrm)
Bathrooms: 2 Ensuite

Enjoy a relaxing holiday in the midst of your trip. The 2 quality smoke-free units in our large home offer comfort, privacy and off-street parking in a central location. The larger Unit 1 is in a private garden setting. A ranchslider opens on to a deck with outdoor furniture. It has an electric stove, microwave, TV, auto washing machine & phone. Unit 2 has a balcony with seating to enjoy sea and mountain views. It has a microwave, hotplate, TV & phone. We have a tonkinese cat.

NELSON   *6km S of Nelson*

Tarata Homestay   *B&B Homestay*
John & Mercia Hoskin
5 Tarata Street, Stoke, Nelson

Tel (03) 547 3426   0800 107 308
hosts@taratahomestay.co.nz
www.taratahomestay.co.nz

Double $90-$105   Single $75-$95
(Continental Breakfast)   Child $25
Credit cards accepted   Children welcome
1 Queen 1 Twin (2 bdrm)
Bathrooms: 1 Private

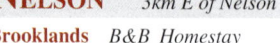

Quiet, secluded and surrounded by gardens and mature trees, Tarata Homestay offers quality accommodation. We cater for up to 4 guests but do not take bookings for others while you are here, giving you exclusive use of all facilities. Just relax and unwind after a day's travel and enjoy a drink in the guest lounge or soak up the sun on the patio. Free internet access to keep in touch with home. Raja is our elderly but friendly golden labrador dog. Qualmark: Three Star Plus.

NELSON   *3km E of Nelson*

Brooklands   *B&B Homestay*
Lorraine & Barry Signal
106 Brooklands Road, Atawhai, Nelson

Tel (03) 545 1423   Fax (03) 545 1423
bsignal@paradise.net.nz
www.bnb.co.nz/brooklands.html

Double $100-$125   Single $70   (Full Breakfast)
Child by arrangement   Dinner $35
Credit cards accepted   Children welcome
1 Queen 2 Double 2 Single (3 bdrm)
Bathrooms: 1 Ensuite 1 Guests share

Brooklands is a spacious, luxurious 4 level home with superb sea views. Guests have exclusive use of 2 levels. The large bathroom has a spa bath for 2. 1 bedroom has a private balcony. There are spacious indoor/outdoor living areas. We enjoy sports, travel and outdoors. Lorraine makes dolls and bears and enjoys crafts, gardening and cooking. We are close to Nelson's attractions - beaches, crafts, wine trails, national parks, lakes and mountains. We enjoy making new friends. Smoke-free. Courtesy transport available.

NELSON   *2km W of Nelson Central*

Jubilee House   *Homestay*
Patsy & Sheridan Parris
107 Quebec Road, Nelson

Tel (03) 54 88 5 11   0800 11 88 91
Fax (03) 54 88 5 11   Mob 027 44 8 77 67
info@jubileehouse.co.nz
www.jubileehouse.co.nz

Double $100-$110 Single $70-$80
(Full Breakfast) Credit cards accepted
2 Double 2 Single (4 bdrm)
Bathrooms: 1 Guests share

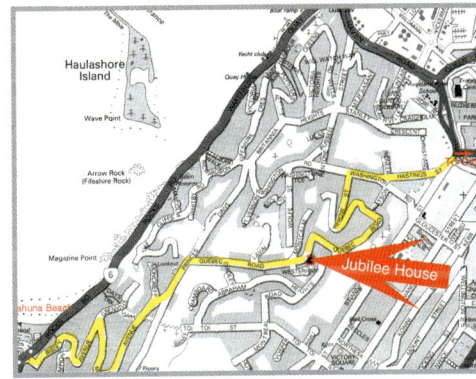

Many of our guests have told us we have
some of the finest views of any Bed &
Breakfast in New Zealand. High on a
ridge overlooking the whole of Nelson
City, beautiful Tasman Bay, mountains and
harbour entrance. Drive downtown in 3
minutes, or try the walkway from the top of Quebec Road to the valley below.

Breakfast is special, our own muesli made with beech honey and cinnamon, home-made yoghurt, breads,
muffins or scones. Taste Sheridan's special blend of coffee. Waffles are our specialities, topped with
seasonal fruit and real Canadian maple syrup. You might like to go savoury with salami, tasty bacon and
fruit. We can serve something traditional or different, or cater for your special diet, with adequate notice.

As Nelson leads the rest of the country in sunshine hours, stay a while in this beautiful region. You may
even get to see one of our spectacular sunsets. We are happy to help or advise you on places of interest,
or on the many great restaurants and cafés we have in our city. Use our freephone to book or advise us
of your arrival. Book-in time after 4pm preferred. We provide a smoke-free environment, off-street
parking. Courtesy pick up from bus depot. KJ our devon rex cat, may grace you with his presence, he is
non-allergenic.

Visit our website: www.jubileehouse.co.nz

NELSON   *2.5km S of Nelson*

Sunset Waterfront B&B   *B&B Self-contained*
Bernie Kirk & Louis Balshaw
455 Rock Road, Nelson

Tel (03) 548 3431   Fax (03) 548 3743
Mob 025 363 500   waterfrontnelson@xtra.co.nz
www.bnb.co.nz/sunsetwaterfrontbb.html

Double $140-$150 Single $110-$120 (Full Breakfast)
Credit cards accepted
2 Queen 1 Twin 1 Single (2 bdrm) Bathrooms: 2 Ensuite

Sunset Waterfront B&B provides wonderful panoramic sea and mountain views of Tasman Bay. Ideally situated to walk to quality seafood restaurants. Stroll along the promenade to enjoy the sunset or take an evening walk along the beach. 10 minutes drive from the airport and bus station. Quiet and secluded location. We provide comfortable bedrooms with ensuites, TV, fridge, and sea views. One room for optional self-catering. Freshly brewed coffee and local fresh produce provided. Home-made fruitbread, scones and muffins. Also freshly picked raspberries and strawberries when in season. Off-street parking. Also holiday cottage next door. Regretfully no children under 12. Pet, Bono our golden retriever.   Come enjoy our paradise!

NELSON   *800m E of Trafalgar/Hardy intersection*

The Baywick Inn   *B&B*
Tim Bayley & Janet Southwick
51 Domett Street, Nelson

Tel (03) 545 6514   Fax (03) 545 6517
Mob 027 454 5823   baywicks@iconz.co.nz
www.baywicks.com

Double $135-$155 Single $105-$120
(Special Breakfast) Dinner $40-$50pp
Credit cards accepted
3 Queen 1 Single (3 bdrm)
Bathrooms: 2 Ensuite 1 Private

Overlooking the Maitai River, Brook Stream and Centre of New Zealand, this elegantly restored 1885 Victorian, offers spacious and luxuriously appointed rooms. Each has its own character and charm with antique furnishings, comfortable beds and modern amenities. Enjoy afternoon tea or cappuccino in the cozy guest lounge, sunroom or garden and chat with Tim about his classic MG's. Janet, a cook by profession, makes breakfast to order, healthy or indulgent, cooked or continental. This Canadian/New Zealand ambiance is enhanced by their lively fox terrier.

NELSON CENTRAL   *0.8km E of Nelson*

Sunflower Cottage   *B&B*
Marion & Chris Burton
70 Tasman Street,
Nelson

Tel (03) 548 1588   Fax (03) 548 1588
marion@sunfloweraccommodation.co.nz
www.sunfloweraccommodation.co.nz

Double $115 Single $75 (Continental Breakfast)
2 King/Twin 2 Twin 2 Single (2 bdrm)
Bathrooms: 2 Ensuite

Welcome to our home on the banks of the Maitai River. Our large bedrooms, with ensuite bathrooms, are serviced daily with fresh flowers, complimentary basket of fruit and contain TV, microwave, fridge, tea/coffee making facilities, and toaster. Breakfast is self-service. We are very close to Queen's Gardens, Suter Art Gallery and the Botanical Hill, where after an easy walk to the centre of New Zealand, you experience wonderful views over Tasman Bay and Nelson township. Courtesy car to airport or bus depot.

NELSON CENTRAL *400 m NE of Nelson Central*

Grove Villa *B&B*
Gerry & Christine
36 Grove Street, Nelson

Tel (03) 548 8895 0800 488 900 Fax (03) 548 8856
gerry@grovevilla.co.nz www.grovevilla.co.nz

Double $85-$140 Single $70-$115
(Continental Breakfast) Credit cards accepted
Children welcome
1 King/Twin 2 Queen 1 Double 2 Twin 2 Single
(6 bdrm)
Bathrooms: 3 Ensuite 1 Private 1 Guests share

Welcome to Grove Villa, a character Victorian home
furnished for comfort in period style. Our relaxed
hospitality, with an emphasis on personal service, aims
to enhance your enjoyment of this beautiful city.

Delicious breakfasts feature home-made breads, freshly
made yoghurt, muffins and jams, with fresh fruit salads
using local produce.

Grove Villa is ideally situated just 5 minutes' walk from
the heart of Nelson and its many attractions. Intercity
Buses can drop you at our door. We will be happy to
share our extensive local knowledge to help you to plan
and book your activities and to select from Nelson's
excellent range of restaurants.

Begin your Abel Tasman National Park excursions with
pick ups from our door.

*• 100 year old villa with period furnishings • 5 minute walk to city centre • Comfortable rooms
with ensuite, private or shared bathrooms • Sunny verandahs and courtyard • Delicious
homemade breakfasts • All day refreshments • Knowledgeable advice of local attractions • Pick
up and drop off point for Abel Tasman National Park and other tours • Baggage storage available*

NELSON   *2km S of Nelson*

Beach Front B&B *B&B*
Oriel & Peter Phillips
581 Rocks Road, Nelson

Tel (03) 548 5299 Fax (03) 548 5299
Mob 025 216 5237 peterp@tasman.net
www.bnb.co.nz/beachfrontbb.html

Double $100-$125 Single $100 (Full Breakfast)
Credit cards accepted
1 Queen 1 Double (2 bdrm)
Bathrooms: 1 Ensuite 1 Private

Our home is situated overlooking Tahunanui Beach, Haulashore Island and Nelson waterfront with amazing daytime mountain views and magnificent sunsets. Enjoy a wine out on the deck with your hosts. Excellent restaurants and cafés within walking distance, stroll to beach or 5 minute drive to city or World of Wearable Art. Golf course, tennis courts and airport nearby. 1 hour drive to Abel Tasman. Both rooms have ensuite/private bathrooms, quality beds, electric blankets, fridge, TV, tea & coffee making facilities, heaters, iron and hairdryers. Kiwi Host. Meet Tigger our cat.

NELSON   *5km S of Nelson / Richmond*

Cherry Trees Bed and Breakfast *B&B*
Ann & John Connor
537 Waimea Road, Wakatu, Nelson

Tel (03) 547 3735 Fax (03) 547 3735
Mob 025 266 7579 cherrytrees@ts.co.nz
www.bnb.co.nz/cherrytrees.html

Double $95-$110 Single $85 (Full Breakfast)
1 King 1 Double 1 Twin (3 bdrm)
Bathrooms: 1 Ensuite 1 Private 1 Guests share

Imagine beautiful sunsets and magnificent views of mountain ranges and Tasman Bay. Private colourful garden to enjoy evening drinks or just relax. Only 5 minutes drive to fine restaurants/cafés, Honest Lawyer Pub, Suburban Club, World of Wearable Arts complex, Tahunanui Beach, Nelson Golf Course, hospital, airport & city. We are retired people and in our home you will find a relaxed friendly atmosphere, good comfortable beds, quality fittings, tea/coffee, robes, hairdryer etc. Most of all, great hospitality and sensitivity to your needs. Don't imagine, come, relax enjoy.

NELSON   *Nelson Central*

Peppertree B&B
Richard Savill & Carolyn Sygrove
31 Seymour Ave, Nelson

Tel (03) 546 9881 Fax (03) 546 9881
c.sygrove@clear.net.nz
www.bnb.co.nz/peppertreebb.html

Double $100 (Continental Breakfast) Child $15
Dinner $25-$35 by arrangement Extra adult $30pp
Credit cards accepted Children welcome
1 Queen 1 Double 1 Single (1 bdrm)
Bathrooms: 1 Ensuite

Enjoy space and privacy in our Heritage Villa, only 10 minutes riverside walk from Nelson's city centre. The master bedroom has an ensuite bathroom and walk in wardrobe. Your private adjoining rooms include a large lounge with double innersprung sofabed, single bed, log fire, Sky TV, fridge, microwave, kettle, etc. and sunroom with cane setting and private entrance. Email/internet/fax facilities and off-street parking available. Children are welcome. We have 2 daughters aged 10 and 8 and a friendly cat, called Chocolate.

NELSON - STOKE   *7km SW of Nelson city centre*

Sakura Bed & Breakfast   *B&B*
Fumio & Sayuri Noguchi
604 Main Road, Stoke, Nelson

Tel (03) 547 0229   Fax (03) 547 0229
Mob 021 547 022   fumio.noguchi@paradise.net.nz
www.sakura-nelson.co.nz

Double $140   Single $75   (Full Breakfast)
Child $20   Children welcome
1 King 4 Single (3 bdrm)
Bathrooms: 1 Ensuite 1 Host share

We serve delicious Japanese breakfast (traditional & healthy! We are friendly Japanese hosts). Also you can enjoy our cooked breakfast with Muffins & Scones (just baked). The choice is yours. Only 5 minutes drive from Nelson Airport and 10 minutes from Nelson City centre. Modern, sunny and comfortable house with peaceful garden area. Situated in a quiet cul-de-sac off the Main Road. Complimentary tea, coffee, Japanese green tea, home-made biscuits, fruits at all times. Sorry, no smoking inside the house.

NELSON - TAHUNANUI   *8km W of Nelson*

Parkside Bed & Breakfast   *B&B Self-contained*
16 Centennial Road,
Tahunanui, Nelson

Tel (03) 548 6629   0800 548 662   Fax (03) 548 6621
parkside.nelson@xtra.co.nz
www.bnb.co.nz/parkside.html

Double $95-$130   Single $75-$110
(Continental Breakfast)
Credit cards accepted Children welcome
1 King 4 Queen 2 Single (4 bdrm)
Bathrooms: 3 Ensuite 1 Private

Welcome to our friendly atmosphere at Parkside. In our separate large modern bedrooms and guest lounge there are TV, fridge, tea/coffee facilities. Close to restaurants, golf course, sporting grounds, beach and airport. Shopping from Nelson City is only 8 minutes drive. Enjoy a deluxe breakfast and a stroll in our garden. All rooms have quality fittings for your comfort. You can be sure of a warm friendly stay in our smoke-free home with our 2 daughters aged 17 and 9 and friendly cat Tigger.

NELSON   *Central*

Mikonui   *B&B*
Elizabeth Osborne
7 Grove Street,
Nelson

Tel (03) 548 3623
bess.osborne@xtra.co.nz
www.bnb.co.nz/mikonui.html

Double $100   Single $70   (Full Breakfast)
Credit cards accepted
1 Queen 1 Double 1 Twin (3 bdrm)
Bathrooms: 3 Ensuite

One hundred metres from the Visitor Information Centre in the heart of Nelson City is the Mikonui. This delightful house built in the 1920's, has been the Blair Family home for more than 50 years. The lovely rimu staircase leads to 3 tastefully appointed guest rooms all with ensuites. A delicious continental or cooked breakfast is served each morning. Just a short stroll to restaurants, cafés, the cinema and the beautiful Queens Gardens. Come and enjoy the hospitality at the Mikonui, you won't be disappointed. Off-street parking.

NELSON   *0.5km Nelson*

Grampian Villa   *B&B*
John & Jo Fitzwater
209 Collingwood Street, Nelson

Tel (03) 545 8209   Fax (03) 548 5783
Mob 021 459 736 (Jo) or 021 969 071 (John)
Jo@GrampianVilla.co.nz GrampianVilla.co.nz

Double **$150-$295** Single $150-$280
(Special Breakfast) Child POA
Credit cards accepted
1 King/Twin 2 King 1 Queen (4 bdrm)
Bathrooms: 4 Ensuite

4 spacious ensuited rooms (3 superking, 1 queen with
clawfoot bath and shower) each have french doors
opening onto the spacious verandahs with views of
Nelson City and the sea.

Facilities: • Spacious tiled showers with heated
floors and large heated towel rails • Wireless DSL
internet access • Writing desk in all rooms. • Fax and
computer available • Toiletries, robes and hairdryer
in all bathrooms • Clawfoot baths in some suites •
Quality Sheridan linen in all rooms • TV, DVD,
In-house movies etc. available in all bedrooms •
Complimentary tea/coffee, port, local chocolates,
cookies • Enjoy a latte/expresso from our professional
coffee machine • Gourmet/Special breakfast changes
every day • TV, VCR, CD, DVD, Sky, and stereo
available in lounge • Central heating for your comfort

We regret that we cannot accommodate children under the age of 12 years or pets.
To check for availability and/or make a reservation please go to:
http://art.globalavailability.com/guests/guest-main.php?pid=271

*Located in the mature tree-lined streets on the lower slopes of The Grampians overlooking
Nelson City, historic Grampian Villa is a pleasant 5 minute walk to Nelson's city centre*

NELSON   *4.5km S of Nelson*

Annesbrook House   *B&B*
Kath and Tony Charlton
201 Annesbrook Drive, Tahunanui, Nelson

Tel (03) 548 5868   Fax (03) 548 5802
tony.kath@paradise.net.nz
www.annesbrookhouse.co.nz

Double $75-$90 Single $65   (Continental Breakfast)
1 Queen 1 Double (2 bdrm)
Bathrooms: 2 Ensuite

Drive up our private drive from Highway 6 to our
peaceful home in a quiet sunny bush setting, with lovely
views of the sea and mountains. Each bedsit has its own separate entrance, safe parking (some covered),
ensuite, TV, fridge, electric blanket, hairdryer, heating, table and chairs, T&T facilities, microwave.
Telephone available. We can book you in to many of the area's tourist attractions including boat trips
and walks in the Abel Tasman National Park. We are centrally situated near Tahuna Beach, golf,
airport, clubs, restaurants. Look for the sign on the lime green letterbox.

NELSON

Lamont B&B   *B&B*
Pam & Rex Lucas
167A Tahunanui Drive, Nelson

Tel (03) 548 5551   Fax (03) 548 5501
Mob 027 435 1678   rexpam@xtra.co.nz
www.bnb.co.nz/lamont.html

Double $105 Single $65   (Full Breakfast)
Child by arrangement   Dinner $30
Credit cards accepted   Children welcome
1 Queen 1 Double (2 bdrm)
Bathrooms: 1 Private 1 Guests share

We are in a position to offer high standard
accommodation having two double bedrooms with own toilet and bathroom facilities. Our house is on
a private property in Tahunanui Drive opposite the Nelson Surburban Club where it is possible to get an
evening meal most nights. A 2 minute drive to Tahuna Beach and 5 minutes to a number of waterfront
restaurants gives plenty of variety and choice. We are a few minutes from the airport. Pick up from
airport and bus. 2 cats in residence

NELSON   *500m S of Nelson central*

Haven Guesthouse B&B   *B&B*
Kathy Perkins
89 Haven Road, Nelson

Tel (03) 545 9321   0800 446 783   Fax (03) 545 9320
havengh@xtra.co.nz
www.havenguesthouse.co.nz

Double $89-$160 Single $75-$90
(Continental Breakfast)   Child $10
Credit cards accepted   Children welcome
Family Room 1 king & single, 2 king, 4 queen,
1 king twin, 1 twin   (9 bdrm)
Bathrooms: 9 Ensuite

Recent extensive renovations to the Haven Guest House, one of Nelson's oldest homes, now provides 9
bedrooms all with ensuite, TV and phone. Originally built circa 1860 for the first collector of customs,
it is situated opposite the Wearable Arts venue, just a 5 minute walk to town and a 5 minute drive to the
beach. A delicious continental breakfast is served and tea/coffee making facilities are available in the
dining room. internet/fax/laundry facilities are also available.

NELSON *Nelson Central*

Approved

SunShine Inn B&B and Tours *B&B*
Sue Mangos
6 Collingwood Street, Nelson

Tel (03) 548 9290 0800 894 783 Fax (03) 548 9296
Mob 027 448 6373 stay@SunShineInn.co.nz
www.SunShineInn.co.nz

Double $95-$195 Single $90-$195 (Continental
Breakfast) $30 extra adult, Credit cards accepted
1 Super King 1 Queen 1 Twin 1 Single (3 bdrm)
Bathrooms: 1 Ensuite 1 Guests share

Welcome to SunShine Inn B&B and Tours. We're
easily found, just 5 minutes walk to Nelson City. Our
Guests Say: "Clean; Warm; Friendly; Comfy beds; Great showers; Quiet; Relaxing; Feel safe; Love
the colours; Beautiful gardens; Love the waterfall; Thanks Mom!...". Not suitable young children. No
pets on property. Smoke-free. Seasonal Rates. Frequent-Stayer Card. Continental breakfast. Cooked
breakfast available by request (additional charge). Small group tours/transfers - 1 hour to 4+ days.
Online bookings: SunShineInn.co.nz - Meet people - have fun - or just relax!

NELSON - CENTRAL *500m S of Nelson Central*

Approved

Kowhai Cottage *Self-contained*
Marion & Andrew James
272 Rutherford Street, Nelson

Tel (03) 548 1272 Mob 025 400 216
marion@kowhaicottage.co.nz
www.kowhaicottage.co.nz

Double $130 Single $110 (Continental Breakfast)
Child rates vary Credit cards accepted
Children welcome
1 King 1 Double (1 bdrm)
Bathrooms: 1 Private

Come and enjoy our well-presented character
accommodation located in the premier residential area of Nelson. Our delightful 1930's bungalow is
situated in a quiet street, 10 minutes walk from the heart of the city, yet right on the doorstep of fabulous
walking tracks, parks and historic houses. Our spacious and comfortable self-contained area has a
double king bedroom, attractive sun room with comfortable double sofa bed, bathroom and large lounge,
kitchen facilities and secure garage parking. Cat and one child in residence.

NELSON *7 km N of Nelson*

Approved

Avonbank Homestay *B&B*
Dale & Clive Cook
3 Seaton Street, Marybank, Nelson

Tel (03) 545 0056 Fax (03) 545 0056
Mob 025 200 2530 clivecook@ts.co.nz
www.bnb.co.nz/avonbank.html

Double $80 Single $55 (Continental Breakfast)
Child $25 Dinner $20 by arrangement
Credit cards accepted Children welcome
1 Queen 1 Twin 2 Single (2 bdrm)
Bathrooms: 1 Guests share

Welcome to our sunny non-smoking home. We are only 5 minutes from central Nelson on the Blenheim
side. Relax in our spa pool and enjoy spectacular sunsets across Tasman Bay or read from our many
books. We have travelled extensively both overseas and in New Zealand and enjoy sharing our special
area of Nelson with others. Children are welcome. Electric blankets on beds. Off-street parking. Bus at
gate. Laundry facilities available. Quiet safe neighbourhood. Taz, our cat, will welcome you with rolly
pollys.

NELSON CENTRAL   *3mins Nelson Central*

Trafalgar Square   *B&B Homestay*
Janine Fisher & Dennis Shacklady
368A Trafalgar Square, Nelson

Tel (03) 546 6659   Mob 021 343 937   021 269 4412
Homestay-Nelson@xtra.co.nz
www.homestay-nelson.co.nz

Double $110   Single $90   (Full Breakfast)
Credit cards accepted
2 Queen (2 bdrm)
Bathrooms: 2 Ensuite

Nestled alongside the Nelson Cathedral in a quiet
cul-de-sac, our classic 1932 home offers you a relaxed
atmosphere only minutes walking distance to central city shopping, restaurants and other attractions.
Off-street parking is provided. Our 2 comfortable guest rooms feature queen-sized beds, ensuite
bathrooms, tea/coffee making facilities, couch and television. Your choice of breakfast, continental or
cooked, using fresh local produce where possible. At Trafalgar Square we offer you a warm welcome to
our home, which is non-smoking.

NELSON - ATAWHAI   *6 km N of Nelson on SH6*

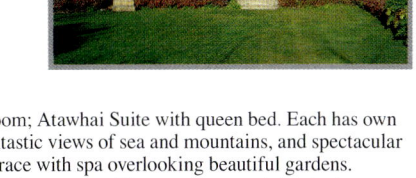

Strathaven Lodge   *B&B Homestay*
Julie & Hugh Briggs
42 Strathaven Place, Atawhai, Nelson

Tel (03) 545 1195   Fax (03) 545 1195
Mob (025) 243 5301   strathavenlodge@xtra.co.nz
www.strathavenlodge.com

Double $125-$175 Single $100-$125
(Full Breakfast) Child $50   Dinner $30pp
Credit cards accepted   Children welcome
1 King 1 Queen 1 Single (3 bdrm)
Bathrooms: 2 Private

2 room Haven Suite with king bed and 1 single bedroom; Atawhai Suite with queen bed. Each has own
private bathroom, TV and option for tea making. Fantastic views of sea and mountains, and spectacular
sunsets. Attractive guest lounge to relax in. Large terrace with spa overlooking beautiful gardens.
Wonderful breakfasts with muesli, breads, yoghurts and conserves. Dinners on request. 6 minutes on
SH6 north of the city. Hugh and Julie look forward to welcoming you.

NELSON - ATAWHAI   *6km N of Nelson*

Five Smooth Stones   *B&B Homestay*
Liz & Chris Chinnery-Jack & Bowyer
784A Atawhai Drive, Nelson
(Second house on right up the drive)

Tel (03) 545 1230 fivesmoothstones@clear.net.nz
www.bnb.co.nz/fivesmoothstones.html

Double $85-$100 (Special Breakfast)
Dinner $35 per person
2 Double (2 bdrm)
Bathrooms: 2 Ensuite

New Zealanders Liz & Chris welcome you to Five Smooth Stones. Not glitzy, up-market or intimidating
just wonderful Nelson views and warm, welcoming Kiwi hospitality with comfortable indoor/outdoor
guest areas. Off-street parking. With prior notice we will cook you a real Kiwi dinner using home
grown and local produce. Guests comments during our first season include; '..lovely stay, great food
and conversation..' '..beautiful view, super comfy bed and great breakfast..' '..lovely to get to know the
Kiwis on a more personal basis..'

NELSON - ATAWHAI *7km N of Nelson*

A Culinary Experience *Boutique B&B*
Kay & Joe Waller
71 Tresillian Avenue, Atawhai, Nelson

Tel **(03) 545 1886** Fax (03) 545 1869
Mob 027 445 1886 kpastorius@xtra.co.nz
www.a-culinary-experience.com

Double $120-$145 Single $105-$130 (Full Breakfast)
Gourmet dinner $35 by arrangement
Credit cards accepted
2 King/Twin (2 bdrm)   Bathrooms: 2 Ensuite

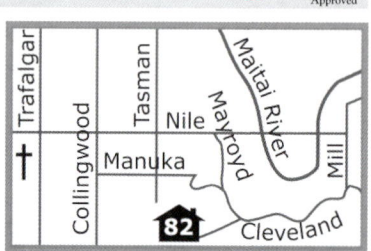

Welcome to our lovely home filled with art, laughter,
great food and our adorable yorkshire terrier. We lead gourmet European tours and enjoy cruising our
boat in North America. Kay, author and former cooking school owner, can provide delightful dinners
or cooking classes. Joe, degreed in naturopathic medicine, offers therapeutic massage. Our boutique
accommodation, near Nelson, is nestled in the hills: beautifully appointed bedrooms, ensuites, spa, sun-
drenched patios, sensational sunsets overlooking bay and mountains. Pets and children by arrangement.
Complementry glass of wine. Two nights recommended.

NELSON *5 mins Nelson Central*

Te Maunga - Historic House *B&B*
Anne Kolless
82 Cleveland Terrace, Nelson

Tel **(03) 548 8605** 0800 548 860
anniegranniekiwi@yahoo.com
www.bnb.co.nz/temaunga.html

Double $90-$120 Single $80 (Continental Breakfast)
Child $20 Credit cards accepted
2 Double 1 Twin 1 Single (3 bdrm)
Bathrooms: 1 Private 1 Host share

Anne welcomes you to her family's Historic Places, character home, built in 1936 by Harry & Dorothy
Atmore. Harry was NZ's first Independant Member of Parliament serving Nelson for 30 years. Still
mainly as original with modern facilities Te Maunga is perched on a knoll, within a rambling garden,
giving commanding views over Nelson city, sea and Matai Valley and only 5 minutes to downtown.
Enjoy your continental style breakfast including local fruits, yoghurts, cheeses and home-made breads,
while taking in the views.

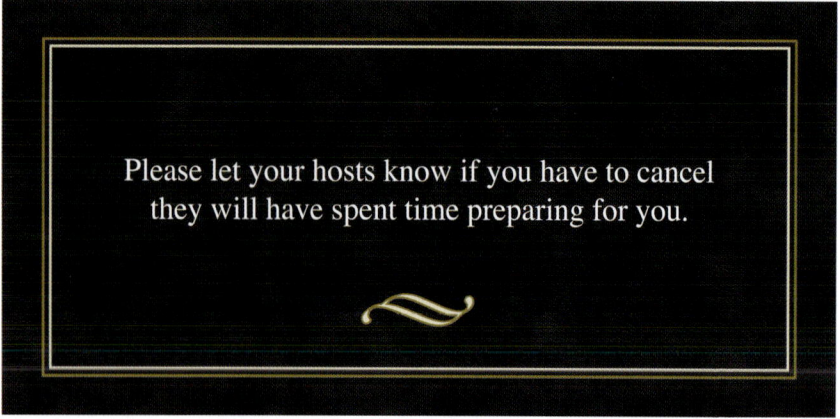

Please let your hosts know if you have to cancel
they will have spent time preparing for you.

NELSON   *500m E of Nelson Central*

Sussex House Bed & Breakfast
Historic Bed & Breakfast House
Victoria & David Los
238 Bridge Street, Nelson

Tel (03) 548 9972   0800 868 687
Fax (03) 548 9975   Mob 027 478 4846
reservations@sussex.co.nz
www.sussex.co.nz

Double $120-$150 Single $100-$130
(Full Breakfast) Credit cards accepted
5 Queen 3 Twin 3 Single (5 bdrm)
Bathrooms: 4 Ensuite 1 Private

Situated beside the beautiful Maitai
River, Sussex House has retained all
the original character and romantic
ambience of the era. It is only minutes'
walk from central Nelson's award

winning restaurants and cafés, the Queens Gardens, Suter Art Gallery and Botanical Hill (The Centre of
NZ) and many good walks, river and bush.

The 5 sunny bedrooms all have TV's and are spacious and charmingly furnished. All rooms have access
to the verandahs and complimentary tea and coffee facilities are provided. Breakfast includes lots of
fresh and preserved fruits, muffins baked fresh every morning, hot croissants and pastries, home-made
yoghurts, cheeses and a large variety of cereals, bagels, rolls, breads and crumpets. Cooked breakfasts
are available.

We regret that we are not suited to children. Other facilities include: Wheelchair suite; Email/internet
station; fax; courtesy phone; laundry facilities; separate lounge for guest entertaining; complimentary
port; tea & coffee facilities; very sociable cat (Riley). We have lived overseas and have travelled
extensively. We speak French fluently.

Experience the peace and charm of the past in our fully restored circa 1880's B&B,
one of Nelson's original family homes

NELSON   *6km W of Nelson Central*

Phoenix Castle Gatehouse   *B&B*
Alie Summer
102 Point Road, Monaco, Nelson

Tel 021 778 607   Fax 03 547 8176
alie_summer@xtra.co.nz   www.bnb.co.nz/phoenix.html

Double $280   (Continental Breakfast)
Credit cards accepted Children welcome Pets welcome
2 Queen (2 bdrm)   Bathrooms: 2 Ensuite

Stand-alone cottage on the waters edge in a sleepy peninsula of Monaco, where we aim to make your stay truely enjoyable. Families welcome, portacot on request. Pets welcome by prior arrangement. Surround sound lounge with DVDs and CDs provided. Sky TV, internet connection, fax, open gas fire, sofa bed. Opens to water front deck. Outside your door is a boat ramp and jetty, where you can launch your complimentary kayaks and dingy and explore the surrounding islands. Flounder net and fish smoker provided. DVDs and TV in both bedrooms. Full kitchen with dishwasher all condiments are complimentary and complimentary drinks.

RICHMOND   *0.5km E of Richmond*

Hunterville   *Homestay*
Cecile & Alan Strang
30 Hunter Avenue, Richmond, Nelson

Tel (03) 544 5852   0800 372 220   Fax (03) 544 5852
strangsa@clear.net.nz.
www.bnb.co.nz/hunterville.html

Double $100   Single $60   (Full Breakfast)
Child ¹/₂ price   Dinner $20 by arrangement
Credit cards accepted   Children welcome   Pets welcome
1 King 1 Twin 1 Single (3 bdrm)
Bathrooms: 1 Private 1 Guests share 1 Host share

A short driveway brings you to our peaceful home where birdsong greets you from the surrounding trees. Here we offer you real 'home hospitality', New Zealand style.

Later, pre-dinner drinks poolside in summer, fireside in winter. Enjoy a generous breakfast, (either full or continental) with home-made preserves and good coffee.

We are on the route to the Abel Tasman/Golden Bay regions, and 15 minutes by motorway from Nelson City. Travelling often overseas, we do appreciate travellers' needs, so have firm, comfortable beds, a good laundry and dinner with local food and wine. Add to that travellers tales and your visit will be memorable.

Our other interests are music, reading, bridge plus Coco our dalmatian and Waldo, both friendly dogs. Our special pleasure is the many travellers who become our friends and return to stay again with us.

A welcome 'cuppa' with home-made biscuits on your arrival

RICHMOND   *10km S of Nelson*

Bay View   *B&B Self-contained*
Janice & Ray O'Loughlin
37 Kihilla Road, Richmond

Tel (03) 544 6541   Fax (03) 544 6541
Mob 021 176 8511
bayview@ts.co.nz
www.bnb.co.nz/bayviewrichmond.html

Double $90-$100   Single $65
(Full Breakfast)   Credit cards accepted
2 Queen 1 Twin (3 bdrm)
Bathrooms: 1 Ensuite 1 Private 1 Guests share

Bayview is a modern, spacious home built on the hills
above Richmond township, with spectacular views of
Tasman Bay and mountain ranges.

We offer rooms that are quiet, private and immaculately
furnished with your complete comfort in mind. A large
guest bathroom has shower and spa bath. The lounge
opens onto a sheltered deck where you can relax, enjoy
a drink or sit and chat. The self-contained suite with
private entrance, off-street parking, kitchen, bathroom/
laundry, lounge area and queen bed offers privacy and all
home comforts.

We have 2 miniature schnauzer dogs, a variety of birds
in a large aviary, tend our colourful garden and enjoy
meeting people from New Zealand and overseas.

By car Bayview is 15 minutes from Nelson, 2 minutes
from Richmond and award-winning restaurants, close
to National Parks, beaches, vineyards and crafts. Be
assured of warm, friendly hospitality and a happy stay in
our smoke-free home.

RICHMOND   *2km S of Richmond*

Nicholls Country Homestay B&B
B&B   Country Homestay
Alison & Murray Nicholls
87 Main Road, Hope, Nelson

Tel (03) 544 8026   Fax (03) 544 8026
m_a.nicholls@xtra.co.nz
www.bnb.co.nz/nicholls.html

Double $80   Single $40   (Full Breakfast)
Child $25   Dinner $12.50   Children welcome
1 Queen 1 Twin (2 bdrm)
Bathrooms: 1 Guests share

We are situated on a kiwifruit orchard on State Highway 6, 2km south of Richmond. A lengthy driveway ensures quiet surroundings in a lovely garden setting, with a pool. We are centrally situated, placing Nelson's many attractions within easy reach. We will happily provide information about these and make arrangements as required. Complimentary tea or coffee is offered to guests upon arrival and dinner may be provided by arrangement. A phone call before arrival would be appreciated. Ours is a non-smoking home.

RICHMOND   *10km W of Nelson*

Chester Le House   *B&B Homestay*
Noelene & Michael Smith
39 Washbourn Drive, Richmond, Nelson

Tel (03) 544 7279   Fax (03) 544 7279
Mob 027 277 6022   n.smith@xtra.co.nz
www.bnb.co.nz/chesterlehouse.html

Double $120   Single $65   (Full Breakfast)
Dinner $35 by arrangement   Flat $125
Credit cards accepted
1 Double 4 Single (3 bdrm)
Bathrooms: 1 Ensuite 2 Guests share 1 Host share

We live in a fantastic part of New Zealand in a lovely modern home that we enjoy sharing with many people. Lovely views and all the comforts of home await you. 2 twin rooms and queen suite with ensuite available. Lock your car in our garage and enjoy a barbecue or evening meal with us. Laundry and drier available. Pick up from terminals available. Only 10 minutes from Nelson City, Richmond is close to wineries and a scenic 40 minutes drive to Abel Tasman National Park.

RICHMOND   *1km E of Richmond*

Antiquarian Guest House   *B&B Guesthouse*
Robert & Joanne Souch
12A Surrey Road, Richmond, Nelson

Tel (03) 544 0253 or (03) 544 0723   Fax (03) 544 0253
Mob 021 417 413   souchebys@clear.net.nz
www.bnb.co.nz/antiquarian.html

Double $95   Single $75   (Full Breakfast) Child $10
Credit cards accepted Children welcome Pets welcome
1 King 1 Queen 1 Twin (3 bdrm)
Bathrooms: 1 Ensuite 1 Guests share

Bob and Joanne Souch welcome you to their peaceful home only 2 minutes from Richmond (15 minutes drive south of Nelson) - excellent base for exploring National Parks, beaches, arts/crafts, ski fields etc. Relax in the garden, beside the swimming pool or in our large TV/Guest lounge. Tea/coffee facilities, home-baking and memorable breakfasts. Our family pet is Gemma (friendly border collie). As local antique shop owners we know the area well.

NELSON, GOLDEN BAY

RICHMOND   *12km SW of Nelson*

Idesia *B&B Homestay*
Jenny & Barry McKee
14 Idesia Grove, Richmond, Nelson

Tel (03) 544 0409   0800 361 845
Fax (03) 544 0402   Mob 025 604 0869
idesian@xtra.co.nz
www.idesia.co.nz

Double $85-$105 Single $75-$85 (Full Breakfast)
Dinner $30 by arrangement Credit cards accepted
1 King/Twin 1 Queen 1 Twin (3 bdrm)
Bathrooms: 1 Ensuite 1 Private

A warm welcome to our home centrally located to explore the Nelson/Tasman region. 2km from Highway 6, in a quiet grove neighbouring the country. Our modern house is elevated to catch the sun and views. For your comfort the bedrooms, recently furnished, have superior beds. Breakfast includes a continental selection and/or a cooked breakfast. Join us for dinner, by prior arrangement, and relax with us in the lounge over coffee. Our aim is to provide a home away from home and to offer tasty meals.

WAKEFIELD   *27km S of Nelson*

Lansfield Bed & Breakfast Homestay
B&B Homestay
Dianne & Malcolm Tillier
133, Eighty-Eight Valley Road, Wakefield

Tel (03) 541 9789   Mob 0274 160 727
mdtillier@xtra.co.nz
www.bnb.co.nz/lansfield.html

Double $110-$130 (Full Breakfast) Dinner $25
Credit cards accepted
1 King/Twin 2 Queen (3 bdrm)
Bathrooms: 3 Ensuite

We welcome you to our comfortable new home set in a tranquil valley, with a lovely view, handy to all the activities that the Nelson region offers. Country hospitality and home produce are part of the welcome. Our interests include gardening and classic cars. We have a burmese cat, called Pheobe. Tea, coffee and home-baking provided, laundry facilities available, dinner by arrangement. Situated on the outskirts of Wakefield Village, 25 minutes from Nelson. We look forward to meeting you.

THORPE   *55km W of Nelson*

Rerenga Rural Homestay   *Rural Homestay*
Joan & Robert Panzer
1637 Dovedale Road, Thorpe, Nelson

Tel (03) 543 3825   Fax (03) 543 3640
Mob 027 543 3825   joan.panzer@xtra.co.nz
www.rerengaruralhomestay.co.nz

Double $95 (Full Breakfast) Dinner $30
Credit cards accepted Children welcome
1 Queen (1 bdrm)
Bathrooms: 1 Ensuite

You are offered a peaceful, rural retreat with international hosts (Dutch and North American). Our 2 children are real 'Kiwis'. The homestead is surrounded by rolling hills, forests and situated along the Dove River. We have a variety of trees, chickens, pigs, sheep, and an outdoor cat and dog. Note: our main business is 'Tailored Travel', personalized New Zealand custom tours (2-4 pax), tailored to your specific requirements and dates.

MAPUA *10km N of Richmond*

Atholwood Country Accommodation
B&B Self-contained Country Accomodation
Robyn & Grahame Williams
Bronte Road East,
off Coastal Highway 60, Near Mapua

Tel (03) 540 2925 Fax (03) 540 3258
Mob 025 310 309 atholwood@xtra.co.nz
www.atholwood.co.nz

Double $180-$200 Single $150 (Full Breakfast)
Child by arrangement Dinner $45pp by arrangement
Self-contained $200 C/C accepted Children welcome
1 King/Twin 2 Queen 3 Single (3 bdrm) Bathrooms: 3 Ensuite

Beauty, seclusion and tranquillity. We welcome you to share our home situated on the shores of the Waimea Inlet with 2 acres of garden and bush. The Gatehouse is self-contained with full amenities, opening out to a terrace. The guest wing is upstairs within the house and has 2 rooms, each with ensuites and a guest lounge.(B&B basis) Start your day with a special breakfast and to finish - award-winning restaurants are close, in Mapua. Our beautiful cat, Carlos, completes the family.

MAPUA *4km S of Mapua*

Kimeret Place Boutique B&B
Luxury Suites & Separate Apartments
Clare & Peter Jones
Bronte Road East (Off SH60), Near Mapua, Nelson

Tel (03) 540 2727 Fax (03) 540 2726
stay@kimeretplace.co.nz   www.kimeretplace.co.nz

Double $175-$340 Single $135-$275
(Special Breakfast)
2 bedroom cottage $240-$320   Credit cards accepted
4 King/Twin (4 bdrm)
Bathrooms: 4 Ensuite

A tranquil coastal setting in the heart of the wine and craft region with stunning views, heated swimming pool and spa. Just 4km to award winning restaurants and 30 minutes from the Abel Tasman National Park. A range of accommodation all with ensuite facilities, (2 with spa-baths), TV, Hi-Fi, tea/coffee, fridge, sitting area and views from either balcony or deck. The 2 bedroom cottage also has a kitchenette and dining area. Light meals, local wines, laundry and internet are also available. Dog lovers may wish to meet our two friendly labradors.

MAPUA VILLAGE *30km W of Nelson*

Mapua Seaview B&B *B&B Homestay*
Murray & Diana Brown
40 Langford Drive,
Mapua Village, Nelson

Tel (03) 540 2006 Fax (03) 540 2006
Mob 025 839 634 seaview@mapua.co.nz
www.mapua.co.nz

Double $110 (Full Breakfast) Credit cards accepted
2 Queen (2 bdrm)
Bathrooms: 2 Ensuite

Mapua Seaview B&B commands special views of the Waimea Estuary and Richmond Mountains (view our website)while overlooking the delightful coastal village of Mapua. The choice of 3 popular waterfront restaurants are all within a few minutes walk. Only a 25 minute scenic drive to the Abel Tasman National Park or Nelson City. Our modern home is sited on elevated sunny garden setting, being off-street and very quiet. Comfortable (queen-size) beds, private bathrooms, TV etc. Full breakfast.

MAPUA   *500m W of Mapua*

Mitch's Place   *B&B Self-contained*
Jan & Kerry Mitchell
7 Iwa Street, Mapua, Nelson

Tel (03) 540 2399
Mitchs_place@xtra.co.nz
www.mitchsplace.co.nz

Double $120   (Full Breakfast)
Single rollaway bed in lounge   Off season rates apply
1 Queen (1 bdrm)
Bathrooms: 1 Private

Cosy, affordable, comfort in Mapua, gateway to
outstanding beauty of Abel Tasman and Kahurangi
National Parks. Self-contained accommodation (1-3 people) in a secluded, sunny setting with world
renowned restaurants, galleries, unique natural attractions, adventure at doorstep. Wake to bird song,
breakfast on private deck, wander down to beach, famous Mapua Wharf. Mapua has a population of
1600, an abundance of boutique art & craft galleries. Hosts Jan & Kerry Mitchell provide you with the
thought and experience that comes from a decade in the accommodation industry and welcome you.

RUBY BAY   *20km W of Nelson*

Broadsea B&B   *B&B*
Rae & John Robinson
42 Broadsea Avenue,
Ruby Bay, Nelson

Tel (03) 540 3511   Fax (03) 540 3511
www.bnb.co.nz/broadseabb.html

Double $120   Single $100   (Full Breakfast)
Unsuitable for children
1 Queen (1 bdrm)
Bathrooms: 1 Ensuite 1 Private

Beach front accommodation, queen room with own
large bathroom and seperate toilet. Lovely walks on
beach and reserve, cafés and tavern close by, as are wineries and restaurants. We are 15 minutes from
Richmond & Motueka, 30 minutes from Nelson and the airport. Abel Tasman and Kaiteriteri are within
40 minutes drive. We want our guests to feel at home and have their privacy in a peaceful and private
setting. A continental and full cooked breakfast are served, with coffee, tea and old fashioned home-
made biscuits available. Our birman cat, Bogart, and labrador, Sally, will greet you in the drive way.
'

RUBY BAY   *32km W of Nelson*

Sandstone House   *B&B*
John and Jenny Marchbanks
30 Korepo Road,
Ruby Bay, Nelson

Tel (03) 540 3251   Fax (03) 540 3251
Mob 025 246 0444   sandstone@rubybay.net.nz
www.rubybay.net.nz

Double $190   Single $170   (Full Breakfast)
Credit cards accepted
2 Queen (2 bdrm)
Bathrooms: 2 Ensuite

Welcome to Sandstone House - the ideal place to relax - stay a few days and explore this delightful
region. We enjoy a maritime and semi-rural situation, ideally situated midway between Nelson and
Motueka. We are handy to all the fine attractions that this region has to offer - National Parks, wineries,
award winning restaurants, beaches, arts and crafts, the famous Mapua Wharf and lots lots more. We
have 35 years local knowledge and are happy to assist you to make the most of your holiday. Please feel
free to relax and enjoy our quality, comfortable facilities.

TASMAN - UPPER MOUTERE   *10mins Mouteka*

Maple Grove
B&B Separate/Suite Self-contained Boutique cottage
Judy Stratford & George Page
72 Flaxmore Road, RD 2,
Upper Moutere, Nelson

Tel (03) 543 2267   Fax (03) 543 2267
Mob 025 623 8631   george1judy@xtra.co.nz
www.maplegrove.co.nz

Double $130-$160 (Full Breakfast)
Child neg   Children welcome
1 Queen 1 Double 1 Twin (2 bdrm)
Bathrooms: 1 Private

The perfect private hideaway on 4 acres in the heart of the wine country and at the gateway to Able Tasman National Park.Enjoy ambience and charm of bygone days. Magnificent views to the grand avenue of mature trees, private pond and the mighty Mount Arthur Range. This 2 bedroom boutique cottage with modern conveniences is designed with your comfort in mind. Indulge in home-baked goodies from the breakfast hamper. Close to vineyards, cafés award winning restaurants.

TASMAN - UPPER MOUTERE   *5km N of Upper Moutere*

Lemonade Farm   *B&B Farmstay Self-contained*
Linda & Ian Morris
Roses Road, (off SH6, turn down Neudorf Road,)
Upper Moutere, RD 2, Nelson

Tel (03) 543 2686   Fax (03) 543 2686
Mob 021 101 7172   stay@lemonadefarm.co.nz
www.lemonadefarm.co.nz

Double $130   Single $110   (Continental Breakfast)
Child neg   Extra person $20pp
Off season rates neg   Credit cards accepted
Children welcome   Pets welcome
1 Queen 1 Double (1 bdrm)   Bathrooms: 1 Private

Experience beautiful rural NZ, yet just 15 minutes to Tasman Bay and Motueka. B&B is a self-contained, self-catering apartment, with own drive/entrance. Your private deck with BBQ faces the gorgeous sunsets. The room is large, open plan and sunny with fabulous Pacific décor. The kitchen is fully equipped. There is a separate sunroom overlooking the lawn where sheep graze. We have 2 friendly labrador dogs.

MOTUEKA VALLEY   *18km S of Motueka*

Mountain View Cottage/Dexter Farmstay
Farmstay Self-contained
A & V Hall
Waiwhero Road, RD 1, Motueka

Tel (03) 526 8857   Fax (03) 526 8857
ajandvhall@xtra.co.nz
www.bnb.co.nz/mountainviewcottage.html

Double $95   Single $60   (Special Breakfast)
Dinner $25   Cottage $95   Credit cards accepted
1 King/Twin 1 Queen (2 bdrm)
Bathrooms: 1 Ensuite 1 Private

Your hosts Alan and Veronica offer B&B Farmstay and separate cottage accommodation on our 35 acre organic property complete with unique dexter cows and native bush covenanted area. Perfectly situated for anglers, close to 3 National Parks and art/craft/garden trails. Mountain View Cottage is completely self-contained while our homestead offers spacious bedroom with own ensuite, tea/coffee & TV facilities. Meals are cooked on our wood-fired range and breakfast comprises choice of home-made muesli, bread, yoghurt, and organic eggs. A very warm welcome completes the picture.

MOTUEKA VALLEY *26km S of Motueka*

Doone Cottage Country Homestay
B&B Homestay
Glen & Stan Davenport
2455 Motueka Valley Highway, RD 1, Motueka

Tel (03) 526 8740 Fax (03) 526 8740
Mob 021 258 7389
doone-cottage@xtra.co.nz
www.doonecottage.co.nz

Double $130-$180 Single $110-$155
(Full Breakfast) Dinner by arrangement
Credit cards accepted
2 King/Twin 1 Queen (3 bdrm)
Bathrooms: 3 Ensuite

Overlooking Motueka River Valley and the Mt
Arthur range, this charming 130 year old cottage
has welcomed homestay guests for 25 years.
Situated in 4 acres of secluded native trees, ferns
and flower gardens on a natural river terrace
looking out across the valley to Kahaurangi
National Park it offers homely hospitality, peace
and tranquillity, friendly, helpful, experienced hosts, very comfortable beds, ensuites, home-cooked
meals, home-made breads, preserves, home-grown produce, free-range eggs, etc.

Comfortably furnished cottage style, guest rooms and private garden chalet have extensive garden/valley
views. Native birds abound, sheep, chickens, ducks and donkeys. Your hostess spins wool from her own
sheep, her weaving studio offers sweaters, blankets, wall hangings, rugs, etc. which she has produced. A
chuckling stream runs through the property, flowing into the Motueka River, famous for its brown trout,
with 5 more trout streams close by. Guiding & licences available.

Our central location offers short distances to excellent day trips/activities in Abel Tasman, Kahurangi
and Nelson Lakes National Parks. Nelson and Golden Bay - mountain and coastal bush walks,
wilderness fishing, golf etc. (Bookings handled for cruising, water taxis, kayaking, horse trekking).
Award winning wineries, arts and crafts. 45 minutes to Nelson; 2.5 hours to Picton; 3 hours to the West
Coast; 5 hours to Christchurch; 20 minutes Motueka (1 Mile north of Woodstock Junction).

Simply relax and soak up the country atmosphere of yesteryear in this special place

MOTUEKA VALLEY   *25km S of Motueka*

The Kahurangi Brown Trout
B&B Farmstay Homestay Self-contained
David Davies & Heather Lindsay
2292 Westbank Road, Pokororo, RD 1, Motueka

Tel (03) 526 8736 0800 460 421
enquiries@kbtrout.co.nz
www.kbtrout.co.nz

Double $95-$125 Single $75-$105 (Full Breakfast)
Child $25 Dinner $18-$35 Credit cards accepted
Children welcome Pets welcome
2 King/Twin 1 Single (2 bdrm)   Bathrooms: 2 Ensuite

Comments from last years visitors book say it all. 'What
a beautiful spot! A piece of heaven. It is truly wonderful.
What a find! What a way to lose our B&B cherry - this is paradise. What a wonderful, relaxing, soul-
nourishing haven. Wish it could be longer. Just the job! Loved the hospitality and the room. Envy your
lifestyle. Really enjoyed the home-grown produce. Hope to come back some day.' Come and see for
yourself. Pets and young children are welcome too.

MOTUEKA   *0.5km S of Motueka*

Rosewood   *B&B*
Barbara & Jerry Leary
48 Woodlands Avenue, Motueka

Tel (03) 528 6750   Fax (03) 528 6718
Mob 021 251 0131
Barbara.Leary.Rosewood@xtra.co.nz
www.accommodation-new-zealand.co.nz/rosewood

Double $100   Single $65   (Full Breakfast)
Child ¹/2 price Credit cards accepted
1 Double 2 Single (2 bdrm)
Bathrooms: 1 Private 1 Guests share

Enjoy a friendly atmosphere in our comfortable spacious
home 5 minutes walk to shops and cafés. We offer a private lounge for relaxation together with Sky TV.
Nearby is the scenic Motueka River renowned for large brown trout or a round of golf on a top quality
golf links. Our interests include golf, fishing, and roses. Barbara is always available to give helpful
advice on your day excursions. She also prepares a delicious country-style breakfast. Love to see you as
will Jasper our cat.

MOTUEKA   *1.4km E of Motueka*

B&B Homestay
Rebecca & Ian Williams
186 Thorp Street, Motueka

Tel (03) 528 9385 Fax (03) 528 9385
Mob 0274 480 466 B&B@motueka-homestay.co.nz
www.motueka-homestay.co.nz

Double $100-$110 Single $60 (Full Breakfast)
Child $20   Dinner by arrangement
Credit cards accepted
1 Queen 1 Double 1 Single (2 bdrm)
Bathrooms: 2 Ensuite

We only look expensive. We are 1.4km to Motueka shopping centre and 1.2km to 18 hole golf course.
Each bedroom has own ensuite. The guest lounge has tea and coffee making facilities and fridge.
Motueka is the stop-over place for visitors to explore Abel Tasman and Kahurangi National Parks.
Golden Bay and Kaiteriteri golden sands beach is 10km away. We have a Jack Russell dog. Visa and
M/C.

Motueka   *2km S of Motueka*

Approved

Grey Heron - The Italian Organic Homestay
B&B Homestay
Sandro Lionello & Laura Totis
110 Trewavas Street, Motueka 7161

Tel (03) 528 0472 Fax (03) 528 0472
Mob 021 266 0345
sandro@greyheron.co.nz
www.greyheron.co.nz

Double $85-$110 Single $50-$80
(Continental Breakfast) Dinner $30
3 Queen 1 Single (4 bdrm)
Bathrooms: 1 Ensuite 1 Guests share

We are a couple recently moved from the
north of Italy to the south of New Zealand,
much travelled and keen on tramping and
mountaineering.

Our beautiful garden faces the Moutere River Estuary: you will enjoy our breakfast (Continental-plus
with Italian specialities, organic home-made bread and jams), overlooking a super tidal view of the
estuary and of the Kahurangi National Park mountain range. Set among native trees and lovely singing
birds. Depending on the season, you will have the chance to see the spectacular White Herons and
Royal Spoonbills feeding in the estuary.

Plan a longer holiday in this region and *profit* by Sandro's experience in geology, outdoor activities and
Italian language teaching. *Book* with us: • one day botanical/geological guided walks along the tracks
of the surrounding National Parks. For those on a *tight schedule* we have a special half-day walking
option in the beautiful Kahurangi National Park. • Rock-climbing lessons by special arrangements. •
Italian language lessons for beginners and advanced.

Our house is close to the beach: you can have a jog or a quiet walk along the quay, safe wind-surfing and
swimming just across the road. The 18 hole golf course is 15 minutes. walking. The ensuite bedroom is
small and cosy and includes a private driveway and ground-floor entrance.

On request we prepare delicious recipes of our Italian cuisine, famous all around the world, using
fresh herbs from our garden. You can enjoy dinner with us, overlooking wonderful sunsets beyond the
mountains. Coffee, tea, laundry facilities. Secure off-street parking. Links with kayaking and trout
fishing companies for booking tours. *Benvenuti Tutti Gli Amici Italiani.*

Directions: From Nelson: at the Southern roundabout in High Street, turn right towards Port Motueka,
then turn left into Trewavas Street. From the West Coast: at the intersection with High Street go
straight, drive up to the end of Old Wharf Road. and turn right into Trewavas Street. Look for our sign.

You will appreciate our Mediterranean atmosphere in the heart of New Zealand nature

MOTUEKA *1km S of Motueka*

Ashley Troubadour *B&B Self-contained*
Coral & John Horton
430 High Street, Motueka

Tel (03) 528 7318 Fax (03) 528 7318
Reservations Call 0800 222 046
www.bnb.co.nz/ashleytroubadour.html

Double $75 Single $52 (Continental Breakfast)
Child $10 Self-contained $85-$110
Credit cards accepted
2 Queen 2 Double 1 Single (4 bdrm)
Bathrooms: 2 Ensuite 2 Guests share

Ashley Troubadour used to be a nunnery. Nowadays it is an adventure base for the Abel Tasman National Park and all other outdoor pursuits available in this area. You name it, we've got it and John and Coral Horton, your friendly Ashley Troubadour hosts, will gladly arrange all bookings to make your stay a pleasure. Laundry facilities, security room and ample off-street parking are available for your peace of mind. Our ensuite rooms are near new and fully self-contained in quiet garden setting.

MOTUEKA *500m E of Motueka*

Golf View Chalet *B&B and Self-contained Apartment*
Kathleen & Neil Holder
20A Teece Drive, Motueka

Tel (03) 528 8353 info@GolfViewChalet.co.nz
www.GolfViewChalet.co.nz

Double $95-$120 Single $75
(Special Breakfast) Child $20
Self-contained apartment $100 double Extra adult $15
Credit cards accepted Children welcome
3 Queen 1 Double 4 Single (4 bdrm)
Bathrooms: 1 Ensuite 2 Private

Welcome to our sunny home on 18 hole golf course, beside the sea. Close to restaurants, National Parks and golden beaches nearby – your choice of the regions attractions. Then sleep well in our comfortable beds. Generous flexitime breakfast is served in hosts dining room. Breakfast option available for self-cater apartment (extra). Complimentary laundry, tea, coffee making facilities, guest fridge, BBQ. Directions: from High Street (main street), State Highway 60, turn into Tudor Street, left Thorp Street, right Krammer Street, left into Teece Drive.

RIWAKA *2km N of Motueka*

Bridge House B&B *B&B*
Michelle & Malcolm Greenwood
274 Main Road, Riwaka RD 3, Motueka

Tel (03) 528 9117 Fax (03) 528 9117
Mob 021 038 2936 bridgehouse@ihug.co.nz
homepages.ihug.co.nz/~malandmichelle

Double $145-$165 (Full Breakfast)
Dinner $25pp Credit cards accepted
3 Queen (3 bdrm)
Bathrooms: 3 Ensuite

Relax in the queen-size suites with big baths. Our guest lounge has Sky TV, video, complimentary beverages, books, games etc. Home-cooked evening meals by arrangement (inclusive May to October). Internet, Fax and Laundry facilities available. Enjoy your generous full cooked breakfast before you take in the local scenery or experience the many varied activities the Tasman region has to offer. Malcolm & Michelle look forward to meeting you with Tui and Tiki our very cuddly birman kittens. Regret no pets.

KAITERITERI   *9km N of Motueka*

Seaview B&B   *B&B*
Jackie & Tig McNab
259 Riwaka-Kaiteriteri Road,
RD 2, Motueka

Tel (03) 528 9341   Fax (03) 528 9341
www.bnb.co.nz/seaviewbb.html

Double $100   Single $85   (Continental Breakfast)
Credit cards accepted
2 Queen (2 bdrm)
Bathrooms: 1 Guests share

Jackie and Tig welcome you to our peaceful and ideally located coastal property just 5 minutes to
Kaiteriteri beach and handy to Abel Tasman and Kahurangi National Parks. Nearby attractions include
sea kayaking, water taxi trips, beach and bush walks, golden sands and safe swimming beaches. Set
against a large area of private native bush with abundant birdlife we offer panoramic views of Tasman
Bay with breathtaking sunrises and sunsets. Large continental breakfast with home-made jams. Guest
lounge with tea/coffee making facilities. Bar and restaurant 4 minutes away.

KAITERITERI   *16km N of Motueka*

Bayview *B&B*
Aileen & Tim Rich
Kaiteriteri Heights,
RD 2, Motueka

Tel (03) 527 8090   Fax (03) 527 8090
Mob 027 454 5835   book@kaiteriteribandb.co.nz
www.kaiteriteribandb.co.nz

Double $150-$180 (Full Breakfast)
Dinner by arrangement   Credit cards accepted
1 King/Twin 1 King 1 Twin (2 bdrm)
Bathrooms: 2 Ensuite

Welcome to our piece of paradise. Our modern house has huge windows with outstanding seaviews
overlooking Kaiteriteri Beach out to Abel Tasman National Park. Large, beautifully furnished guest
rooms have every convenience you could want. Enjoy delicious home-cooked breakfast with your
hosts or on your terrace. Laundry, email and booking facilities for boat trips, walking and kayaking are
available. We are happy to share our home, extensive book collection and general lifestyle with you so
stay a while and enjoy this unique area.

KAITERITERI   *10km N of Motueka*

Bracken Hill B&B *B&B Not Suitable for Children*
Grace & Tom Turner
265 Kaiteriteri Road, RD 2, Motueka

Tel (03) 528 9629 Fax (03) 528 9629
Mob 027 224 7110 gracet@ihug.co.nz
www.bnb.co.nz/brackenhillbb.html

Double $120-$130 Single $100
(Continental Breakfast)   Credit cards accepted
2 Queen 1 Twin (3 bdrm)
Bathrooms: 3 Private

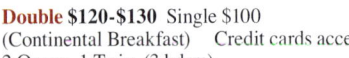

Coastal Luxury. Welcome to our tasteful, spacious modern home. Cosy rooms all have wonderful
sea views over Tasman Bay. Enjoy mountains, native bush, magical sunrises, sunsets & stars. A large
viewing sundeck leads to a unique natural rock garden. Guests TV lounge, tea/coffee, fridge, pool table,
laundry facility. Experience (5-15minutes) golden Kaiteriteri Beach, Marahau, Kahurangi/Abel Tasman
National Parks; (1 hour) Golden Bay. Kayaking, walks, water taxis. Restaurants close. Interests:
Service Clubs, travel & delight in a refreshing breakfast, at our Peaceful Haven. Grace & Tom.

KAITERITERI *13km N of Motueka*

Everton B&B *B&B*
Martin & Diane Everton
Kotare Place, Little Kaiteriteri,
RD 2, Motueka

Tel (03) 527 8301   Fax (03) 527 8301
Mob 027 450 5944   everton@xtra.co.nz
www.evertonbandb.co.nz

Double $110   Single $90   (Continental Breakfast)
Credit cards accepted
1 Queen 2 Twin (2 bdrm)
Bathrooms: 1 Guests share

We live 2 minutes walk from the golden sands of Little Kaiteriteri Beach with wonderful sea views. Breakfast includes fresh home baked bread or muffins. Our interests include golf, music, travel, walking, conversation and reading. The Abel Tasman National Park is right here where you can kayak, walk and take boat trips. Nearby are excellent restaurants, wineries and craft shopping. Trout and sea fishing can be arranged. We are licensed to take you on a personalised trip in our boat if you choose. Email is offered and even a piano to play! We have no pets and are non-smokers.

KAITERITERI *15km N of Motueka*

Bellbird Lodge *B&B*
Anthea & Brian Harvey
Sandy Bay Road, Kaiteriteri, RD 2, Motueka

Tel (03) 527 8555   Fax (03) 527 8556
Mob 025 678 8441   stay@bellbirdlodge.com
www.bellbirdlodge.com

Double $150-$225 Single $100-$150
(Special Breakfast) Dinner by arrangement (May-Sept)
Credit cards accepted
1 King/Twin 1 Queen 1 Twin (3 bdrm)
Bathrooms: 1 Ensuite 1 Private

Situated in a tranquil hillside setting with panoramic sea views, Bellbird Lodge is close to Kaiteriteri Beach and Abel Tasman National Park. The tastefully furnished guest rooms are on the ground floor and have tea/coffee making facilities. Enjoy a buffet breakfast with sumptuous hot course of the day served in the dining room or alfresco on the terrace with its stunning view, accompanied by songs of bellbirds and tuis. Welcome to our home where warm, friendly hospitality, superb food and fine accommodation await you.

KAITERITERI *13km N of Motueka*

The Haven *B&B Self-contained*
Tom & Alison Rowling
Rowling Heights, RD 2,
Kaiteriteri, Motueka

Tel (03) 527 8085   Fax (03) 527 8065
thehaven@internet.co.nz   www.thehaven.co.nz

Double $150   (Continental Breakfast)
House B&B $100 per room
Self-contained extra person $50   Credit cards accepted
1 King 1 Queen 4 Twin (4 bdrm)
Bathrooms: 3 Ensuite 1 Private

The Haven - the name says it all. Just the sound of the waves, bird song, and the occasional haunting cry of the big black back gulls as they soar overhead. Self-contained, 2 bedrooms, the Captain's Cabin with king-size bed and ensuite, the Crew's Quarters with 2 large single beds and private bathroom. The galley kitchen has generous breakfast provisions and 2 decks provide outdoor living. Also available B&B in our home, queen or twin rooms with ensuites. Informal relaxed family atmosphere, spectacular views, swimming pool, private bush track to the beach. Minimum stay 2 nights. Not suitable for small children.

KAITERITERI *15km N of Motueka*

Ngaiomi *Separate/Suite*
Julie & Allan Hunter
Kaiteriteri / Sandy Bay, Motueka RD 2, Nelson

Tel (03) 527 8274 Fax (03) 527 8309
Mob 025 543 009 homes@goldensands.co.nz
www.bnb.co.nz/ngaiomi.html

Double $85-$135 (Continental Breakfast)
Credit cards accepted
1 Queen 1 Double (1 bdrm)   Bathrooms: 1 Ensuite

Welcome to Ngaiomi. Your private villa set in our garden has
ensuite facilities, kitchenette and TV. You will wake to the song
of the bellbird and tui. Partake of breakfast on your deck while
enjoying the sea views. We are just minutes away from the golden
sands of Kaiteriteri Beach and start of the Abel Tasman National
Park. This area offers kayaking, bush walks and marvellous boat
trips. Top rated wineries, restaurants and craft shopping beckon.
Hosts Julie and Allan and friendly cat Ben.

KAITERITERI *13km N of Motueka*

Robyn's Nest B & B *B&B Self-contained*
Robyn & Mike O'Donnell
1 Rowling Road, Kaiteriteri

Tel (03) 527 8466 Fax (03) 527 8466
Mob 021 431 735 robynod@ihug.co.nz
www.accommodationkaiteriteri.co.nz

Double $110-$150 Single $100
(Continental Breakfast)   Child negotiable
Credit cards accepted   Children welcome
2 Queen 1 Single (2 bdrm)
Bathrooms: 2 Ensuite

Take the track through our garden and walk 100 metre
to the beautiful Kaiteriteri Beach with golden sand, clear and safe swimming. Kaiteriteri is also the
departure point for launches, water-taxis and kayaking into the Abel Tasman National Park. Both
our rooms have private entry via your own terrace, television, hairdryer, refrigerator and tea, coffee &
toast making facilities. We have off-street parking, guests BBQ area and petanque court. Continental
breakfast includes homemade muesli and preserves. No pets

KAITERITERI - TAPU BAY *12km N of Motueka*

Maison Luc *B&B Self-contained*
Angie & Martin Lucas
Tapu Bay, Kaiteriteri Road, RD 2, Motueka

Tel (03) 527 8247 0800 468 815 Fax (03) 527 8347
Mob 027 221 6090 maison_luc@hotmail.com
www.bnb.co.nz/maisonluc.html

Double $80 Single $70 (Continental Breakfast)
Cottage Single $110 Double $130 Extra people $15
(breakfast not included) Children welcome
2 Queen 1 Double 1 Twin (4 bdrm)
Bathrooms: 1 Private 1 Guests share

Angie, Martin and Lu (dog) welcome you to Maison Luc. 2 minute walk to Tapu and Stephens
Bays, 1km to Kaiteriteri beaches. Gateway to Abel Tasman. Self-contained separate unit in peaceful
orchard garden. Sleeps 4 (2 on sofa), children welcome. B&B: 2 double bedrooms upstairs. Guests
share bathroom. Continental breakfast served in dining room or on terrace with views across the bay.
Swimming pool. Good restaurants nearby. Hunting/fishing guiding available. We look forward to
meeting you and introducing you to the magic of this special area.

view is taken from guest balcony

ABEL TASMAN NATIONAL PARK *17km NW of Motueka*

B&B
Approved

Twin Views *B&B*
Ellenor & Les King
Tokongawa Drive, Split Apple Rock,
RD 2, Kaiteriteri

Tel (03) 527 8475 Fax: (03) 527 8479
Mob: 025 318 937
twinviews@xtra.co.nz www.twinviews.co.nz

Double $135-$145 (Special Breakfast)
Credit cards accepted
1 king/twin 1 queen (2 bedrooms) 2 ensuite

Wake to the sound of waves breaking on the beach below
in this new architect designed home with magnificent
sea views overlooking Tasman Bay. Each room has
panoramic sea views, ensuite, fridge, tea/coffee making
facilities, TV, hair dryer, heated towel rails, comfortable
seating, private entrance and sliding doors on to your
own private deck. We are only a few minutes walk from
two beaches, bush walks and 5 minutes drive to start of
Abel Tasman Track.

Enjoy a delicious buffet breakfast with fresh organic fruit
from our own garden whenever possible.

Breakfast can be served in the guest lounge or on your
own private balcony.
We have had over 10 years in the accommodation
industry and are born and bred Kiwis.
We are located at Split Apple Rock in a quiet, peaceful,
spectacular location, 1 hour from Nelson, 2.5 hours from
Picton Ferry.

Directions:
*Proceed past Kaiteriteri Beach for 4km, turn
right onto Tokongawa and go right to the top.*

ABEL TASMAN NATIONAL PARK - MARAHAU *18km NW of Motueka*

Abel Tasman Bed & Breakfast
B&B Homestay Self-contained Motels
George Bloomfield
Abel Tasman National Park, Marahau

Tel (03) 527 8181 Fax (03) 527 8181
abel.tasman.stables.accom@xtra.co.nz
www.abeltasmanstables.co.nz

Double $95-$120 Single $65 (Special Breakfast)
Self-contained motels $120 Credit cards accepted
5 Queen 2 Double 3 Single (6 bdrm)
Bathrooms: 5 Ensuite 1 Private 1 Guests share 1 Host share

Great views, hospitality, peaceful garden setting are yours at Abel Tasman Stables accommodation. Closest ensuite facility to Abel Tasman National park. Guests comments include 'I know now that hospitality is not just a word', TH, Germany. 'Wonderful place, friendly hospitality. The best things for really special holidays. We leave a piece of our hearts', P&M, Italy. 'The creme-de-la-creme of our holiday. What a view', MN & JW, England. Homestay bed & breakfast or self-contained options. Café close by.

ABEL TASMAN NATIONAL PARK *17km NW of Motueka*

Split Apple Rock Homestay *B&B Homestay*
Thelma & Rodger Boys
Tokongawa Drive, Split Apple Rock,
RD 2, Motueka

Tel (03) 527 8182 splitapplerock@hotmail.com
www.bnb.co.nz/splitapple.html

Double $130-$140 Single $115-$120 (Full Breakfast)
Dinner $30 by arrangement
1 Queen 1 Twin (2 bdrm)
Bathrooms: 2 Ensuite

Enjoy 180 degree panoramic sea views of Tasman Bay and Abel Tasman National Park. Our Eco-log home rooms have private entrances and decking. We are within walking distance of 2 golden beaches, 5 minutes drive to Marahau and the start of Abel Tasman National Park where walking, kayaking, boating, swimming and more are available. 2 cats in residence. Directions: on the Marahau/Kaiteriteri Road take the Tokongawa Drive turn-off, 1.2km up Tokongawa Drive the 'Split Apple Rock Homestay' sign is on your right.

PATONS ROCK BEACH - TAKAKA *10km W of Takaka*

Patondale
Farmstay Separate/Suite Self-contained 4 villas
Vicki & David James
Patons Rock,
RD 2, Takaka

Tel (03) 525 8262 0800 306 697 Fax (03) 525 8262
Mob 025 936 891 patondale@xtra.co.nz
www.patonsrockbeachvillas.co.nz

Double $120 Single $120 (Continental Breakfast)
Child $10 Credit cards accepted Children welcome
Breakfast provisions supplied for first morning
4 King 8 Single (8 bdrm) Bathrooms: 4 Private

Golden Bay's newest villas. 4 sunny, spacious, deluxe self-contained units, own attached carports. 2 bedrooms. Peaceful rural setting at the seaward end of our dairy farm yet only a few minutes walk to beautiful Patons Rock beach. Central location. "Simply the Best." Your Kiwi hosts David & Vicki invite you to be our guests.

TAKAKA - TATA BEACH *15km NE of Takaka*

The Devonshires *B&B Homestay*
Brian & Susan Devonshire
32 Tata Heights Drive, Tata Beach, R.D 1, Takaka

Tel (03) 525 7987 Fax (03) 525 7987 Mob 025 463 118
devs.1@xtra.co.nz www.bnb.co.nz/thedevonshires.html

Double $90 Single $60 (Full Breakfast) Child not suitable
Dinner $25-$30 by arrangement Credit cards accepted
1 Queen (1 bdrm) Bathrooms: 1 Ensuite

The Devonshires live at Tata Beach and invite you to enjoy their
new home and stroll to the nearby beautiful golden beach. A
tranquil base for exploring the truly scenic Golden Bay, the Abel
Tasman Walkway, Kahurangi National Park, Farewell Spit,
amazing coastal scenery, fishing the rivers or visiting interesting
craftspeople. Brian, an educator, wine and American Football
buff is a keen fisherman. Susan enjoys crafts, painting, gardening
and practising her culinary skills. Charlie Brown and Hermione
are the resident cats. Longer visits welcomed.

TAKAKA *5km S of Takaka*

Rose Cottage *B&B Self-contained*
Margaret & Phil Baker
Hamama Road,
RD 1, Takaka

Tel (03) 525 9048 Fax (03) 525 9043
www.bnb.co.nz/rosecottage.html

Double $77-$87 Single $60-$67
(Continental Breakfast) Self-contained units $97-$127
Credit cards accepted
1 Queen 2 Single (2 bdrm)
Bathrooms: 1 Guests share

Rose cottage, much loved home of Phil and Margaret situated in the beautiful Takaka valley, in 2.5
acres of garden amongst 300 year old Totara trees, is ideally situated to explore Golden Bay's many
attractions. Our 3 self-contained units have full kitchens, private sun decks and quality furniture made
by Phil in his craft workshop. The 12 metre indoor solar-heated swimming pool is available to our
guests. Our interests are travel, photography, gardening, arts and crafts and helping to make our guests'
stay a memorable one.

TAKAKA *2km S of Takaka*

Croxfords Homestay *Homestay*
Pam & John Croxford
Dodson Road, RD 1, Takaka, Golden Bay

Tel (03) 525 7177 0800 264 156 Fax (03) 525 7177
croxfords@xtra.co.nz
www.bnb.co.nz/croxfordshomestay.html

Double $100 Single $70 (Full Breakfast) Child $10
Dinner $25 Credit cards accepted Children welcome
1 Double 3 Single (2 bdrm)
Bathrooms: 2 Ensuite

You are welcome to our spacious home in a peaceful
rural setting close to Takaka. Views of Kahurangi
National Park are spectacular. Pam loves cooking evening meals, including special diets, using home
grown produce. Breakfasts include home made bread, muesli, yoghurt and preserves. We enjoy
assisting visitors make the most of their visit. We are near beaches and national parks. We have many
New Zealand books. No children at home, or pets. Non-smokers preferred. We offer guided walks in
the Abel Tasman and Kahurangi national parks.

TAKAKA   *6.5km N of Takaka*

Golden Bay Grove Retreat   *B&B*
Jocelyn Kemp & Brad Harwood
The Grove, Rocklands Road, RD 1, Takaka

Tel (03) 525 7011   Mob 021 884 773 or 021 522 279
bradnet22@yahoo.com
www.bnb.co.nz/goldenbaygroveretreat.html

Double $140-$198 Single $100   (Full Breakfast)
Dinner $35   Honeymoon cottage $100
Bike rentals $20
2 Queen 1 Single (2 bdrm)
Bathrooms: 1 Private

An unspoiled setting amongst a backdrop of native forest in a labyrinth of ancient limestone rock formations. Come to feel the peace, quiet and natural beauty of this extensive setting framed by tall nikau palms and ancient rata forest. Located 1km from Pohara Beach next to scenic Grove Reserve. We offer solar heated swimming pool with optional massage/healing treatments on request. Guests choosing to dine in house will experience a range of cultural food preferences such as organic Mediterranean, Middle Eastern and Asian cuisine.

PARAPARA   *20km NW of Takaka*

Hakea Hill House   *B&B*
Vic & Liza Eastman
PO Box 35, Collingwood 7171

Tel (03) 524 8487   Fax (03) 524 8487
vic.eastman@clear.net.nz
www.bnb.co.nz/hakeahillhouse.html

Double $120 Single $80   (Full Breakfast) Child $40
Dinner by arrangement   Credit cards accepted
Children welcome
2 Double 6 Single (3 bdrm)
Bathrooms: 1 Guests share

Hakea Hill House at Parapara has views from its hilltop of all Golden Bay. The 2 storey house is modern and spacious. 2 guest rooms have large balconies; the third for children has 4 bunk beds and a cot. American and New Zealand electric outlets are installed. Television, tea or coffee, and telephone lines are available in rooms. Vic is a practising physician with an interest in astronomy. Liza is a quilter and cares for 2 outdoor dogs. Please contact us personally for reservations and directions.

COLLINGWOOD   *25km N of Takaka*

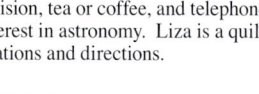

Skara Brae Garden Motels and
Bed & Breakfast   *B&B Self-contained*
Joanne & Pax Northover
Elizabeth Street, Collingwood

Tel (03) 524 8464   0800 752 722   Fax (03) 524 8474
skarabrae@xtra.co.nz
www.accommodationcollingwood.co.nz

Double $130 Single $100   (Continental Breakfast)
2 self-contained units $95   Credit cards accepted
2 Queen 1 Double 1 Twin 2 Single (4 bdrm)
Bathrooms: 1 Ensuite 3 Private

Skara Brae, the original police residence in Collingwood built in 1908, has been tastefully renovated over the years. Our historic home is in a quiet, peaceful garden setting. Join us in the house for bed and breakfast or our 2 self-contained motel units. Either way you will experience a warm welcoming atmosphere and individual attention. We are a minute away from the excellent Courthouse Café and local tavern bistro bar and it is a short stroll to the beach. Farewell Spit trips depart close by.

COLLINGWOOD   *25km SE of Takaka*

Win's B&B   *B&B Homestay*
Heather Margaret Win
State Highway 60,
Plain Road, RD 1

Tel (03) 524 8381   www.bnb.co.nz/wins.html

Double $70-$80 Single $35   (Full Breakfast)
Child $20
Dinner by arrangement
Children welcome
1 Queen 2 Double 1 Twin (4 bdrm)
Bathrooms: 2 Guests share 1 Host share

A warm welcome to Win's Bed & Breakfast. Win's backs onto a sheep and cattle farm with mountain range in the background, close to walking tracks and beach. 3km from Collingwood where there are 2 excellent cafés and a tavern bistro bar; also bookings for Farewell Spit trips. We are at the start of Plain Road.

PAKAWAU BEACH - COLLINGWOOD   *12km N of Collingwood*

Pakawau Homestay   *Homestay Self-contained*
Val & Graham Williams
Pakawau Beach, RD,
Collingwood

Tel (03) 524 8168
Fax (03) 524 8168
www.bnb.co.nz/pakawauhomestay.html

Double $90-$100 Single $80   (Continental Breakfast)
Dinner $25 Self-contained $80
2 Queen 1 Double 1 Single (2 bdrm)
Bathrooms: 1 Ensuite 1 Host share

We are the northern most homestay in the South Island, 9km from Farewell Spit. We offer self-contained accommodation from $80 per night. The Farewell Spit Tours will pick you up from our gate. You only have to walk a few metres through our garden to a safe swimming beach. Local seafoods available, eg. whitebait, scallops, or you can walk across the road to a licensed café. We are non-smokers, have 2 cats and look forward to sharing our lifestyle with you.

GOLDEN DOWNS   *26km SW of Wakefield*

Golden Downs Lodge   *Lodge*
William Cameron
Corner Valley Road and Kerr Hill Road,
Kohatu, State Highway 6, Wakefield

Tel (03) 522 4175   Fax (03) 522 4611
thelodge@goldendowns.co.nz
www.goldendowns.co.nz

Double $95 Single $50   (Full Breakfast)
Child $20 Dinner $25 $35
Children welcome Pets welcome
2 Double 6 Single (3 bdrm)
Bathrooms: 3 Private

Golden Downs lodge is a quirky, homely retreat at the heart of Golden Downs forest. Set on 30 acres of tree covered grounds, the lodge occupies the old Golden Downs Village Hall. We are proud of our fine food prepared from local produce, and an atmosphere of intelligent and entertaining hospitality. Snowy the dog, Puss the cat, and Hazel the child may be in residence too.

TOPHOUSE   *9km N of St Arnaud*

Tophouse   *Farmstay Self-contained*
Melody & Mike Nicholls
RD 2, Nelson

Tel (03) 521 1848   Fax (03) 521 1848
tophouse@clear.net.nz   www.bnb.co.nz/tophouse.html

Guest House:
Double $80   Single $40   (Continental Breakfast)
1 Queen 1 Double 6 Single (5 bdrm)
Dinner $25
Bathrooms: 3 Guests share

Four Self-contained cottages:
Double $90   plus $15 per extra person
Each cottage includes: 1 Double 1 twin   (2 bdrm)
                          1 Private bathroom

Credit cards accepted   Child rates available

*We invite you to share
our unique home with its
huge open fires*

*Lovely setting and
homely atmosphere*

Tophouse, a cob (mud) building, dating from the 1880's when it was a hotel, and re-opened in 1989 as a Farm Guest House, has that 'good old days' feel about it.

Situated on a golf course on 300 hectare (730 acres) of picturesque high country farm running cattle, with much native bush and an abundance of bird life, a popular holiday spot for its peace and beauty, bush walks, fishing, and in the winter serves the local ski field. Tophouse is only 9km from St Arnaud, gateway to Nelson Lakes National Park.

A typical farmhouse dinner is taken with the family and since the fire's going, 'real' toast for breakfast.

Cottages are two bedroom, fully self contained including kitchen, with great views of the surrounding mountains.

Directions:
Just off State Highway 63 between Blenheim and Murchison and 9km from St Arnaud is Tophouse, that's us! The area took its name from the building.

If travelling from Nelson, leave State Highway 6 at Belgrove and travel towards St Arnaud, we're signposted from the main road and looking forward to your visit.

NELSON LAKES - ST ARNAUD   *85km S of Nelson*

Nelson Lakes Homestay   *Homestay*
Gay & Merv Patch
RD 2, State Highway 63, Nelson

Tel (03) 521 1191   Fax (03) 521 1191
Mob 021 261 8529   Home@Tasman.net
www.nelsonlakesaccommodation.co.nz

Double $125   Single $90   (Full Breakfast)
Dinner $35pp by arrangement
Credit cards accepted
2 King/Twin 1 Queen (2 bdrm)
Bathrooms: 2 Ensuite

Nestled on the sunny slopes of the St Arnaud Mountain Range, Nelson Lakes National Park, our spacious modern home is designed for the comfort and convenience of our guests. Spacious ensuite rooms, with doors opening on to our garden, large comfortable lounge and terrace to relax on at the end of the day and admire the magnificent mountain views. Laundry facilities are available and three course meals by prior arrangement. We have a house cat. Directions: State Highway 63, 4km east of St Arnaud.

NELSON LAKES - ST ARNAUD   *85km SW of Nelson*

St Arnaud House - a sub-alpine retreat
Debbie & Justin Murphy   *Boutique B&B Lodge*
Corner Bridge, Holland & Lake Road,
PO Box 88, St Arnaud
Tel (03) 521 1028   Fax (03) 521 1208 Mob 027 668 7544
info@st-arnaudhouse.co.nz   www.st-arnaudhouse.co.nz

Double $185-$215 Single $125-$150 (Special Breakfast)
Dinner $45   Single share with 1 x double $55
Credit cards accepted
2 King/Twin 1 King 2 Queen 1 Single (4 bdrm)
Bathrooms: 3 Ensuite 1 Private

A secluded sub-alpine haven amid the native beech forest of Nelson Lakes National Park. Abundant and vocal native birdlife adds a musical background to lake, forest and mountain excursions suiting all fitness levels. NZ's great spotted kiwi re-introduced May 2004, furthering the successful Mainland Island Conservation Project. Lake Rotoiti, skiing, world class trout fishing, Buller river adventures, wine and art trails among many other local & regional attractions. We live in an adjacent classic Kiwi cottage, giving guests a hosted, boutique lodge accomodation experience.

MURCHISON   *16km S of Murchison*

Awapiriti Farmstay   *Farmstay*
Jean Hayward & Andrew Motte-Harrison
Highway 65, Maruia Valley, Murchison

Tel (03) 523 9466   Fax (03) 523 9777
awapiriti@ihug.co.nz
www.bnb.co.nz/awapiriti.html

Double $140   Single $110   (Full Breakfast)
Dinner by arrangement Credit cards accepted
Pets welcome
1 King/Twin 1 Queen 2 Single (3 bdrm)
Bathrooms: 2 Ensuite 1 Private

Experience something special: visit Awapiriti, nestled between the Maruia River and bush-clad hills. Share our home and enjoy good New Zealand food and wine. Spot the trout from our own swing bridge. Take a guided walk in the native bush or a farm tour to see the elk, cattle, sheep, etc. Meet the dogs and cats. Fishing/hunting guides or massage by arrangement. 3 hours approx from Picton/ Christchurch/Hokitika and 2 hours from Nelson, Awapiriti is a haven for adults, unsuitable for children.

MURCHISON *0.5km N of Murchison*

B&B Approved

Murchison Lodge *B&B Homestay*
Shirley & Merve Bigden
15 Grey Street, Murchison, 7191

Tel (03) 523 9196 Fax (03) 523 9196
Mob 021 266 7016 info@murchisonlodge.co.nz
www.murchisonlodge.co.nz

Double $140-$160 Single $110-$135 (Full Breakfast)
Dinner by arrangement Credit cards accepted
2 Queen 1 Twin (3 bdrm)
Bathrooms: 3 Ensuite

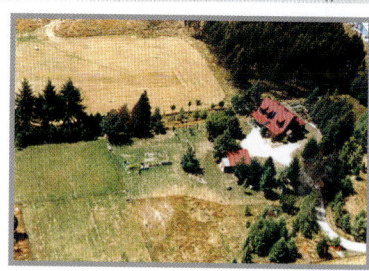

Come and enjoy our warm and relaxed hospitality, comfortable beds and hearty breakfasts. Murchison Lodge (formerly known as Coch-y-Bondhu) is a uniquely crafted timber home set on 3 acres bordering the mighty Buller river. We are just 10 minutes walk from Murchison township but you will get the feeling you are in the middle of the wilderness in the quiet and secluded garden of mature trees. We have a friendly dog, several cows and hens and we encourage and see many native birds.

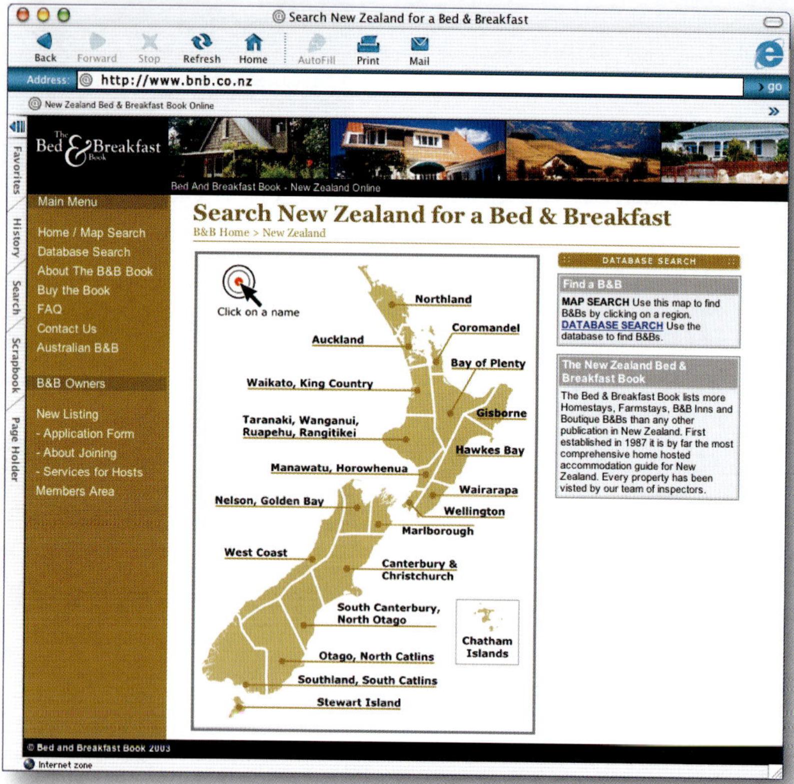

West Coast

Towns listed generally follow
a north to south route. Refer
to the index if required.

Karamea

67

Carters Beach

Cape Foulwind
Westport

6

Charleston

69

Punakaiki

Reefton

Barrytown

7

Nine Mile Creek
Greymouth

Moana

Hokitika

Lake Brunner

Ruatapu

0   Kilometres   60

0   Miles   36

6

Harihari

Castle Hill Village

Whataroa

Lake Coleridge

Franz Josef

Darfield

Fox Glacier

Mt Hutt

Bruce Bay

Staveley   Methven

Paringa

Rakaia

Mount Cook

Ashburton

6
Haast

Lake Tekapo

Burkes Pass   Fairlie   Geraldine   Ealing

KARAMEA   *84km N of Westport*

Beachfront Farmstay B&B   *B&B Farmstay*
Dianne & Russell Anderson
Karamea, SH67, Karamea

Tel (03) 782 6762 Fax (03) 782 6762
Mob 021 782 676   farmstay@xtra.co.nz
www.WestCoastBeachAccommodation.co.nz

Double $130-$150   Single $100   (Full Breakfast)
Child $35   Dinner $40
Credit cards accepted Children welcome
1 king 1 queen 1 twin (3 bdrm)
Bathrooms: 2 ensuite 1 shared

Welcome to a spectacular area of the West Coast. Our home is 2 minutes walk to a beautiful sandy beach, ideal for walking, jogging or just beachcombing. We milk 420 friesian cows on our undulating pasture. Join us for delicious country cuisine, organic vegetables, homemade desserts and NZ wine. Special farmhouse breakfasts include fresh baked bread, whitebait, fish, homemade preserves. Our area offers day walks, guided tours in limestone caves, unique limestone arches, golf, horse riding, bird watching, trout fishing. Come and relax in our spacious home and garden.

KARAMEA   *0.5km Karamea*

Bridge Farm   *Farmstay Self-contained*
Rosalie & Peter Sampson
Bridge Street, Karamea, RD 1, Westport

Tel (03) 782 6955   0800 KARAMEA
Fax (03) 782 6748   Enquires@karameamotels.co.nz
karameamotels.co.nz

Double $85-$120 (Continental Breakfast)
Child $10   Extra adult $20   Credit cards accepted
Children welcome
6 Queen 8 Single (10 bdrm)
Bathrooms: 8 Private

Since relinquishing their dairy farm to daughter Caroline and son-in-law Bevan, Rosalie and Peter have purpose-built on the property accommodation that neatly bridges the gap between motel and farm stay. Both are happy to share their extensive knowledge of their district, its people and environment and introduce guests to the many short walks that Karamea offers. Each quality suite is self-contained and has a private lounge that overlooks the farm to Kahurangi National Park beyond. A small mob of deer and alpaca graze nearby.

WESTPORT - CAPE FOULWIND   *11km SW of Westport*

Steeples Cottage & B&B Homestay
B&B Homestay Self-contained
Pauline & Bruce Cargill
Lighthouse Road, RD 2, Cape Foulwind, Westport

Tel (03) 789 7876   0800 670 708   Mob 021 663 487
steepleshomestay@xtra.co.nz
www.bnb.co.nz/steepleshomestay.html

Double $90   Single $50   (Full Breakfast)   Child $15
Fully self-contained cottage $110   Children welcome
1 Queen 2 Single (2 bdrm)   Bathrooms: 1 Private

Enjoy our peaceful rural home or cottage with magnificent views of the Tasman Sea, rugged coastline, beautiful beaches & tranquil sunsets. Great swimming, surfing, fishing & walking. Within 5 minutes, walk the very popular seal colony walkway, or dine at The Bay House Restaurant or the friendly local, Star Tavern. Other local attractions include full golf course, Coaltown Museum, blo-carting, horse riding, underworld & white water rafting, bush walks & Punakaiki National Park. We are keen gardeners and enjoy all sports. We have a Jack Russell dog and a cat. All laundry facilities available and off-street parking. Self-contained cottage includes continental breakfast.

WESTPORT *Westport Central*

Havenlee Homestay *Homestay*
Jan & Ian Stevenson
76 Queen Street, Westport

Tel (03) 789 8543 0800 673 619 Fax (03) 789 8502
Mob 025 627 2702 info@havenlee.co.nz
www.havenlee.co.nz

Double $95-$120 Single $60-$75 (Continental plus)
Child neg Credit cards accepted
Children welcome
2 Queen 1 Double 1 Twin (3 bdrm)
Bathrooms: 1 Private 1 Guests share suite

Peace in Paradise - this is Havenlee, offering tranquil location 300 metres from town centre. Born and bred West Coasters - hospitality is part of our heritage. Share our quality, spacious home set amongst native and exotic trees and shrubs, idyllic for exploring our environmental wonderland. Check out the outdoor adventure experiences and local attractions. Soak up the nature, rest and restore body and soul. Enjoy a generous continental-plus breakfast. Bathroom (with tub), shower room, toilet each separate. Laundry facilities, local knowledge in a friendly relaxed, smoke free environment.

WESTPORT *2km N of Westport*

Chrystal Lodge *Separate/Suite*
Ann & Bill Blythe
Corner Craddock Drive and Derby Street, Westport

Tel (03) 789 8617 0800 259 953 Fax (03) 789 8617
blythea@xtra.co.nz
www.bnb.co.nz/chrystallodge.html

Double $85 Single $65 (Continental Breakfast)
Child neg Continental breakfast $10 optional
Credit cards accepted Children welcome
2 Queen 1 Single (2 bdrm) Bathrooms: 2 Ensuite

Ann and Bill would like to welcome you to Chrystal Lodge. We are established on 20 acres beside a beach ideal for walking, surfing and fishing. Our separate self-contained units have a fully equipped kitchen/lounge with ensuite bedrooms. The garden setting has ample off-street parking. Free guest laundry. Pony available for children. We have one shy cat. Seasonal rates. Directions: turn right at the post office, continue down Brougham Street, turn left at Derby Street until at the beach.

WESTPORT - CAPE FOULWIND *11km W of Westport*

Clifftop Homestay B&B *B&B Homestay*
Paddy & Gail Alexander
Clifftop Lane, Cape Foulwind, RD 2, Westport

Tel (03) 789 5472 0800 328 472
clifftophomestay@yahoo.com
www.bnb.co.nz/clifftophomestay.html

Double $110-$150 (Continental Breakfast) Child $15
Cooked breakfast $15pp b/a (whitebait in season)
Children welcome
2 Double 1 Single (2 bdrm)
Bathrooms: 1 Private 1 Guests share

We warmly invite fellow travellers to discover the magic of The Cape. Our boutique clifftop B&B offers peace and seclusion with breathtaking views of sea, Steeples and mountains. The private guest wing has a luxurious spa bathroom. Relax on our balcony with complementary refreshments, after exploring stunning beaches, seal colony and lighthouse walkway. Great dining nearby, (Bayhouse Café or country pub). Clifftop is the perfect haven to restore body and soul. Directions: first right past Star Tavern, right into Clifftop Lane, second house.

WESTPORT - CAPE FOULWIND   *10km W of Westport*

Lighthouse Homestay
B&B Farmstay Homestay Self-contained
Derek Parsons & Helen Jenkins
32 Lighthouse Road, Cape Foulwind, Westport

Tel (03) 789 5352   Mob 021 432 472
hj.jenkins@xtra.co.nz
www.bnb.co.nz/lighthousehomestay.html

Double $90-$150 Single $80   (Continental Breakfast)
Self-contained cottage $120
1 King/Twin 2 Queen 1 Double 1 Twin 2 Single (3 bdrm)
Bathrooms: 2 Ensuite 1 Private 1 Guests share

Enjoy the soothing tranquillity of amazing sea views from your bedroom/patio. Walk the impressive Cape Foulwind Walkway with its seals and captivating coastline, ending at the magic Bay House Restaurant overlooking Tauranga Bay. Numerous outdoor activities and attractions nearby. Helen and Derek can take you out on the farm shifting cattle or walking through native rainforest. Let Poppy our fox terrier take you beachwalking below the cliffs. Self-contained cottage option. Short walk to friendly country pub. Smoke-free inside.

WESTPORT - CARTERS BEACH   *3km S of Westport*

Bellaville   *B&B*
Marlene & Ross Burrow
No 10 on SH67, Carters Beach / PO Box 157, Westport

Tel (03) 789 8457   0800 789 845   Mob 025 6131 689
fairhalls@xtra.co.nz
www.bnb.co.nz/bellaville.html

Double $90   Single $60   (Full Breakfast) Child $15
Children welcome
1 Queen 1 Twin (1 bdrm)
Bathrooms: 1 Private

Come stay with us at Carters Beach. Wake to the sound of the waves pounding on our safe walking and swimming beach. Plenty off-street parking. Quiet sunny extra large, spacious studio room with private entrance, own patio, private bathroom with spa bath, shower and separate toilet. Sleeps 4 people in comfort. Ideal for a family. Laundry available, Electric blankets, TV, tea & coffee and home-baking. Close to all activities coastal walks, seal colony. Short walk to friendly licensed country café bar, golf course, beach, airport.

WESTPORT

Archer House   *B&B*
Kerrie Fairhall
75 Queen Street, Westport

Tel (03) 789 8778   0800 789 877   Fax (03) 789 8763
Mob 025 260 3677   accom@archerhouse.co.nz
www.archerhouse.co.nz

Double $150   Single $140   (Full Breakfast)
Credit cards accepted   Children welcome
3 Queen 2 Single (3 bdrm)
Bathrooms: 2 Ensuite 1 Private

3 large bedrooms, 2 with ensuites, 1 with private facilities. All bedrooms have TVs and tea/coffee facilities. Bathrooms have a hair dryer, heated towel rail and toiletries. Sunny balconies and relax in a sheltered private conservatory or one of the two guest lounges. New Zealand Heritage Home, with outstanding historic significance to the West Coast created by leadlighting masterpieces and antique furniture. Short stroll to all town amenities including Victoria Square and heated swimming pool. Whole home is available for rental for those who prefer privacy.
See website for more details, www.archerhouse.co.nz.

WESTPORT - CARTERS BEACH   *4km S of Westport*

Approved

Carters Beach B&B   *B&B*
Sue & John Bennett
Main Road Carters Beach, On SH67A, Westport

Tel (03) 789 8056   0800 783 566   Mob 027 589 8056
cartersbeachaccom@xtra.co.nz
www.bnb.co.nz/cartersbeachbb.html

Double $90   Single $60-$70
(Continental Breakfast) Children welcome
2 Queen 1 Twin (3 bdrm)
Bathrooms: 1 Ensuite 1 Private

Carters Beach B&B has a lovely relaxed atmosphere, situated only 4kms south of Westport. A 3 minute walk will take you to our beautiful beach, with fully licenced Resturant/Café and home bakery.

A golf links, the world famous Seal Colony and Bay House Café within a few minutes drive. 20 minutes drive south take in the magnificent scenery from the Charleston Nile Rain Forest Train, then on to the popular Truman Track before the ever popular Punakaiki Pancake Rocks. North of Westport you can visit Karamea, the start of the Heaphy Track or take in the view from Denniston being the old coal mining town or just visit the Coal Town Museum.

Our rooms are very spacious with TV and tea/coffee making facilities. Own private entrance ways to the rooms with own sun decks. Laundry facillities available by arrangement. Ideal accommodation for couples travelling togeather. We look forward to listening to your travel tales and sharing our local knowledge with you. Cheers, Sue and John Bennett.

WESTPORT   *14km S of Westport*

Okari Lake Hideaway   *Self-contained*
Marie Dickson
Virgin Flat Road, Westport

Tel (03) 789 6841   0800 H D AWAY
Fax (03) 789 6841   Mob 0274 452 410
marie.greg@xtra.co.nz   www.hideaway.com

Double $150-$200 (Full Breakfast)
Children welcome
1 Queen (1 bdrm)
Bathrooms: 1 Private

If you are looking for peace and tranquillity this private exclusive cottage, which is built over a private lake, is the perfect place for you. There is a boat moored on the cottage jetty for your use. The location of the lake allows for all-weather trout fishing. This is a bird watches paradise – there are many varieties of native birds and water foul. A book on native birds and binoculars are to help identify them. We are only 35 minutes from Punakaiki and 30 minutes from the Bay House.

WESTPORT   *4km SW of Westport Central*

Lakeside Terrace B&B   *B&B*
Anne & Wynne Goldie
12 Lakeside Terrace, RD 2, Westport

Tel (03) 789 7438   Fax (03) 789 6269
wa.goldie@xtra.co.nz
www.bnb.co.nz/lakeside.html

Double $100-$120 Single $85-$95
(Continental Breakfast)
1 Queen 1 Double 1 Single (3 bdrm)
Bathrooms: 1 Private

We offer quality accommodation for one party of guests at a time in our new and modern sunny home, set in a peaceful rural area, surrounded by native trees and shrubs and the native ducks on nearby lakes. Experience the amazing outdoor activities and attractions our district has to offer, or just relax and enjoy the tranquillity of your 'back to nature' surrounds with magical panoramic views. Hospitality is our heritage – you can be assured of a warm welcome and a memorable stay. Resident cat.

WESTPORT - CAPE FOULWIND   *11km S of Westport*

Cape House   *B&B Homestay*
Dave Low
Tauranga Bay Road, Cape Foulwind, Westport

Tel (03) 789 6358   Mob 027 481 8672
stay@capehouse.co.nz
www.capehouse.co.nz

Double $80-$100 Single $55-$65
(Continental Breakfast) Child $20
Dinner $20-$25 by arrangement Extra person $20
Children welcome
2 Queen 2 Single (2 bdrm)
Bathrooms: 1 Ensuite 1 Private

Cape House is a large and warm open style house in a secluded environment with a funky and friendly atmosphere. Your hosts are Dave the surfer and fisherman and Mark the technical guy. Chill out or enjoy the outdoors. Very near by are the Cape Foulwind walkway, seal colony, beaches, surfing and fishing. Options for eating out are a stroll to the local tavern, or the award winning Bayhouse café. Free internet access is available. We have an old outside dog and an inside cat.

WEST COAST

WESTPORT - CARTERS BEACH   *3km N of Westport*

Beach Haven   *B&B*
Leslie & Gary Broderick
35 Marine Parade,
Carters Beach, Westport

Tel (03) 789 8207   0800 111 585
Fax (03) 789 8207   leslie.gary@xtra.co.nz
www.bnb.co.nz/beachhaven.html

Double $110-$120   Single $60   (Continental Breakfast)
2 Queen 1 Single (3 bdrm)
Bathrooms: 1 Ensuite 1 Private 1 Host share

As our name implies Beach Haven is situated on the shoreline of Carters Beach. Your hosts Leslie & Gary will endeavour to make your stay as enjoyable as possible. Gary, a born coaster can impart his knowledge of all things local and places of interest to visit. Take a stroll on the beach, enjoy a glass of wine whilst watching the sun go down. Be lulled to sleep by the sound of the waves. We have beautiful walks, underwater rafting, horse treking and much more. Be as relaxed or as busy as you choose. Don't rush, stay a day or two. You'll be glad you did.

WESTPORT   *3km N of Westport*

Haven of Tranquility   *B&B Homestay*
Margaret Broderick
89 Snodgrass Road, RD 2 Ext, Westport

Tel (03) 789 8655   Mob 025 245 7258
marg.b@xtra.co.nz
www.bnb.co.nz/havenoftranquility.html

Double $100-$120   Single $100-$110
(Continental Breakfast)   Child neg Dinner neg
Credit cards accepted
1 Queen 2 Twin (2 bdrm)
Bathrooms: 1 Private 1 Host share

A Haven of Tranquility and much more. Nestled on the bank of the Orowaiti River, 3km north of central Westport, a perfect location for a restful stay. Make it your base for exploring the Buller District or enjoy the river view, the fishing or many walks. We assure you of a friendly welcome, top facilities and a willingness to do all we can to ensure your stay is memorable. Kevin can be your personal guide by arrangement. No pets, children by arrangement

CHARLESTON   *8km N of Charleston*

Bird's Ferry Lodge   *Lodge B&B*
Alison & Andre Gygax
Bird's Ferry Road, Charleston 7650

0800 212 207   Mob 021 337 217
fishax2@yahoo.co.nz
www.bnb.co.nz/birdsferry.html

Double $110-$165   Single $90-$145   (Full Breakfast)
Child free under 12 years Dinner $45
Ask about our winter rates
Credit cards accepted Children welcome
3 Queen (3 bdrm)   Bathrooms: 3 Ensuite

Welcome to our newly built lodge. Awaiting your visit are tranquility, 360 degree views of the Tasman Sea, Paparoa Mountains and native bush. Spacious ensuite rooms with luxury touches. Step onto the deck from your room and enjoy the ocean sunset from the heated spa. Guest lounge features house bar and central log fire. Breakfast includes freshly baked bread and home baking. Gourmet dinner using home-grown produce. We will be happy to assist with a huge range of local activities. We share our lodge with two norfolk terriers.

REEFTON   *Reefton Central*

Historic Reef Cottage B&B and Café
Susan & Ronnie Standfield   *B&B Self-contained*
51-55 Broadway, Reefton

Tel **(03) 732 8440**   0800 770 440   Fax (03) 732 8440
reefton@clear.net.nz   www.reefcottage.co.nz

Double $80-$135 Single $65-$115 (Full Breakfast)
Child 1/2 price Dinner $10-$35 Credit cards accepted
1 King/Twin 1 Queen 2 Double (4 bdrm)
Bathrooms: 2 Ensuite 2 Private

Built in 1887 from native timbers for a local barrister.
This historical Edwardian home has been carefully
renovated to add light and space without losing its
olde world charm. Elegantly decorated, the house
features charming character rooms serviced daily. Reefton is nestled in historic gold/coal mining
country between native beech forests and the Inangahua River, Reef Cottage is unrivalled as the finest
accommodation in Reefton. Reef Café next door offers casual dining, specialist coffees and decadent
desserts. Trout fishing, hiking, 4WD and tours available.

REEFTON   *Reefton central*

Quartz Lodge   *B&B*
Toni and Ian Walker
78 Sheil Street, Reefton, West Coast

Tel **(03) 732 8383** 0800 302 725 Fax (03) 732 8083
Mob 027 619 4520 quartz-lodge@xtra.co.nz
www.quartzlodge.co.nz

Double $100-$130 Single $75-$95 (Full Breakfast)
Child $35 Credit cards accepted Children welcome
1 King 1 Queen 1 Twin 1 Single (3 bdrm)
Bathrooms: 1 Ensuite 1 Private 1 Guests share

You will be sure of a friendly welcome when you arrive
at Quartz Lodge, in the heart of Reefton. Guests only
entrance will take you upstairs to huge picture windows in every room. Luxurious beds, robes and so
much more. We are surprised how often our guests compliment us on our comfortable beds. Laundry
service available. Complimentary coffee and a selection of teas are available in your private lounge/
dining area. We pride ourselves on making you feel at home. Quality and comfort says it all.

PUNAKAIKI   *45km N of Greymouth*

The Rocks Homestay   *B&B Homestay*
Peg & Kevin Piper
No. 33 Hartmount Place, PO Box 16,
Punakaiki 7850 West Coast

Tel **(03) 731 1141** 0800 272 164 Fax (03) 731 1141
therocks@minidata.co.nz www.therockshomestay.com

Double $110-$175 Single $100-$120
(Special Breakfast) Child $40-$60
Dinner $35-$45 by arrangement S/C House $140-$180
Credit cards accepted
2 Queen 2 Twin (3 bdrm) Bathrooms: 3 Ensuite

At Punakaiki, in view of the Pancake Rocks and Blowholes, adjacent Truman Track and beach,
The Rocks Homestay sits above the forest - comfortable, modern, well-appointed, warm, friendly
- unique in its wilderness location. Huge windows provide astounding panoramic views - coast, sea,
crags, rainforest, National Park. Healthy breakfasts with home baking. Home-cooked evening meals
(by arrangement). Take time to experience unspoiled New Zealand. Walk a track, stroll on a beach,
photograph limestone gorges, enjoy the reference library. Midway Greymouth and Westport, turn 200
metres north of Truman Track.

PUNAKAIKI - BARRYTOWN

Golden Sands Homestay   *Homestay*
Sue & Tom Costelloe
4 Golden Sands Road, Barrytown, Runanga

Tel (03) 731 1115 Fax (03) 731 1116
goldensands@paradise.net.nz
www.bnb.co.nz/goldensandshomestay.html

Double $85-$95 Single $50   (Continental Breakfast)
Child by arrangement   Dinner by arrangement
Credit cards accepted
2 Queen 1 Twin (3 bdrm)
Bathrooms: 1 Ensuite 2 Private

Nestled between the Paparoa Range and the Tasman Sea on the Greymouth to Westport Scenic Highway, Golden Sands Homestay offers a friendly atmosphere and comfortable rooms. It is handy to Punakaiki, the Pancake Rocks, and the Paparoa National Park to the north, with Greymouth a 25 minute drive to the south. As well as stunning views and wonderful sunsets, Golden Sands Homestay has Sky TV, internet facilities, a cosy fire in winter and a contented cat. Access and facilities for disabled people. Nearby restaurants.

PUNAKAIKI - BARRYTOWN

Kallyhouse   *B&B Homestay Self-contained*
Kathleen & Alister Schroeder
13A Cargill Road,
Barrytown RD 1, Westland

Tel (03) 731 1006   Fax (03) 731 1106
kallyhouse@xtra.co.nz
www.bnb.co.nz/schroeder.html

Double $100-$120 Single $75   (Continental Breakfast)
Credit cards accepted
3 Queen 1 Twin (4 bdrm)
Bathrooms: 2 Guests share

We have a new spacious home on a quiet rear section, a garden setting, with native bush backdrop and sea views. We offer a self-contained flat downstairs, with queen-size waterbed, twin beds in spacious living area, full kitchen, washing machine, parking and separate entrance. We also have two queen rooms upstairs. Breakfast with host. Punakaiki pancake rocks and adventure activities in Paparoa National Park, 15 minutes north. Greymouth is 20 minutes south. Turn at Barrytown Hotel corner, past 3 houses on left, up the lane, house on left.

NINE MILE CREEK

The Breakers   *B&B Homestay*
Frank & Barbara Ash
PO Box 188,
Greymouth, Westland

Tel (03) 762 7743   0800 350 590 Fax (03) 762 7733
stay@breakers.co.nz
www.breakers.co.nz

Double $150-$235 (Full Breakfast)
Credit cards accepted
2 King 2 Queen 2 Twin (4 bdrm)
Bathrooms: 4 Ensuite

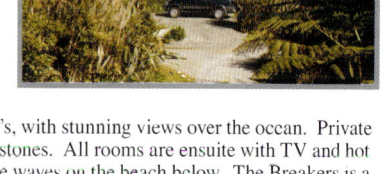

One of the West Coast's most spectacularly located B&B's, with stunning views over the ocean. Private beach access allows you to fossick for jade and beautiful stones. All rooms are ensuite with TV and hot beverage making facilities. Fall asleep to the sound of the waves on the beach below. The Breakers is a wonderful base to visit the Pancake Rocks, the Paparoa National Park and the best stretch of coastline in NZ. Sorry, unsuitable for children.

GREYMOUTH *4km S of Greymouth*

Tides *Homestay*
Ib Pupich
5 Stanton Crescent,
Greymouth

Tel (03) 768 4348 Fax (03) 768 4348
IbPupich@xtra.co.nz
www.bnb.co.nz/pupich.html

Double $100-$110 Single $90-$95 (Full Breakfast)
Credit cards accepted
1 King/Twin (1 bdrm)
Bathrooms: 1 Ensuite

We offer warm hospitality in our lovely home overlooking the Tasman Sea and south to Mount Cook and Tasman. You can be assured of a relaxed stay in this quiet street only 5 minutes walk from the beach. Your room, with its private deck is spacious and comfortable with lovely sea views. There is much to do and see in the area; lakes, rivers, wonderful bush and coastline walks. Trout fishing and golf or just laze on the deck and watch the sun go down.

GREYMOUTH *Greymouth Central*

Ardwyn House *Homestay*
Mary Owen
48 Chapel Street, Greymouth

Tel (03) 768 6107   Fax (03) 768 5177
Mob 027 437 6027   ardwynhouse@hotmail.com
www.bnb.co.nz/ardwynhouse.html

Double $80-$85 Single $50 (Full Breakfast)
Child ¹/2 price Credit cards accepted
Children welcome
2 Queen 3 Single (3 bdrm)
Bathrooms: 1 Guests share

Ardwyn House is 3 minutes walk from the town centre in a quiet garden setting offering sea, river and town views. The house was built in the 1920's and is a fine example of an imposing residence with fine woodwork and leadlight windows, whilst being a comfortable and friendly home. Greymouth's ideally situated for travellers touring the West Coast being central with good choice of restaurants. We offer a courtesy car service to and from local travel centres and also provide off-street parking.

GREYMOUTH *6km S of Greymouth*

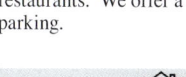

Paroa Homestay (formerly Pam's Homestay)
Pam Sutherland
345 Main South Road, Greymouth

Tel (03) 762 6769 Fax (03) 762 6765
Mob 021 118 6591 paroahomestay@xtra.co.nz
www.bnb.co.nz/paroahomestay.html

Double $100-$125 Single $79-$99
(Special Breakfast) Child neg Credit cards accepted
Children over 5 years welcome
1 King/Twin 1 King 1 Double (3 bdrm)
Bathrooms: 1 Ensuite 1 Private 1 Guests share

Relax on terraces overlooking the sea and watch incredible sunsets. 3 minutes walk to the beach. Towering trees, native bush surrounds spacious classic home with luxurious guest lounge. Excellent restaurants within 3-6 minutes drive. Experience superb continental breakfast as baking and cooking is Pam's forté (previously owning Greymouth's busiest café/bar). Pam enjoys hospitality, antiques, china, organic gardening and bush walking. Courtesy transport from train/bus (including complimentary drive to Shantytown). Off-street parking. Pam has operated this homestay for 10 years. Guests comments: 'best breakfast in NZ', 'wonderful hospitality'.

GREYMOUTH   *1km S of Greymouth*

Rosewood   *B&B*
Rhonda & Stephan Palten
20 High Street, Greymouth

Tel (03) 768 4674   0800 185 748   Fax (03) 768 4694
Mob 027 242 7080   rosewoodnz@xtra.co.nz
www.rosewoodnz.co.nz

Double $110-$150   Single $85-$125 (Full Breakfast)
Child $20   Credit cards accepted Children welcome
1 King/Twin 4 Queen 1 Twin 2 Single (5 bdrm)
Bathrooms: 3 Ensuite 1 Private 1 Guests share

Rosewood is one of Greymouth's finest old restored
homes, a few minutes walk from the town centre with
its restaurants & cafés. Rooms are well appointed and
feature quality king and queen beds with modern ensuites or bathroom. Separate guest lounge/dining
room with complimentary tea/coffee and homemade biscuits. Hosts Rhonda, her German husband
Stephan and their 2 children allow you to recover from your journey or activities of the day and offer a
superb breakfast making a perfect start to your day.

GREYMOUTH   *3km S of Greymouth*

Maryglen Homestay   *Homestay*
Allison & Glen Palmer
20 Weenink Road, Karoro, Greymouth

Tel (03) 768 0706   0800 627 945   Fax (03) 768 0599
Mob 027 4380 479   mary@bandb.co.nz
www.bandb.co.nz

Double $105-$130   Single $85-$95
(Continental Breakfast)   Child neg   Dinner $30pp
Credit cards accepted   Children welcome
2 King/Twin 1 Queen 1 Single (3 bdrm)
Bathrooms: 3 Ensuite

What an amazing location - Guests comments about our home set in bush overlooking the sea.
Downstairs rooms have their own entrance onto large deck where you can enjoy the bush and amazing
sunsets. Each bedroom has hot drink facilities, TV and reading materials. Our dog, Lady, and cat, Misty,
enjoy our guests company. Allison enjoys gardening and playing bridge (games can be arranged) while
Glen is a jigsaw fan. We are off main road, level access, parking. Complimentary pick up from bus/train.
Scenic tours arranged.

GREYMOUTH   *6km S of Greymouth*

Sunsetview   *Homestay*
Russell & Jill Fairhall
335 Main South Road,
Greymouth 7801

Tel (03) 762 6616   Fax (03) 762 6616
sunsetview@xtra.co.nz
www.bnb.co.nz/sunsetview.html

Double $100-$140   Single $90   (Full Breakfast)
Credit cards accepted
1 King/Twin 1 King 1 Queen (3 bdrm)
Bathrooms: 2 Ensuite 1 Private

Russell and Jill welcome you to our sunny modern home with amazing sea and mountain views. We
offer well-appointed superior bedrooms. TV in rooms. Home cooked meals available on request. Tea,
coffee and laundry facilities available. Outdoor areas with pool and barbecue. Short walk to beach.
Trips arranged to visit modern and old gold mining sites. Fishing trips can be arranged. We offer a
courtesy car service to and from local travel centres and provide off-street parking.

GREYMOUTH   *12km N of Greymouth*

Westway   *Homestay*
John Best & Wayne Margison
58 Herd Street, Dunollie, Greymouth

Tel (03) 762 7077   Fax (03) 762 7377
Mob 027 495 2844   westway@xtra.co.nz
www.westway.co.nz

Double $100-$120 Single $85-$95 King/Twin $100
(Continental Breakfast) Child neg Dinner $25-$40
Credit cards accepted Children welcome
1 King/Twin 2 Queen (3 bdrm)
Bathrooms: 1 Ensuite 1 Private 1 Guests share

Just minutes from Greymouth, Westway is situated in a native forest clad valley, including an historic tunnel and glow worms. Only 5 minutes drive from a sandy beach. There are private places in the garden where you can experience nature and the tranquility of Westway. We have a friendly and relaxing lifestyle; take pleasure in sharing our local knowledge and in creating an environment that visitors enjoy. There's space for your leisure equipment Evening meals available. Complimentary transport. Come and let us spoil you.

GREYMOUTH   *15km S of Greymouth*

Chapel Hill   *B&B Farmstay Homestay*
Gay Sweeney
783 Rutherglen Road, Paroa, Greymouth

Tel (03) 762 6662   Fax (03) 762 6664
Mob 025 816 736
gay@chapelhill.co.nz   www.chapelhill.co.nz

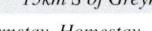

Double $90-$110 Single $75 (Full Breakfast)
Dinner $25   Credit cards accepted
2 Queen 1 Double 2 Single (3 bdrm)
Bathrooms: 1 Ensuite 1 Private 2 Guests share

Touch the ferns out your window! Spectacular architect-
designed country stay in a rainforest/lifestyle farm
setting, 15 minutes south of Greymouth on the Christchurch/Glaciers highway. Huge log fire, free email, and big comfy beds with electric blankets. Hearty country breakfasts included. Superb day trips to Punakaiki Blowholes, Lakes Brunner, Kaniere and Mahinapua (30-45 minutes) and skiing at Porters Pass (2 hours). Non-smoking. Pets, farm and forest wildlife on the property. Unusual multi-level design is unsuitable for children under 12 or disabled.

GREYMOUTH   *3km N of Greymouth*

Oak Lodge   *B&B Homestay*
Colette and Brian MacKenzie
Coal Creek, State Highway 6, Greymouth

Tel (03) 768 6832   0800 351 000   Fax (03) 768 4362
oaklodgenz@xtra.co.nz
www.oaklodge.co.nz

Double $130-$290 Single $110 (Full Breakfast)
Credit cards accepted Children welcome
2 King/Twin 2 Queen 1 Twin (5 bdrm)
Bathrooms: 4 Ensuite 1 Private

This 100 year old farmhouse is full of character, and
only 3 minutes from Greymouth. It is surrounded by extensive gardens, has a spa/jacuzzi, swimming pool, sauna, tennis court, billiard room, guest lounge and laundry facilities. This 20 acre hobby farm has an unusual collection of black sheep, hens, and a very friendly donkey called Finias. Colette and Brian, who have travelled themselves, extend a very warm welcome to you. A generous farmhouse breakfast is served. "We came as guests and leave as friends"

MOANA - LAKE BRUNNER   *35km E of Greymouth*

Lancewood   *B&B Homestay*
Jan & Simon Wilkins
2177 Arnold Valley Road, Moana, Lake Brunner

Tel (03) 738 0844   Mob 027 436 9706
lancewood.upon.moana@paradise.net.nz
www.bnb.co.nz/lancewood.html

Double $90-$130   Single $65-$120
(Continental Breakfast)   Bunk room for older children
Credit cards accepted   Child by arrangement
1 Queen 1 Twin (2 bdrm)
Bathrooms: 1 Ensuite 1 Host share

A very warm welcome awaits you at Lancewood. Relax with us enjoying captivating views of Lake Brunner, amidst a scenic backdrop of the Southern Alps. Spend time enjoying bush walks, gold panning, trout fishing or a scenic launch trip. Your choice of accommodation is either a double queen bed with ensuite, complimentary tea and coffee facilities plus TV and fridge or a twin single room with a host share bathroom. A continental breakfast is served at a time suitable to you. A bunk room is also available for older children.

LAKE BRUNNER - MOANA   *35km E of Greymouth*

Lake View B&B   *Self-contained*
Brent & Madeline Beadle
18 Johns Road, Moana, Westland

Tel (03) 738 0886   Fax (03) 738 0887
Mob 027 431 8022   browntrout@minidata.co.nz
www.fishnhunt.co.nz/guides/brunner/index.htm

Double $100-$120   Single $90-$100
(Continental Breakfast)   Child $20
Credit cards accepted   Children welcome
1 King 2 Single (2 bdrm)
Bathrooms: 1 Private

Lake View B&B offers guests fantastic views of Lake Brunner from the lounge, the decking or while lying in bed. Accommodation is a very private self-contained cottage adjacent to our house only 5 minutes walk to the village centre, café or hotel. The lake is famous for its trout fishing 365 days and Brent is a fishing guide. Lake tours, canoe hire, bush walks and a pottery are all close by. The Tranz Alpine stops at Moana. Christchurch is 3 hours away by road.

HOKITIKA   *3km S of Hokitika*

Meadowbank   *Rural Homestay*
Alison & Tom Muir
Takutai Road,
RD 3, Hokitika

Tel (03) 755 6723   Fax (03) 755 6723
www.bnb.co.nz/meadowbank.html

Double $80   Single $50   (Full Breakfast)
Child ¹/₂ price Dinner by arrangement
Children welcome
1 Double 2 Single (2 bdrm)
Bathrooms: 1 Guests share

Tom and Alison welcome you to their lifestyle property, situated just minutes south of Hokitika. Our large home, which we share with 2 cats, is modern, sunny and warm, and has a large garden. Nearby we have the beach, excellent golf-links, an old gold mine, river, and of course Hokitika, with all its attractions. Directions: travel south 2km from south end of Hokitika Bridge on SH6, turn right - 200 metres on right. North-bound traffic - look for sign 1km north of Golf-links and Paddleboat.

HOKITIKA CENTRAL   *Hokitika central*

Teichelmann's Bed & Breakfast   *B&B*
Frances & Brian Ward
20 Hamilton Street, Hokitika

Tel (03) 755 8232   0800 743 742 Fax (03) 755 8239
teichel@xtra.co.nz   www.teichelmanns.co.nz

Double $165-$185   Single $120-$140
(Full Breakfast)
Visa and Mastercards accepted
1 King/Twin 4 King 1 Double 1 Single (6 bdrm)
Bathrooms: 5 Ensuite 1 Private

Teichelmanns for fine accommodation. Frances
and Brian welcome you to 'catch your breath and
breakfast' at our quiet yet central location in the
heritage area of Hokitika. Our large historic home
offers ensuite rooms with king beds.

Outside, 'Teichy's Garden Cottage' our premium studio
ensuite unit features a double spa bath overlooking a
private garden area.

Close by are many interesting craft galleries, restaurants
and cafés. Stroll to the beach in the evening and enjoy a
West Coast sunset.

HOKITIKA *1.5km N of Hokitika*

Hokitika Heritage Lodge *B&B Homestay*
Dianne & Chris Ward
46 Alpine View, Hokitika

Tel (03) 755 7357   0800 261 949
Fax (03) 755 8760   Mob 0274 371 254
hokitikaheritage@xtra.co.nz
www.bnb.co.nz/hokitikaheritage.html

Double $145-$185 Single $145-$185
(Full Breakfast) Dinner by arrangement
Credit cards accepted
3 Queen 1 Single (3 bdrm)
Bathrooms: 3 Ensuite

Your hosts, Chris and Dianne, have loved hosting B&B guests for 10 years at our previous address: Terrace View Homestays Hokitika.

We now invite you to stay at our attractive newly created heritage themed lodge/home, specifically planned for comfort and experience of our guests. You can enjoy the choice of 3 West Coast themed rooms each providing queen beds and ensuites. The *Gold Room* also provides for those guests who like separate beds.

Our *Gold and Heritage Rooms* allow you to take in views of the mountains, sea and town, while the Jade Room gives you bush and morning sun views. All rooms include views, ensuites, tea / coffee making facilities, Sky TV. Internet service is available.

Our stunning *Dining Room* gives you the opportunity to continue enjoying the views along with a four course dinner, while breakfast will be served in our sunny *Living Room* with homemade jams, breads and breakfast treats.

Chris and I are happy to transport you to the glowworms at night and include a short town history tour; also to a restaurant if desired. Our animals are really aging now: Whippy our white cat, and Cinders our black, well, grey, Lab, who both live mainly outside the lodge/home.

Find us by following the signs from the main road to the airport along Tudor Street, turning left into Airport Drive. Turn right at the top of the hill into Alpine View. Travel to the end of the street, turning left into our drive. Follow the road around the house to a parking area, and our main entrance, where you will be warmly welcomed.

Relax with a complimentary drink in our lounge while experiencing magnificent views from the sea to the mountains. Sunsets are magical.

HOKITIKA   *1km N of Hokitika*

Montezuma   *Homestay*
Russell & Alison Alldridge
261 Revell Street,
Hokitika, Westland

Tel (03) 755 7025
www.bnb.co.nz/montezuma.html

Double $95 Single $65   (Continental Breakfast)
1 Queen 1 Double (2 bdrm)
Bathrooms: 1 Ensuite 1 Host share

Welcome to Montezuma by the sea. So named after
a ship that was wrecked here in 1865. Alison a
Queenslander, Russell a genuine West Coaster. Enjoy a
leisurely walk along the beach, watch the breathtaking sunset, visit the nearby glowworm dell and take
time out to enjoy our West Coast hospitality. Directions: when travelling to Hokitika from north take
first turn to your right (Richards Drive). Our house is the last on the street. When travelling from south
turn left at the last street out of town.

HOKITIKA   *0.9km E of Hokitika*

Larry's Rest *B&B Homestay Self-contained*
Linda & Paul Hewson
188 Rolleston Street, Hokitika

Tel (03) 755 7636   Mob 021 220 3295
info@larrysrest.co.nz   www.larrysrest.co.nz

Double $110-$150   Single $100-$125   (Full Breakfast)
Apartment $130 double
Credit cards accepted   Children welcome
2 Queen 2 Twin (4 bdrm)
Bathrooms: 1 Ensuite 2 Private

Receive a warm welcome at Larry's Rest where outdoor enthusiasts Linda and Paul will willingly share
their extensive knowledge of South Island walks, activities and attractions, enabling you to make the
most of your holiday. Choose from our queen room (ensuite), twin room (own bathroom) or secluded
self-contained apartment with twin room and queen room, opening onto a private garden/outdoor living
area. Spacious living area, kitchen/dining, laundry. Wheelchair friendly bathroom. Families welcome.
Signposted from the main highway opposite the Four Square store.

HOKITIKA - UPPER KOKATAHI   *28km E of Hokitika*

Farmstay Self-contained
Trish & Terry Sheridan
Middle Branch Road,
Upper Kokatahi RD 1, Hokitika

Tel (03) 755 7967   tpsheridan@xtra.co.nz
www.bnb.co.nz/sheridan.html

Double $100   Single $60   (Full Breakfast)
Child neg   Dinner $30 by arrangement
Self-contained unit from $75
Children welcome   Pets welcome
1 Queen 2 Double 3 Twin (6 bdrm)
Bathrooms: 1 Ensuite 2 Guests share

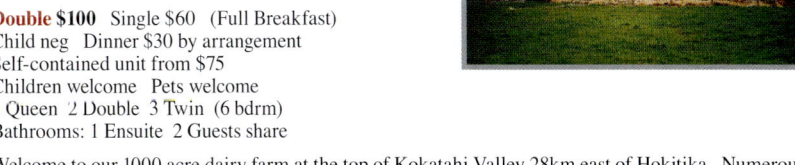

Welcome to our 1000 acre dairy farm at the top of Kokatahi Valley 28km east of Hokitika. Numerous
day walks, 3 rivers with trout fishing and kayaking and Lake Kaniere are all minutes away. Share our
newly renovated home or stay in our fully serviced self-contained unit. We enjoy meeting people and
love travelling. Terry enjoys current affairs and all sports while Trish is happy in the kitchen or garden.
Enjoy dining with us in peaceful surroundings.

HOKITIKA   *1km N of Town*

Ocean Crest B&B   *B&B*
Lesley Staniland
8 Whitcombe Terrace, Seaview, Hokitika

Tel (03) 755 7125   Fax (03) 755 7125
Mob 027 220 7620   thewordsmith@xtra.co.nz
www.bnb.co.nz/oceancrest.html

Double $95-$120 Single $75-$95
(Continental Breakfast)
Child $50   Pets welcome
1 King 1 Twin 1 Single (3 bdrm)
Bathrooms: 1 Ensuite 1 Host share

Absolutely stunning views of Alps, Hokitika and Tasman
Sea. Our interests: arts, aviation, history, travel, meeting people. Easels, loom and spinning wheels available for use. Make up a small group and relax in soothing surroundings. Small group arts, history tours. Visit the Coast's wonders with friendly, informative hosts, or be independent. Not suitable elderly or toddlers. Pets by negotiation. Close to airport. Bus, airport and Tranz Alpine pickup from Greymouth and Hokitika. From Main Road turn into Tudor Street then left 3 times.

HOKITIKA   *7km E of Hokitika*

Riverside Villa   *B&B Homestay*
Margaret & Alan Stevens
Woodstock-Rimu Road, RD 3, Hokitika

Tel (03) 755 6466   Mob 0274 371 515
amstevens@actrix.co.nz
www.bnb.co.nz/riversidevilla.html

Double $80-$110 Single $65 (Full Breakfast)
Dinner $25 by arrangement
1 Queen 1 Twin (2 bdrm)
Bathrooms: 1 Guests share

Set in extensive grounds with tranquil river and
mountain views, Riverside Villa is a haven for relaxation a short drive away from Hokitika. We combine the elegance of a 100 year old villa with the warmth of large open plan lounge and sunny verandahs. An ideal place for peaceful stopover. With the Hokitika river on the boundary, it is a fisherman's paradise with our own glowworm grotto. We are keen travellers, have an extensive knowledge of NZ outdoors and enjoy meeting people. Warm hospitality assured.

HOKITIKA   *2km E of Hokitika*

Craidenlie Lodge   *B&B Separate/Suite*
Janette & Laurie Anderson
Hau Hau Road, Blue Spur, Hokitika

Tel (03) 755 5063   0800 361 361   Fax (03) 755 5063
Mob 025 201 6126   l.anderson@xtra.co.nz
www.craidenlielodge.co.nz

Double $180-$280 Single $180-$280 (Full Breakfast)
Credit cards accepted
5 Queen 2 Twin (5 bdrm)
Bathrooms: 3 Ensuite 1 Guests share

Our 6500 square foot lodge is located on 21 acres and is
surrounded in native kahikatea trees providing complete quiet and privacy. A great place for a retreat or just time out. Most guests base themselves in Hokitika for visits to the glaciers and Punakaiki, allow two nights. Laurie and Janette welcome you to Craidenlie Lodge, both are widely travelled and have many experiences to share with you. Laurie a retired police officer and commercial pilot, Janette is a health professional with a keen interest in quilting.

RUATAPU
12km S of Hokitika

Berwick's Hill *B&B Country Stay*
Eileen & Roger Berwick
Ruatapu, Ruatapu-Ross Road,
State Highway 6, RD 3, Hokitika

Tel (03) 755 7876 Fax (03) 755 7870
Mob 025 673 7387 berwicks@xtra.co.nz
www.bnb.co.nz/berwickshill.html

Double $100-$120 Single $70 (Full Breakfast)
Dinner $40 by arrangement Credit cards accepted
1 Queen 2 King single (2 bdrm)
Bathrooms: 1 Ensuite 1 Private

Welcome to Berwick's Hill. We offer you a warm and relaxed stay in our comfortable home. Magnificent views of the Tasman Sea and the Southern Alps are seen from the main living areas. Experience the sunsets and sunrises. We are close to Lake Mahinapua, bush walks, the beach and golf course. We run sheep and cattle and grow pine trees on our hobby farm. We have one farm dog and we share our home with our cat and our house dog.

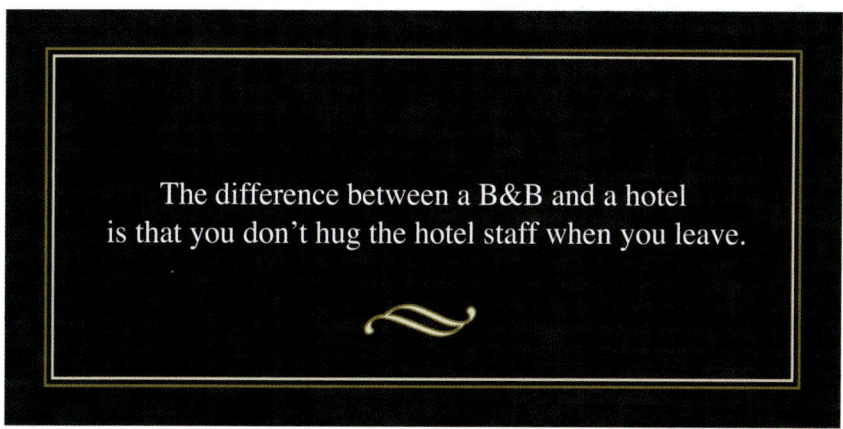

The difference between a B&B and a hotel
is that you don't hug the hotel staff when you leave.

HARIHARI
1km N of Harihari

Carrickfergus Rural Homestay
B&B Homestay Self-contained
Lindsay Grenfell & Catherine Healy
432 Robertson Road, Harihari 7953, South Westland

Tel (03) 753 3124 Fax (03) 753 3124
Mob 021 152 9406 info@carrickfergus.co.nz
www.carrickfergus.co.nz

Double $146 Single $85 (Continental Breakfast)
Dinner $40 -3 course b/a Credit cards accepted
3 Queen 1 Double 2 Single (4 bdrm)
Bathrooms: 2 Ensuite 1 Private

Welcome to our home which is north facing enjoying panoramic mountain & rural views 5km off SH6. Enjoy tranquil surrounds, hear native birds, meet our aged Basset. Landscape gardens clad with native trees, ferns & orchids adjoin our farmlet where we care for calves and sheep. Breakfast in the privacy of your self-contained suite or with us. Take time out to explore Harihari Coastal Walkway, local walks, La Fontaine stream for trout, glacier flights or White Heron Colony.

HARIHARI   *0.5km S of Hari Hari*

Approved

Wapiti Park Homestead   *Luxury Farmstay / Country Lodge*
Bev & Grant Muir
RD 1, Hari Hari 7953, South Westland

Tel (03) 753 3074 0800 WAPITI Fax (03) 753 3024
wapitipark@xtra.co.nz www.wapitipark.co.nz

Spoil yourself!

Double $165-$345 Single $125-$295

(Special Breakfast) Dinner $65 Credit cards accepted
3 King/Twin 2 King 4 Single (5 bdrm)
Bathrooms: 4 Ensuite 1 Private

Hosts Grant and Beverleigh invite you to join them and discover the unique experience of staying at Wapiti Park Homestead. Enjoy a special combination of elegance, informal sophistication, and warm hospitality. Relax in complete comfort and affordable luxury.

Nestled beneath the forest-clad foothills of the Southern Alps and set in tranquil surroundings amid extensive gardens, our modern colonial style Lodge is built on the site of the original Hari Hari accommodation house, coaching stop and post office. The Homestead overlooks its own small farm which specialises in the breeding of wapiti (Rocky Mountain elk). Join Grant on the 6pm tour to handfeed the wapiti, meet the farm pet Vicki, and learn about elk antler velvet and it's potential health benefits.

Enjoy spacious indoor/outdoor areas; large bedrooms with superior comfort beds and ensuites or private facilities; two lounges and a trophy games room; a well stocked bar fridge and selection of NZ wines; and our renowned *all you can eat* country style five course dinners. Special diets catered for by prior arrangement.

Our location on State Highway 6 makes us the ideal stopover between the Nelson/Christchurch - Wanaka/Queenstown areas. However to explore this scenic wonderland of rainforests, glaciers, lakes and National Parks; to pursue the challenges of our renowned brown trout fishery; to hunt; or to simply catch your breath and relax, a minimum two night stay is recommended. Log-on to our website www.wapitipark.co.nz for our suggested activities programs and more information. Unsuitable for children under 12. Advance booking recommended.

"Outstanding - five star at its best" (E&L Aust).
"Well above expectations. Fantastic food and hospitality" (M&J UK).
"We loved it. Best stay of our whole trip. Super food, wonderful elk and hosts" (S&J USA)

WHATAROA   *35km N of Franz Josef*

Matai Lodge   *Farmstay*
Glenice & Jim Purcell
Whataroa, South Westland

Tel (03) 753 4156   0800 787 235   Fax (03) 753 4156
Mob 021 395 068   jpurcell@xtra.co.nz
www.bnb.co.nz/matailodgewhataroa.html

Double $150-$180 Single $120
(Full Breakfast) Dinner $40pp
1 King/Twin 1 King 2 Single (3 bdrm)
Bathrooms: 1 Ensuite 1 Private

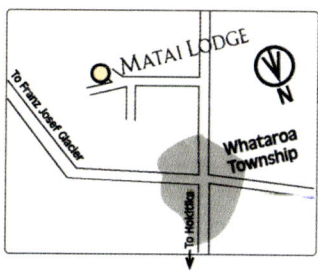

Matai Lodge rests in the tranquil valley 20 minutes north
of Franz Josef Glacier in the small farming community of Whataroa.

You are welcome to share with us our modern spacious home on the 400 acre farm of sheep, cows, and
farm dog. Upstairs is a suite of a king-size room and twin room with conservatory and private bathroom
and downstairs a king-size ensuite. You are welcome to join us for a home cooked dinner with NZ wine,
over which we enjoy hearing tales from your home, and we will help you discover ours.

With local advice and activity bookings available our motto
is *'A Stranger Is A Friend We Have Yet To Meet'*. You will
need at least two days to see the glaciers, walk in the World
Heritage Park, kayak on the Okirito Lagoon, or visit the White
Heron Bird Sanctuary by jet boat and see the spectacular
scenery, or go horse trekking.

Glenice and Jim play golf at the scenic golf course in
Whataroa, green fees $10, clubs available. Glenice has
travelled to Japan teaching felting, weaving and spinning and
enjoyed Japanese customs and language and being hosted
by her many friends there. Jim and Glenice look forward to
sharing their home and tranquil scenic paradise with you.

Driving time from Matai Lodge to: Christchurch 5 hours, Picton 6 hours, Nelson 6 hours,
Queenstown 6 hours, Wanaka 4 hours, Greymouth 2 hours, Whataroa 3km, and Franz Josef 20
minutes. Also available: Tel/fax, email, Sky TV.

WHATAROA - SOUTH WESTLAND
13km N of Whataroa/10 mins

Mt Adam Lodge   *B&B Farmstay*
Elsa & Mac MacRae
State Highway 6, Whataroa,
South Westland

Tel (03) 753 4030   0800 675 137   Fax (03) 753 4264
mtadamlodge@paradise.net.nz
www.mountadamlodge.co.nz

Double $90-$120 Single $75-$90
(Continental Breakfast) Credit cards accepted
2 Queen 1 Double 4 Twin (7 bdrm)
Bathrooms: 5 Ensuite 1 Guests share

If you're wanting to escape the crowds in the busy tourist centres then we are an ideal place for you to stay. Just a short 35 minute drive north of Franz Josef Glacier. We are situated on our farm at the foot of Mt Adam surrounded by farmlands and beautiful native bush. Our lodge is just newly established and offers comfortable accommodation and a fully licensed restaurant. You can stroll along the river bank and the farm tracks meeting our variety of animals along the way.

WHATAROA
30km N of Franz Josef Glacier

Heritage Gateway B&B   *B&B Homestay*
Clare & Rob Shaw
State Highway 6, Whataroa, South Westland

Tel (03) 753 4158   0800 466 108   Fax (03) 753 4159
heritage.gateway@xtra.co.nz
www.bnb.co.nz/heritage.html

Double $100-$130 Single $70-$100
(Continental Breakfast)
Credit cards accepted Children welcome
3 Queen 1 Twin (4 bdrm)
Bathrooms: 2 Ensuite 1 Private

Rob and Clare invite you to Whataroa, gateway to South Westland's World Heritage Area. We are just 20 minutes north of Franz Josef Glacier village. Here we offer a friendly quiet retreat from the busy Glacier towns in our very comfortable, spacious 1930's home. We both enjoy meeting people and with our experience in the tourist information industry we can provide you with lots of local knowledge. Just relax and enjoy the scenery or experience some of the many local activities. Pet cat on property.

WHATAROA
3.6km N of Whataroa

Whataroa Country Home Stay   *B&B Homestay*
Stellamaris & Bruce Graham
360 Whataroa Flat Road,
RD 1, Whataroa

Tel (03) 753 4130
bruceandstell@hotmail.com
www.bnb.co.nz/whataroa.html

Double $110-$115 Single $80-$100
(Continental Breakfast)
1 Queen 2 Twin (3 bdrm)
Bathrooms: 1 Guests share 1 Host share

Stay with us on our 85 hectare, 200 cow dairy farm, with a recently renovated homestead. Take in a visit to the local native White Heron colony, or travel 30 minutes south to Franz Josef and view its magnificent glacier. Skiplane or Helicopter up to a landing on the snow, or take one of the many walks. The farm has a 450 metre gravel airstrip so why not fly in, though phone first. We have 2 cats, would not mind children over 12, but no pets please.

FRANZ JOSEF GLACIER

1.5km N of Franz Josef Glacier

Holly Homestead B&B *Boutique B&B*
Gerard & Bernie Oudemans
State Highway 6, Franz Josef Glacier, South Westland

Tel **(03) 752 0299** Fax (03) 752 0298
stay@hollyhomestead.co.nz
www.hollyhomestead.co.nz

Double $190-$260 Single $160-$230 (Full Breakfast)
Credit cards accepted
2 King/Twin 2 Queen (4 bdrm)
Bathrooms: 4 Ensuite

Bernie & Gerard were both born in New Zealand and are the proud owners of one of Franz Josef's finest old timber homesteads. You are invited to share the ambience and charm of their 1920's character home - lovingly restored and extended. Spacious farmhouse style kitchen/dining with spectacular view from breakfast table, clouds permitting! Allow yourself time to enjoy this magnificent region. Relax in the comfortable guest lounge featuring native timber. 2 minute drive or 20 minute walk to/from Franz Josef township. Children 12 and over welcome.

FRANZ JOSEF

4km N of Franz Josef Glacier

Ribbonwood Retreat *B&B Separate/Suite*
Julie Wolbers & Jo Crofton
26 Greens Road, Franz Josef Glacier

Tel **(03) 752 0072** Fax (03) 752 0272
ribbon.wood@xtra.co.nz
www.ribbonwood.net.nz

Double $160-$220 Single $120
(Continental Breakfast) Credit cards accepted
2 King/Twin 1 Queen 1 Single (4 bdrm)
Bathrooms: 2 Ensuite 2 Private

Our unique Ribbonwood Retreat is set in majestic West Coast scenery. We welcome you to our home and new private cottages set in regenerating rainforest. You will love glacier and mountain views from your room! Enjoy our outdoor bath, gardens and home-made breakfast. Hosts Julie and Jo are keen outdoor enthusiasts and can give expert advice on places of interest to visit. Ribbonwood Retreat is located in quiet farmland several minutes drive north of Franz Josef Village and just 10 minutes drive to the glacier.

FRANZ JOSEF

3km S of Franz Josef Glacier

Knightswood Bed and Breakfast *B&B*
Sheryl Pearson and Gerry Findlay
State Highway 6, Franz Josef Glacier

Tel **(03) 752 0059** Fax (03) 752 0061
Mob 027 4330312 knightswood@xtra.co.nz
www.knightswood.co.nz

Double $160-$210 Single $130-$170 (Full Breakfast)
Child price dependent on age
Dinner by arrangement   Credit cards accepted
2 King/Twin 1 Queen 1 Single (3 bdrm)
Bathrooms: 2 Ensuite 1 Host share

Enjoy our modern home on 24 acres, with spectacular alpine views. 3km from Franz Josef Town, we assure you peace and tranquility. Ensuite rooms have private entrances and outdoor area. Gerry, a helicopter pilot and former wildlife ranger, and Sheryl, a teacher, are well travelled and enjoy convivial conversations and sharing experiences. Enjoy an interpretive guided walk through our own native bush, view the prolific bird life or venture further for a scenic glacial flight or hike.

Fox Glacier *0.5km W of Fox Glacier*

The Homestead *B&B Farmstay*
Noeleen & Kevin Williams
PO Box 25,
Cook Flat Road,
Fox Glacier

Tel (03) 751 0835
Fax (03) 751 0805
foxhmstd@xtra.co.nz
www.bnb.co.nz/thehomestead.html

Double $130-$160 (Full Breakfast)
Cooked Breakfast $7pp
1 King/Twin 2 Queen (3 bdrm)
Bathrooms: 2 Ensuite 1 Private

Kevin and Noeleen, welcome you to our
2200 acre beef cattle and sheep farm.

Beautiful native bush-clad mountains surround on 3 sides, and we enjoy a view of Mt Cook. Our spacious 105 year old character home, built for Kevin's grandparents has fine stained glass windows.

The breakfast room overlooks peaceful pastures to the hills, and you are served home-made yoghurt, jams, marmalade, scones etc, with a cooked breakfast if desired. The guest lounge, with its beautiful wooden panelled ceiling, has an open plan fire for cool autumn nights.

It is our pleasure to help you with helihikes, helicopter scenic flights and glacier walks. Unsuitable for small children. Bookings recommended. Smoke-free.

Directions: On Cook Flat Road, fifth house on right, 400 metres back off road before church.

*A rural retreat within walking distance of village facilities,
with Matheson (Mirror Lake) and glacier nearby.*

Fox Glacier *0 km N of Fox Glacier*

Roaring Billy Lodge *Homestay*
Kathy & Billy
PO Box 16, 21 State Highway 6,
Fox Glacier

Tel (03) 751 0815 Fax (03) 751 0085
kathynz@xtra.co.nz
www.bnb.co.nz/roaringbillylodge.html

Double $85-$100 Single $70-$90 (Special Breakfast)
Credit cards accepted
1 King/Twin 1 Double 1 Twin (2 bdrm)
Bathrooms: 1 Private 1 Guests share

Welcome to the comfort, warmth and hospitality of our 2 storey home. Our livingroom, kitchen, diningroom and veranda are upstairs and lined with local timbers, with 360 degree views of glacier valley, mountains, farms and the township. We're the closest homestay to the glacier and 2 minutes walk to all eating and tourist facilities. We are happy to book your local activities. The bus goes past our home. We offer a special cooked vegetarian breakfast. We have one cat, Koko and one dog, Angel.

Fox Glacier

Fox Glacier Homestay *Homestay*
Eunice & Michael Sullivan
64 Cook Flat Road, Fox Glacier

Tel (03) 751 0817 Fax (03) 751 0817
Mob 021 239 4212 euni@xtra.co.nz
www.bnb.co.nz/foxglacier.html

Double $90-$110 Single $70-$90
(Continental Breakfast)
Children welcome Pets welcome
1 Queen 1 Double 1 Twin 1 Single (3 bdrm)
Bathrooms: 1 Guests share 1 Host share

Eunice and Michael are third generation farming and tourism family. We have three grown children, 1 dog (Ruff), 2 cats (Bushy Tail & Tig). Our grandparents were founders of the Fox Glacier Hotel. We are a couple who enjoy meeting people and would like to share the joys of living in our little paradise (rain and all). Our home is surrounded by a large garden and have views of the mountains and Mt Cook. A 5 minute walk from township.

Fox Glacier *2km W of Fox Glacier*

Mountain View *B&B Self-contained*
Julene & Phil Silcock
Williams Drive,
Fox Glacier

Tel (03) 751 0770 Fax (03) 751 0774
gingephil@actrix.co.nz
www.bnb.co.nz/user104.html

Double $120-$140 (Continental Breakfast)
1 King 1 Double 1 Twin (3 bdrm)
Bathrooms: 3 Ensuite

Our family welcomes you to our piece of paradise. Set on 8 acres our 6 year old country home has it all, spectacular views of Mt Cook and Mt Tasman surrounded with bush clad hills and our own pond which reflects the mountains. Being fourth generation we have extensive knowledge of the area and can help organise Glacier flights and walks. Situated 2km from the village we are only minutes from cafés and restaurants. We have 2 school age children Harry, 10 and Katie, 8. 1 cat, 2 horses, 2 ponies.

Fox Glacier *160km S of Hokitika*

Misty Peaks *Homestay Boutique Accommodation*
Lea & Dave Bentley
Cook Flat Road, Fox Glacier, South Westland

Tel (03) 751 0849 Fax (03) 751 0849
davidbentley@xtra.co.nz mistypeaks.co.nz

Double $250
(Special Breakfast) Credit cards accepted
4 King/Twin 4 King (4 bdrm)
Bathrooms: 4 Ensuite 4 Private

Lea & Dave Bentley welcome you to Misty Peaks our
new purpose-built boutique accommodation. Misty
Peaks offers 4 private guest suites each with luxurious
bedding, private ensuites, hairdryers, telephone, TV
and complimentary gift basket to enjoy. Each suite has
double-opening doors to veranda, double glazing and
individual guest access.

The veranda around Misty Peaks provides a comfortable
setting to take in breathtaking views of Mt Cook and
Mt Tasman, stunning sunsets and the delightful ever-
changing rural setting.

A well appointed guest lounge with wood fire
provides a quality atmosphere to relax in and enjoy
a complimentary drink with other guests. An à la carte dinner, offering quality fresh New Zealand
produce and wines, is available every evening with all guests dining together.

Breakfast is available at a time to suit your plans for the day. Fresh fruit, hot muffins and bread, a
delicious full cooked or continental. Complimentary tea and coffee available at all times.

Our aim is to make your stay at Misty Peaks one to rememeber, and hopefully one day you will return to
our little part of paradise to share it with us again.

Offering you the very best in quality, comfort and genuine Kiwi hospitality

BRUCE BAY   *50km S of Fox Glacier*

Mulvaney Farmstay   *Farmstay*
Peter & Malai Millar
PO Box 117, Bruce Bay,
South Westland

Tel (03) 751 0865   0800 393 297   Fax (03) 751 0865
mulvaney@xtra.co.nz
www.bnb.co.nz/millar.html

Double $80-$95 **Single** $65   (Continental Breakfast)
Child n/a Dinner $30
1 Queen 1 Double 1 Twin (3 bdrm)
Bathrooms: 2 Guests share 1 Host share

Welcome to Mulvaney Farmstays! We run a beef farm consisting mainly of hereford and limosin cattle.
Our house was built in the 1920's by my Great Uncle Jack Mulvaney, for his bride to be but she never
arrived. Jack Mulvaney was of Irish descent, just as the rest of his family was who settled in this valley
130 years ago. So he lived here by himself until 1971 raising hereford cattle. We have now lived here
for 20 years with our children (who are all grown up and studying away from home).

PARINGA   *70km S of Fox Glacier*

home

Condon Farmstays   *Farmstay Homestay*
Glynis & Tony Condon
NZ Post Ltd, Lake Paringa, South Westland

Tel (03) 751 0895   Fax (03) 751 0001
condonfarms@xtra.co.nz
www.bnb.co.nz/condonfarmstays.html

Double $90 **Single** $50   (Full Breakfast)   Child $20
Dinner $30 by arrangement   Children welcome
1 Double 4 Single (3 bdrm)
Bathrooms: 1 Guests share 1 Host share

We run a 4th generation working beef farm, with a few sheep. We enjoy meeting people and have
travelled to America, England, Kenya, Australia and some parts of Europe. Our farm is nestled beneath
the bush clad foothills of the Southern Alps, close to Lake Paringa and the Paringa River. We have 3
adult children and 3 grandchildren. Our interests include hunting, jet boating, fishing, spinning, knitting
and reading.Tony is a civil marriage celebrant. We have 1 house cat and a small dog. We are members
of @home New Zealand Directions: 70km south of Fox Glacier, 50km north of Haast, 4 hours drive
from Queenstown on State Highway 6.

HAAST   *16km S of Haast*

Okuru Beach   *B&B Homestay Self-contained*
Marian & Derek Beynon
Okuru, Haast, South Westland

Tel (03) 750 0719   Fax (03) 750 0722
okurubeach@xtra.co.nz
www.okurubeach.co.nz

Double $75-$80 **Single** $50   (Continental Breakfast)
Child $20 Dinner $20 by arrangement
Self-contained $85-$90   Credit cards accepted
4 Double 6 Single (7 bdrm)
Bathrooms: 1 Ensuite 2 Private 1 Guests share

Okuru Beach gives you the opportunity to stay in a unique part of our country, in a friendly relaxed
environment. Enjoy coastal beaches with driftwood, shells and penguins in season. Walk in the
rainforest and view the native birds. We and our friendly labrador dog enjoy sharing our comfortable
home and local knowledge. Dinner served with prior notice. Our interests are our handcraft shop, coin
collecting, fishing and tramping. Also available - Seaview Cottage, self-contained sleeps 8 persons.
Directions - turn into Jacksons Bay Road, drive 14km turn into Okuru.

WEST COAST

Canterbury

Kaikoura

Hanmer Springs

7

1

Waiau

Culverden

Waikari

Castle Hill Village

Amberley

73

Oxford

Rangiora

Waikuku Beach

Lake Coleridge

Kaiapoi

Darfield

West
Melton

Christchurch,
see next page

Mt Hutt

72

Methven

Selwyn

Okains Bay

Staveley

Lincoln

Rakaia

Banks
Peninsula

Akaroa

1

Ashburton

Akaroa
Harbour

Reefton

Inchbonnie

Towns listed generally follow
a north to south route. Refer
to the index if required.

0   Kilometres   40

0   Miles   24

Christchurch
City

Ohoka
Kaiapoi
1

Christchurch
International
Airport
1
Harewood
Bryndwr
Burnside
Yaldhurst
Fendalton
St Albans
Avondale
Avonhead
Dallington
New Brighton
Ilam
Merivale
Richmond
Avonside
Christchurch
Central
Woolston
Hoon Hay
St Martins
Redcliffs
Broadfield
Mt Pleasant
Westmorland
Huntsbury
Sumner
Halswell
Cashmere
75
Lansdowne
Lyttelton
Governors Bay
Diamond
Harbour
Lyttelton
Harbour
Purau
Church Bay
Tai Tapu

0   Kilometres   5
0   Miles   3

Let Our Home be Your Home

KAIKOURA   *130km S of Blenheim*

BℬB Approved

Bay-View   *Homestay*
Margaret Woodill
296 Scarborough Street, Kaikoura

Tel (03) 319 5480   Fax (03) 319 7480
bayviewhomestay@xtra.co.nz
www.bnb.co.nz/bayviewkaikoura.html

Twin $85   Single $55 Queen ensuite $95   (Full Breakfast)
Child $15 under 14 Dinner $25   Children welcome Pets welcome
1 Queen 1 Twin 1 Single   (3 bedrooms)
Bathrooms: 1 Ensuite 1 Private 1 Guests share

Our spacious family home on Kaikoura Peninsula has splendid
mountain and sea views and is exceptionally quiet. Only 5 minutes
from the Kaikoura township, off the main highway south. The
house nestles in an acre of colourful garden and there is plenty of
off-street parking.

A guest lounge is available or you are more than welcome to
socialise with the host. Laundry facilities and tea/coffee with home-
made baking available. Traditional breakfast with home-baked
bread, muesli, home preserves, available early as required for whale/
dolphin watching guests. Enjoy breakfast in the dining area or out
on the sunny deck whilst taking in the magnificent mountain view.

We book local activities and happily meet bus or train. Margaret,
your friendly host, has lived in the area for most of her life. She
has a grown family of 4 and 7 grandchildren. Margaret enjoys
gardening, golf, bowls, sewing, choir and her amusing burmese cat.
She especially enjoys warmly welcoming guests into her home.

Guests comments: *"This B&B is an unforgettable memory for me
in NZ 5 weeks travel"* (Japan). *"Beautiful place, beautiful food,
fabulous hospitality, Margaret. Thank you for opening up your
home and welcoming us. Be back again"* (Wellington). *"Thank
you for meeting the train and showing us the area. You were highly
recommended and we absolutely endorse this"* (UK). *"Many thanks for your generous hospitality.
You and your lovely home are a credit to B&B Homestays"* (UK). *"We felt like family! Thank you
for such a lovely visit and wonderful, delicious meals. We thank you a million!"* (USA).

*"The most amazing breakfast in all of New Zealand. The views are amazing
too and so is Margaret's hospitality"* (Australia).

KAIKOURA   *5km N of Kaikoura*

Ardara Lodge   *B&B Self-contained*
Alison & Ian Boyd
233 Schoolhouse Road, RD1, Kaikoura

Tel (03) 319 5736   0800 226 164   Fax (03) 319 5732
aemboyd@xtra.co.nz   www.ardaralodge.com

Double $100-$120   Single $80-$120   Child $20
(Continental Breakfast)   Credit cards accepted
Cottage, 2-6 persons $130-$220   Children welcome
6 Queen 2 Twin 3 Single (6 bdrm) Bathrooms: 5 Ensuite

You will enjoy a relaxed and peaceful stay in a beautiful
rural setting near the magnificent Kaikoura mountains.
Relax on our deck and enjoy Alison's colourful garden
which completes the panoramic view. Enjoy our outdoor
hot tub (spa), view the Kaikoura mountains by day and
the stars by night.

Ian's great, great, Uncle Jim, left Ardara, Ireland in
1876. He bought our land here in Kaikoura in 1883 and
milked cows. He established an orchard and planted
macrocarpa trees for shelter One macrocarpa tree was
milled and used to build the cottage which was designed and built by Ian in 1998. The cottage has an
upstairs bedroom with a queen and 2 single beds. Downstairs there is a bedroom with a queen bed, a
bathroom with a shower, and a lounge, kitchen, dining room. The deck is private with a great view of
the mountains. It has been very popular with groups, families and honeymoon couples.

The house has ensuite bathrooms with queen beds, TV, fridge, settee and coffee/tea facilities. You have
your own private entrance and you can come and go as you please. We offer laundry facilities, off-street
parking, courtesy car from bus/train.

Bookings for local tourist attractions, restaurants and farm tours can be arranged. Ian's brother Murray,
has Donegal House, an Irish garden bar and restaurant, which is within walking distance. Ian is a retired
teacher and Alison a librarian. Our hobbies are tennis, golf, designing and building houses, gardening,
handcrafts, spinning and we like to travel. No smoking indoors please. We look forward to your company.
Directions: driving north, 4km from Kaikoura on SH1, turn left, 1.5km along Schoolhouse Road.

Harbour Lights - Peninsula

Ian and Alison welcome you to our two up market apartments
with one of the best views in Kaikoura. Large deck to view the
stunning sea and mountain panorama. Walk from the lounge
onto the deck and soak up the view while having breakfast.

The accommodation comprises of two self-contained suites,
both having quality beds with electric blankets, TV, DV.D,
kitchen/dining room/ lounge. Continental breakfast supplied.
Laundry facilities are shared. Undercover parking. Computer
access. Tariff: Double: $130-$160 Single $130-$160.

CANTERBURY

KAIKOURA - OARO   *22km S of Kaikoura*

Waitane Homestay   *B&B Homestay Self-contained*
Kathleen King
Oaro, RD 2, Kaikoura

Tel (03) 319 5494   Fax (03) 319 5524
waitane@xtra.co.nz
www.bnb.co.nz/waitane.html

Double $75   Single $45   (Full Breakfast) Child $20
Dinner $20 by arrangement   Credit cards accepted
1 Double 4 Single (3 bdrm)
Bathrooms: 2 Private

Waitane is 48 acres, close to the sea and looking north to the Kaikoura Peninsula. Enjoy coastal walks to the Haumuri Bluff with bird watching, fossil hunting etc, or drive to Kaikoura along our beautiful rocky coast. This is a mild climate and we grow citrus and sub-tropical fruits – mainly feijoas. Guest room in house has 2 single beds. Self-contained unit has 2 bedrooms, sleeps 4. 2 friendly cats live with us. Join me for dinner – fresh vegies, home preserves and homemade ice cream.

KAIKOURA   *Kaikoura Central*

Bevron   *B&B Homestay*
Bev & Ron Barr
196 Esplanade, Kaikoura

Tel (03) 319 5432   Fax (03) 319 5432
bevronhouse@hotmail.com
www.bnb.co.nz/bevron.html

Double $100-$110 Single $90   (Continental Breakfast)
Child 1/2 price
1 Queen 1 Double 2 Twin (2 bdrm)
Bathrooms: 2 Ensuite

We are a friendly active retired couple who enjoy meeting new people and sharing the delights of our home on the beachfront. The view from our balcony is breathtaking, giving an unobstructed panorama of sea and mountains. We have guest TV lounge and games room. There is a swimming beach opposite, with children's play area and BBQ. Kaikoura has many tourist attractions, we are happy to help with bookings. Our home is centrally located, being a short walk to restaurants, galleries and scenic attractions.

KAIKOURA   *20km SW of Kaikoura*

The Kahutara Homestead   *Farmstay*
Nikki & John Smith
PO Box 9, Kaikoura

Tel (03) 319 5580   0800 273 351   Fax (03) 319 5580
kahutarahomestead@xtra.co.nz
www.bnb.co.nz/thekahutara.html

Double $190-$210 Single $150   (Full Breakfast)
Dinner $50-$70 Credit cards accepted
2 Queen 3 Single (3 bdrm)
Bathrooms: 1 Ensuite 1 Private

The Kahutara - a haven in the hills. An award winning homestay situated on the Inland Kaikoura Route. The Alpine Pacific Triangle linking Kaikoura with the Hamner Springs thermal pool resort or fish the Clarence River for trout; 1 1/2 hours drive. We operate a 2600 acre beef cattle and sheep farm with a small thoroughbred stud. Enjoy quality homestead accommodation in well-appointed rooms, and experience country hospitality. Complimentary pre-dinner drinks and local Marlborough/Canterbury wines served with dinner. Walk the surrounding valley or enjoy lawn croquet. Whale watching, dolphin swimming, horse trekking reservations made.

KAIKOURA *130km S of Blenheim*

Churchill Park Lodge *B&B Separate/Suite*
Moira & Stan Paul
34 Churchill Street, Kaikoura, Marlborough

Tel (03) 319 5526 0800 363 690
Fax (03) 319 5526
cplodge@ihug.co.nz
www.churchillparklodge.co.nz

Double $95 Single $95
(Continental Breakfast)
Child $20 Credit cards accepted
Children welcome
1 Queen 1 Double 1 Single (2 bdrm)
Bathrooms: 2 Ensuite

We proudly offer you the choice of 2 separate
upstairs suites with ensuite bathrooms, TV, fridge,
lounge settee, dining suite, and tea/coffee making
facilities including coffee percolator, heater and
electric blankets. We have designed your room
to guarantee your stay with us is comfortable and
enjoyable. Our rooms are smoke-free.

Take time to relax and enjoy your continental
breakfast while watching the sunrise out of the
sea. We offer laundry facilities and off-street
parking.

Our home is only 5 minutes walk through
Churchill Park to the town centre where you will
find a restaurant that will suit your taste buds,
souvenir shops, Visitor Information Centre and
a walk along the beach. We are in close walking
distance to Whale Watch and Dolphin Encounter
Tour Departure Stations and are happy to book
local tours and offer a courtesy pick up from train
or bus stations.

We are a Christian couple and like Muffy, our cat, are friendly and welcoming and look forward to
making your stay a time to remember.

*We believe the sea and mountain views we offer from your room
and balcony is unbeatable in Kaikoura*

KAIKOURA   *3km N of Kaikoura*

Carrickfin Lodge   *B&B Lodge*
Roger Boyd
Mill Road, Kaikoura

Tel (03) 319 5165   0800 265 963
Fax (03) 319 5162   Mob 025 575 0760
rogerboyd@xtra.co.nz
www.carrickfinlodge.co.nz

Rates: double/single $100 (full breakfast)
Not suitable for children
5 rooms with ensuite

Carrickfin Cottage   Self-contained
Rate from $100-120   Sleeps 6
Minimum stay 2 nights

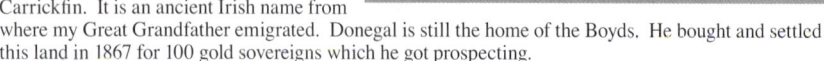

Welcome to Kaikoura (*Kai* = food   *Koura* = crayfish). My name is Roger and I'm the fourth generation Boyd to live and farm Carrickfin. It is an ancient Irish name from where my Great Grandfather emigrated. Donegal is still the home of the Boyds. He bought and settled this land in 1867 for 100 gold sovereigns which he got prospecting.

The Lodge is built on 100 acres adjoining the Kairkoura township. It is a large and spacious place with an open fire and a guests' bar. It was built well back from the road amidst 2 acres of lawns and shrubs to give complete privacy and security.

There are breathtaking views from all rooms looking directly at the Seaward Kaikouras a spectacular mountain range which rises to 8500 feet. These mountains are home to a unique and variety of wild life. Our sea and coastline is also unique for the whales, dolphins, seals and many ocean going birds including the wandering albatross. It is one place in the world where whales are found all the year round.

As well as fattening heifers I am a professional wool classer by trade and have worked in shearing sheds throughout the South Island high country. Another feature of Carrickfin Lodge is the big English breakfast which is legendary. I am 3km from Whale Watch, Dolphin Encounter and some of the best restaurants.

Directions: At the north end of town turn west into Mill Road. I am up on the left.

Easy to find - hard to leave

One Hundred Thousand Welcomes

KAIKOURA *5km N of Kaikoura*

BnB Approved

Donegal House *B&B Farmstay*
Licenced Rest & Accomodation

Murray Boyd
Schoolhouse Road, Kaikoura

Tel (03) 319 5083
0800 346 873
Fax (03) 319 5083
Mob 027 534 6873
donegalhouse@xtra.co.nz
www.donegalhouse.co.nz

Double $130   Single $100
(Continental Breakfast)
Child $15   Dinner $27.50
Credit cards accepted
12 Queen 3 Single (13 bdrm)
Bathrooms: 13 Ensuite

Donegal House, the little Irish Hotel in the country, brimming with warmth and hospitality, open fires and accordion music.

Set on an historical dairy farm which has been farmed by the Boyd family since their arrival from Donegal, Ireland in 1865, *Donegal House* offers, accommodation, full bar facilities and a public licensed restaurant. The a-la-carte menu, specialising in Kaikoura's famous crayfish and seafood, plus locally farmed beef. NZ beers, Kilkenny and Guinness are on tap along with a good selection of Marlborough wines. Two spring fed lakes, home to chinook salmon, mute and black swans, blue teal, paradise and mallard ducks, are feature in the extensive lawns and gardens which surround *Donegal House.*

The towering Kaikoura Mountains make a perfect backdrop to this unique setting. The Restaurant and Bar facilities at *Donegal House* have become a very popular place for visitors staying at the nearby Carrick-finn Lodge, Ardara Lodge, The Old Convent and Dylans Country Stay, to meet the Kaikoura locals and enjoy the rural hospitality in a unique Irish atmosphere.

We book whale watching, dolphin and seal swimming and horse trekking etc.

Directions: Driving North 4kms from Kaikoura on SH1 turn left at Large transit signs, 1.6km along Schoolhouse Road.

Even if you're not Irish - this is the place for you! A home away from home!

CANTERBURY

KAIKOURA *180km N of Christchurch*

Austin Heights *B&B Separate/Suites*
Lynley & John McGinn
19 Austin Street, Kaikoura, New Zealand

Tel (03) 319 5836 0800 080 324 Fax (03) 319 6836
Mob 021 295 7031 austinheights@xtra.co.nz
www.bnb.co.nz/austinheightsb&b.html

Double $125-$160 Single $80-$100
(Full Continental Breakfast) Child neg
Credit cards accepted Children welcome
1 Super King 1 Queen (2 bdrm)
Bathrooms: 2 Ensuite

Austin Heights is close to Kaikoura's unique attractions, with whale watching and the towns centre only a few minutes away. We have 2 new ensuite units elevated above our home,which is situated in a prime location on the Kaikoura peninsula looking towards the magnificent mountains and sea view, each unit has doors opening onto a balcony. Each unit has kitchenette, fridge, microwave, TV, stereo, hairdryers, bathrobes, excellent beds, and complimentary fruit & chocolates. We serve a generous continental breakfast. Cooked is available.

KAIKOURA *Central Kaikoura*

Bendamere House *B&B Homestay*
Ellen & Peter Smith
37 Adelphi Tce, Kaikoura

Tel (03) 319 5830 0800 107 770 Fax (03) 319 7337
bendamerehouse@xtra.co.nz
www.bendamere.co.nz

Double $80-$120 Single $70 (Full Breakfast)
Child $15 Children welcome
2 Queen 1 Twin 3 Single (3 bdrm)
Bathrooms: 2 Ensuite 1 Private

We are retired dairy farmers and fourth generation Kaikourians with extensive knowledge of the area. Our 1930's restored home and large garden are just minutes from the township, beach, Whale Watch and other attractions. Incredible views of the Pacific Ocean and Seaward Kaikoura Mountains. Well appointed rooms offer electric blankets, heaters, hairdryers, television and tea making facilities. Fax and laundry available. We enjoy helping visitors get the most of our their stay in our lovely seaside town. True country breakfast and other homemade treats. Courtesy car available to meet buses and trains.

KAIKOURA *4km Kaikoura town centre*

The Point *B&B*
Peter & Gwenda Smith
Fyffe Quay, Kaikoura

Tel (03) 319 5422
Fax (03) 319 7422
pointsmith@xtra.co.nz
www.bnb.co.nz/thepoint.html

Double $90 Single $75 (Continental Breakfast)
1 Queen 1 Double (2 bdrm)
Bathrooms: 2 Ensuite

We offer you a warm and friendly welcome to our family home, which we share with our 2 daughters. Enjoy the quietness and unique location of this beautiful 125 year old farmhouse. On the waterfront and surrounded by 90 acres of farmland (part of Kaikoura Peninsula) Spectacular views of the sea and mountains. Ideally situated for walks around the Kaikoura peninsula and seal colony. 5 minutes walk to one of Kaikoura's top restaurants. We run daily sheep shearing shows, have farm dogs and one cat.

KAIKOURA   *6km S of Kaikoura*

Approved

Fyffe Country Lodge   *B&B*
Chris Rye
State Highway One, Kaikoura,

Tel (03) 319 6869   Fax (03) 319 6865   Mob 021 161 1625
fyffe@xtra.co.nz   fyffecountrylodge.com

*Fyffe has a class
all of its own*

Double $270   Single $160   Suites from $495
(Continental Breakfast)   Dinner $32   Credit cards accepted
4 King 2 Queen 1 Twin (7 bdrm)
Bathrooms: 7 Ensuite

Fyffe Country Lodge is a small luxury lodge with an award winning restaurant close to whale watching in Kaikoura. The lodge is beautifully created of rammed earth with Canadian cedar shakes on the roof; its rustic charm gives the property a timeless atmosphere. At Fyffe you can expect to find the finest of linens, individually décor'd rooms/suites, a superb menu sporting fresh local delicacies. Excellent service and gracious hosts. Not suitable for young children or pets

CANTERBURY

KAIKOURA   *200km N of Christchurch*

Endeavour Heights Boutique B&B   *B&B*
Janice & Grant Dreaver
1 Endeavour Place, Kaikoura

Tel (03) 319 5333   Fax (03) 319 5333
Mob 025 224 0549
dreavers@xtra.co.nz   www.endeavourheights.co.nz

Double $150-$180 Single $120   Child $20
(Full Breakfast)   Credit cards accepted
2 Queen (2 bdrm)
Bathrooms: 2 Private

Endeavour Heights truly portrays magnificence in
hospitality, scenic views and quality accommodation,
all nestled within the Kaikoura Peninsula, where the
mountains meet the sea. Travellers can experience
a warm welcome from their Kiwi hosts Janice
and Grant, whilst relaxing from a private seaward
facing balcony enjoying the unsurpassed ocean and
mountainous views.

Endeavour Heights is centrally located amidst all of
Kaikoura's major attractions, including the township
with its great local craft shops, trendy cafés and very
own local winery. Endeavour Heights also overlooks
the very popular peninsular walkway and seal colony,
both of which are accessible by foot.

All bedrooms are tastefully decorated, with a private
bathroom. The rooms are equipped with Sky TV, tea
and coffee making facilities, luxurious bathrobes and a hairdryer. Complimentary laundry facilities
and pick up or drop off are also offered to ensure your stay is pleasant and carefree. A freshly
prepared continental or cooked breakfast will be served in the upper level of the house or in your
own room on request.

We welcome you to Endeavour Heights, warm, relaxing and peaceful.
Easy to find but hard to leave.

KAIKOURA

Nikau Lodge   *Boutique/Deluxe B&B*
John & Lilla Fitzwater
53 Deal Street,
Kaikoura (central)
Tel (03) 319 6973   Fax (03) 319 6973
Mob 021 682 076   stay@NikauLodge.com
www.NikauLodge.com

Double $100-$195 Single $90-$180   (Full Breakfast)
Credit cards accepted
1 King/Twin 4 Queen 1 Twin (6 bdrm)
Bathrooms: 5 Ensuite 1 Private

Conveniently located in the heart of Kaikoura on SH1 with magnificent hilltop views of sea and mountains, Nikau offers high quality affordable B&B accommodation. 5 minutes walk takes you to Kaikoura's main street where you can enjoy local Rock Lobster. Relax in the hot-tub or garden with a glass of wine and gaze at the stars and snow-capped mountains. Internet access, Sky TV, complimentary tea/coffee, laundry, in-room TV/movies etc. Friendly new owners John & Lilla Fitzwater welcome the opportunity to make your stay enjoyable and memorable.

KAIKOURA   *NW of Kaikoura Central*

Driftwood Villa   *B&B Homestay*
Suzy James & Chris Valkhoff
166A Beach Road, Kaikoura

Tel (03) 319 7116   Fax (03) 319 7116
Mob 027 476 7000   chrisandsuzy@xtra.co.nz
www.driftwoodvilla.co.nz

Double $105-$155 Single $90-$110 (Full Breakfast)
Child $20   Credit cards accepted Children welcome
1 King 3 Queen 1 Twin 4 Single (4 bdrm)
Bathrooms: 4 Ensuite

Welcome to our lovingly restored 1900's Colonial Villa. You are guaranteed to enjoy your stay in one of our elegantly appointed bedrooms, each with their own ensuite, tea & coffee making facilities, electric blanket, bathrobe, and TV. Our character villa is set in a secluded garden with countless roses and flowers. Either enjoy a game of petanque or sit back and take in the view of the Kaikoura Mountains from our hot tub. Our hearty breakfast will fire you up for a magical Kaikoura experience!

KAIKOURA   *Central Kaikoura*

Admiral Creighton B&B   *B&B*
Yvonne & Tony Steadman
191 Beach Road, Kaikoura

Tel 0800 742 622   (03) 319 7111   Fax (03) 319 7111
admiral.creighton.b2b@ihug.co.nz
www.admiral-creighton.com

Double $100-$150 Single $95   (Full Breakfast)
Dinner $30   Credit cards accepted
4 Queen 1 Twin (5 bdrm)
Bathrooms: 3 Ensuite 2 Private

Admiral Creighton B&B is situated inside the Kaikoura Township. Close to everything including the Whale Watch departure, restaurants and shops. We are easy to find and offer a rural peaceful atmosphere with mountain views. Feed the trout, eels & ducks in our stream boundry. Ideal small conference venue with spacious living and BBQ area. Enjoy a continental and fully cooked breakfast. Dinners by prior arrangement. A courtesy car is available and off-street parking. Our well behaved cockatoo, Creighton, will welcome you warmly. On line booking at www.admiral-creighton.com

WAIAU - MT LYFORD   *21km N of Waiau*

Mason Hills   *Farmstay Homestay*
Averil & Robert Leckey
Inland Kaikoura Road, Waiau, RD, North Canterbury

Tel (03) 315 6611   0800 101 961   Fax (03) 315 6611
Mob 021 157 1035   mason_hills@xtra.co.nz
www.bnb.co.nz/masonhills.html

Double $120   Single $100   (Full Breakfast)
Dinner $30 by arrangement   Credit cards accepted
Children welcome
1 Queen 2 Single (2 bdrm)
Bathrooms: 1 Ensuite 1 Private

Conveniently situated midway between Kaikoura and Hanmer Springs on the Alpine Pacific Triangle (SH70), Mason Hills Station offers a real New Zealand rural experience: • Fourth generation New Zealanders • Commercial Sheep and Beef Hill Country Station • Large character homestead in a genuine alpine setting • 21km north of Waiau, 1km south of Mt Lyford ski field turn-off • 4WD farm tour encompassing spectacular alpine to Pacific views available as an extra. Averil, Robert and Gracie the Labrador look forward to welcoming you.

HANMER SPRINGS   *5km SW of Hanmer Springs*

Mira Monte   *Country Homestay*
Anna & Theo van de Wiel
324 Woodbank Road, Hanmer Springs

Tel (03) 315 7604   Fax (03) 315 7604
Mob 021 043 1218   vdwiel@xtra.co.nz
www.miramonte.co.nz

Double $110-$130   Single $85-$100   (Full Breakfast)
Child neg Dinner $35 by arrangement
Credit cards accepted
2 King 1 Single (2 bdrm)
Bathrooms: 2 Ensuite

Close to the thrills of Hanmer Springs, at the foot of the mountains, lies our peaceful home. Our guest rooms have been tastefully decorated to make your stay special. Relax in your own sitting room or join us. We make a great espresso! Years in the hospitality trade have taught us how to pamper you. There is a grand piano and our large garden has a swimming pool. We speak Dutch and German. Mindy, our Jack Russell, is part of the family. Come as a stranger! Leave as a friend!

HANMER SPRINGS

Cheltenham House   *B&B Self-contained*
Maree & Len Earl
13 Cheltenham Street, Hanmer Springs

Tel (03) 315 7545   Fax (03) 315 7645
cheltenham@xtra.co.nz   www.cheltenham.co.nz

Double $160-$200   Single $130-$170
(Special Breakfast) Child by arrangement
Extra person $30   Credit cards accepted
Children Welcome by arrangement
2 King/Twin 4 Queen 2 Single (6 bdrm)
Bathrooms: 5 Ensuite 1 Private

Cheltenham House offers luxury B&B accommodation, 200 metres from the thermal pools, restaurants and forest walks. This gracious 1930's home was renovated with the guests comfort paramount. The 4 spacious, sunny suites in the house and 2 cottage suites in the extensive garden, are all centrally heated. Enjoy breakfast of your choice, served in your suite, and local wine in the original rimu panelled billiard room in the evening. Together with our gentle labrador and sociable siamese, we look forward to meeting you.

HANMER SPRINGS
130km N of Christchurch

Albergo Hanmer
LODGE & ALPINE VILLA

Bascha & Beat Blattner　　　*B&B Self-contained*
88 Rippingale Road, Hanmer Springs

Tel (03) 315 7428　**Tollfree** 0800 342 313
Fax (03) 315 7428　　Mob 021 217 2411

albergo@paradise.net.nz
www.AlbergoHanmer.com
Check our website for specials & packages!

Cost　Double **$130-$220**　Villa $250-$425
　　　　Single from $100,　Dinner by prior arrangement
　　　　All major credit cards accepted
Beds　3 Super King/Twin　1 American King/Twin
Baths　3 Ensuite (SPA) / JACUZZI

BREAKFASTS - WELLNESS - CUISINE

RENOWNED three course gourmet breakfasts, the wafting smell of freshly baked Swiss mini-loaves & superb Italian coffee! Dine by candle light – tailormade menu features Pacific Rim & European cuisine, surprise Swiss desserts. Set in a magic mountain arena with VIEWS from all windows, Albergo Hanmer offers PEACE, PRIVACY AND ALL DAY SUN, yet only 2 minutes drive from the Thermal Pools/cafes/shops and 18 hole golf.

The eclectic styling is modern, creating a fresh, light & comfortable feel (underfloor heating). CHOOSE from the spacious suites in the main lodge guest wing: In-room TV/tea&coffee/fridges with large ensuites/spa, (great water pressure!). Relax in the 3 guest living spaces, providing internet, latest mags, CD's, & Feng Shui courtyard with waterfall. Enjoy a drink from the Albergo in-house beverage list. Chefs kitchen & laundry available.

OR for ultra decadence, experience the new stand alone ALPINE VILLA: Self-contained with PRIVATE OUT-DOOR JACUZZI and includes: American king bed, marbled ensuite with panorama window (views while you shower!), bidet, IN-ROOM CINEMA, air condition. Dedicated hosts, Bascha & Beat Blattner are a young couple (NZ & Swiss origins) with 19 years experience in hospitality & tourism. Bascha's background is in fashion & design. Beat is a tourism expert. We speak English, Swiss/German, French, Spanish and Italian. WE CAN ARRANGE YOUR HUNTING & FISHING TOURS, ON SITE MASSAGES/FACIALS.

Guest comments: *'Thank you – you have delighted us. You have a gift for knowing how to provide the 'WOW' factor.'* Irene & Graham Blair, QLD, AU *'Loved the in-room (in-bed) DVD and would come back just for Beat's hand-made bread'* Sharon and John King, Banora Point, AU *'Wonderful eclectic design mix and warm hospitality – who could ask for more? The best views from the loo! (anywhere!) and aah, those breakfasts.'* Colin & Maureen Rice, Kent, UK.

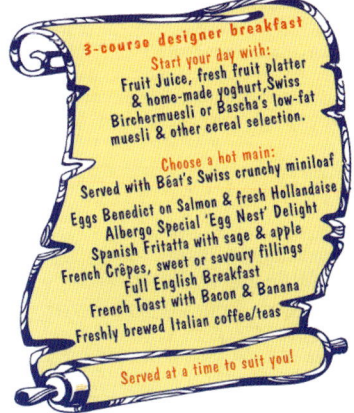

3-course designer breakfast
Start your day with:
Fruit Juice, fresh fruit platter
& home-made yoghurt, Swiss
Birchermuesli or Bascha's low-fat
muesli & other cereal selection.

Choose a hot main:
Served with Beat's Swiss crunchy miniloaf
Eggs Benedict on Salmon & fresh Hollandaise
Albergo Special 'Egg Nest' Delight
Spanish Fritatta with sage & apple
French Crêpes, sweet or savoury fillings
Full English Breakfast
French Toast with Bacon & Banana
Freshly brewed Italian coffee/teas

Served at a time to suit you!

DIRECTIONS: At junction before main village, 300 metres past Shell Garage, take *ARGELINS ROAD* (Centre branch), go past Hanmer Golf Club, take next road left RIPPINGALE ROAD. Albergo Hanmer is 900 metres down on the right hand side (sign at drive entrance).

HANMER SPRINGS *Hanmer Springs*

Hanmer View *B&B*
Will & Helen Lawson
8 Oregon Heights, Hanmer Springs, 8273

Tel (03) 315 7947   0800 920 800   Fax (03) 315 7958
hanmerview@xtra.co.nz
www.hanmerview.co.nz

Double $140-$170 Single $110-$130 (Full Breakfast)
Dinner by arrangement Credit cards accepted
1 King/Twin 2 Queen (3 bdrm)
Bathrooms: 3 Ensuite

Hanmer View, surrounded by beautiful forest and adjoining Conical Hill track. Stunning panoramic alpine views. Purpose built to ensure guests enjoy quiet, relaxing stay in warm, spacious quality ensuite rooms. Individually decorated with TV, wool duvets and hand made patchwork quilts. Tea, coffee and cake always available and your hosts, Will and Helen delight in serving you a generous scrumptious cooked and continental breakfast. No one goes away hungry. Short stroll to village, thermal pools and tourist attractions. See letterbox sign, on right, end Oregon Heights.

HANMER SPRINGS *7km S of Hanmer*

Charwell Lodge *Homestay*
Judy & Bill Clarkson
74P Medway Road, Hanmer Springs

Tel (03) 315 5070   Fax (03) 315 5071
Mob 021 347 905
charwell.countrystay@xtra.co.nz
www.bnb.co.nz/charwell.html

Double $150   Single $120
(Full Breakfast)
Credit cards accepted
1 King 2 Queen (3 bdrm)
Bathrooms: 3 Ensuite

Our new home is built to enjoy magnificent mountain and river views from an elevated sunny and secluded position. Just 7km to Hamner Springs thermal pools and cafés. Nestled among wilding pines with an abundance of birdlife. A large open fire, home baked delicious full breakfast included. With our own small flock of sheep, an explanation and demonstration of working NZ sheepdogs may be given by arrangement.

HANMER SPRINGS *1.5hrs N of Christchurch*

Cheshire House *B&B*
Jan & Chris Ottley
164C Hanmer Springs Road,
Highway 7A, Hanmer

Tel (03) 315 5100   0800 337 332   Mob 021 269 2737
janandchris@xtra.co.nz
www.bnb.co.nz/cheshirehouse.html

Double $110-$140 Single $89   (Full Breakfast)
Child over 10 years Children welcome
2 Queen 1 Twin (3 bdrm)
Bathrooms: 3 Ensuite

Cheshire House is conveniently situated 1 minute drive from Hanmer township. Come and be spoilt with our English hospitality and relax in one of our 3 beautifully furnished ensuite bedrooms with private guest entrance and stunning mountain views. Jan & Chris will ensure that you have a memorable stay and breakfast in Hanmer Springs where many activities can also be enjoyed if you wish. Experience Hanmer's delightful thermal pools and relax by indulging into health, body and mind.

HANMER SPRINGS   *130km NW of Christchurch*

Oakview Hanmer Springs   *B&B Self-contained*
Michael Malthus
46 Jacks Pass Road, Hanmer Springs

Tel **(03) 315 7757**   Fax (03) 315 7746
Mob 021 577 570
m.j.malthus@xtra.co.nz
www.bnb.co.nz/oakview.html

Double $150   Single $110   (Full Breakfast)
Child $50   Credit cards accepted
3 Queen 1 Twin (4 bdrm)
Bathrooms: 3 Ensuite

Well appointed accommodation within a modern
gracious home overlooking large gardens through a vista of oak trees onto the golf course. Only 250
metres easy walk to the thermal pools, shops and a great selection of restaurants. Your hosts Jenny
and Michael will do everything possible to make your stay welcome and enjoyable. The choice of
accommodation varies from 2 bedroom self-contained apartments with kitchens, to 1 bedroom suites all
with their own spa baths and showers.

HANMER SPRINGS   *140km N of Christchurch*

Alpine B&B Hanmer   *B&B*
Cobie & Gavin Bickerton
21A Leamington Street, Hanmer Springs,
North Canterbury 8273

Tel **(03) 315 5051**   Fax (03) 315 5051
gavinandco@callplus.net.nz
www.bnb.co.nz/alpinebb.html

Double $110-$130   Single $90-$110   (Full Breakfast)
Credit cards accepted
1 King/Twin 1 Queen (2 bdrm)
Bathrooms: 2 Ensuite

Please come and stay at our purpose designed brand new B&B home which will open in November
2004. We are in a very tranquil residential street with views across the Hanmer valley to the mountains
and a short level walk to the famed Hot Springs, forest walks, restaurants, and shops. Each of our 2
guest rooms has their own ensuite, entrance, tea and coffee making facilities, and deck. Breakfast will
be served in your room. Your hosts (NZ and Dutch) believe they can offer you complete unobtrusive
hospitality.

CULVERDEN   *3km S of Culverden*

Ballindalloch   *Farmstay*
Diane & Dougal Norrie
Culverden, North Canterbury

Tel **(03) 315 8220**   Fax (03) 315 8220
Mob 027 4 37 3184
dianedougal@xtra.co.nz
www.bnb.co.nz/ballindalloch.html

Double $110   Single $60   (Full Breakfast)
Child $30   Dinner $30   Children welcome
1 Queen 2 Single (2 bdrm)
Bathrooms: 1 Guests share

Welcome to Ballindalloch, 2090 acre irrigated farm 3km south of Culverden. We milk 1400 cows
(2 herds) through a new 70 bail rotary dairy and a floating dairy. We have 1000 Corriedale sheep stud.
We are just over 1 hour north of Christchurch; half hour to Hanmer Springs, Kaikoura whales 1.5 hour
drive. Having travelled extensively overseas we appreciate relaxing in a homely atmosphere - this we
extend to our guests. I am involved in the nutrition field and enjoy discussing health care. Our cat is
Thomas. Guests are welcome to smoke outdoors. We look forward to welcoming you.

CANTERBURY

WAIKARI   *28km NW of Amberley*

Tullach Glas Motel B&B
B&B Homestay Separate/Suite Self-contained
Patsy & Ivor McMillan
38 Princes Street, Waikari, North Canterbury

Tel (03) 314 4931   0800 373 030
Fax (03) 314 4936   info@countrystay.co.nz
www.countrystay.co.nz

Double $75   Single $45   (Continental Breakfast)
Child $10   Dinner $20pp b/a   Credit cards accepted
3 Queen 1 Twin (4 bdrm)
Bathrooms: 2 Ensuite 2 Private 1 Guests share

Welcome to our country home. We are 50 minutes from Christchurch International Airport and an ideal stop off point to major tourist attractions nearby. We have our own small farm, Biddy the sheep dog and BC our very aloof black cat. Rest awhile with us, lunch at local wineries, fish in our lakes and river, walk, horse trek, play golf or just admire the view.

AMBERLEY   *1km S of Amberley*

Bredon Downs Homestay   *Farmstay Homestay*
Bob & Veronica Lucy
Bredon Downs, Amberley, RD 1,
North Canterbury

Tel (03) 314 9356 or (03) 314 8018   Fax (03) 314 8994
Mob 025 494 517   lucy.lucy@xtra.co.nz
www.bnb.co.nz/bredondownshomestay.html

Double $110-$130   Single $75   (Full Breakfast)
Dinner $40 (including wine)   Credit cards accepted
1 Queen 1 Twin 1 Single (3 bdrm)
Bathrooms: 1 Ensuite 1 Private

Our drive goes off SH1 and so we are conveniently en route to and from the Interisland Ferry, just 48km north of Christchurch and 100km south of the Kaikoura whales, and easy to find. The house is surrounded by an English style garden with swimming pool, and close to the Waipara wineries, beach and attractive golf course. We breed ostriches which we are pleased to show visitors, have travelled extensively and lived abroad, and now share our lives with a newfoundland and a labrador, two geriatric donkeys and Hugo the cat!

AMBERLEY   *1km W of Amberley*

Kokiri B&B   *B&B Self-contained*
Pat & Graham Shaw
65 Douglas Road, Amberley, North Canterbury

Tel (03) 314 9699   Fax (03) 314 9699
Mob 021 033 3173
grahampat@actrix.co.nz
www.bnb.co.nz/kokiri.html

Double $120-$100   (Continental Breakfast)   Child $15
Children welcome Pets welcome
1 King 1 Queen 1 Single (2 bdrm)
Bathrooms: 1 Ensuite 1 Private

Turn off SH1 in centre of Amberley, 1km along Douglas Road you will find Kokiri. Set in the countryside opposite Amberley Domain with views of Mount Gray our colonial home awaits you with doves, fish and labrador. Centrally heated throughout. Relax and enjoy strolling around large gardens or play croquet! Good restaurants within walking distance. 5 minutes from wineries, 1 hour to Hanmer Springs and Mount Lyford skiing.
40 minutes to Christchurch, marine interests at Kaikoura 100km north.

WAIKUKU BEACH *30km N of Christchurch*

Emmanuel House *B&B*
Graham and Mary Dacombe
20 Allin Drive, Waikuku Beach,
North Canterbury 8254

Tel **(03) 312 7782** Fax (03) 312 7783
emmanuel.house@xtra.co.nz
www.bnb.co.nz/emmanuelhouse.html

Double $95 Single $55 (Full Breakfast)
Child under 12 ¹/₂ price, under 5 free
Dinner $20 by arrangement
1 Double 1 Twin 1 Single (3 bdrm)
Bathrooms: 1 Guests share

You are special to us, and we warmly invite you to our new one level purpose built home in its park-like setting with wheelchair access throughout. Emmanuel House is 2km from the main highway, within walking distance of the beach and 30km north of Christchurch. Close by is the thriving rural township of Rangiora. Amateur radio ZL3NZ and ZL3MD, music, correspondence, and people are our interests. Complimentary tea/coffee/home baking always available.

RANGIORA *30km N of Christchurch*

Willow Glen *B&B*
Glenda & Malcolm Ross
419 High Street, Rangiora

Tel **(03) 313 9940** Fax (03) 313 9946
Mob 025 984 893 rosshighway@xtra.co.nz
www.willowglenrangiora.co.nz

Double $110 Single $75 (Full Breakfast)
Credit cards accepted
1 Queen 1 Double (2 bdrm)
Bathrooms: 1 Ensuite 1 Private

Nestled on the northern side of Rangiora township on Highway 72, towards Oxford 30 minutes from Christchurch, 90 minutes to Mt Hutt. Walking distance to cafés, restaurants. We invite you to share our enchanting English style home for Kiwi hospitality. Off-street parking available. Comfortable beds, electric blankets, quality linen, hearty home style continental or cooked breakfast. Bedrooms overlook garden and surrounding countryside. Relax in the spa with a glass of wine. Meet Lucy, our foxy, and Millie, our personable british blue cat. Email available.

RANGIORA *25km N of Christchurch*

Silverlea B&B
B&B Homestay Self contained on upper floor
Geoff & Shirley Cant
12 Janelle Place, Rangiora

Tel **(03) 313 0001** Fax (03) 313 0304
Mob 021 299 1705 silverlea@paradise.net.nz
homepages.paradise.net.nz/thecantz

Double $85-$105 Single $75 (Full Breakfast)
Child $25 Dinner $25 Children welcome
2 Queen 1 Single (2 bdrm)
Bathrooms: 1 Private 1 Guests share

Our place is located a short distance north of Christchurch. Our home is a modern house, comfortable with all mod cons. Children welcome. Breakfast includes home-made bread, jams and preserves. Your hosts are semi-retired with a hospitality background. We are 2.5 hours from Kaikoura for whale watching and central to Marlborough and North Canterbury wine areas. Hanmer Springs is 1.25 hours away for year-round hot baths and winter skiing. Plentiful off-steet secure parking. Airport transfers arranged.

CANTERBURY

RANGIORA *7km W of Rangiora Town*

Springbank Vineyard *B&B*
Daphne Robinson
1035 Oxford Road, RD1, Rangiora

Tel (03) 312 5653 Fax (03) 312 5623
springbankvineyard@hotmail.com
www.bnb.co.nz/springbankvineyard.html

Double $100-$125 Single $50 (Full Breakfast)
Credit cards accepted
2 Queen 2 Twin 1 Single (5 bdrm)
Bathrooms: 1 Ensuite 1 Guests share 1 Host share

Historic Springbank Homestead, originally one of Canterbury's great estates, is encircled by spacious grounds and vineyards, with sheep, deer, horses and exquisite lavender fields nearby. Lovely large sunny bedrooms overlook the grounds and gardens, and many colonial antiques and paintings grace the 140 year old homestead. Situated just 30 minutes from Christchurch between Rangiora and Cust on AA's Scenic Highway 72, Springbank is close to golf courses, ski fields and good fishing rivers. Rangiora's shops and restaurants are just 10kms away.

RANGIORA *25km W of Christchurch*

Oakleigh *Homestay*
Philip Holden & Leon Mary Russell-White
148 King Street, Rangiora

Tel (03) 313 0420 Fax (03) 313 0421
leonmrussell@xtra.co.nz www.bnb.co.nz/oakleigh.html

Double $180 Single $75 (Full Breakfast)
Extra adults $60 per person Child $50
Dinner $50 Credit cards accepted
Children welcome Pets welcome
1 King 2 Single (2 bdrm)
Bathrooms: 1 Ensuite

Oakleigh is a charming historic home upgraded for modern living, situated in the heart of Rangiora on Route 72, 30 minutes from Christchurch and 10 minutes from SH1 if travelling south. Your host Philip is a well known author/photographer, Leon Mary has many interests, her aim is to make your stay memorable. We are close to ski fields, golfing, fishing, tramping, beaches and wineries. We offer excellent off-street parking, access to the internet, TV and telephone. We have one resident west highland terrier.

RANGIORA - OHOKA *24km N of Christchurch*

Stockbridge Country Bed & Breakfast
B&B Private guest wing
Peta Purdy
10 Wilson Drive, Ohoka, North Canterbury

Phone/fax 03 312 6924
Mob 021 591 266 alan.purdy@clear.net.nz
www.bnb.co.nz/stockbridge.html

Double $120 Single $70 (Full Breakfast)
Dinner $30 per person Credit cards accepted
Children welcome
1 Queen 2 Twin (2 bdrm) Bathrooms: 1 Private

Peta, Alan and Molly, the cat, will make you welcome, in rural Ohoka, 5 minutes off SH1 and 20 minutes from the airport and Christchurch. Set in 2 acres of lawns and gardens, Stockbridge has beautiful garden or mountain views from all rooms. The sunny, self contained and fully equipped guest wing opens onto the courtyard and terrace. A perfect place to relax! Local attractions include golf, fishing, walking, skiing, vineyards and Christchurch City. We enjoy overseas travel, outdoor activities, music, food and wine.

OXFORD   *60km W of Christchurch*

Country Life   *B&B Homestay Self-contained*
Helen Dunn
137 High Street, Oxford, North Canterbury

Tel (03) 312 4167
www.bnb.co.nz/countrylife.html

Double $60-$70 Single $35-$40 (Full Breakfast)
Dinner $20 by arrangement
Children welcome Pets welcome
Smoking area inside

3 Double (3 bdrm)
Bathrooms: 1 Ensuite 1 Guests share 1 Host share

Country life has been operating since 1987, the house is 80 years old and has a spacious garden, warm and sunny. Helen enjoys meeting people from far and wide – whether overseas visitors or those wanting a peaceful break away from Christchurch – all are welcomed at Country Life. High Street is off the Main Road – left. Sign outside the gate.

OXFORD   *40mins W of Christchurch Airport*

Hielan' House   *B&B Homestay*
Shirley & John Farrell
74 Bush Road, Oxford, North Canterbury

Tel (03) 312 4382 0800 279 382 Fax (03) 312 4382
Mob 025 359 435 hielanhouse@ihug.co.nz
www.hielanhouse.co.nz

Double $115-$130 Single $95 (Special Breakfast)
Child price on application Dinner by arrangement
Credit cards accepted Children welcome Pets welcome
1 King/Twin 1 Queen 1 Twin (2 bdrm)
Bathrooms: 1 Ensuite 1 Private

Nestled on 6 acres in peaceful rural surroundings with Oxford foothills as a backdrop, we have 2 quality upstairs guest rooms with their own relaxing areas, ensuites, separate entrance. TV, tea/coffee facilities. Inground swimming pool, laundry, fax/internet facilities. Christchurch 45 minutes away. Delicious menu breakfasts, dinners, organic meat and home grown vegetables in season. Your warm welcome includes home baking and cup of coffee/tea. Friendly farm animals. From Inland Scenic Route 72 (Oxford's main street) turn into Bay Road and then left into Bush Road.

OXFORD   *40min W of Christchurch Airport*

Leo's on Oxford   *B&B Homestay*
Judy & Tom Delaney
218 High Street, Oxford

Tel (03) 312 1350 Fax (03) 312 1350
leosonline@xtra.co.nz
www.bnb.co.nz/oxford.html

Double $130 Single $95 (Full Breakfast)
Child price on application Dinner $35 (3 course)
Credit cards accepted Children welcome Pets welcome
1 King/Twin 1 Queen (2 bdrm)
Bathrooms: 1 Private 1 Host share

A coffee, a friendly welcome, attention to guests comfort and privacy awaits you at Leo's. Enjoy the ambience and peacefulness of Country Oxford. Relax, unwind, stroll through the garden. Settle down with a book in the library, catch up with emails and faxes, switch on the big screen. Curl up beside the cosy log fire. Retire to your room in the comfort of the private guest wing, crash out between sun dried sheets. In the morning breakfast awaits you and is served in the family dining room.
Laundry facilities included.

CANTERBURY

WAIMAKARIRI *10km NE of Oxford*

Waimakariri Lodge *B&B*
Sharon & Ian Moore
Depot Gorge Road, Oxford, North Canterbury

Tel **(03) 312 3662** Fax (03) 312 3662
Mob 027 437 1096 sharonian@xtra.co.nz
www.waimakaririlodge.co.nz

Double $220-$165 Single $130 (Full Breakfast)
Child $70 Dinner $45pp Credit cards accepted
1 King/Twin 1 King 1 Queen 1 Twin 1 Single (4 bdrm)
Bathrooms: 2 Ensuite 2 Private

Waimakariri Lodge is situated on Route 72 and very easy to find. A Farmstay with panoramic views of gorge and mountains. Enjoy our scrumptious breakfasts, warm hospitality, home gym, relaxing private spa, and beaiutiful quiet location. An 18 hole golf course is adjacent to property, golf clubs available for hire. Private guest lounge, private entrance, tea/coffee making facilities in rooms, email facilities, guest laundry. Children over 12 are welcome. Bedrooms have warm cosy beds, electric blankets, fresh flowers, fluffy towels, chocolates and french doors opening out to your own balcony. Our two Jack Russells love to socialize with guests. Come and stay with us, your welcome.

KAIAPOI *15km N of Christchurch*

Morichele *B&B*
Helen & Richard Moore
25 Hilton Street,
Kaiapoi

Tel **(03) 327 5247** Fax (03) 327 5247
morichele@xtra.co.nz
www.bnb.co.nz/morichele.html

Double $90 Single $60 (Full Breakfast)
Child negotiable Dinner by arrangement
1 Double 1 Twin (2 bdrm)
Bathrooms: 1 Guests share

Your hosts Helen and Richard provide comfortable accommodation in a beautiful garden setting, close to rivers, beaches, golf course and walks. With off-street parking, your own entrance, sitting/dining area with fridge, tea and coffee making facilities, TV and video. Cafés and restaurants within walking distance and approx 2 hour drive will take you to ski fields, Hanmer Springs, Akaroa and Kaikoura each with their own attractions. Extra bed, email, fax and laundry available.

KAIAPOI *20km N of Christchurch*

Fairway View Kaiapoi B&B Motel
B&B Self-contained New motel
Christine & Michael Cole
465 Williams Street (formally Main North Road),
RD1, Kaiapoi, Christchurch

Tel **(03) 327 5688** Fax (03) 327 5629
stay@fairwayviewkaiapoi.co.nz
www.fairwayviewkaiapoi.co.nz

Double $95-$125 Single $95-$115 (Continental Breakfast) New motel $135 for 2 C/Cs accepted
3 King/Twin 1 Queen 1 Single (4 bdrm)   Bathrooms: 1 Ensuite 1 Private

Travellers retreat/golfers delight. 20 minutes north of Christchurch and international airport. Turn off SH1 at Kaiapoi River Town exit, drive along Williams Street past golf course, look for blue B&B sign, Fairway View is at end of drive (house cannot be seen from road). Set in 1 acre of quiet, tranquil gardens overlooking golf course, separate guest entrance, lovely guest lounge with CD, DVD, TV, fridge and dining area where we serve breakfast. New 2 bedroom (twin /king beds) motel. Golf packages. Spa pool. Friendly warm welcome assured. 3 minutes drive to several restaurants.

CHRISTCHURCH - HAREWOOD   *7.5km N of Christchurch Centre*

St James B&B   *B&B*
Margaret & David Frankish
125 Waimakariri Road, Harewood, Christchurch 8005

Tel (03) 359 6259   Fax (03) 359 6299
Mob 025 224 4982   dj.frankish@xtra.co.nz
www.bnb.co.nz/stjames.html

Double $100-$140   **Single** $75-$90   (Full Breakfast)
Child $40   Dinner $30   Credit cards accepted
Children welcome
1 King 1 Queen 1 Twin (2 bdrm)
Bathrooms: 1 Guests share

Located 5 minutes from Christchurch Airport, 10 minutes from city. Begin/end your South Island trip in our warm, modern home with its tranquil garden setting, and the horses who live on the 3 acre property. Our lovely guest rooms include private lounges with a spa bath/ bathroom upstairs. Rooms have tea/ coffee facilities and TV. Internet access is available. We have 2 teenage children and a spaniel. Close by are golf courses, excellent restaurants, shopping, Wildlife Reserve, McLeans Island Recreation Area and Antarctic Centre.

CHRISTCHURCH - WEST MELTON   *25km W of Christchurch*

Hopesgate   *B&B Farmstay*
Yvonne & Robert Overton
Hoskyns Road, RD 5, Christchurch

Tel (03) 347 8330   Fax (03) 347 8330
Mob 0274 31 1234   robove@free.net.nz
www.bnb.co.nz/hopesgate.html

Double $90   **Single** $60   (Full Breakfast)
Dinner $20 by arrangement
Credit cards accepted
1 Queen 2 Single (2 bdrm)
Bathrooms: 1 Guests share

We have a 30 hectare property where we farm sheep and grow lavender. Close to all amenities, in a quiet rural setting with magnificent views of the mountains. Countless day trips can be taken from our home. We have enjoyed entertaining folk from different parts of the world and look forward to meeting and caring for many more. Relax with us and enjoy a farmhouse dinner. Begin or end a memorable holiday with us. 15 minutes from Christchurch Airport. Smoke-free home. Friendly cat.

CHRISTCHURCH - WEST MELTON   *15km W of Christchurch*

Shettleston Farm   *Rural Homestay*
Cherry & Donald Moffat
Bells Road, West Melton,
RD 1, Christchurch

Tel (03) 347 8311   Fax (03) 347 8391
Mob 027 527 7217
shettlestonfarm@xtra.co.nz
www.bnb.co.nz/shettlestonfarm.html

Double $95   **Single** $75   (Continental Breakfast)
Dinner $25pp
1 Double 1 Twin (2 bdrm)   Bathrooms: 1 Private

Enjoy the best of both worlds, 15 minutes from Christchurch Airport, 25 minutes from City Centre, yet a world away on our 10 acre country retreat. Our modern home is furnished with colonial furniture and our grounds display a collection of vintage farm machinery to complete the nostalgic atmosphere. We share our paradise with a flock of black and coloured sheep, Poppyseed our cow, goats, 3 donkeys, and a collection of waterfowl on our pond. Smoke-free home.

CHRISTCHURCH - WEST MELTON

15km W of Christchurch

Hillcrest *B&B Homestay*
Averil Dyke
Manna Place, West Melton, Christchurch

Tel (03) 318 1948 Fax (03) 318 1948
Averil.A.Dyke@xtra.co.nz
www.bnb.co.nz/hillcrest.html

Double $100 Single $60 (Full Breakfast) Dinner $30
Credit cards accepted
1 King 1 Double (2 bdrm)
Bathrooms: 1 Ensuite 1 Host share

Your hosts, Averil and David offer warm and friendly hospitality on our 2 acre property. We are situated 15 minutes from the Airport and 30 minutes from Christchurch City Centre. We offer a super king bed in the main bedroom and ensuite facilities with french doors to verandah. There is a guests lounge with a home theatre system. Evening meals can be provided by prior arrangements. We look forward to sharing our non-smoking home with you.

CHRISTCHURCH - YALDHURST

8km W of Christchurch CBD

Gladsome Lodge *B&B Homestay*
Stuart & Sue Barr
314 Yaldhurst Road, Avonhead, Christchurch 4

Tel (03) 342 7414 0800 222 617 Fax (03) 342 3414
Mob 025 299 1684 sue@gladsomelodge.com
www.gladsomelodge.com

Double $80-$100 Single $70 (Continental Breakfast)
Child neg Dinner $25 Credit cards accepted
Children welcome
2 Queen 2 Double 2 Twin 3 Single (5 bdrm)
Bathrooms: 1 Ensuite 3 Guests share

Located close to Airport with easy access to key attractions. Be assured of professional, attentive hosting in a friendly environment. Enjoy our property which has a tennis court, swimming pool and sauna available. We are able to accommodate couples travelling together as a group. Have knowledge of Maori history and culture. We are centrally heated. On bus route to city. On route to ski fields and West Coast Highway. Hosts Sue and Stuart, New Zealanders who have travelled and have a wide variety of interests.

CHRISTCHURCH - YALDHURST

10km W of Christchurch

GP's Place *Homestay*
Gwenda & Peter Bickley
164 Old West Coast Road, RD 6,
Christchurch

Tel (03) 342 9196 Fax (03) 342 4196
Mob 021 158 6208 gpsplace_@hotmail.com
www.bnb.co.nz/gpsplace.html

Double $100 Single $60 (Full Breakfast)
1 Queen 1 Twin (2 bdrm)
Bathrooms: 1 Private

We invite you to come and enjoy the ambience of our warm and spacious home set in a large garden with magnificent views of the Southern Alps. Our home is situated on 7 1/2 acres where we farm ostriches and various other farm animals. We are ideally located just 7 minutes from the airport and 10 minutes from the city. Also closely situated to ski fields, beautiful lakes, fine wineries and golf courses. A full sized tennis court is available for guests use.

CHRISTCHURCH - AVONHEAD *10 min W of Christchurch CBD*

Ash Croft *Self-contained holiday houses*
Sky & Raewyn Williams
6 Fovant Street, Avonhead, Christchurch

Tel (03) 342 3416 Fax (03) 342 3415
Mob 0275 663 724 bookings@ashcroftgroup.com
www.ashcroftgroup.com

Double $100-$120 (Continental Breakfast)
Child under 5 free $10 each additional person
Credit cards accepted Children welcome
2 Queen 2 Twin (3 bdrm)
Bathrooms: 1 Private

Quality accommodation for the visitor to Christchurch, offering privacy and comfort, off-street parking and a child-friendly environment. Modern facilities, full kitchen, dining area, lounge with comfortable furnishings, TV, VCR, CD/radio/tapeplayer, collection of videotapes, book library and childrens games/ toys. Bathroom includes full bath and separate shower. Laundry with washing machine and dryer. Easy access to airport, city centre, local shopping centres and tourist attractions. Contact us or see our website for details of either of our 2 holiday homes.

CHRISTCHURCH - AVONHEAD *10km W of Christchurch Central*

Russley 302 *B&B Homestay*
Helen and Ron Duckworth
302 Russley Road, Avonhead, Christchurch 8004

Tel (03) 358 6510 Fax (03) 358 6470
Mob 021 662 016
haduck@ducksonrussley.co.nz
www.bnb.co.nz/russley302.html

Double $110-$120 Single $70-$110 (Full Breakfast)
Credit cards accepted
1 King 1 Twin 1 Single (3 bdrm)
Bathrooms: 1 Ensuite 1 Private 1 Host share

3 minutes from Christchurch Airport, 15 minutes from the city centre you will find a warm welcome at Russley 302, an ideal location for visitors arriving and departing Christchurch. Each well appointed guest room has refreshment facilities, refrigerator, television and electric blanket. Laundry options available on request. Alfresco dining on warm summer evenings and a log fire in winter create a relaxing atmosphere. Email and fax facilities available. Stay awhile, Christchurch is an ideal base for excursions to Canterbury's hinterland.

CHRISTCHURCH - BURNSIDE *8km NW of Christchurch*

Burnside Bed & Breakfast *B&B*
Elaine & Neil Roberts
31 O'Connor Place, Burnside 8005,
Christchurch

Tel (03) 358 7671 Fax (03) 358 7761
elaine.neil.roberts@xtra.co.nz
www.bnb.co.nz/burnside.html

Double $90 Single $65 (Continental Breakfast)
1 Queen 1 Twin (2 bdrm)
Bathrooms: 1 Guest share

Welcome to our comfortable, modern home in a quiet street, 5 minutes from the airport and 15 minutes to the city centre. You are greeted with fresh flowers and sweets in your bedroom. Relax in the garden with tea or coffee and freshly baked muffins. Enjoy a generous continental breakfast. Off-street parking and laundry facilities are available. We have travelled in New Zealand and overseas. Our interests include sport, walks, gardening and local history. We enjoy sharing our home with guests and look forward to meeting you.

CANTERBURY

CHRISTCHURCH - BURNSIDE

Stableford *B&B*
Margaret & Tony Spowart
2 Stableford Green, Burnside,
Christchurch 8005

Tel (03) 358 3264 Mob 027 415 0834
stableford@xtra.co.nz
www.stableford.co.nz

Double $100-$120 Single $100-$120
(Continental Breakfast $10 per person)
Credit cards accepted
2 Queen 1 Twin (3 bdrm)
Bathrooms: 1 Ensuite 1 Private 1 Guests share

Welcome to Stableford, the closest B&B to the Christchurch airport, making it ideal for arriving or departing visitors. City bus stop at door. We are situated adjacent to the prestigious Russley Golf Club.

Stableford is new, clean and comfortable with a separate guest lounge available. Our rates include tea, coffee and toast, a continental breakfast is available at $10 per person. Good restaurants are close by. Snacks by request.

Our interests are travel, music, antiques, golf and fishing. Golf, hunting and fishing tours arranged.

CHRISTCHURCH - ILAM   *7.5 km from Christchurch Central*

Anne & Tony Fogarty Homestay   *Homestay*
Anne & Tony Fogarty
7 Westmont Street, Ilam,
Christchurch 8004

Tel (03) 358 2762   Fax (03) 358 2767
tony.fogarty@xtra.co.nz
www.bnb.co.nz/fogartyhomestay.html

Double $80   Single $50   (Continental Breakfast)
Dinner $30 by arrangement Credit cards accepted
4 Single (2 bdrm)
Bathrooms: 1 Guests share 1 Host share

Our home is in the beautiful suburb of Ilam, only minutes from Canterbury University and Christchurch College of Education. Close to Christchurch Airport (7 minutes by car) and the railway station (10 minutes). Bus stop to central city (with its many attractions) 50 metres from our home. Willing to arrange transport from airport or train. Guests are welcome to use our laundry. We have a wide range of interests. Complimentary tea and coffee at any time. Stay with us and get value for money.

CHRISTCHURCH - BRYNDWR   *5km NW of Christchurch Central*

Rowan House   *B&B Homestay*
Patricia & Win Clancey
89A Aorangi Road, Bryndwr, Christchurch

Tel (03) 351 6092   Fax (03) 351 6092
wclancey@xtra.co.nz
www.geocities.com/w_clancey/

Double $110   Single $85   (Full Breakfast)
Child by arrangement Credit cards accepted
Children welcome
1 Queen 1 Twin (2 bdrm)
Bathrooms: 2 Ensuite

We warmly welcome you to our spacious, comfortable home set in quiet attractive gardens. The queen bedroom has a balcony overlooking a secluded outdoor swimming pool, the twin bedroom opens into the gardens. A sunroom/TV room is available as a second (private) lounge. Tea/coffee, juice, home baking, always available. Generous breakfasts. We have both travelled, have wide ranges of interest and enjoy talking to people. If needed, we are happy to help with travel plans. Courtesy pick up, off-street parking and laundry facilities are available.

CHRISTCHURCH - BRYNDWR   *5km NW of Christchurch*

Bryndwr B&B   *B&B Homestay*
Kathy & Brian Moore
108 Aorangi Road,
Christchurch

Tel (03) 351 6299   eroom.b@clear.net.nz
www.bnb.co.nz/bryndwrbb2.html

Double $85   Single $65   (Full Special Breakfast)
1 Double 1 Single (2 bdrm)
Bathrooms: 1 Guests share

Welcome, share our comfortable home with relaxing
outdoor garden. Located Northwest corner of Christchurch 5km from airport off Wairakei Road or via Memorial Avenue, left onto Ilam Road, past Aqualand, on to Aorangi Road. Walking distances to local shops and restaurants. Welcome to bring home takeaways. Complimentary tea, coffee. laundry, ironing facilities available. 3 minute walk to bus route, 10 minutes ride to city centre, passing Botanical Gardens, museum, Art Centre. Inspection welcomed. Ring if you have questions, we may be able to help.

CHRISTCHURCH - FENDALTON *5 min NW of Christchurch CBD*

Ambience on Avon *B&B Boutique*
Lawson & Helen Little
9 Kotare Street, Fendalton, Christchurch

Tel (03) 348 4537 0800 22 66 28 Fax (03) 348 4837
Mob 0274 333 627 lawsonh@amcom.co.nz
www.ambience-on-avon.co.nz

Double $160-$190 Single $150-$180
(Special Breakfast) Credit cards accepted
1 Queen 1 Double (2 bdrm)
Bathrooms: 1 Ensuite 1 Private

Ambience on Avon in a private, picturesque garden on the Avon. Helen & Lawson, your gracious hosts enjoy welcoming guests into their home with its elegant comfortable understated furnishings, guest lounge with a large open fire, TV. Enjoy homebaking, complimentary wine and refreshments antipasto under the large elm tree or in the river garden, or relax in leather therapeutic chairs in family room opening into garden. Art, comfortable beds, fine linen, electric blankets, room heaters and all modern conveniences for a relaxing friendly-hosted stay. Courtesy pick up. Off-street parking, no pets, no children.

CHRISTCHURCH - FENDALTON *4 min NW of Christchurch CBD*

Anselm House *Boutique B&B*
Jan & Leigh Webber
34 Kahu Road, Fendalton, Christchurch

Tel (03) 343 4260 0800 267 356 Fax (03) 343 4261
anselm@paradise.net.nz
www.anselmhouse.co.nz

Double $120-$150 Single $100-$120 (Full Breakfast)
Dinner $45 each Credit cards accepted
2 Queen (2 bdrm)
Bathrooms: 2 Ensuite

Anselm House is beside the Avon River; a landmark building built of pink Hanmer marble and designed

by the famous architect Heathcote-Helmore. Special attractions include: 4 minute walk to Riccarton for restaurants, banks and mall; private, courtesy airport and TranzAlpine pick up and drop off; safe off-street parking; within easy walking distance of Hagley Park, art galleries, city centre; adjacent to historic Riccarton House; close to university; on city centre bus route; friendly, family atmosphere. Not suitable for pets or children under 12.

CHRISTCHURCH - DALLINGTON *4km NE of Christchurch*

Killarney *B&B Separate/Suite*
Lynne & Russell Haigh
27 Dallington Terrace, Dallington, Christchurch

Tel (03) 381 7449 Fax (03) 381 7449
Mob 025 235 2409
haigh.killarney@xtra.co.nz
www.bnb.co.nz/killarney.html

Double $95 Single $75 (Full Breakfast) Child neg
2 Double (2 bdrm)
Bathrooms: 1 Ensuite 1 Private

Peace, tranquillity and a cottage garden on the banks of the river Avon. Detached double (ensuite) accommodation is warm and cosy with fridge, microwave, TV, extra single couch-bed available, and private garden. Double accommodation, lounge and private bathroom available inside. Tea/coffee, home baking and laundry service always available. Scenic river walks or borrow our dinghy and row! 6 minutes drive to city centre. Buses stop nearby. Ensuite room only rate available if you provide own breakfast. Both of us and our cat look forward to meeting you.

CHRISTCHURCH - MERIVALE *2km N of Christchurch*

Leinster Homestay B&B   *B&B Homestay*
Kay and Brian Smith
34B Leinster Road, Merivale, Christchurch

Tel (03) 355 6176   Fax (03) 355 6176
Mob 0274 330 771   brian.kay@xtra.co.nz
www.bnb.co.nz/leinsterhomestaybb.html

Double $120-$125 Single $120
(Continental Breakfast) Child neg
Credit cards accepted Children welcome
1 Queen 1 Double 1 Single (2 bdrm)
Bathrooms: 1 Ensuite 1 Private

At Leinster Bed & Breakfast we pride ourselves on creating a relaxed friendly atmosphere in our modern sunny home. Only 5 minutes to city centre (art gallery, museum, Botanical Gardens, Cathedral Square, casino, town hall etc), 10 minutes from the airport. For evening dining convenience there are excellent restaurants just a leisurely stroll away at Merivale Village. Laundry, email, fax and off-street parking facilities makes us your home away from home. Bedrooms have TV, electric blankets, heaters, tea/coffee. Well behaved puss & pooch in residence.

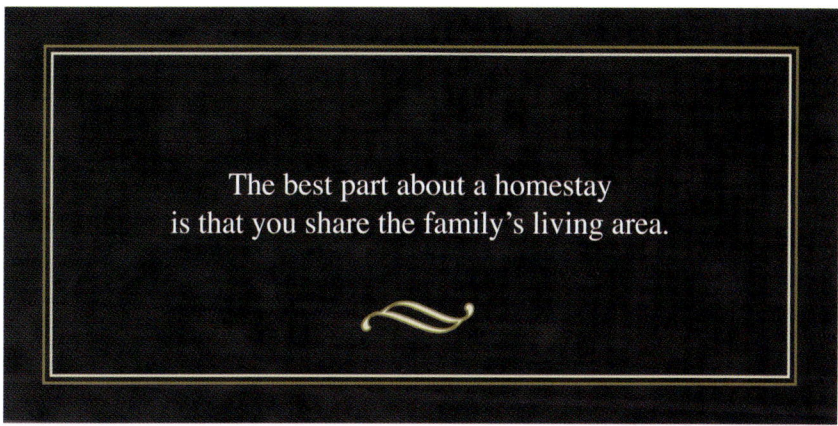

The best part about a homestay
is that you share the family's living area.

CHRISTCHURCH - MERIVALE *3min Christchurch*

Melrose   *B&B*
Elaine & David Baxter
39 Holly Road, Merivale, Christchurch

Tel (03) 355 1929   Fax (03) 355 1927
Mob 025 647 5564   BaxterMelrose@xtra.co.nz
www.melrose-bb.co.nz

Double $120   Single $75   (Full Breakfast)
Child $30   Credit cards accepted Children welcome
3 Queen (3 bdrm)
Bathrooms: 1 Private 2 Guests share

A warm welcome awaits you at Melrose, a charming character home (1910) located in a small quiet street, just off Papanui Road only minutes away from the city and all the shops, restaurants and cafés of Merivale. Our house is spacious, we offer large rooms with tea and coffee making facilities and a private dining room/lounge. We have many interests and having travelled extensively, are keen to accommodate your needs. Our family comprises of 2 daughters and a boxer, Milly. Off-street parking. Children are welcome.

CHRISTCHURCH - ST ALBANS   *1.6km N of Christchurch Centre*

Barrich House   *B&B Homestay*
Barbara & Richard Harman
82 Caledonian Road, St Albans, Christchurch 8001

Tel **(03) 365 3985**   Mob 025 659 5787
r.harman@ext.canterbury.ac.nz
www.bnb.co.nz/barrichhouse.html

Double $90-$120 Single $60-$90 (Special Breakfast)
Child neg Dinner by arrangement
Children welcome
1 Queen 1 Twin (2 bdrm)
Bathrooms: 1 Ensuite 1 Private

Our welcoming home, startlingly alive and furnished with strong but tasteful interior colours, is in a quiet street within easy walking distance of the city and tourist amenities. Both rooms are well appointed and have very comfortable beds. The spacious queen room has armchairs and overlooks a lovely courtyard. Excellent breakfast menu. Tea, coffee and biscuits are always available. Friendly hosts willing to help you plan your visit for best value. Use of laundry and pick up transport available. Please contact us in advance.

CHRISTCHURCH - ST ALBANS   *3km N of Christchurch City*

Severn St B&B   *B&B*
Tina & Peter Reynolds
15 Severn Street, St Albans
Christchurch 8001

Tel **(03) 960 3185**   Fax (03) 960 3186
tina.reynolds@paradise.net.nz
www.bnb.co.nz/severn.html

Double $105 Single $75 (Full Breakfast)
Child $20 Credit cards accepted Children welcome
2 King/Twin 1 Queen (2 bdrm)
Bathrooms: 2 Private

Severn Street B&B is a warm character home in a tree lined street, 5 minutes drive from town, and close to the bus route. Facilities include; large warm bedrooms, guest kitchen, cot, highchair, fax/email, off-street parking, hot spa, tea and coffee, courtesy pick up, Deutsche sprache. Peter and I and our cat are well travelled New Zealanders. Peter is an English language teacher, and I am a retired OT. I now have time for weaving, painting and potting.

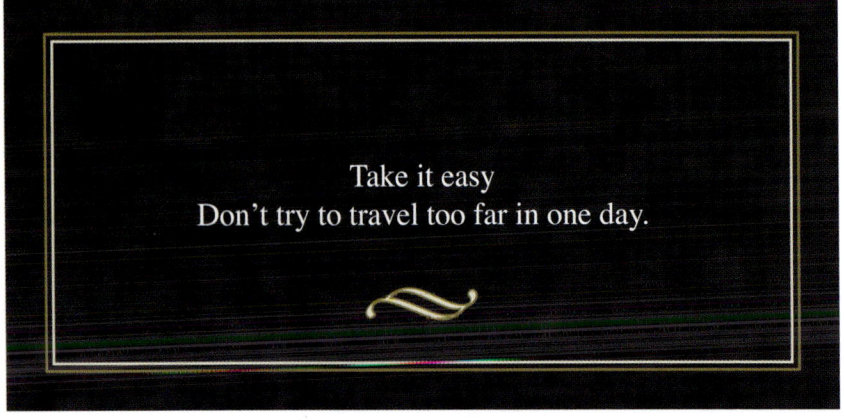

Take it easy
Don't try to travel too far in one day.

CHRISTCHURCH - AVONDALE *8km NE of Christchurch Central*

Hulverstone Lodge *B&B*
Diane & Ian Ross
18 Hulverstone Drive, Avondale, Christchurch

Tel (03) 388 6505 0800 388 6505
Fax (03) 388 6025 Mob 025 433 830
hulverstone@caverock.net.nz
www.canterburypages.co.nz/hulverstone

Double $100-$130 Single $80-$110
(Full Breakfast) Credit cards accepted
3 King/Twin 1 Single (4 bdrm)
Bathrooms: 1 Ensuite 1 Private 1 Guests share

Gracing the bank of the Avon River in a quiet suburb, yet only 10 minutes from the city centre, stands picturesque Hulverstone Lodge. From our charming guest rooms watch the sun rise over the river, catch glimpses of the Southern Alps or enjoy views of the Port Hills. Delightful riverside walks pass the door. Numerous golf courses and the QEII leisure complex are close at hand.

Located just off Christchurch's Ring Road system, Hulverstone Lodge offers easy access to all major tourist attractions, while frequent buses provide convenient transport to the city. An ideal base for holidays year-round, Hulverstone Lodge is only a couple of hours from quaint Akaroa, Hanmer Hot Springs thermal attraction, Kaikoura's Whale Watch, and several ski fields.

How to find us

Follow the Ring Road (marked with an **R** on the big blue/green road signs) clockwise until it crosses the Avon River. Turn left then left again.

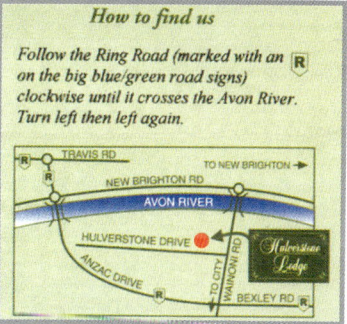

You are guaranteed warm hospitality and quality accommodation at Hulverstone Lodge. All our rooms are decorated with fresh flowers from our garden. We regret our facilities are not suited to young children.

We offer: Complimentary pick up; Fax and email facilities; king or twin beds; Advice on onward travel planning; French and German languages spoken; A delicious breakfast. Come and experience the ambience of Hulverstone Lodge.

A pleasant stroll along the riverbank leads to New Brighton with its sandy Pacific Ocean beach and pier.

CHRISTCHURCH - NEW BRIGHTON

8km E of Christchurch

Tudor House *B&B*
Rosa Rijk & Alex Isherwood
17 Hood Street, New Brighton, Christchurch

Tel (03) 382 1077 Fax (03) 382 1177
Mob 021 113 2401 and 021 233 1093
alexish@xtra.co.nz
www.bnb.co.nz/tudorhousebb.html

Double $100 Single $80 (Full Breakfast)
3 Queen 2 Double (5 bdrm)
Bathrooms: 2 Guests share

Welcome to Tudor House, our beautiful and comfortable 1920's residence which offers a homely atmosphere, created by Alex and Rosa. You are guaranteed quality accommodation furnished with old worlde charm. Rooms are heated and all beds have electric blankets.

We have laughed and cried during our restoration of the property and look forward to the pleasure of hosting guests in our bed and breakfast.

It is one minute to New Brighton's sandy beaches, offering fantastic shoreline walks where native birds can be spotted.

We can offer, within easy reach, leisure complexes, numerous golf courses and our village is full of interesting cafes and bars. There is easy access to Christchurch City with its tourist attractions and a regular bus service is available. A swimming pool available to guests is on the property. Tea and coffee facilities are always on tap, and as neither of us smoke we prefer guests to do so outside.

We look forward to sharing our home with you.

CHRISTCHURCH - RICHMOND *1.5km NE of Christchurch centre*

Willow Lodge *B&B Self-contained*
Grania McKenzie
71 River Road, Avonside, Christchurch 1

Tel (03) 389 9395 Fax (03) 381 5395
willow@inet.net.nz   www.willowlodge.co.nz

Double $100-$150 Single $70-$100 (Full Breakfast)
Child $25 Credit cards accepted Children welcome
1 King/Twin 2 Queen 1 Single (3 bdrm)
Bathrooms: 1 Ensuite 2 Private

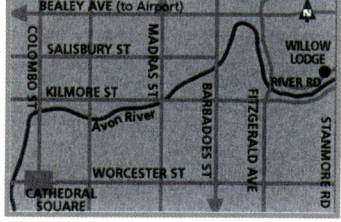

Relax and unwind, read or chat, make yourself at home here at Willow Lodge. Enjoy the 1920's architecture and style, and contemporary NZ art and books. Our views over the river are unsurpassed, and lovely in all seasons. Excellent large, firm beds. Breakfast is generous, fresh and changes with the seasons. Organic breads, good coffee & teas.

We hope you will enjoy Christchurch - 400,000 people, a wonderful new art gallery and a lively arts scene. We also boast good bookshops, fashion, antiques and excellent food and wine choices. Christchurch is well located for day trips - Akaroa and Banks Peninsula, Arthurs Pass, Hanmer Springs, Kaikoura and several ski fields.

Mountain bike, offstreet parking and laundry available. Shuttle or taxi service to the gate from air/rail/ coach. Times: central city is five minutes by car, and a 20 minute walk. Airport or rail is 20 minutes by car. For those wanting self-contained or longer stays (three day minimum) our fully furnished 2 bedroom apartment is available. Central city location in quiet Avon Loop.

- *Beautiful river setting*
- *Stroll into town*
- *1928 Art Deco house*
- *Also a funky S/C apartment*

CANTERBURY

CHRISTCHURCH CITY *Christchurch Central*

Windsor B&B Hotel   *Private Hotel*
Carol Healey & Don Evans
52 Armagh Street, Christchurch 1

Tel (03) 366 1503   0800 366 1503   Fax (03) 366 9796
reservations@windsorhotel.co.nz
www.windsorhotel.co.nz

Double $120, Single $85, Triple $150, Quad/Family $164
(Full Breakfast)   Child $15 under 12 years with adult
Credit cards accepted
(40 bdrm)
Bathrooms: 25 Guests share

Built at the turn of the century this inner city residence
is located on the Tourist Tram Route and is within 5-10
minutes walk of the city centre, restaurants, convention
centre, casino, galleries, museum and Botanical
Gardens.

Guests are greeted on arrival by our pet dachshund *Miss Winnie* and
shown around our charming colonial style home. Often described
as *traditional* this family operated Bed & Breakfast Hotel prides
itself on the standard of accommodation that it offers. The warm and
comfortable bedrooms are all decorated with a small posy of flowers and
a watercolour by local artist Denise McCulloch.

The shared bathroom facilities have been conveniently appointed with
bathrobes provided, giving warmth and comfort in the Bed & Breakfast
tradition. Such things as *hotties* and *brollies* add charm to the style of
accommodation offered, as does our 1928 Studebaker sedan.

Our generous morning breakfast (included in the tariff) offers fruit juice, fresh fruits, yogurt and cereals
followed by bacon and eggs, sausages, tomatoes, toast and marmalade, and is served in the dining room
each morning between 6:30 - 9:00am. The 24 hour complimentary tea and coffee making facilities
allow guests to use them at their own convenience. *Supper* (tea, coffee and biscuits) is served each
evening in the lounge at 9:00pm. As part of our service the Hotel offers laundry facilities, off street
parking for the motorist and bicycle and baggage storage. *Quote this book for 10% discount*

Looking for Bed & Breakfast in Christchurch, then try The Windsor

CHRISTCHURCH CITY

B&B Approved

Turret House *B&B*
Michael and Pam Hamilton
435 Durham Street North, Christchurch

Tel (03) 365 3900   0800 488 773
Fax (03) 365 5601
turretb.bchch@xtra.co.nz   www.turrethouse.co.nz

Double $95-$130 Single $75-$130
(Continental Breakfast) Credit cards accepted
3 King/Twin 3 Queen 1 Twin 1 Single (8 bdrm)
Bathrooms: 8 Ensuite

Turret House is a gracious superior Bed &
Breakfast accommodation located in downtown
Christchurch. It is within easy walking distance
of Cathedral Square, the Botanical Gardens,
museum, art gallery, Arts Centre and Hagley Park 18 hole golf course. Also the casino, new
convention centre and the town hall.

Built around 1900 this historic residence is one of only 3 in the area protected by the New Zealand
Historic Places Trust. It has been restored to capture the original character and charm. Situated
within the grounds is one of Christchurch's best examples of our native kauri tree.

Attractively decorated bedrooms with heaters and electric blankets combine comfort and old world
elegance, with private bathrooms, some with bath and shower, all offering a totally relaxed and
comfortable environment. Tea, coffee and biscuits available 24 hours. Cots and highchairs are also
available. Family room sleeps 4.

If you're looking for a place to stay where the accommodation is superior and the atmosphere friendly
- experience Turret House. Non-smoking policy. Just 15 minutes from Christchurch Airport.
Situated on the corner of Bealey Avenue and Durham Street. Off-street parking.

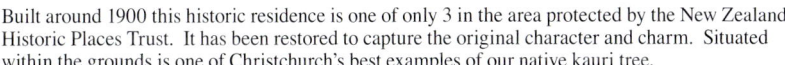

'Céad Míle Fáilte'   One hundred thousand welcomes

CHRISTCHURCH CITY *Christchurch Central*

Riverview Lodge *B&B Self-contained*
Holiday houses
Ernst and Sabine Wipperfuerth
361 Cambridge Terrace, Christchurch 1

Tel (03) 365 2860 Fax (03) 365 2845
riverview.lodge@xtra.co.nz   www.riverview.net.nz

Double $160-$195 Single $100-$150
(Full Breakfast) S/C suites/holiday house $225
Credit cards accepted Children welcome
3 Queen 1 Double 1 Twin 1 Single (5 bdrm)
Bathrooms: 4 Ensuite 1 Private

If you like quality accommodation in a relaxed and
quiet atmosphere, still just minutes walking away
from the centre of an exciting city: this is the place
to stay.

Riverview Lodge is a restored Edwardian residence
that reflects the grace and style of the period with
some fine kauri carvings. Balconies provide
wonderfull river views.

The Edwardian townhouse next door has 2 very
spacious (80 square metres) apartments (1 or 2
bedrooms) for a private stay. Guests find antiques
and quality furniture, a fully equipped kitchen,
lounge, bathroom, TV and private telephone.

For full breakfast we invite guests into the lodge or
if requested supply a continental breakfast in the
suite. For information on our inner city holiday
cottages please look up www.moacottages.co.nz. As ex-tour operators we'll be happy to help you with
planning and bookings. Kayaks, bicycles and golf clubs are for guests to use. We are multilingual.

Guest rooms are elegant combining modern facilities with colonial furnishings

CHRISTCHURCH CITY

Approved

Croydon House *B&B Hotel*
Nita Herbst
63 Armagh Street, Christchurch

Tel (03) 366 5111 0800 276 936 Fax (03) 377 6110
welcome@croydon.co.nz www.croydon.co.nz

Double $120-$150 Single $90-$110 (Full Breakfast)
Child $20 under 12 years Self-contained apartment $180-$220
Credit cards accepted Children welcome
1 King 4 Queen 2 Double 3 Twin 2 Single (12 bdrm)
Bathrooms: 10 Ensuite 2 Guests share

*'Community Pride'
Garden Award winner
for the last four years*

Croydon House is a charming hotel offering fine accommodation in the heart of New Zealand's Garden City. All bedrooms are tastefully refurbished with share or ensuite bathroom. Start your day with our scrumptious buffet and indulge yourself in a deliciously cooked breakfast prepared especially for you.

Explore the city's major attractions, great restaurants, conference venues and the famous Botanical Gardens are within easy walking distance. Also visit the historic tram, art gallery, casino and art centre. We provide internet access. For more information visit our home page on the internet with on-line booking form. Croydon House has received the 'Community Pride' Garden Award for the last 4 consecutive years.

CANTERBURY

CHRISTCHURCH CITY *Christchurch Central*

Home Lea B&B
Pauline & Gerald Oliver
195 Bealey Avenue, Christchurch

Tel (03) 379 9977 0800 355 321 Fax (03) 379 4099
homelea@xtra.co.nz   www.homelea.co.nz

Double $90-$115 Single $65-$90
(Continental Breakfast) Child neg
Dinner by arrangement Credit cards accepted
Children welcome
1 King 3 Queen 3 Single (5 bdrm)
Bathrooms: 2 Ensuite 1 Private 1 Guests share

Home Lea offers the traveller a comfortable and enjoyable stay. Built in the early 1900's, Home Lea has the charm and character of a large New Zealand home of that era: rimu panelling, leadlight windows, and a large lounge with a log fire. Tea, coffee, biscuits and fruit are available at all times. Off-street parking, and email/fax facilities available for guests. Pauline and Gerald are happy to share their knowledge of local attractions and their special interests are travel, sailing and music.

CHRISTCHURCH CITY *Christchurch Central*

Orari B&B *B&B*
Ashton Owen
42 Gloucester Street, Christchurch 1

Tel (03) 365 6569 Fax (03) 365 2525
orari.bb@xtra.co.nz
www.orari.net.nz

Double $160-$190 Single $130-$150
(Special Breakfast) Credit cards accepted
1 King/Twin 9 Queen 5 Single (10 bdrm)
Bathrooms: 8 Ensuite 2 Private

Orari was built in 1893. Of kauri construction with beautifully proportioned rooms, Orari is located in the heart of the city directly opposite the new Christchurch Art Gallery. Orari is within easy walking distance of the Art Centre, the Botanic Gardens, museum, Hagley Park, town hall, casino, convention centre and Cathedral Square. Featuring 10 bedrooms with private bathrooms, off-street parking and wheel chair access, it provides comfortable, friendly accommodation for travellers, business people and small group conferences. Enjoy the convenience of the inner city in an elegant heritage home.

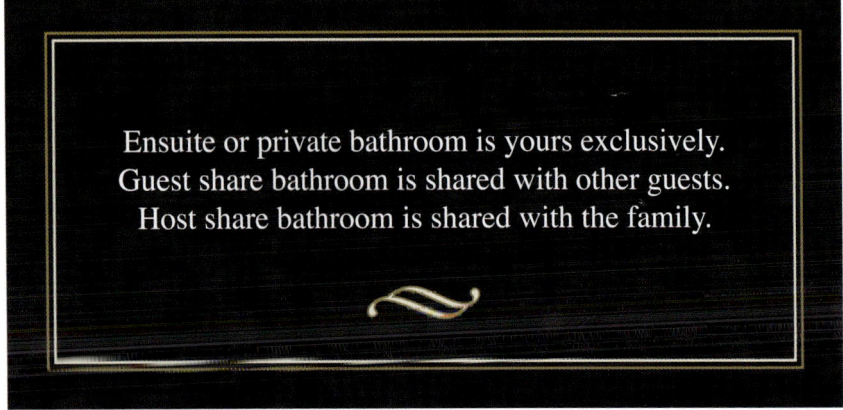

Ensuite or private bathroom is yours exclusively.
Guest share bathroom is shared with other guests.
Host share bathroom is shared with the family.

CHRISTCHURCH CITY *Christchurch Central*

Apartment 37 B&B *B&B*
Lynne & David
Apartment 37, PO Box 177, Old Government Buildings,
Cathedral Square, Christchurch

Tel (03) 377 7473 Fax (03) 377 7863
Mob 027 622 0849 apartment37@xtra.co.nz
www.bnb.co.nz/apartment.html

Double $145-$175 Single $145-$160 (Special Breakfast)
Credit cards accepted
1 Queen 1 Twin (2 bdrm) Bathrooms: 2 Ensuite

In the heart of Christchurch (Cathedral Square), Apartment
37 is unique offering warm friendly hospitality and elegant
accommodation in a grand historic building with central city
convenience. In addition enjoy many extras including Sky TV, tea/coffee making facilities, and access
to in-building facilities (lap pool, gymnasium, spa, sauna, restaurant). Walk to Christchurch's vibrant
attractions - Arts Centre, museum, Botanic Gardens, Hagley Park, shops, cafés, conference centre, and
entertainment or use transport right on door step. Perfect for holidays, conferences or business.

CHRISTCHURCH CITY *Christchurch Central*

The Manor *B&B*
Ann Zwimpfer & Harold Williams
82 Bealey Avenue, City Central, Christchurch

Tel (03) 366 8584   0800 366 859
Fax (03) 366 4946
info@themanor.co.nz
www.themanor.co.nz

Double $187-$347 Single $167-$327 (Full Breakfast)
Credit cards accepted
5 King/Twin 4 Queen 4 Single (9 bdrm)
Bathrooms: 9 Ensuite

The Manor is a beautifully restored Victorian mansion,
built in 1860. The original architecture includes a magnificent entrance foyer, lead light windows and
wood panelling. The tariff includes a full continental and cooked breakfast. We are a short drive from
the airport and a 10-15 mins level walk to the Art Centre, Botanical Gardens, art galleries, museums,
city centre, golf course and restaurants. Free parking and internet access is available to guests. We are a
day trip to Hanmer Springs, Akaroa, and Kaikoura.

CHRISTCHURCH CITY *Christchurch Central*

The Devon B&B *B&B Guesthouse*
Sandra & Benjamin Humphrey
69 Armagh Street, Christchurch

Tel (03) 366 0398   0800 283 386
Fax (03) 366 0392
bandbdevonhotel@xtra.co.nz
www.devonbandbhotel.co.nz

Double $115-$150 Single $80-$99 (Full Breakfast)
Child under 12 $1 per year of age Dinner $20
$35 Extra Adults Credit cards accepted
6 Queen 3 Twin 2 Single (11 bdrm)
Bathrooms: 6 Ensuite 1 Private 4 Guests share

The Devon is a personal guest house located in the heart of beautiful Christchurch City, which offers
elegance and comfort in the style of an olde worlde English manor. Just 5 minutes' walk to Christchurch
Cathedral, town hall, convention centre, casino, museum, art gallery, hospital and Botanical Gardens in
Hagley Park. TV lounge, tea & coffee making facilities. Off-street parking.

CHRISTCHURCH CITY

Holly House *B&B*
Erica & Allister Stewart
1/337 Cambridge Terrace, Inner City,
Christchurch

Tel (03) 371 7337
a.e.stewart@xtra.co.nz
www.bnb.co.nz/hollyhouse.html

Double $120 Single $110 (Special Breakfast)
1 King/Twin (1 bdrm)
Bathrooms: 1 Private

We would be pleased to welcome you to our home which is within walking distance to anywhere in the inner city. We have one lovely bedroom which can be arranged as twin beds or one king-size bed. The guests' bathroom is adjacent to the bedroom. The sitting room overlooks the beautiful tree-lined Avon River. A comment from our visitors' book: "Holly House is an absolute gem." Erica is an artist working with stained glass, and clay sculpture. Allister is a retired school teacher.

CHRISTCHURCH CITY - EAST *1.5km E of Christchurch*

Lanslow Lodge
B&B Homestay Separate/Suite Self-contained
Lance Ching & Dennis Munslow
564 Cashel Street, City East, Christchurch

Tel (03) 942 9842 (4.15pm mon-fri)
Fax (03) 942 9842 Mob 021 262 4377
lanslowlodge@xtra.co.nz
www.bnb.co.nz/lanslow.html

Double $80-$150 Single $50-$80 (Cont. Breakfast)
Dinner $20 Video hire $5 Credit cards accepted
6 Queen 1 Double 1 Twin 2 Single (6 bdrm)
Bathrooms: 1 Ensuite 1 Private 2 shared

Lanslow Lodge (House) character 1930's villa. Home away from home atmosphere, where you can relax, read or just stroll around garden with Amy & Chelsea, our friendly west highland terriers. Join us for a chat over pre-dinner drinks by the fire. 10 minutes to city center. Bus at gate. 5 minutes walk to Eastgate Mall. We do our best to suit everyone and if we don't offer a service please ask and we will endeavor to provide it. Not suitable for children. The house is smoke-free.

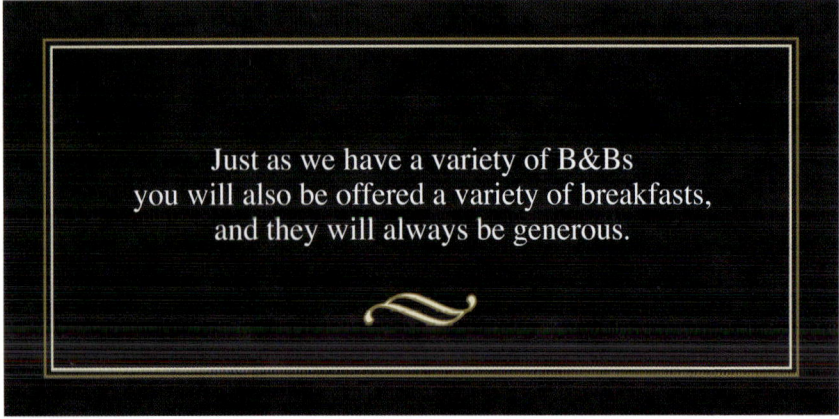

Just as we have a variety of B&Bs
you will also be offered a variety of breakfasts,
and they will always be generous.

CHRISTCHURCH CITY *0.5km Cathedral Square*

Martina Bed & Breakfast *B&B*
Sunny Morley
302 Gloucester Street, Central City, Christchurch

Tel (03) 377 7150 Fax (03) 377 7476
martinabedandbreakfast@ihug.co.nz
www.bnb.co.nz/martinab&b.html

Double $85 Single $75 (Continental Breakfast)
Credit cards accepted
1 Queen (1 bdrm) Bathrooms: 1 Host share

Martina is a charming, victorian house with a peaceful garden,
4 blocks from Cathedral Square. A short walk takes you to
all the city has to offer - restaurants, shopping, museum, arts
centre, art galleries, Botanical Gardens, movies and theatre.
Your downstairs room has a queen bed, bay window, TV, video,
telephone. Toilet in laundry downstairs. We have off street
parking and a bus stop at the gate. Martina has a family yet
international atmosphere. Host is well travelled, lived on 4 continents; also speaks Spanish.

CHRISTCHURCH CITY *1km E of Centre*

The Chester *B&B Separate/Suite*
Jennifer & Jan van den Berg
Suite 3/173 Chester Street East, Christchurch City

Tel (03) 366 5777 Fax (03) 366 5777
Mob 021 365 495
thechester@clear.net.nz
www.bnb.co.nz/thechester.html

Double $95 Single $65 (Continental Breakfast)
Credit cards accepted
1 King/Twin (1 bdrm)
Bathrooms: 1 Ensuite

The Chester B&B Apt 3, situated in the historic Old Wards Brewery Building, dates back to the 1850's.
Now converted into elegant apartments, this unique suite offers all modern comforts and amenities in
close walking distance of the city centre, restaurants, banks, town hall, Arts Centre, casino & convention
centre. Perfect for holiday or business. Your hosts Jan & Jennifer van den Berg will ensure your stay is
comfortable and memorable. Courtesy airport transfers, theatre and concert bookings can be arranged
on request.

CHRISTCHURCH - AVONSIDE *4km E of Christchurch*

Avon Park Lodge
B&B Separate/Suite Garden Studio
Murray & Richeena Bullard
144A Kerrs Road, Avonside, Christchurch

Tel (03) 389 1904 Fax (03) 389 1904
Mob 027 641 9692 avonparklodge@clear.net.nz
www.avonparklodge.bizhosting.com

Double $85-$95 Single $60-$85 (Full Breakfast)
Child by arrangement Dinner by arrangement
Garden studio $95-$100 Credit cards accepted
2 Queen 2 Twin (3 bdrm)
Bathrooms: 1 Ensuite 1 Guests share

Enjoy quiet surroundings in our beautiful garden and 2 storey home close to the Avon River, Porritt Park
rowing and hockey and QE2 leisure centre. The 2 upstairs guest bedrooms are comfortably furnished
with tea and coffee making facilities, etc. Our garden studio has ensuite, fridge and microwave. Close
to frequent public transport (including bus to the railway station). 5 minutes drive to the city. Your hosts
and their lovable boxer dog, Gus, assure you of a warm, friendly welcome. Complimentary pick up.

CANTERBURY

CHRISTCHURCH - WOOLSTON *4km E of Christchurch*

Treeview *B&B Homestay*
Kathy & Laurence Carr
6 Lomond Place, Woolston,
Christchurch 6

Tel (03) 384 2352
www.bnb.co.nz/treeview.html

Double $90   Single $50   (Continental Breakfast)
Child $20   Dinner $20
1 Double 2 Single (2 bdrm)
Bathrooms: 1 Guests share

Welcome. Kiwi hospitality. Smoke-free sunny home in quiet cul-de-sac. Garden with seating. Guests carport. Comfortable beds, electric blankets, hair drier. Generous breakfast in dining room with cathedral ceilings. 10 minutes by car to city and beaches. Bus handy. Courtesy transport from railway station. Airport shuttle service. From Cathedral Square take Gloucester Street to traffic lights at Linwood Avenue. Turn right. Pass Eastgate Mall to traffic lights end of avenue of trees. Right into Hargood Street. First left into Clydesdale, first left Lomond Place.

CHRISTCHURCH - ST MARTINS *4km S of Christchurch City Centre*

Kleynbos B&B *B&B Self-contained*
Gerda De Kleyne & Hans van den Bos
59 Ngaio Street, Christchurch

Tel (03) 332 2896   Mob 027 422 7444
KLEYNBOS@xtra.co.nz
www.bnb.co.nz/kleynbosbb.html

Double $80-$90 Single $75   (Continental Breakfast)
Credit cards accepted
1 Queen 1 Double 1 Single (2 bdrm)
Bathrooms: 1 Ensuite 1 Guests share

Especially for you, quality accommodation with a personal touch. Close (4km) to the city centre, in an easy to find, friendly, tree-lined, residential street. That's us! Your large room with ensuite bathroom is $90 and has its own microwave, fridge, water boiler etc. Gerda works in Mental Health. Having guests is like family who have come to stay.   Directions: SH74 Barbadoes Street, Waltham Road, Wilsons Road, right into Gamblins Road, first left.   (We have for longer term, a large stand-alone house for rent, as well as self-catering accommodation.)

CHRISTCHURCH - ST MARTINS *Christchurch Central*

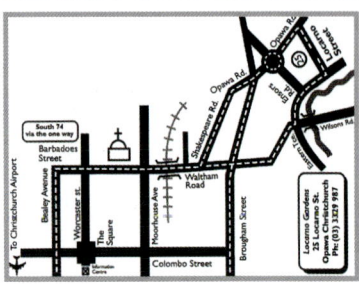

Locarno Gardens   *B&B Self-contained two luxury self-catering apartments*
Aileen & David Davies, 25 Locarno Street, St Martins, Christchurch 8002
Tel (03) 332 9987   Fax (03) 332 9687   Mob 027 4399 747
locarno@xtra.co.nz   www.cottagestays.co.nz/begonia/cottage.htm
Double $85-$115 Single $85-$115   (Continental breakfast optional extra)   Extra person $30
1 SuperKing 1 Queen 1 Twin (3 bdrm)   Bathrooms: 2 Ensuite 1 Private

CHRISTCHURCH - MT PLEASANT *7km E of Christchurch*

Plains View *B&B Homestay*
Robyn & Peter Fleury
2 Plains View, Mt Pleasant,
Christchurch 8

Tel (03) 384 5558 Fax (03) 384 5558
Mob 027 460 8582 Fleury@inet.net.nz
www.bnb.co.nz/fleury.html

Double $80-$95 Single $65 (Continental Breakfast)
1 Queen 1 Double 1 Single (3 bdrm)
Bathrooms: 1 Guests share

Enjoy our warm hospitality in the comfort of our modern home, spacious and sunny with wonderful views of the city and Southern Alps. Relax in our separate guests lounge or join us in our famliy room. Close by is Sumner Beach, Ferrymead Historical Park, Mt Cavendish Gondola and numerous walking tracks. There are many excellent restaurants nearby in Sumner. Complimentary tea and coffee provded. Please phone for directions.

CHRISTCHURCH - MT PLEASANT *7km E of Christchurch CBD*

The Cotterage *B&B Homestay*
Jennifer Cotter
24B Soleares Avenue, Mt Pleasant, Christchurch 8008

Tel (03) 384 2898 Fax (03) 384 2898
jen@e3.net.nz www.bnb.co.nz/thecotterage.html

Double $110 Single $70 (Continental Breakfast)
Child neg Dinner $20 by arrangement Twin $95
Credit cards accepted
1 Queen 1 Twin 1 Single (3 bdrm)
Bathrooms: 1 Ensuite 1 Guests share 1 Host share

Away from the city smog. Quiet secluded comfort in homely cottage down private lane. Charming tranquil garden. Sunny bedrooms opening on to covered terrace (for breakfast alfresco!) Tea and coffee always available. Many cafés, pubs, good restaurants 5 minutes drive. Estuary where bird life abounds 2 minutes walk. Nearby scenic attractions include Sumner Beach, hills, walks, gondola, Lyttelton Harbour. City centre is 15 minutes. We enjoy company, have travelled extensively, enjoy creative pursuits, gardening, books. 2 resident cats. Laundry facilities. Smoking outdoors. Please phone for directions.

CHRISTCHURCH - MT PLEASANT *8km SE of Christchurch CBD*

Santa Maria *B&B*
Anne & Ian Harris
57 Santa Maria Avenue, Mt Pleasant,
Christchurch

Tel (03) 384 1174 Fax (03) 384 6474
Mob 021 673 549 the-harris-family@xtra.co.nz
www.bnb.co.nz/santamaria.html

Double $110 Single $80 (Continental Breakfast)
2 Queen (2 bdrm)
Bathrooms: 1 Ensuite 1 Private

Santa Maria with its swimming pool and astroturf tennis court has panoramic views of the Pacific Ocean through to the Southern Alps. Our comfortable guestroom has ensuite bathroom, tea/coffee making facilities and access to a sunny courtyard. A second bedroom and bathroom is available if desired. Visit the nearby beach village of Sumner with its excellent selection of cosy cafés, restaurants, bars and movie theatres. 2 minutes to windsurfing / kitesurfing / yachting / kayaking. Ride the Gondola or explore the walkways of the Port Hills.

CANTERBURY

CHRISTCHURCH - MT PLEASANT
7km E of Central Christchurch

A Nest on Mount Pleasant *B&B Self-contained*
Kathryn & Kai Tovgaard
15 Toledo Place, Mount Pleasant, Christchurch 8

Tel (03) 3849 485 Fax (03) 3848 385
thenestonMP@xtra.co.nz
www.PlacesToStay.co.nz/places/5011.asp

Double **$85-$115** Single $75-$105 (Full Breakfast)
Child discounted Dinner by arrangement
Credit cards accepted Children welcome
2 Queen 2 Twin (3 bdrm)
Bathrooms: 1 Ensuite 1 Guests share

Unique self-contained home (including full kitchen and laundry facilities) yet with all the service of a homestay: this is the promise of The Nest. Warm hospitality guaranteed with hosts next door. Situated in one of Christchurch's most exclusive hill suburbs set in native bush. Views of estuary, sea and mountains beyond. Tranquil and secure, with garage parking. TV, stereo and BBQ. Very close to Chistchurch's best beaches with excellent cafes and restaurants, Ferrymead Historic Park, Lyttelton Harbour, and hillside walks with breathtaking views to the Southern Alps.

CHRISTCHURCH - MT PLEASANT
8km E of Christchurch

Mt Pleasant Homestay *B&B Homestay*
Jan Neilsen
106A Mt Pleasant Road, Christchurch

Tel (03) 384 1940 Fax (03) 384 1940
janneilsen_me@xtra.co.nz
www.bnb.co.nz/mtpleasanthomestay.html

Double **$120** (Full Breakfast) Child $30
$80 (for single person in twin) Credit cards accepted
Children welcome Pets welcome
1 Queen 1 Twin (2 bdrm)   Bathrooms: 2 Private

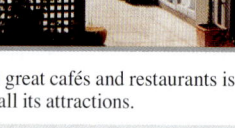

Come park your car at the front door and relax. Enjoy warm hospitality, peace and wonderful sea views. Upstairs in this modern home is where you will have breakfast and share family life. The ground floor is devoted to guests. Bedrooms have private bathrooms. If you wish for privacy there is a guest lounge and kitchen. All rooms open into the garden. Sumner beach, with great cafés and restaurants is 5 minute drive. A 10 minute drive will have you in our beautiful city with all its attractions.

CHRISTCHURCH - MT PLEASANT
8km E of City Centre

Paradise Hills *Homestay*
Sijing & Damon Rutherford
347 Mt Pleasant Road, Mt Pleasant,
Christchurch 8008

Tel (03) 384 5085 0800 709 375
Fax (03) 384 5095 Mob 021 359 376
info@paradise-hills.com   www.paradise-hills.com

Double **$120-$140** Single $80 (Continental Breakfast)
Credit cards accepted
2 Queen 1 Single (3 bdrm)
Bathrooms: 1 Private 1 Guests share

Breathtaking views and fresh sea air - 15 minutes from city centre and 5 minutes to beach. Located on the hills and surrounded by a 200 acre sheep farm, our spacious 500 square metre home offers relaxation in resort type surroundings. Take picturesque walks to meet lambs and rabbits or explore ancient caves. Main bedrooms have mountain and coastline views. Large tennis/squash court, professional pool table, heated swimming/diving pool (Nov-Mar) and indoor spa. Your Chinese hostess offers superb Chinese cuisine (by arrangement). Complimentary airport/city pickup.

CHRISTCHURCH - REDCLIFFS *8km E of Christchurch*

Redcliffs on Sea *B&B Homestay*
Cynthia & Lyndsey Ebert
125 Main Road, Redcliffs,
Christchurch 8

Tel (03) 384 9792 Fax (03) 384 9703
redcliffsonsea@xtra.co.nz
www.redcliffsonsea.co.nz

Double $120 Single $75 (Continental Breakfast)
Credit cards accepted
1 Queen 1 Single (1 bdrm)
Bathrooms: 1 Ensuite

Relax and enjoy our comfortable home by the sea, situated approximately 15 minutes from the city, our home is absolute water front, on the Avon-Heathcote Estuary with magnificent views of the sea, birds and boating. We are non-smoking and our guest facilities include a sunny queen and single bedroom with its own ensuite and TV. Local restaurants offer a choice of cuisine, continental breakfast is included in the tariff, laundry facilities and off-street parking. What more could you wish for?

CHRISTCHURCH - REDCLIFFS *8km E of Christchurch centre*

Pegasus Bay View *B&B*
Denise & Bernie Lock
121A Moncks Spur Road, Redcliffs, Christchurch

Tel (03) 384 2923 Mob 021 254 2888
pegasusbay@slingshot.co.nz
www.pegasusbayview.co.nz

Double $110-$120 Single $100
(Continental Breakfast) Credit cards accepted
1 Queen 1 Double (2 bdrm)
Bathrooms: 1 Private

Relax and enjoy spectacular views over the South Pacific and to the Southern Alps. We offer modern quality accommodation, just 15 minutes from Christchurch City centre and 3 minutes from the seaside suburb of Sumner. Tea and coffee making facilities are provided and breakfast can be enjoyed alfresco on our decked area or in our dining room. The private guest lounge can be converted to a second bedroom for additional friends or family. Relaxation, a warm welcome and marvellous scenery awaits you. One friendly cat.

CHRISTCHURCH - SUMNER *10km E of Christchurch*

Villa Alexandra *B&B Homestay Self-contained*
Wendy & Bob Perry
1 Kinsey Terrace,
Christchurch 8

Tel (03) 326 6291 Fax (03) 326 6096
villa_alexandra@xtra.co.nz
www.villaalexandra.co.nz

Double $85-$110 Single $70 (Full Breakfast)
Child $15 over 12yrs Dinner $35 by arrangement.
1 Queen 1 Double 1 Twin 1 Single (4 bdrm)
Bathrooms: 2 Ensuite 2 Private

Enjoy the warmest hospitality in our spacious turn of the century villa overlooking Sumner Bay. Our home retains the graciousness of a bygone era while offering all modern comforts. In winter enjoy open fires, cosy farmhouse kitchen and on sunny days the verandah and turret. Spectacular sea views from Sumner to the Kaikouras. We enjoy food, wine, music, gardening, tramping, travel. The children have flown, but we still have 3 hens. 5 minutes walk to beach; off street parking; laundry. Also self-contained beach front apartment, 2 double bedrooms, $135 per night, minimum 3 nights.

CANTERBURY

CHRISTCHURCH - SUMNER BEACH   *8km E of Christchurch*

Cave Rock Bed & Breakfast   *B&B Guesthouse*
Gayle & Norm Eade
16 Esplanade, Sumner, Christchurch

Tel **(03) 326 6844**   Fax (03) 326 5600
Mob 027 436 0212   eade@chch.planet.org.nz
www.caverockguesthouse.co.nz

Double $120   Single $95   (Continental Breakfast)
Child $15   Credit cards accepted   Children welcome
4 Queen (4 bdrm)
Bathrooms: 4 Ensuite

The Cave Rock B&B is Christchurch's ultimate seafront
accommodation opposite Sumner's famous Cave Rock. Hosts Gayle and Norm Eade have been in the
industry for 18 years and enjoy meeting people from overseas and within NZ. Our large double rooms
all have seaviews, colour TV, heating and ensuite bathrooms, and can sleep up to 4. Kitchen facilities
available. Sumner is an ideal location, 15 minutes from Christchurch City, we have café/bars, shops,
cinema, all within walking distance. We have a friendly dalmatian dog.

CHRISTCHURCH - SUMNER   *9km E of Central Christchurch*

Abbott House Sumner Bed & Breakfast   *B&B Self-contained*
Janet & Chris Abbott
104 Nayland Street, Sumner, Christchurch

Tel **(03) 326 6111**   For Reservations 0800 020 654
Fax (03) 326 7034   Mob 021 654 344
info@abbotthouse.co.nz   www.abbotthouse.co.nz

Double $70-$125   Single $70-$125   (Continental Breakfast)
Child $5   Credit cards accepted   Children welcome
2 King/Twin 1 Double 1 Single (2 bdrm)
Bathrooms: 1 Ensuite 1 Private

Your hosts, Chris and Janet Abbott welcome you to our historic
restored 1870's villa in Christchurch's unique seaside village. Our
home is one block from the beach, and an easy 10 minute walk
along the beach to Sumner's many cafés, restaurants, boutique
shops and cinema. Both suite and studio have king-sized beds, own kitchen areas, TV and video or DVD,
internet access. Off-street parking. Laundry facilities. We also have nearby a 3 bedroom 2 livingroom
house that sleeps 8 for holiday rentals.

CHRISTCHURCH - SUMNER   *12km E of Christchurch*

Scarborough-Heights   *B&B*
Barbara and Brian Hanlon
21 Godley Drive, Scarborough, Christchurch 8008

Tel **(03) 326 7060**   Fax (03) 326 7060
Mob 027 229 7312   stay@scarborough-heights.co.nz
www.scarborough-heights.co.nz

Double $150   Single $90   (Full Breakfast)
Child $50   Dinner $40 by arrangement
Credit cards accepted   Children welcome
1 Queen 2 Single (2 bdrm)
Bathrooms: 1 Ensuite 1 Private

Scarborough-Heights is a striking, modern architecturally designed home set in an award winning
garden, high on Scarborough Hill and offering luxurious bed & breakfast accommodation. All rooms
offer spectacular views of the Southern Alps, Christchurch City and South Pacific Ocean. We provide
friendly hospitality in peaceful, quiet surroundings yet are only 20 minutes from the city centre and 5
minutes from the seaside village of Sumner with its many cafés, speciality shops and cinema. We have
no children living at home, only 2 cats.

CHRISTCHURCH - SUMNER *8km E of Christchurch*

Tiro Moana *B&B*
Helen Mackay & Brian Lamb
89 Richmond Hill Road, Sumner, Christchurch

Tel (03) 326 6209 Fax (03) 326 6203
enquiries@tiromoana.co.nz
www.tiromoana.co.nz

Double $100-$140 Single $80-$115 (Full Breakfast)
Child $25 Dinner by arrangement
Credit cards accepted Children welcome
1 King/Twin 1 Queen 1 Double (3 bdrm)
Bathrooms: 1 Ensuite 1 Private

Sumner, only 15 minutes from the city, with interesting restaurants, cinema, specialty shops and walks. Tiro Moana – built 1904 in a splendid position overlooking the beach. A perfect spot to relax, wander the garden have a bath outside under the stars and sleep to the sound of the sea. The atmosphere is friendly, relaxed and informal providing guests' lounge, tea and coffee facilities, a fresh and generous breakfast. Laundry facilities are available. We look forward to welcoming you.

CHRISTCHURCH - SUMNER *10km E of Christchurch*

Clifton Hill B&B
B&B Separate/Suite Self-contained
Dean & Raelene Rees
112 Panorama Road, Clifton Hill, Sumner, Christchurch

Tel (03) 326 7275 Fax (03) 377 0830
Mob 027 224 4972 stay@cliftonhill.co.nz
www.cliftonhill.co.nz

Double $150-$165 (Continental Breakfast)
Child by arrangement Dinner by arrangement
Credit cards accepted Children welcome
1 Queen (1 bdrm) Bathrooms: 1 Ensuite

Enjoy our hospitality at our peaceful property, your own deck and our swimming pool and spa to use. Situated 20 minutes drive from the city, 3 minutes from Sumner village and beach with its many restaurants, cafés and cinema. At the end of our road are the walkways of the Port Hills and nearby are the Port of Lyttelton, Ferrymead Historic Park & Mt Cavandish Gondola. We are non-smoking and have a 5 year old son, 2 cats and a dog. Phone for directions.

CHRISTCHURCH - HOON HAY *5km SE of Christchurch*

Sparks Road *B&B*
Micky & Alistair Watson
330 Sparks Road, Hoon Hay,
Christchurch

Tel (03) 339 0138 Fax (03) 339 0139
Mob 021 145 9597 alandmic@xtra.co.nz
www.bnb.co.nz/hoonhay.html

Double $85-$100 Single $70-$85 (Full Breakfast)
1 Queen (1 bdrm)
Bathrooms: 1 Private

A touch of country 10 minutes from the city, our 8 acre property has spacious gardens for you to enjoy. We offer you a suite with your own lounge, tea/coffee making facilities, laundry, shower & bath. Your comfort is our priority and you will be our only guests. The main highway to Akaroa is close, plus several wineries and golf courses. We have travelled extensively in NZ and may be able to help with trips away from tourist routes. Courtesy pick up. 1 cat.

CANTERBURY

CHRISTCHURCH - WESTMORLAND *7km SW of CBD*

Slippers *B&B Homestay*
Large separate guest suite with own entrance
Georgie & Ron McKie
66 Penruddock Rise, Westmorland 8002, Christchurch

Tel (03) 339 6170 Fax (03) 339 6170
Mob 021 114 2198 mckiepic@paradise.net.nz
www.bnb.co.nz/slippers.html

Double $190 Single $120   (Continental Breakfast)
Dinner $50 including wine Credit cards accepted
1 King/Twin 1 Single (2 bdrm)
Bathrooms: 1 Private

Pure New Zealand wool slippers are ready for your use the moment you arrive at Slippers. We invite you to relax in our beautiful Port Hills home with stunning views of the Alps, the Canterbury Plains and Christchurch City.

Specializing in single party bookings we offer 2 bedrooms, a lounge, private bathroom and private entrances in a smoke-free environment. All rooms have central heating, electric blankets, bathrobes, hair dryers, access to full service Sky TV, and an extensive library. The house features a superb collection of museum quality artefacts from Papua New Guinea as well as spectacular antique maps and photographs by leading NZ photographers.

A fruit bowl, home baking, wonderful PNG plunger coffee and Twinings teas are available at all times. Dinner is available on 24 hours notice, and features fine wines. Complimentary email and internet are available, and we have 2 friendly cats, Mangi and Liklik. Parking is off-street and a bus service to the central city is at the gate.

We are internationally recognized photographers and photographer guests are welcome to use our superbly equipped chemical darkroom, and digital scanning and CD burning facilities. Lessons can be arranged on request.

With our extensive knowledge of the South Island we can offer great advice on photographic opportunities as well as introductions to local camera clubs. We are widely travelled and enjoy meeting people with similar interests.

CHRISTCHURCH - CASHMERE *5km S of Christchurch*

City Lights *B&B Homestay*
Jan & Bob Thayer
34 Harry Ell Drive, Cashmere, Christchurch

Tel (03) 332 5566 Fax (03) 337 0038
Mob 021 105 8593   jancitylights@xtra.co.nz
www.bnb.co.nz/citylightschristchurch.html

Double $130-$160 Single $100 (Full Breakfast)
Dinner by arrangement Credit cards accepted
1 King/Twin 1 Queen 1 Twin (3 bdrm)
Bathrooms: 1 Private

Enjoy the quiet and private gardens, beautiful heated
saltwater swimming pool (Oct-April), piano, home gym,
and the nearby Port Hills walkways. Relax in any of the
sundrenched outdoor areas and enjoy the million dollar
views from the mountains to the sea or curl up with a book
in the spacious warm and well appointed living areas or
private lounge. Bedrooms have comfortable excellent
quality beds and linen including cosy luxurious robes in
which to relax.

Delicious full breakfasts with fresh locally grown produce,
great coffee and freshly baked bread. Superb dinners
available by arrangement and special diets catered for.
Alternatively we can tell you about some great Christchurch
restaurants in this area. Our home is smoke-free inside and
we share it with our lovely cat Tabby.

Our interests include sports (armchair), walking, gardening, kayaking, Rotary, travel, good food and
wine, and most importantly our grandchildren We prefer to host one couple or group of people at
a time. This ensures your privacy and enables us to focus on your requirements. Bob and Jan have
travelled a lot and really appreciate our beautiful country. It would be our privilege to help you plan
to get the very best our of your time here whether you are on holidays or business. We look forward to
welcoming you to our home with tea/coffee and fresh baking or a cool drink. Directions will be given at
time of booking.

*Stunning panoramic views and a warm welcome await you in our spacious modern
Mediterranean style home nestled in the Cashmere Hills.*

CHRISTCHURCH - CASHMERE *5km S of Christchurch Centre*

Janet Milne *B&B*
12A Hackthorne Road, Cashmere, Christchurch

Tel (03) 337 1423
www.bnb.co.nz/milne.html

Single $50 (Continental Breakfast)
1 Queen 1 Single (1 bdrm)
Bathrooms: 1 Ensuite 1 Guests share 1 Host share

2 storeyed home in quiet back section on Cashmere Hills.
Lower storey is an independent suite comprising 2 hand basins,
shower, lavatory, kingsize bed with electric blanket, 2 single
bunks, television, telephone, heaters, and table and chairs. Tea/
coffee making facilities. Non-smokers only. I am a registered
general nurse; obstetrics nurse; a university student studying for a
degree in linguistics; and an English language teacher. The piano
loves attention. Spanish and English are my favourite languages.
'Explorer' of foreign countries.

CHRISTCHURCH - HALSWELL *6km SE of Christchurch Central*

Overton *B&B Self-contained*
Judi & Joe Brizzell
241 Kennedys Bush Road, Halswell, Christchurch 3

Tel (03) 322 8326 Fax (03) 322 8350
Mob 025 623 0831 brizzell.accom@xtra.co.nz
www.bnb.co.nz/overton.html

Double $85-$110 Single $60-$85 (Full Breakfast)
Child neg Dinner $30 Credit cards accepted
Children welcome
1 Queen 4 Twin (3 bdrm)
Bathrooms: 1 Private 1 Host share

Tranquil, cosy and convenient. Only 20 minutes from the city and near the Akaroa Highway, our
extensive garden on the Port Hills overlooks the rural Canterbury Plains to the Southern Alps. Enjoy
a warm hosted experience. The self-contained, exclusive-to-you Garden Lodge is fully equipped – 2
bedrooms (1 queen, 2 twin), private bathroom, kitchen and TV. Twin bedroom in our home. New
Zealand cuisine, featuring seasonal home-grown produce. Interests include our garden, fishing, fibre-
arts, walking in the adjacent park and our friendly dog.

CHRISTCHURCH - BROADFIELD *16km SW of Christchurch Central*

Huntingdon Grange
B&B Farmstay Separate/Suite Self-contained
Gaye & Lindsay Johnson
Shands Road, RD6, Broadfield, Christchurch

Tel (03) 344 5899 Fax (03) 344 5533
Mob 027 446 6144 stay@huntingdongrange.co.nz
www.huntingdongrange.co.nz

Double $100-$175 Single $90 (Continental Breakfast)
(Full Breakfast) Credit cards accepted
2 King/Twin 1 King 3 Queen (5 bdrm)
Bathrooms: 3 Ensuite 1 Guests share

Just minutes from Christchurch City or airport, enjoy the ambience of our small country estate.
Nestled amongst established trees and gardens, Huntingdon Grange is the ideal place to stay while
visiting Christchurch or on your journey around the South Island. Quality furnishings and tasteful
décor enhance your relaxation and enjoyment. Unwind in our stylish lounge with open fire, or in the
conservatory or in a heated swimming pool in summer. Enjoy tennis, petanque, croquet or visit the
wineries, golf courses and country cafés close by.

CHRISTCHURCH - LINCOLN
20km S of Christchurch CBD

Menteith Country House   *Country B&B*
Fay & Stephen Graham
961 Springs Road, RD 6, Christchurch 8021

Tel **(03) 325 2395**   Fax (03) 325 2396
Mob 021 131 5523   menteith@paradise.net.nz
www.bnb.co.nz/menteithcountryhomestay.html

Double $150-$180   Single $135-$150   (Full Breakfast)
Child neg   Credit cards accepted
2 King/Twin 1 Queen (3 bdrm)
Bathrooms: 3 Ensuite

Our tranquil farmlet with easy city/airport access
supports a small sheep flock for Fay's spinning (try
your hand!) and 8 beehives. Attractive guests rooms surround the heated spa and swimming pool
conservatory with robes provided. Be pampered with crisp linen, large fluffy towels, refrigerator, tea/
coffee and cookies, TV, phone, hairdryer, computer jack, plenty of heat and warm cosy beds. Hearty
breakfasts are served in our sunny dining room. Delightful reasonably priced restaurants nearby. Golf
course and university 3km. Resident cat, Muffin.

CHRISTCHURCH - LANSDOWNE VALLEY *10km S of Christchurch*

Lansdowne   *Farmstay*
Susan & Colin Sinclair
203 Early Valley Road,
Lansdowne Valley RD2, Christchurch

Tel **(03) 322 1207**   Fax (03) 322 1208
colnsue@ihug.co.nz
www.bnb.co.nz/lansdowne.html

Double $130   (Full Breakfast) Dinner $30pp
Credit cards accepted
1 Queen 2 Single (2 bdrm)
Bathrooms: 1 Guests share

Lansdowne farm offers country peace only 20 minutes from the centre of Christchurch. Relax on
our verandah or sunroom while enjoying our garden and native birds. A great base for exploring
Christchurch, Banks Peninsula, Akaroa, mountains or nearby wineries. Susan enjoys needlework and
patchwork. Colin is a member of Lions. Guests are welcome to share our home overnight or for longer
stays to enjoy the surrounding attractions. Full board can be provided. Our cat and spaniel also enjoy
the garden and verandah.

CHRISTCHURCH - TAI TAPU   *15km S of Christchurch*

Pear Drop Inn   *B&B Homestay*
Erik & Paula Gray
Akaroa Highway 75, Tai Tapu, RD 2, Christchurch

Tel **(03) 329 6778**   Fax (03) 329 6661
Mob 021 126 6873   peardropinn@clear.net.nz
www.bnb.co.nz/peardropinn.html

Double $100-$120   Single $60   (Continental Breakfast)
Child $30 under 5 years free Dinner $30
Credit cards accepted Children welcome
1 King 2 Queen 6 Single (3 bdrm)
Bathrooms: 1 Ensuite 1 Guests share 1 Host share

Welcome to our comfortable country home, nestled in 2.5 acres. Superbly located for city and country
activities. Relaxed Kiwi hospitality and home cooked meals. Sprayfree vegetables/produce from our
garden. Meal times flexible. Our rooms are spacious, and comfortably appointed. We include fresh
fruit and goodies in each room. Local wineries, restaurants, walking tracks, golf, all within 5 minutes.
Christchurch City centre 15 minutes. Akaroa Village 1 hour drive.
Free pick up and drop off to airport, bus, train.

CANTERBURY

LYTTELTON *9km E of Christchurch*

Shonagh O'Hagan's Guest House *B&B*
Shonagh O'Hagan
Dalcroy House, 16 Godley Quay, Lyttelton

Tel **(03) 328 8577** Mob (025) 346 351
shonagh.ohagan@xtra.co.nz
www.bnb.co.nz/shonaghohagans.html

Double $115 Single $90 (Full Breakfast)
Child $25 Dinner $35
Credit cards accepted Children welcome
1 King/Twin 2 Queen 1 Double (4 bdrm)
Bathrooms: 3 Guests share 2 Host share

Dalcory House built 1859, has been a boarding school, private residents, rental property, and hostel for naval rating's in WW2. Shonagh your hostess is a cook, nurse, educator, health manager and mother. Have a comfortable nights sleep in pleasant surroundings with a clear view of Lyttelton Port and Harbour, 5 minutes' walk from the centre of Lyttelton and 1 minute's drive to the centre of Christchurch. Shonagh and her son will ensure your stay is comfortable and memorable.

LYTTELTON - CHURCH BAY *25km SE of Christchurch*

The Priory *Homestay*
Anne Prior
177 Marine Drive, Main Road, Church Bay, RD 1, Lyttelton

Tel **(03) 329 4441** Fax (03) 329 4441 Mob 021 262 2046
thepriory@xtra.co.nz   www.bnb.co.nz/thepriory.html

Double $85 Single $60 (Full Breakfast) Child $10
Dinner $20 by arrangement Credit cards accepted Children welcome
1 Queen 1 Double 2 Single (1 bdrm) Bathrooms: 1 Host share

The Priory at Church Bay is just 30 minutes from Christchurch city, located on the southern edge of Lyttelton Harbour. Upstairs studio sleeps 6, with great elevated views overlooking Church Bay and the harbour. Pretty cottage garden. Shared bathroom, cooked and continental breakfast available, evening meals on request (complimentary homemade fruit wines from The Priory.) Be playing golf in just 5 minutes, good swimming a short walk away and other activities close by. Close boat ramp makes it ideal for sailing holidays. Woolcraft workshop weekends available.

GOVERNORS BAY *13km SE of Christchurch*

Governors Bay Bed & Breakfast
B&B Self-contained
Karen & Kevin McGrath
14 Hays Rise, Governors Bay, Lyttelton RD 1

Tel **(03) 329 9930** Mob 021 622 657
karen@gbbedandbreakfast.co.nz
www.gbbedandbreakfast.co.nz

Double $110-$130 Single $100
(Continental Breakfast)
Credit cards accepted Pets welcome
1 Queen (2 bdrm) Bathrooms: 1 Private

Unique timber home designed to accommodate our B&B private guest wing. Separate entrance with sunny morning deck. Enjoy brekky (self-contained) in your room or on the deck. Queen room with picture window has panoramic views of Lyttelton Harbour. TV, fridge, and CD player. Private guest lounge optional extra, or convert for more sleeping. 20 minute drive to Christchurch, 15 minutes to Lyttelton, only 2 minutes to local hotel and café/wine bar. Karen operates Earth Healer Aromatherapy and offers complimentary aromatherapy baths. Full treatments and Reiki by appointment. We and our labrador cross Bella-Brae look forward to welcoming you soon.

TEDDINGTON - LYTTELTON HARBOUR *20km S of Christchurch*

Bergli Hill Farmstay   *Farmstay*
Rowena & Max Dorfliger
265 Charteris Bay Road, Teddington, R.D.1 Lyttelton

Tel (03) 329 9118   Fax (03) 329 9118
Mob 027 482 9410   bergli@ihug.co.nz
www.vmacgill.net/bergli

Double **$105-$125**   Single $70-$90   (Full Breakfast)
Child $7 less   Dinner from $25 by arrangement
Credit cards accepted Children welcome
1 King/Twin 1 Queen 1 Double
2 Twin 3 Single (3 bdrm)   Bathrooms: 2 Ensuite 1 Host share

Lyttelton Harbour and the Port Hills create a dynamic panorama you can enjoy from our custom-built log chalet. Rowena speaks Japanese (but is a Kiwi) and Max speaks German. We are both self-employed (woodworker and shadow puppeteer) and enjoy sharing a sail on Max's yacht. Our pet cat, alpacas and sheep, welcome guests enthusiastically. Whether relaxing on the veranda at Max's hand-crafted table or sipping wine in the spa bath, we are sure you will make good memories.

DIAMOND HARBOUR - CHURCH BAY   *35km S of Christchurch*

Kai-o-ruru Bed & Breakfast
B&B Separate/Suite   Self-contained
Robin & Philip Manger
32 James Drive, Church Bay,
Lyttelton, RD 1

Tel (03) 329 4788   Fax (03) 329 4788
manger@xtra.co.nz
www.bnb.co.nz/kaiorurubedbreakfast.html

Double **$90**   Single $50   (Full Breakfast)
Dinner $25
2 Single (1 bdrm)
Bathrooms: 1 Ensuite

Explore Banks Peninsula from Church Bay. Our cosy, ensuite unit overlooks Quail Island and our coastal garden. The room has a tea/coffee tray, home-made biscuits, books, TV, fridge. We are a non-smoking household with an unobtrusive cat. Philip and I are travelled, retired teachers who enjoy welcoming travellers to our wonderful area. Languages: German, Dutch (some Italian, Spanish).

LYTTELTON HARBOUR - PURAU   *35km SE of Chrsitchurch*

Mt Evans B&B   *B&B Separate/Suite*
Pauline Croft & Barry Kendall
53 Purau - Port Levy Road,
Purau, Lyttelton Harbour

Tel (03) 329 4414   Fax (03) 329 4414
kendallcroft@hyper.net.nz
www.bnb.co.nz/mtevans.html

Double **$75-$95**   Single $70-$90
(Continental Breakfast)   Child $15
Dinner by arrangement   Two separate cottages
2 Queen 2 Single (3 bdrm)   Bathrooms: 2 Private

Our home is situated on 1.5 hectares, amongst mature trees on the gentle slopes of Mt Evans. Just 500 metres from the beach, we offer tranquil rural accommodation in 2 separate and sunny modern cottages. A perfect base for exploring Banks Peninsula and Christchurch (ferry 7 minutes to Lyttelton) or to relax and unwind. Local attractions include swimming, boating etc, wildlife cruises in the harbour. Mountain biking, tramping (we are experienced outdoor people happy to share our knowledge) abundant bird life and wonderful views.

SELWYN - DUNSANDEL   *30km SW of Christchurch*

Selwyn Bed and Breakfast   *B&B*
Susan Askew & John Baker
Camden Street, Selwyn Village,
Near Dunsandel, Canterbury

Tel (03) 325 4184 Fax (03) 325 4195
selwyn@baskcontrol.co.nz
www.bnb.co.nz/selwynbandb.html

Double $100-$115 Single $75-$85 (Full Breakfast)
Child neg
2 Queen 1 Single (2 bdrm)
Bathrooms: 2 Ensuite

Our modern home with half-acre garden is in historic Selwyn Village, off SH1 south of Christchurch. Surrounded by farmland, we are also close to vineyards, skiing and world class salmon fishing. Newly appointed upstairs guest rooms, each with large ensuite, comfortable bed, TV and radio/alarm, open onto a guest lounge with tea/coffee facilities, or feel at home in our family lounge with two quiet children and friendly cats and dog. Continental or cooked breakfast; choice of nearby restaurants. email, facsimile and laundry facilities.

AKAROA - BARRY'S BAY   *12km before Akaroa*

Rosslyn Estate   *B&B Farmstay Homestay*
Ross, Lynette, Kirsty (12) & Matt (10) Curry
Barry's Bay, RD 2, Akaroa

Tel (03) 304 5804 Fax (03) 304 5804
Rosslyn@xtra.co.nz
www.bnb.co.nz/rosslynestate.html

Double $115-$135 Single $100 (Full Breakfast)
Child negotiable Dinner $30pp Laundry no charge
Credit cards accepted
2 Queen (2 bdrm)   Bathrooms: 2 Ensuite

Rosslyn is a large historic homestead built in the 1860's, overlooking the serene Akaroa Harbour. It has been our family home and dairy farm for 4 generations. 2 large ground floor rooms have been refurbished to accommodate you in comfort. A spa room, pool and laundry are also available. We have enjoyed sharing our life style with guests for the past 17 years and look forward to welcoming you too. Directions: SH75, Rosslyn Estate sign behind red picket fence on left travelling to Akaroa.

AKAROA - PAUA BAY   *12km E of Akaroa*

Paua Bay Farmstay   *B&B Farmstay*
Murray & Sue Johns
Postal, C/- 113 Beach Road,.
Akaroa, Banks Peninsula

Tel (03) 304 8511 Fax (03) 304 8511
Mob 021 133 8194 info@pauabay.com
www.pauabay.com

Double $100 Single $70 (Full Breakfast)
Child neg Dinner $30
1 Queen 1 Twin (2 bdrm)
Bathrooms: 1 Guests share

Set in a private bay, our 900 acre sheep, deer and cattle farm is surrounded by coast-line, native bush and streams. You are spoilt for choice - walk to the beach, enjoy seals and extensive bird life, join in seasonal farming activities or horse riding. Swim in the pool, laze in the hammock and don't miss the secluded moonlit bath under the stars overlooking the pacific ... In the evening share a meal of fresh farm produce with relaxed conversation gathered around the large kitchen table.

BANKS PENINSULA - OKAINS BAY *20km N of Akaroa*

Kawatea *Farmstay*
Judy & Kerry Thacker
Okains Bay, Banks Peninsula

Tel (03) 304 8621 Fax (03) 304 8621
kawatea@xtra.co.nz   www.bnb.co.nz/kawatea.html

Double $100-$130 Single $65-$90 (Full Breakfast)
Child by arrangement Dinner $25-$30 Credit cards accepted
3 Queen 2 Single (3 bdrm)
Bathrooms: 1 Ensuite 1 Private 1 Guests share

Experience the grace and charm of yesteryear, while enjoying
the fine food and wine of NZ today. Revel in the peace of
country life, but still be close to sights and activities. Escape
to Kawatea, an historic Edwardian homestead set in spacious
gardens, and surrounded by land farmed by our Irish ancestors
since the 1850s. Built in 1900 from native timbers, it features
stained glass windows and handcrafted furniture, and has been
carefully renovated to add light and space without losing its old
world charm.

Linger over your choice of breakfast in the sunny conservatory.
Join us for barbeques on the expansive verandahs, savouring
seafood from the bay, and creative country fare from our garden
and farm. Gather around the dining table by the fire, sharing
experiences with fellow travellers.

Participate in farm activities such as moving stock, feeding
pet sheep, lambing, calving or shearing. Wander our 1400

acre hillside farm, climbing to enjoy a panoramic view of Banks Peninsula. Relax or swim at Okains
Bay, observe the birdlife on the estuary, or walk along the scenic coastline to secluded beaches and
a seal colony with excellent photographic opportunities. Learn about Maori culture and the life of
early settlers at the acclaimed Okains Bay Museum. Explore Akaroa, with its strong French influence,
visit art galleries and craft shops. Play golf, go horse riding, sample local wines and watch traditional
cheeses being made. Take a harbour cruise or swim with the rare Hector's dolphin.

We have been providing farmstays since 1988, and pride ourselves on thoughtful personal service.
Romantic weekends and special occasion dinners are also catered for. We hope you come as a visitor
but leave as a friend. **Directions:** Take Highway 75 from Christchurch through Duvauchelle. Turn
left at signpost marked Okains Bay. Drive to the top of the bay - we are 6km downhill on the right.

AKAROA *5km N of Akaroa*

Farmstay Separate/Suite
Hanne & Paul LeLievre
Box 4, Akaroa, Banks Peninsula

Tel (03) 304 7255   Fax (03) 304 7255
Mob 027 4942 070
Double.L@Xtra.co.nz
www.sealsafari.com

Double $95   Single $50   (Full Breakfast)
Dinner $25   Children welcome
1 Queen 1 Single (1 bdrm)
Bathrooms: 1 Ensuite

Our home is situated 1.5km up the Takamatua Valley and 5km from Akaroa. We farm sheep, cattle and deer, and usually have a menagerie of dogs, cats and orphaned pets around. Hanne is Danish and speaks that language fluently. Our interests include golf and bridge. We offer spacious accommodation in a sheltered position and invite you to enjoy some good old fashioned country hospitality. A trip to the Akaroa Seal Colony Safari which includes a farm and scenic tour, should be considered a must.

AKAROA *1km N of Akaroa*

Loch Hill Country Cottages
Self-contained individual cottages
Jill and Murray Gibb (resident managers)
PO Box 21, Main Highway75, Akaroa

Tel (03) 304 7195   0800 456 244   Fax (03) 304 7672
lochhill@xtra.co.nz   www.lochhill.co.nz

Double $125-$165   Single $125
(Continental Breakfast $10pp)   Child $15 under 12 years
Credit cards accepted   Children welcome
2 King/Twin 4 King 8 Queen 4 Single (13 bdrm)
Bathrooms: 7 Ensuite 3 Private

Loch-Hill with magnificent sea views overlooking Akaroa, and cluster of fully self-contained luxurious cottages, nestled in surrounding bush, park and garden setting, offers privacy and tranquillity. Some large cottages have air-conditioning. Try our new romantic honeymoon cottages with cozy log-fires and double spa-baths. Enjoy wonderful views form your balcony. Experience the hospitality of Loch-Hill "Caid Mile Failte" (One hundred thousand welcomes). Explore or relax in these idyllic, secluded surroundings. Perfect for your holiday retreat, smaller business conference, or wedding group. Special rates available.

AKAROA *80km SE of Christchurch*

The Maples *B&B*
Lesley & Peter Keppel
158 Rue Jolie, Akaroa

Tel (03) 304 8767   Fax (03) 304 8767
maplesakaroa@xtra.co.nz
www.themaplesakaroa.co.nz

Double $110-$120   Single $85   (Full Breakfast)
Credit cards accepted
3 Queen 1 Single (3 bdrm)
Bathrooms: 3 Ensuite

The Maples is a charming historic 2 storey home built in 1877. It is situated in a delightful garden setting, 3 minutes walk from the cafés and waterfront. We offer 2 queen bedrooms with ensuites upstairs and a separate garden room with a queen and single bed also ensuited. You can relax in the separate guests lounge where tea and coffee is available. Our delicious continental and cooked breakfasts usually include freshly baked brioche and croissants.

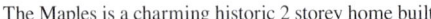

408

AKAROA   *5km S of Akaroa*

Onuku Heights - Historic Farmstay   *B&B Farmstay*
Eckhard Keppler
Onuku Heights, Akaroa

Tel (03) 304 7112 Fax (03) 304 7116
onuku.heights@paradise.net.nz
www.onuku-heights.co.nz

Double $140-$240 (Full Breakfast)
Dinner $40-$60 by prior arrangement
Credit cards accepted
3 King (3 bdrm)
Bathrooms: 3 Ensuite

Onuku Heights is a charming, carefully restored 1860's homestead overlooking the Akaroa Harbour. Nestled in orchard and tranquil gardens with an abundance of bird life, it is surrounded by native bush reserves, streams and waterfalls on a 309 hectare working sheep farm.

Enjoy spacious rooms furnished with antiques, comfortable firm king-size beds and exquisite ensuite bathrooms. The 2 guest rooms in the homestead have majestic sea views and the sunny cottage room has quaint garden views. There is a separate well-appointed guest lounge with an open fire and verandah. Indulge yourself at the heated pool; soak up the sun, listening to the trickling fountain and basking in the stunning views.

Explore the beautiful scenery on well maintained walking tracks, going up to 700 metres altitude with breathtaking panoramic views of the Akaroa Harbour, the ocean and the Alps. Our property is part of the Banks Peninsula Track.

In the morning we prepare you a delicious breakfast with freshly baked bread, home-made jam, cereals, fruits from the orchard; bacon and eggs if you like. In the evening you may choose one of Akaroa's fine restaurants, a mere 15 minute drive away or we can spoil you with a three course candle lit dinner by prior arrangement. Then relax on the veranda with a glass of wine, enjoy the sunset and beautiful birdsong.

Join us in the farm activities, recline in a sun-lounger,
or just dream the day away under an apple tree

AKAROA *80km SE of Christchurch*

Maison de la Mer
B&B Homestay Self contained apartment
Laurice & Alan Bradford
1 Rue Benoit, Akaroa, Banks Peninsula

Tel (03) 304 8907   Fax (03) 304 8907
Mob 025 376 982   maisondelamer@xtra.co.nz
www.maisondelamer.co.nz

Double $150-$200 Single $130   (Full Breakfast)
breakfast provisions in apartment $220
Credit cards accepted
4 Queen 1 Single (4 bdrm)   Bathrooms: 4 Ensuite

Maisondelamer is a 1910 2 storey villa sited directly opposite the beach. Guests can easily walk to the shops, restaurants, and cafes. 2 rooms have harbour views, 1 has a double spa bath, and 1 has a private sitting room. All rooms are elegantly furnished and have TV and tea/coffee facilities. The Loft is a seperate apartment that sleeps 2 with views of the harbour. Enjoy a glass of wine in our lounge or on the verandah in summer. It is our aim to provide a warm welcome, and we can assure you of an enjoyable stay.

AKAROA *80km SE of Christchurch*

Wilderness House   *Boutique B&B*
Jim & Liz Coubrough
42 Rue Grehan, Akaroa

Tel (03) 304 7517   Fax (03) 304 7518   Mob 021 669 381
info@wildernesshouse.co.nz
www.wildernesshouse.co.nz

Double $195-$220 Single $160-$180 (Full Breakfast)
Dinner by arrangement Credit cards accepted
1 King/Twin 3 Queen (4 bdrm)
Bathrooms: 3 Ensuite 1 Private

Wilderness House is a beautiful historic home set in a large traditional garden containing protected trees, old roses and a private vineyard. Charming bedrooms, with their own character, feature fine linen, fresh flowers, tea/coffee and home baking. Elegant lounge opens to verandah and garden. Delicious continental and cooked breakfasts. We take particular care to make you feel comfortable, relaxed and welcome in our home. Join us for a glass of wine in the evening. Short stroll to harbour, restaurants and shops. Resident cats, Beethoven and Harry.

AKAROA HARBOUR - FRENCH FARM *70km SE of Christchurch*

Bantry Lodge   *B&B Self-contained*
Dolina & David Barker
French Farm, RD 2 Ext, Akaroa

Tel (03) 304 5161   Fax (03) 304 5162
Mob 025 284 8260   barker.d@xtra.co.nz
www.bantrylodge.co.nz

Double $120-$140 Single $80-$100
(Full Breakfast) Dinner $40 by arrangement
Self contained cottage Credit cards accepted
1 Queen 1 Double 1 Single (3 bdrm)
Bathrooms: 2 Private

Our historic home has uninterrupted views across Akaroa Harbour 50 metres away. Groundfloor double room has french doors to verandah and sea views, private bath. Upstairs queen room with balcony overlooks harbour and hills, private bath. Coffee and tea facilities provided with home baking. Our comfortable sitting room is for relaxing or joining us for a drink. Full breakfast is served in our elegant dining room. We offer comfort, tranquillity, space. A self-contained cottage sleeps 4, linen, breakfast supplies available.

AKAROA   *3km N of Akaroa*

Akaroa Country Lodge
B&B Separate/Suite Self-contained
David & Sue Thurston
19 Bells Road, Takamatua, Akaroa

Tel (03) 304 7499   0800 492 568   Fax (03) 304 7499
Mob 025 370 664   takamatua@xtra.co.nz
www.akaroacountrylodge.com

Double $160-$185 Single $150
(Continental Breakfast) Walnut Cottage
Credit cards accepted Children welcome
3 Queen (3 bdrm)   Bathrooms: 3 Ensuite

A peaceful rural retreat set amongst bush, birds and creeks. Enjoy the private swimming pool, croquet or petantque. All rooms are private and ensuite, the provencial style French hut set in the bush beside the creek with an outside bath. David a cabinetmaker built the house which has many examples of his work including 2 sleigh beds in the guest rooms, he is happy to welcome visitors to his workshop. Sumptuous breakfast includes fresh fruit from the orchard, croissants, home-made preserves and freshly ground coffee.

AKAROA   *80km SE of Christchurch*

La Belle Villa   *B&B*
Maureen and Barry
113 Rue Jolie, Akaroa

Tel (03) 304 7084   Fax (03) 304 7084
Mob 021 339 304   bookings@labellevilla.co.nz
www.bnb.co.nz/labellevillaakaroa.html

Double $115-$125 Single $85-$95 (Special Breakfast)
Credit cards accepted
1 King 2 Queen 1 Twin (4 bdrm)
Bathrooms: 4 Ensuite

A warm welcome awaits you. Relax in the comfort of a bygone era, and appreciate the antiques in our picturesque historic villa with separate guest lounge. Built in the 1870's as the first doctor's surgery in Akaroa it is now established on beautiful, mature grounds. Enjoy the indoor/outdoor living, and gently trickling stream. We offer to make your stay with us special. Breakfast alfresco with real coffee. Being centrally situated, restaurants, cafés, wine bars and beach are all in walking distance.

AKAROA   *80km SE of Christchurch*

Chez Fleurs   *B&B*
Jan & Paul Wallace
15 Smith Street, Akaroa 8161

Tel (03) 304 8674   Fax (03) 3048974
Mob 021 155 7727   chezfleurs@xtra.co.nz
 www.chezfleurs.co.nz

Double $150 Single $100   (Continental Breakfast)
Credit cards accepted
2 Queen 1 Twin (3 bdrm)
Bathrooms: 2 Ensuite 1 Private

Bonjour! Chez Fleurs is ideally situated 200 metres up from the beach and 3 minutes walk to cafés, galleries, restaurants, shops and Information Centre. Enjoy our stunning waterfront views, beautiful garden and native birdlife, while relaxing on your own private balcony. We offer superior accommodation with private tea/coffee making facilities, fridge, TV, hairdryers and fresh flowers in suites. Complimentary guest laundry and BBQ. Secure off-street parking. Your delicious breakfast, using fresh home-grown produce is served alfresco, on your own balcony. 'A Bientot'. See you soon!

CANTERBURY

AKAROA   *80km SE of Christchurch*

Mullberry House   *B&B Homestay*
Separate/Suite Summerhouse
Anne Craig & Jack Clark
9 William Street, Akaroa 8161

Tel (03) 304 7778 or (03) 304 7793   Fax (03) 304 7778
Mob 021 610 456
anneandjacknz@yahoo.com www.mulberryhouse.co.nz

Double $100-$150 Single $80   (Special Breakfast)
1 King 1 Queen 1 Twin 1 Single (3 bdrm)
Bathrooms: 2 Ensuite 1 Private

Experience the very best in homestyle accommodation
and delight in the setting of *Mulberry House,* which
accommodates up to 6 guests. There is a choice of
double rooms, with or without ensuite, and a twin room
which will delight children. The romantic poolside
summerhouse has its own kitchen, ensuite and garden to
provide total privacy if desired.

Breakfasts are a specialty and feature a choice of
American, European, English, and New Zealand styles.
Champagne breakfasts and other meals by arrangement.
Meals can be served outside in the summer months
overlooking the pool.

Your Hosts: Well travelled and semi retired Anne Craig and Jack Clark offer unparalleled hospitality.
Fussy about food, both Anne and Jack love to cook: Anne preserves and bakes, and Jack adds his
American expertise to breakfasts of pancakes, waffles, omelettes, fresh fruits, and delicious coffee from
the espresso machine.

Guest Comments: Desmond Balmer (LondonGuardian/Observer Travel) recommends Mulberry House
as amoungst New Zealand's Top Twenty. Featured on Sydney's channel 7 'Ernie Dingo's Getaway' as
the place to stay in Akaroa. Featured in Autumn 2000 European *Wining and Dining.*

All rooms are beautifully decorated and feature quality beds and fine linen

AKAROA *80km SE of Christchurch*

Lavaud House *B&B, Homestay*
Alison & Gavin Porteous
83 Rue Lavaud, Akaroa

Tel (03) 304 7121
Fax (03) 304 7121
lavaudhouse@xtra.co.nz
www.nzhomestay.co.nz/lavaudhouse.html

Double $130-$190 (Continental Breakfast)
Credit cards
1 king 2 queen 1 twin (4 bedrooms)
Bathrooms: 3 ensuite 1 private

'Lavaud House' is a gracious, historic home which overlooks the beach and harbour. Being centrally located, you are only 5 minutes walking distance from restaurants, galleries and shops. Relax in the comfort of elegant furnishings, or wander in our peaceful garden with its magnificent harbour views and enchanting native birds. In the evening I invite you to enjoy a complimentary glass of wine with us and, in the morning, a delicious continental breakfast.

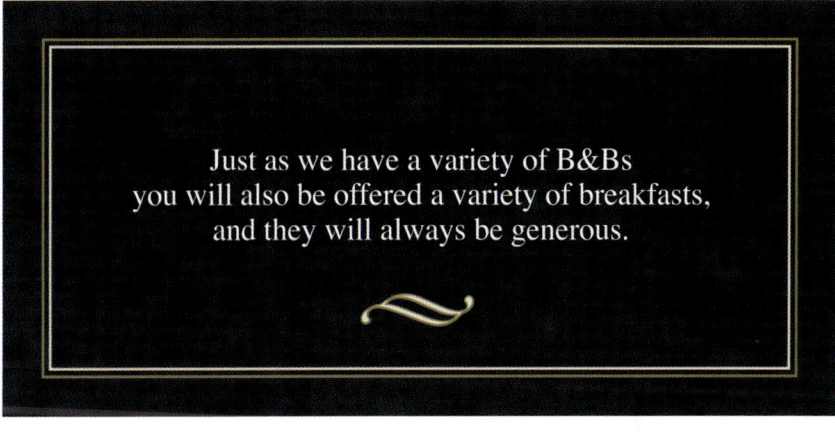

Just as we have a variety of B&Bs
you will also be offered a variety of breakfasts,
and they will always be generous.

DARFIELD *4km W of Darfield*

The Oaks Historic Homestead *Boutique accommodation*
Madeleine de Jong
State Highway 73, Corner Clintons Road, Darfield

Tel (03) 318 7232 Fax (03) 318 7236
Mob 021 046 0840 theoaks@quicksilver.net.nz
www.bnb.co.nz/oakshistoric.html

Double $150-$275 Single $125
(Continental Breakfast) Dinner $38pp on request
Credit cards accepted Children welcome Pets welcome
3 Queen 1 Single (4 bdrm) Bathrooms: 1 Ensuite 2 Private

One of Canterbury's oldest and most beautiful homesteads. Located amidst the stunning scenery of the Southern Alps on State Highway 73. The Oaks features; 4 guest rooms with ensuite/private bathrooms; a guest dining and living room featuring stunning open fires and a traditional large homestead kitchen. Children welcome, cot, highchair,stroller available at no cost. Pets on request. Your host Madeleine de Jong speaks 5 languages including German, French and Dutch. Wherever possible I try to use organic produce fresh out of my mother's garden. Madeleine would love to invite you to join her in the farm kitchen for either a hot cuppa or a glass of wine.

Heritage & Character Inns,
Boutique Lodgings 4 1/2 star

DARFIELD   *35km W of Christchurch*

Meychelle Manor Luxury Bed & Breakfast
Brian & Michelle Walker   *Homestay Luxury B&B*
State Highway 73, Main West Coast Road, Darfield

Tel (03) 318 1144   0800 181 144
Fax (03) 318 1965   Mob 027 226 0118
stay@meychellemanor.co.nz   www.meychellemanor.co.nz

Double $190-$220 Single $130-$150 (Full Breakfast)
Dinner negotiable   Child $20-$80 up to 12 years
Super single, rollaway airbed / portacot   Family rate available
Credit cards accepted   Children welcome
3 King/Twin (3 bdrm)
Bathrooms: 2 Ensuite 1 Private

Meychelle Manor Luxury Bed & Breakfast offers you a warm and friendly environment in magnificent accommodation only 30 minutes from Christchurch City and airport, and only 4 minutes from Darfield, the gateway to several ski and golf areas and other superb recreation opportunities in the close by foothills, high country and the Southern Alps.

Guests enjoy beautifully appointed super king/twin ensuite rooms with balconies providing panoramic views of snow-capped mountains and pastoral farmlands with deer grazing. Views of our tree-lined lake with trout and goldfish amongst our extensive grounds in a farm-park setting with birds roaming and a selection of exotic and farmyard animals.

Meychelle Manor (winner of 'House of the Year' 2000 for Canterbury/Westland) is a Mediterranean styled home offering stunning views and outstanding facilities including heated indoor swimming pool, weight gym, 2 guest lounges with DVD and music, telescope for viewing the southern stars, guest bar and barbecue and many complimentaries. Beauty, massage and health therapy can be arranged. The home is centrally heated throughout. A full laundry is available and communication facilities include telephone, internet, email and fax. Family needs are catered. Outside activities include a farm tour, feeding of animals & birds, putting green and playground.

Each morning guests may choose from a scrumptious menu selection of a continental or home-cooked farm-style breakfast whilst in the evening you can enjoy complimentary New Zealand wine and warm conversation with Michelle and Brian or taste the highly recommended local cuisine (courtesy transport is available).

Whether to enjoy the many adventure sports of the region, a taste of rural life in luxury or simply some relaxation, you can be assured of a special experience at Meychelle Manor.

DARFIELD *35km W of Christchurch*

Oakden Manor *B&B Homestay*
Pam & Alister Duncan
33 Oakden Drive, Darfield, Canterbury

Tel (03) 317 9226 Fax (03) 317 9246
Mob 027 441 6941 pamandal@actrix.co.nz
www.bnb.co.nz/oakden.html

Double $90-$110 Single $60 (Full Breakfast)
Child $45 Dinner by arrangement
Credit cards accepted Children welcome
1 King 1 Double 2 Single (3 bdrm)
Bathrooms: 1 Private 1 Host share

Genuine Kiwi hospitality awaits. We are semi-retired farmers with a friendly cairn terrier. We enjoy growing our own fruit and vegetables and like to share the tranquility of the garden with you. Jet boating, skiing, fishing, golf close by. Take a trip on the Tranz Alpine to the West Coast from Darfield. Complete your day with a pre-arranged meal with us or at one of the local eateries. Guests have tea/coffee /TV facilities in each bedroom. A comfortable lounge for relaxing in.

HIGHCOUNTRY CANTERBURY - CASTLE HILL *33km W of Springfield*

The Burn Alpine B&B *B&B Homestay*
Bob Edge & Phil Stephenson
11 Torlesse Place, Castle Hill Village, Canterbury

Tel (03) 318 7559 Fax (03) 318 7558
theburn@xtra.co.nz
www.theburn.co.nz

Double $100 Single $60 (Continental Breakfast)
Child 1/2 price Dinner $25 Dinner and B&B $85pp
Credit cards accepted Children welcome
3 Double 2 Single (4 bdrm)
Bathrooms: 2 Guests share

One hour west of Christchurch a carefree atmosphere prevails at The Burn. Nestled in the heart of the Southern Alps, it's arguably New Zealand's highest B&B. We designed and built our alpine lodge to maximise mountain vistas. Centered in the mystic Castlehill basin, surrounded by native forest, this is a fantastic place to return after a days activity or just kick back and relax on the sunny deck. A host of outdoor sports include skiing, snowboarding, hiking, mountain biking and flyfishing. Professional flyfishing guiding available in house.

MT HUTT - METHVEN *6km E of Methven*

Pagey's Farmstay *Farmstay*
Shirley & Gene Pagey
Chertsey Road, Methven Mt Hutt Village,
12 RD Rakaia

Tel (03) 302 1713 Fax (03) 302 1714
pageysfarmstay@wave.co.nz
www.bnb.co.nz/pageysfarmstay.html

Double $100 Single $70 (Full Breakfast)
Child 1/2 price under 12 years Dinner $25pp
Children welcome
1 King 1 Queen 4 Single (3 bdrm)
Bathrooms: 2 Private

Come as guests and leave as friends. Enjoy our hospitality and beautiful 4500 square foot home set amidst aged oak trees, 1.5 acres of rose garden and lawn and/or watch our 47" TV. Relax with pre-dinner drinks, home grown cuisine and fine wine. Experience farm activities, clean air and mountain views. Surrounding activities include wonderful bush walks, 2 golf courses, ballooning, skiing. You may never want to leave. Directions: From Methven town centre, turn down Methven Chertsey Road, 6km on left.

CANTERBURY

Mt Hutt - Methven   *8km N of Methven*

Tyrone Deer Farm   *Self-contained Country-Stay*
Pam & Roger Callaghan
Mt Hutt Station Road, RD 12, Rakaia,
Methven-Rakaia Gorge Alternative Route

Tel (03) 302 8096   Fax (03) 302 8099
tyronedeerfarm@xtra.co.nz
www.bnb.co.nz/tyronedeerfarm.html

Double $130-$140 Single $90   (Full Breakfast)
Dinner $40 by arrangement
Self-contained $140 double
1 Queen 1 Double 1 Twin (3 bdrm)
Bathrooms: 2 Ensuite 1 Private

Welcome to *Tyrone Deer Farm,* centrally situated
in the Mount Hutt, Rakaia Gorge, Methven area
in the middle of the South Island, 5 kilometers
from the Inland Tourist Route (Highway 72) and
1 hour from Christchurch International Airport,
making *Tyrone* an ideal stopover heading south to
Queenstown.

Our home is positioned with mountain views (Mt
Hutt) and deer grazing a few metres away, and
has ensuite bedrooms with electric blankets, wool
underlays and duvets on the beds, also heaters and
hair dryers. The lounge has open fire, TV, tea &
coffee making facilities and guest fridge.

Come meet Guz, our pet deer, her daughter $$s and
10:30 our cat. Evening meal is by arrangement and
served with New Zealand wines.

We are able to arrange professional guides
for fishing (salmon and trout) and for hunting;
especially thar, red deer, and chamois. Skiing at Mt
Hutt, hot-air ballooning, jet-boating, golf on nearby
18 hole courses. Numerous walks - scenic, bush,
garden, alpine.

Laze in the garden, swim in the pool - relax

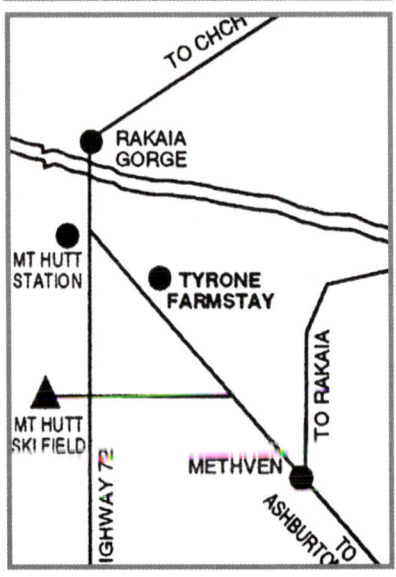

Mt Hutt - Methven *4km NW of Methven - Mt Hutt Village*

Green Gables Deer Farm *B&B Farmstay*
Roger & Colleen Mehrtens
185 Waimarama Road, Methven-Mt Hutt Village,
Postal No 12 R.D. Rakaia

Tel (03) 302 8308 New Zealand 0800 466 093 Fax (03) 302 8309
greengables@xtra.co.nz www.nzfarmstay.com

Double $140-$180 Single $110-$140
(Special Breakfast) Child $55.00 Dinner $50pp
Super King Beds Credit cards accepted Children welcome
2 King 2 Twin (3 bdrm)
Bathrooms: 2 Ensuite 1 Private

Green Gables is a 4 Star Qualmarked Bed and Breakfast Country House. 1 hour from Christchurch International Airport and 3 hours from Kaikoura Whale Watching where you can swim with dolphins. 3 ¹/₂ Mt Cook and 5 ¹/₂ (approximately) to Queenstown. Relax with a welcome cup of tea on arrival with your hosts, meet pet deer and our semi retired, portly Labrador.

Tranquil surroundings, private entrances, electric blankets, clock radios, ensuites, heaters, hair dryers, curling wands, toiletries, bathrobes and tea & coffee facilities. Iron and ironing boards. Laundry available free with 2 nights or more accommodation. Sumptuous breakfasts. Dinner by arrangement. Complimentary pre-dinner drinks when dining in. Or visit superb restaurants. 4km to Methven-Mt Hutt village.

ACTIVITIES: Golf International golf courses - Methven & Terrace Downs (club & cart hire available). Hot air ballooning; bush, mountain & rhododendron walks. 4WD scenic tours are available by arrangement. Some of the many activities include: fishing, jet boating, scenic flights, ecotours, bird watching, horse trekking, heliski, snowboarding, skiing. There are 7 club-fields all nearby.

LOCATION: Situated on SH77 4km north west of Methven. From the Inland Scenic-Route 72, turn into SH77 and travel 5km, Green Gables Deer Farm is on the right.

Visit the nearby Edoras from the Lord of the Rings film site at Mt Sunday

MT HUTT - METHVEN *11km W of Methven*

Glenview Farmstay *B&B Farmstay*
Separate unit with ensuite
Helen & Mike Johnstone
142 Hart Road, Methven

Tel (03) 302 8620 Fax (03) 302 8620
helenmikejohnstone@yahoo.com
www.bnb.co.nz/glenviewfarmstay.html

Double $100 Single $60
(Full Breakfast) Child $25 Dinner $25
Children welcome
2 Queen 1 Double 2 Twin 1 Single
(5 bdrm)
Bathrooms: 1 Guests share

Glenview farmstay is situated at the base of
Mt Hutt Ski Field, with the house designed
to look at the mountains and down the
Canterbury plains to the Port Hills.

Our 1200 acre farm consists of mainly cattle
with a few sheep. We have a golden labrador
and a cat.

There is a peaceful unit in the garden which is suitable
for a couple or a family which has 1 queen and 2 single
beds, ensuite, TV, tea & coffee making facilities and
wonderful views. The rooms in the house have seperate
access, good heating and are non-smoking. Dinner by
arrangement. Free farm tours on request.

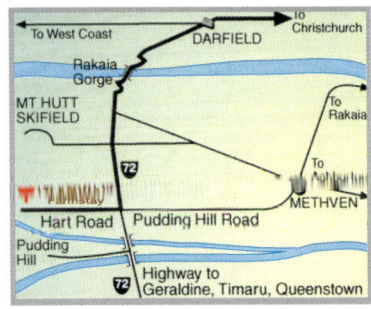

*Methven is only ten minutes away and we are
very close to good fishing, golf, ballooning,
bush walks and jet boating*

STAVELEY - MT SOMERS *20km SW of Methven*

Korobahn Lodge *B&B Homestay*
Caroline & John Lartice
Burgess Road, Staveley

Tel (03) 303 0828 Mob 021 183 4418
carolinel@xtra.co.nz
www.korobahnlodge.co.nz

Double $110-$150 Single $90-$120 (Full Breakfast)
Dinner $40 Credit cards accepted Children welcome
2 Queen 1 Twin (3 bdrm)
Bathrooms: 3 Ensuite

Welcome to our unique North American barn style homestead. Korobahn is tucked into the foot of Mt Somers and stands in several acres of gardens, surrounded by farmland. The property has recently been totally refurbished to a very comfortable standard. Korobahn Lodge is on Inland Scenic Highway 72, approximatly 110 kilometres SW of Christchurch Airport and on the way to Mt Cook and Queenstown. Local activites inculde bush walking, horse treks, jet boating, fishing, eco tours and skiing. (Close to Mt Hutt Ski Field.)

RAKAIA *50km S of Christchurch*

St Ita's Guesthouse *B&B Homestay Guesthouse*
Miriam & Ken Cutforth
11 Barrhill-Methven Road,
Rakaia Township, Canterbury

Tel (03) 302 7546 Fax (03) 302 7546
Mob 027 4888673 stitas@xtra.co.nz
www.stitas.co.nz

Double $110-$120 Single $70 (Full Breakfast)
Child $30 Dinner $30pp
Credit cards accepted Children welcome
1 Queen 1 Double 4 Single (3 bdrm) Bathrooms: 3 Ensuite

Relax in our elegant and comfortable historic former convent, 600 metres from SH1 in small town New Zealand. Excellent base for exploring Ashburton District. Excellent first and last stop from Christchurch International Airport. All bedrooms have ensuites and garden views. Walking distance to local shops, hotels, crafts and winery. Close to golf and salmon fishing, 30 minutes to skiing, jet boating and more. Dinner based on local produce served with wine. Full breakfasts. Share the open fire with our cat and golden retriever.

ASHBURTON *Ashburton Central*

Homestay
Pat & Dave Weir
1 Sudbury Street,
Ashburton

Tel (03) 308 3534
d&pweir@xtra.co.nz
www.bnb.co.nz/weir.html

Double $70 Single $40 (Full Breakfast) Dinner $20
Credit cards accepted
1 Double 2 Single (2 bdrm)
Bathrooms: 1 Guests share 1 Host share

Our comfortable home is situated in a quiet street with the added pleasure of looking onto a rural scene. We are 10-15 minutes walk from town or 3-5 minutes to riding for the disabled grounds or river walkway. Guest rooms have comfortable beds with electric blankets. We welcome the opportunity to meet and greet visitors and wish to make your stay a happy one. Your hosts are semi-retired, hobbies general/varied from meeting people to walking etc. Request visitors no smoking inside home. Laundry facilities available.

CANTERBURY

ASHBURTON *8km W of Ashburton*

Carradale Farm *B&B Farmstay*
Karen & Jim McIntyre
Ferriman's Road (Rapid number 200), RD 8, Ashburton

Tel (03) 308 6577   Fax (03) 308 6548   Mob 027 433 8044
jkmcintyre@xtra.co.nz   www.ashburton.co.nz/carradale

Double $100-$120 Single $70   (Full Breakfast)
Child ½ price under 12 years Dinner $30 by arrangement
Caravan powerpoint $25   Credit cards accepted
1 Double 2 Twin (3 bdrm)
Bathrooms: 1 Ensuite 2 Private

Our homestead, which captures the sun in all rooms,
is cosy and inviting. It is situated in a sheltered garden
where you can enjoy peace, tranquillity and fresh country
air or indulge in a game of tennis.

All guest rooms have comfortable beds, electric blankets,
reading lamps and tea/coffee making facilities. Laundry
and ironing facilities available.

Dinner is by arrangement and features traditional
New Zealand cuisine including home-grown meat and
vegetables. Breakfast is served with delicious home-
made jams and preserves.

We have a 220 acre irrigated sheep and cattle farm.
You may like to be taken on a farm tour or enjoy a walk
on the farm. As we have both travelled extensively in
New Zealand, Australia, United Kingdom, Europe,
North America and Zimbabwe. We would like to offer
hospitality to fellow travellers. Our hobbies include
meeting people, travel, reading, photography, gardening,
sewing, cake decorating, rugby, cricket, Jim belongs to
the Masonic Lodge and Karen is involved in community
affairs.

For the weary traveller a spa pool is available. For young
children we have a cot and high chair. There is a power
point for camper vans.

We are 1 hour from Christchurch International Airport.

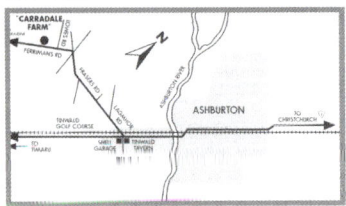

Carradale farm "Where people come as strangers and leave as friends"

ASHBURTON   *1km S of Ashburton Centre*

A Welcome Inn   *B&B Homestay*
Betty & Bruce Arnst
13 Thomson Street, Tinwald, Ashburton

Tel **(03) 308 7297**   Fax (03) 308 7297
bb_arnst@xtra.co.nz
www.bnb.co.nz/awelcomeinn.html

Double $100-$120 Single $60-$70   (Full Breakfast)
Child neg by age   Dinner $30pp
Children welcome
1 Double 1 Twin (2 bdrm)
Bathrooms: 1 Guests share

We are a retired couple who have travelled overseas and in New Zealand and love sharing experiences with travellers. We provide a warm friendly stay in our comfortable modern home with an opportunity for travellers to meet New Zealanders in a family setting. We have two elderly pets, both living outdoors. We have a small private lounge for guests, but join us in our large lounge, or in our pleasant garden. 5 minutes from Lake Hood. 1 hour south from Christchurch International Airport. Near sports facilities.

ASHBURTON   *Ashburton Central*

Falcutt House   *B&B*
Nola & Stuart Lovett
23 Falcon Drive, Ashburton

Tel **(03) 308 9253**
Mob 025 685 4317
www.bnb.co.nz/falcutthouse.html

Double $90   Single $50   (Full Breakfast)
Child $30 under 12
Dinner $30 by arrangement
2 Twin (2 bdrm)
Bathrooms: 1 Private

A new house situated in a quiet cul-de-sac surrounded by pleasant garden, with private areas. 2 comfortable twin bedrooms. Guests' private bathroom with separate toilet. Visit farm upon request. Close to town and restaurants. Off-street parking available.

ASHBURTON   *1km N of central Ashburton*

Ferriman House   *B&B Homestay*
Gail Cooper & Neville Gutsell
10 Ferriman Street, Ashburton

Tel **(03) 307 2600**
Mob 027 241 6371   or   025 672 8514
gailcook@xtra.co.nz
www.bnb.co.nz/ferrimanhouse.html

Double $100-$120 Single $85-$95 (Full Breakfast)
Dinner $30 by arrangment
1 King/Twin 1 King (2 bdrm)
Bathrooms: 1 Ensuite 1 Private

A warm welcome to our new sunny home built 2004. We are situated on a quiet street just off the main road and close to motels and town centre. Retired moteliers of 21 years we enjoy golf, fishing, boating and travelling. We have 2 comfortable rooms; one is purpose built with ensuite and access to a private lounge or join us in our large dining room. Both bathrooms have heated towel rails, underfloor heating, TV in rooms. Directions from Christchurch: second left turn off East Street to King Street, then first right.

South Canterbury & North Otago

Fox Glacier

e Bay

Mount Cook

80

Lake Tekapo

Kimbell

Geraldine

Ealing

ley

Burkes Pass

Fairlie

79

1

8

Lake Pukaki

8

Temuka

Twizel

Seadown

8

Timaru

Omarama

Kingsdown

Makihikihi

Kurow

Waimate

82 1

85

Oamaru

Waianakarua

Moeraki

Towns listed generally follow
a north to south route. Refer
to the index if required.

0   Kilometres   30

0   Miles   18

Palmoroton

GERALDINE   *3km N of Geraldine*

The Crossing   *Boutique Bed & Breakfast Guest Lodge*
Richard & Barbara Sahlie
124 Woodbury Road, RD 21, Geraldine

Tel (03) 693 9689   Fax (03) 693 9789
srelax@xtra.co.nz   www.thecrossingbnb.co.nz

Double $160-$190   Single $140-$170 (Full Breakfast)
Dinner by arrangement Extra person $30
Children over 12 welcome Credit cards accepted
2 Queen 1 Double 2 Single (3 bdrm)
Bathrooms: 3 Ensuite

The Crossing is a beautifully restored and furnished
English style manor house built in 1908. Our spacious
lounges have open fires and comfortable seating. A
shaded verandah overlooks the lovely gardens, where
you can relax and read or enjoy a leisurely game of
croquet or petanque. Enjoy dinner and your choice of
beverages in our fully licensed restaurant. Dinners by
prior arrangement.

The Crossing is your perfect base for exploring the
central South Island. Local attractions include fishing
for salmon and trout, white water rafting, nature treks in
Peel Forest, and ski fields are nearby. Golfers, spend a
week and play 14 uncrowded courses each within 1 hours
drive. All have low green fees and welcome visitors.

We are located on the main route between Christchurch
and Queenstown or Mount Cook.

Directions: signposted on SH72/79 approx 3km north
of Geraldine, turn into Woodbury Road, then 1km on
right hand side.

*Experience New Zealand history on 37 tranquil
acres near the base of the Four Peaks Range*

GERALDINE *0.5km S of Geraldine*

Victoria Villa *B&B Self-contained*
Leigh & Jerry Basinger
55 Cox Street, Geraldine 8751

Tel (03) 693 8605 0800 537 533 Fax (03) 693 8605
Mob 027 482 1842 jbasinger@xtra.co.nz
www.bnb.co.nz/aoteavilla.html

Double $80-$120 Single $80-$100 (Full Breakfast)
Child $10-15 Dinner by arrangement
Detached studio unit Credit cards accepted
3 Queen 2 Double 2 Single (4 bdrm)
Bathrooms: 3 Ensuite 1 Private

Welcome to our historical villa, completely refurbished - spacious bedrooms with ensuites or private bathroom. Off-street parking, private entrance and lounge. Molded ceilings, native woods. Also, separate studio with ensuite and light cooking area; ideal for family up to 5 people. On Highway 79 to Mt Cook and Queenstown. 7 minutes walk to Geraldine Village which has a boutique movie theatre, fine restaurants, sports pub, antiques, world class glass blower, boutique shops, 2 golf courses. Adjacent to domain. Personality pet dog and cat. Your hosts will assist to make your stay enjoyable.

GERALDINE *0.2km S of Geraldine*

Lilymay *B&B*
Lois & Les Gillum
29 Cox Street, Geraldine

Tel (03) 693 8838 0800 LILYMAY (0800 545 9629)
elgillum@chc.quik.co.nz
www.bnb.co.nz/lilymay.html

Double $80-$95 Single $55-$60 (Full Breakfast)
Child $15-20 Credit cards accepted Children welcome
2 Queen 1 Double 3 Twin 3 Single (3 bdrm)
Bathrooms: 2 Guests share

A charming character home set in a large garden where Sammy, the cat, plays. A friendly, warm welcome is assured with tea/coffee and Lois' home-baked cookies. Ample off-street parking and separate guest entrance. Teas, coffee, etc available at all times in the guest lounge with cosy open fire. The village, shops, cafés, restaurants, crafts a short stroll away. We are on the main highway to the Southern Lakes and mountains and the ideal stopover from Christchurch (137km).

GERALDINE *0.5km S of Geraldine*

Forest View *B&B Sleep-out*
Joyce & John Leverno
128 Talbot Street, Geraldine

Tel (03) 693 9928 0800 572 740 Fax (03) 693 9928
Mob 021 440 349 forest.view@xtra.co.nz
www.bnb.co.nz/forestview.html

Double $80-$110 Single $55-$75 (Full Breakfast)
Child neg Dinner $30 by arrangement Sleep out $45
Credit cards accepted Children welcome
1 King 1 Queen 1 Double 1 Twin 1 Single (4 bdrm)
Bathrooms: 1 Ensuite 1 Private 1 Guests share

We have a charming 2 storey, character home set in a cottage garden where our dogs, Oscar and Emmy love to play. You will be warmly welcomed on arrival and a refreshing cup of tea or coffee is available in the guest lounge at all times. We are a short stroll to the cafés and restaurants in the charming village of Geraldine which is the ideal first stop from Christchurch (137km) as you travel towards the Southern Lakes and mountains.

GERALDINE *3km N of Geraldine*

Rivendell *B&B Homestay Self-contained*
Erica & Andrew Tedham
Woodbury Road, RD 21, Geraldine

Tel (03) 693 8559 Fax (03) 693 8559   Mob 021 264 1520
rivendellnz@xtra.co.nz www.bnb.co.nz/rivendellbb.html

Double $100-$110   Single $85 (Full Breakfast)
Child neg   Credit cards accepted
Children welcome Pets welcome
1 Queen 1 Single (2 bdrm)
Bathrooms: 1 Ensuite 1 Host share
Self contained/motel, 1 Queen bed & 1 sofa bed, $100-$120

Set in over 3 acres Rivendell is a traditional New Zealand villa and has beautiful secluded gardens that can be enjoyed relaxing on the large verandah or in the spa pool. Our home provides all modern facilities including internet and laundry. The delightful village of Geraldine with its numerous cafés, restaurants, shops and cinema is only 5 minutes drive. We offer you a truly warm welcome together with our dogs, Lady Lou (collie) & Sophie Pippin (New Zealand huntaway) horse Bracken and peacocks Aragorn & Arwen.

GERALDINE *10 km SW of Geraldine*

Moor Crichel *B&B Farmstay*
Robyn Askin
279 Winchester Hanging Rock Road, Geraldine

Tel (03) 693 9367   0800 693 936   Fax (03) 693 9368
Mob 0274 926 009   crichel@xtra.co.nz
www.bnb.co.nz/moorcrichel.html

Double $120-$140 Single $70-$85
(Special Breakfast)   Child $20-$30
Twin room has 2 king single beds
Credit cards accepted   Children welcome   Pets welcome
1 King 1 Queen 2 Twin (3 bdrm)
Bathrooms: 2 Private

A warm welcome awaits you at Moor Crichel. Our dairy farm also has sheep, goats & pigs. Relax in the lounge/patios, wander in the garden or stroll to the adjoining river. We can help make arrangements for off-farm activities, eg fishing, skiing and rafting, golf, day trips (picnic lunches by arrangement) or a 4WD trip to "Lord of Rings" Middle Earth region. Dinner is available by arrangement. Let us help you to enjoy the holiday of a lifetime.

TEMUKA *20km N of Timaru*

Ashfield B&B *B&B Homestay*
Ray & Wendy Pearson
71 Cass Street, Temuka

Tel (03) 615 6157   Fax (03) 615 9062
ashfield@paradise.net.nz
www.bnb.co.nz/ashfieldbb.html

Double $100-$150 Single $65-$75 (Full Breakfast)
Child neg Credit cards accepted Children welcome
1 King 2 Queen 1 Double (4 bdrm)
Bathrooms: 1 Ensuite 1 Guests share

Ashfield, a Victorian villa built in 1883 is set in 4 acres of woodlands and features the original marble fireplaces, gilt mirrors, and full size snooker table. Only 10 minutes walk from shops and restaurants and close to ski fields, salmon and trout fishing. Two of our upstairs bedrooms open out to a balcony with lovely views of the mountains. We enjoy spending the evening with guests by the open fire. Join us with our cats and newfoundland dogs for a wonderful stay in a lovely setting.
Guests welcome to use laundry.

TIMARU CENTRAL

Homestay
Margaret & Nevis Jones
16 Selwyn Street, Timaru

Tel (03) 688 1400   Fax (03) 688 1400
www.bnb.co.nz/jonestimaru.html

Double $100   Single $60   (Full Breakfast)
Child ¹/2 price   Dinner $25   Credit cards accepted
2 Double 1 Twin (3 bdrm)
Bathrooms: 2 Ensuite 1 Guests share

Welcome to our spacious character brick home built in
the 1920's and situated in a beautiful garden with a grass tennis court. A secluded property with off-
street parking and views of the surrounding sea and mountains. Centrally situated, only 5 minutes from
the beach and town with an excellent choice of cafés and restaurants. On arrival tea is served on our
sunny verandah. Hosts have lived and worked extensively overseas, namely South Africa, UK and the
Middle East, and enjoy music, theatre, tennis and golf. Dinner by arrangement.

TIMARU - SEADOWN   *4.8km N of Timaru*

Country Homestay   *Homestay Country Homestay*
Margaret & Ross Paterson
491 Seadown Road, Seadown, RD 3, Timaru

Tel (03) 688 2468   Fax (03) 688 2468
Mob 021 213 7434
www.bnb.co.nz/countryhomestay.html

Double $80   Single $50   (Full Breakfast)
Child ¹/2 price   Dinner $20   Credit cards accepted
1 Double 2 Single (3 bdrm)
Bathrooms: 1 Guests share

Our homestay is approximately 10 minutes north of Timaru, situated 4.8km on Seadown Road off State
Highway 1 at Washdyke - second house on left past Pharlap Statue. We have hosted on our farm for 11
years - now retired and have a country farmlet with some farm animals, with views of farmland and
mountains. Day trips to Mt Cook, hydro lakes and ski fields, fishing, golf course few minutes away.
Electric blankets on all beds - laundry facilities available. Interests are farming, gardening, spinning
and overseas travel.

TIMARU   *Timaru Central*

Bidwill House   *Homestay*
Dorothy & Ron White
15 Bidwill Street, Timaru

Tel (03) 688 5856   Fax (03) 688 5870
Mob 027 238 8122   bidwillhouse@xtra.co.nz
www.bnb.co.nz/bidwillhouse.html

Double $100   Single $80   (Full Breakfast)
Child ¹/2 price   Dinner $15-$25 by arrangement
Credit cards accepted
1 King/Twin 2 Single (2 bdrm)
Bathrooms: 1 Ensuite

Bidwill House offers superior personalised homestay in a classic two storeyed home with a delightful
garden in a quiet street in central Timaru. 5 minutes walk to the town centre, restaurants and Caroline
Bay. The guest bedroom has a super king/twin with a smaller bedroom with 2 single beds. The 2 rooms
are only available to the one booking. Laundry facilities and a courtesy car are available. We look
forward to welcoming guests to our home, and offer our hospitality to those who prefer a homestay.

TIMARU

Okare Boutique Accommodation *B&B Homestay*
Malcolm Smith
11 Wai-iti Road, Timaru

Tel (03) 688 0316 Fax (03) 688 0368
Mob 027 229 7301   okare@xtra.co.nz
okare.co.nz

Double $95-$125 Single $85-$100 (Full Breakfast)
Child $45 Credit cards accepted Children welcome
1 King/Twin 1 Queen 1 Double 1 Twin 4 Single (4 bdrm)
Bathrooms: 1 Ensuite 1 Private 1 Host share

Okare is a substantial Edwardian brick residence built in
1909 and offers discerning travellers and small families visiting the region comfortable accommodation
with warm welcoming hospitality. Okare offers substantial sunny living spaces for our guests, upstairs
there is a super king/twin and one twin room with share bathroom and a double with twin spa-bath
ensuite, downstairs a queen room with private facilities. We are situated only 5 minutes walk from
a selection of restaurants. Our own restaurant, Boudicca's, offers a charge back facility. We have 2
children and 2 huskies for your entertainment.

TIMARU   *5km N of Pleasant Point*

Ballyagan *B&B Homestay*
Gail & Bill Clarke
State Highway 8 Levels, RD 4, Timaru

Tel (03) 614 8221   Fax (03) 614 8221
Mob 025 653 7663
ballyagan@xtra.co.nz   www.bnb.co.nz/ballyagan.html

Double $90-$120 Single $60 (Full Breakfast)
Child 1/2 price Dinner $25 by arrangement
Children welcome
1 Queen 1 Double 4 Single (4 bdrm)
Bathrooms: 1 Ensuite 1 Private 1 Guests share

Welcome to Ballyagan. Our home is among trees and gardens with native birds, small farm walk, pet
sheep, cat. Bedrooms have electric blankets and bedside lamps. Restaurants 5 minutes to Pleasant
Point vintage trains and golf course. We serve Devonshire afternoon tea, herbal tea and fresh percolated
coffee. Sample our local wine. Mount Cook ski fields and fishing within reasonable distance. Tea
making, laundry facilities available. We enjoy meeting and hosting guests. Directions: SH8 7km from
Washdyke. 5km from Pleasant Point. B&B Homestay sign at gate.

TIMARU   *3.5km NW of Central/City Timaru*

Ranui *B&B Farmstay Homestay Separate/Suite*
Margaret & Kevin Cosgrove
5 Kellands Hill, Timaru

Tel (03) 686 1288 Fax (03) 686 1285
Mob 027 432 1458 or 027 291 9311
ranui@timaru.com   www.ranuihomestay.co.nz

Double $95-$120 Single $75 (Full Breakfast)
Child 1/2 price Dinner $30   Separate/Suite $150
Credit cards accepted Children welcome
3 Queen 2 Single (4 bdrm)
Bathrooms: 1 Ensuite 1 Private 1 Guests share

Our spacious home on 5 acres enjoys the best of both worlds - country living only 3.5km from the
centre of Timaru. Set in 1.5 acres of established gardens with a magnificent view of Mt Cook we offer a
relaxed atmosphere, heated swimming pool (summer), Sky TV in bedroom, dinner by arrangement. We
run coloured sheep, the wool of which Margaret spins and knits. We enjoy golfing, boating and meeting
people. Our family are all away. Children welcome. Phone for directions.

TIMARU   *3km S of Timaru*

Mountain View B&B   *B&B Farmstay Homestay*
Marlene & Norman McIntosh
23 Talbot Road, RD 1 Kingsdown, Timaru

Tel (03) 688 1070   Fax (03) 688 1069
Mob 021 113 8517   mvhomestay@xtra.co.nz
www.bnb.co.nz/mtview.html

Double $90   Single $60   (Full Breakfast)
Child $20 under 13   Dinner $25 by arrangement
Credit cards accepted   Children welcome
1 Queen 1 Double 1 Twin (3 bdrm)
Bathrooms: 2 Private

Mountain View is a farmlet on Talbot Road, 200 metres from State Highway 1. Blue and white Bed & Breakfast signs on highway 3km from Timaru. Semi-retired farmers - pet deer and sheep. Home is situated in tranquil garden overlooking farmland with views of mountains. Private bathrooms - laundry facilities available. Tea, coffee. Nearby fishing, golf courses, swimming and walk to sea coast. Day trips comfortably taken to Mt Cook, hydro lakes and ski fields. We enjoy meeting people and look forward to offering our hospitality.

TIMARU - KINGSDOWN   *7km S of Timaru*

Kingsdown Manor   *B&B*
Lynne Harper
10 Bristol Road, RD 1, Timaru
Tel (03) 684 9612   Fax (03) 684 9613
Mob 027 221 5306   lynnedeane@xtra.co.nz
www.kingsdownmanor.co.nz
Double $120-$130   Single $60   (Full Breakfast)
Child $15   Dinner $25   Credit cards accepted
Children welcome
2 Queen 1 Twin 1 Single (4 bdrm)
Bathrooms: 1 Ensuite 2 Guests share

Deanne & Lynne welcome you to our B&B. Kingsdown Manor is built around a small chapel and hall on State Highway 1, just south of Timaru. Home is situated in tranquil gardens surrounded by farmland and views of the mountains and sea. In the area are ski fields, golf courses, fishing and access to the ocean and beach. Tea & coffee in rooms, laundry facilities, a wonderful court yard to sit in the sun or relax in the large lounge with open fire burning. Deane & Lynne have a wealth of NZ farming knowledge between them and still own a small sheep stud farm in North Canterbury. We have a much loved cat, 2 dogs and 2 wonderful children, Jody 18 and Billie 16, who have both now left home.

MAKIKIHI - WAIMATE   *37km S of Timaru*

Alford Farm   *Farmstay*
June & Ken McAuley
Lower Hook Road, RD 8, Waimate

Tel (03) 689 5778   Fax (03) 689 5779
Mob 027 267 6008   alfordfarmstays@paradise.net.nz
www.bnb.co.nz/alfordfarm.html

Double $90   Single $60   (Continental Breakfast)
Dinner $25
Credit cards accepted
1 double and 2 long deluxe single beds. (2 bdrms)
Bathrooms: 1 Host share

Halfway between Dunedin and Christchurch: stop over to enjoy the peaceful surroundings on our deer and cattle farm. Guests are offered a farm tour or can participate in farm activities if time permits. Hosting since 1985 we enjoy sharing our home, farm, attractive garden and native birds with visitors. Attractions: trout and salmon fishing, penguin colony, two golf courses, bush walks and day trips to Mount Cook. Directions: 4km south of Makikihi, turn inland into Lower Hook Road. Second on the right (2km). Rapid number 202.

FAIRLIE   *3km W of Fairlie*

Fontmell   *B&B Farmstay Homestay*
Anne & Norman McConnell
Nixons Road 169, RD 17, Fairlie

Tel (03) 685 8379 Fax (03) 685 8379
www.bnb.co.nz/fontmell.html

Double $90-$110 Single $65 (Full Breakfast)
Child $35 Dinner $25
2 King/Twin 1 Queen 1 Double 2 Twin 1 Single (4 bdrm)
Bathrooms: 1 Private 1 Guests share

Our farm consists of 400 acres producing fat lambs, cattle and deer, with numerous other animals and bird life. The house is situated in a large English style garden with many mature trees in a tranquil setting. In the area are 2 ski fields, golf courses, walkways and scenic drives. Informative farm tours available. Our interests include golf, gardening and music. Directions: Travel 1km from town centre, along Tekapo highway, then turn left into Nixon's Road when two more kilometres will bring you to the Fontmell entrance.

FAIRLIE   *1.5km NW of Fairlie*

Ashgrove   *B&B Separate/Suite*
Maria & Stewart Evans
Mt Cook Road, Fairlie

Tel (03) 685 8797   Fax (03) 685 8795
Mob 025 289 5323   maria@ashgrove.co.nz
www.ashgrove.co.nz

Double $120-$150 Single $80 (Continental Breakfast)
Child neg Credit cards accepted
Children welcome Pets welcome
1 King/Twin 1 Double (2 bdrm)
Bathrooms: 1 Ensuite 1 Private

Enjoy a restful stopover on your South Island journey at our 3 acre farmlet. Our house is set amongst established trees and gardens. Guest facilities include a private sunny sitting room. Microwave, fridge, TV, tea & coffee are available. We also offer refreshments for sale. Only 10 minutes walk to award winning restaurants. We are happy to share our knowledge of the South Island, especially to trampers and those keen to fish the clear lakes and rivers of the region.

KIMBELL   *8km W of Fairlie*

Rivendell Lodge   *Country Homestay*
Joan Gill
15 Stanton Road, Kimbell, RD 17, Fairlie

Tel (03) 685 8833   Fax (03) 685 8825
Mob 027 481 9189   Rivendell.lodge@xtra.co.nz
www.fairlie.co.nz/rivendell

Double $110-$130 Single $70 (Full Breakfast)
Child neg Dinner $40   Credit cards accepted
Children welcome
2 Queen 3 Single (3 bdrm)
Bathrooms: 2 Private 1 Host share

Welcome to my 1 acre paradise; a haven of peace and tranquility offering quality country comfort and hospitality. I am a well travelled writer with a passion for mountains, literature and good conversation. I enjoy cooking and gardening and use home grown produce wherever possible. Take time out for fishing, skiing, walking, golf or water sports. Relax in the garden, complete with stream and cat, or come with us to some of our favourite places. Complimentary refreshments on arrival. Laundry facilities and internet access available.

BURKES PASS   *23km E of Lake Tekapo*

Dobson Lodge   *Country Homestay*
Margaret & Keith Walter
Dobson Lodge, RD 17, Burkes Pass,
Mackenzie Country

Tel (03) 685 8316   Fax (03) 685 8316
dobson_lodge@xtra.co.nz   www.dobsonlodge.co.nz

Double $120-$160 Single $70-$100
(Continental Breakfast) Child neg Dinner $25pp
S/C railway carriage $40-$60 Credit cards accepted
2 Queen 1 Double 1 Single (3 bdrm)
Bathrooms: 2 Ensuite 1 Host share

Come and share our unique glacier stone cottage with exceptional character set in 17 acres. We are nestled in a picturesque valley, with views of Mount Dobson and are close to Lake Tekapo. We are on the main tourist route, approximately halfway between Christchurch and Queenstown or Dunedin. There are small restaurants close by. Our interests include photography, crafts and animals. We have one cat, a friendly collie and pet sheep. As well as the lodge, self contained railway accommodation is available.

LAKE TEKAPO   *40km W of Fairlie*

Freda Du Faur House   *B&B Homestay*
Dawn & Barry Clark
1 Esther Hope Street, Lake Tekapo

Tel (03) 680 6513 dawntek@xtra.co.nz
www.bnb.co.nz/fredadufaurhouse.html

Double $105 Single $70   (Continental Breakfast)
Child neg Credit cards accepted
1 Queen 1 Double 2 Single (3 bdrm)
Bathrooms: 1 Guests share

Experience tranquillity and a touch of mountain magic. A warm and friendly welcome. Comfortable home, mountain and lake views. Rimu panelling, heart timber furniture, attractive decor, blending with the McKenzie Country. Bedrooms in private wing overlooking garden, 2 opening onto balcony. Refreshments on patio surrounded by roses or view ever changing panorama from lounge. Walkways nearby. Mt Cook 1 hour away. Views of ski field. Our cat Missy welcomes you. 5 minutes to shops and restaurants. From SH8 turn into Lakeview Heights and follow green B&B sign into Barbara Hay Street. Then right and see our Freda Du Faur sign.

LAKE TEKAPO   *43km W of Fairlie*

Creel House   *B&B*
Grant & Rosemary Brown
36 Murray Place, Lake Tekapo

Tel (03) 680 6516   Fax (03) 680 6659
creelhouse.l.tek@xtra.co.nz
www.bnb.co.nz/creelhouse.html

Double $140-$150 Single $75   (Special Breakfast)
$110 double/twin Off-season tariff
Credit cards accepted Children welcome
2 Queen 1 Twin (3 bdrm)
Bathrooms: 1 Ensuite 2 Private

Built by Grant, our 3 storied home with expansive balconies offers panoramic views of the Southern Alps, Mt John, Lake Tekapo and surrounding mountains. All rooms are spacious and comfortable, with guest lounge and separate guest entrance. A NZ native garden adds an attractive feature. Restaurants in township. Our two daughters are 14 and 16 years old. We live on the ground floor with 2 cats thus separate from our guest accommodation. Grant is a professional flyfishing guide (NZPFGA) and offers guided tours.

LAKE TEKAPO   *43km W of Fairlie*

Alpine Vista   *B&B*
Gillian & Peter Maxwell
12 Hamilton Drive, Lake Tekapo

Tel (03) 680 6702   0800 390 637
Fax (03) 680 6707   Mob 021 415 544
info@alpinevista.co.nz
www.bnb.co.nz/alpinevista.html

Double $170-$195   Single $120   (Full Breakfast)
Credit cards accepted
1 King/Twin 2 King (3 bdrm)
Bathrooms: 3 Ensuite

Welcome to Alpine Vista, our recently renovated home offering amazing views of the Southern Alps, beautiful Lake Tekapo and a panorama of Mt John. Our warm modern home offers 3 fully ensuited guests rooms, tea & coffee making facilities, email facilities, laundry and large lounge where we encourage you to meet with us and fellow guests. Having lived in the Mackenzie Country for 30 years we would enjoy sharing our knowledge of what this area has to offer. We assure you of a warm and comfortable stay.

LAKE PUKAKI - MT COOK   *7km N of Twizel*

Rhoborough Downs, Pukaki   *Homestay*
Roberta Preston
State highway 8 Tekapo / Twizel,

Tel (03) 435 0509
Fax (03) 435 0509
ra.preston@xtra.co.nz
www.bnb.co.nz/rhoboroughdowns.html

Double $100   Single $50   (Continental Breakfast)
Child $30
1 Double 3 Single (3 bdrm)
Bathrooms: 1 Guests share

A quiet place to stop, halfway between Christchurch and Queenstown or Christchurch and Dunedin via Waitaki Valley. 40 minutes to Mt Cook. The 18,000 acre property has been in the family 85 years. Merino sheep graze to 6000 feet, hereford cattle. Views of the southern sky the homestead is set in tranquil gardens afternoon tea/drinks served on the veranda, We have a black lab. Twizel has a bank, doctor, restaurants, shops. Dinner by arrangement. Please phone for bookings and directions. Cot available.

LAKE PUKAKI   *27km Lake Tekapo*

Tasman Downs Station   *Farmstay*
Linda, Bruce & Ian Hayman
Lake Tekapo

Tel (03) 680 6841   Fax (03) 680 6851
samjane@xtra.co.nz
www.bnb.co.nz/tasmandownsstation.html

Double $110-$130   Single $85   (Full Breakfast)
Dinner $40pp
1 Queen 1 Twin (2 bdrm)
Bathrooms: 1 Private 1 Guests share

A place of unsurpassed beauty located on the shores
of Lake Pukaki with magnificent views of the lake, Mount Cook and Southern Alps. Our local stone home blends in with the natural peaceful surroundings. This high country station has been in our family since 1914 and runs mainly angus cattle. Bruce, an ex-RAF pilot, and Linda enjoy sharing their knowledge of farming with guests. An opportunity to experience true farm life with friendly hosts and a good natured corgi.

SOUTH CANTERBURY, NORTH OTAGO

TWIZEL - MT COOK   *2km W of Twizel Info Centre*

Artemis B&B   *B&B*
Jan & Bob Wilson
33 North West Arch,
Twizel

Tel (03) 435 0388
Fax (03) 435 0377   artemistwizel@paradise.net.nz
www.bnb.co.nz/user188.html

Double $125 Single $95 (Special Breakfast)
Credit cards accepted
2 Queen 1 Single (2 bdrm)
Bathrooms: 1 Ensuite 1 Private

Welcome to the magnificent Mackenzie Basin. Our modern home has stunning mountain views along with peace and tranquility. We are only 45 minutes from Mount Cook and 3 minutes drive to nearby restaurants. A guest sitting room with balcony - tea, coffee and complimentary snack and television. Our special continental breakfast includes a choice of juices, fruits, cereals, cheeses and homemade croissants, toast and jams. A selection of teas and coffees. We look forward to sharing our home with you.

TWIZEL - MT COOK   *2km W of Twizel*

Heartland Lodge   *Homestay Self-contained Loft*
Kerry & Steve Carey
19 North West Arch, Twizel, South Canterbury

Tel (03) 435 0008   0800 164 666 Fax (03) 435 0387
Mob 021 230 7502   heartland@xtra.co.nz
www.heartland-lodge.co.nz

Double $200-$220 Single $150 (Full Breakfast)
Child neg Dinner $50 by arrangement
Credit cards accepted   Children welcome
4 King/Twin 1 Queen (5 bdrm)
Bathrooms: 4 Ensuite
Loft from $120 double

Welcome to our lovely, large Homestay Lodge, only 40 minutes from the Aoraki/Mt Cook World Heritage Park. Luxuriously appointed guest rooms feature ensuites with spa baths or therapeutic saunas. Relax with your friendly Kiwi hosts. Kerry is of Maori descent and would love to share her culture and history with you; and Steve is a world renowned fishing guide. We also offer The Loft - a large self-service apartment above our garage, which is ideal for families. It sleeps up to 6 people

TWIZEL

Aoraki Lodge
Oksana & Vlad Fomin
32 Mackenzie Drive,
Twizel / Mt Cook 8773

Tel (03) 435 0300   Fax (03) 435 0305
Mob 027 414 9646   aorakilodge@xtra.co.nz
www.aorakiadventure.co.nz

Double $145-$150 Single $95 (Continental Breakfast)
Child $30   Credit cards accepted
Children welcome
2 Queen 1 Double 1 Twin 4 Single (5 bdrm)
Bathrooms: 4 Ensuite 1 Private 1 Host share

Haere mai ki Aoraki (Welcome to Aoraki Lodge). If you prefer a casual informal atmosphere with friendly hosts then Aoraki Lodge is the place for you. Relax in our warm, sunny home and enjoy our private garden. Native birds can be seen and heard. Vlad is a well known fishing guide and can offer helpful advice and information on all the attractions in the area. We look forward to meeting you.

TWIZEL - LAKE RUATANIWHA   *4km SW of Twizel*

Lake Ruataniwha Homestay   *Homestay*
Robin & Lester Baikie
146 Max Smith Drive, Twizel

Tel (03) 435 0532   Fax (03) 435 0522
Mob 025 321 532   robinandlester@xtra.co.nz
www.bnb.co.nz/lakeruataniwhahomestay.html

Double $120-$150   Single $70-$90 (Full Breakfast)
Child neg   Dinner $30pp
Credit cards accepted   Children welcome
2 Queen 2 Twin (3 bdrm)
Bathrooms: 1 Ensuite 1 Guests share

Welcome to our new home, built on four hectares overlooking Lake Ruataniwha with 360 degree views of the lake and mountains. We have travelled overseas and enjoy meeting people. Kitchen/living area opens onto large decks to relax on and enjoy the view. We have a variety of farm animals close to our house, which our grandchildren delight in feeding when they visit. Our interests are farming, horse trekking, sport and CWI. Email and fax facilities available. An ideal stopover between Christchurch and Queenstown.

TWIZEL

Hunters House   *B&B Homestay*
Anne & Matt Hunter
58 Tekapo Drive, Twizel

Tel (03) 435 0038   Fax (03) 435 0038
Mob 021 154 9859   annehunter@xtra.co.nz
www.bnb.co.nz/amhunter.html

Double $140   Single $90   (Full Breakfast)
Dinner $40   Self contained cottage
Credit cards accepted
2 King/Twin (2 bdrm)   Bathrooms: 2 Ensuite

Hunters House was built in 2003. It is architecturally designed for guests and features every comfort and a warm welcoming environment. It overlooks the native tussocks and trees of the Green Belt. Guest privacy is assured. All rooms are sited for sun and views. The unique attractions of the Mackenzie Country and Aoraki Mt Cook are well known to the Hunters, and they are always happy to share their knowledge. Cead mile failte.

OMARAMA   *1km S of Omarama*

Omarama Station   *Farmstay*
Beth & Dick Wardell
Omarama, North Otago

Tel (03) 438 9821
Fax (03) 438 9822
wardell@paradise.net.nz
www.omaramastation.co.nz

Double $110   Single $60   (Full Breakfast)
Child $20-$50   Dinner by arrangement $35
2 Queen 2 Single (3 bdrm)
Bathrooms: 1 Ensuite 1 Private

Omarama Station is a merino sheep and cattle property adjacent to the Omarama township. The 100 year old homestead is nestled in a small valley in a tranquil parklike setting of willows, poplars and a fast flowing stream (good fly fishing), pleasant walking environs, and interesting historical perspective to the high country as this was the original station in the area. Swimming pool and a pleasant garden. An opportunity to experience day to day farming activities.

SOUTH CANTERBURY, NORTH OTAGO

KUROW *60km W of Oamaru*

Approved

Glenmac Farmstay
Farmstay Self-contained Campervans or tents
Kaye & Keith Dennison
RD 7K, Oamaru

Tel (03) 436 0200   Fax (03) 436 0202   Mob 027 222 1119
glenmac@farmstaynewzealand.co.nz
www.farmstaynewzealand.co.nz

Double $80-$100   Single $40-$50   (Full Breakfast)
Child ¹/2 price under 13 years   Dinner $25
S/C price on application   Credit cards accepted
Children welcome   Pets welcome   Smoking area inside
1 Queen 2 Double 2 Twin (4 bdrm)   Bathrooms: 1 Ensuite 1 Host share

A peaceful situation, away from traffic noises, enjoy home cooked meals, a comfortable bed, relax and be treated as one of the family. Explore our 4000 acre high country farm. Either on farm or nearby enjoy horse riding, four wheel drive farm tour, walking/tramping, fishing (guide available), mountain biking, golf or explore the new Fossil Trail. Self-contained cottage also available. Directions: Situated at end of Gards Road which is 10km east of Kurow on right or 13km west of Duntroon on left.

KUROW *2.7km E of Kurow*

Approved

Western House *B&B Self-contained Homestyle*
Bernadette & Michael Parish
Highway 83, Kurow,
North Oago

Tel (03) 436 0876   Fax (03) 436 0872
mbparish@xtra.co.nz
www.westernhouse.co.nz

Double $100-$120   Single $90-$120   (Full Breakfast)
Dinner $40   Credit cards accepted
2 Queen 1 Double 1 Twin (4 bdrm)
Bathrooms: 1 Ensuite 1 Private 1 Guests share

Western House, built in 1871 as an accomodation house, is surrounded by extensive garden and orchard with mountain views. Enjoy wood fires, fresh flowers, hearty breakfasts and wholesome dinners. A warm welcome awaits guests for an enjoyable stay with us and our cat Simba. Attractions: trout and salmon fishing (guide available), golf (clubs on-site), tennis, squash, walks, mountain biking, 4WD, swimming pool, beehive tours, and historic water wheel built 1899.

OAMARU

Approved

Wallfield *Homestay*
Pat & Bill Bews
126 Reservoir Road,
Oamaru

Tel (03) 437 0368
Mob 025 284 7303
b&pbews@xtra.co.nz
www.bnb.co.nz/wallfield.html

Double $80   Single $45   (Continental Breakfast)
1 Double 2 Single (2 bdrm)
Bathrooms: 1 Guests share

Our modern home is situated high above the north end of Oamaru with superb views to the east. We have 4 children, all happily married,. We have been home hosting for the last 13 years and although now retired from farming, still enjoy the buzz of meeting new friends. Our interests include gardening and tramping.

WAIANAKARUA - OAMARU *27km S of Oamaru*

Glen Dendron *B&B Farmstay*
Anne & John Mackay
284 Breakneck Road, Waianakarua, 9 - ORD, Oamaru

Tel (03) 439 5288 Fax (03) 439 5288 Mob 021 615 227
anne.john.mackay@xtra.co.nz
www.glenhomestays.co.nz

Double $120-$145 Single $80-$100
(Full Breakfast) Child $45
Dinner $35 with wine
Credit cards accepted Children welcome
2 King/Twin 2 Queen (4 bdrm)
Bathrooms: 2 Ensuite 1 Guests share

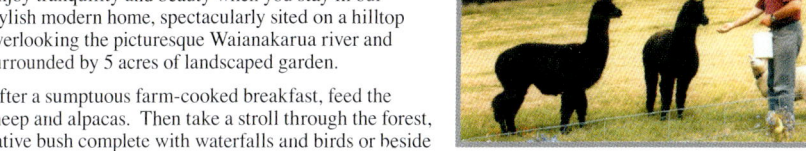

Whitestone Waitaki Tourism Award Winner 2003.
Enjoy tranquility and beauty when you stay in our
stylish modern home, spectacularly sited on a hilltop
overlooking the picturesque Waianakarua river and
surrounded by 5 acres of landscaped garden.

After a sumptuous farm-cooked breakfast, feed the
sheep and alpacas. Then take a stroll through the forest,
native bush complete with waterfalls and birds or beside
the river. Play a round on our private golf course. Later, watch the seals and penguins on a beach
nearby. Then, complete a perfect day with our gourmet three-course dinner with fine NZ wine before
snuggling down for a peaceful sleep in the fresh country air.

After a lifetime spent in farming and forestry we relish the opportunity to share our home and semi-
retired lifestyle with guests. Our adult family lives overseas so we travel frequently and have a great
interest in other countries and cultures. We are very keen gardeners, read widely and enjoy antiques.
Anne is a floral artist and John is involved with the Lions organization.

We can plan customised itineraries of the area's many attractions: • Oamaru's historic architecture •
Garden, heritage and fossil trails • Beaches, fishing, seals and penguins • Famous Moeraki Boulders
and other interesting geological features. Use us as a base for day visits to Oamaru, Dunedin, Waitaki
Valley and Mt Cook. **Christchurch International Airport - 3.5 hours. We don't mind short notice!**

*An overnight stay is not enough to do justice to this lovely area -
with so much to see, why not stay awhile!*

OAMARU *8km SW of Oamaru*

Tara *Homestay*
Marianne & Baxter Smith
Springhill Road, 3 ORD,
Oamaru

Tel (03) 434 8187 Fax (03) 434 8187
smith.tara@xtra.co.nz
www.tarahomestay.com

Double $100 Single $60 (Full Breakfast)
Dinner $30 by arrangement
2 Single (1 bdrm)
Bathrooms: 1 Private

Want to be pampered? Tara is the place for you. Enjoy the comfort and luxuries of our character Oamaru stone home. Tara boasts all day sun and the privacy to soak up the country atmosphere. Nestled amongst eleven acres of roses, mature trees and rural farmland Tara is the perfect place to unwind. Our livestock include alpacas, coloured sheep, donkeys and an aviary. We also have a burmese cat and a lassie collie. My husband Baxter and I will ensure your visit is an enjoyable experience. Please phone for directions.

OAMARU *3km S of Oamaru, just off SH1*

Springbank *Homestay Self-contained full kitchen*
Joan & Stan Taylor
60 Weston Road, Oamaru

Tel (03) 434 6602 Fax (03) 434 6602
Mob 025 669 2902 www.bnb.co.nz/springbank.html

Double $85 Single $50 (Continental Breakfast)
Child $10 Credit cards accepted
1 Double 1 Twin (1 bdrm)
Bathrooms: 1 Private

We look forward to sharing our retirement haven
with visitors from overseas and New Zealand. Our modern home and separate guest flat are set in a peaceful and private large garden. Feed the goldfish and pamper Oscar, our cat. Our guest flat is sunny, warm, spacious and comfortable. We enjoy helping visitors discover our district's best kept secrets! Penguins, gardens, Moeraki Boulders, beaches, pool, fishing and golf. Our interests - travel, gardening, grandchildren. Stan's - Lions and following sports. Joan's - patchwork, floral design and all handcrafts.

OAMARU *1.3km N of Oamaru town centre*

Highway House Boutique B&B *B&B Homestay*
Stephanie & Norman Slater
43 Lynn Street, Orana Park, Oamaru
(Corner Thames Highway and Lynn Street)

Tel (03) 437 1066 0800 003 319 Fax (03) 437 1066
Mob 025 200 2976 cns@ihug.co.nz
www.bnb.co.nz/highway.html

Double $100-$120 Single $80-$100 (Full Breakfast)
Child neg Dinner by arrangement
Credit cards accepted Children welcome
2 King 1 Twin (3 bdrm) Bathrooms: 1 Guests share 1 Host share

Our character residence on Thames Highway, the main north road (1.3km from town centre), has been entirely refurbished to the highest standard. We provide a full cooked breakfast and other refreshments as required. We can assist with tours of historic Oamaru or visits to the nature sites. Our courtesy car can collect or take you to nearby dining establishments. If you appreciate a quality ambiance and particular assistance from Stephanie and Norman who have travelled widely overseas, Highway House will be ideal for you.

OAMARU   *10km S of Omaru*

Sunnyside B&B   *B&B*
Andrina & Tony Butcher
3 Kakanui Road, 5 ORD,
Oamaru 8921

Tel (03) 439 5442   Fax (03) 439 5442
Mob 025 285 3342   tonyandrina@xtra.co.nz
www.bnb.co.nz/sunnyside.html

Double $80 Single $50   (Continental Breakfast)
1 Queen (1 bdrm)
Bathrooms: 1 Ensuite

Kakanui is a pretty coastal village on the Vanished World Fossil Trail. You can walk, swim, surf, fish, kayak on the river or fossick for interesting stones or just relax. There is a shop with takeaway and café nearby. We are centrally located for historic Oamaru, Moeraki Boulders, Central Otago Goldfields, Waitaki Valley Hydro-lakes, penguins and much more. We are semi-retired from forestry and urban tree management. You can be assured of a warm welcome from us, our two cats and one dog.

OAMARU   *2km N of Oamaru Central*

Coral Sea Cottage & Ocean View
B&B   Self-contained   Semi-rural Cottage
Nicola & Peter Mountain
34 Harlech Street, Oamaru

Tel (03) 437 1422   Fax (03) 437 1422
Mob 021 659 757 or 021 042 6997
nmountainnz@hotmail.com   www.bnb.co.nz/coralsea.html

Double $75-$112 Single $30-$66   (Special Breakfast)
Child (5-16) $23   Children welcome   Pets welcome
3 King/Twin 1 Single (4 bdrm)
Bathrooms: 1 Ensuite 1 Private

Come and relax in our delightful, newly equipped, cosy cottage with secluded garden or in new self-contained accommodation in our home, Ocean View, with magnificent panoramic views. In a 5 acre hillside setting with sheep, chickens, pheasants, pet cow, dogs (small), cats and teenage boys. Breakfast provisions include eggs. Near local shops and restaurants and only 5 minutes drive to historic town centre, art galleries and famous blue penguin colony. We look forward to welcoming you and offering help with planning your visit to our area.

OAMARU   *.5 km W of Oamaru centre*

Homestay Oamaru   *Homestay*
Doug Bell
14 Warren Street, Oamaru

Tel (03) 434 1454   Fax (03) 434 1454
Mob 027 408 2860
homestayoamaru@paradise.net.nz
www.bellview.co.nz

Double $65-$95 Single $40-$55   (Full Breakfast)
Dinner $25
2 Queen 1 Double (3 bdrm)
Bathrooms: 2 Ensuite 1 Host share

Sweeping views over the town and harbour. Warm, spacious and comfortable accommodation for the travelling enthusiast, with books, maps, atlases and guides for you perusal. Quiet, private site, close to town centre. (see map on website). Off-street parking. Southern scenic walkway access at property boundary. Some of the area's attractions include sea and river fishing, historic architecture, unique geological features and eco-tourism. Host has detailed local knowledge. Site unsuitable for young children or pets.

SOUTH CANTERBURY, NORTH OTAGO

MOERAKI - OAMARU   *38km S of Oamaru*

Moeraki Boulder Downs Farmstay and B&B
B&B Farmstay
Jan & Ken Wheeler
State Highway 1, Moeraki,
RD 2, Palmerston, North Otago

Tel (03) 439 4855 Fax (03) 439 4355
Mob 025 614 6396 farmstay@moerakiboulders.co.nz
www.moerakiboulders.co.nz

Double $90-$120 Single $70 (Full Breakfast)
Child $40 Dinner by arrangement C/C accepted
1 Queen 2 Twin (2 bdrm) Bathrooms: 1 Guests share

Indulge yourself and enjoy warm hospitality at our country retreat by the sea. We invite you to join us for a traditional New Zealand dinner - then relax by the fire in our charming 1920's homestead. Breakfast with the bellbirds - then stroll along the beautiful beach to Moeraki Boulders and quaint fishing village. Sheep farm tours available. Stay two nights and experience the Moeraki penguins, seals, historic Oamaru, golf courses and antique shops nearby. We are enroute to Christchurch, Dunedin, Queenstown and Mt Cook.

---

visit... www.bnb.co.nz

For the most up-to-date information from our hosts, and links to our other web sites around the world.

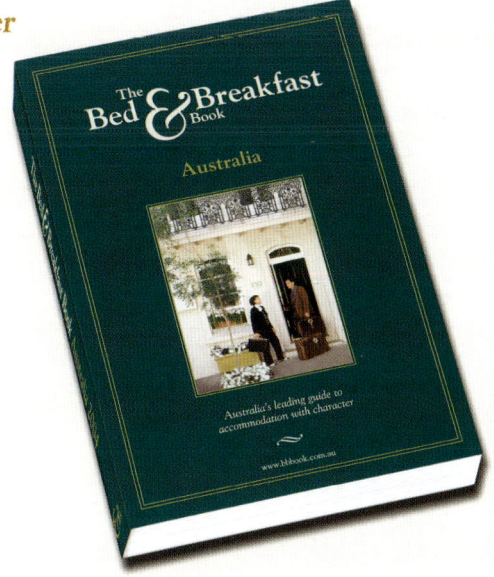

Otago &
North Catlins

Towns listed generally follow
a north to south route. Refer
to the index if required.

Makarora

Hawea
Albert Town
Wanaka

Glenorchy

Arrowtown
Cromwell
Queenstown

Alexandra

Middlemarch
Waikouaiti

Roxburgh

Ettrick
Millers Flat

Port Chalmers
Mosgiel
Lawrence
Dunedin

Otago
Peninsula
Waihola

Balclutha

Koka Point
The Catlins
Owaka
Nuggets

MAKARORA *65km N of Wanaka*

Larrivee Homestay
Homestay Self-contained Cottage
Andrea and Paul
Makarora, via Wanaka

Tel (03) 443 9177 andipaul@xtra.co.nz
www.larriveehomestay.co.nz

Double $100-$150 Single $80 (Full Breakfast)
Child ¹/2 price under 12 years Dinner $35 BYO
Credit cards accepted
2 Double 2 Single (3 bdrm)
Bathrooms: 1 Ensuite 1 Private

Nestled in native bush bordering Mt Aspiring National Park, our unique home and cottage are secluded, quiet and comfortable. Originally from the USA, we have lived in Makarora for over 25 years and like sharing our mountain retreat and enjoying good food and conversation. Many activities are available locally, including fishing, bird watching, jet boating, scenic flights and bush walks - including the wonderful Siberia Experience, fly/walk/boat trip. We are happy to help make arrangements for activities.

MAKARORA *65km N of Wanaka*

Makarora Homestead *Self-contained*
Kenna Fraser
53 Rata Road, Makarora

Tel (03) 443 1532
bnb@makarora.com
www.makarora.com

Double $95-$105
(Continental Breakfast)
Children welcome
7 Queen 1 Double 7 Twin (8 bdrm)
Bathrooms: 2 Ensuite 3 Guests share

Makarora Homestead offers a secluded retreat in the midst of the Southern Alps and is perfect for travellers looking for the warmth and ambience of a home. A self-contained comfortable house with a private sunny deck leads into the open plan kitchen/dining/living area. 2 new detached bedrooms have queen beds, ensuite bathrooms and verandah. With tame farm animals to feed Makarora Homestead provides a fun rural experience for any age.

WANAKA *Wanaka Central*

Lake Wanaka Homestay *B&B Homestay*
Gailie & Peter Cooke
85 Warren Street, Wanaka

Tel (03) 443 7995 0800 443 799 Fax (03) 443 7945
wanakahomestay@xtra.co.nz
www.lakewanakahomestay.co.nz

Double $100-$110 Single $60-$70
(Full Breakfast) Credit cards accepted
2 Double 1 Twin 2 Single (3 bdrm)
Bathrooms: 2 Guests share 1 Host share

Welcome to our home. Relax with us enjoy breathtaking views of lake and mountains, just 5 minutes walk to shops, restaurants, lake. Peter keen fly fisherman happy to show guests where to find "the big ones". Complimentary tea, coffee, home-made cookies during your stay. Warm home-cooked breakfast, comfortable beds, electric blankets. We have shared our home with guests for many years, made wonderful friendships, both enjoy meeting, helping people, fishing, golf, skiing, walking, gardening. Kate, our labrador dog, is everyone's friend. Freephone 0800 443 799.

WANAKA   *Wanaka*

Aspiring Images   *Homestay*
Betty & George Russell
26 Norman Terrace, Wanaka

Tel **(03) 443 8358**   Fax (03) 443 8327
stay@aspiringimages.co.nz   www.aspiringimages.co.nz

Double $120-$140   Single $80-$100
(Full Breakfast) Child by arrangement
Dinner by arrangement Credit cards accepted
1 King/Twin 1 Queen (2 bdrm)
Bathrooms: 1 Ensuite 1 Private

The challenge - portray Wanaka and our homestay in 85 words! Wanaka is: magical; tranquil; dramatic; refreshing; exhilarating; captivatingly beautiful. Wanaka has: activities both challenging and restful, fascinating history, distinctive micro-climate, ecological diversity, mountain light ever changing. Our homestay offers: informative welcoming hosts, warmth and comfort, lake and mountain views, adjacent park with lake access, mountain bikes to ride. We are: ex-teachers with musical, sporting, photographic and Rotary interests; well travelled both nationally and internationally, qualified to help with NZ itineraries.

LAKE WANAKA   *Wanaka*

Beacon Point   *B&B Homestay Self-contained*
Diana & Dan Pinckney
302 Beacon Point Road, PO Box 6, Lake Wanaka

Tel **(03) 443 1253**   Fax (03) 443 1254
Mob   Di 025 246 0222 or Dan 027 435 4847
dan.di@lakewanaka.co.nz www.beaconpoint.co.nz

Double $90-$120 (Continental Breakfast)
Child $30 Dinner $40 Children welcome
1 Queen 1 Twin (2 bdrm)
Bathrooms: 2 Private

Beacon Point B&B is surrounded by one acre of lawn and garden for your enjoyment. Leads to a walking track to the village around the edge of the lake with snow capped mountains in winter. Private spacious studio with ensuite, queen and single beds (2 rooms), kitchen, TV, sundeck and BBQ area. Studio equipped with every need for a perfect stay. We are flexible and enjoy planning your days with you. Our intrests include farming, forestry, fly fishing, real estate, boating, gardening and grandchildren. Turn right at lake - Lakeside Road - then to Beacon Point Road 302.

WANAKA   *Wanaka*

Harpers   *B&B Homestay*
Jo & Ian Harper
95 McDougall Street, Wanaka

Tel **(03) 443 8894**   Fax (03) 443 8834
harpers@xtra.co.nz
www.harpers.co.nz

Double $120   Single $80
(Continental Breakfast) Credit cards accepted
1 King/Twin 2 Single (2 bdrm)
Bathrooms: 1 Ensuite 1 Private

We take pride in offering a friendly, comfortable home.
Share breakfast and awesome lake and mountain views with us. Also explore our extensive garden, which provides a tranquil environment for relaxing. We offer a drink and muffins on your arrival. This is a smoke-free home. Recent guests' comments: "A wonderful stay - hot bath, hot pancakes, hot view and such a welcome. The best yet." "Thanks for your warm and friendly hospitality, very high standard of service and lovely pancakes." "Lovely stay, wonderful views, pancakes delicious."

WANAKA *10km N of Wanaka*

Approved

The Stone Cottage *B&B Self-contained*
Belinda Wilson
Wanaka, RD 2, Central Otago

Tel (03) 443 1878 Fax (03) 443 1276
stonecottage@xtra.co.nz www.stonecottage.co.nz

Double $230-$260 Single $210
(Full Breakfast) Child $^1/_2$ price under 12 years
Dinner $65 Credit cards accepted
1 King 1 Queen 1 Double 2 Single (2 bdrm)
Bathrooms: 1 Ensuite 1 Private

50 years ago, a spectacular garden was created at
Dublin Bay on the tranquil shores of Lake Wanaka.
Its beauty still blooms today against a backdrop of
the majestic Southern Alps. Accommodation is
private, comfortable and elegantly decorated.

The Stone Cottage offers two self-contained loft
apartments with breathtaking views over Lake
Wanaka to snow clad alps beyond. Featuring your
own bathroom, bedroom, kitchen, living room
and balcony. Television, fax and email available.
Private entrance.

Enjoy breakfast at leisure, made from fresh
ingredients from your well stocked fully equipped kitchen, Pre-dinner drinks, delicious three course
dinner and NZ wines or a gourmet picnic hamper is available by arrangement.

Walk along the beach just 4 minutes from The Stone Cottage or wander in the enchanting garden.
Guests can experience trout fishing, nature walks, golf, boating, horse riding, wine tasting and ski fields
nearby. Only 10 minutes from Wanaka, this is the perfect retreat for those who value privacy and the
unique beauty of this area.

*Relax in the magic atmosphere at The Stone Cottage and awake to the dawn
bird chorus of native bellbirds and fantails.*

OTAGO, NORTH CATLINS

WANAKA   *4km S of Wanaka*
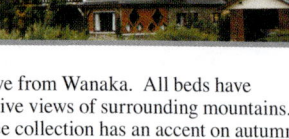

Stonehaven   *Homestay Rural*
Deirdre & Dennis
Halliday Lane, RD 2, Wanaka

Tel (03) 443 9516 Fax (03) 443 9513
moghul@xtra.co.nz
www.stonehaven.co.nz

Double $95 Single $75   (Full Breakfast)
Child $20 neg portacots & high chairs available
Credit cards accepted Children welcome
2 Queen 2 Single (2 bdrm)
Bathrooms: 1 Ensuite 1 Private

Our home is set in a slightly developed 2 acres about 5 minutes drive from Wanaka. All beds have electric blankets, tea and coffee is freely available. We have extensive views of surrounding mountains. Children are welcome. Child care by arrangement. Our nearby tree collection has an accent on autumn colour. Local walks a speciality. Organic fruit both in season and preserved. We have twin 15 year old girls, a small dog, and 2 cats. No smoking inside please. Please phone for directions.

WANAKA   *2min N of Wanaka*

Hunt's Homestay   *Homestay*
Bill & Ruth Hunt
56 Manuka Crescent, Wanaka 9192, Central Otago

Tel (03) 443 1053 Fax (03) 443 1355
Mob 025 265 0114
relax@huntshomestay.co.nz
www.huntshomestay.co.nz

Double $110 Single $70   (Continental Breakfast)
Child by arrangement Credit cards accepted
1 Queen 2 Single (2 bdrm)
Bathrooms: 1 Guests share

Welcome to our modern home in Wanaka where we will greet you with tea or coffee in our smoke-free house and settle you in your spacious ground floor accommodation. After farming near Wanaka, we built this house over looking the mountains and lake, and so have a good knowledge of the area. Through our membership of Lake Wanaka Tourism we are kept informed of all tourist activities in the area. Our interests are golf, gardening, travel and meeting people. We have no resident children or pets.

WANAKA   *2km NW of Wanaka Central*

Lake Wanaka Home Hosting   *B&B Homestay*
Joyce & Lex Turnbull
19 Bill's Way, Wanaka

Tel (03) 443 9060 Fax (03) 443 1626
Mob 027 228 9160 lex.joy@xtra.co.nz
www.lakewanakahomehosting.co.nz

Double $100-$140 Single $65
(Full Breakfast) Child under $25 10 years
Dinner $40 Children welcome
1 King/Twin 1 Double 1 Twin (3 bdrm)
Bathrooms: 2 Private

We welcome visitors to Wanaka, enjoy sharing our natural surroundings with others. We have a large peaceful home where our guests can experience not only the austerity of the lake and mountains around them, but also experience the ambience of Wanaka itself. Guest room with super king bed has adjoining TV lounge with TV, tea coffee facilities, private bathroom. Good laundry facilities. We wish your stay in Wanaka will be a very happy one. Directions: please ring for directions. We enjoy your company.

WANAKA *Wanaka Central*

Te Wanaka Lodge *B&B Separate/Suite*
Boutique Accommodation
Graeme & Andy Oxley
23 Brownston Street, Wanaka

Tel (03) 443 9224 0800 WANAKA (926 252)
Fax (03) 443 9246
tewanakalodge@xtra.co.nz   www.tewanaka.co.nz

Double $145-$185 Single $135-$175
(Full Breakfast) Garden Cottage Room $200
Credit cards accepted
9 Queen 4 Twin (13 bdrm)   Bathrooms: 13 Ensuite

Nestled in the heart of Wanaka, Te Wanaka Lodge
is a 2 minute walk to the lake, restaurants, shops
and golf course. Tastefully decorated with fishing
and skiing memorabilia, Te Wanaka Lodge has a
distinctive alpine ambience.

On a hot summers day laze under our walnut tree
with a cool drink from the house bar, or in winter
relax by the warmth of our log fire after enjoying a
soak in our secluded garden hot tub.

• All bedrooms with ensuite and private balcony
• Full cooked breakfast included
• House Bar specialising in local beers and wines
• Sky TV, video, CD and book library
• Off-street parking
• Ski drying room and laundry service
• Full business facilities
• In-house massage therapy
• Mountain bike & equipment available

OTAGO, NORTH CATLINS

WANAKA

Northridge *B&B Homestay*
Sue Atkinson & Richie Heathfield
11 Botting Place, PO Box 376, Wanaka

Tel (03) 443 8835 Fax (03) 443 1835
Mob 025 950 436 stay@northridgewanaka.co.nz
www.northridgewanaka.co.nz

Double $140-$160 Single $140
(Full Breakfast) Credit cards accepted
2 Queen 2 Single (3 bdrm)
Bathrooms: 1 Ensuite 2 Private

Looking for quality accommodation with spectacular views? Northridge is the place for you. Situated in a prime location on a ridge overlooking Lake Wanaka, the mountains and within walking distance to restaurants, shops and the lakefront. Our quality 2 storey native timber and schist stone home lends itself to indoor/outdoor living, where you can wander through the garden or sit on the patio with refreshments and take in the everchanging scenery. The rooms all with views are spacious and have quality linen, wool underlays and feather duvets. Northridge is centrally heated to keep us all cosy in winter.

WANAKA   *2.5km E of Wanaka*

Riverside *B&B*
Lesley & Norman West
11 Riverbank Road, RD 2, Wanaka

Tel (03) 443 1522 Fax (03) 443 1522
Mob 0274 640 333 n.l.west@paradise.net.nz
www.bnb.co.nz/riverside.html

Double $110-$130 Single $75-$85 (Full Breakfast)
Dinner by arrangement Credit cards accepted
1 Queen 2 Twin (2 bdrm)
Bathrooms: 1 Guests share

We welcome guests to the tranquility of our quality brick home with lovely timber interior finishing. Set on six acres overlooking the Cardrona River we are just 100 metres off SH84, 5 minutes (2.5km) from Lake Wanaka. We offer you a friendly, peaceful environment with extensive mountain and rural views. Guests are welcome to relax by the open fire in winter, or enjoy shady terraces in summer. 2 well-appointed guest rooms, quality linen and central heating ensures your stay will be relaxing and enjoyable. Courtesy vehicle available. We have 2 cats and a small friendly dog (outdoors).

WANAKA - ALBERT TOWN   *6km N of Wanaka*

Riversong *B&B Homestay*
Ann Horrax
5 Wicklow Terrace, Albert Town, RD 2, Wanaka

Tel (03) 443 8567 Fax (03) 443 8564
Mob 021 113 6397 info@happyhomestay.co.nz
www.happyhomestay.co.nz

Double $110-$140 Single $85-$90 (Full Breakfast)
Child $25 Dinner $35pp by arrangement
Credit cards accepted Children welcome
1 King/Twin 1 Queen 1 Single (3 bdrm)
Bathrooms: 1 Ensuite 1 Private

Riversong is 5 minutes from Wanaka Township, at historic Albert Town, on the banks of the magestic Clutha River. At our secluded haven all rooms have river and mountain views, with immediate access to the river. My background is healthcare and Ian's law. We invite you to share all the comforts of our home and garden and Ian's knowledge of the region's fishing. We aim to provide a peaceful and friendly atmosphere (books galore!) where you can unwind. We have 2 outside lab dogs.

LAKE WANAKA *2.3km NW of Wanaka Centre*

Peak-Sportchalet *B&B Self-contained*
Alex and Christine Schafer
36 Hunter Crescent, Lake Wanaka

Tel (03) 443 6990 Fax (03) 443 4969
stay@peak-sportchalet.co.nz
www.Peak-Sportchalet.co.nz

Double $90 $125 Single $70 (Special Breakfast)
Children welcome
1 King/Twin 1 King 1 Twin (3 bdrm)
Bathrooms: 2 Ensuite 1 Private

Welcome at Peak-Sportchalet. Our well designed home
and chalet inviting you to stay and discover beautiful Lake Wanaka. Relax in the chalet or in a king-size double with own entrance. Enjoy a breakfast you will remember, great mountain views and great hospitality. Chalet has 1 or 2 bedroom option with lounge, full kitchen, bathroom with underfloor-heating and super king-size beds. Double ensuite with kitchennette ajoining a native garden area. All rooms have great mountain views and own sundeck - close to lake and walking tracks. You can be most asure to experience a memorable time out.

WANAKA *2km S of Wanaka*

Mountain Range *B&B Boutique B&B*
Lindsey and Matthew Brady
Heritage Park, Cardrona Valley Road,
PO Box 451, Wanaka

Tel (03) 443 7400 Fax (03) 443 7450
Mob (021) 443 741 stay@mountainrange.co.nz
www.mountainrange.co.nz

Double $225-$280 Single $195
(Full Breakfast) Credit cards accepted
2 King/Twin 1 King 4 Queen (7 bdrm)
Bathrooms: 7 Ensuite

Set on 10 acres of private parkland, Mountain Range draws its name and inspiration from the breathtaking mountain views that provide a unique backdrop for this peaceful and relaxing retreat. The lodge benefits from total seclusion and privacy, yet is only 2 minutes from the local amenities and restaurants. 7 spacious guestrooms with luxury ensuite bathrooms. Delicious continental and cooked breakfast. Sumptuous guest lounge with elegant furnishings and log fire. Complimentary tea, coffee and cookies. Gourmet breakfast, afternoon tea and aperitifs incl in tariff.

WANAKA *1.5km Wanaka central*

Temasek House *B&B Homestay*
Vivien Reid & Mandy Madin
7 Heuchan Lane, Wanaka 9192

Tel (03) 443 1655 Fax (03) 443 1655
temasek.house@xtra.co.nz
www.bnb.co.nz/temasek.html

Double $95-$110 Single $65
(Full Breakfast) Twin $95
Credit cards accepted Children welcome
1 Queen 1 Twin 1 Single (3 bdrm)
Bathrooms: 1 Ensuite 1 Guests share

Only 1.5km from the town centre, Temasek House offers guests a friendly, homely atmosphere. Our home is ideally situated for the local ski fields and Mount Aspiring National Park. A large comfortable lounge opens on to a balcony with mountain views. A gentle stroll to local restaurants and lakeside. Tea and coffee complimentary with home-made treats. Internet/email and laundry facilities available for small extra charge. One small dog on property.

OTAGO, NORTH CATLINS

WANAKA *2km E of Wanaka*

Oregon Hollow *B&B Self-contained*
Robyn & Gene Clements
426 Aubrey Road, RD 2, Wanaka, Otago

Tel (03) 443 4086 Fax (03) 443 4086
Mob 021 418 878 gene.c@clear.net.nz
www.bnb.co.nz/oregonhollow.html

Double $165-$185 Single $140
(Full Breakfast) Credit cards accepted
1 Queen (1 bdrm)
Bathrooms: 1 Private

Oregon Hollow is a luxury 1 bedroom apartment
(renovated 2003) attached to our house. Set in a
peaceful location yet less than 2 kilometres to Wanaka's restaurants and amenities. The apartment has a
separate entrance, private bathroom, and large living area with a kitchenette and log burner, TV, DVD
and stereo. Quality bed linen, furnishings are fitted throughout. A private patio is set in our 1 acre
of country garden. A speciality breakfast hamper is provided. We have a son, Oliver, 2 Jack Russell
terriers. Bookings essential.

WANAKA *2.4km E of Wanaka*

The Cedars *B&B Homestay*
Mary & Graham Dowdall
7 Riverbank Road, RD 2,
Wanaka 9192, Central Otago

Tel (03) 443 1544 Fax (03) 443 1544
Mob 021 120 8960 thecedarswanaka@xtra.co.nz
www.bnb.co.nz/cedars.html

Double $110-$150 Single $70-$100 (Full Breakfast)
Dinner by arrangement   Credit cards accepted
Children welcome   Smoking area inside
2 Queen 1 Single (2 bdrm) Bathrooms: 1 Guests share

Céad Míle Fáilte – One hundred thousand welcomes. A warm Irish/Kiwi welcome awaits at 'The
Cedars', by Mary, Graham and pet English collie, Flipper. Our stone home set on 11 acres includes
panoramic views, expansive gardens, guest lounge with large open fire. Nearby attractions include
The Maze, The Warbirds Museum (both internationally acclaimed), golf, ski fields, walking tracks,
paragliding, lakes and rivers for water pursuits: shops and restaurants. Full breakfast is served with
fresh and home-made produce. We offer evening meals or BBQ by prior arrangement.

WANAKA *300m Wanaka Central*

Wanaka Springs Boutique Lodge
Boutique B&B Lodge
Lyn & Murray Finn
21 Warren Street, Wanaka, Central Otago

Tel (03) 443 8421 Fax (03) 443 8429
Mob 027 2414113
relax@wanakasprings.com www.wanakasprings.com

Double $250-$330
(Full Breakfast) Credit cards accepted
2 King/Twin 5 Queen 1 Twin (8 bdrm)
Bathrooms: 8 Ensuite

Welcome to Wanaka's in-town retreat, a purpose built, boutique lodge set in the tranquility of natural
springs and native gardens. It is within a 5 minute stroll to the lakefront, golf course and Wanaka's
shops, cafés, bars and restaurants. 8 spacious guestrooms, each with private ensuite, have superior king,
queen or twin beds. The guest lounge has a welcoming log fire, quality furnishings, book collection and
entertainment systems. Full breakfast, afternoon tea, pre-dinner drinks and nightcaps are included in
the tariff.

WANAKA   *Wanaka Central*

Blackpeak Lodge   *B&B*
Dean Smith
38 Kings Drive, Wanaka

Tel (03) 443 4078   Fax (03) 443 4038
Mob 021 295 0046
relax@blackpeaklodge.co.nz
www.blackpeaklodge.co.nz

Double $130-$195   Single $120-$155
(Full Breakfast) Child neg
3 Queen (3 bdrm)
Bathrooms: 2 Ensuite 1 Private

Come and soak up the magnificent views from the hot
tub on the deck to the guest rooms. Warm and friendly hospitality where our aim is to make your stay
unforgettable and as relaxing as possible. Underfloor heating and a feature fireplace ensures warmth
in the winter months and in the summer, the living room opens up onto the decking for a great place to
have a BBQ and admire the sunset. A truly alpine feel with charm and ambience amid comfort and
style. Tea, coffee, chocolates, cookies and muffins are always available during your stay.

WANAKA   *2km W of Wanaka*

Sequora Lodge   *B&B Homestay*
Lew Crawford
137 Anderson Road, RD 2, Wanaka

Tel (03) 443 1961   Fax (03) 443 1964
Mob 021 166 6450
stay@sequoralodge.co.nz   www.sequoralodge.co.nz

Double $120-$160   Single $90-$100
(Continental Breakfast)
Child neg   Credit cards accepted
3 Queen (3 bdrm)
Bathrooms: 3 Ensuite

Sequora Lodge is a quality purpose built B&B in a large
new home set on 2 acres, 2 minutes drive to town, with spectacular lake and mountain views. Quiet and
spacious guest rooms. The guest lounge has a piano, open fire, TV, VCR and DVD player. Facilities
include guest verandah, ski drying room, central heating, library, email access, laundry facilities, and
complimentary classic/vintage car tour of Wanaka. Mountain bikes and fishing rods available. 2
children at home, pet on property. A warm welcome assured.

WANAKA   *13km N of Wanaka*

Green Gables   *Self-contained*
Caroline & Dave Wigg
458 Camp Hill Road, Hawea Flat, Wanaka

Tel (03) 443 4221   Fax (03) 443 4221   Mob 021 116 8935
carolinestudio@xtra.co.nz
www.bnb.co.nz/greengablesbb.html

Double $110   Single $70   (Continental Breakfast)
Child $10   1 double sofa bed in cottage
Children welcome Pets welcome
1 Queen 1 Double (1 bdrm)
Bathrooms: 1 Ensuite

The Green Gables homestead was built in the 1920's in an
established garden setting. We welcome you to stay in our self-
contained guest cottage. The cottage sleeps 2-4 with a queen-
size bed (and sofa converts to a bed). It has an ensuite shower, toilet and under floor heating. A modern
lounge with tea and coffee facilities, microwave and fridge. We also have a spa pool for you to relax in.
Our 2 children love the ponies and trampoline and our elderly labrador Tessa.

WANAKA   *2km S of Wanaka*

Wanaka Cottage   *Self Contained Cottage*
Linzi & Brian Ebbage-Thomas
11 Orchard Road, Wanaka

Tel (03) 443 8425   Fax (09) 353 1390   Mob 027 490 3175
info@wanakacottage.co.nz   www.wanakacottage.co.nz

Cottage $250 plus $55 one-off cleaning fee (Min 2 nights)
Credit cards accepted Children welcome Pets welcome
1 Super King/Twin 1 Super King (2 bdrm)
Bathrooms: 1 Private   Alfresco Hot Tub

Surrounded by mountain views this gorgeous new 2
bedroomed self-contained cottage has been built and
furnished with sumptuousness and character in mind.
The master bedroom features a super king oak sleigh
bed and luxurious linens - timber shutters open into the
vaulted ceiling over the living/dining areas with its open
log fire. The second bedroom can either be a king twin
or a super king. The classicly tiled bathroom has an
extravagant french tub with ceiling rose shower.

The facilities include: Sky TV, DVD and CD player,
fully equipped kitchen, full laundry, under floor heating,
heaters, electric blankets, telephone and internet
connection. The patio, with seating and a cedar hot tub,
captures the all day sun.

The Cottage is located on the edge of 20 acres of parkland
just off the Cardrona Valley Road - only a 2 minute drive
from the lakefront and town centre. 100 metres away is an
excellent espresso, breakfast and lunch café, and 200 metres
away is a superb evening dining restaurant. The hosts live
on site with their 2 children and friendly cocker spaniel
dog. Directions: once in Wanaka, drive along the lake front
and turn left into MacDougall Street. Orchard Road is
approximately 2.5km on the left hand side. Turn left onto
Orchard Road and Wanaka Cottage is the second turning
(50 metres) on the left.

*This gorgeous, fully-equipped cottage is ideal for
couples and families and a perfect base from which
to explore the surrounding area*

WANAKA   *Wanaka Central*

Wanaka Homestead Lodge & Cottages
B&B Self-contained
Roger North
1 Homestead Close, Wanaka

Tel (03) 443 5022   Fax (03) 443 5023
stay@wanakahomestead.co.nz
www.wanakahomestead.co.nz

Double $225-$275   Single $190
(Full Breakfast)
Cottages $310-$420 all facilities included
Credit cards accepted Children welcome
5 King/Twin (5 bdrm)
Bathrooms: 5 Ensuite

Wanaka Homestead warmly welcomes you to our brand new luxury lodge and cottage accommodation, just 200 metres from the shores of Lake Wanaka. The homestead lodge provides informal luxury in a friendly 5 bedroom boutique bed & breakfast, which during winter has a ski lodge feel.

WANAKA - HAWEA   *13km N of Wanaka*

Mount Maude - Solar Powered - Lodge
B&B Farmstay
Lee & Nigel Buckingham
SH 6 Te Awa Road, RD 2, Wanaka

Tel (03) 443 6882   Fax (03) 443 6882
Mob 025 677 1852   mtmaudelodge@msn.com
www.bnb.co.nz/mountmaude.html

Double $120-$170 Single $90   (Continental Breakfast)
Child $25   Fishing & hunting guiding by arrangement
Credit cards accepted Children welcome
2 Queen 1 Single (2 bdrm)   Bathrooms: 2 Ensuite 2 Private

Location: 10 minutes from Wanaka and 2 minutes from Hawea on Wanaka-Haast Highway (SH6). This modern 480 square metre lodge has it's own guest wing, with 2 rooms with ensuites. Rooms lead to 2 large lounges with open fires in the winter, and BBQ on deck in summer. All modern comforts available, TV, computer, library. 2 children, 2 cats, 1 dog and other farm animals roam the grounds (50 acres) and enjoy the company of guests. Nigel is a keen fisherman/hunter and tramper and will guide if requested.

CROMWELL

Stuart's Homestay   *Homestay*
Elaine & Ian Stuart
5 Mansor Court, Cromwell

Tel (03) 445 3636   Fax (03) 445 3617
Mob 027 252 9823   ian.elaine@xtra.co.nz
www.bnb.co.nz/stuart.html

Double $100-$120 Single $70-$80 (Full Breakfast)
Dinner $20-$30 by arrangement Credit cards accepted
2 Queen 2 Single (3 bdrm)
Bathrooms: 1 Ensuite 1 Guests share

Welcome to our home which is situated within walking distance to most of Cromwell's amenities. We are semi-retired Southland farmers who have been home hosting for over 10 years. Now enjoying living in the stone fruit and wine region of Central Otago. Cromwell is a quiet and relaxed town which is known for historic gold diggings, vineyards, orchards, trout fishing, boating, walks and close to ski fields. 45 minutes to Wanaka or Queenstown. Share dinner with us or just Bed & Breakfast. Tea & coffee available at all times with home-made cookies. We enjoy sharing our home and garden with visitors and a friendly stay is assured.

OTAGO, NORTH CATLINS

CROMWELL   *1km N of Cromwell*

Cottage Gardens   *B&B Homestay*
Jill & Colin McColl
3 Alpha Street, Corner State Highway 8b,
Cromwell, Central Otago

Tel (03) 445 0628   Fax (03) 445 0628
cottage.gardens@ihug.co.nz
www.fiordland.gen.nz/jill.htm

Double $90   Single $40-$60 (Continental Breakfast)
Dinner $20   Credit cards accepted
1 Twin 2 Single (3 bdrm)   Bathrooms: 1 Ensuite 2 Host share

Hospitality is our specialty. For 10 years we have offered travellers good food and company, and welcome you to join us. Our spacious guest room has ensuite, TV, fridge, tea making facilities, private entrance with verandah overlooking garden and Lake Dunstan. Cromwell is surrounded by orchards, vineyards, ever-changing scenery and has excellent sporting facilities. Accompany labrador Jessica May on lakeside walks. Fritter is a retired pre-school cat. Members of Lion International: retired orchardists. Free laundry. Queenstown and Wanaka 45 minutes, Te Anau 2 - 2 1/2 hours drive.

CROMWELL - NORTHBURN   *4km N of Cromwell*

Quartz Reef Creek Bed and Breakfast   *B&B*
Separate/Suite Self-contained
June Boulton
Quartz Reef Creek, RD 3, Northburn,
State Highway 8, Cromwell

Tel (03) 445 0404   Fax (03) 445 0404
june-boulton@xtra.co.nz www.bnb.co.nz/boulton.html

Double $100-$120 Single $70-$80
(Continental Breakfast) Twin room/single $100
Credit cards accepted
1 Queen 1 Twin 1 Single (3 bdrm)   Bathrooms: 1 Ensuite 1 Private

You are invited to stay at my peaceful and modern lakeside home located in Central Otago, a rapidly expanding wine growing region. Panoramic views from your sunny room include Lake Dunstan and surrounding mountains. Both rooms have total privacy with their own entrances. One has its own deck, tea making facilities, fridge, microwave and TV. Another room has twin beds, TV and sitting room with another single bed. I enjoy making pottery in my studio and supply local galleries. I have 2 friendly pets, a dog Guinness and cat, Tom.

CROMWELL   *5km N of Cromwell*

Lake Dunstan Lodge   *Homestay Lodge*
Judy & Bill Thornbury
Northburn, RD 3, Cromwell

Tel (03) 445 1107   Fax (03) 445 3062
Mob 027 431 1415   william.t@xtra.co.nz
www.lakedunstanlodge.co.nz

Double $110-$130 Single $80   (Full Breakfast)
Child neg Dinner $25pp by arrangement
Credit cards accepted Children welcome
2 Queen 3 Single (3 bdrm)
Bathrooms: 1 Ensuite 1 Guests share

Friendly hospitality awaits you at our home privately situated beside Lake Dunstan. We are ex-Southland farmers and have a cat Ollie. Our interests include Lions, fishing, boating, gardening and crafts. Bedrooms have attached balconies, fridge, tea and coffee facilities. Guests share our living areas, spa pool and laundry. Local attractions: orchards, vineyards, gold diggings, fishing, boating, walks, 4 ski fields nearby. Enjoy dinner with us or just relax in the peaceful surroundings. No smoking indoors please. Directions: 5km north of Cromwell Bridge on SH8.

CROMWELL - BANNOCKBURN   *6km Cromwell*

Aurum   *B&B Homestay Self-contained*
Janette & Maurice Middleditch
RD 2, Bannockburn, Lawrence Street - Short Street

Tel (03) 445 2024   Fax (03) 445 2027
Mob 025 693 8248
aurumgallery@xtra.co.nz
www.nzsouth.co.nz/aurumhomestay

Double $110   Single $75 (Continental Breakfast)
Child negotiable   Dinner by arrangement
Credit cards accepted
1 Queen 1 Double (3 bdrm)
Bathrooms: 1 Private

Situated in Bannockburn and surrounded by local wineries and historic gold mining sites, Aurum provides private guest living. Maurice is a scenic artist who exhibits throughout the country and Janette speaks Dutch and loves meeting people. 2 bedrooms and bedsitting room with big bathroom and bath, hairdryer, TV, tea and coffee, and laundry facilities available. A continental breakfast will be served at a time suitable to you. Reservations essential.

CROMWELL   *5km W of Cromwell*

Serendipity Vineyard
B&B Farmstay Self-contained Vineyard
Joanna Lewis
229 Ripponvale Road, R D 2, Cromwell

Tel (03) 445 1864   Fax (03) 445 1864
Mob 021 215 9809
serendipityvineyard@xtra.co.nz
www.bnb.co.nz/serendipityvineyard.html

Double $100   Single $80 (Continental Breakfast)
Family self-contained $100 per night Children welcome
1 Queen 2 Double 6 Single (2 bdrm)
Bathrooms: 1 Ensuite 2 Private

Situated 5 minutes from Cromwell on our family vineyard. Self-contained queen bedsit unit with luxurious ensuite bathroom and private courtyard. Separate self-contained family accommodation sleeping up to 10 people with private garden, 2 modern toilets and showers, full cooking and laundry facilities, telephone and internet. No pets.

ARROWTOWN   *18km NE of Queenstown*

Bains Homestay
Homestay Separate/Suite Self-contained
Ann & Barry Bain
R32 Butel Road, Arrowtown 9196, Otago

Tel (03) 442 1270   Fax (03) 442 1271
bainshomestay@ihug.co.nz
www.dotco.co.nz/bainshomestay

Double $100-$120 (Full Breakfast)   Child neg
Bunkroom $70 double   Credit cards accepted
Children welcome   Pets welcome
1 Queen 4 Single (3 bdrm)   Bathrooms: 1 Ensuite 2 Private

We are a retired business couple who have travelled extensively. We welcome our guests to a peaceful, spacious, sunny self-contained upstairs suite complete with kitchen, and a balcony with panoramic views of surrounding mountains and the famous Millbrook golf resort. Meet our friendly cocker spaniel. Extra continental breakfast with freshly baked bread, jams etc is provided in your suite; or join us for a cooked starter. Complimentary laundry, road bikes, gold mining gear, BBQ etc. Our courtesy car is an Archbishop's 1924 Austin drophead coupe.

OTAGO, NORTH CATLINS

ARROWTOWN *20km N of Queenstown*

Polly-Anna Cottage *B&B Self-contained*
Daphne & Bill Maclaren
43 Bedford Street, Arrowtown

Tel (03) 442 1347 Fax (03) 442 1307
Mob 027 220 3974
daphneandbill@pollyannacottage.co.nz
www.pollyannacottage.co.nz

Double $100 Single $80 (Continental Breakfast)
Dinner $30 by arrangement Credit cards accepted
1 Double 2 Single (2 bdrm)
Bathrooms: 1 Ensuite 1 Private

Daphne and Bill, retired business couple, have restored and renovated their quaint, cute and cosy 100 year old cottage, nestled in an attractive garden, surrounded by spectacular mountains. Bill retired from Ford Dealer Industry; Have both travelled widely; Can inform on all local attractions and offer our warm hospitality, completely private ensuite facilities. 3 minutes from historic Arrowtown, 15 minutes to Queenstown. Try Daph's home preserves. Comments: "Highlight of our trip". "Thanks for Memory". Cat named Maggie. Come in, be surprised. Directions: Polly-Anna sign at front gate.

ARROWTOWN *19km E of Queenstown*

Rowan Cottage *Homestay*
Elizabeth & Michael Bushell
9 Thomson Street,
Arrowtown

Tel (03) 442 0443
Mob 025 622 8105
www.bnb.co.nz/rowancottage.html

Double $90 Single $60
(Continental Breakfast) Dinner $25pp
1 Double 2 Single (2 bdrm)
Bathrooms: 1 Guests share

Rowan Cottage is situated in a quiet tree lined street with views to the mountains and hills. We are 10 minutes walk to the town and 20 minutes drive to Queenstown. We have a lovely cottage garden to relax and have coffee and home-made goodies. We are well travelled and can advise you on things to see and do in our beautiful part of the country. Guests comments: Wonderful Hospitality - Very Comfortable - Excellent Breakfasts.

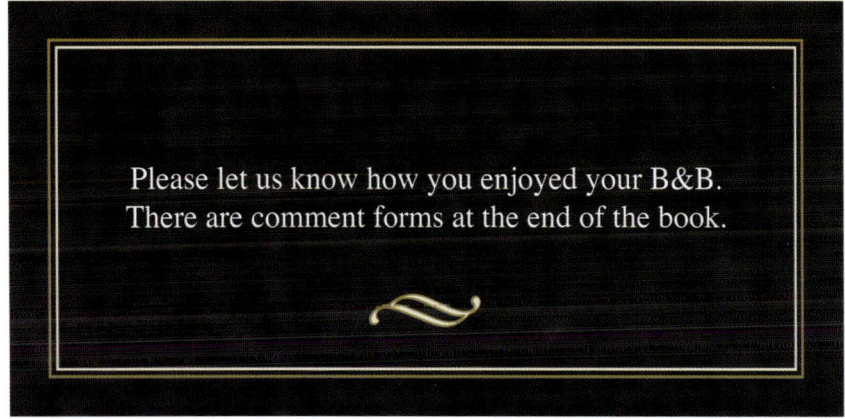

Please let us know how you enjoyed your B&B.
There are comment forms at the end of the book.

ARROWTOWN *Arrowtown Central*

Arrowtown Lodge & Hiking Co *B&B Lodge*
John & Margaret Wilson
7 Anglesea Street, Arrowtown

Tel (03) 442 1101 0800 258 802 Fax (03) 442 1108
hiking@queenstown.co.nz
www.arrowtownlodge.co.nz

Double $150-$180 Single $100-$150
(Full Breakfast) Credit cards accepted
Children welcome
2 King/Twin 2 Queen (4 bdrm)
Bathrooms: 4 Ensuite

Located in the historic part of Arrowtown. Arrowtown Lodge and Hiking Company is only 200 metres from the centre of the village where guests can enjoy a good selection of restaurants, cafés and pubs. Arrowtown Lodge is built in the old style using schist and mud brick. The 4 cottage style suites have king or queen-size beds, TV, tea and coffee making facilities, hair driers, heated floors, guest phones, private guest entrance and off-street car parking. Children welcome. Advise on hiking available.

ARROWTOWN *Arrowtown Central*

Separate/Suite
Pam Miller
23 Berkshire Street, Arrowtown

Tel (03) 442 1126
www.bnb.co.nz/miller.html

Double $110 Single $90
(Full Breakfast) Credit cards accepted
1 Queen (1 bdrm)
Bathrooms: 1 Private

You will be made very welcome at my home which is centrally located on the main road, entering Arrowtown from Queenstown. I am 3 blocks from the Arrowtown Village centre. My accommodation for guests has a private entrance, double bedroom, small sitting room with TV and tea/coffee making facilities. Also a private bathroom with laundry facilities. Delicious continental or full breakfast is served in the dining room upstairs. Off-street parking. Only 20 minutes drive to Queenstown.

ARROWTOWN - QUEENSTOWN *14km Arrowtown*

Crown View *B&B Farmstay*
Caroll & Reg Fraser
457 Littles Road, Dalefield, Queenstown 9197

Tel (03) 442 9411 Fax (03) 442 9411
Mob 025 495 156
info@crownview.co.nz
www.crownview.co.nz

Double $150-$170 (Full Breakfast)
Credit cards accepted Children welcome
2 King (2 bdrm)
Bathrooms: 1 Ensuite 1 Private

Peaceful and quite rural setting with views of Remarkables and Crown Range. 15 minutes from either Queenstown and Arrowtown. 2 double bedrooms both with super king-size beds, that can be made into single beds if required. Both rooms have tea & coffee facilities, TV & radios. Breakfast can be had on upstairs balcony or outside on our secluded terrace both with views of the mountains. Relax and enjoy our rural lifestyle, along with our 2 white highland westies (Dougal & Archie) sheep and chickens. Come as a guest leave as a friend.

OTAGO, NORTH CATLINS

Willowbrook is within easy reach of four ski fields and three very picturesque golf courses

ARROWTOWN - QUEENSTOWN *4km W of Arrowtown*

Willowbrook *B&B Self-contained*
Tamaki & Roy Llewellyn
Malaghan Road, RD 1, Queenstown

Tel (03) 442 1773 Fax (03) 442 1773 Mob 025 516 739
info@willowbrook.net.nz   www.willowbrook.net.nz

Double $140-$165 Single $115-$135 (Continental Breakfast)
Cottage: $295 (4 persons/night) BBQ: $15
Credit cards accepted
2 King 2 Queen 3 Twin (7 bdrm)
Bathrooms: 5 Ensuite 1 Private

Willowbrook is a 1914 homestead at the foot of Coronet Peak
in the beautiful Wakatipu Basin. The setting is rural, historical
and distinctly peaceful, and with the attractions of Queenstown
and Arrowtown only 15 and 5 minutes away respectively,
Willowbrook can truly claim to offer the best of both worlds.
4 acres of mature garden contain a tennis court, luxurious spa
pool and several outhouses.

The former Shearers Quarters have been rebuilt and a hay
barn renovated allowing Willowbrook to offer varied styles
of accommodation: *Bed & Breakfast in the Main House*
– centrally heated double rooms, ensuite bathrooms, guest
lounge with open fires and Sky TV.

The Barn – offers warm, spacious ensuite accommodation
with kitchenette, separate from the *Main House*. Super king
bed, bunks for children, TV and BBQ deck. Annex available
for extra members of same party.

The Cottage – is a delightfully cosy two bedroom cottage
with full kitchen and laundry facilities. Ensuite bathrooms,
underfloor heating throughout, spacious sundecks and private
lawn.

*Kate and Allan are your hosts. Expect a warm welcome,
friendly advice and traditional South Island hospitality.*

QUEENSTOWN   *Queenstown Central*

The Stable   *Homestay*
Isobel & Gordon McIntyre
17 Brisbane Street, Queenstown

Tel (03) 442 9251   Fax (03) 442 8293
gimac@queenstown.co.nz
www.thestablebb.com

Double $160-$180   Single $120
(Full Breakfast) Credit cards accepted
1 King/Twin 1 Double (2 bdrm)
Bathrooms: 1 Ensuite 1 Private

A 130 year old stone stable, converted for guest accommodation, and listed by the New Zealand Historic Places Trust, shares a private courtyard with our home.

The Garden Room is in the house, providing convenience and comfort with lake and mountain views. Our home is in a quiet cul-de-sac and set in a garden abundant with rhododendrons and native birds. It is less than 100 metres from the beach where a small boat and canoe are available for guests' use.

The famous Kelvin Heights Golf Course is close and tennis courts, bowling greens and ice skating rink are in the adjacent park. All tourist facilities, shops and restaurants are within easy walking distance, less than 5 minutes stroll on well lit footpaths. Both rooms are well heated with views of garden, lake or mountains. Tea and coffee making facilities are available at all times.

Guests share our spacious living areas and make free use of our library and laundry. A courtesy car is available to and from the bus depots. We can advise about and are booking agents for all sightseeing tours. Do allow an extra day or two for all the activities in the Queenstown region.

No smoking indoors. Your hosts, with a farming background, have bred welsh ponies and now enjoy weaving, cooking, gardening, sailing and the outdoors.

We have an interest in a successful vineyard and enjoy drinking and talking about wine. We enjoy meeting people and have travelled extensively overseas.

Directions: Follow State Highway 6A (Frankton Road) to where it veers right at the Millenium Hotel. Continue straight ahead. Brisbane Street (no exit) is second on left. Phone if necessary.

OTAGO, NORTH CATLINS

QUEENSTOWN *8km NE of Queenstown*

Collins Homestay *Semi self contained*
Pat & Ron Collins
Grant Road, RD 1, Queenstown

Tel (03) 442 3801
rcollins@queenstown.co.nz
www.bnb.co.nz/collins.html

Double $100-$120 Single $80
(Special Breakfast)
2 Queen 2 Single (3 bdrm)
Bathrooms: 1 Ensuite 1 Private

Relaxed Kiwi hospitality in rural environment with mountain views, lovely gardens. Accommodation: garden cottage with queen bed, ensuite, patio; Guest wing with queen or twin, private bathroom. Laundry facilities. Able to help with sightseeing arrangements. Our interests are golf, gardening, family, fishing and walking our dog Meg. Directions: Grant Road sign on mailbox on SH 6 from North 2km before Frankton. From south right at Frankton on SH6 to Grant Road 2km on gravel road left turn. Second house end of lane.

QUEENSTOWN *1.5km Queenstown Central*

Birchall House *B&B Self-contained*
Joan & John Blomfield
118 Panorama Terrace, Larchwood Heights,
Queenstown

Tel (03) 442 9985 Fax (03) 442 9980
Mob (03) 442 9985 birchall.house@xtra.co.nz
www.zqn.co.nz/birchall

Double $135-$150 Single $100-$110
(Full Breakfast) Child $50 Children welcome
1 Queen 2 Twin (2 bdrm)
Bathrooms: 1 Ensuite 1 Private

Welcome to our home in Queenstown, purpose built to accommodate guests in a beautiful setting. At Birchall House, enjoy a magnificent 200 degree view of lake and mountains within walking distance of town centre. Guest accommodation is spacious, private, separate entrance, centrally heated, electric blankets, smoke-free. Continental or cooked breakfast available. From Frankton Road, turn up Hensman Road, left into Sunset Lane. Or Frankton Road, turn up Suburb Street, right into Panorama Terrace. Access via Sunset Lane. Off-street parking. Visit our website: www.zqn.co.nz/birchall.

QUEENSTOWN CENTRAL *200m N of Queenstown*

Queenstown House *Boutique Hotel*
Louise Kiely, Family and Friends
69 Hallenstein Street, Queenstown

Tel (03) 442 9043 Fax (03) 442 8755
queenstown.house@xtra.co.nz
www.queenstownhouse.co.nz

Double $250-$595 Single $225
(Special Breakfast) Credit cards accepted
10 King/Twin 4 Queen (14 bdrm)
Bathrooms: 14 Ensuite

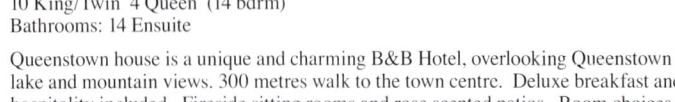

Queenstown house is a unique and charming B&B Hotel, overlooking Queenstown Bay with majestic lake and mountain views. 300 metres walk to the town centre. Deluxe breakfast and pre-dinner hospitality included. Fireside sitting rooms and rose scented patios. Room choices include 5 luxurious villa suites and studio rooms with private lakeview decks hospitality and ambience specialists. 'Your memories make us famous'.

Queenstown
Bed & Breakfast
NUMBER 12
.... a quiet convenient location

QUEENSTOWN   *Queenstown Central*

Number Twelve   *B&B Homestay Self-contained*
Barbara & Murray Hercus
12 Brisbane Street, Queenstown

Tel **(03) 442 9511**   Fax (03) 442 9755
hercusbb@queenstown.co.nz
www.number12bb.co.nz

Double $140-$150 Single $100-$110
(Full Breakfast) Credit cards accepted
2 King 2 Twin (2 bdrm)
Bathrooms: 1 Ensuite 1 Private

We would like you to come and share our conveniently situated house in a quiet no-exit street. You only have a 5 minute stroll to the town centre. We have mountain and lake views.

Our home is warm and sunny, windows double glazed and we have central heating for the winter months. Our bedrooms have TVs, coffee/tea making facilities, hair dryers and instant heaters. Our downstairs studio apartment has a separate entrance with a view of our rose garden. Email & laundry is available. No smoking indoors.

We have a solar heated swimming pool (Dec-March) the sun deck and BBQ are for your use. Our sun room is available for your comfort. Guests have the choice of either a full or continental breakfast in our dining room with its panoramic views.

Once settled in you will seldom need to use your car again. There are several easy walking routes into the town centre, restaurants, shops and tourist centres. We are very close to the lake and our Botanical Gardens.

Whilst you are with us we will be happy to advise on tourist activities and sightseeing and make any arrangements you would wish.

Barbara has a nursing/social work background and Murray is a retired chartered accountant. We have travelled extensively within our country and overseas. We have an interest in classical/choral music.

Directions:
Highway 6a into Queenstown - the Millennium Hotel will be on your right, do NOT turn right at the sign Town Centre but continue straight ahead. Brisbane Street is second on the left and we are on the left.

QUEENSTOWN *800m Queenstown*

Monaghans *B&B*
Elsie & Pat Monaghan
4 Panorama Terrace, Queenstown

Tel (03) 442 8690 Fax (03) 442 8620
patmonaghan@xtra.co.nz
www.bnb.co.nz/monaghans.html

Double $100 Single $90
(Continental Breakfast)
1 Queen (1 bdrm)
Bathrooms: 1 Ensuite

Welcome to our home in a quiet location, walking distance to town. Enjoy this panoramic view while you breakfast. One couple - personal attention. Spacious comfortable room with separate entrance and garden patio. Queen bed, own bathroom, TV, fridge and tea/coffee biscuits. Interests - music, gardening, sport, travel. We will enjoy your company but respect your privacy. Off-street parking. Airport and bus transfers. Directions: turn right up Suburb Street off Frankton Road which is the main road into Queenstown then first right into Panorama Terrace.

QUEENSTOWN *Queenstown Central*

Anna's Cottage & Rose Suite *Self-contained*
Myrna & Ken Sangster
67 Thompson Street, Queenstown

Tel (03) 442 8994 Fax (03) 441 8994
Mob 025 693 3025
www.bnb.co.nz/annascottage.html

Double $120-$145 Single $90
Continental breakfast available $12
Credit cards accepted
1 King/Twin 2 Queen (2 bdrm)
Bathrooms: 2 Private

A warm welcome to Anna's Cottage. Myrna a keen gardener and golfer, Ken with a love of fishing. Enjoy the peaceful garden setting and mountain views. Full kitchen facilities and living room combined. Washing machine. Tastefully decorated throughout, the bedroom is furnished with Sheridan linen. Only a few minutes from the centre of Queenstown. Private drive and parking at cottage. Attached to the end of our home The Rose Suite, self-contained, 1 queen bed with ensuite, small kitchen, washing machine, furnished with Sheridan linen.

QUEENSTOWN *1.5km NE of Queenstown*

Campbells B&B *B&B Self-contained*
Ruth Campbell
10 Wakatipu Heights, Queenstown

Tel (03) 442 9190 Fax (03) 442 4404
Mob 021 116 8801
roosterretreat@xtra.co.nz
www.bnb.co.nz/campbell.html

Double $120 Single $80 (Continental Breakfast)
S/C unit $250 Credit cards accepted Children welcome
1 King/Twin 1 Queen 1 Double 1 Single (3 bdrm)
Bathrooms: 2 Private

Our tranquil home has off-street parking, relaxing garden, outstanding views over Lake Wakatipu and the Remarkables. Option 1: super king/twin room with private bathroom, down duvets etc. Complimentary tea, coffee, laundry facilities. Option 2: fully self-contained 2 bedroom unit, sleeps 4-5. Unit faces sun and has own garden. Fully equipped kitchen, laundry, books, hair dryer etc. No stairs, all guest facilities on ground level. Enjoy a generous continental breakfast with fresh baked bread and real coffee, at your leisure.

QUEENSTOWN   *Queenstown Central*

Larch Hill Homestay B&B   *B&B Homestay*
Maria & Chris Lamens
16 Panners Way, Goldfields, Queenstown

Tel **(03) 442 4811**   Fax (03) 441 8882
info@larchhill.com www.larchhill.com

Double $110-$190 Single $100 (Special Breakfast)
Dinner $60   Apartment (twin share) $190-$260
Credit cards accepted
2 King 1 Queen 1 Twin 2 Single (4 bdrm)
Bathrooms: 2 Ensuite 2 Private

A warm welcome awaits you at Larch Hill. Our comfortable and relaxing homestay is just 3 minutes drive from the centre of town. Public transport stops at the drive way. All rooms have lake and mountain views. In winter there is a roaring log-fire awaiting your return from a days skiing or sightseeing. Maria provides 3 course dinners by prior arrangement. We have pleasure in organising any Queenstown experiences. We speak Italian, German. Directions: from HW6A turn into Goldfield Heights at Sherwood Manor. Second left is Panners Way.

QUEENSTOWN   *0.8km NW of Central Queenstown*

Coronet View Apartments and B&B
B&B Self-contained Apartments
Karen, Neil, Dawn & Warrick
30 Huff Street, Queenstown

Tel **(03) 442 6766**   0800 896 766
Fax (03) 442 6767   Mob 027 432 0895
stay@coronetview.com www.coronetview.com

Double $130-$300   Apartments from $180-$900
Dinner $25-$70   Child price on application
Credit cards accepted   Children welcome
8 King/Twin 1 Queen 1 Twin (10 bdrm)   Bathrooms: 9 Ensuite 1 Private

We welcome you to our beautifully appointed rooms that offer every comfort in either hosted accommodation or private apartments. Superb views of Coronet Peak, The Remarkables and out to Lake Wakatipu. Guest areas include elevated and spacious dining and living areas, outdoor decks, a sunny conservatory, outdoor BBQ, pool and jacuzzi area and computers with internet access. Apartments feature fully equipped kitchens and laundries and generous living areas. Full booking and/or tour guide service. Friendly persian cats on property.

QUEENSTOWN   *300m NW of Central Queenstown*

Browns Boutique Hotel   *B&B Boutique Hotel*
Bridget & Nigel Brown
26 Isle Street, Queenstown

Tel **(03) 441 2050**   Fax (03) 441 2060
stay@brownshotel.co.nz www.brownshotel.co.nz

Double $240-$260 Single $200-$220
(Continental Breakfast) Credit cards accepted
10 King/Twin (10 bdrm)
Bathrooms: 10 Ensuite

Located only 2 blocks walk from downtown Queenstown with views over Queenstown Bay to the Remarkables. Every guest room is well appointed, spacious and boasts a super king-size bed along with french doors opening onto balconies over the courtyard. All rooms have their own generous sized ensuite including showers and baths. The guest lounge and dining room feature leather couches, open fireplace and mahogany dining tables and chairs. Nigel and Bridget believe they are offering a unique product in Queenstown with a quality built and furnished hotel with superior service.

QUEENSTOWN

Delfshaven *Homestay*
Irene Mertz
11 Salmond Place (off Kent Street), Queenstown

Tel (03) 441 1447 Fax (03) 441 1383
Mob 025 659 2609
irenemertz@xtra.co.nz
www.bnb.co.nz/mertz.html

Double $165 Single $150
(Special Breakfast)   Credit cards accepted
1 Double (1 bdrm)
Bathrooms: 1 Private

Nestled at the base of Queenstown is my sunny warm modern home, offering magnificent unobstructed 180 degree views over town, lake and mountains. The comfortable guest room, with its own TV and tea making facilities, opens out to the garden and those beautiful views. It is only a 5 minute downhill walk to the town. I am a retired teacher, widely travelled, enjoy good food and wine, love art, music and enjoy meeting people. A piano is waiting to be played. Welcome to Salmond Place.

QUEENSTOWN *14km no of Queenstown*

Kahu Rise *B&B Separate guest wing*
Angela & Bill Dolan
455 Littles Road, RD 1, Queenstown

Tel (03) 441 2077   0800 436 111
Fax (03) 441 2078   Mob 021 104 0009
info@kahurise.co.nz   www.kahurise.co.nz

Double $190 Single $140
(Special Breakfast) Dinner by arrangement
Teenage sleepout also available.   Additional person $50
Credit cards accepted Children welcome
1 Queen 2 Single (2 bdrm)   Bathrooms: 1 Private

In the country, yet close to Queenstown, local attractions and ski fields we offer tranquility and convenience. Catering exclusively for single party bookings (1-4) our guest wing has a private bathroom, underfloor heating, tea and coffee facilities, refrigerator, TV, hairdryer etc. Rooms enjoy mountain views and open directly onto the lawn. Laundry facilities available. We prepare you a delicious home-cooked breakfast each morning and are happy to offer dinner with complimentary wine, by arrangement. Angela, Bill and Tess, our friendly dog, warmly welcome you.

QUEENSTOWN *100m Queenstown*

The Dairy Guest House *Boutique Accommodation*
Elspeth Zemla
10 Isle Street, Queenstown

Tel (03) 442 5164   0800 333 393
Fax (03) 442 5166   Mob 025 204 2585
info@thedairy.co.nz   www.bnb.co.nz/thedairy.html

Double $295-$355 Single $265-$290
(Full Breakfast) Credit cards accepted
10 King/Twin 1 King 2 Queen (13 bdrm)
Bathrooms: 13 Ensuite

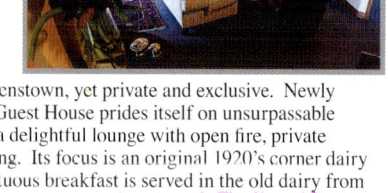

A unique, boutique B&B just a 1 minute walk from Queenstown, yet private and exclusive. Newly refurbished and completely upgraded in May 2004, the Guest House prides itself on unsurpassable personal service. It has 13 private rooms with ensuites, a delightful lounge with open fire, private library, ski storage, 6 seater hydrotherapy spa, and parking. Its focus is an original 1920's corner dairy - from which the guesthouse takes its name. Your sumptuous breakfast is served in the old dairy from where you can view the beautiful surrounding mountains. Recent Tourism Awards Finalists, this special place has to be seen to be believed.

QUEENSTOWN *10km E of Queenstown*

Milestone *B&B Self-contained*
Betty & John Turnbull
Ladies Mile, RD 1, SH6,
Queenstown

Tel (03) 441 4460 Fax (03) 441 4460
jcturnbull@xtra.co.nz   www.themilestone.co.nz

Double $165-$225 Single $125-$165 (Full Breakfast)
Dinner by arrangement Credit cards accepted
Children welcome
1 King 3 Queen 1 Single (4 bdrm)
Bathrooms: 2 Ensuite 1 Private

Milestone, built of Queenstown stone, is set in 3 acres of gardens and water features. Located on the main highway, SH6, the outlook is rural with sheep and deer grazing over the fence but still only 10 minutes from downtown Queenstown. Close to 3 ski fields and 4 golf courses, Milestone is also 4 minutes from the airport, supermarket, shops and lakes.

Guests, including children, are welcome to relax in the garden or we can help them plan their serious adventure activities that Queenstown is famous for. The rooms are warm and well appointed with antique furniture, televisions, tea and coffee making facilieites, and amazing views . The rose-covered stone schist cottage is adjacent to the house and beside the orchard and is self-contained, the romantic bedroom is a favourite with honeymooners and the living room has a custom built queen divan for extra guests.

The *Coronet ensuite* has its own private deck where the guests can relax in the swing seat and gaze at a working water wheel set in ruins, garden and lilly-pond. Up stairs the Remarkables suite has a king and a single bed in a large room with dressing room and sitting area. There is also the *Crown Range room* which has a queen bed and can be part of the suite. Accommodation for a large family group.

Betty is a marriage celebrant and has arranged and officiated at many weddings in the garden and house, up on the surrounding mountains, by the rivers and lake, in the local churches, on the golf courses and ruins. John has been a climber, tramper and fly-fisherman and can advise those keen to experience the area first hand. They love their garden and enjoy sharing it with guests, their old labrador Kali, and hundreds of birds that visit every day.

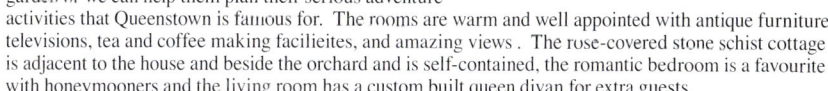

Encircled by The Remarkables, Coronet Peak, and the Crown Range

QUEENSTOWN   *500mtr N of Queenstown*

Approved

Chalet Queenstown   *B&B*
Dianalyn Kaahu & Murray Colson
1 Dublin Street, Queenstown

Tel (03) 442 7117   0800 222 457   Fax (03) 442 7508
chalet.queenstown@xtra.co.nz   www.chalet.co.nz

Double $125-$185   Single $99-$150
(Continental Breakfast)
4 King/Twin 1 Queen (5 bdrm)
Bathrooms: 5 Ensuite

You will love the location of Chalet Queenstown, a
sunny site, 500 metres from the central post office,
and Botannical Gardens, an easy stroll will take you
to the lakeside walking track and the millenium walk,
Queenstown Hill is on our doorstep.

Other features of our home:
* *complimentary mountain bike use*
* *off-street parking*
* *laundry facilities*
* *filtered water*
* *relaxed and friendly atmosphere*

Murray and Dianalyn have been involved in the tourism
industry for many years and have a great knowledge of
Queenstown and all its activities. We enjoy meeting
people, very keen outdoor enthusiasts, especially
tramping, fishing, sightseeing. Dianalyn is also a
qualified therapeutic masseuse, cranial sacral therapist
and Reiki instructor. We also have on-site our own
healing room (appointments essential).

Our well appointed rooms all have views of lake or mountains, ensuite facilities (shower), TV,
refrigerator, tea/coffee, hair dryer, oil heating, electric blankets, lovely linen and super comfortable beds,
where a good nights sleep is assured.

We endeavour to provide guests with wholesome organic preservative free food and beverages. You will
enjoy the hearty continental breakfast consisting of lots of fresh fruit, organic and flavoured yoghurts,
your choice of milk, home made muesli, seeds, nuts and dried fruits, 100% juices. Fresh baked
croissants, cereals, toast, tea, good quality coffee and herbal teas.

We are more than happy to assist with all your reservations for Queenstown's
activities and onward bookings through the NZ B&B Book.

QUEENSTOWN *Queenstown Central*

Cameo Cottage *B&B Self-contained*
John and Jean Lindsay
41 Goldfield Heights Road, Queenstown

Tel (03) 442 5649 Fax (03) 442 5684
cameo_cottage@hotmail.com
www.bnb.co.nz/cameocottage.html

Double $120-$160 Single $90 (Continental Breakfast)
Child $30 Self-contained cottage $180-$240
Credit cards accepted Children welcome
2 King 1 Single (2 bdrm)
Bathrooms: 1 Guests share

Welcome to Cameo Cottage where you will experience real home comforts, with warm friendly atmosphere. Just 10 minutes from central Queenstown with an idealic view of Deer Park Heights and the Remarkable Mountains. We are close to all amenities and tourist attractions. We offer good hearty breakfasts, child safe facilities and equipment, complimentary laundry, ample off-street parking. Rooms are serviced daily. John and I have been involved in the tourism industry for over 27 years and really love sharing our home and meeting people from all walks of life.

QUEENSTOWN *1.3km Queenstown*

Matterhorn Chalet Lodge *B&B Homestay*
Maria & Joe Arnold
20 Wakatipu Heights, Queenstown

Tel (03) 441 3935 Fax (03) 441 3935 Mob 021 951 577
info@matterhornchalet.com
www.matterhornchalet.com

Double $190-$200 Single $160 (Full Breakfast)
Visa & Mastercard accepted
2 King 2 Queen 2 Single (4 bdrm)
Bathrooms: 1 Ensuite 2 Guests share

Imagine a European alpine lodge magically moved to the shores of Lake Wakatipu. Matterhorn Chalet is a luxury B&B with views as breath-taking as any in Europe (all rooms have lake views). Only 15 minutes walk to the bustling heart of downtown Queenstown. For peace and tranquility stay; this is the place for you. Great breakfasts. Maria and Joe speak English, Swiss, German and Dutch. For the most panoramic views over Remarkables and Lake Wakatipu. We provide a courtesy shuttle to Queenstown Airport.

QUEENSTOWN - GLENORCHY *40mins Queenstown*

Lake Haven *B&B Homestay*
Ronda
Benmore Place, Glenorchy

Tel (03) 442 9091 Fax (03) 442 9801
lakehaven@xtra.co.nz
www.bnb.co.nz/lakehaven.html

Double $120 Single $80
(Full Breakfast) Child by arrangement
Dinner by arrangement Credit cards accepted
Children welcome
2 King/Twin (2 bdrm)
Bathrooms: 2 Ensuite

Lake Haven offers quality accommodation and warm hospitality at our secluded Lakefront property with stunning lake and bush clad mountain views. Glenorchy is the base for several world famous walking tracks, eg Routeburn, renowned for its trout fishing and a large range of activities. Ronda is a longtime local and is happy to assist you in exploring and enjoying our unique and beautiful area. Children welcome. Laundry facilities. Fishing guide available. Glenorchy - Gateway to paradise.

OTAGO, NORTH CATLINS

GARSTON *50km S of Queenstown*

B&B Homestay Self-contained
Bev & Matt Menlove
17 Blackmore Road,
Private Bag, Garston 9660

Tel (03) 248 8516
mattmenlove@xtra.co.nz
www.bnb.co.nz/menlove.html

Double $80 Single $50 (Continental Breakfast)
Dinner $25 by arrangement
1 Double 1 Single (1 bdrm)
Bathrooms: 1 Ensuite

We are organic gardeners and our other interests include lawn bowls, sailing, gliding and alternative energy. Garston is New Zealand's most inland village with the Mataura River (famous for its fly fishing) flowing through the valley, surrounded by the Hector Range and the Eyre Mountains. A fishing guide is available with advance notice. For day trips, Garston is central to Queenstown, Te Anau, Milford Sound or Invercargill. We look forward to meeting you.

ALEXANDRA - EARNSCLEUGH *6km W of Alexandra*

Iversen Separate/Suite Orchardstay
Robyn & Roger Marshall
47 Blackman Road, RD 1 Alexandra, Central Otago

Tel (03) 449 2520 Fax (03) 449 2519
Mob 025 384 348 r.r.marshall@xtra.co.nz
www.bnb.co.nz/iversen.html

Double $150 Single $100
(Continental Breakfast) Child by arrangement
Dinner $25 by arrangement Credit cards accepted
2 Queen (2 bdrm)
Bathrooms: 2 Ensuite

Our separate guest accommodation offers you privacy and comfort. Combined with a warm welcome into our home, you can share with us, the peaceful and relaxing setting our our cherry orchard. While at Iversen , you can experience the grandeur and contrasts of the Central Otago landscape, walk the thyme covered hills, visit local wineries or just relax. Directions: from Alexandra or Clyde, travel on Earnscleugh Road, turn into Blackman Road and look for our sign on the left. Advanced bookings preferred.

ALEXANDRA *3.5km N of Alexandra*

Duart Homestay
Mary & Keith McLean
Bruce's Hill Lane, Rapid No. 356
Highway 85, RD 3, Alexandra

Tel (03) 448 9190 Fax (03) 448 9190
duart.homestay@xtra.co.nz
www.duarthomestay.co.nz

Double $90 Single $70 (Continental Breakfast)
Child $50 Dinner $25 by arrangement
Credit cards accepted Children welcome Pets welcome
1 Double 1 Twin 1 Single (3 bdrm) Bathrooms: 1 Ensuite 1 Guests share

Your accredited Kiwi Hosts, Mary and Keith, welcome you to our secluded home, 5 minutes from Alexandra. Your privacy is assured, but we enjoy company and conversation if that is your wish. Relish the spectacular views from our extensive stone terraced garden, or relax on the verandahs, sitting room or library. Revel in the myriad activities and experiences Alexander offers; we pick you up from the Rail Trail, bus depot, Grape Escape. Laundry, Sky TV, complimentary tea, coffee, biscuits, fruit anytime. Complimentary pre-dinner drink and nibbles. Children and pets welcome.

ALEXANDRA   *2km S of Alexandra*

Quail Rock   *B&B Homestay*
Robyn & Geoff McKenzie
5 Fairway Drive, Bridge Hill,
Alexandra, Central Otago

Tel (03) 448 7224   Mob 021 169 4173
quailrok@ihug.co.nz   www.bnb.co.nz/quailrock.html

Double $125   Single $75
(Continental Breakfast) Child neg
Dinner by arrangement
1 King/Twin 1 Queen (2 bdrm)
Bathrooms: 1 Ensuite 1 Private

Welcome to our new home overlooking Clyde, Alexandra to the Hawkdun Ranges. We offer you first class accommodation surrounded by beautiful gardens complimented by the natural schist rock of Central Otago. We have 2 bedroom accommodation with separate entrance plus guest TV, tea/coffee room and laundry. We can assist with wine, art tours, fishing and 4WD trips. We are an hours drive from Wanaka and Queenstown. With Bonnie & Clyde, our 2 cats we look forward to sharing with you Kiwi hospitality.

ROXBURGH - MILLERS FLAT   *16km S of Roxburgh*

The Studio   *B&B Separate/Suite*
Sheena & Wallace Boag
Millers Flat, RD 2, Roxburgh, Central Otago

Tel (03) 446 6872   Fax (03) 446 6872
www.bnb.co.nz/thestudio.html

Double $75   Single $45   (Continental Breakfast)
Child $20   Dinner $20 by arrangement
Double bed settee (upstairs)   Credit cards accepted
2 Single (1 bdrm)
Bathrooms: 1 Ensuite

An easy 2 hour drive from Dunedin, Wanaka, Queenstown and Invercargill, Millers Flat is an attractive village in farming and fruitgrowing country, well-equipped with recreational facilities, easy access to fishing, walking tracks, gardens to visit, and the well known community owned store, Faigan's. We live on 10 acres in a 110 year old house of rammed-earth construction. Our guest accommodation is a 2 storey building of more recent vintage, formerly Wallace's architectural studio, an interesting composition of space and light, comfortably-heated, with tea/coffee making facilities. Please phone ahead for directions.

ROXBURGH - ETTRICK   *15km SW of Ettrick*

Wilden Station Homestead
B&B Farmstay Homestay
Sarah & Peter Adam
Wilden School Road, Near Dunrobin,
West Otago

Tel (03) 204 8115   Fax (03) 204 8116
wildenstation@xtra.co.nz   www.bnb.co.nz/wilden.html

Double $140   Single $100   (Special Breakfast)
Child $50   Dinner $30   Credit cards accepted
Children welcome
2 Queen 2 Single (3 bdrm)   Bathrooms: 1 Ensuite 1 Private

Wilden Station is a large scale high country sheep & cattle property. This gracious historic 2 storied homestead (some accomodation upstairs) is set in private grounds with a walk through forest to a small lake. Your hosts, Peter & Sarah, have travelled extensively overseas and very much enjoy meeting people. We have 2 young boys, 2 cats and working dogs. Highlights include farm tours (and historic buildings), horsetreks, fishing the Pomahaka River, musterers' hut visits, dinner, all by prior arrangement. Families most welcome. Please telephone for directions.

LAWRENCE   *45 min Balclutha*

The Ark   *B&B*
Frieda Betman
8 Harrington Place (Main Road), Lawrence

Tel (03) 485 9328
the.ark@xtra.co.nz
www.theark.co.nz

Double $90   Single $50
(Full Breakfast)   Child $15
2 Double 1 Twin 1 Single (4 bdrm)
Bathrooms: 1 Guests share 1 Host share

My home is situated on the main road near the picnic
ground with its avenue of poplars. My garden is special
to me, the home is 100 years old, has character, charm and a lived-in feeling. It's home to Ambrose
& Pumpkin, my cats and Holly a miniature foxie. Guestrooms are restful with fresh flowers, fruit,
and breakfast includes hot bread, croissants, home-made jams. Free-range eggs. There is a lovely
peaceful atmosphere in our early gold mining town. Approx. 45 minutes to Dunedin airport, just over
an hour to Dunedin.

MIDDLEMARCH   *4km SW of Middlemarch*

The Farm   *Farmstay Homestay*
Lynley & Glynne Smith
Farm Road, RD2, Middlemarch

Tel (03) 464 3610   Fax (03) 464 3612
Mob 027 436 2423
glynley@xtra.co.nz   www.bnb.co.nz/thefarm.html

Double $95   Single $70   (Full Breakfast)
Dinner $15pp by arrangement (24 hours notice)
Credit cards accepted Children welcome Pets welcome
1 King 1 Twin (2 bdrm)
Bathrooms: 1 Guests share

Set amongst mature oaks and gardens is our 100 year old stone farmhouse. Glynne and Lynley came to
Middlemarch from the high country, interested in horses and hunting, they have 200 acres of land which
they use to raise sheep, cattle, and horses with 2 family cats and Jack Russell dog. On the Central Otago
Rail Trail, 1 hour from Dunedin, they find Middlemarch a convenient and interesting area. October
2004 they will have a self-contained stone cottage on the property for guest use.

WAIKOUAITI   *5km N of Waikouaiti*

Boutique Country Cottage
B&B Self contained studio suites
Barbara Morgan
107 Jefferis Road, Flag Swamp, Waikouaiti RD 2

Tel (03) 465 7239   Fax (03) 465 7239
Mob 027 224 8212
jbmorgan@xtra.co.nz
www.boutiquecountrycottage.co.nz

Double $120-$180   Single $120-$150   (Full Breakfast)
3 Queen (3 bdrm)
Bathrooms: 3 Ensuite

Relax in peaceful private surroundings on a deer farm. 1km off SH1. 30 minutes north of Dunedin.
Private driveway. Established trees and gardens. Observe deer grazing while breakfasting on the
verandah. Boutique Country Cottage was built in the 1870's. Now this facade houses 3 completely new
luxury studios with ensuites. Tasteful décor. TV, fridge, microwave, toaster, sink, tea/coffee facilites.
Fresh fruit bowl, home-baking. Tennis court. Farm tour. Short drive to 2 golf courses, Waikouaiti Beach,
Tavora Nature Reserve, restaurants. We welcome you.

DUNEDIN *2km W of Dunedin*

Magnolia House *B&B*
Joan & George Sutherland
18 Grendon Street, Maori Hill,
Dunedin 9001

Tel (03) 467 5999   Fax (03) 467 5999
mrsuth@paradise.net.nz
www.bnb.co.nz/magnoliahouse.html

Double $100 Single $80
(Full Breakfast)
1 Queen 1 Double 2 Single (3 bdrm)
Bathrooms: 2 Private

Our quiet turn of the century villa sits in broad, flower bordered lawns backed by native bush with beautiful, tuneful birds. All rooms have electric heating, comfortable beds with electric blanket, and antiques, while the queen room has an adjoining balcony. Close by is Moana Pool, the glorious Edwardian house, Olveston, and Otago Golf Course. Our special breakfast will set you up for the day. We have a courtesy car, a burmese and a siamese cat. It is not suitable for children or smokers.

DUNEDIN *7km NE of Dunedin*

Harbourside B&B *B&B Homestay*
Shirley & Don Parsons
6 Kiwi Street, St Leonards, Dunedin

Tel (03) 471 0690   Fax (03) 471 0063
harboursidebb@xtra.co.nz
www.bnb.co.nz/harboursidebb.html

Double $80-$95 Single $60
(Full Breakfast) Child $20 Dinner $25
Credit cards accepted Children welcome
1 King/Twin 2 Queen 3 Single (3 bdrm)
Bathrooms: 1 Ensuite 1 Guests share

We are situated in a quiet suburb overlooking Otago Harbour and surrounding hills. Within easy reach of all local attractions. Lovely garden or harbour views from all rooms. Children very welcome. Directions: Drive into city on one-way system watch for Highway 88 sign follow Anzac Avenue onto Ravensbourne Road. Continue approx 5km to St Leonards turn left at Playcentre opposite Boatshed into Pukeko Street then left into Kaka Road, straight ahead to Kiwi Street turn left into number 6.

DUNEDIN *Dunedin Central*

Deacons Court *B&B*
Keith Heggie & Gail Marmont
342 High Street, Dunedin

Tel (03) 477 9053   0800 268 252   Fax (03) 477 9058
Deacons@es.co.nz
www.deaconscourt.co.nz

Double $100-$130 Single $60-$80
(Full Breakfast) Child $20-$30
Credit cards accepted Children welcome
1 King 2 Queen 3 Single (3 bdrm)
Bathrooms: 2 Ensuite 1 Private

Deacons Court is a charming superior spacious Victorian Villa 1km walking distance from the city centre and on a bus route. We offer you friendly but unobtrusive hospitality in a quiet secure haven. Guests can relax in our delightful sheltered rose garden and conservatory. All our bedrooms are large, have ensuite or private bathrooms, heaters, TV & electric blankets. Complimentary 24 hour tea or coffee, free parking and laundry service available. We cater for non-smokers and have a quiet cat. Family groups welcome.

DUNEDIN - OTAGO PENINSULA   *8km Dunedin City*

Captains Cottage   *Homestay*
Christine & Robert Brown
422 Portobello Road, RD 2, Dunedin

Tel **(03) 476 1431**   Fax (03) 476 1431
Mob 0274 352 734
wildfilm@actrix.co.nz www.wildfilm.co.nz

Double $145   Single $100
(Special Breakfast) Dinner $30   Credit cards accepted
1 King/Twin 1 Queen (3 bdrm)
Bathrooms: 1 Ensuite 1 Private

Enjoy the spectacular view from our waterfront home, in a bush setting beside Glenfalloch Gardens, on the ruggedly beautiful Otago Peninsula. En route to albatross, penguin and seal colonies. Christine and Robert are wildlife film makers, having filmed for BBC, National Geographic and Discovery. Our local knowledge can help make your stay. Wildlife/photography day trips, by arrangement, include a picnic lunch and an opportunity to share Robert's experience with wildlife and filming. Great food, hospitality, barbeques, or relax by the fire in our comfortable, character filled home.

DUNEDIN   *3.2km N of Dunedin Central*

Dalmore Lodge   *B&B Homestay*
Loraine Allpress & Mike Ravenwood
9 Falkirk Street, Dalmore, Dunedin

Tel **(03) 473 6513**   Fax (03) 473 6512
Mob 025 287 1517   bookings@dalmorelodge.co.nz
www.dalmorelodge.co.nz

Double $110-$140   Single $85-$100 (Special Breakfast)
Child neg   Credit cards accepted   Children welcome
* 1 Queen + single bed   * 1 Queen
* 2 King Singles   * 1 Single   (4 bdrm)
Bathrooms: 1 Private 1 Guests share

In its peaceful setting, 2 minutes off the Northern Motorway you'll find Dalmore Lodge, offering views of the harbour, Pacific Ocean/Otago Peninsula. The balcony leads out onto a sheltered garden, relax/enjoy watching/listening to native birds along with our cat Teagan. Public transport at gate. Off-street parking. A 3 minute drive takes you into the city centre. We look forward to meeting you and sharing delights of Dunedin and its local attractions. Dunedin City Council Building Code Compliant – allowing accommodation for up to 8 guests.

DUNEDIN   *4.5km SE of Dunedin Central*

Alloway   *B&B Homestay*
Lorraine & Stewart Harvey
65 Every Street, Andersons Bay, Dunedin

Tel **(03) 454 5384**   0800 387 245   Fax (03) 454 5364
alloway@xtra.co.nz   www.alloway.co.nz

Double $110-$180   Single $105-$175
(Continental Breakfast) Child neg Credit cards accepted
2 Queen 2 Single (2 bdrm)
Bathrooms: 1 Private 1 Guests share

We are situated on the gateway to the Otago Peninsula, which features wildlife, walking tracks, Taiaroa Head Albatross Colony, Disappearing Gun, seal colonies, yellow-eyed penguins, Glenfalloch Gardens and much more. We are 7 minutes to town centre. Our home is a modern interpretation of a traditional Scottish house, and set in 1 acre of gardens and lawns, with indoor/outdoor living. Awake to the sound of abundant bird life in a quiet and secure neighbourhood. We serve delicious healthy breakfasts. 2 luxury bedrooms complete with 1 queen and 1 single bed. All rooms have tea making facilities, TV, heaters, electric blankets. Separate facilities with modern guest bathroom. Business people are welcome. All non smoking, no pets and not suitable for young children.

DUNEDIN - PORT CHALMERS   *20km NE of Dunedin*

Atanui   *Farmstay Homestay*
Betty & Bob Melville
Heywards Point Road, RD 1, Port Chalmers, Dunedin

Tel (03) 482 1107   Fax (03) 482 1107
atanui@actrix.gen.nz www.bnb.co.nz/atanui.html

Double $100-$120 Single $80-$100
(Continental Breakfast) Child ¹/² price
Dinner $25   Credit cards accepted
1 King/Twin 1 Queen 1 Twin (2 bdrm)
Bathrooms: 1 Ensuite 1 Guests share

Betty & Bob welcome you to our spacious stonehouse in a peaceful rural setting, 30 minutes from Dunedin, with a spectacular view across the Otago harbour. Feed the emus, aplacas, peacocks etc. Good surfing beach and walking tracks. Relax in our spa pool. 3 friendly cats. 3 course farm-style meals available. Morning and afternoon teas complimentary. Children and campervans welcome. We look forward to meeting you. Directions: from north: left at Waitati; follow signs to Port Chalmers; at crossroads, turn left (no exit); next junction Heywards Point Road (metal) 4km on right. From south: Port Chalmers Highway 88 follow sign up hill to Longbeach, at Heyward Point Road (metal) 4km on right.

DUNEDIN   *2km N of central*

Arden St B&B Dunedin Central   *B&B Homestay*
Joyce Lepperd
36 Arden Street, North East Valley, Dunedin Central

Tel (03) 473 8860   Fax (03) 473 8861
Mob 027 404 6550
joyce-1@clear.net.nz   www.ardenstreethouse.co.nz

Double $75-$120 Single $45-$90
(Continental Breakfast) Child $10-15 Dinner $10 - $25
Children welcome
3 Double 2 Twin 3 Single (5 bdrm)
Bathrooms: 1 Ensuite 1 Private 1 Guests share

Comfortable Quiet 1930s character homestay built by a sea captain with stained glass themes. Guests describe as having a warmth far beyond temperature! Good parking. Close Botanical Gardens, Otago University, Knox College, city, hospice. Arty, quirky, sunny, great views, birdsong, garden. Modern bathrooms, ensuite. Social dinners (meet the locals) using organic produce from Joyce's garden. Good guests' piano. Children welcome. We practice recycling! Cat called QT! From the north turn left towards North East Valley. North Road, first right (Glendining Avenue up to 36 Arden Street).

DUNEDIN   *1 km Dunedin Central*

Highbrae Guesthouse   *B&B Homestay*
Fienie & Stephen Clark
376 High Street, City Rise, Dunedin

Tel (03) 479 2070   Fax (03) 479 2100
Mob 64 025 328 470
highbrae@xtra.co.nz   www.highbrae.co.nz

Double $85-$110 Single $65-$85
(Continental Breakfast) Child $15-$20
Credit cards accepted Children welcome
1 King 1 Queen 1 Twin (3 bdrm)
Bathrooms: 1 Guests share 1 Host share

Experience a taste of early Dunedin. This heritage home in the heart of the city was built on the High Street Cable Car route in 1908 to provide first class accommodation to its residents. Today it is still an impressive home with spectacular views of the city and harbour. The 3 upstairs guest rooms are carefully restored to preserve their character for visitors, who delight in the many features in the home. A courtesy van can meet you at the bus or train if required.

DUNEDIN   *Dunedin Central*

Approved

Albatross Inn   *B&B*
Glynis Rees
770 George Street, Dunedin

Tel (03) 477 2727   0800 441 441   Fax (03) 477 2108
albatross.inn@xtra.co.nz
www.bnb.co.nz/albatrossinn1.html

Double $100-$140   Single $85-$95
(Continental Breakfast) Child $15
Credit cards accepted Children welcome
1 King 4 Queen 3 Double 5 Single (9 bdrm)
Bathrooms: 8 Ensuite 1 Private

Welcome to Dunedin and Albatross Inn! Our beautiful
late Victorian House is ideally located on the main street
close to the university, gardens, museum, shops and
restaurants.

Our attractive rooms have ensuite/private bathrooms,
telephone, TV, radio, tea/coffee, warm duvets and
electric blankets on modern beds. Extra firm beds upon
request. Very quiet rooms at rear of house. Several
rooms have kitchenette and fridge.

Enjoy your breakfast in front of the open fire in our lounge. We serve freshly baked bread and muffins,
fresh fruit salad, yoghurt, juices, cereals, teas, freshly brewed coffee. We are happy to recommend and
book tours for you. All wildlife tours pick up and drop off here. We can recommend many great places
to eat, most just a short walk down George Street. Nearby laundry, non-smoking, cot and highchair.
Winter special $75 double - special conditions apply. Complimentary email and internet.

Some comments from our visitors book: *The right balance of everything location, breakfast and
lovely room. Delightfully different. Absolutely fantastic as always. Home away from Home. A
touch of class, lovely home beautifully presented. Perfecto!*

www.albatross.inn.co.nz

DUNEDIN *Dunedin Central*

Grandview *B&B Homestay*
Steve Scott
360 High Street, Dunedin 9001

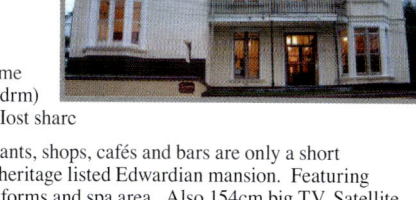

Tel (03) 474 9472 0800 749 472 Fax (03) 474 9473
Mob 021 101 9857 nzgrandview@msn.com
www.grandview.co.nz

Double $80-$170 Single $60-$125
(Continental Breakfast) Child $10 under 13
Dorm Room $30pp C/C accepted Children welcome
2 King 6 Queen 1 Double 1 Twin 10 Single (10 bdrm)
Bathrooms: 3 Ensuite 1 Private 3 Guests share 1 Host share

Grandview is centrally located! The casino, restaurants, shops, cafés and bars are only a short stroll away! Relax in luxury in this charming 1901 heritage listed Edwardian mansion. Featuring magnificent panoramic views from our viewing platforms and spa area Also 154cm big TV, Satellite TV, videos, internet, laundry facilities, mountainbikes and scrumptious continental breakfasts are all a complimentary part of the Grandview experience. 10 rooms to suit all budgets! From $30pp share accomodation to our luxury trendy spa suites for your pleasure!

DUNEDIN *4km S of Dunedin*

Aberdeen B&B *B&B Homestay*
Robert O'Shea
43A Aberdeen Road, St Clair, Dunedin

Tel (03) 487 8217 or (03) 479 7617
43AAR@bigfoot.com
www.bnb.co.nz/aberdeenbb.html

Double $115-$135 Single $80-$110
(Continental Breakfast) Child $25
Credit cards accepted Children welcome
2 Queen 1 Single (2 bdrm)
Bathrooms: 2 Ensuite

Aberdeen B&B is a large, warm house, set in a quiet, sunny enclave on St Clair headland with spectacular views of beach and peninsula. It's 2 minutes drive from St Clair Beach and about 8 minutes drive from the Visitor Centre. There are 2 large ensuite rooms, 1 with a large spa bath. My son Joel (13) and I enjoy meeting people; we've travelled in USA, Canada, Europe, and Australia. We offer peace and privacy with the comforts of home.

OTAGO PENINSULA - BROAD BAY *16km E of Dunedin*

Chy-an-Dowr *B&B*
Susan & Herman van Velthoven
687 Portobello Road, Broad Bay, Dunedin

Tel (03) 478 0306 Fax (03) 478 0306
Mob 021 036 5190
hermanvv@xtra.co.nz
www.chy-an-dowr.co.nz

Double $140-$175
(Special Breakfast) Credit cards accepted
1 King 1 Queen 1 Double 1 Single (3 bdrm)
Bathrooms: 1 Ensuite 1 Private

Chy~an~Dowr (House by the Water), a quality B&B located midway on scenic Otago Peninsula. Our character 1920's home with its harbourside location has panoramic views, is situated opposite a small beach and enroute to the albatross & penguin colonies. The upstairs guest area is spacious and private with comfortable rooms, bathrobes, tea/coffee, TV, fridge, ensuite/private facilities and sunroom. Enjoy a delicious breakfast at your leisure. Originally from Holland, we enjoy welcoming people and sharing our wonderful location with them.

OTAGO PENINSULA - MACANDREW BAY   *11km E of Dunedin*

Mac Bay Retreat   *B&B Self-contained*
Jeff & Helen Hall
38 Bayne Terrace, Macandrew Bay,
Dunedin 9003

Tel (03) 476 1475   Fax (03) 476 1975
Mob 021 897 243   jhall9@ihug.co.nz
www.otago-peninsula.co.nz/macbayretreat.html

Double $105 Single $85
(Continental Breakfast) Credit cards accepted
1 King 1 Double (2 bdrm)
Bathrooms: 1 Ensuite

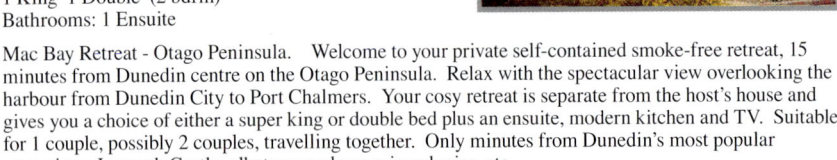

Mac Bay Retreat - Otago Peninsula.   Welcome to your private self-contained smoke-free retreat, 15 minutes from Dunedin centre on the Otago Peninsula. Relax with the spectacular view overlooking the harbour from Dunedin City to Port Chalmers. Your cosy retreat is separate from the host's house and gives you a choice of either a super king or double bed plus an ensuite, modern kitchen and TV. Suitable for 1 couple, possibly 2 couples, travelling together. Only minutes from Dunedin's most popular attractions, Larnach Castle, albatross and penguin colonies, etc.

OTAGO PENINSULA - BROAD BAY   *16km E of Dunedin*

Broad Bay White House   *B&B Homestay*
Chris & Margaret Marshall
11 Clearwater Street, Broad Bay, Dunedin

Tel (03) 478 1160 Fax (03) 478 1159
maheno@paradise.net.nz
www.broadbaywhitehouse.co.nz

Double $140-$165
(Full Breakfast) Dinner $30 by arrangement
Credit cards accepted
2 Queen 1 Double 1 Single (3 bdrm)
Bathrooms: 2 Ensuite 1 Private

Looking for peace and quiet, privacy, panoramic views
over the harbour, superb meals with silver service? Look no further. We are a 3.5 hectare tranquil rural hideaway located on the Otago Peninsula. Handy to albatross, penguin and seal colonies. All bedrooms enjoy spacious decks and panoramic views over the harbour.House is centrally heated throughout. Relax and wander through gardens and enjoy the abundant bird life. Have fun with a game of petanque (no experience required).

OTAGO PENINSULA - PORTOBELLO   *20km W of dunedin*

Ty yr Mor   *Self-contained*
Fiona Owens
34 Allan's Beach Road, Portobello, Dunedin

Tel (03) 478 1089   Mob 021 174 9413
Ty_yr_mor@hotmail.com
www.bnb.co.nz/tyyrmor.html

Double $110 Single $100 Child $10
Children welcome Pets welcome
2 Queen (1 bdrm)
Bathrooms: 1 Private

Gaze at the stars in your fire bath nestled between the
native bush. Stroll along the golden sands; admire
the yellow-eyed penguins, seal lions and seals. Visit the only land based albatross colony. Have a professional massage and enjoy your own private cottage. For the energetic, mountain bikes and kayaks are for hire. Pets and children are very welcome. Book library. Full equipped kitchen, cot available. Futon sofa bed in lounge. BBQ available. Babysitting available.

OTAGO PENINSULA - HARINGTON POINT

30km NE of Dunedin

Harington Point Accommodation
B&B Separate/Suite Self-contained Motels
Dave and Marie Rodger
932 Harington Point Road, RD 2, Dunedin

Tel (03) 478 0287   Fax (03) 478 0089
mdrodger@ihug.co.nz
www.wildlifetours.co.nz

Double $85-$120 (Continental Breakfast)
S/C cottages/motels From $85 Credit cards accepted
3 Queen 1 Double 2 Twin 2 Single (5 bdrm)
Bathrooms: 5 Ensuite

Enjoy very comfortable self-contained cottages or B&B units, looking out to Otago Harbour. Closest accommodation to world-famous albatross and penguin colonies. Local wildlife includes albatross, penguins, seals, shags and sealions. The area has many historic features including The Disappearing Gun and Larnach Castle' 2 minutes walk to the beach for a leisurely stroll and spectacular sunsets. Golf course, restaurants and cafés close by. The Otago Peninsula offers many scenic walks and drives. Let our local knowledge enhance your stay on the Peninsula.

OTAGO PENINSULA - PORTOBELLO

20km NE of Dunedin

Peninsula B&B   *B&B*
Toni & Stephen Swabey
4 Allans Beach Road, Portobello, Dunedin

Tel (03) 478 0909   Fax (03) 478 0909
Mob 021 252 4970   toni@peninsula.co.nz
www.peninsula.co.nz

Double $105-$165 Single $85-$125
(Full Breakfast) Child price on application
Dinner Apr-Oct by arrangement Credit cards accepted
1 King 2 Queen 1 Twin (4 bdrm)
Bathrooms: 2 Ensuite 1 Guests share

Relax and enjoy your time out in our comfortable guest lounge. Take in the harbour views from our sun-drenched garden. Unwind in one of our luxury bedrooms - including ensuite if you wish. Enjoy your choice from our superb breakfast menu. Catch up with our complimentary newspaper and make yourself at home with tea and coffee making facilities, plus home-baking. If you really need it - laundry and internet access. Central to wildlife and scenic attractions. Meet Charlie, the cat, and our 5 chickens.

DUNEDIN - MOSGIEL

14km S of Dunedin

The Old Vicarage   *Homestay*
Lois & Lance Woodfield
14 Mure Street, Mosgiel, Otago

Tel (03) 489 8236   Fax (03) 489 8236
l.l.woodfield@clear.net.nz
www.bnb.co.nz/theoldvicarage.html

Double $65-$85 Single $45
(Continental Breakfast) Credit cards accepted
Children welcome
1 Queen 2 Single (2 bdrm)
Bathrooms: 1 Private

Welcome to our English style cottage home. Built in 1913 and used as the vicarage for 46 years, before passing to private owners who made sympathetic restorations. The outstanding feature is the exquisitely balanced garden, laid out in 'rooms'. 2 upstairs guest rooms and bathroom enjoy a commanding view of the garden. Warm Oregan panelling and leadlight windows enhance the atmosphere. Situated in Mosgiel, close to the airport, just 15 minutes from Dunedin. We are a retired Christian couple who enjoy gardening, architecture, tramping and history.

OTAGO, NORTH CATLINS

WAIHOLA *40km S of Dunedin*

B&B Homestay Self-contained
Lillian & Trevor Robinson
Sandown Street, Rapid No 13, Waihola, South Otago

Tel (03) 417 8218 Fax (03) 417 8287
Mob 025 545 935
www.bnb.co.nz/robinson.html

Double $80 Single $50
(Full Breakfast) Dinner $25 by arrangement
Credit cards accepted
1 Queen 2 Single (2 bdrm)
Bathrooms: 1 Ensuite 1 Guests share 1 Host share

We have a very comfortable home situated in a quiet street, only 15 minutes drive to Dunedin Airport. Our double room has queen-sized bed with ensuite, tea making facilities, TV, fridge and heater. Lake Waihola is popular for boating, fishing and swimming. We enjoy meeting people and ensure a very pleasant stay. Please phone.

WAIHOLA *40km S of Dunedin*

Lakeside Cottage *B&B Homestay Lakeside Cottage*
Robin & Bryan Leckie
Rapid No. 7, State Highway 1, Waihola, Otago 9057

Tel (03) 417 8946 0800 112 996 Fax (03) 417 8966
ivycottage@xtra.co.nz
www.bnb.co.nz/lakesidecottage.html

Double $80-$90 Single $60-$65 (Full Breakfast)
Child price on application Dinner $25 by arrangement
Long stay discount C/C accepted Children welcome
1 Double 3 Single (2 bdrm) Bathrooms: 2 Ensuite

Our 'Lakeside' property is on SH1 near Dunedin Airport (15km). Guests enjoy unobstructed scenic views of Lake Waihola, farmlands and forests. Excellent base for day trips. North - Dunedin's albatross colony, heritage. South - The Catlins, scenic beauty, wild life. West – Central Otago orchards and vineyards. East – Taieri Mouth and Pacific beaches. Waihola features wetlands, whale fossils, walkways, and aquatic recreation. We have many interests. Our detached accommodation, The Shed, has ensuites, tea facilities, TV, laundry, etc. Dining options include our cuisine with wine or Waihola restaurants. Bud is our friendly gold retriever.

BALCLUTHA *26km W of Balclutha*

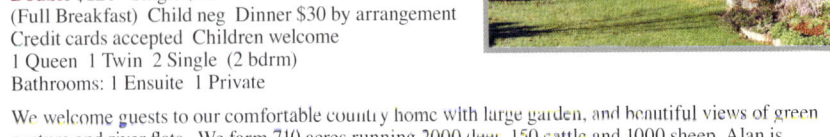

Argyll Farmstay *Farmstay*
Trish & Alan May
246 Clutha River Road, Clydevale, RD 4, Balclutha

Tel (03) 415 9268 Fax (03) 415 9268
Mob 027 431 8241
argyllfm@ihug.co.nz
www.bnb.co.nz/argyllfarmstay.html

Double $120 Single $60
(Full Breakfast) Child neg Dinner $30 by arrangement
Credit cards accepted Children welcome
1 Queen 1 Twin 2 Single (2 bdrm)
Bathrooms: 1 Ensuite 1 Private

We welcome guests to our comfortable country home with large garden, and beautiful views of green pasture and river flats. We farm 710 acres running 2000 deer, 150 cattle and 1000 sheep. Alan is a experienced fisherman who is happy to share his knowledge of our local rivers. We are centrally located for people travelling to the Catlins, Queenstown or Te Anau. Directions: please telephone.

BALCLUTHA   *4km N of Balclutha/Catlins*

Lesmahagow   *B&B Boutique accommodation*
Noel & Kate O'Malley
Main Road, Benhar, RD 2, Balclutha

Tel (03) 418 2507   0800 301 224   Mob 025 578 465
lesmahagow@xtra.co.nz   www.lesmahagow.co.nz

Double $100-$150
(Full Breakfast) Dinner $35   Lunches on request
Credit cards accepted Children welcome
2 Queen 2 Double 1 Single (4 bdrm)
Bathrooms: 2 Private 1 Guests share

Lesmahagow offers excellent accommodation in an historic homestead and garden setting. Centrally situated, discerning travellers can make Lesmahagow their base to explore the Catlins region, Dunedin and the Otago Penninsula or the historic goldfields of Lawrence. Centrally heated, with delightful bedrooms and gorgeous bathrooms you can be sure of wonderful hospitality, and a truly memorable stay. Evening dining is always available and our special breakfasts will satisfy all taste buds! Teas, coffees, fruit and homebaking there for the taking. Come as strangers, leave as friends

BALCLUTHA - NORTH CATLINS   *8 km E of Balclutha*

Balmoral   *Country Homestay*
Yana & Barry Eaton
147 Chicory Road, Inchclutha RD1, Kaitangata

Tel (03) 418 1444   Mob 025 533 446
barrye2000@xtra.co.nz
www.bnb.co.nz/balmoral.html

Double $100-$125 (Full Breakfast) Child $15
Dinner $40 BYO Children welcome
2 Queen 3 Twin (3 bdrm)
Bathrooms: 1 Private 1 Guests share

Taste the Catlins! Relax at historic Balmoral, your luxurious 1862 totara homestay nestled on the river island near Balclutha. Stroll rhododendron gardens and nature tracks. Go birding. Pet lambs and horses. Fish onsite! Dayhop to Catlins beaches, lighthouse, forest parks. Barry is a veteran wilderness guide; get tips on hidden wonders of Catlins, Otago, Fiordland. Yana is a former Alaskan, keen on herbs, organic gardens, art, and helping Barry build his amphibian plane. We warmly welcome you as guests!

NUGGETS - THE CATLINS   *24km Balclutha & Owaka*

Nugget Lodge   *Self-contained*
Kath & Noel Widdowson
Nugget Road 367, RD 1, Balclutha, South Otago

Tel (03) 412 8783   Fax (03) 412 8784
lighthouse@nuggetlodge.co.nz
www.nuggetlodge.co.nz

Double $110-$125
(Continental Breakfast $15pp)
Extra person $25pp   Credit cards accepted
1 King/Twin 1 Queen 1 Single (2 bdrm)
Bathrooms: 2 Ensuite

A unique position above the incoming tide on a deserted beach. Sleep to the roar of the waves, breathe the sea air from modern, private, centrally heated units. Guests may choose to rest and rejuvenate the soul or the eco-enthusiasts can experience magnificant unspoilt scenery, seals, sealions, penguins, birds and walk tracks. Stay a while as one day is not enought to experience all the Catlins magic. Host: wildlife ranger/photographer. Pets not welcome, not suitable for children. Restaurants nearby. Our motto: Educate/inform/protect.

OTAGO, NORTH CATLINS

KAKA POINT - THE CATLINS   *21km S of Balclutha*

Rata Cottage   *B&B Self-contained*
Jean Schreuder
31 Rata Street,
Kaka Point, South Otago

Tel (03) 412 8779
www.bnb.co.nz/ratacottage.html

Double $70   Single $60
(Continental Breakfast) Child $7
Extra adult $15 each
1 Twin (1 bdrm)
Bathrooms: 1 Ensuite

A fully self contained sunny Bed & Breakfast unit in a tranquil bush garden setting, with sea view, bell birds and tuis. Bedroom with twin beds, plus double divan in lounge. Wheelchair facilities. 5 minutes from a beautiful sandy beach for swimming or long walks. next door to scenic reserve and bush walks. You can have breakfast in the garden with the birds, or a visit from Baxter the cat if you wish. Non smoking. Laundry facilities available. Cooking facilities.

KAKA POINT - THE CATLINS   *20kms Balclutha & Owaka*

Cardno's Accommodation   *B&B Self-contained*
Lyn & Selwyn Cardno
8 Marine Terrace, Kaka Point - The Catlins,
RD1, Balclutha

Tel (03) 412 8181   Fax (03) 412 8101
cardnos@xtra.co.nz
www.cardnosaccommodation.co.nz

Double $95-$150 Single $95-$120
(Continental Breakfast $10pp)
Extra person $25pp Credit cards accepted
2 Queen 1 Single (2 bdrm)   Bathrooms: 2 Ensuite

Kaka Point with its long white sandy beaches is an ideal base to access the Catlins spectacular scenery, consisting of Nugget Point Lighthouse, yellow-eyed penguins, seals, sealions petrified forest, native birds and bush walks. We offer new quality, modern contempory furnished accommodation of either a self-contained unit with cooking facilities or B&B, each with own ensuite, both with magnificient views of the beach and Nugget Point Lighthouse. Complimentry chocolates, tea/coffee, filtered water, television and stereo. The Restaurant/bar/shop and beach are 1 minute walk.

OWAKA - THE CATLINS   *15km S of Owaka*

Greenwood Farmstay   *Farmstay Self-contained*
Helen-May & Alan Burgess
739 Purakaunui Falls Road, Owaka, South Otago

Tel (03) 415 8259   Fax (03) 415 8259
Mob 027 438 4538   greenwoodfarm@xtra.co.nz
www.bnb.co.nz/greenwood.html

Double $110   Single $70   (Full Breakfast)
Child $35   Dinner $40pp (3 course)
Self-contained house at Papatowai Beach $70 double
Extra person $10   Children welcome
1 Queen 1 Twin 3 Single (3 bdrm)   Bathrooms: 1 Ensuite 1 Private 1 Guests share 1 Host share

Welcome... Situated within walking distance to beautiful Purakaunui Falls, Alan enjoys taking people around our 1900 acre sheep, cattle and deer farm. Our home offers warm, comfortable accommodation. One guest bedroom with ensuite and day-room opening to a large garden. A private bathroom services other guest rooms. We enjoy dining with our guests. The Catlins features the yellow-eyed penguin. Directions: take Highway 92 to Owaka from Balclutha or Invercargill. From Owaka follow the signs to Purakaunui Falls. Our name is at gate entrance.

OWAKA - THE CATLINS *6km N of Owaka*

Hillview *B&B Farmstay Self-contained*
Kate & Bruce McLachlan
Rapid 161 Hunt Road, Katea, RD 2,
Owaka, South Otago

Tel **(03) 415 8457** Fax (03) 415 8650 Mob 025 334 759
hillviewcatlins@xtra.co.nz
www.bnb.co.nz/hillview.html

Double $85-$95 Single $60 (Continental Breakfast)
Child $40 Dinner from $20 Credit cards accepted
Children welcome
2 Queen 4 Single (4 bdrm) Bathrooms: 2 Guests share

Our 450 acre cattle grazing unit is situated 15 minutes from Nugget Point, 10 minutes from Cannibal Bay. Relax in our cosy private cottage set in a large developing garden, or enjoy the relaxed atmosphere of our home. Our burmese cat and miniature poodle live outside. Our interests are varied. Bruce is a shepherd who enjoys working with horses and training sheepdogs. Kate is a school librarian who enjoys reading, gardening, and various handcrafts. We both enjoy our grandchildren and meeting people. Breakfast with us or in private. Meals by arrangement. Bookings essential. Please phone after 4pm.

OWAKA - THE CATLINS *1/2 km N of Owaka*

J T's Catlins B&B *B&B Homestay*
John & Thelma Turnbull
Main Road, Owaka

Tel **(03) 415 8127** Fax (03) 415 8129
Mob 025 649 7693
jtowaka@ihug.co.nz www.jtscatlinsbnb.co.nz

Double $75-$90 Single $60
(Full Breakfast) Child half price
Dinner by arrangement Children welcome
1 Queen 1 Twin (2 bdrm)
Bathrooms: 1 Guests share

Welcome to our warm and comfortable home, which is situated on a 25 acre farmlet, surrounded by colourful, peaceful gardens with splendid unspoilt views. Located in the heart of the Catlins, renowned for its wildlife and spectacular scenery, we are within walking distance of Owaka township with its restaurants, museum and other amenities. Our guests are encouraged to dine with us for the evening meal when we enjoy quality local food and wine. We look forward to meeting you. Travel safely.

OWAKA - THE CATLINS *6km E of Owaka*

Kepplestone by the Sea
B&B Homestay Separate/Suite
Esther & Jack Johnson
9 Surat Bay Road, Newhaven, The Catlins, Owaka 9251

Tel **(03) 415 8134** 0800 105 134 Fax (03) 415 8137
Mob 025 242 4235 kepplestone@xtra.co.nz
www.bnb.co.nz/kepplestone1.html

Double $100-$110 Single $85 (Full Breakfast)
Dinner by arrangement Children welcome
1 King/Twin 1 Queen 2 Twin (3 bdrm)
Bathrooms: 2 Ensuite 2 Guests share

There are no strangers here, only friends we haven't met. Situated metres from Surat Bay, with hooker sealions basking. Close to Catlins scenery, waterfalls, royal spoonbills, golf. Private yellow-eyed penguin viewing with Catlins Natural Wonders. Delicious homemade breakfasts. Fabulous meals served with Organically grown vegetables from garden. Alergy diets catered for, every care taken. Directions: Owaka, (Royal Terrace) Follow signs towards Pounawea, at golf course go across bridge, right to Newhaven, go 3km on metal road, at Surat Bay Road, right first house on left.

OWAKA - THE CATLINS *20 S of Balclutha*

PJ's Bed & Breakfast *B&B*
Jenny O'Connell
32 Waikawa Road, Owaka

Tel (03) 415 8711 jennyandpeter@xtra.co.nz
www.bnb.co.nz/pjs.html

Double $80-$100 Single $80
(Full Breakfast) Credit cards accepted
1 Queen 1 Double 1 Twin (3 bdrm)
Bathrooms: 1 Guests share 1 Host share

Residential and rural outlook. Owaka is a small country town with a big heart fully serviced to cater for tourists, walk from PJ's. We invite you to share the comfort and warmth off our humble home. Our guest rooms have qualty linen, cosy beds, fully redecorated inside. Beaches, seals, penguins, walking tracks, waterfalls, and more within 15 minutes from here. Local fishing trips sea/trout. PJ's B&B is oppisite the Owaka Police Station entrance to the southern senic route. All enquiries wellcome. Regards Peter & Jenny (and Tina the cat.)

OWAKA - THE CATLINS *10 E of Owaka*

Catlins Dairy Farmstay
B&B Farmstay Self-contained
Margaret Anderson
981 Owaka Valley Road, RD 2, Owaka

Tel (03) 415 8776 Fax (03) 415 8776
anders@ihug.co.nz
www.bnb.co.nz/catlinsdairy.html

Double $160 (Continental Breakfast) Child $20
Bed-sit $75 Credit cards accepted
Children welcome Pets welcome
2 Queen 1 Twin (4 bdrm) Bathrooms: 1 Private

We are located 10km out of Owaka in a quiet valley. Supermarket, hotel, restaurants, craft shop are 10 minutes away. All the natural wonders of the Catlins are at your fingertips. The perfect hideaway if you want privacy with comfort, with just our dairy cows for company. We have a 4 bedroom house and a small bed-sit available, fully self-contained and there is always a special little 'something' added to make your stay special. Evening meals are available by prior arrangement.

FOR LISTINGS IN THE SOUTH CATLINS AREA, SEE PAGE 495

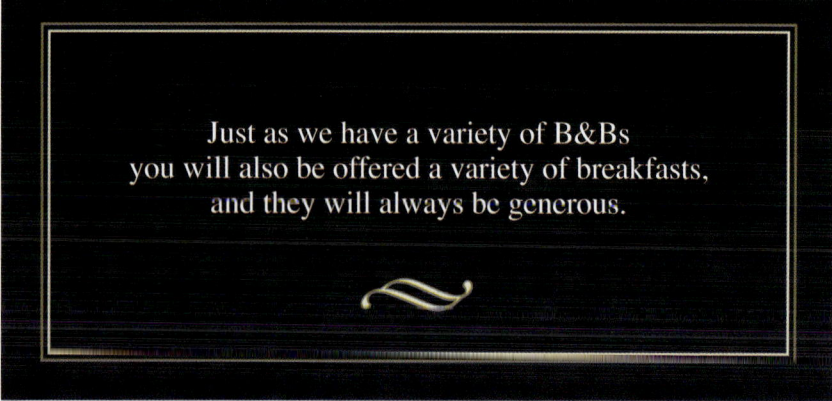

Just as we have a variety of B&Bs
you will also be offered a variety of breakfasts,
and they will always be generous.

Planning a trip around Australia?

Ask for ...

The Bed & Breakfast Book
Australia 2005

Accommodation with Character

- Small Hotels
- Romantic Hideaways
- Pet Friendly Getaways
- Self-Contained Cottages
- Short Breaks for the less able
- Farmstays and Retreats for Families and Children

Available on-line at www.bnb.co.nz and good book shops

$19.95

Moonshine Press
PO Box 6843, Wellington, New Zealand
Phone (04) 385 2615, Fax (04) 385 2694, info@bnb.co.nz

Southland, South Catlins & Stewart Island

Te Anau

94

Manapouri

99

Mossburn

Wendonside

Lumsden

Waikaka

Balfour

96

6

Gore

Pukerau

Mataura

Waimatuku

Waianiwa

99

Riverton

Wyndham

Invercargill

1

Mokotua

Fortrose

92

Progress Valley

Tokanui

Bluff

Stewart Island

Towns listed generally follow a north to south route. Refer to the index if required.

0   Kilometres   30

0   Miles   10

TE ANAU   *20km E of Te Anau*

Tapua   *Farmstay*
Dorothy & Donald Cromb
RD 2, Te Anau

Tel (03) 249 5805
Fax (03) 249 5805
Tapua.Cromb@xtra.co.nz
www.fiordland.org.nz/html/tapua.html

Double $110-$120 Single $110   (Full Breakfast)
Dinner $35pp Credit cards accepted
1 King 1 Twin (2 bdrm)
Bathrooms: 1 Guest shared

You are surrounded by million dollar views while enjoying the comfort of our large modern family home. Electric blankets, heaters in rooms. Traditional farm style meals. Excellent base for day trips to Milford or Doubtful Sound. A two night stay is recommended. Farm tour prior to dinner of our 348 hectare farm which has 3700 sheep and some cattle. Excellent fishing rivers within a few minutes drive as are great walking tracks, golf course etc. We have a cat. Smoke-free home.
Directions: please phone.

TE ANAU

Rob & Nancy's Place   *Homestay Self-contained*
R & N Marshall
13 Fergus Square,
Te Anau

Tel (03) 249 8241   Fax (03) 249 7397
Mob 025 226 1820   rob.nancy@xtra.co.nz
www.bnb.co.nz/robnancysplace.html

Double $125   Single $125   (Full Breakfast)
Credit cards accepted
2 King (2 bdrm)
Bathrooms: 1 Ensuite 1 Private

Rob, Nancy and Chardonnay, our burmese cat, welcome you to our quiet and tranquil home facing a park, 5 minutes walk to the lake and town centre. We are a couple retired from farming and enjoy meeting people. Our modern home includes a courtyard barbecue and gardens. Te Anau is a special place to visit with the magnificent scenery of the Fiordland National Park including spectacular Milford and Doubtful Sounds. All tours are picked up and delivered to the door. Off-street parking and storage available.

TE ANAU - MANAPOURI   *20 min E of Manapouri*

Crown Lea   *Farmstay*
Florence & John Pine
Gillespie Road,
RD 1, Te Anau

Tel (03) 249 8598   Fax (03) 249 8598
Mob 025 227 8366   crownlea@xtra.co.nz
www.bnb.co.nz/crownlea.html

Double $140-$160 Single $140   (Full Breakfast)
Dinner $35
1 King/Twin 1 Queen 1 Twin (3 bdrm)
Bathrooms: 1 Ensuite 2 Private

Our 900 acre sheep, cattle and deer farm offers a farm tour after 6pm, and views of Lake Manapouri, Fiordland mountains, and the Te Anau Basin. Day trips to Doubtful and Milford Sounds, visits to Te Anau, glowworm caves, or hikes on the many walking tracks in Fiordland are all within easy reach. Having travelled in the UK, Europe, Canada, Hong Kong and Singapore, we enjoy meeting guests from all over the world. We, and Harriet the cat, look forward to welcoming you to our home.

TE ANAU - MANAPOURI   *20km S of Te Anau*

The Cottage *B&B Homestay*
Don & Joy MacDuff
Waiau Street,
Te Anau - Manapouri

Tel (03) 249 6838   Fax (03) 249 6839
don.joymacduff@xtra.co.nz
www.thecottagefiordland.co.nz

Double $100-$120 Single $90-$110 (Special Breakfast)
Credit cards accepted
2 Queen 1 Single (2 bdrm)
Bathrooms: 2 Ensuite

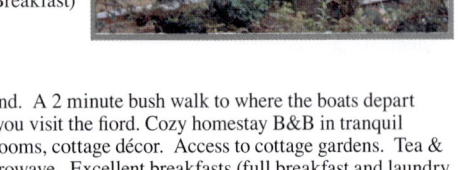

Gateway to the scenic wonders of Doubtful Sound. A 2 minute bush walk to where the boats depart for Doubtful Sound. Leave your car here while you visit the fiord. Cozy homestay B&B in tranquil bush setting, with lovely views. Warm ensuite rooms, cottage décor. Access to cottage gardens. Tea & coffee, TV in room. Shared lounge, fridge, microwave. Excellent breakfasts (full breakfast and laundry extra charge). We, with Rosie our skye terrier, extend a warm welcome to all who choose to stay with us. Come as strangers, leave as friends.

TE ANAU - MANAPOURI   *10km N of Manapouri*

Christies' Cottage *B&B Farmstay Self-contained*
Murray Christie
Hillside/Manapouri Road,
Te Anau

Tel (03) 249 6695   Mob 212594973
mchristie@xtra.co.nz
www.christiescottage.co.nz

Double $115 (Continental Breakfast)
Child negotiable Extra adult $15 Children welcome
1 Double 1 Single (2 bdrm)
Bathrooms: 1 Private

Exclusively yours, in a tranquil setting, is a delightful sunlit self-contained cottage with courtyard garden, beautiful mountain backdrop overlooking the (famous trout fishing) Mararoa River. Murray, with two teenage children, lives on a sheep/cattle farm close to both Te Anau and Manapouri, Murray enjoys sharing his extensive knowledge of fishing and the region. I love gardening and helping with your travel plans if you wish. Bookings can be made for local tourist excursions. Looking forward to meeting you; travel safely.

TE ANAU   *5km S of Te Anau*

Kepler Cottage *B&B Farmstay Country Homestay*
Jan & Jeff Ludemann
William Stephen Road, Te Anau

Tel (03) 249 7185   Fax (03) 249 7186
Mob 027 431 4076   kepler@teanau.co.nz
www.fiordlandaccommodation.co.nz

Double $150-$200 Single $100-$120 (Full Breakfast)
Credit cards accepted
1 Queen 3 Single (3 bdrm)
Bathrooms: 1 Ensuite 1 Private

Jeff, an aircraft engineer and Jan, who works from home as a marketing consultant, welcome you to their small farmlet on the edge of Fiordland, just 5 minutes drive from Te Anau. Relax outdoors in the garden and enjoy the peace and comfort of our rural location between visiting Milford or Doubtful Sounds, or walking one of the many nearby tracks. Our family includes a cairn terrier, and 2 cats. We can advise tours and sightseeing and make bookings where needed.

TE ANAU   *26km E of Te Anau*

Country Cottage   *Farmstay Self-contained*
Carolyn & John Klein
The Key,
RD 2, Te Anau

Tel (03) 249 5807   Fax (03) 249 5807
kleinbnb@ihug.co.nz   www.fishfiordland.com

Double $95   Single $75   (Continental Breakfast)
Child negotiable   Credit cards accepted
Children welcome   Pets welcome
1 Queen 3 Single (2 bdrm)
Bathrooms: 1 Private

We live at The Key, a tiny village on the main Queenstown-Te Anau highway, nestled under the Takitimu mountains, just 15 minutes drive from Te Anau. Our modern self-contained cottage is exclusively yours, well-equipped, very warm and comfortable with a beautiful country view. We all enjoy meeting people and sharing our extensive knowledge of the region with you. John offers guided fishing on many of our local rivers. If you're looking for a real country experience, come and see us, we'd love to see you!

TE ANAU   *1km N of Te Anau Centre*

Shakespeare House   *B&B Self-contained Guesthouse*
Margaret & Jeff Henderson
10 Dusky Street,   PO Box 32, Te Anau

Tel (03) 249 7349   0800 249 349 Fax (03) 249 7629
marg.shakespeare.house@xtra.co.nz
www.shakespearehouse.co.nz

Double $100-$115   Single $85-$95 (Full Breakfast)
Child $5-$15 Self-contained 2 bedrooms (sleeps 5)
Credit cards accepted Children welcome
4 King 3 Queen 4 Single (8 bdrm)
Bathrooms: 8 Ensuite

Shakespeare House is a well established Bed & Breakfast, where we keep a home atmosphere with personal service. We are situated in a quiet residential area yet are within walking distance of shops, lake and restaurants. Our rooms are ground floor and have the choice of king, queen or twin beds. Each room has private facilities, TV, tea/coffee making. Tariff includes continental or delicious cooked breakfast. Guest laundry available, internet and payphone facilities on site. Winter rates May to September.

TE ANAU   *8km S of Te Anau*

Lynwood Park   *B&B Farmstay Homestay*
Trina & Daniella Baker
State Highway 94, Te Anau

Tel (03) 249 7990   Fax (03) 249 7990
Mob 021 129 5626 lynwood.park@xtra.co.nz
www.bnb.co.nz/lynwoodpark.html

Double $80-$130   Single $50-$80   (Full Breakfast)
Child $40   Winter rates May-Oct
Credit cards accepted   Children welcome
2 Queen 1 Double 3 Single (3 bdrm)
Bathrooms: 2 Ensuite 1 Private

Lynwood Park is set amidst our family's 450 acre sheep, cattle and deer farm in a lovely quiet rural oasis. Each guest room has a private entrance, TV and tea/coffee. Cooked or continental breakfast available. We offer the use of laundry facility and childrens' play area which Daniella, my 6 year old, looks forward to sharing with you. We have 3 pet sheep, and a cat on the property. I am able to advise or arrange most activities to make your holiday a memorable experience.

SOUTHLAND, SOUTH CATLINS

TE ANAU   *2km E of Te Anau*

Rose 'n' Reel   *B&B Farmstay Self-contained*
Lyn & Lex Lawrence
Ben Loch Lane, RD 2, Te Anau

Tel (03) 249 7582   Fax (03) 249 7582
Mob 025 545 723   rosenreel@xtra.co.nz
www.rosenreel.co.nz

Double $90-$100   Single $60-$70
(Continental Breakfast)   Credit cards accepted
1 Queen 1 Double 1 Single (3 bdrm)
Bathrooms: 1 Private 1 Guests share

Genuine Kiwi hospitality in a magic setting 5 minutes from Te Anau. Hand feed tame fallow deer, meet our friendly cat and dog. Sit on the veranda of our fully self-contained cabin and enjoy watching deer with a lake and mountain view. The 2 room cabin has cooking facilities, fridge, microwave, TV, one queen, one double plus bathroom. Our modern 2 storey smoke-free home is set in an extensive garden. 2 downstairs guest bedrooms. Lex is a fishing guide and average golfer, while I love to garden. Directions: please phone.

TE ANAU   *Te Anau Central*

Cosy Kiwi   *B&B*
Virginia and Gerhard Hirner
186 Milford Road, Te Anau 9681

Tel (03) 249 7475   0800 249 700   Fax (03) 249 8471
info@cosykiwi.com   www.cosykiwi.com

Double $100-$150   Single $80-$110   Triple $135-$160
(Special Breakfast)   Child neg   Credit cards accepted
Children welcome
4 King/Twin 3 Queen 9 Single (7 bdrm)
Bathrooms: 7 Ensuite

Virginia and Gerhard and our 2 children welcome you to our new Bed & Breakfast (20 years experience in hospitality, we speak German). Privacy with comfort, quiet spacious, ensuited bedrooms, quality beds, individual heating and television. Gourmet breakfast buffet of home-made breads, jams, fresh fruits, home-bottled fruits, yoghurt, brewed coffee, special teas, mouth watering pancakes with maple syrup and more. Centrally located, bookings arranged for all tours, pick up at gate. Guest lounge with internet access, laundry, off-street parking and luggage storage.

TE ANAU   *1.5km N of Te Anau*

The Croft   *B&B Self-contained Rural Lifestyle*
Jane & Ross McEwan
Te Anau Milford Sound Road,
RD 1, Te Anau

Tel (03) 249 7393   Fax (03) 249 7393
Mob 027 682 0061   jane@thecroft.co.nz
www.thecroft.co.nz

Double $130-$145 (Continental Breakfast)
Credit cards accepted
2 Queen 1 Single (2 bdrm)
Bathrooms: 2 Ensuite

Warm hospitality and quality accommodation are guaranteed at The Croft, a small lifestyle farm only minutes from Te Anau. Our 2 recently built self-contained cottages are set in private gardens and enjoy magnificent lake and mountain views. Timber ceilings, large ensuite bathrooms, window seats and elegant furnishings are some of the highlights. Microwaves, fridges, sinks, TV's and CD Mini systems. Enjoy breakfast with Jane & Ross or have it served in your cottage. Pets include Dolly the sheep, Mac the Jack Russell, and Kitty. Lake and river access from our farm.

TE ANAU

Edgewater XL B&B *B&B Self-contained*
Mark Excell
52 Lakefront Drive, Te Anau

Tel (03) 249 7258 0800 433 439
Fax (03) 249 8099
edgewater.xl.motels@xtra.co.nz
www.bnb.co.nz/edgewaterxl.html

Double $150 (Continental Breakfast)
Credit cards accepted Children welcome
1 Queen 2 Single (2 bdrm)
Bathrooms: 1 Ensuite 1 Private

Situated on the lakefront, Edgewater XL B&B provides unobstructed views of the lake and Fiordland National World Heritage Park. From your bedroom and private lounge, sliding doors open on to a balcony. Your unit has coffee and tea making facilities and ensuite with spa bath. Tariff includes continental breakfast. We are a booking agent for all activities. Ian has good local knowledge of trout fishing areas. This magic setting is only 3 minutes from the town centre. Off-season rates apply.

TE ANAU *5km E of Te Anau*

Stonewall Cottage *B&B Self-contained*
Nicky Harrison & Jim Huntington
36 Kakapo Road, RD 2, Te Anau

Tel (03) 249 8686 Fax (03) 249 8686
Mob 027 260 3414 stonewall@hprojects.co.nz
www.bnb.co.nz/stonewallcottage.html

Double $140 Single $100 (Continental Breakfast)
Child $20 neg Credit cards accepted
Children welcome
1 Queen (1 bdrm)
Bathrooms: 1 Ensuite

Come up the driveway passed the pond and dry stonewalls to our self-contained guest studio. It is sited at our home amidst our deer farm in Kakapo Road, only 5 minutes out of Te Anau. You have your own private accomodation, including ensuite bathroom and kitchen. Your courtyard overlooks our organic vegetable garden to the mountains of Fiordland. It is peaceful and quiet, we hope you will enjoy the environment as we do. Breakfasts include home produce and seasonal fruit. Great kids play area as well.

TE ANAU - MANAPOURI *19km S of Te Anau*

Rose Cottage B&B *B&B Self-contained*
Mary & Rennie McRae
1809 Te Anau, Manapouri Highway, RD 1, Te Anau

Tel (03) 249 6691 Fax (03) 249 6690
Mob 027 435 9512 or 025 656 0404
renniemac@xtra.co.nz
www.bnb.co.nz/rosecottagebb.html

Double $125 Single $95 (Continental Breakfast)
Child $15 Credit cards accepted
Children welcome Pets welcome
1 Queen 2 Twin (2 bdrm) Bathrooms: 1 Private

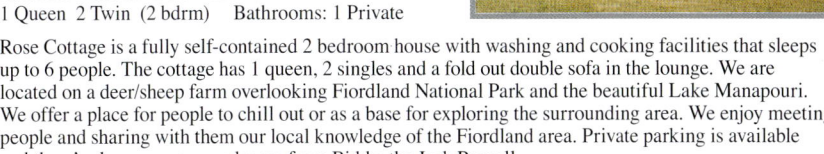

Rose Cottage is a fully self-contained 2 bedroom house with washing and cooking facilities that sleeps up to 6 people. The cottage has 1 queen, 2 singles and a fold out double sofa in the lounge. We are located on a deer/sheep farm overlooking Fiordland National Park and the beautiful Lake Manapouri. We offer a place for people to chill out or as a base for exploring the surrounding area. We enjoy meeting people and sharing with them our local knowledge of the Fiordland area. Private parking is available and there's always a warm welcome from Biddy, the Jack Russell.

SOUTHLAND, SOUTH CATLINS

TE ANAU   *1 km N of Town Te Anau*

Approved

Te Anau Lodge   *B&B*
Kerry Carey
52 Howden Street, Te Anau

Tel (03) 249 7477   Fax (03) 249 7487
Mob 021 230 7502   info@teanaulodge.com
www.teanaulodge.com

Double $180-$220 Single $150   (Full Breakfast)
Child $80   Credit cards accepted   Children welcome
1 King/Twin 5 Queen 2 Twin 2 Single (7 bdrm)
Bathrooms: 6 Ensuite 1 Private

Step into a charming jewel of Southland history.
Originally a convent, it was moved to Te Anau, near the tranquil lake in 2003 where it retains the
peaceful atmosphere and warm wood interior, but with the added attractions of modern conveniences
and central heating. Laundry facilities and luggage storage is provided. Enjoy complimentary drinks
and nibbles in our spacious library/lounge, or wander around our 3 hectares of newly established
parkland, and breakfast in our chapel at a time that suits you.

TE ANAU   *Te Anau central*

Approved

Antler Lodge   *B&B Self-contained*
Helen & Chris Whyte
44 Matai Street, Te Anau

Tel (03) 249 8188   Fax (03) 249 8188
Mob 025 684 1385   antler.lodge@xtra.co.nz
www.antlerlodgeteanau.co.nz

Double $120-$155   (Continental Breakfast)
Credit cards accepted
1 King 2 Queen (3 bdrm)
Bathrooms: 3 Ensuite

Helen, Chris and daughter Hayley invite you to enjoy
their comfortable bed & breakfast accommodation. Situated in a quiet residential area close to shops,
restaurants and within walking distance of the lake. From a farming background, we have a deer farm
on the outskirts of Te Anau. We have 2 friendly Jack Russell dogs. We offer 3 spacious smoke-free guest
rooms, each with a private ensuite. The 2 cottages each have full kitchen facilities, electric heating and
comfortable furnishings. Our third room is an upstairs suite with its own entrance and sunroom dining
area. This suite has beautiful views of Mt Luxmoore.

TE ANAU   *1km S of Central Te Anau*

Approved

Cat's Whiskers   *B&B*
Anne Marie & Lindsay Bernstone
2 Lakefront Drive, Te Anau

Tel (03) 249 8112   Fax (03) 249 8112
bookings@catswhiskers.co.nz
www.catswhiskers.co.nz

Double $145-$150 Single $95-$100 (Full Breakfast)
Child neg   Credit cards accepted
Children welcome
2 King 2 Queen 4 Single (4 bdrm)
Bathrooms: 4 Ensuite

On the lakefront opposite Fiordland National Park Visitor Centre. A short walk to the town centre.
Guest rooms offer comfortable king, queen and twin beds. All rooms have ensuites, TV, tea and coffee
making facilities. A cooked or continental breakfast is served in our dining room. Booking service for
local trips. Off-street parking available. Guest laundry and short term luggage storage is also available.
Our cat, Lucy, and a small maltese dog, Elle, live with us.

TE ANAU *5km E of Te Anau*

Glacial Rock Cottages
B&B Farmstay Self-contained
Sarah & Finn Murphy
Rapid 141, Tutoko Lane, Te Anau

Tel (03) 249 9141   Fax (03) 249 9143
Mob 021 640 046
mail@glacialrock.com www.glacialrock.com

Double $160-$180 Single $140-$160
(Continental Breakfast) Child neg
Breakfast provisions provided
Credit cards accepted Children welcome
1 King/Twin 1 Double (1 bdrm)
Bathrooms: 1 Ensuite

Glacial Rock farm is situated down Tutoko
Lane, a private sealed lane 4km from Te
Anau on SH94. The farm is terraced with the
cottages situated 200 metres above Lake Te Anau. The farm is bordered by the Upukeroa River.
We are only 5 minutes to town yet free from hustle and traffic noise of Te Anau.

Two purpose built cottages designed with your every comfort in mind, finished inside with rimu,
complete with heated tiled kitchen and bathroom floors. These cosy yet spacious cedar cottages are
situated on our 70 acre deer farm on a elevated site with 180 degree alpine panorama and ideally
situated for stunning views up the Southern Arm of Lake Te Anau.

Watch the wapiti and red deer along with the highland cattle grazing from your sunny window
seat, or from the swing seat on your spacious verandah. Where possible guests are welcome to
participate in farm activities such as feeding and moving stock, subject to seasonal requirements.

No expense has been spared in the cottage construction and set up. Complete with Sky TV, outside
BBQ, underfloor heating, computer jackpoints. Your super king bed can be converted to 2 singles if
preferred, and a double pullout sofa is avaliable in the lounge if required. By arrangement: gluten
free provisions, laundry. We are happy to discuss and assist you with booking your sightseeing
arrangements anywhere in the spectacular Fiordland area.

Your hosts are Finn & Sarah; Finn is one of the local police officers, while Sarah coordinates
their 3 enthusiastic children and the day to day running of the farm. Pets currently include a very
friendly italian spinone and 3 cats. The Cottages are due for completion July 2004; check out our
web site for pictures and more information.

Stunning views over the mountains and lake with magic sunsets

TE ANAU   *5km N of Te Anau*

Lochvista B&B   *B&B*
Viv Nicholson
454 State Highway 94, Te Anau

Tel (03) 249 7273   Fax (03) 249 7278
Mob 0274 559 949   lochvista@xtra.co.nz
www.bnb.co.nz/lochvista.html

Double $140-$150   Single $130-$140
(Continental Breakfast) Full breakfast on request $15pp
2 Queen (2 bdrm)   Bathrooms: 2 Ensuite

Welcome to Fiordland. Lochvista is situated on Te
Anau Milford Highway 5km from the town centre,
overlooking Lake Te Anau and Murchison mountains. 2 rooms each with queen beds and ensuite, tea/
coffee making facilities, fridge, TV, hairdryer. French doors onto the patio where you can sit and take
in spectacular views. Fiordland has a great deal to offer and I am more than happy to help guests with
any booking to make their stay more relaxing. Directions: travel along Milford Road 4.6km from the
100kmph sign. Take first right after Sinclair Road and the blue lodge sign. 300 metres up road, turn right
at 3 letterboxes, follow driveway down to house. A cat called Mischief.

TE ANAU   *200m central Te Anau*

House of Wood   *B&B Homestay*
Merle & Cliff Buchanan
44 Moana Crescent, Te Anau

Tel (03) 249 8404   Fax (03) 249 7676   Mob 021 2500 802
houseofwood@xtra.co.nz www.bnb.co.nz/houseofwoodbb.html

Double $100-$125   Single $90-$110 (Full Breakfast)
Credit cards accepted   Dinner by arrangement
2 Queen 1 Double 1 Twin (4 bdrm)
Bathrooms: 3 Ensuite 1 Private

A warm welcome is assurred when you arrive at our home, the
House of Wood. We really enjoy meeting guests from overseas
(and locals). Our house is a unique architecturally designed home
of native and exotic timber. Sit at the outdoor tables and enjoy
the beautiful views from our balconies. Our interests are boating,
fishing, golf and gardening. We can help you plan your activities
and book trips, with pick-up at the door. We are 2 minutes walk
from town centre and 5 minutes to the Lake.

TE ANAU - MANAPOURI   *10 km S of Manapouri*

Connemara   *B&B Farmstay Self-contained*
Bev & Murray Hagen
415 Weir Road,
Manapouri, Te Anau

Tel (03) 249 9399   Fax (03) 249 9399
Mob 027 292 3651   hagen@southnet.co.nz
www.bnb.co.nz/connemara.html

Double $115   Single $90 (Continental Breakfast)
Child $15   Breakfast ingredients supplied
1 Queen 1 Double (1 bdrm)
Bathrooms: 1 Ensuite

Connemara is a newly renovated, cosy self contained cottage with electric heating and TV, a separate
bedroom with ensuite and a double fold out sofa-bed. Our deer farm is 5 minutes from Manapouri
on the Southern Scenic Route and borders the lower Waiau River with magnificent mountain views.
Your hosts Bev and Murray enjoy motorbike touring and Murray is an enthusiastic microlight pilot.
Angel is our curiously friendly cat. A tranquil place to stay while enjoying our magnificent Fiordland
scenery.

MOSSBURN   *25km S of Mossburn*

Farmstay
Joyce & Murray Turner
RD 1, Otautau, Southland

Tel (03) 225 7602   Fax (03) 225 7602
murray.joyce@xtra.co.nz
www.innz.co.nz/host/e/etalcreek.html

Double $80   Single $50   (Full Breakfast)
Child 12 years & under $20   Dinner $30
1 Queen 4 Single (3 bdrm)
Bathrooms: 1 Private

Our modern home on 301 hectares, farming sheep & beef cattle, is situated halfway between Invercargill and Te Anau, which can be reached in 1 hour. We enjoy meeting people, will provide quality accommodation, farm fresh food in a welcoming friendly atmosphere. You can join in farm activities, farm tour or just relax. The Aparima River is adjacent to the property. Murray is a keen fly fisherman. Guiding available. Pet bichon frise. Evening meal on request. Directions: please phone/fax. 24 hours notice to avoid disappointment.

MOSSBURN   *1km W of Mossburn*

Kowhai Lodge   *B&B Farmstay Self-contained*
Ailsa Broughton
5665 Highway 94,
Mossburn

Tel (03) 248 6137   Fax (03) 248 6137
kowhailodge@xtra.co.nz
www.nzhomestay.co.nz/broughton.html

Double $150   Single $120   (Special Breakfast)
Child $25   Credit cards accepted Children welcome
1 King/Twin 1 Queen (2 bdrm)
Bathrooms: 1 Private

Our beautifully restored cottage features a hand-built stone chimney and large open fire, with comfortable beds and cosy atmosphere. It is surrounded by red deer including a pet hind to feed. The Oreti River on our boundary provides top fishing. You can join us on the farm with the sheep, or plan some hunting, fishing or tramping. We offer a wonderful family atmosphere to enrich any child's holiday. We look forward to meeting you and sharing our 100% pure New Zealand Hospitality.

LUMSDEN   *9km S of Lumsden*

Josephville Gardens
Farmstay self-contained room available
Annette & Bob Menlove
Rapid sign 824, State Highway 6,
RD 4, Lumsden

Tel (03) 248 7114   Fax (03) 248 7114
Mob 021 494 149
bobannette@menlove.net
www.bnb.co.nz/josephvillegardens.html

Double $130-$150   (Full Breakfast) Dinner $30
1 King/Twin 2 Double 1 Twin (4 bdrm)
Bathrooms: 1 Ensuite 1 Private 1 Guests share 1 Host share

We have a 480 hectare farm which runs sheep, cattle and deer. Surrounding our comfortable warm home, we have a large garden with a selection of specimen trees, rhododendrons, roses, peonys and perennials. The golf course is 3km away - golf clubs are available. A good fishing river nearby. We have hiked in our mountains a lot and can give advise on where and what to see. If you wish a four wheel drive trip is available.

SOUTHLAND,
SOUTH CATLINS

BALFOUR *3km N of Balfour*

Hillcrest *Farmstay*
Liz & Ritchie Clark
206 Old Balfour Road, RD 1, Balfour

Tel (03) 201 6165 Fax (03) 201 6165 clarkrl@esi.co.nz
www.bnb.co.nz/hillcrestbalfour.html

Double $120-$150 Single $120-$150 (Full Breakfast)
Dinner $40pp Children welcome
2 King/Twin (2 bdrm)
Bathrooms: 1 Private 1 Host share

Welcome to our 650 acre sheep and deer farm. Relax
in our garden; enjoy a farm tour with mountain views
or a game of tennis. Trout fishing in the Mataura, Oreti
and Waikaia rivers. Fishing guide can be arranged with notice. Enjoy a relaxing dinner with fine food,
wine and conversation. Breakfast is served with fresh baked bread, yoghurt, muesli, jams and preserves.
Interests include handcrafts, tennis, photography and fishing. We have 3 children attending boarding
school/tertiary education and a cat. Directions: at Balfour crossroads, take the road to Waikaia, then
first left Old Balfour Road and travel 2.06km, we are on right. Please phone.

WENDONSIDE *15km N of Riversdale*

Ardlamont Farm *Farmstay*
Dale & Lindsay Wright
110 Wendonside Church Road North,
Wendonside, RD 7, Gore

Tel (03) 202 7774 Fax (03) 202 7774
ardlamont@xtra.co.nz
www.bnb.co.nz/ardlamontfarm.html

Double $120 Single $80 (Full Breakfast)
Dinner $40
1 King/Twin 1 Double (2 bdrm) Bathrooms: 1 Private

Experience Ardlamont, a fourth generation 1200 acre sheep and beef farm offering panoramic views of
northern Southland. Gourmet meals a specialty, served with fine New Zealand wines. Tour the farm,
then return to the renovated comforts of our 95 year old homestead. Having travelled widely we enjoy
welcoming visitors into our home. Our 3 teenage children attend university/boarding school. 2 of New
Zealand's best trout rivers only 5 minutes away. 15 minutes off SH94 (Queenstown - Gore - Dunedin
route) Well worth the detour.

WAIKAKA *30km N of Gore*

home
NEW ZEALAND

Blackhills Farmstay *B&B Farmstay*
Dorothy & Tom Affleck
192 Robertson Road, RD 3, Gore, Southland

Tel (03) 207 2865 Fax (03) 207 2865
Mob 025 2091 563 afflecks@ispnz.co.nz
blackhillsfarmstay.co.nz

Double $100 Single $50 (Full Breakfast)
Child $25 Dinner $25 by arrangement
Credit cards accepted Children welcome
2 King/Twin 1 Queen (3 bdrm)
Bathrooms: 1 Private 1 Guests share 1 Host share

Rest between Dunedin and Te Anau gateway to Milford Sound. 15 minutes from SHW90 means no
traffic noise. Dorothy and Tom have farmed 800 acre Blackhills for 35 years. Dorothy: "We treat you as
friends we haven't met and want you to feel at home" That means as much privacy as you like, home-
grown vegetables, and meat, in home-cooked meals, established tree and shrub gardens. Take Tom's
farm tour, walk rolling green hills, catch trout, play golf, meet NZer's. Tom: "See you soon." Ask for
directions please.

PUKERAU - GORE   *12km E of Gore*

Connor Orchids   *Country Homestay*
Dawn & David Connor
1158 State Highway 1, Pukerau, Southland

Tel (03) 205 3896   0800 372 484
Fax (03) 205 3896   Mob 027 669 1362
ddconnor@esi.co.nz
www.bnb.co.nz/connororchids.html

Double $80-$100 Single $45   (Full Breakfast)
Dinner by arrangement Credit cards accepted
1 King/Twin 1 Queen (2 bdrm)
Bathrooms: 1 Private 1 Guests share

Relax with us in our warm comfortable home set in a mature garden with a rural outlook. We are just minutes away from several rivers including the Mataura which is well known for brown trout fishing. Fishing guide available on request. Growing a variety of orchids is our main interest, we run a few pet sheep. We enjoy meeting people and have travelled extensively ourselves. Complimentary tea & coffee available. Smoke-free accommodation.

GORE   *1km S of Gore*

Charlton Lodge   *B&B*
Judy & Jim Milne
Corner Charlton Road and Main Street, Gore

Tel (03) 208 9279   0800 95 63 43   Fax (03) 208 0161
info@charltonlodge.co.nz
www.charltonlodge.co.nz

Double $75-$85 Single $60   (Full Breakfast)
Child neg   Credit cards accepted   Children welcome
2 King/Twin 1 Queen 2 Double 6 Single (11 bdrm)
Bathrooms: 1 Ensuite 3 Guests share

Charlton Lodge B&B Hotel offers southern hospitality in a smoke-free centrally heated environment with complimentary tea and coffee, providing off street parking, laundry services, a full cooked breakfast in our cosy dining room. We are situated on State Highway 1 close to the heart of Gore. On site café caters for day and evening meals from a traditional roast to lighter meals. Fish the world renowned Mataura River and have your catch cooked by your able host or peruse the arts, sport or gardens.

MATAURA - GORE   *12km S of Gore*

Kowhai Place   *Farmstay*
Helen & John Williams
291 Glendhu Road, RD 4, Gore

Tel (03) 203 8774   Fax (03) 203 8774
kowhaiplace@xtra.co.nz
www.southland-homestays.co.nz

Double $80-$95 Single $50   (Full Breakfast)
Child ½ price   Dinner $20 by arrangement
Children welcome   Pets welcome
2 Queen 4 Single (4 bdrm)
Bathrooms: 1 Private 1 Guests share 1 Host share

John & Helen farm sheep and deer, on our 50 acre farmlet. We live 5 minutes from one of the best brown trout fishing rivers in the world. Drive 1 hour south to Bluff, and 90 minutes to Queenstown's ski fields. We both play golf, and enjoy gardening. Fishing guide, and garden tours can be arranged with prior notice. Children and outside pets welcome. Over the past years we have enjoyed sharing our spacious home and garden with lots of overseas guests. Enjoy the south.

WYNDHAM   *3.65km E of Wyndham*

home

Smiths Farmstay   *Farmstay*
Beverly and Doug Smith
365 Wyndham - Mokoreta Road,
RD 2, Wyndham, Southland

Tel (03) 206 4840   Fax (03) 206 4847
Mob 025 286 6920
beverly@smithsfarmstay.co.nz
www.bnb.co.nz/smithsfarmstay.html

Double $110-$140 Single $100
(Full Breakfast) Child neg Dinner $40
Credit cards accepted Children welcome
2 King/Twin 1 Queen 1 Twin (4 bdrm)
Bathrooms: 1 Ensuite 1 Private 1 Guests share

Beverly and Doug assure you of a warm welcome to the
modern farm house set in 265 hectare sheep farm. We
are situated on the hills above Wyndham only 3.65km,
set in quiet and peaceful surroundings.

Farm tour included in tariff. Feeding the animals and
sheep shearing when in season. Doug will demonstrate
his sheep dogs working. Beverly a registered nurse
enjoys cooking, floral art, knitting, gardening and travel.
We enjoy meeting people and both are of a friendly
deposition, with a sense of humour.

• Each bedroom has a view and is tastefully furnished to
meet your needs. • Genuine home-cooking. • Special diets on request. • Packed Lunches if required.
• You are most welcome to join us for the evening meal, which is $40pp. Prior booking required please.

Fishermans Retreat: The Mataura, Wyndham and Mimihau Rivers are renowned for their abundance
of brown trout. Each of these Rivers is only a short 5km away. Doug, a keen experienced fisherman
is only too happy to share his knowledge of these rivers with you. Enjoy the Mad Mataura evening
Rise, a site to experience. Gateway to Catlins, Only 2 hours from Queenstown, Te Anau and Dunedin.
Laundry and fax available.

Directions: come to Wyndham, follow signs to Mokoreta. Sign at gate, number 365.

PROGRESS VALLEY - SOUTH CATLINS *6km N of Waikawa*

Catlins Farmstay B&B *B&B Farmstay*
June & Murray Stratford
174 Progress Valley Road, South Catlins, Southland

Tel (03) 246 8843 Fax (03) 246 8844
catlinsfarmstay@xtra.co.nz
www.catlinsfarmstay.co.nz

Double $160-$220 Single $100 (Full Breakfast)
Child neg Dinner $40 Self-contained
Credit cards accepted Children welcome
1 King 2 Queen 2 Single (4 bdrm)
Bathrooms: 3 Ensuite 1 Private 1 Guests share

Ours is a great location close to fossil forest at Curio Bay. Superior new guest rooms plus king self-contained suite available with private entrances. I specialise in dinners using homegrown venison, beef or lamb, and organic vegetables, (vegetarians catered for) followed by delicious desserts - and breakfasts. We farm 1000 acres, running 2500 sheep, 500 deer, 150 cattle with 3 sheepdogs. Farm tours by arrangement. Directions: turn off at Niagara Falls into Manse Road, drive 2km. Ask about our self-contained cottages at Waikawa and Curio Bay (www.cottagestays.co.nz/curio/cottage.htm)

FORTROSE - THE CATLINS *50km SE of Invercargill*

Greenbush *B&B Farmstay*
Ann & Donald McKenzie
298 Fortrose - Otara Road,
Fortrose, RD 5, Invercargill

Tel (03) 246 9506 Fax (03) 246 9505
Mob 021 395 196
info@greenbush.co.nz
www.greenbush.co.nz

Double $130 Single $100 (Full Breakfast) Child neg
Dinner $40 by arrangement Credit cards accepted
1 King/Twin 1 Double 1 Twin (3 bdrm)
Bathrooms: 1 Ensuite 1 Private

Greenbush Bed & Breakfast is ideally located off the Southern Scenic Route from Fortrose. Within 30 minutes drive from Greenbush you can enjoy Curio Bay, Waipapa Point and Slope Point, the southern most point in the South Island. Greenbush is nestled in 2 acres of garden. You will wake to the song of birds and magnificent views of green rolling countryside. Enjoy our private beach access, lake and farm tour. Directions: at Fortrose take Coastal Route drive 4km.

MOKOTUA *20km NE of Invercargill*

Fernlea *B&B Farmstay Self-contained cottage*
Anne & Brian Perkins
Mokotua, RD 1,
Invercargill on Southern Scenic Route

Tel (03) 239 5432 Fax (03) 239 5432 Mob 025 313 432
fernlea@southnet.co.nz www.fernlea.co.nz

Double $120 (Full Breakfast) Child $10
Dinner $30 by arrangement Children welcome
2 Double (1 bdrm)
Bathrooms: 1 Private

Proof of Fernlea's success was winning both the 'Hosted Accommodation' section and the 'Supreme Tourism Award for Southland'. Anne's cottage, nestled in its own private olde world garden, is completely self-contained and can sleep 4. Our dairy farm of 300 acres is home to 300 holstein friesian cows - farm tour included. Interests include golf, travel, tramping, fishing and people. Relax and enjoy a taste of real NZ farm life on your journey to discover the Catlins, or en route to Stewart Island, Te Anau or Queenstown. Directions: 20 minutes from Invercargill on SH92, turn left at Mokotua Garage.

INVERCARGILL *5km N of Invercargill city*

Glenroy Park Homestay *B&B Homestay*
Margaret & Alan Thomson
23 Glenroy Park Drive, Invercargill

Tel (03) 215 8464 Fax (03) 215 8464
home_hosp@actrix.co.nz
www.bnb.co.nz/glenroypark.html

Double $100-$115 Single $65-$75
(Continental Breakfast) Child $12
Dinner $30 Children welcome
1 Queen 1 Twin 1 Single (3 bdrm)
Bathrooms: 1 Private 1 Guests share

Exclusively yours in a quiet retreat with restaurants and parks nearby. Be our special guests and share an evening of relaxation and friendship. Our interests are golfing, meeting people, travel and cooking. We look forward to having you visit us. Invercargill is the gateway to Queenstown, Fiordland, Catlins and Stewart Island. Directions: from Queenstown turn left at first traffic lights (Bainfield Road), take first left, third house on left. From Dunedin turn right at first traffic lights (Queens Drive), travel to end, turn left, first street right, third house on left.

INVERCARGILL *15km N of Invercargill*

Tudor Park *Farmstay Country stay and Garden*
Joyce & John Robins
21 Lawrence Road, RD 6, Invercargill

Tel (03) 221 7150 Fax (03) 221 7150 Mob 025 310 031
tudorparksouth@hotmail.com
www.tudorpark.co.nz

Double $160 Single $90 (Full Breakfast)
Child neg Dinner From $40 Twin $130
Credit cards accepted Children welcome
1 King/Twin 2 Queen (3 bdrm)
Bathrooms: 2 Ensuite 1 Private

When travelling in the scenic south enjoy the peace and tranquility of a comfortable country home set in a large prize winning garden. Peonies and Hellebores are also being grown comercially. Fresh flowers, cotton sheets, private facilities and the 'best beds in NZ'. Close to Invercargill, Stewart Island, SH6 to Te Anau and Queenstown. We have spent most of our life farming and still have many rural involvements. We enjoy overseas travel. Please book ahead if possible. We also have a house available at Riverton.

INVERCARGILL

The Oak Door *B&B*
Lisa & Bill Stuart
22 Taiepa Road, Otatara, RD 9,
Invercargill 9521

Tel 64 3 213 0633 Fax 64 3 213 0633
blstuart@xtra.co.nz
www.bnb.co.nz/theoakdoor.html

Double $100 Single $80 (Full Breakfast)
Child price on application
2 Queen 2 Twin 1 Single (3 bdrm)
Bathrooms: 2 Guests share

Bill (Kiwi) & Lisa (Canadian) welcome you to their warm, self built, unique home. Enjoy attractive gardens and native bush setting, minutes from: Invercargill CBD, Scenic-route amenities, airport. Coffee/tea awaits you on arrival at The Oak Door. Guests comment on a warm comfortable visit, where beds, breakfast & hospitality are quality plus! A warm welcome! (No smoking and no pets). Directions: Drive past the airport entrance. Take first left (Marama Avenue South). Take first right Taiepa Road second drive on right (#22).

INVERCARGILL   *3 N of Invercargill City Centre*

Gimblett Place   *B&B*
Alex & Eileen Henderson
122 Gimblett Place,
Kildare, Invercargill

Tel (03) 215 6888   Fax (03) 215 6888
the_grove@xtra.co.nz
www.bnb.co.nz/thegrovedeerfarm.html

Double $90   Single $65   (Full Breakfast)
Child neg Credit cards accepted
1 Queen 2 Single (2 bdrm)
Bathrooms: 1 Guests share

Eileen and Alex are experienced hosts who are ex-farmers and offer comfortable accommodation in a quiet cul-de-sac close to city amenities, golf, parks, restaurants. We are pleased to assist with local and tourist information and can guide if required. (ie Catlins) Alex is a vintage car and machinery enthusiast and can arrange good veiwing. Close to famous trout fishing rivers. Bus and airport courtesy pick up. Directions: find Queens Drive, Gimblett Street is first left north of Thomsons Bush, fourth right into Gimblett Place.

INVERCARGILL   *10km E of Invercargill on Southern Scenic Rte*

Long Acres Farmstay   *Farmstay Self-contained*
Helen & Graeme Spain
Waimatua, RD 11, Invercargill

Tel (03) 216 4470   Fax (03) 216 4470
Mob 025 228 1308   longacres@xtra.co.nz
www.longacres.co.nz

Double $100-$120 Single $70-$80 (Full Breakfast)
Child neg Dinner $30 Self-contained $120-$140
Credit cards accepted Children welcome
1 Queen 1 Double 1 Twin 2 Single (4 bdrm)
Bathrooms: 1 Private 1 Guests share 1 Host share

Southland hospitality at its best awaits you at our warm and friendly home. Our farm is 850 acres carrying 3000 sheep and 80 cattle. We are a farming and shearing family. Shearing videos available to watch. Farm tour available. Our farm is 30 minutes from Bluff. Transport to Stewart Island can be arranged. Our home and garden is relaxing and very peaceful. Being travellers ourselves, we enjoy meeting visitors. Stay as long as you wish. Home cooked meal always available. A welcome assured. Directions: from Invercargill east on Southern Scenic Route approx 15 minutes. Look for Long Acres Farmstay Sign.

INVERCARGILL - WAIANIWA   *18km W of Invercargill*

Annfield Flowers   *B&B Homestay*
Margaret & Mike Cockeram
126 Argyle-Otahuti Road,
Waianiwa, RD 4, Invercargill

Tel (03) 235 2690   Fax (03) 235 2745
Mob 021 385 134   annfield@ihug.co.nz
www.bnb.co.nz/annfieldflowers.html

Double $90-$105   (Full Breakfast)
Dinner $30   Light meal $20   Credit cards accepted
1 King/Twin (1 bdrm)
Bathrooms: 1 Ensuite

We are 1km from the Southern Scenic Route (signposted Waianiwa/Drummond) and well placed for sightseeing, fishing and golf. Dating from 1866, Annfield has been renovated to retain character and include modern facilities. Our sunny guest room opens into the garden. 2 cats and a dog have limited access inside. We are semi-retired, grow flowers for export, keep coloured sheep and alpacas. We enjoy meeting people and love to share dinner or a light meal, including our own produce. Complimentary laundry facilities.

SOUTHLAND,
SOUTH CATLINS

INVERCARGILL *Invercargill Central*

Gala Lodge *B&B Homestay*
Jeanette & Charlie Ireland
177 Gala Street, Invercargill

Tel (03) 218 8884 Fax (03) 218 9148
charlie.ireland@xtra.co.nz
www.bnb.co.nz/galalodge.html

Double $100 Single $60 (Full Breakfast) Child neg
Dinner $25 by arrangement Budget backpacker's room
1 Queen 2 Twin 1 Single (3 bdrm)
Bathrooms: 2 Ensuite 2 Guests share 1 Host share

Gala Lodge, ideally situated for visitors to Invercargill, overlooks beautiful Queens Park, city centre, museum and information centre. The home has well appointed upstairs bedrooms (electric blankets provided). Downstairs, kitchen and two guest lounges. Spacious gardens, ample car parking. Hosts background - farming, police work, education & training, gardening. Interests - reading, genealogy, handcrafts, travel. Many years hosting students of many nationalities including Japan and China. We provide a relaxing, friendly base, support in welfare and travel arrangements. Courtesy car available. Most buses stop here. You are very welcome.

INVERCARGILL *4km N of Invercargill Central*

Stoneleigh Homestay *B&B Homestay*
Joan & Neville Milne
15 Stoneleigh Lane, Invercargill

Tel (03) 215 8921 Fax (03) 215 8491
nevm@bowdens.co.nz
www.bnb.co.nz/stoneleighhomestay.html

Double $90-$110 Single $65-$75 (Full Breakfast)
Dinner $30 Credit cards accepted
1 Queen 3 Single (3 bdrm)
Bathrooms: 1 Guests share

We welcome guests to share our warm comfortable new home, which has underfloor heating. Neville owns a wholesale fruit and vegetable market and Joan enjoys cooking so we would love to share an evening meal with you. We are keen golfers and members of the Invercargill Golf Club; rated in the top 10 courses in NZ. Our home is 5 minutes drive from the city centre, on the main highway to Queenstown and Te Anau. City and airport pick-ups can be arranged.

INVERCARGILL *6km NE of Invercargill*

The Manor *B&B Homestay*
Pat & Frank Forde
9 Drysdale Road, Myross Bush, RD 2, Invercargill

Tel (03) 230 4788 Fax (03) 230 4788
Mob 025 667 0904 the.manor@xtra.co.nz
www.bnb.co.nz/themanor.html

Double $90-$110 Single $65-$75 (Full Breakfast)
Child neg Dinner $30 by arrangement
Credit cards accepted Children welcome
2 Queen 2 Single (3 bdrm)
Bathrooms: 1 Guests share

Relax and enjoy our warm and comfortable home in a sheltered garden setting. Our 10 acre farmlet (sheep, lambs, horses & hens) is situated on the outskirts of Invercargill. We are retired farmers, our interests include: golfing, gardening, horses, travel and meeting people. We have underfloor heating, electric blankets, pleasant outdoor areas and meals of fresh home grown produce, private guest area with television, fridge, tea and coffee making facilities. We are 5 minutes drive from Invercargill along State Highway 1. Sign at Kennington corner.

INVERCARGILL

Montecillo Lodge *B&B Self-contained*
Bevron Sinclair
240 Spey Street, Invercargill

Tel (03) 218 2503   0800 666 832   Fax (03) 218 2506
montecillo@hyper.net.nz
www.bnb.co.nz/montecillolodge.html

Double $100 Single $80   (Full Breakfast)
Child $15 Dinner $25   Four motel units $70
Credit cards accepted
4 Queen 2 Double 8 Single (14 bdrm)
Bathrooms: 6 Ensuite 1 Guests share

Your friendly hosts Bevron & Ray extend you a warm welcome to our comfortable lodge. We are situated in a quiet street just 5-10 minutes walk from the city centre, museum, park, golf course and swimming centre. Each of our centrally heated rooms has it's own ensuite, telephone, TV, tea and coffee making facilities. Cooked breakfast is available in our dining room. Dinner by arrangement. We can arrange trips to Stewart Island and your next nights accommodation. We go that extra step to make your stay more enjoyable.

INVERCARGILL   *Invercargill central*

Victoria Railway Hotel *B&B Boutique Hotel*
Trudy & Eian Read
3 Leven Street, off Picadilly Place,
Invercargill

Tel (03) 218 1281   0800 777 557   Fax (03) 218 1283
Mob 025 347 170   vrhotel@xtra.co.nz
www.bnb.co.nz/victoriahotel.html

Double $95-$140 Single $48-$60 (Full Breakfast)
Child $15 Dinner $16-$25 Credit cards accepted
8 Queen 2 Double 1 Twin 8 Single (19 bdrm)
Bathrooms: 11 Ensuite 2 Guests share

Come and enjoy old world charm and southern hospitality in a boutique hotel in the heart of the city. Built in 1896 we are a Class 1 Historic Places heritage building and we completed our architecturally designed upgrade and refurbishment in May 2004. We offer a variety of accommodation options including Executive, VIP, and 2 ground floor accessible units. Guests can relax in our bar before dining and then enjoy traditional home-cooked meals and a selection of fine NZ wines.

BLUFF   *25km S of Invercargill*

The Lazy Fish
Self-contained continental breakfast optional
Robyn & Roy Horwell
35 Burrows Street, Bluff

Tel (03) 212 7245   Fax (03) 212 8868
Mob 021 211 7424
thelazyfish@es.co.nz
www.thelazyfish.co.nz

Double $95   Continental breakfast $8.50pp
1 Double (1 bdrm)
Bathrooms: 1 Private

Very homely fully self-contained unit attached to our home, in a peacefull garden setting. Sleeps 4, double bed in bedroom and sofa bed in lounge. Sunny shelterd courtyard. Animals in residence. Gateway to Stewart Island and Southern Scenic Route. Take a break and absorb our deep sea and fishing port. Coastal and native bush walks, maritime museum, restaurants and supermarket all within walking distance. 5 minutes walk to Stewart island ferry. Continental breakfast by arrangement.

RIVERTON   *35km S of Invercargill*

River Lodge Bed & Breakfast
B&B Self-contained
Jocelyn and Russell Dore
93 Towack Street, Riverton

Tel (03) 234 8732   Fax (03) 234 8732
rbjmdore@actrix.co.nz www.bnb.co.nz/dore.html

Double $85-$140   Single $50
(Continental Breakfast)   Credit cards accepted
1 King 2 Queen 2 King single (4 bdrm)
Bathrooms: 2 Ensuite 1 Guests share

Relax and enjoy our comfortable home by the sea,
situated on the waterfront with our 3 double bedrooms
opening onto a sunny veranda with peaceful water and
garden views. We also have a private, spacious upstairs
studio unit with spa bath and views from the mountains
to the sea.

Come and enjoy a relaxed homestyle stay. We are only
20 minutes from Invercargill on the Southern Scenic
Route. Enjoy a meal at Riverton's great cafés. Laundry
facilities available. We look forward to meeting you.

RIVERTON - WAIMATUKU *25km NW of Invercargill*

Kildonan Farm *Farmstay*
Jacqui & Bruce Fallow
83 Fraser Road, Waimatuku

Tel (03) 224 6269 Fax (03) 224 6284
Mob 025 284 6882 fallow@southnet.co.nz
www.bnb.co.nz/kildonan.html

Double $90-$100 Single $55 (Full Breakfast)
Child neg Dinner $30 Credit cards accepted
Children welcome Pets welcome
1 Queen 1 Double 1 Twin (3 bdrm)
Bathrooms: 1 Guests share

Looking forward to meeting you and sharing this unique part of New Zealand. Our home has modern facilities, is warm and comforable, and set in a peaceful established garden on a 200 hectare deer and cropping farm. Our interests include people, cooking, travel, gardening, fashion. Pets stay outside. Dinner by arrangement. Directions: Waimatuku is 16km west along SH99 (Southern Scenic Route) or 14km east of Riverton. Travel 3km north along Thornbury-Waimatuku Road, turn right onto Fraser Road. We are at 83 Fraser Road.

RIVERTON *40min W of Invercargill*

Reo Moana *B&B*
Jean & Alan Broomfield
192 Rocks Highway,
Riverton, Southland

Tel (03) 234 9044 Fax (03) 234 9047
www.bnb.co.nz/reomoana1.html

Double $140 Single $100 (Full Breakfast) Child neg
2 nights or more $120 per night Children welcome
1 King 1 Twin (2 bdrm)
Bathrooms: 2 Ensuite

Reo Moana, meaning 'language of the sea', overlooks a beautiful secluded swimming and surfing beach with extended views to the open sea beyond, and northward to the mountains and hills of Southland. Reo Moana, recently completed, was built to take advantage of the sea views and sun. Tastefully decorated, the warm and spacious guest rooms each have ensuite bathrooms and sea views. Your hosts Jean and Alan have many years experience in the tourism industry. We welcome you to Riverton, on the Southern Scenic Route and just 45 minutes from Tuatapere and the Humbridge track.

STEWART ISLAND *One km Oban*

Glendaruel Bed & Breakfast *B&B*
Raylene & Ronnie Waddell
38 Golden Bay Road, Oban, Stewart Island

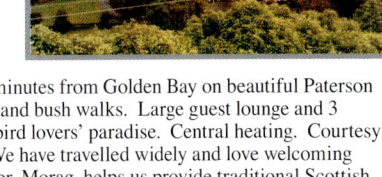

Tel (03) 219 1092 Fax (03) 219 1092
r.r.waddell@xtra.co.nz
www.glendaruel.co.nz

Double $170 Single $90-$110 (Full Breakfast)
Dinner $25 b/a Credit cards accepted
1 King/Twin 1 Queen 1 Single (3 bdrm)
Bathrooms: 3 Ensuite

Peaceful bush setting, 10 minutes walk from village, 3 minutes from Golden Bay on beautiful Paterson Inlet. Handy for water taxis, kayak hire, sandy beaches and bush walks. Large guest lounge and 3 balconies with bush and sea views. Colourful garden - bird lovers' paradise. Central heating. Courtesy transfers. Advice and assistance with local activities. We have travelled widely and love welcoming guests from around the world. Our friendly Cairn Terrier, Morag, helps us provide traditional Scottish and Kiwi hospitality. "A Hundred Thousand Welcomes!"

Welcome to the tranquillity of our sunny open-plan home 'On the Beach' with panoramic views of Horseshoe Bay

STEWART ISLAND   *1km N of Oban*

B&B Approved

Thorfinn Charters & Accommodation   *B&B Homestay Self-contained*
Barbara McKay & Bruce Story
PO Box 43, Halfmoon Bay, Stewart Island

Tel (03) 219 1210   Fax (03) 219 1210   Mob 027 201 1336
thorfinn@southnet.co.nz   www.thorfinn.co.nz

Double $160   Single $110   (Full Breakfast)   Dinner by arrangement
3 self-contained units from $120   Credit cards accepted
2 Queen 3 Single (2 bdrm)   Bathrooms: 1 Private 1 Guests share 1 Host share

Welcome to the tranquillity of our sunny open-plan home 'On the Beach' with panoramic views of Horseshoe Bay out to the offshore islands from all rooms. Guest bedrooms on the second floor are spacious with queen and single bed in each. You may join us downstairs, or use the upstairs sitting area for reading, writing or quiet reflection in privacy.   With central heating, Sky TV, and transfers, you are assured a comfortable stay. Evening meals are by arrangement and feature local seafood.

For groups and families we offer 3 self-contained houses just 10 minutes walk from the village. Two quality houses, each 2-bedroom, sleep up to 7, while our 'Premium' house has 3 bedrooms, 2 ensuite, dishwasher, etc. Sleeps up to 10. All feature Sky TV, central heating, superb sea views, conservatory, bush surrounds and native birds. Thorfinn, our luxury 12 metre launch provides 15 passengers with a comfortable ride, and great visibility. Our specialities are pelagic (seabirds) and terrestrial endemic birds and mammals with commentary on island history, everywhere magnificent scenery, and always the option to catch a fish. The highest number of available birds in any one place in NZ makes 30-40 species per day a possibility.

For 10 years we have operated nature trips with a guided nature walk on Ulva Island to explore unspoilt forest, rare and endangered birds. We also do private charters including exclusive charters for up to six pax with deluxe seafood meal and fine wine luncheon. BJ, from the US East Coast and Hawaii, a medical doctor, brings botanical skill, while Bruce is a former hill-country farmer with 40+ years' experience of the flora and fauna of Fiordland, the Catlins and Stewart Island. Both are DoC Concessionaires, can access 'off the beaten track' areas, and are foundation members of the NZ Birding Network. It will be our privilege to help you discover Stewart Island.

STEWART ISLAND *500m Oban township*

B&B Approved

Sails Ashore & Kowhai Lane *B&B*
Self Contained Flat
Iris and Peter Tait
11 View Street, Stewart Island

Tel (03) 219 1151 Fax (03) 219 1151
tait@taliskercharter.co.nz
www.taliskercharter.co.nz

Sails Ashore Double $350
(Continental Breakfast)
2 King/Twin ensuite

Kowhai Lane Double $170
(Continental Breakfast)
2 King/Twin Ensuite 1 Queen Ensuite
Self-contained flat $150

Iris, Anne & Peter welcome you to Stewart Island. Both houses overlook Halfmoon Bay township and each is about four minutes stroll from the waterfront. Both have delightful sea views and private gardens for you to enjoy. All rooms are centrally heated and either just built or newly furnished. Each house has a large sitting or sun room where you can enjoy our extensive library of books, photos and local interest DVD's. Phone and internet is available, as is a guest laundry.

We have a hire car or guests may prefer to explore the roads with us on an exclusive scenic tour. We need to know your arrival details so we can meet you off the plane and are happy to assist with travel and activity planning. This can be especially useful if planning something a little different, for example kiwi watching at Mason's Bay.

For evening meal you have the option of eating out at one of the excellent local restaurants or alternatively have one deliver to you from their menu. At Sails Ashore our border terriers will be absolutely delighted. to take you for a walk.

Guests may come as strangers,
we hope they leave as friends.

Stewart Island offers everything that is excellent about natural New Zealand. Virgin forest, deserted beaches undisturbed bird and marine life. The Island is all about relaxing, enjoying the natural history and savouring the scenery. We have lived here for some 35 years, initially as Ranger in Charge and then commercial fisherman and as District Nurse. Anne is a senior paediatrics registrar.

Sails Ashore and Kowhai Lane are complemented by our 17 metre charter yacht Talisker offering day exploration and liveaboard charters around Stewart Island. We hold a marine mammal watch permit and are DoC Concessionaires, which together with many years experience ensures you a truly memorable Island experience. An absolute must do is a guided walk with us on Ulva Island, open sanctuary and conservation showpiece. You may choose to extend this to include a leisurely exploration of Paterson Inlet, either as a private charter or as part of a larger group.

SOUTHLAND, SOUTH CATLINS

INDEX

General
Friendly, warm greeting at door by host
Local tourism and transport information available to guests
Property appearance neat and tidy, internally and externally
Absolute cleanliness of the home in all areas used by the guests
Absolute cleanliness of kitchen, refrigerator and food storage areas
Gate or roadside identification of property
Protective clothing and footwear available for farmstay guests
Hosts accept responsibility to comply with local body bylaws
Host will be present to welcome and farewell guests
Hosts' pets and young children mentioned in listing
Smoke alarms in each guest bedroom and above each landing
Evacuation advice card displayed in each bedroom (recommended)
Working torch beside every bed
Suitable fire extinguisher in kitchen and on landing of each upper floor (recommended)
Fire blanket in kitchen (recommended)

Hosts accept responsibility to comply with applicable laws and regulations
Fire safety laws and requirements
Insurances
Swimming and spa pool regulations
Other laws impacting on operation of a B&B

Bedrooms
Each bedroom solely dedicated to guests with...
Bed heating
Heating
Light controlled from the bed
Wardrobe space with variety of hangers
Drawers
Good quality floor covering
Mirror
Power point near a mirror
Waste paper basket
Drinking glasses
Clean pillows with additional available
No Host family items stored in the room
Night light for guidance to w.c. if not adjacent to bedroom
Blinds or curtains on all windows where appropriate
Good quality mattresses in sound condition on a sound base
Clean bedding appropriate to the climate, with extra available

Bathroom & toilet facilities
At least one bathroom adequately ventilated and equipped with...
Bath or shower
Wash handbasin and mirror
Covered wastebasket in bathroom
Extra toilet roll
Lock on bathroom and toilet doors
Electric razor point if bedrooms are without a suitable power point
Soap, towels, bathmat, facecloths, fresh for each new guest
Towels changed or dried daily for guests staying more than one night
Sufficient bathroom and toilet facilities to serve family and guests

The New Zealand
Bed & Breakfast
Book

PLEASE HELP US
KEEP OUR STANDARDS HIGH

To help maintain the high reputation of *The New Zealand Bed & Breakfast Book* we ask for your comments about your stay. You can simply stick a stamp on this form or save all your comment forms and return them in an envelope.

Alternatively, leave your comment at our website
www.bnb.co.nz

Name of Host or B&B__ __ __ __ __ __ __ __ __ __ __ __

Address __ __ __ __ __ __ __ __ __ __ __ __ __ __ __

__ __ __ __ __ __ __ __ __ __ __ __ __ __ __ __

Considering things such things as breakfast, meals, beds, cleanliness, hospitality, value for money, what is your overall *satisfaction rating*, with 1 being the lowest and 10 being the highest rating?

1	2	3	4	5	6	7	8	9	10
☹				☺					☺

Do you have any comments?

We may display your comments on our website. The rating will be confidential and will be kept for administrative purposes.

Fill in your details to go into our regular prize draws!
Your details will not be passed on to anyone else. If you do not have email we suggest you use a friend's email address.

Your name __ __ __ __ __ __ __ __ __ __ __ __ __ __

Your town/city
and country __ __ __ __ __ __ __ __ __ __ __ __ __

Email __ __ __ __ __ __ __ __ __ __ __ __ __ __ __

Please post this form to:
The New Zealand B&B Book,
PO Box 6843, Wellington, New Zealand

Place stamp
here or send
forms in one
envelope.

Moonshine Press
PO Box 6843
Wellington
New Zealand

ORDER FORM

Extra copies of *The Bed & Breakfast Book*
may be ordered at www.bnb.co.nz
or use this form...

Please mail me ☐ copies of *The Bed & Breakfast Book - Australia* and
☐ copies of *The Bed & Breakfast Book - New Zealand* at a cost of
NZ$19.95 plus postage as applicable.
Postage is free within New Zealand and Australia or NZ$10 per book
airmail to the rest of the world.

Please charge my Visa/ Mastercard _____/_____/_____/_____
Exp ____/____ for NZ$_____ including postage.

Signature _____

Name   _____
Address   _____
            _____
            _____

Please email, post or fax your order to...
email info@bnb.co.nz
PO Box 6843, Wellington, New Zealand
Fax +64 4 385 2694

NOTES